The Life and Legend of
the Sultan Saladin

Perceptions of the Crusades from the Nineteenth to the
Twenty-First Centuries (2018, co-editor)

The Crusades, 1095–1204 (second edition, 2014)

Caffaro, Genoa and the Twelfth-Century Crusades
(2012, with Martin Hall)

Holy Warriors: A Modern History of the Crusades (2009)

The Second Crusade: Extending the Frontiers of Christendom (2007)

The Fourth Crusade and the Sack of Constantinople (2004)

The Experience of Crusading: Volume 2 (2003, co-editor)

The Crusades, 1095–1197 (2002)

The Second Crusade: Scope and Consequences (2001, co-editor)

The First Crusade: Origins and Impact (1997, editor)

Defenders of the Holy Land: Relations Between the
Latin East and the West, 1119–1187 (1996)

The Life and Legend of the Sultan Saladin

JONATHAN PHILLIPS

THE BODLEY HEAD
LONDON

1 3 5 7 9 10 8 6 4 2

The Bodley Head, an imprint of Vintage,
20 Vauxhall Bridge Road,
London SW1V 2SA

The Bodley Head is part of the Penguin Random House group of companies
whose addresses can be found at global.penguinrandomhouse.com.

Penguin
Random House
UK

First published in the UK by The Bodley Head in 2019

www.vintage-books.co.uk

A CIP catalogue record for this book is available from the British Library

Hardback ISBN 9781847922144
Trade paperback ISBN 9781847926012

Typeset in 11.5/14pt Dante MT Std
by Integra Software Services Pvt. Ltd, Pondicherry

Printed and bound in Great Britain by Clays Ltd, Elcograf S.p.A.

Penguin Random House is committed to a sustainable future for our business,
our readers and our planet. This book is made from Forest Stewardship
Council® certified paper.

FSC
www.fsc.org

MIX
Paper from
responsible sources
FSC® C018179

For Sophie and John

Contents

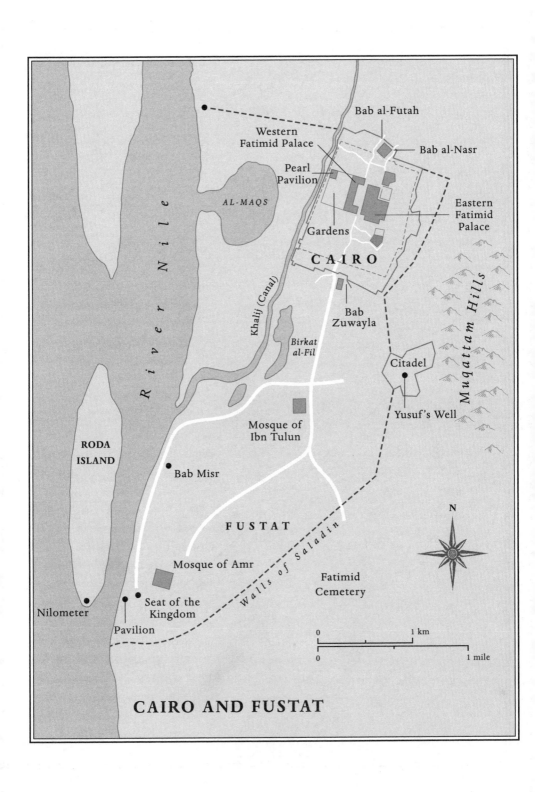

Bab al-Futah

Western
Fatimid Palace

Bab al-Nasr

Pearl
Pavilion

AL-MAQS

Eastern
Fatimid
Palace

Gardens

River Nile

CAIRO

Khalij (Canal)

*Birkat
al-Fil*

Bab
Zuwayla

Muqattam Hills

Citadel

Yusuf's Well

**RODA
ISLAND**

Mosque of
Ibn Tulun

● Bab Misr

FUSTAT

Walls of Saladin

Mosque of Amr

Fatimid
Cemetery

N

Nilometer

Seat of the
Kingdom

Pavilion

0   1 km

0   1 mile

CAIRO AND FUSTAT

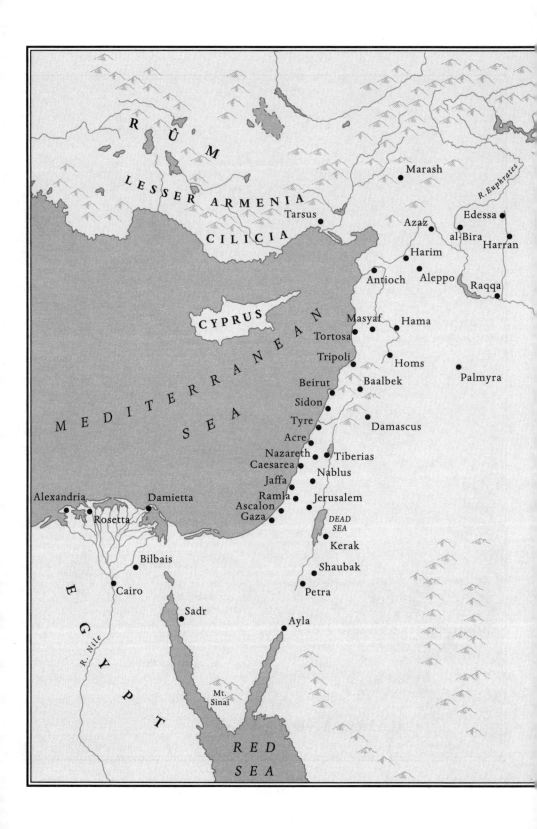

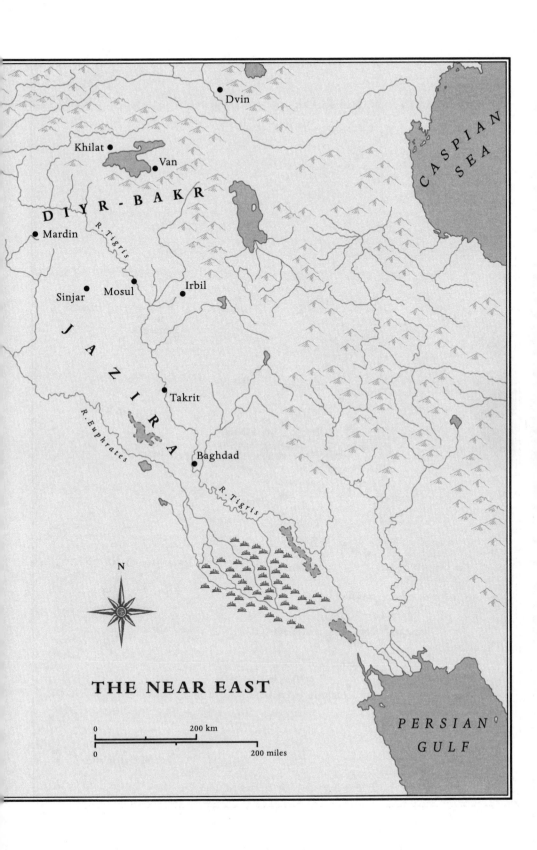

CASPIAN SEA

Dvin

Khilat

Van

D I Y R - B A K R

Mardin

R. Tigris

Sinjar   Mosul   Irbil

J A Z I R A

R. Euphrates

Takrit

Baghdad

R. Tigris

N

THE NEAR EAST

0   200 km

0   200 miles

PERSIAN GULF

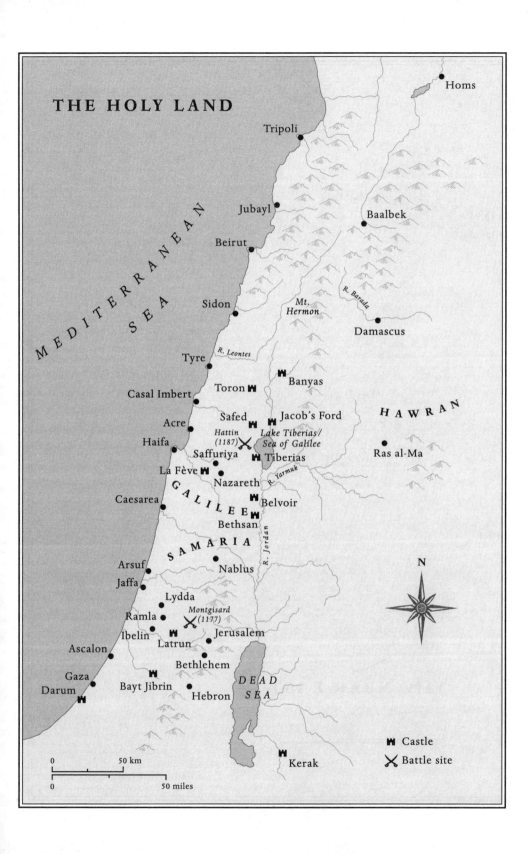

THE HOLY LAND

Homs

Tripoli

Jubayl

Baalbek

Beirut

MEDITERRANEAN

SEA

Sidon

Mt.
Hermon

R. Barada

Damascus

Tyre

R. Leontes

Toron

Banyas

Casal Imbert

HAWRAN

Safed

Jacob's Ford

Acre

Hattin
(1187)

Lake Tiberias/
Sea of Galilee

Haifa

Saffuriya

Tiberias

Ras al-Ma

La Fève

Nazareth

R. Yarmuk

Caesarea

GALILEE

Belvoir

Bethsan

SAMARIA

R. Jordan

Arsuf

Nablus

Jaffa

Lydda

Ramla

Montgisard
(1177)

Ibelin

Jerusalem

Ascalon

Latrun

Gaza

Bethlehem

Darum

Bayt Jibrin

DEAD

Hebron

SEA

N

Kerak

⊞ Castle

✕ Battle site

0   50 km

0   50 miles

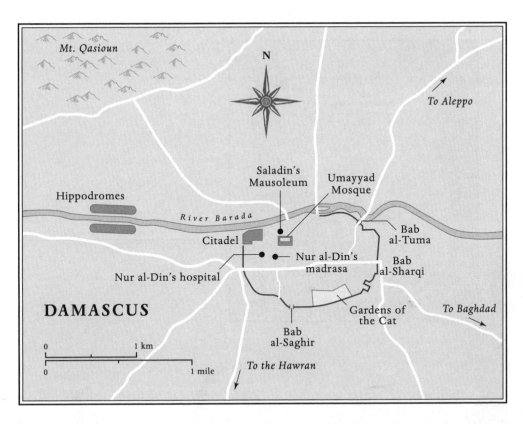

DAMASCUS

Mt. Qasioun

To Aleppo

Hippodromes

River Barada

Saladin's Mausoleum

Umayyad Mosque

Bab al-Tuma

Citadel

Nur al-Din's madrasa

Bab al-Sharqi

Nur al-Din's hospital

Bab al-Saghir

Gardens of the Cat

To Baghdad

To the Hawran

0   1 km

0   1 mile

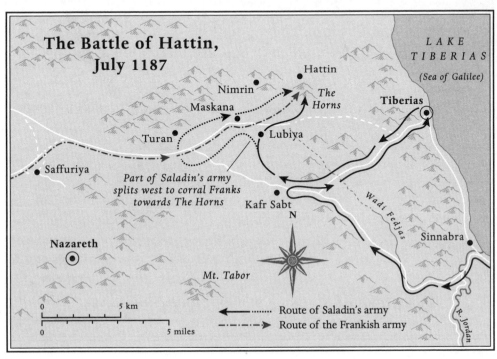

The Battle of Hattin, July 1187

LAKE TIBERIAS
(Sea of Galilee)

Hattin

Nimrin

The Horns

Tiberias

Maskana

Turan

Lubiya

Saffuriya

Part of Saladin's army splits west to corral Franks towards The Horns

Kafr Sabt

Wadi Fedjas

Nazareth

Sinnabra

Mt. Tabor

R. Jordan

0   5 km

0   5 miles

━━━━ ·········· Route of Saladin's army
━ · ━ · ━▶ Route of the Frankish army

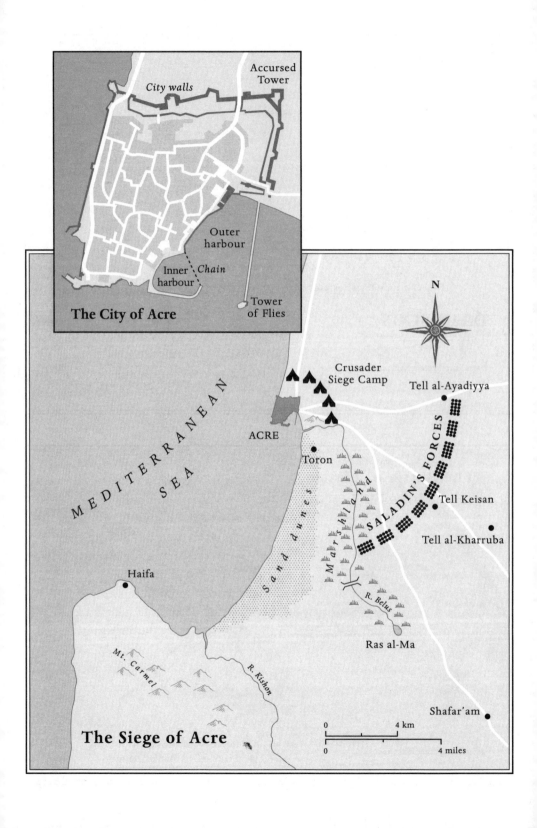

The City of Acre

City walls

Accursed Tower

Outer harbour

Inner harbour · *Chain*

Tower of Flies

N

Crusader Siege Camp

Tell al-Ayadiyya

MEDITERRANEAN SEA

ACRE

Toron

Sand dunes

Marshland

SALADIN'S FORCES

Tell Keisan

Tell al-Kharruba

Haifa

Mt. Carmel

R. Kishon

R. Belus

Ras al-Ma

Shafar'am

The Siege of Acre

0   4 km

0   4 miles

Dramatis Personae
and a Note on Names

Some of the names here are not easy for a western reader to distinguish. My main aim has been to promote clarity and so I have often adopted a name in simplified form or chosen to use a particularly distinctive part of it; similarly, if a nickname exists, I have sometimes selected it. Muslim names are properly a combination of a given name, a lineage, a parental honorific, an honorific or title, and an ascription (geographical or ethnic origin, profession or a distinctive attribute). Breaking down Saladin's name is an interesting example of this:[1] Al-Malik al-Nasir Salah al-Din Abu'l Muzaffar Yusuf ibn Ayyub al-Tikriti al-Kurdi.

Thus: the king who supports/aids (an honorific); righteousness of the faith (another honorific); father of the victorious (parental honorific); Joseph (given name, in Quranic form of a biblical name); son of Job (lineage, in Quranic form of a biblical name); of Tikrit (ascription of birthplace); the Kurd (ascription of ethnicity). Our familiar 'Saladin' is a Latin corruption of 'Salah al-Din', just as his brother, known to us as 'Saphadin', is a blur of 'Sayf al-Din', meaning 'Sword of the Faith'.

I have also chosen to use the phrase 'counter-crusade'. This can suggest an overly strict parity in the concepts of crusade and jihad. The definitions and discussions in the main text draw out important distinctions (as well as the similarities) between the two ideas. A more precise phrase in the context of Saladin's labours would be 'anti-Frankish jihad', although with the caveat above duly noted, the more readable 'counter-crusade' has been employed. As will also be apparent, Arabic diacritics are rarely used; with apologies to the purist, the issue of ease of reading overturned strict linguistic practice.

Al-Adid – last of the Shi'ite Fatimid caliphs (d.1171).

Al-Afdal – Saladin's eldest son.

Amalric – king of Jerusalem (r.1163–74).

Ayyub – Saladin's father (d.1173).

Baldwin IV – leper-king of Jerusalem (r.1174–85).

Beha al-Din Ibn Shaddad – Saladin's army judge, and one of his chief officials and biographers.

Ibn al-Athir – Mosuli historian, generally very pro-Zengid (d.1233).

Imad al-Din al-Isfahani – secretary to Nur al-Din and, from 1175 onwards, to Saladin. He was with the latter for most of the remainder of the sultan's life; historian and poet (d.1201).

Imad al-Din Zengi – a nephew of Nur al-Din who married one of his daughters, also lord of Sinjar and an important contributor to Saladin's armies.

Isa al-Hakkari – instrumental in getting Saladin chosen as vizier of Egypt, a famous jurist and a closely trusted advisor to the sultan (d.1189).

Ismat al-Din Khatun – wife of Nur al-Din and then (from 1176) of Saladin; she died in 1186.

Izz al-Din Mas'ud – lord of Mosul, a Zengid who resisted Saladin's authority until 1186.

Keukburi ('Blue Wolf'), Muzaffar al-Din – lord of Harran, senior commander.

Al-Mashtub ('The Scarred') – long-time supporter of Saladin and a senior general during the siege of Acre.

Nur al-Din – Zengi's son and ruler of Aleppo, Damascus and Mosul; the man who gave real impetus to the counter-crusade, and Saladin's theoretical overlord (d.1174).

Nur al-Din Muhammad – Artuqid Turkish ruler of Hisn Kayfa and Diyar Bakr, ally of Saladin.

Qadi al-Fadil – head of the Fatimid administration who joined Saladin's chancery in 1171 and was one of his inner circle until the sultan's death; a prolific writer.

Qaraqush ('Blackbird') – former Fatimid official and Saladin's master-builder of Cairo, as well as one the generals inside Acre when it surrendered.

Al-Salih Ismail – Nur al-Din's son and successor in Aleppo (d.1181).

Sanjar Shah – lord of Jazirat Ibn Umar and a nephew of Imad al-Din Zengi, the lord of Sinjar.

Saphadin (al-Adil) – Saladin's brother and the holder of many important political and advisory roles. Later ruler of Syria and Egypt (d.1218).

Shawar – vizier of Egypt, responsible for inviting in both the Franks and the Syrians to his country as he sought to hold on to power (d.1169).

Shirkuh – Saladin's uncle, briefly vizier of Egypt and a key general to Nur al-Din (d.1169).

Taqi al-Din – Saladin's nephew, son of an elder brother of the sultan and one of his most important generals (d.1191).

Turanshah – one of Saladin's older brothers (d.1180).

Al-Zahir Ghazi– Saladin's third and seemingly favourite son.

Zengi – father of Nur al-Din, founder of the Zengid dynasty; a brutal warrior who conquered Frankish Edessa in 1144 (d.1146).

Introduction

Damascus 2009

Early morning, October 2009. I am strolling alongside the bustling, horn-honking traffic of downtown Damascus when a poster catches my eye. A bearded face looks out calmly from under a decorated conical helmet: Saladin. The text, in both Arabic and English, names a dance company and states a place and a time: the Damascus Opera House, a twelve-night run starting, by coincidence, the following evening. I carry on walking, moving into the quieter residential areas. A modern dance production about Saladin. I'm not convinced that's quite my cup of tea. But the further I walk, the more the idea appeals. Look, I reason to myself, how often are you going to be in Damascus with this sort of event taking place? What's to lose? It's only one evening. I'm attending an academic conference and in the course of the day I find a friend and colleague intrepid enough to come along. We get tickets for the opening night.

It is dark by the mid-evening start time. There is an energising buzz as the audience funnels into the modern concrete Opera House; local television crews interview the director, and then men whom I take to be government ministers arrive too. Before the show begins there are speeches that include a couple of denunciations of Israel, greeted with warm approval from the audience. Then the dance commences, a vigorous, contemporary production with segments of film, blended with drama and singing. It depicts Saladin's resolve to recover Jerusalem from western crusaders, who had captured it in 1099, and his uniting of the Arab people to take on the crusaders' untrustworthy (and in one case, drunk) leaders. Next, a great whirling of swords and banners portrays the Battle of Hattin, Saladin's historic victory over the

Christian armies in July 1187. The magnanimous sultan regains Jerusalem for Islam and the Arab people and, at the moment of triumph, he spares its population from a massacre of the sort inflicted by the First Crusaders eighty-eight years earlier. The show ends with a celebratory dance, by which time the audience is enthusiastically cheering and clapping along as they enjoy their hero's success.[1]

It was a revelatory evening. I'm not sure it kindled a lifelong love of the genre, but it set me thinking about why the event had been staged, not least in the most prominent location in the city, the House of Asad Opera House. Today Saladin is familiar to all Damascenes through schoolbooks and television drama series. There is a fine equestrian statue of him outside the citadel, and his tomb complex lies adjacent to the city's Great Mosque. Yet what this modern representation of the story seemed to demonstrate was that his relevance is not merely historical but urgently contemporary. The symbolism of Saladin's achievement in recovering Jerusalem from an occupying army was manifest from the very start of the evening, and the show celebrated a well-known episode to reach a conclusion the government of the day aspires to.

Watching this musical set me off on a journey that led, ultimately, to this book. Even while it describes the life and deeds of a twelfth-century warrior leader, a Kurdish outsider who came to rule Egypt, the wealthiest land in the Near East; who usurped the Syrian lands of his overlord; who managed to draw together a fragile coalition to defeat the crusader states and recover Jerusalem for the people of Islam – and then to resist the might of King Richard the Lionheart – this is a book that was inspired not by the past but by the present.

As I was to discover in the years following my visit to Damascus, Syria is far from the only place where the legacy of Saladin is alive and well. In fact, over the last few years the sultan has emerged in a number of wildly different guises – in both the Middle East and the West – almost all of them, glowingly positive. A couple of years after the Damascus dance production, the Baalbek Arts Festival in Lebanon hosted a musical called *From the Days of Saladin*. A local newspaper summarised: 'In this portrayal of the conflict between West and East, the former stands opposed to justice, fairness, courage, wisdom and kindness. Saladin is, on the other hand, perfect.'[2] In Oslo, the House of Literature hosts the annual 'Saladin Days' event, a gathering inspired by the sultan's merciful behaviour towards the defenders of Jerusalem and designed to promote religious tolerance.[3] More recently, in 2014, the Globe Theatre in London saw *Holy Warriors: A Fantasia on the Third Crusade and the History of Violent Struggle in the Holy Lands* by David Eldridge. An elegant and charismatic Saladin (played by Alexander Siddig) reached out across the centuries as a symbol of hope and compromise, denied by an inflexible Richard the Lionheart (John Hopkins): 'What a tragedy it is for our people when you or I cannot imagine a different future even as we weigh the triumphs and failures of our times', lamented the sultan.[4]

Comfortably the most high-profile exposure for Saladin was in Ridley Scott's movie *Kingdom of Heaven* (2005), an international blockbuster shown across the western world and presented to great acclaim in the Near East too.[5] In the wake of 9/11, this was a determined effort to tone down the religious rhetoric in its depiction of the crusades and to massage them into a chivalric enterprise. Saladin was played with great poise by the Syrian actor Ghassan Massoud, who described the sultan as a Muslim hero 'who returned to Arabs and Muslims their pride and dignity, an example for our people, our leaders, our society'.[6] A few years later, Saladin became the subject of a multi-part animated cartoon series for Malaysian children, commissioned by the then prime minister himself, and later translated into English. Here Saladin was an exemplar for young people; as the advertising material stated: 'Saladin: the ultimate hero – courageous in the face of danger, never willing to admit defeat and funny when he needs to be. In a world of danger, there's only one man you'll want in your corner ...'

In fact, both in the Near East and the West, Saladin has been the subject of a number of television programmes. During the holy month of Ramadan families gather to watch serials. In 2001, rival productions in Syria and Egypt aired at this time, dramatising Saladin's deeds. More straightforward documentaries were also produced in Syria and elsewhere in the Near East.[7] Most recently, Al Jazeera Egypt broadcast a major four-part series on the crusades. In the West, there have been *Richard and Saladin: Holy Warriors* (BBC, 2005), *The Cross and the Crescent* (History Channel, 2009) and *The Crusades* (BBC, 2011), as well as a BBC Radio profile of the sultan in a series on *The Islamic Golden Age*.

Saladin has provided material and inspiration for contemporary musicians too. Soon after President Obama won the US presidential election in 2008 he announced plans to visit the Middle East. The wave of admiration for the new American president prompted concerns in some quarters that this energetic leader might too easily be seen as the saviour for all Arab issues. Shaaban Abdel Rahim, a highly polemical rap artist, came out with a warning:

> Bush, may his years be ruined, has caused us losses for days and years
> And Obama, people are imagining him to be Saladin
> What will Obama do for the catastrophes of Bush and his father?[8]

Saladin is also the subject for *nasheed*, a form of instrument-free vocal music that is popular online in the Islamic world. Some songs have footage from *Kingdom of Heaven* to accompany their message: 'O Salah al-deen, you are a hope we'll wait for forever.'[9]

In the second part of the book I will explore more fully what that cultural legacy means and where it has come from. But as we shall also see, it is in the political arena that Saladin appears most frequently. In 2011, when President Recep Tayyip Erdoğan of Turkey was pushing for Palestinian membership of the United Nations, he was hailed on his arrival in Cairo with the words: 'Welcome, Erdoğan, Saladin', and was described as 'Erdoğan, who angers Israel, will liberate Palestine like Saladin.'[10] Back home Erdoğan developed the theme further. In 2015, along with Prime Minister Davutoğlu, he opened a new airport in eastern Turkey named after Saladin. The opening ceremony was an opportunity to make some particular points: 'We are naming this airport Selaheddine Ayyubi,' he said, 'to send a message of solidarity and brotherhood and to say that Jerusalem belongs to Kurds, Turks, Arabs and Muslims forever.'[11]

Saladin was of Kurdish origin, and partly Erdoğan's speech was for domestic consumption, an attempt to win the support of Turkey's Kurdish population for an upcoming election. In Irbil, meanwhile, capital of Iraqi Kurdistan, there is the well-established Salahaddin University. In this region, an image of the sultan takes precedence on their coinage. Clearly it remains a source of immense pride to Kurds that he achieved what hitherto Turks and Arabs had been unable to do, namely, to defeat the crusaders. But a few express frustration. A Swedish-based exile from Syria said: 'I feel proud about him, but I also get mad at him because he did nothing for Kurdistan or the Kurds.' But in the twelfth century Saladin was not fighting on behalf of his own ethnic group, but in the name of Islam (and for the advantage of his own family, the Ayyubids). At the same time Saladin's appeal ran across ethnic lines to include Turks and Arabs in his army and it continues to do so today.[12] The Free Syrian Army features the 'Descendants of Saladin Brigade', while ISIS frequently casts its conflict with the West as a struggle against 'crusaders'.[13] In Egypt in March 2015, the Egyptian military cracked down on the Muslim Brotherhood with an order that banned Saladin from school textbooks on the grounds that he could be used by extremists to incite violence.[14] Saladin has taken a prominent role in school textbooks across the Near East and North Africa since the 1920s, with his moral and military success heavily contrasted with the imperialistic greed of the westerners. This ban was a stark, if backhanded, compliment to his ability to act as a powerful rallying call even in the context of a political-religious struggle within a Sunni Muslim country.

Cumulatively, across politics, theatre, music and television, Saladin today has a formidable profile. How has this happened? And despite the fact that the crusaders are viewed completely differently in the Near East and the West, it is notable that Saladin is largely conveyed in a positive light in both places. Why is this?[15] In the West runs a deep sense that the history of the crusades is something very distant and long gone. Paradoxically, however, the man who defeated the westerners to recover Jerusalem is, and has been for over 800 years now, a figure often hugely admired. The Royal Navy named a vessel HMS *Saladin* in the First World War, and between 1959 and 1994 the British Army had an armoured car named the Saladin – hardly signs of hostility to the sultan's memory. The crusaders remain knights of old, the brave and impetuous King Richard clanks around in his heavy, uncomfortable chainmail, leading his troops into battle. Centuries of using crusading as a metaphor for a good cause have compounded this to blunt the edge of the sword and Saladin's relatively benign persona massages this further into the distance. But this romanticised and chronologically remote view is the disjuncture, the point where the understanding of much of the West does not mesh with, for example, the ongoing struggle for a Palestinian state and control over Jerusalem. More broadly, in the eyes of the Muslim and Arab Near East, the crusaders were motivated by greed and/or religious fervour, invading and conquering their lands, killing their people. And the man who defeated them was Saladin.

Watching the dance musical in Damascus set me seeking the various ways in which Saladin's image and achievements have been adopted and recast in the modern age, but it also prompted me to ask how he has come to have such a predominantly heroic character. As one reviewer of the 1963 Egyptian film *El-Naser Salah al-Din* wrote, the problem with the movie is that Saladin starts as a good man, becomes a great man and ends up as a legend; within such a framework there is little chance of character development. Yet as one explores Saladin's life and career it is apparent that in reality, he was as capable of mistakes, of self-interest and cruelty as anyone else in such a position. Saladin has become a man famous for his faith, generosity, mercy and justice – personal qualities that drew people to him and did much to explain his success. To some of his contemporaries, though, he was a usurper and simply out to build a dynastic power base. And in attaining such heights, he was also, it must be said, the beneficiary of considerable good fortune.

What I hope to convey in the pages that follow is some sense of the man within these various images, whose story repeatedly takes us beyond the crude stereotypes of the 'Clash of Civilisations', of Christianity against Islam, even while its legacy returns us to it. As Saladin gathered an empire that stretched from North Africa through the Holy Land and Syria, and over to the River Tigris in modern Iraq, his life involved people from a bewildering variety of religious, ethnic and political backgrounds. His is a story rich with bloody conflict but not always across the neat divisions of faith which were only inconsistently observed at the time: we will see Christians fighting Christians and Muslims fighting Muslims. We have Christians and Muslims fighting different Christians and Muslims. They might well make a truce, switch sides, and carry on their conflict, or even exist together for a period. Then as now, the reality of the situation on the ground was always far more complicated than it appears from a distance, a cocktail of ethnic, political, economic and personal factors, not just religious beliefs.

The Near East in the twelfth century saw these various factors combined in a particularly unstable blend. Today, Saladin is often presented for political reasons as a man who united his peoples under a common cause, but the turbulent conditions of the time promoted only a limited sense of unity or shared purpose. Arguably Saladin's most extraordinary achievement was to conjure up just such a coalition, to hold in check the bubbling range of interests and priorities of those whom he had gathered, and then to steer it to victory at Jerusalem in 1187. But in conquering a place of such unique religious significance to such a huge array of people, that variety of motives, not all of which were religious, easily slipped out of sight.

This book begins by tracing Saladin's emergence into the rich religious and cultural environment of the Near East. It places his rise in the context of dynastic ambition, holy war and family politics, and describes how Saladin accomplished his great and defining victory at Jerusalem. It narrates his epic confrontation with the armies of Richard the Lionheart and the Third Crusade, but it also goes further. After his death it explains how he has come to be a figure of such renown and respect in the West and of such major significance in the Muslim Near East. We will trace his story through contemporary histories, poems and letters, and later through newspapers, plays, films and novels. Following their telling and retelling leads us down the centuries, back to the Damascus Opera House and beyond to the present day.

PART I

The Life of Saladin

I

The Muslim Near East and the First Crusade

*'How many a mosque have they
made into a church!'*

In March 1132 a group of horsemen hurtled up to the gates of Takrit, a town perched on the banks of the River Tigris. At their head was Zengi, a dynamic and brutal Turkish warlord set upon carving out a power base in northern Syria and Iraq. Zengi's ambition and desire for independence frequently brought him into conflict with his nominal superiors; loyalty and consistency of allegiance were not his modus operandi, a pattern of behaviour replicated by many of his contemporaries and successors. Yet sometimes even Zengi could be defeated, and in this instance, he was on the run. In these desperate circumstances he had a stroke of good fortune: the governor of Takrit let him into the town and then gave him the boats and provisions to escape over the river.[1]

The governor was Najm al-Din Ayyub, later to become Saladin's father. From this impromptu starting point began a relationship that set the Ayyubid family on a path that took them from minor local administrators to the dominant dynastic power of the eastern Mediterranean and, in the person of Saladin himself, a figurehead whose name became known from western Europe to the borders of Asia.

Flux and division characterised the medieval Near East, a region running from Egypt through the Holy Land and Syria, up to Asia Minor, over to the Jazira (meaning 'island', the area between the Tigris and the Euphrates rivers), and across to Persia. A population of extraordinary ethnic and religious variety lived largely under

Muslim rule, although the confessional split within Islam formed just one of the many fault lines in this complex environment. Back in the seventh century a dispute arose as to who should lead the people of Islam following the death of the Prophet Muhammad in 632 ('caliph' means the 'successor' to Muhammad and is the spiritual and legal head of the Sunni believers). This generated the break that crystallised in the Sunni–Shi'ite divide that has been a cause of so much bitterness and tension down the ages.[2] By the eleventh century the split was apparent in political form through the Sunni Abbasid regime based in Baghdad and the Shi'ite Fatimid dynasty in Cairo. It would be a mistake, however, to regard everyone living under either of these powers to be followers of the same denomination, or even the same faith. The natural movement of people caused by politics, trade and the environment, coupled with the extensive pre-Islamic heritage of, for example, Jews, Christians, Zoroastrians and pagans (some polytheists, some monotheists), added a plethora of further ingredients to the mix. Other particularly important fissures were the multiple forms of Eastern Christianity, such as the Greek Orthodox, the Armenians, the Maronites and the Jacobites, or in the case of Islam, divisions amongst the Shi'ites. Back in the eighth century, a dispute saw the emergence of the Isma'ilis, a group who supported the claim of the son of the sixth Imam* to succeed his father. This party came to prominence in North Africa and emerged as a political force in the shape of the Fatimid dynasty who established Cairo as their capital from 969. At the end of the eleventh century, a further splinter group, the Nizaris, known more famously as the Assassins, also come into being, as we will see later.[3]

Urban environments, such as the great cities of Cairo, Alexandria, Aleppo and Damascus, encouraged an especially polyglot population. Religious rivalry could generate conflict, but by reason of habit, economic expediency and indifference, people often just rubbed along. Moments of tension could be for any number of reasons beyond faith alone, such as ethnic differences or short-term political aims; immense

---

*For Shi'ites, the term 'Imam' refers to a descendant of the Prophet chosen by God to lead them. For Sunnis, the term is sometimes interchangeable with 'caliph' or with prayer leader, or is used to honour a scholar. In this book, the term is capitalised when used in its Shi'ite meaning.

linguistic diversity, amplified in trading cities by the presence of merchants, added yet another layer of complexity.

In the case of the Sunni caliph of Baghdad, religious authority did not translate seamlessly to political power. In the course of the early eleventh century (1020s to 1050s) periods of extreme cold, coupled with a relentless will to conquer, saw the nomadic Seljuk Turks leave their homelands on the central Eurasian steppe and move westwards. These tough warriors, recent converts to Islam, quickly imposed their power over the Iranian world, including the caliph and, with their families and livestock, came to settle across the region. By the 1090s the Seljuk Empire stretched from the Holy Land over to Kashpur in what is now China. For a couple of decades, it was reasonably cohesive, but in the early 1090s, a catastrophic spate of deaths – both by murder and through natural means – shattered the existing hierarchies and the Sunni lands of the Near East broke into a series of regional political entities, based in the big urban centres of Aleppo, Damascus and Mosul. Smaller city states, such as Hama, Tripoli or Harran, also emerged, each looking to assert their own independence and to advance their position at the expense of neighbours. Familial ethnic groups, such as the Turkish Artuqids or the Zengids, the Kurdish Hakkaris, or the Bedouin (tribes of nomadic Arab pastoralists), were amongst the fluctuating candidates to rule a city or district, or be brought into a larger polity.[4]

The ongoing churn of this rich blend of peoples and faiths was precisely the situation in which ambitious newcomers could thrive. The Ayyubids were ethnic Kurds, a clan based around the small city of Dvin in the broad Araxes valley in western Azerbaijan (now modern Armenia). Their skill as mounted warriors meant that they were in demand to join the forces of the various Seljuk Turkish warlords in the area. The relationship between the Turks and the Kurds was one of pragmatism peppered with occasional bouts of tension and bigotry; much of the time, however, it suited them to work together, hence Ayyub's position as governor of Takrit.[5]

A few years after his escape across the Tigris, Zengi was able to return the favour to the Ayyubids. While he was clearly a ruthless warrior, another fundamental facet of leadership was the ability to dispense patronage. In 1137–8 the Kurdish clan hit trouble in Takrit. Ayyub's brother, Shirkuh, took offence at the insulting remarks made by the local army commander to a young woman. A confrontation ensued and Shirkuh killed the man. The family's good standing insulated them from physical punishment by the authorities, but Ayyub was stripped of the governorship and the group was forced into exile; now was the moment for Zengi to repay that help. The family sought refuge with him in Mosul where he awarded them lands.[6]

Amidst all this upheaval, and just before the clan left Takrit, Salah al-Din ibn Ayyub was born. While westerners know and refer to him as Saladin, these parts of his name have an honorific meaning, 'Righteousness of the Faith, son of Ayyub', a form of title widely used at the time. His birth name was Yusuf (Joseph), a choice resonant with ties to the Quran. The story of Yusuf occupies Sura 12 of the holy book and narrates his life and role as a Prophet, the son of Jacob. At one point this pious, calm and forgiving character provides advice that preserves Egypt from disaster, in this case famine. The notion that an individual called Yusuf saves Egypt means this came to prove a prescient choice by Saladin's family, and in the course of his career the name Yusuf was frequently employed in letters and poems about him, often to highlight the parallels with his Quranic namesake and to enhance his image.[7]

Although Zengi continued to fight his fellow Muslims, his territorial ambitions inevitably brought him into conflict with the other major players in the Levant – the Franks (Ifranj or Firanj in Arabic), the term adopted for the Christian settlers who had set up a series of independent states in the aftermath of the conquest of Jerusalem by the First Crusade in 1099. In doing so these westerners, themselves a heady blend of southern Italians, Provençals and northern Europeans, added more layers to the cultural and linguistic complexity of the Near East.[8]

Zengi's wars against the Franks brought a further dimension to the fore, that of jihad, the concept commonly equated with holy war. The idea of the crusade, an armed pilgrimage to liberate Jerusalem from the Muslims, was invented by the papacy in the late eleventh century. In contrast, the notion of jihad was a basic element of the Islamic faith, enshrined in the Quran and hadith (the sayings of the Prophet), that dated back to the age of the Prophet in the seventh century. Jihad, which literally means 'striving', exists in two forms: the 'greater jihad', which is the spiritual struggle of every Muslim to live according to the teachings of Allah, and the 'lesser jihad' which by the ninth century had evolved to be both a communal and an individual obligation 'to engage in defensive and then offensive warfare for the benefit of the community'.[9]

By the later decades of the twelfth century, the call to jihad and the duty of able-bodied Muslims to engage in holy war constituted a fundamental part of Saladin's success, but when the armies of the First Crusade reached the Near East in the late 1090s it was barely in evidence. The crusade had emerged in western Europe through an alliance of the motives and interests of the religious and noble classes. The pope called for the liberation of Christ's tomb, the Holy Sepulchre, and offered participants remission of all confessed sins. The nobility (the warriors, in other words), responded vigorously to that message, capturing Jerusalem in 1099. In the highly fragmented Near East no such partnership between the religious classes and the fighting classes existed. Furthermore, the disastrous series of deaths across the Muslim world (including Fatimid Egypt) in the early 1090s eliminated a layer of senior leadership that could well have stopped the crusade in its tracks. In 1105, a Damascene religious scholar called al-Sulami preached the jihad in a small village on the edge of the city. He lambasted the nobles of the day for their failure to defend their subjects against the crusaders. He also emphasised the duty of free, adult, healthy men to participate and insisted on the need for spiritually correct intention; that is, the precedence of the greater jihad over the lesser, citing the important contemporary theologian, al-Ghazali, in support of this idea.[10] Threats, both material and spiritual, followed, as well as an outline of heavenly and earthly rewards, especially plunder. At the time of the First Crusade the majority of the Muslims in Syria had not recognised the campaign as, in part, a conquest of religious colonisation, although al-Sulami pointed out that recent Christian advances in Spain and Sicily perhaps (erroneously) suggested a more systematic programme of conquest. In 1105 al-Sulami's audience was tiny, only a handful of other scholars, an indication that his message was falling on stony ground, but the text survived and the core tenets of his appeal would, decades later, ring out loudly across the Muslim Near East.[11] Not even in Baghdad, the seat of Sunni Islam, was there much interest in, or understanding of, the events on the western edge of the caliph's lands. Far closer to home the serial convulsions within the Seljuk world fully absorbed the attention of Baghdad.

We catch intermittent references to crusade and jihad in the early decades of the twelfth century. A few poets castigated their leaders and angrily lamented events in Syria and the Holy Land:

> The sword is cutting and blood is spilt.
> How many Muslim men have become booty?
> And how many Muslim women's inviolability has been plundered?
> How many a mosque have they made into a church!
> The cross has been set up in the *mihrab* [the niche inside a mosque
>   indicating the direction of Mecca].
> The blood of the pig is suitable for it.
> Qurans have been burned under the guise of incense.[12]

In a more aggressive tone, a Seljuk poet in Baghdad called for a war 'to make polo-balls of the Franks' heads and polo sticks from their hands and feet'.[13] In 1111 a band of religious scholars and merchants from Aleppo travelled to Baghdad and burst into Friday prayers in the Seljuk sultan's mosque and in the caliphal mosque. These acts of calculated disrespect were a sign of their fury at the inadequacy of any response to the Frankish conquests. Muslim rulers in Syria had, of course, fought the settlers, but very much in the framework of their own individual political needs. One indication of some stirrings of holy-war mentality was prior to the Battle of the Field of Blood in northern Syria in 1119. There a Shi'ite judge from Aleppo preached to the troops and urged them to victory. A few years later, Balak of Aleppo died fighting the Franks and inscriptions on his tomb describe him as a martyr who fought the holy war, 'leader of the army of the Muslims, vanquisher of the infidel and the polytheists'.[14]

A stronger trail emerges in the final years of Zengi's career in the early 1140s. Inscriptions on a Damascus madrasa (a college of theology and law that trained religious scholars and state officials) describe him as 'the fighter of jihad, the defender of the frontier, the tamer of the polytheists and the destroyer of the heretics'.[15] In other words, notwithstanding the fact that he spent the bulk of his time in conflict with other Muslims, the religious classes of Syria eventually seem to have found in him a figure who periodically could take on the mantle of a holy warrior in wars against the Christians. In 1137 he hammered a

Frankish army at the Battle of Montferrand and took towns and castles from the Frankish principality of Antioch; the following year he fended off a major invasion from the Byzantine emperor, John Komnenos.[16] It was in 1144, however, that he struck the most substantial blow to date in the counter crusade.

The city of Edessa was captured by the First Crusaders in 1098. A later northern Syrian writer described it as a place that 'inflicted great harm on the Muslims around it ... Edessa was like the eye of the territories of the Jazira', lying on a large plain, about sixty-five miles east of the River Euphrates.[17] It had an important position in the history of Christianity as the first city to convert to Christianity under King Abgar, and as the burial place of the apostles Thomas and Thaddeus. Even after the crusader conquest, the bulk of its population remained Armenian, although there was some degree of intermarriage with the western newcomers.[18]

Zengi's activities against Muslim rivals up towards the River Tigris encouraged Count Joscelin II, the ruler of Edessa, to leave his city and travel many miles west. The Turk's formidable network of intelligence operatives informed him of this and Zengi 'moved forward fast, like an arrow leaving its bow or like a flood running its course', calling upon the 'tribes of the Turkmen to assist him and to carry out the obligation of the Holy War'.[19] A powerful army besieged the citadel of Edessa and specialist mining engineers from Khurasan (northeastern Persia, today's eastern Iran and Uzbekistan) created an elaborate system of mines. On 23 December 1144, a section of the wall collapsed. The defenders fought hard to plug the gap but the following day, the attackers swarmed in. The terrified population fled to the citadel and in the panic the aged archbishop was trampled to death at the gate. A few days later the citadel itself surrendered; the men were killed or tortured and the women and children enslaved. Churches were destroyed, as was the silver coffin that held the bones of Thaddeus and King Abgar.[20]

'[Zengi] afflicted everyone inside with evil. He captured the city and damned it. He crushed its semen, inverted its crosses, exterminated its monks and priests, killed its knights and heroes.'[21]

The taking of a major Frankish city, indeed the capital of one of their four states, was a breakthrough moment for the Muslim Near East and a feat recognised by the caliph of Baghdad with the award of a series of honorific titles to the successful warlord: 'the adornment of Islam, the victorious prince, the helper of the believers'.[22]

> The victory of Edessa had outshone all other victories
> By the deeds of Zengi, Islam is reawakened
> If justice be done, he should be called caliph
> Tomorrow he will invade Jerusalem.[23]

The poet's predictions regarding Jerusalem proved wide of the mark, but his sense of triumph reflects the feelings that Zengi's success had aroused. The man himself may have had a more pragmatic next step in mind, however. In the latter half of 1145 he was known to be gathering levies and stockpiling siege weapons in Baalbek. Some said that this was for the purposes of holy war, but rumours in nearby Damascus suggested that they were the next target.[24] As so often, however, events to the east demanded his attention and, with Shirkuh, Saladin's uncle, amongst his troops, he marched away to besiege Qa'lat Jabar, over 220 miles north-east on the Euphrates. There, in September 1146, Zengi met an unexpected, but predictably violent, end. The accounts vary in detail, but most agree that he engaged in a heavy drinking session and then passed out. Some versions say that he was murdered by a slave of Frankish origin, others that he awoke to find his eunuch servants drinking the leftover alcohol and that he threatened them with punishment in the morning. Fearing for their lives, the servants (literally) struck first and killed him in his bed.[25]

At the time Zengi emerged onto the scene, much of the political power in the Near East was highly localised, but he was the first Muslim ruler in the twelfth century to have the aggression, the ambition and the ability to take on a range of foes. His appointment as an *atabeg* (tutor or regent for a young prince) notwithstanding, Zengi asserted his independence from the Seljuk sultans of Iraq, periodically fought the Abbasid caliph, and was certainly intending to usurp power in Damascus from its existing Muslim rulers. Even the historian Ibn al-Athir, a real acolyte of the Zengid dynasty, wrote that its founder had orchestrated numerous rebellions against the Seljuk Sultan Mas'ud 'in order to keep the sultan distracted so that he [Zengi] would have a free hand in expanding his frontiers and consolidating his power'.[26] By the later stages of his career we can discern some flickering signs that the jihad was part of contemporary discourse, but as an individual Zengi was not particularly known for his personal piety. It was through the next generation of Zengids that a wider and more systematic diffusion of ideas of holy war would take place – and it was in this same environment that Saladin himself grew up.

Back in 1139 Zengi had captured the Damascene-controlled city of Baalbek about thirty-five miles to the north. After massacring the garrison, he installed Saladin's father, Ayyub, as governor. But after the *atabeg*'s death, the Damascene ruler Unur took the chance to besiege Baalbek. Once water supplies ran low, surrender was inevitable. In November 1146 Ayyub handed the town to Unur in return for a few villages in the countryside near Damascus, and thus it was in these rather awkward circumstances that the Kurdish family came to be in and around the metropolis of Syria.

Within a couple of years the Ayyubids had direct experience of the jihad when the armies of the Second Crusade laid siege to Damascus in the summer of 1148. The fall of Edessa had prompted the Franks to send appeals for help to western Europe and by the summer of 1147 the kings of France and Germany led the largest armies for fifty years to set out for the East. This aroused grave concerns in Muslim lands, although the crusaders' poor discipline and the robust oppos-ition of the Seljuk Turks of Anatolia drained much of their military strength before they even reached the Levant.[27] By this time an earlier alliance between Damascus and Jerusalem had soured, meaning that while the recovery of Edessa had been the crusaders' original aim, a council of crusaders and Franks now felt it acceptable to attack Damascus. In late June 1148 the armies of Jerusalem and the western crusaders set out to besiege the Muslim city.

Following early progress through the dense orchards that protected the city, the Christians had paused in front of the walls where they met stern resistance. With Jerusalem now hostile, the Damascenes had conducted an about-turn and looked to the Zengids for help against the outside invaders.[28] Perplexingly, the crusaders had brought little in the way of supplies or siege equipment and, fearing being caught between the defenders of Damascus and the advancing northern Syrians, they withdrew. This was a terrible humiliation. It was the first time that kings had been on a major crusade, and preachers in the West had whipped up an expectation of victory. St Bernard of

Clairvaux, the greatest orator of the age in Europe, had cried out 'lucky is this generation' to have such a chance of divine reward. Utterly convinced they would follow in the successful footsteps of the heroes of the First Crusade, they had instead feebly collapsed, not even suffering some epic defeat from which to derive a claim of heroism.[29]

This victory over the western forces was a huge boost to morale in the Muslim Near East. Understandably the large crusading armies had been feared, but now they had been completely faced down. As a Frankish chronicler wrote: 'From this time the condition of the Latins in the East became visibly worse. Our enemies saw that the labours of our most powerful kings and leaders had been fruitless and all their efforts in vain ... hence [the Muslims'] presumption and boldness rose to such heights that they no longer feared the Christian forces and did not hesitate to attack them with unwonted vigour.'[30] It is likely that Saladin, aged around eleven years old, was inside Damascus during the siege. Ayyub had moved to the city after the surrender of Baalbek in 1146 and members of the family took part in fighting the crusaders, in the course of which Saladin's elder brother was killed.[31]

By this stage, another figure was poised to seize the ascendancy in the Muslim Near East: Zengi's younger son, Nur al-Din, meaning 'light of the faith', an appropriate name for the man who would do so much to energise the counter-crusade.[32]

2

Nur al-Din and the City of Damascus

'Gardens encircle it like the halo
around the moon'

Nur al-Din became one of the central players in the history of the Muslim counter-crusade. As an overlord, patron, and later a rival, he exerted a huge influence on Saladin's life for almost three decades, providing in many ways a blueprint for much of what the Ayyubid would do. Writers describe him as a handsome man with charming eyes; tall and swarthy, bearded only on his chin. He was greatly admired for his piety, learning and asceticism. The Franks, too, came to respect and fear an opponent who was a formidable warrior as well as a great leader. He was said to have carried two bows and two quivers into battle, a choice of weapon that emphasised his heritage as a Turkish warrior whose method of fighting was based around horse archers.[1] Just like Zengi, Nur al-Din coveted Damascus and wished to take the city from its Burid rulers.[2]

He soon demonstrated his military skills at the Battle of Inab in northern Syria on 29 June 1149. The Frankish knights launched their famous charge, but the Muslims deliberately gave ground, divided in two and then turned upon their enemies. The result was a complete and utter rout. The leading Frankish warrior of the day was Prince Raymond of Antioch, a man who 'had acquired special repute by the dread which he inspired by his great severity, and excessive ferocity', yet he too was amongst the slain. When his body was found, a delighted Nur al-Din sent Raymond's head to the caliph of Baghdad. Nur al-Din's credentials as a holy warrior, 'the Fighter of the Holy War, the

Champion of the Faith', were starting to build. Inscriptions on build-ings in Aleppo from this time extol the virtues of the jihad, although this did not prevent him from looking to increase his personal and family power at the expense of other Sunni Muslims.[3]

In April 1150 Nur al-Din brought his forces down to Damascus, nominally in response to appeals from the inhabitants of the Hawran region to protect their flocks and villages from Christian raiders. As before, the Damascene leaders feared the intentions of outsiders and now doubled back to their former policy of asking the Franks of Jerusalem for help. This inevitably opened them to charges of colluding with the infidel and failing to protect their people and to engage in holy war: 'This is displeasing in the sight of God.'[4] In the event, in May 1150 a diplomatic solution was reached because Nur al-Din was said by Ibn al-Qalanisi, a contemporary Damascene poli-tician and writer, to be unwilling to shed the blood of Muslims, a stark contrast to the approach of his father. A cynic might note that the chances of taking such a strong city as Damascus – likely to be reinforced by troops from Jerusalem – were slight. The inherent tension for those claiming to be fighting the enemies of the faith yet engaging in warfare against their fellow Sunni Muslims is a recurrent theme in this story and is an issue that would prove particularly chal-lenging for Saladin.

An acknowledgement of Nur al-Din's overlordship and the insertion of his name in the *khutba* – the ritual address given in the Friday sermon that included an invocation to the recognised leaders of the community, meaning the caliph and also the emir or sultan – gave him a nominal hold over Damascus. His name was also put on the coins, the other customary sign of authority (the *sikka*). He presented senior figures from the city with garments known as robes of honour as a mark of their submission, while the poor and needy were given gifts too. This was all standard practice for a ruler and proved a form of behaviour that Saladin would take to vastly higher levels. The arrival of some of Nur al-Din's religious advisors in the city was another signal of his longer-term aims, although for the moment the emir's power there was still largely theoretical.

A year later, in April 1151, Nur al-Din's troops once more marched towards the city. Ibn al-Qalanisi again proclaimed the aspiring ruler had a scrupulous aversion to slaying Muslims and prioritised fighting polytheists (Franks) instead. After further negotiations a truce was made, a process that necessitated a prominent role for the Ayyubids. They were in the curious position of having one brother (Shirkuh) in Nur al-Din's camp, and the other (Ayyub, Saladin's father) now living under Damascene authority. The latter's surrender of Baalbek to Unur back in 1146 was simple pragmatism, rather than betrayal, and with the help of a prominent local jurist the brothers formulated a treaty, an early instance of the family's diplomatic skills.[5]

For a short period all was well, but in 1153 the Franks besieged the vital port of Ascalon. This was the only coastal city that remained in Muslim hands, albeit under the authority of the Egyptian Fatimid Shi'ite regime. It was also important as the location of the shrine of Husayn, the Prophet's grandson and the son of Ali, the first Shi'ite Imam.[6] Now, however, the city faced a major crisis in the form of a full Frankish assault, including a naval blockade.[7]

Setting aside sectarian differences with the Fatimids, both Nur al-Din and the Damascenes hoped to prevent the Christians from seizing this powerful city, but before the plan took effect they quarrelled. Such was the intensity of the siege it was likely Ascalon would have fallen anyway, but this division hardly helped. After seven months, the city capitulated in August 1153, marking a significant achievement for the Franks and providing a boost in morale after the failure of the Second Crusade five years earlier.[8]

For Nur al-Din the breakdown of this proposed campaign was the final straw. Ibn al-Qalanisi reported that political dissensions continued to simmer with a flurry of changes amongst the ruling elite signalling growing instability.[9] In the early months of 1154, Nur al-Din employed another means to generate pressure, namely an economic blockade. Grain prices soared and the poor and the weak struggled badly. Shirkuh led an advance guard southward and by 25 April Nur al-Din had joined him at Damascus. Fighting broke out but resistance was half-hearted as a combination of lack of food and disapproval of the regime's close relationship with Jerusalem took its toll. A Jewish woman let down a rope and one of the troops scrambled up to hoist Nur al-Din's standard above the walls. Next a woodcutter smashed the bolts on the great East Gate, the doors were thrown open and Nur al-Din's warriors surged in. The people welcomed them warmly and the emir swiftly assumed control, promising safety to the leadership and acting firmly to prevent any looting.[10]

Nur al-Din used the opportunity of the first Friday prayers after his takeover to confirm the abolition of taxes that were un-Quranic, as well as those that were simply unpopular, including those on the melon market and the vegetable market, and the collection of taxes on using the canals.[11] The removal of hated financial impositions of a previous regime is a standard course of action for most new rulers and, as in this instance, usually meets with enthusiasm and an expectation of better times. In Nur al-Din's case, his wish to improve the living conditions of Damascenes really did prove to be genuine and this, coupled with a concerted policy of encouraging religious foundations, became the hallmarks of his domestic rule.

Under his authority, Damascus became the hub of the counter-crusade. It is one of the great cities of the world, a place saturated in layer upon layer of history, a past absorbed within its narrow streets, alleyways, minarets, markets and monuments, and is one of the oldest continuously inhabited cities on the planet, dating back 3,000 years. Prominent during the Assyrian, Persian, Hellenistic and Roman periods, with the rise of Islam it became a centre for the Umayyad caliphate from 661 to 750. Next the Abbasids, then the Fatimids held the city and in the latter half of the eleventh century an offshoot of the Great Seljuks moved eastwards to assert themselves over much of Syria, taking Damascus in 1076. A few decades later it became the seat of the Burids, a semi-independent Turkish dynasty who sought to remain free of other local power-players such as Aleppo and the kingdom of Jerusalem.[12] With such a kaleidoscopic past, the population was a religious and ethnic melting pot of Sunnis and Shi'is, Jews and Eastern Christians, Arabs, Bedouin and Turks.

Medieval writers extolled its beauty and especially its sanctity; it was God's Paradise on Earth. In later decades it was the place that Saladin returned to most often and was where he and his family clearly felt at home.[13] The city lies on a plain a couple of kilometres south of the towering ridge of Mount Qasioun, revered as the birthplace of Abraham, while on the same hillside sits a cave containing traces of the blood of Abel, known as the Grotto of Blood. Although Damascus is not mentioned by name in the Quran, writers associated it with verses from the holy text. Traditions describe it as the stage for the coming of the Messiah before the Day of Judgement with some asserting that this would occur in the Great Umayyad Mosque, one of Islam's holiest sites. Writers claim that Damascus was where God gave asylum to Jesus and his mother, while it was also the burial place of companions of the Prophet, such as his muezzin, and members of his family, including Ruqayya, the daughter of Ali.[14]

Below the mountainside of Qasioun runs the River Barada. This precious waterway rises in the Anti-Lebanon Mountains around twenty-five kilometres to the north-west and in spring it surges down a gorge into a fertile valley to spread out and bring life to an area of about thirty square kilometres, upon which the city lies. In medieval times the river also refreshed dozens of irrigation channels that nurture a vast girdle of orchards that almost surrounded the settlement. A visitor in the 1180s marvelled that 'the gardens encircle it like the halo around the moon ... wherever you look on its four sides its ripe fruit holds the gaze'.[15] Nineteenth-century images show a similar vista, and even in the modern age a view from Mount Qasioun reveals swathes of trees still visible in the distance, pushed back by the concrete sprawl of the modern city.

The mighty Mount Hermon (around 2,700 metres high) and the Golan Heights around forty kilometres south-west of the city create a formidable barrier to the Mediterranean Sea, itself only about seventy-five kilometres due west. Further north lies the bulk of Syria with, on the River Orontes, the cities of Hama and Homs and, about 350 kilometres north, the other great metropolis of Syria, Aleppo. Travellers heading south of Damascus pass through the Hawran region where fertile volcanic soil supports a vital wheat-growing area before this gives way to a more rugged landscape down into Transjordan. To the east of Damascus, the life-giving River Barada runs into a lake providing irrigation to a further stretch of rich agricultural land before that surrenders to dry grasslands and then desert.

Trade and pilgrimage helped shape the city, in the latter instance because Damascus was one of the prime gathering places for haj caravans heading south to Mecca and Medina in the Arabian peninsula. Multiple trade routes from as far away as India came through the Jazira, while goods produced there and in Anatolia and northern Syria also came to Damascus where they could either funnel west to the Frankish ports on the coast, or go down to Egypt, Arabia and the Red Sea.[16]

Through a combination of his political and religious will, Nur al-Din was able to create a city that became the theological engine room for the jihad. With Jerusalem in the hands of unbelievers, Damascus stepped forwards to generate the spiritual energy to recover it; arguably in doing so, it supplanted Baghdad as the principal centre of Sunni religious thought at the time. This powerful combination of the city's deep religiosity and its important strategic location came to exert a powerful pull on Saladin down the years.

The walled city of Damascus is roughly oval-shaped, about 1,600 metres long and 900 metres wide. Ten gates punctuate this girdle with the old Roman artery known as 'the Street Called Straight' bisecting the city east–west just below its mid-point; most of the key buildings lie north of this. The dominant structures, then and now, are the citadel and, the real jewel, the Great Umayyad Mosque, or the Congregational Mosque as it is also known, a building admired by all down the centuries. The Spanish pilgrim Ibn Jubayr was awestruck when he visited in 1184: 'For beauty, perfection of construction, marvellous and sumptuous embellishment and decoration, it is one of the most celebrated mosques of the world.'[17] An institution of such size and prestige was obviously a spiritual focus and it ranks amongst the holiest mosques in Islam. As with all mosques it was a place of daily worship, but it also acted as a repository for sacred objects and as a base for preachers, reciters, jurists, theologians and teachers. Precious items such as the Quran of Uthman (a companion of the Prophet and the third caliph), which helped to inspire the defence of the city against the Second Crusade in 1148, were housed there for people to venerate, while the shrine of the head of the prophet known to us as John the Baptist stands in the main prayer hall.[18]

The main courtyard is a broad open area, fifty metres wide and over 140 metres long, colonnaded on three sides. On the south is the prayer hall, a wonderful space with its three aisles raised on a forest of over sixty pillars, all complementing a richly ornamented *mihrab*. In the central aisle is a great lead dome standing high and proud on the city's skyline and likened by the locals to the head of a mighty eagle; Ibn Jubayr was thrilled to be allowed to climb up into the roof space and rhapsodised that this was 'a spectacle that sends the senses reeling ... stupendous, so miraculously constructed ... more astounding than what is told of the wonders of the world'.[19] The mosque was a social space too, and within the courtyard and the hall groups of locals and pilgrims sat, talked, listened and learned, as they still do today. Above the entrance to the main prayer hall the gold, green and blue mosaics depicting fine buildings, trees and rivers continue to catch the afternoon sun. An ablutions fountain, the eighth-century treasury building, also wrapped in mosaic, along with an ingenious water clock (no longer extant) all inhabited this space. But it was the preachers who took centre stage, men from across the Islamic world from Iberia to western Asia, representing the different and rival schools of Sunni jurisprudence, addressing audiences at set-piece moments, especially the Friday prayers, but also teaching, debating and studying. Mosques were very much places of education in religion, grammar, law, logic and history.[20] The Friday sermon was the optimum moment to deliver news as well as religious instruction, not least in the progress of the holy war. Here, and in reaction to other sermons, the audience itself might then respond, question, assimilate and disseminate what they had heard.[21]

Of course, there were other mosques in Damascus; Ibn Asakir, a contemporary cleric and writer, listed 242 within the walls. These were not just the grand buildings endowed by the political elite, but could be much more humble institutions sponsored by artisans, such as butchers, or camel-dealers.[22] Under Nur al-Din, madrasas saw an enormous expansion. At the start of his time in power, there were sixteen madrasas across his lands; by his death in 1174, a further fifty-six had been added. Similarly, khanqahs – buildings that housed Sufi mystics, ascetics who lived in communities and prayed and chanted – grew up. Ibn Jubayr witnessed some of these holy men listening to music and attaining 'an abstracted state of rapture' during his stay in the city.[23]

Damascus was more than a religious centre. The citadel was a formidable rectangular complex in the north-western corner of the city, a place that acted as a base for government containing, for example, a treasury and a prison, and a barracks for troops fighting the counter-crusade. Nur al-Din soon reinforced the defences, strengthening the walls and further fortifying some of the towers and gatehouse, adding a small mosque to the latter.[24]

The admiring pen of Ibn Asakir gives us a glimpse into the daily life of the city that Saladin came to know so well.[25] The provision of

water was essential in such a dense urban environment and the
Damascenes prided themselves on their complex canal systems with
over a hundred sub-channels delivering water to baths, mosques and
khanqahs, houses and gardens, and to commerce, as well as public
latrines. Fine air and good water were real marks of status for a city,
and Damascus confidently asserted its standing in these respects. As
the Quran says, water is a gift from God, and a hadith notes that there
is no greater gift of alms than to give a drink of water. Bathhouses
were of special note as one place for the ritual ablutions central to
religious practice. They were run by a master of the house, with a
bather, a water-carrier, a cleaner and a man to heat the water. In Nur
al-Din's time there was a ratio of one bathhouse to six mosques and
the hammam that he founded still exists deep in the old city of
Damascus offering a vigorous experience to today's visitors.[26] Water
fountains provided refreshment and a way to clean the streets; public
toilets were plentiful, a contrast to the contemporary West. In
Damascus, no less than forty public toilet facilities could be counted
in the mid-1180s, with one thirty-seater facility attracting particular
praise from Ibn Jubayr.[27]

Stepping away from the central thoroughfares and the grander stone
buildings, a visitor would be drawn down much narrower streets and
passages, twisting and turning past the smaller mosques, madrasas
and marketplaces. As a major metropolis the range of trades was
considerable; we read of main markets for fruit, wheat, grain and
vegetables, supplemented by the presence of the money-changers
needed to cope with the multiple coinages that swirled around the
trade routes of the Near East.[28] Other foodstuffs had specialised districts
too, such as sugar or roasted meat, yoghurt and cheese. Clothing
markets for hats and furs were noted, as well as districts that dealt in
more exotic products such as perfumes, pearls, birds, novelties and
gifts, and ice. Some of these little enclaves had bathhouses too, hence
the Bath of the Pearlers, or the Bath of the Cheese sellers. The distinctive noises and smells of each street, along with the push and shove
of traders, pilgrims, clerics and soldiers, made for an energised community that impressed contemporary tourists; Ibn Jubayr thought the
markets 'the finest in the world'.[29]

Other essential institutions, such as orphanages, were also
commented upon by writers. Orphanages could be places of teaching,

and Ibn Jubayr observed approvingly that in contrast to his own homeland in Spain the Damascene boys learned the Quran by memory and practised writing through poetry. Thus, if they made a mistake their error would not defile the sacred text.[30] The production of books was undoubtedly stimulated by the religious institutions supported by Nur al-Din, and literature, both sacred and secular, was a prime trade in the al-Kallasa district of Damascus where there was a market for booksellers every Friday. The breathtaking calligraphy in various surviving texts testifies to the skill and technique of some of these artisans. This was also a trade practised by women; Ibn al-Athir recorded with sadness the passing of Shuhda, known as Fahkr al-Nisa, meaning 'the Pride of Women', a renowned calligrapher. Book production is also a sign and a stimulus to the creation of libraries; the Near East was, in comparison to the contemporary West, an immensely literate society, and the survival of a later Ayyubid library catalogue from Damascus gives an extraordinary glimpse into this world.[31]

A beautiful example of Nur al-Din's contribution towards the well-being of his people still exists in the old city: his *bimaristan* or hospital, founded in 1154. Wonderful wooden doors, studded with bronze nails forming geometrical astral patterns, announce an institution of real prestige. The doors were designed by a man known as al-Muhandis (the geometer), a carpenter, a stonemason, a writer on science and literature, and a man who read hadith, grammar and poetry; a powerful combination, and in its range not unrepresentative of so many amongst the creative classes of the Near East.[32] A tall *muqarnas* facade (made up of small prisms that form a honeycomb-style structure) towers above this doorway drawing the visitor into an oasis of calm after the energy of the markets outside. After walking under a spectacular square dome of descending *muqarnas*, pierced by natural light, the visitor is in a courtyard dominated by a rectangular pool flanked by four *iwans*, arched structures each leading to rooms for staff and patients. A thirteenth-century writer who learned and worked in the building recorded that Nur al-Din ensured the hospital bearing his name was endowed with numerous medical texts, indicating again the importance he attached to it, and that it was a place of study, as well as one of physical and spiritual healing. It treated men and women and also had a room for the mentally unwell, in addition to a library and teaching room. The place survived as a hospital until the late nineteenth century when it became an orphanage for girls; it is now a museum.[33]

Not all of the city was fine buildings; many of the lesser houses were built of mud and reeds, rendering them extremely vulnerable to fire. Public spaces were essential too. Areas in the south of the walled city contained the fragrant flowers and trees of the Garden of the Cat. To the north-west, either side of the River Barada, lay two large open spaces 'so green as to seem to be rolls of silk brocade, enclosed by a wall with the river between them, and bordering them is a large wood of poplars forming a very pleasant sight'. These hippodromes were suitable for archery, horse racing and for polo, a passion shared by Nur al-Din and Saladin. Even though the former has a rather austere reputation he was not entirely without a lighter side, and such was his abiding passion for polo that as Imad al-Din (Nur al-Din's and then Saladin's secretary) wrote, 'he would often go out in the dark and play by the light of candles as the day began to break and Saladin would ride out to play with him every morning. He was knowledgeable in the etiquette of the game at court and in the accepted rules.'[34]

The social elite of the Kurdish and Turkmen tribes were practically raised in the saddle and the fiercely competitive environment of the polo pitch was a favourite recreation, as well as encouraging the equestrian skills so essential in contemporary warfare.[35]

Nur al-Din's takeover of Damascus marked a significant advance in his power. For the first time since the foundation of the Latin East the cities of Aleppo, Mosul and Damascus were under the control of the same family, the Zengids, representing a serious increase in the threat level to the Franks. With Damascus firmly in his grasp, the conflict with the Christians became more aggressive. After the defeat of a Frankish force in the north in 1156, the severed heads of the slain were sent to Damascus and carried in procession around the city.[36] A subsequent truce suited both sides but when the Christians foolishly savaged Arab and Turkmen grazing their horses and cattle near Banyas, Nur al-Din was livid, partly because an oath had been broken but also because it did little for his credentials as a new local ruler. In the spring of 1157 preparations began for a campaign against 'the accursed enemies of God'. This included the decoration of the citadel and royal palace with swords, spears, armour and shields; with captured Frankish armour, and with banners, flags, drums and trumpets. In other words, a symbolic showing of the weapons of war, the means by which the conflict would be taken to the infidel. Ibn al-Qalanisi wrote that such a ceremony was unknown in Damascus (and he was from an established family in the city), but it patently excited the population who all pressed to view the spectacle and to express their admiration.[37] By the end of April they could see the results of this display when, after a resounding victory over the forces of Jerusalem, Nur al-Din called a public holiday. Once more the heads of the slain, prisoners and captured equipment were processed around Damascus to the delight of the citizens and, as Ibn al-Qalanisi wrote, manifested God's punishment on the shameless polytheists.[38]

Nur al-Din's holy war was beginning to gather momentum. Shirkuh commanded a large contingent of Turkmen warriors, said to be full of ardour for the jihad, while in Damascus itself, a public appeal for volunteers to fight met with an enthusiastic response from young men, Sufis, lawyers and others. An emphatic victory over the forces of the kingdom of Jerusalem at Jacob's Ford, just north of the Sea of Galilee (Lake Tiberias), in June 1157 offered the chance to refine further the victory-parade format. This time, captured Frankish horsemen were set in pairs upon camels, accompanied by an unfurled standard decorated with the scalps of the slain. Castellans were kept on horseback in their armour and helmets but had to carry these grotesque standards; lesser men such as foot soldiers and turcopoles, were roped together in threes and fours and bundled through the streets. Also on view were huge quantities of equipment, including something intriguingly described as 'their church with its famous apparatus'.[39] Signs of God's support and the overt humiliation of the Franks were the orders of the day. Within the writings of Ibn al-Qalanisi the language of religious conflict steps up. Nur al-Din urged proclamations to be made to the people of Damascus to commit themselves to the jihad, to fight the Franks, 'the upholders of polytheism and heresy'.[40] Those Muslims killed in the conflict were lauded as martyrs.

The geographical extent of his dominions inevitably required Nur al-Din's presence in the north, with danger from the Frankish principality of Antioch and various attacks by the Turkish sultan of Iconium. Tough a warrior as he was, in October 1157 Nur al-Din was afflicted by a severe fever. It looked to be fatal and so he summoned his brother, Nusrat al-Din, along with Shirkuh and other leading emirs. He gave Aleppo to his sibling and directed that Shirkuh was to hold Damascus as his lieutenant.[41] As the illness intensified Nur al-Din was carried by litter to Aleppo while Shirkuh hurried southwards to protect Damascus should the Franks seek to exploit this turn of events. In the end the crisis passed but it took a couple of months for Nur al-Din to recover. When he did, Shirkuh headed back north to join him in Aleppo 'in the holy war against the enemies of God'. Ibn al-Qalanisi notes how Shirkuh was received with honour and praised for his zeal; the Ayyubid warrior had risen far under the Zengid banner. This was an impressive transformation for a family that had needed to seek refuge with Zengi in the late 1130s. Two decades later their senior figure now stood as Nur al-Din's most trusted lieutenant, charged with governing one of the greatest cities in the Near East. It showed adaptability, as well as military and diplomatic talent; not a bad exemplar for the young Saladin.

Diplomacy had its place too, especially when an opponent was particularly strong or when one faced a number of threats simultaneously. The arrival of the Byzantine emperor Manuel Komnenos (r.1143–80) in northern Syria in early 1159 generated near-panic amongst all the local powers, Frankish, Armenian and Muslim. The Byzantine Empire, Greek Orthodox in faith, was well past its peak, but in contemporary terms it still represented a genuinely heavyweight entity and Manuel wished to re-establish some of the authority, both religious and political, that his predecessors had enjoyed.[42] Given the obvious power of the Greeks, Nur al-Din prudently released a number of captives from the prisons of Aleppo. Some had been there since the Second Crusade ten years before, others had arrived more recently, such as a captive from Jacob's Ford, the master of the Templars. These were the warrior monks sworn to defend Christian lands against the Muslims and who would become one of Saladin's most deadly enemies. In response to the prisoner release the Greek emperor sent robes, jewels, a brocade tent (objects of particular esteem given how long rulers of the day spent on campaign) and many horses. Of greater use to Nur al-Din was an alliance against their mutual enemies, the Seljuks of Asia Minor, although troubles back towards Constantinople drew Manuel home.[43] After the uncertainties of his illnesses Nur al-Din wanted to mark his achievement in resisting the emperor with a huge feast for his commanders and warriors.[44]

A brief period of calm ensued, not least because a series of major players died. The caliph of Baghdad passed away after a twenty-four-year reign in March 1160. A month earlier, his Shi'ite counterpart, the eleven-year-old Fatimid caliph, had died in Cairo leaving the vizier, Ibn Ruzzik, to choose a youth, al-Adid, as his successor. Ibn Ruzzik had, however, alienated many of the Egyptian nobility and he was murdered in September 1161. The vizierate, which by this stage was, de facto, the position of ultimate political and military authority in Egypt, became the focus of a bitter contest. The Fatimid state was vulnerable anyway, but when this internal power struggle started to cascade outwards to involve the Franks and Muslim Syria, the ramifications were immense. Such instability offered these ambitious neighbours the chance to transform their own standing and potentially to achieve a position of supremacy.[45]

The fight for Egypt would dominate the military scene in the Levant for decades. Put simply, relative to Syria or the kingdom of Jerusalem, Egypt was fabulously wealthy. Alexandria was, by a fair margin, the prime commercial port in the Mediterranean for trade routes from the Maghreb, the Red Sea, India, sub-Saharan Africa and the gold mines of West Africa. It was attractive to the Christian merchants of Byzantium and the Italian cities of Venice, Genoa and Pisa, as well as catering for the nearer markets of Syria and the Latin East. A contemporary Frankish historian, William of Tyre, provides this glowing description of Alexandria and, by extension, the riches of Egypt itself:

> Alexandria is most conveniently situated for carrying on extensive commerce. It has two ports that are separated from one another by a very narrow stretch of land. At the end of that tongue rises a tower of marvellous height called the Pharos. By the Nile, Alexandria receives from Upper Egypt an abundance of food supplies of every kind and, indeed, a wealth of almost every commodity. If there is anything that the country itself lacks, it is brought by ships from the lands across the sea in profuse abundance. As a result, Alexandria has the reputation of receiving a larger supply of wares of every description than any other maritime city. Whatever part of the world lacks in the matter of

pearls, spices, Oriental treasures, and foreign wares is brought hither from the two Indies; Saba, Arabia, and both the Ethiopias, as well as from Persia and other lands nearby ... People from East and West flock thither in great numbers, and Alexandria is a public market for both worlds.[46]

Whoever succeeded in gaining power in Egypt would have this at their disposal and the capability to hold sway over the eastern Mediterranean. One candidate for the vizierate was Shawar, the former governor of Upper Egypt, who had murdered Ibn Ruzzik's successor and then taken his clan's money and possessions for himself. The emergence of a rival, Dirgham, caused Shawar to flee to Syria seeking help from the court of Nur al-Din; in other words, giving the Damascene ruler a ready-made entry into the affairs of Egypt. Dirgham, meanwhile, established himself as vizier of Egypt, although in consolidating his own position he killed many other emirs, removing a layer of experienced leadership and increasing the regime's vulnerability down the line. In the short term, one potential aggressor – the kingdom of Jerusalem – had to deal with a succession issue too. On 10 February 1163, aged only thirty-two, Baldwin III died of dysentery leaving no children. The throne fell to his brother, Amalric, a tall, overweight man with receding blond hair and a taciturn disposition. He was, however, an energetic and proactive ruler who would certainly engage directly with his myriad opponents.[47]

This change of characters set the scene for the Ayyubids to emerge onto a wider political stage. Of Saladin's activities at this time we know almost nothing. In 1160 his uncle Shirkuh chose to go on the haj to Mecca, the duty of all Muslims at least once in their lives.[48] As a young noble at court, most likely based in Damascus, Saladin enjoyed games of polo and hunting. He is described as a carefree individual, contrasting with his later devotion and personal austerity. It would be logical for him to take part in some of the military expeditions of the time and we learn that he joined Shirkuh, who seems to have been far more warlike than Saladin's father, in a visit to Aleppo in the early 1150s. Saladin would likely have seen the processions of Frankish prisoners through Damascus and been exposed to the increasing intensity of jihad propaganda, both in sermons and via the physical surroundings of the city.

This was the religious and political climate in which Saladin grew up. His Kurdish clan had moved from the rural Jazira to the more densely populated land of Syria and the great city of Damascus. Through military and administrative skill and by adherence to two powerful and successful patrons they had seen their own standing grow and grow. This in turn enabled them to show patronage of their own to relatives and supporters alike. In broader terms, the complexities of the Muslim Near East were omnipresent, although Nur al-Din's developing authority had at least brought a good number of towns, regions and groups under one banner and the Zengid Empire was taking shape. The polyglot nature of the region, and its rich and complex recent history, meant the inhabitants had become accustomed to a succession of new masters who were often – as in the case of the Zengids – outsiders. The Christians of Armenia and Byzantium also had to be reckoned with and, through the prism of the holy war, so did the Franks. Yet adherence to the Sunni caliphate did not just mean fighting Christians but sometimes to an even sharper extent the Shi'ites (themselves variously subdivided) who were labelled heretics by the Sunni and therefore appropriate targets. In a modern context, fighting a jihad or a crusade tends to signal notions of extremism, concepts that by their very nature are markers of inflexibility. In the terms of twelfth-century Syria and the Holy Land, to assume such rigidity would be a mistake. Truces, alliances, agreements, betrayals, co-operation and dynastic ambition saturated the political atmosphere, delivering opportunities and flexibility to all. It was in just such an environment that Shirkuh and the Ayyubids were able to transform their fortunes.

3

Nur al-Din and the Rise of the Jihad

*'May God grant [Nur al-Din] success ... fulfilling
what is best for people ... exalt him in victory
with his army'*

In the spring of 1163, near the fortress of Hisn al-Akrad – later known
to the world as Krak des Chevaliers, the finest of all crusader castles –
Nur al-Din and his forces were utterly thrashed by the Franks. The
Zengid commander was rarely ousted in open battle and being put
roundly to flight was a profound shock; so great was the panic that
he even abandoned his own sword. Such a defeat represented a significant blow to his standing. While being careful to guard against
contemporary reports overdramatising the impact of this loss, the
reverse seems to have had a cathartic effect on the emir and prompted
him to sharpen his focus on the jihad, in both its internal and external
forms. Ibn ad-Adim, an Aleppan chronicler, reports a story in which
a man asked Nur al-Din how the sultan would ever have success
when, in his camp, one could find bottles of alcohol, hear the tambou-
rine and the flute played, and see other objects abhorred by God.
Poets scorned him: 'And do not think that glory is found in alcohol
and female singers; there is no glory except in a sword and in fighting.'[1]
A chastened Nur al-Din promised to perform penance and discarded
luxurious clothing for coarse materials, a far more appropriate image
for the holy warrior. He also abolished practices that were contrary
to divine law and punished immoral behaviour. Instructions to this
effect were dispatched to his governors forthwith.[2] He had been
fighting under the banner of the jihad for well over a decade but from
now onwards his programme of religious patronage and engagement

with holy war ramped up considerably. In doing so, he shaped much of the spiritual and strategic environment that Saladin grew up in, and which the latter was then able to take forwards.

The strategic balance between the Syrian Muslims, the Franks and the Egyptians was at a delicate point too. The exiled vizier Shawar offered Nur al-Din one-third of Egypt's vast revenues if he helped him to regain authority and the Syrians kept an army there to support him – a tantalising prospect, but one that needed careful thought. On the one hand Nur al-Din was worried about Shawar's trustworthiness and the scale of the commitment required, but equally he could appreciate the potential to transform the geopolitical situation in the Near East. Eventually, he agreed to act; the leader of the expedition was to be Shirkuh. 'He alone was fit for this mighty matter', and was said to be very energised by the prospect.[3]

In following these events we have, alongside the Muslim sources, the voice of a particularly close observer from the Christian perspective. William of Tyre was the great chronicler of the twelfth-century crusader states. Born in the Holy Land, but educated extensively in Europe, he returned home to hold high church offices and to act as a trusted royal diplomat. He later rose to become archbishop of Tyre and royal chancellor, and compiled his lengthy narrative between 1170 and his death in 1185.[4] He was, therefore, an ideally placed contemporary: often an eyewitness, and certainly in a position to talk to many of those involved. He also provided engaging physical descriptions and character sketches of several of the central players. Shirkuh was praised for his energy and military abilities, for his considerable generosity 'far beyond the resources of his patrimony', and he was beloved by his followers for this munificence. The emir was depicted as short but very stout with a cataract in one eye, and as a man capable of huge endurance even in his later years. William also commented that Shirkuh had risen by merit from lowly origins to his current wealth and power.[5]

In May 1164 Shirkuh's forces invaded Egypt and soon enabled their ally to take hold of the vizierate once more. Not for the last time, however, Shawar showed himself to be deeply untrustworthy and now he tried to throw off the shackles of Damascene power. Thus, much to the delight of the Franks he turned for help to Jerusalem. Fears that Syrian control of Egypt would prevent 'Christians from entering

Jerusalem by land and sea' had prompted a flurry of desperate appeals to western Europe seeking military assistance; this was a chance to prevent such a disaster.[6]

King Amalric hurried into Egypt to assist Vizier Shawar, and in July 1164 together they besieged Shirkuh at Bilbais, around fifty-five kilometres north-east of Cairo. This was an unpromising defensive site with no ditch and only low walls. Nonetheless, Shirkuh fought ferociously and managed to hold out for three months before agreeing to return to Syria. As his troops departed from the town, a visiting crusader asked the emir if he feared being surrounded and attacked at this vulnerable moment. Shirkuh responded that if this happened 'By God, I would wield my sword and not one of our men would be killed until he had killed several of them.' He said that Nur al-Din would then attack and take Frankish lands, eliminating any survivors. The crusader made the sign of the cross and said 'We used to wonder at the Franks of these lands and their exaggerated description of you and their fear of you. Now we excuse them!'[7]

It is around this time we get the first indications of Shirkuh's wider ambitions. Interestingly, the Franks registered this sentiment, and a letter to the West in September 1164 stated that Shirkuh wanted to claim Egypt 'for himself', an opinion repeated by William of Tyre who commented that this was so 'in spite of the sultan and the caliph' (meaning Shawar and al-Adid respectively).[8] A subsequent Muslim author pointedly noted that now Shirkuh had seen Egypt and understood its vulnerability, the 'ambition to win the land implanted in his heart'.[9] Quite how this would stand in respect of his relationship with Nur al-Din is unclear. Was it as a loyal lieutenant, as an independent ally, or as a potential competitor? At this early stage, the first of these roles seems the most likely, but Shirkuh's interest and determination to conquer Egypt would only grow and grow, a desire that came increasingly to involve and influence his nephew Saladin.

Nur al-Din, meanwhile, had multiple aims for his own campaigns in the north. In part he wished to avenge the humiliation of Hisn al-Akrad the previous year, in part he wished to distract Amalric from Egypt and to prevent him defeating Shirkuh, let alone taking control of the country. Nur al-Din soon showed the resources available to him as the ruler of Aleppo and Damascus, as well as the reach of his appeal across the Jazira, as he gathered troops from Mosul, Mardin and Hisn Kayfa. The lord of the last of these towns had been rather sceptical of Nur al-Din's approach, dismissing his excessive prayers, fasting and aggressive battle plans. Initially this man declined to join the campaign but almost immediately changed his mind, much to the confusion of his senior nobles who asked him to explain; he responded:

> If I do not aid him [Nur al-Din] my subjects will rebel … he has written to the local ascetics telling them what the Muslims have met from the Franks, the killing and the captivity they have suffered, and begging the support of their prayers and asking them to urge the Muslims to take up the struggle. Each one of these men has taken his place in public, with his supporters and followers, and is reading out Nur al-Din's letters, while weeping and delivering curses against me. I have to go to him.[10]

In other words, Nur al-Din's message of holy war was starting to gain traction across parts of the Near East.

With his forces assembled, in August 1164 Nur al-Din's siege engines began to pound the castle of Harim, to the north-east of Antioch. Two months later the castle surrendered, and with his victory burnished by the capture of Prince Bohemond III of Antioch and Count Raymond III of Tripoli, Nur al-Din had reaffirmed his credentials to lead the holy war.[11] Not to miss an opportunity the Syrian ruler quickly headed south and, exploiting Amalric's absence in Egypt, in late October he besieged the long-disputed castle of Banyas on the north-eastern edge of the kingdom of Jerusalem. A letter to the king of France bemoaned the situation: Nur al-Din 'can attack [Antioch, Tripoli, Jerusalem and Egypt] all four at one and the same time if he so desires, so great is the number of his dogs'.[12] Events at Harim and now Banyas had, from Nur al-Din's perspective, served their purpose in that they forced Amalric to leave Egypt. With Shirkuh headed back to Syria, Vizier Shawar was left in control of Bilbais and, more importantly, without foreign presence in Egypt – for the time being at least. He had hardly endeared himself to either side, yet both Syrians and Franks had grasped the wider benefits of working with this fickle figure who could – as he kept promising – deliver such wealth and advantage to whomsoever his ally happened to be.

Over the next decade or so Nur al-Din did much to energise the spiritual agenda of the Sunni Near East, laying the real groundwork of the holy war for Saladin to build upon. As the jihad began to gather momentum, and with, for example, the defeat of the Second Crusade, Muslim hopes of regaining the holy city of Jerusalem became plausible. Jerusalem is, of course, central to all three monotheistic religions as a temporal sacred space and as an eternal space. For Christians, the presence, resurrection and expected return of Christ provide a permanent link to the site. For Jews, the city is the location of the Old Temple and its centrality is made paramount in the Jewish literary tradition, including apocalyptic works. For Muslims the city is held to be the third most important city in Islam after Mecca and Medina, the places of the Prophet's birth and burial. Jerusalem was the location of the Prophet's Night Journey into the heavens, marked by the Dome of the Rock as the place from which he ascended.[13] It is also important as the site of the resurrection on the Last Day. References to the Holy Land (*al-ard al-muqaddasa*) in the Quran, as well as to the al-Aqsa Mosque, the farthest place of worship, along with many appearances in collections of hadith, reinforce this. Furthermore, associations with prophets of the past such as Abraham (buried in nearby Hebron) and David all combined to make this a place of huge sanctity and a focus for pilgrimage; it was also a notably meritorious site of burial. It was, therefore, unacceptable to Muslims for the Franks, in the language used by both sides, to pollute the holy places; there was a duty to restore Jerusalem to Islam.[14]

To transmit his message the emir made particularly striking use of buildings, monuments and sacred objects. In the city of Hama, he initiated a series of inter-related projects that displayed his ideas of Islamic unity and holy war. He created a complex consisting of a large mosque, a madrasa and a *bimaristan*, as well as the huge waterwheels that still sit on the banks of the River Orontes, a playground for the hefty local river rats. The architecture of the mosque incorporated objects taken from the crusaders, better to broadcast successes over their enemies; a seven-metre dedicatory inscription also survives. The intent of such inscriptions was to act as a giant advertisement: beginning with the name of God and the profession of faith, the Hama text described Nur al-Din himself as a 'fighter for the faith', 'keeper of the outposts', 'saviour of the public', 'vanquisher of the rebels' and 'killer of the infidels and polytheists'. Unlike the titles given to his father Zengi, those of Nur al-Din were Arabic, rather than Turkish and Persian in origin, indicating where his political interests lay. He affirmed this shift in artistic terms as well. Most public inscriptions under the Seljuks had used a Kufic script, a form that was not always easy to make out. Almost as soon as he started receiving honorific titles from the caliph of Baghdad, Nur al-Din adopted a cursive script which was much more legible and helped to signify and to push the Sunni revival and the orthodox message that both he and the Abbasid caliph so desired.[15] The Hama mosque also sported prominent Quranic inscriptions relating the sacrifice of home and possessions, intolerance to non-Muslims and commitment to the jihad. Complementing this message was a beautiful wooden *minbar* (pulpit), covered in geometric designs and calligraphy, dating from this period. Inscriptions emphasise a testimony of the faith and note the patronage of Nur al-Din himself.[16]

Around the same time (probably 1168) Nur al-Din commissioned another *minbar* in Aleppo. Once completed this beautiful object was placed in the Great Mosque there, but this was meant only as a temporary home. Nur al-Din was quoted as saying 'we have made this to set up in Jerusalem'; its ultimate destination was intended to be the al-Aqsa Mosque, although Nur al-Din himself would not live to realise his dream. This stunning piece of monumental art was a clever and powerfully constructed statement of intent. The work of five Aleppan artisans, the *minbar* contained no less than twenty-five different geometric patterns on its panels and every surface was smothered with various shapes as well as inscriptions, such as:[17]

> May God make his [Nur al-Din's] victories glorious and preserve his power; may He raise his signs and spread in the two sides of the earth his standards and emblems, may He strengthen the supporters of his reign and humiliate those ungrateful of his favour; may He grant him conquest at his own hands and delight his eyes with victory and closeness to Him.[18]

Nur al-Din's explicit wish that God grant him the honour of taking the holy city gave the *minbar* a specific purpose, and its construction acted as an offering to God to allow him this triumph. The Spanish Muslim pilgrim Ibn Jubayr saw the *minbar* as he passed through Aleppo in 1184. He wrote that: 'the art of ornamental carving had exhausted itself in its endeavours on the pulpit for never in any city have I seen a pulpit like it or of such wondrous workmanship. The woodwork stretches from it to the *mihrab* beautifully adorning all its sides in the same marvellous fashion ... the eyes consider [this] the most beautiful sight in the world.'[19] In conjunction with a particularly talented group of skilled geometers this artistic florescence was an interesting side effect of Nur al-Din's actions.[20] The emir himself was known to be a fine calligrapher, a skill immensely valued in contemporary Islam given that 'writing was the means by which the divine scriptures were transmitted to humanity'.[21] In September 1167 he dedicated a beautiful copy of the Quran to the Damascene madrasa where he would later be entombed. This is a rich piece of workmanship, parts of which survive in museums in Damascus, Istanbul and Dallas. Golden patterned frames house chapter headings: decorative gold, red and blue ink palmettes embellish these rectangles with the main parts of the text produced in a clear cursive script, easily legible for reciters.[22] Such a gift both reflected his personal piety and enhanced the prestige of his own madrasas.

Contemporary politics was not simply a question of fighting the Christians but about asserting the pre-eminence of Sunni orthodoxy over the Shi'ites as well. To get people to engage in warfare, both spiritual and physical, on the scale and commitment needed was a tall order. It required both religious and material incentives, and clear leadership. Nur al-Din was astute enough to use his broad patronage to connect with intellectual, social and visual media, demonstrating an impressive ability to direct and deliver his message.

A crucial figure in the creation of this material was Ibn Asakir, one of the foremost Sunni scholars in Syria and an arch exponent of jihad writings against both internal and external enemies of Sunni Islam. Probably in a spirit of religious intensification after the disaster of 1163, Nur al-Din commissioned him to write his text *Forty Hadith for Inciting Jihad*.[23] Hadith are statements attributed to or about Muhammad and number in their thousands; concise collections were, therefore, popular because they were easy to memorise. Ibn Asakir's compendium could be directed against a broad range of enemies. and enjoined his audience, through these special texts, to fulfil their duty and to emulate Muhammad as an exemplar of jihad. Given that Nur al-Din himself spent much of his career in conflict with Muslims, both Sunni and Shi'ite, he needed easily understandable hadith (some of which include passages from the Quran as well) which could be relayed in public teaching sessions and then out through the many scholars and preachers who were added to the armies of the day. Such texts also, of course, had the effect of underpinning and endorsing Nur al-Din's wars. Ibn Asakir wrote:

> [Nur al-Din] the just king, the ascetic, the jihad fighter, and the garri-soned warrior – may God grant him success in that which is proper, fulfilling what is best for people, grant him favour against the recalci-trant, exalt him in victory with his army, and support him with aid – expressed his desire that I collect for him forty hadith relating to jihad that have clear texts and uninterrupted sound chains of transmission so that they could stimulate the valiant jihad fighters, the ones with strong determination and mighty arms, with sharp swords and piercing spears, and stir them up to uproot the unbelievers and tyrants who, because of their unbelief, have terrorised the land, proliferated oppres-sion and corruption – may God pour on them all kinds of torture, for He is all-watching.[24]

The texts themselves elaborate on four themes: the importance of the obligation of jihad to God and his messenger, Muhammad; the ghastly punishments for those who do not carry out these everlasting obligations; the rewards for those who participate in and even support the jihad; and the requirements that as good Muslims jihad fighters must fulfil prior to waging holy war. Hadith 31 says: 'Fight the poly-theists with your wealth, with your lives, with your tongues.' This shows the heart of Nur al-Din's purpose, to rally all of society to help, be they scholars, artisans, sponsors, as well as those directly engaged in armed conflict.[25] Perhaps in reward for this composition, in 1170 Nur al-Din ordered the construction of a school in Damascus dedicated to the study of hadith, and under Ibn Asakir this institution became the intellectual heart of his holy war. It also engaged closely in the production of texts known as *Fada'il al-Quds*, or *Merits of Jerusalem*, a literary genre that proliferated at this time and was impor-tant in the counter-crusade because it did much to emphasise the sanctity of the holy city.[26]

Many other poets wrote in praise of Nur al-Din, such as Ibn al-Munir, who lauded the emir as well as worrying should he perish: 'You are always a sword that does not become rusty, and you are always active in striking ... O Nur al-Din, the horizons will darken if you do not illuminate them.'[27]

Amongst the attributes most admired and required of a Muslim ruler of the age was the provision of justice. The 'Mirrors for Princes' advice books laid heavy emphasis on this basic tenet, supporting the hadith: 'The reward for a single hour of justice is as great as that for sixty years of pious worship, and the punishment for a single hour of injustice is as great as that for sixty years of disobedience.' A text composed in Aleppo around 1165, probably based on a Persian model, wrote at length on the importance of justice: 'Know that every rule marked by justice brings happiness and good fortune in both worlds, and any rule marked by injustice brings wretchedness in both worlds.'[28] Nur al-Din embraced this with genuine enthusiasm, creating a House of Justice in Damascus as soon as he assumed control of the city and sitting in session twice a week on Tuesday and Thursday. The knowledge that their leader was accessible and, by all accounts, fair, did much to enhance his standing with the wider population and showed his concern for correct Islamic procedure. His titles also reflected this with 'al-malik al-adil' ('the just king') coming at the top of his list of honorifics soon after he took power in Damascus, and another, 'protector of the oppressed against oppressors', speaking to the same theme.[29]

Nur al-Din's concern with good government meant the circle of people around him was important and he drew upon a cosmopolitan group. Most visible in our story was Imad al-Din al-Isfahani, a widely travelled man of immense intellectual distinction whose ability to move amongst and across the courts of the Near East testifies to yet another aspect of the fluidity and permeability of contemporary life.[30] Born in Isfahan in Persia in 1125, his uncle (who died only a few years later) had known Ayyub and Shirkuh which, when they rose to positions of power in Syria, provided a connection that proved both fortuitous and fruitful for all concerned. He studied jurisprudence in Baghdad and collected poetry, as well as acting as an important administrator. The vicissitudes of regional politics saw him leave Baghdad in 1167 and move to Damascus. Connections from his student days brought him into the administration of Nur al-Din for whom he also wrote jihad poetry. At this point he became reacquainted with the Ayyubids, meeting and forming a lifelong friendship with Saladin, as we will see later. Characteristic confidence saw him write: 'I had thought the craft of secretary, especially in the chancery, difficult, until I read the letters and documents coming in from other parts and found them very feeble.' He also informs us that he created a new style of chancery practice which 'bewitched and astounded' rulers far and wide.[31] Notwithstanding this robust assessment of his own abilities, he was a well-connected diplomat, a great writer as well as a hugely powerful and effective government official. In the course of the 1160s Saladin himself briefly acquired some administrative experience succeeding his elder brother Turanshah as the *shihna* or police chief of Damascus, an event that attracted the praise of a local poet, doubtless seeking patronage from the up-and-coming young nobleman.[32] Later western writers knew that Saladin had held such a role, although it was described in disparaging terms as the licensing of prostitutes as a device to make money.[33]

As we saw earlier, Saladin had served with Shirkuh as a youth and at some point this seems to have metamorphosed towards an involvement with the close circle of Nur al-Din himself, 'so he was always at his side whether he was away or in residence at court'. Such a position gave him the vantage point to absorb the gathering impetus of the jihad, to witness the dispensation of patronage and justice, and to watch the calculation and complexities of high-level diplomacy. Nur al-Din was a great ruler, and for the observant young Kurd, he offered a lot to admire.

He had blended the political ambitions of a warlord with the aims and image of a holy warrior. His intensive patronage of the religious classes did much to create this image. But this environment was not simply about Nur al-Din; those around him, be they clerics, administrators or servants, were all part of his rule and some of the family connections and relationships formed here became vital to Saladin's own success in later years. The jihad gave both legitimacy and purpose to Nur al-Din's actions, particularly after the defeat at Hisn al-Akrad, and the level of resource poured into the support of the holy war and the recovery of Jerusalem had a visible effect on the environment across Muslim Syria, in Aleppo, Mosul, Hama and al-Raqqa and, most especially, in Damascus.

4

Shirkuh, Saladin and the Conquest of Egypt

*'Do not merely cut the snake's tail and
leave the snake to escape. My wish is that
you also cut the head along with the tail'*

All the while Shirkuh, as Nur al-Din's military commander and 'a man bent on destroying the Christians', continued to take the fight to the Franks, capturing a castle near the port of Sidon and the cave fortress of al-Habis Jaldak to the east of the River Jordan. Yet the lure of Egypt remained; Beha al-Din (an important official and close associate of Saladin) wrote of the commander 'dreaming of how to return to Egypt' and being 'ambitious to seize the country'. Ibn Khallikan, the later compiler of a vast biographical dictionary, mentioned 'hopes [of the] prospect of founding there an empire for himself'. Intriguingly, a contemporary Christian source echoes, and indeed, amplifies this point. The Frankish author William of Tyre was especially well informed about events in Egypt at this time, and he claimed that Shirkuh went in person to the caliph of Baghdad in order to boost his case. The emir gave a fulsome description of Egypt's inestimable wealth and the annual revenues available; he described the weakness and sloth of the people, and he emphasised the challenge posed by the Shi'ites to the authority and interpretation of the Sunni Abbasid caliphate. None of this would have been news to the caliph, of course, but the general's purpose was to get the spiritual leader of the Sunni world to encourage support for his campaign to Egypt; in this he duly succeeded.[1]

By the autumn of 1166 it appears that Nur al-Din was in no position to refuse his commander's wishes. 'Nur al-Din disliked the plan but when he saw how serious Shirkuh was about going it was impossible to do other than send a force with him.'[2] There is a creeping sense that such was his strength, Shirkuh was starting to act as his own man; not yet an outright challenger to his leader, but an individual whose ambitions could not be ignored. A throwaway line from Nur al-Din's great admirer Ibn al-Athir, writing in his *History of the Atabegs of Mosul*, described Shirkuh as possessing such influence that he was thought to be a partner in government with Nur al-Din.[3]

In early 1167 a large Syrian force headed deep into Egypt and set up camp at Giza, near Cairo on the western side of the Nile. The Franks had anticipated this crisis and quickly summoned all their available troops, pushing into Egypt, past Bilbais to reach Fustat, known later as Old Cairo. Fustat was the first Islamic capital of Egypt (founded 640), until al-Qahira (Cairo) was established adjacent to it in the latter half of the tenth century. It nonetheless remained the primary centre for commerce and manufacturing, specialising in ceramics, glass and paper with a busy port that attracted traders from far and wide. The city itself was densely populated with dark, narrow streets wriggling between brick tenement blocks up to seven storeys high. Public hygiene was legendarily terrible, with latrines that drained directly into the Nile, which also happened to be the main water supply, polluting it so badly that the fish died and putrefied.[4]

At this point, both Frankish and Syrian forces were outside Cairo. Vizier Shawar was so fearful that Shirkuh would seize power if the Christians departed that he struck a deal with them. Such was the level of anxiety in Cairo that the terms of the agreement were said to be a perpetual and inviolable peace, a controversial concept in Islam, with some jurists favouring a ten-year maximum for a *hudna* (meaning armistice or peace).[5] Underpinning this were, probably unsustainable, promises of huge payments of annual tribute. Amalric shook hands on this arrangement with Shawar but, mistrusting the vizier, he sent a representative to meet the caliph himself. Count Hugh of Caesarea was one of a number of Frankish nobles, perhaps third-generation settlers, who spoke fluent Arabic. This contradicts any impression that the Christians remained aloof from the local population, and reflects that interaction with the Muslims took many forms beyond just warfare.[6] William of Tyre talked to Count Hugh at length and this permitted him to provide a remarkably detailed narrative because, as he wrote, 'to have an accurate understanding of all this will surely be of no slight advantage to my readers'. For us, it shows what was at stake between the two sides and gives an insight into the realm that Shirkuh seemed so determined to acquire for himself. William also enjoyed telling his readers of the splendour of the caliphal palaces. He himself was soon to visit Constantinople where he saw buildings of astounding beauty and riches, but the great Christian metropolis was moderately well known to westerners after the advent of the crusades. Cairo, in contrast, would have been unfamiliar to almost everyone, and in fact the campaigns of 1167 and 1168 were the only occasions Frankish armies reached or entered the city in the history of the crusades.

In accordance with a diplomatic mission, the guests were steered well clear of the less salubrious area of Fustat and instead were guided to the caliphal palace complex. As intended, the polychrome splendour of the decorations – marble columns, gilded ceilings, lavish fish-pools and an assortment of beautiful, brightly coloured exotic birds – thrilled and awed the visitors. Multiple buildings and courtyards led to the inner palace where they were confronted with a sumptuous set of curtains embroidered with gold and pearls. Shawar immediately pros-trated himself on the ground and after three demonstrations of subser-vience the curtains whisked open to reveal Caliph al-Adid seated on a golden throne and surrounded by his chief counsellors.

The caliph was described as an affable young man, aged about eighteen, tall, with a dark complexion and a slight beard. Following a brief discussion, he duly agreed to the treaty. But Hugh requested the arrangement be confirmed with a handshake. To suggest that the caliph might deign to touch a foreign envoy provoked incomprehen-sion amongst the courtiers, yet Shawar, realising the need to give way, insisted. Al-Adid extended his gloved hand, but Hugh intimated this still conveyed a lack of sincerity. Finally, 'with extreme unwillingness, as if it detracted from his majesty, yet with a slight smile which greatly aggrieved the Egyptians, he put his uncovered hand into that of Hugh' to seal the agreement. The envoys duly returned to the Frankish camp bearing generous gifts.[7]

After a period of skirmishing the Christians and their Egyptian allies managed to cross the Nile and Shirkuh retreated many miles south-wards. Battle was finally joined far upriver at al-Babayn, important as the first occasion we see Saladin taking a leading role in warfare.[8] Shirkuh appointed him as commander of the central cohort, the group expected to absorb a charge from the Frankish heavy cavalry. The Christian horsemen duly smashed into the Muslim troops, but Shirkuh had asked Saladin to give way and in doing so, to break up the cohesion of the Christian charge. Once dispersed, Shirkuh could then come in from the flank with his own heavy cavalry and rout the Franks. The scheme worked perfectly with, ironically, Hugh of Caesarea being taken prisoner.[9]

The Syrians moved quickly to capitalise on this success; they headed north to the Mediterranean coast and entered Alexandria. Shirkuh extracted an undertaking from the population that neither he nor his troops would be handed over to their enemy. Shawar countered by trying to barter with the city elite and setting the surrender of Saladin and the Turkish heavy troops against big financial incentives. He received a crisp response: 'God forbid that we should surrender Muslims to Franks and Isma'ilis [Shi'ites]; this shall never be', a reaction that highlights some of the tensions created by Shawar having Christian allies; it also underlines the point that the Sunnis were the majority denomination in Alexandria.[10]

Shirkuh had slipped out of the city to leave Saladin in charge; this was his first major test and it proved a tough challenge. Frankish catapults pounded the walls for weeks and the Christians used ships' masts to construct a huge siege tower. Pisan ships prevented supplies arriving by sea and the land forces barred foodstuffs from coming down the Nile. Saladin had to work hard to keep morale going and William of Tyre praised his considerable generosity to the poor and the wounded.[11] Eventually, Shirkuh realised that he could neither take Cairo nor relieve the siege of Alexandria and so he decided to negotiate for peace. Hugh of Caesarea remained his prisoner and the Frank was brought before him to discuss a possible deal. This may well be the event that yielded the physical description of the Ayyubid warlord, and the conversation is recounted in some detail. Shirkuh is represented as admitting his ambition and greed: 'I frankly acknowledge that I, eager for glory like all mortals, was attracted by the wealth of the kingdom and relying upon the helpless character of the native population, at one time conceived the hope that this realm might sometime fall into my hands.' While this feels too neat a series of sins for a

Muslim warlord in a Christian chronicle, we have seen that the emir harboured designs on Egypt and registered that the country was certainly wealthy and not especially strong. Shirkuh saw the need to withdraw from Alexandria and wanted Hugh to act as an intermediary with King Amalric. The proposal provided for the end of the siege, for Saladin and his men to go free and the subsequent departure of Shirkuh and all the Syrian troops from Egypt. The defenders of the city and their attackers, formerly at war, now mingled freely with one another, a phenomenon that may seem strange but was sometimes seen after the peaceful resolution of a siege. They also witnessed an exceptionally rare event – a Frankish banner flying above the ancient Pharos lighthouse. Excepting a couple of days during the crusade of King Peter I of Cyprus in 1365, this was the only occasion prior to the British occupation of the late nineteenth century that this great port fell under Christian control.

Alexandria was back in Egyptian hands on 4 August 1167. Vizier Shawar victoriously paraded into the city and promptly imposed heavy financial penalties as a punishment for assisting the Syrians. Saladin meanwhile went to Amalric's camp where he was 'treated with all respect and furnished with a guard to protect him from insults that might be offered to him by audacious spirits'. The Kurd was, in effect, a high-status hostage until the Christians were ready to march away. It is hard to think of a moment in the history of the crusades when the Franks held such a distinguished detainee (even at this stage in Saladin's career) from the Muslim Near East. It is unclear whether the insults mentioned were from supporters of Shawar, or simply because Saladin was a Muslim. In any event, his relationship with Amalric seemed cordial enough because he later recalled the king in fond terms in a letter to Amalric's son, Baldwin IV, after the monarch died in 1174.[12]

While the Franks were to leave the countryside, a garrison remained in Cairo. As Ibn al-Athir noted, Caliph al-Adid's role in this had been purely symbolic; he was effectively powerless. Shirkuh returned to Syria 'having added to his strong desire to win the country'.[13] Nur al-Din, however, needed to keep a bigger picture in mind. As well as events in Egypt and war with the Franks, the imposition and extension of his authority over the archipelago of ethnic and regional groupings of northern Syria, the Jazira and beyond, remained a constant juggling act. From time to time emirs would rebel, local lords would look to him for protection against others, while the need to give lands and rewards to supporters meant either further conquests or confronting and dispossessing those within his existing orbit. All the while, however, Egypt stood as a tempting, paradigm-shifting prospect, waiting for the Franks or the Syrians to make their next attempt to win this great prize.

From time to time in history we can see the effect of good or bad fortune, of careful planning, of duplicity or good faith. We can also see moments of error; pure poor decision-making that has calamitous consequences. Amalric's next invasion of Egypt, in late 1168, was just such an episode. Muslim sources indicate that some of the Franks in Cairo told the king the city was ripe to fall. He supposedly responded that it would be foolish to attempt to take it because the people would simply give it to Shirkuh and 'that means death to the Franks and their expulsion from the lands of Syria'.[14] Remaining satisfied with an annual payment and a buffer against Nur al-Din's dominance of the country seemed a good enough position to be in, for the short term at least. But this proved not to be the case.

Christian sources round out the picture considerably, adding anger and moral condemnation to the decision to attack, not least because the Franks were in the process of successfully negotiating a joint invasion of Egypt with the Byzantine emperor Manuel Komnenos. The support of this international superpower would theoretically transform their chances of victory and bring about the conquest of Egypt or the imposition of a more permanent form of Christian authority. In spite of this, a group within the royal court persuaded Amalric to attack on his own, without waiting for the Greeks. There was also the matter of breaking the oath obtained with such ceremony from the caliph by Hugh of Caesarea. In other words, two very sound reasons existed as to why no invasion should take place. The culprits were the Knights Hospitaller, an organisation of warrior-monks sworn to defend the Holy Land. Their eccentric leader had embarked upon an aggressive castle-building policy that plunged the Order into debt. If they took the town of Bilbais and its surrounding area this would provide them with vital income. Many advised that 'Egypt had kept good faith and did not deserve such treatment', but the hawks won the day and in late October 1168 the invasion began.[15]

On 4 November the Franks ripped into Bilbais. If the decision to attack Egypt had been poor, then the Franks' behaviour here vastly compounded it. The populace was put to the sword; men of fighting age were slaughtered wholesale, everyone else was enslaved and the place stripped of all movables. This was a sack perpetrated with a savagery not seen for decades. Episodes of this sort were often the consequence of a long and bitter siege, but no such engagement had taken place here; it was a matter of pure greed.[16]

A few days later Amalric's troops arrived at the edge of Cairo but their conduct had only stiffened subsequent resistance. The Cairenes, quite plausibly, feared a repeat of events at Bilbais and predictably enough Caliph al-Adid appealed to Nur al-Din. One Muslim commentator suggested that had the Franks not destroyed Bilbais in such a vicious fashion they would have been able to take Cairo.[17]

Vizier Shawar panicked at the Frankish approach. He ordered the commercial centre of Fustat emptied of its goods and inhabitants and then set the city on fire to prevent the Christians taking such an asset.[18] He did not, however, have time to move the ships of the Egyptian navy. In spite of being far from the sea Fustat was the main base and construction yard for the Fatimid fleet, and the destruction of these vessels created a long-term problem. Meanwhile to the north a Frankish fleet had taken the town of Tinnis, adding yet more pressure on the Egyptian regime. Vizier Shawar plunged into frantic deal-making mode and he tried hard to persuade the Franks to accept huge money payments to make peace. The lure was taken but with Fustat still burning and its population dispersed it was hard to raise the cash. Notwithstanding this set of negotiations, he was, all the time, also reaching out to the Syrians, offering Shirkuh one-third of the country's revenues to come and drive the Franks away and then stay to protect him.

As before, Nur al-Din and Shirkuh could appreciate the high stakes. Amalric's invasion was an unexpected move and they now reacted rapidly, although Nur al-Din was, as usual, required to maintain order in Syria. Shirkuh took 2,000 of the elite heavy cavalry; he also signed up 6,000 men from the enlisted cavalry, each with a twenty dinars bonus payment, as well as his own elite Kurdish regiment, the Asadiyya.[19] Given his involvement in the previous Egyptian campaign, Saladin was expected to take part, yet sources suggest that he was profoundly unwilling to do so, citing the stress of the siege of Alexandria and a lack of money and equipment. Neither his uncle nor his overlord took much notice of this and told him that he was coming along regardless, although they did provide him with some material resources. This is an odd episode to read. Showing the hero of Islam not wanting to fight is a curious line to take, although it may be a way of downplaying his later achievements in Egypt by depicting him as a reluctant invader, thereby removing any suggestion of a long-term ambition to rule the country.[20] As with so many of these situations there is a lot of second-guessing as to the agenda of the writer. Every source had his or her own purposes, patron and audience to work around. In the case of a man of such historic achievements as Saladin it can become an understandable compulsion to read too much into a particular narrative moment; it is, as ever, a balance between evaluation and subjective judgement. In this case, it might be that he just did not wish to be involved. With the benefit of hindsight, though, this campaign was to be transformative for the Ayyubids.

Shirkuh left Ras al-Ma, the main Syrian muster point thirty miles south of Damascus, on 17 December. The Franks remained outside Cairo, waiting for Vizier Shawar to pay them off. It seems they had little strategic vision beyond assuming that the initial shock of their invasion would deliver Cairo. When this stalled there was no Plan B; the controversy over the campaign (with the Templars refusing to take part) hardly helped. It was blindingly obvious that Shirkuh would appear soon, and once news of his advance reached the Christians, they duly slunk back to Jerusalem.[21]

Egypt's deliverance from a second Frankish invasion in two years merited proper acknowledgement. Al-Adid met Shirkuh at Cairo on 8 January 1169 and gave him a splendid robe of honour, the quintessential symbol of recognition in the Muslim world. But for Vizier Shawar, this was the end of the line. He had turned, weaved and triangulated so many times between the Franks, the Syrians and within his own lands that his integrity was in tatters. Stalling on promised rewards to the Syrian army meant that he had finally overstepped the mark. The ultimate demise of the vizier is a mystery. One writer claimed that he planned to murder Shirkuh and Saladin and to use their troops to defend the land from the Franks, but the plot was discovered and he was killed. Others placed a more direct onus on Shirkuh in deciding to eliminate the isolated vizier, with some writers adding Saladin as an active player who seized the mercurial official and brought the prisoner to his uncle. When Caliph al-Adid heard of this he chose to put his hopes in the invaders; he asked for Shawar's head, and on 18 January the vizier was killed.[22]

While the Syrian forces were patently the best-armed troops in Cairo, they were, by reason of serious numerical inferiority, potentially vulnerable. The removal of a vizier in such circumstances triggered deep instability. A fearful Shirkuh astutely distracted a gathering mob by encouraging them to ransack Shawar's palace. In the meantime, he went to the caliph who, thinking of his own self-preservation, promptly appointed the portly Kurdish warlord as vizier and commander of the army and invested him with further robes of honour. Foreigners and/or non-Shi'ites had held the role before, but coming in as the head of an invading force was a different scenario. Shirkuh rapidly regained the vizier's palace and started to cement his status by appointing his own followers to govern the provinces and assigning them lands.[23]

With the title of the highest secular authority in Egypt now his, Shirkuh held an extraordinary position. Those in his entourage could appreciate this advance and also the chance to enjoy the associated rewards. Poems both celebrated his ongoing achievement and also saw it as part of a journey towards Jerusalem, reflecting the message that was pulsing through Nur al-Din's religious revival:

> You [Shirkuh] liberated Egypt and I hope that while you are a liberator of Egypt, you will ease the way to liberate Jerusalem.
> We raised our hands to God in thankfulness, since Islam will not be harmed because of you.
> In every home of the Franks you will find a wailing woman; because of what struck them they spend their nights in grief.
> You have saved Muslims from the evil of Shawar.
> So consider just how much you have achieved for the party of God [Hizbullah].
> He [Shawar] is the one who made the Franks aspire to the lands of Islam, until they reached the level of confidently putting forth their ambitions.

He [Shirkuh] returned the caliphate to the Abassids; leave the claimant
   [of the Fatimid caliphate] to meet the worst enemy.
Do not merely cut the snake's tail off and leave the snake to escape.
My wish is that you also cut off the head along with the tail.[24]

For the Franks, the success of Shirkuh was the realisation of their
very worst fears. As William of Tyre wrote so eloquently:

O blind cupidity of men! From a quiet state of peace into what a
turbulent and anxious condition has an immoderate desire for possessions plunged us! All the resources of Egypt and its immediate wealth
served our needs; the frontiers of our realm were safe on that side;
there was no enemy to be feared from the south. The sea afforded a
safe and peaceful passage for those wishing to come to us ... our people
could trade under advantageous conditions. On their part the Egyptians
brought to the realm foreign riches ... the large sums spent by them
every year among us enriched the fiscal treasury. But now, all things
have changed for the worse ... Wherever I turn I find only reasons for
fear and uneasiness ... all the regions around us are subject to the
enemy, and the neighbouring kingdoms are making preparations to
destroy us.[25]

Nur al-Din's reaction to these events is intriguing. While he wanted
to deny the Franks the strategic and financial advantages of Egypt,
his relationship with the openly ambitious Shirkuh was suddenly and
sharply at issue. The Kurd's rapid acquisition of the vizierate and the
huge power that came with such a role constituted a tense, potentially
toxic, combination. Ibn Abi Tayy wrote that Nur al-Din nullified
Shirkuh's and Saladin's landholdings in Syria, presumably as a sign of
his anxiety.[26]

Shirkuh set about ruling, with Saladin taking on a senior administrative post. But the new vizier had barely settled into his role when,
on 22 March 1169, he succumbed to an illness brought on by overeating.
The Kurdish warrior had a reputation for a huge appetite with a
particular predilection for rich meats. Excessive indulgence provoked
agonising bouts of indigestion, complicated further by serious throat
abscesses. Coupled with his substantial weight, the combination swiftly
carried him to his grave.[27]

Shirkuh's interest in Egypt dated from the campaigns of 1164 and 1167 and the sources give us a sense of his intentions, both in practical terms and at a more intangible level. One writer reported that because the Kurd and his men were 'seduced by the beauty of the Egyptian sun, by its fertility and riches the Syrian army strongly desired to stay there and to establish residency'.[28] Regardless of his premature demise, Shirkuh's accomplishments and career bear immense respect. A Kurdish Sunni warrior from the Jazira had briefly become de facto the most powerful man in Egypt, the wealthiest land in the Near East and home to the Shi'ite caliphate. He was a great general who did much to advance the cause of the Sunni counter-crusade; 'shirkuh' is a Persian word meaning 'lion of the mountain', an appropriate name for this tough character. He was also known for his generosity and for religious foundations such as a madrasa in Damascus.[29] Ibn Khallikan's biographical dictionary noted that in 1167 Shirkuh had entered Egypt 'with the design, that he had already formed during his first expedition, of getting that country into his own possession'. In his actions he had presented Saladin – or whoever else succeeded him as vizier – with a pretty clear template.[30]

5

Saladin's Succession in Egypt

*'An animal which dug up with its
hoof the instrument of its death'*

A Kurdish Sunni warlord's brutal acquisition of the most powerful office in Egypt was a transformative moment, but Shirkuh's unexpected death, just two months after he became vizier, prompted a crisis in Cairo. While Shirkuh was best known for his military prowess, the elimination of his predecessor Shawar had been an incisive political move. Lacking such an uncompromising background, his successor could be highly vulnerable on several fronts: the Franks of Jerusalem were desperate to strike back before the Syrians consolidated their hold on Egypt; in Cairo itself factions within the city remained deeply hostile to the Fatimids' current rapprochement with their Syrian neighbours, not least because Nur al-Din's role as a flag-bearer for the Sunni caliphate meant that he posed an obvious threat to the Shi'ite regime. The view from Damascus was important too. While Nur al-Din may have grudgingly acquiesced to his long-time associate Shirkuh becoming vizier, the appointment of a replacement remained entirely the prerogative of the caliph and those present in Cairo.

Saladin's maternal uncle was one potential candidate but, lacking personal support, he suggested instead his nephew, partly because 'if [Saladin] held the office, it would be in his family'. The caliph quickly concurred because he was said to admire Saladin's intelligence and the boldness and obedience he had shown in the removal of Shawar.[1] A contemporary court poet and commentator, al-Wahrani, admittedly

likely to have written in search of patronage, emphasised the decision
to opt for a member of the Ayyubid clan and then to pick Saladin
'because of his fine innate qualities, because of his love of justice and
fairness, because in him kingly characteristics were combined with
the humility of a pauper, and because of his noble mindfulness and
open-handedness'.[2] Beha al-Din, who later became one of his closest
confidants and key officials, indicated that Saladin's competence as an
administrator meant that he handled the bulk of daily affairs during
Shirkuh's short vizierate and this had helped to demonstrate his credibility.[3] Another writer took a different approach and claimed the caliph
saw Saladin as a weak, political lightweight. While several senior figures
aspired to the title, al-Adid quickly offered the post to Saladin, intending
to install a person who could be dominated or removed at will; after
all, the newcomer would owe his promotion to the caliph. If this was
al-Adid's assessment of the relationship then, with the benefit of
hindsight, he proved to be very, very wrong.[4]

It took a little while for the other senior commanders to come
around to Saladin's candidacy, but two of the key individuals in this
process clearly believed in their man and would remain prominent
amongst his inner circle of officials and advisors for decades to come,
an indication of the bonds of trust and patronage forged at this early
stage of his career. First to make the case for the Ayyubid was Shirkuh's
former imam (meaning prayer leader for followers of the Sunni
doctrine) and a notable Kurdish jurist, Isa al-Hakkari; in fact, one
source ascribes to him the initiative in raising Saladin to the vacancy.
Another previous associate of Shirkuh's was the eunuch Qaraqush
(meaning 'blackbird' in Turkish), who was highly influential amongst
the Asadiyya, the emir's regiment of heavy troops.[5]

It is interesting that most of the other candidates were of Kurdish
origin and it was this ethnic solidarity, then focused or refined down
to the Ayyubid clan, that did much to shape their actions here and in
future. Shirkuh's long-standing ambition to conquer Egypt meant he
had brought with him a core group of associates. His potential successors included, as noted, Saladin's maternal uncle, as well as the emir
Qutb al-Din al-Hadhbani. Isa sought to persuade the emir to step aside
by arguing that 'both you and Saladin are Kurds and you will not let
the power pass into the hands of the Turks'. The Hadhbani were a
Kurdish tribe that included the Ayyubids, so the link was clear. Another

candidate was the Kurd al-Mashtub al-Hakkari ('al-Mashtub' meaning 'the scarred', a figure whom the crusaders would get to know very well), but he believed himself insufficiently popular and so, encouraged by the promise of appropriate rewards, he duly came on side. Al-Mashtub also became an immensely important figure in Saladin's career and, like Isa and Qaraqush, featured prominently in his inner circle. The only possible alternative to a Kurdish vizier was a Turkmen, al-Yaruqi, member of a group that had settled under Nur al-Din near Aleppo; unwilling, however, to serve the new Kurdish clique he returned to Syria. Thus Shirkuh's followers had prevailed and Saladin, his nephew and protégé, was in the ascendancy.[6]

Clan loyalty is a theme that appears again and again in this story. As one writer put it, emphasising this, Saladin was 'the central and finest pearl of that brilliant necklace'.[7] Reliance on close family members was one cornerstone for his achievements down the decades. Inevitably there were moments of high tension amongst the Ayyubids, although nothing on the ruinous scale repeatedly experienced by contemporaries in Seljuk lands or in western Europe.[8] But first on Saladin's agenda was the matter of basic survival. During the brief period of Shirkuh's rule he would have gained some appreciation of what was involved in ruling Egypt, but now the task was his.

Military strength was essential. Qaraqush steered the Asadiyya, numbering perhaps 500 men, in support of their former commander's nephew. As well as family loyalty they must have seen Saladin as a man who would generate rewards for them. He could therefore expect, in the short term at least, robust military backing to get his vizierate underway.[9]

Fatimid Egypt was a hugely ceremonial society where public events played a considerable element in the exercise and maintenance of authority. The vizier held an extremely powerful role but in the circumstances of the day it was also an especially vulnerable one; prior to Shirkuh the previous three incumbents had all died violently. Taking the symbols of office was an important early step. Caliph al-Adid summoned Saladin to the palace where he was given the vizier's robes, suitably splendid items consisting of a white garment (white being the Fatimid colour) with gold edging and wide sleeves, a white turban and a large scarf. Particularly striking was the golden neckband, studded with jewels and pearls, fastened by a silk ribbon itself decorated by a pearl 'bigger than a chickpea'. He was also awarded the title 'al-Malik al-Nasir', meaning 'the king who supports', a name that would prove deeply ironic given what transpired later.[10] The cumulative weight of Ayyubid ambition and military muscle seems to have made a strong impression on the caliph and his administrators, because Saladin's letter of investiture to the vizierate included a clause that stated he was following in the footsteps of his uncle, emphasising succession within the clan.[11] Al-Wahrani endorsed this view, claiming that 'in view of their qualities of leadership and governance' and their magnanimity and military skills, the leadership should 'be made perpetual in [Shirkuh's] family'.[12]

The investiture document was written by the highly experienced Fatimid official Qadi al-Fadil (meaning 'the talented qadi'*), a man plainly aware of the need to ingratiate himself with the new regime. The circumstances were especially sensitive because the Shi'ite Caliph al-Adid was being joined by an assertively Sunni vizier. This skilfully formulated document linked the young caliph (the 'Commander of the Faithful') to Abu Bakr, the first leader to follow the Prophet back in the seventh century, and also to Saladin. In making these connections, theoretically the author represented a phase in Islamic history prior to the Sunni–Shi'ite division, although the decision to choose Abu Bakr as the Prophet's successor did of itself pass over the claim of the young Ali, a context apparent to those hearing the proclamation, whichever strand of Islam they adhered to.[13]

Saladin's career in Egypt was the springboard for his later success and it would shape, hone and demonstrate his ambitions and capabilities. He proved brilliantly adaptable to the challenges of the task and dealt deftly with a vast array of different problems; his time as vizier was characterised by generosity, good fortune, considerable firmness, and, as with many great rulers, a major building programme. Years later Beha al-Din observed that when appointed vizier Saladin was said to have become more serious, giving up wine – an interesting indication that he had imbibed in the first place – and 'vain pastimes', although the latter certainly did not include polo. Now he 'donned the garments of seriousness and pious endeavour'. As with reports

---

*Qadi was an honorific for high-ranking officials that usually referred to a judicial status.

of Nur al-Din's reappraisal following his defeat at Hisn al-Akrad in 1163, we may be dealing here with a touch of literary gilding, but the sense of grasping the need to move into a different phase of life and recognising what a leadership role required is certainly apt. Beha al-Din continued: 'I have heard him say, "After God enabled me to gain Egypt, I understood that He planned the conquest of the coast because He planted that idea in my mind."'[14] While this gives a divine blessing to Saladin's later actions it may be an acknowledgement that from this point onwards, however discreetly at first, he had high aspirations, even greater than those of his recently departed uncle. That said, he started out carefully enough by having the *khutba*, the address at Friday prayer, recited in the name of his Syrian master. Nur al-Din remained understandably cautious at the unexpected advance of this relatively junior figure and he pointedly addressed letters jointly to Saladin and the other emirs of Egypt, rather than to the new vizier alone.[15]

Saladin's principal tactic at this time was to lavish money and gifts on those prepared to support him, especially his clansmen, that is, Shirkuh's former emirs, the senior Kurdish warriors and nobles from Syria. Such behaviour was endorsed in contemporary advice manuals and it was a logical way to bind these men to him.[16] But soon he needed to ask al-Adid for funds and the caliph could not refuse, or in the words of a harsh contemporary proverb, 'having now become like an animal which dug up with its hoof the instrument of its death'.[17] News of his generosity spread to Frankish lands and William of Tyre wrote of the new vizier's need to borrow money.[18]

Saladin wanted his brothers to come and bolster his position, and when Nur al-Din learned that the Franks intended another attack on Egypt, he agreed.[19] As this group travelled to Cairo, however, the first serious challenge to Saladin's standing unfolded. Inevitably some of Caliph al-Adid's officials resented the presence and power of the Sunni Kurds and Syrians. A black eunuch with the title 'Commissioner of the Caliphate' planned to write to the Franks and link up with them to overthrow Saladin. The commissioner's messenger got out of Cairo but on the road north-east a sharp-eyed soldier noticed this scruffy traveller wore brand-new sandals. Suspicions aroused, he investigated further and unstitched the footwear to reveal the letter. The bearer was said to be a Jew, but facing punishment, he converted to Islam and confessed his crime, thereby earning Saladin's forgiveness. The commissioner was a person of some influence and so Saladin dealt carefully with the situation. Rather than rushing to arrest the man he kept his knowledge of the plot to himself and waited until the traitor went to an outlying village. There, safely isolated, the vizier's men seized and slew the rebel, bringing his head back to Saladin. A good story indeed, and once circulated it certainly provided a reason to deal harshly with the Fatimid troops. Duly empowered, Saladin installed his trusty aide Qaraqush as the head official of the palace and he in turn dismissed the other eunuchs.[20]

The decapitation of their leader enraged the so-called 'Black Regiments'. These men, recruited from the Sudan, Nubia and Ethiopia as infantrymen, spearmen and archers, were a central element of the Fatimid regime. Thousands gathered in the square in front of the Great Eastern Palace where they were joined by another group of outsiders also integral to the Fatimid forces, namely an Armenian regiment.[21] The aim of this bubbling mass was, of course, to topple the new regime. Fighting broke out for two days in late August 1169 before Saladin, with the caliph's encouragement, acted to break the deadlock. He sent troops into the al-Mansura district south of Cairo where the Nubians and their families lived, and ordered it put to the torch. The tactic pushed the Nubians back into a series of dense alleyways where a party of the new vizier's troops waited to seal the exit routes. Realising their position was hopeless the Nubians negotiated their way across the Nile over to Giza, but Saladin was determined to eradicate the threat and dispatched his elder brother Turanshah to wipe out this last contingent.[22] Al-Wahrani gives a powerful account of this:

The state was … packed with disturbances and dangers, while the scorpions of its soldiers were creeping and the cauldrons of hearts were boiling … the incentives of envy induced them to wrest authority from the claws of the lion. Then he gripped power with his right hand … until he destroyed them and cut their livers. After that their live coals burned amongst the people. But he leapt on them like a bone-crushing lion and pounced upon them like a glowering hero until he had expelled every mischief-maker and fighter and killed all vipers and scorpions.[23]

This decisive savagery gave Saladin the opportunity to billet his own troops in the city. More importantly, because by now so many Fatimid nobles and officials had been deprived of their *iqtas* (grants of the right to collect tax from a specfic area of land), he could continue to lavish rewards on his own emirs. *Iqtas* were, in effect, the basic currency of patronage in the Muslim Near East and the ability to award, confirm or remove these rights was an essential lever of power.[24] As the new holders of *iqtas*, Saladin's family, emirs and officials accrued considerable wealth and in the early days of Ayyubid rule this system of rewards was one way to put down foundations to assure the longer-term security of the dynasty. Such riches also provided a source of funding for Sunni religious institutions.[25]

One major reason why he was able to survive in power was the administrative skills of those at the heart of the regime. The presence and the nurturing of a talented group of secretaries and officials was a hallmark of his entire career. Unlike the largely Kurdish core of his military associates, those who – very self-consciously – wielded the pen rather than the sword were a more cosmopolitan group. Qadi al-Fadil was a central player in the Fatimid government machine. He provided vital, highly qualified continuity in the early stages of Ayyubid rule. Trained in the chancery of Cairo he had worked in Alexandria too. Importantly, he was a Sunni Muslim and some of his writings from this period reflect the decline of the Fatimids.[26] He had been employed by vizier Shawar and like many of his fellow administrators, needed to demonstrate great flexibility and to count on the value of his talents, to pilot his way through a series of employers and patrons. He had established relations with Shirkuh during the turbulence of Shawar's office, and when the latter was murdered and the Kurdish warlord took over his position, Qadi al-Fadil became the logical choice to run his chancery. When Shirkuh died, he remained in post and came to forge a close bond with Saladin.[27]

Men such as al-Fadil helped to steer the sultan through the complexities of the Egyptian political and diplomatic scene. The Franks were, of course, a familiar challenge. Saladin would have known of the various kingdoms and political entities to the south (Nubia, the Sudan and Ethiopia) and to the west (the Almohads and the Banu Ghaniyya in North Africa), but as vizier of Egypt he needed actively to engage with all of these entities, to evaluate what could change, or not; to assess how these groups might view the new regime in religious, political and economic terms. He then had to blend this with his own needs and agenda. In other words, the new man was required to grasp and to navigate a hugely complex geopolitical arena.

As the author of hundreds of letters on Saladin's behalf, in reporting, announcing and interpreting events, Qadi al-Fadil would be the sultan's greatest propagandist; he was also a highly accomplished poet. His skill as a compositor won him enormous regard from contemporaries: 'as a writer of epistles he reached pre-eminence and surpassed every predecessor'. A colleague wrote: 'He was the master of the pen and of lucid expression, of eloquence, and of language; his genius was brilliant, his sagacity penetrating and his style marked by originality and beauty ... to him belonged novelty of thought ... displays of brilliance, and production of the fairest flowers; it was he who conducted the empire by his counsels and fastened the pearls of style on the thread of discourse.'[28]

As well as the talents of al-Fadil there were men such as al-Makhzumi, a senior Fatimid official who compiled a great report on Egypt's land and finances in the year that Saladin became vizier, no coincidence perhaps.[29] Structurally, Egypt was very different to Syria and the Jazira. The basic well-being of the country was dictated by the annual flood of the River Nile. Exerting the greatest possible control over this natural phenomenon and then maximising its life-giving power had been an essential priority for its different rulers over hundreds of years. As a result, institutions and practices had evolved to mean the government of Egypt was much larger and far more centralised in comparison to the smaller and sometimes fragmented structures that existed in the lands Saladin had grown up in.[30] As vizier, Saladin could, to whatever extent he wished, direct or interact with this great administration. We can see his determination to make the best of the unexpected situation in which he found himself through his serious engagement with the apparatus of government. Dry bureaucracy may not sound synonymous with becoming the hero of Islam, but it would be vital for the survival and consolidation of Ayyubid power. Saladin needed to understand exactly what resources were available for him in order to distribute rewards to his followers and to finance his regime; in doing so he would gain an essential insight into how the region functioned, something that could only enhance his ability to both adopt and adapt the Fatimid system for his own ends.

Al-Makhzumi's book explains the many financial (and tax) institutions of what had been Fatimid Egypt, the workings of the annual agricultural calendar, the different types of crops and the times they should be harvested. When the flood receded, the area of land available to be cultivated could be assessed (this would vary every year according to the extent of the flood), the best type of crop to be grown and the tax (*kharaj*) then due calculated. The fecundity of the Nile Delta could support crops ranging from flax and cotton to sugar cane, cumin, turnips, aubergines, lettuce, wheat, barley and chickpeas. Orchards and vineyards were dealt with separately as the land they stood on tended to be less affected by flooding, and note was taken of the different harvest from saplings and mature trees.[31] Al-Makhzumi also wrote about the mint in Cairo and Alexandria, the Office of the Army, and the taxes paid by overseas traders in the ports of Alexandria, Damietta and Tinnis.[32] Finally, he advised Qadi al-Fadil to convince Saladin to properly synchronise the timing of the tax collection with the harvest, something that had fallen away badly under the Fatimids and again had a detrimental effect on incomes.[33]

No sooner had the danger of internal rebellion been dealt with than Saladin had to confront a Frankish invasion. Shirkuh's conquest of Egypt had deeply alarmed the settlers and they sent envoys off to western Europe, pleading for help and highlighting the danger to Jerusalem now that, for the first time in the history of the Latin East, Syria and Egypt were, in theory, under the same ruler. Given the usual rate of response to such pleas (at least a year to preach a crusade, take the Cross and prepare an expedition), plus ongoing tensions between the kings of England and France, little could be expected from northern Europe in the short term.[34]

If Saladin was not to face the prospect of a major crusade from the West, the settlers' increasingly close links with Manuel Komnenos constituted another potent threat. The Byzantine emperor had noted the turmoil in Egypt. He saw an opportunity to step in and, in conjunction with the Franks of Jerusalem, to seize the immense economic advantages on offer and to strengthen the position of Christianity in the eastern Mediterranean. The two parties had agreed a treaty back in the autumn of 1168, and in spite of Amalric's foolish campaign that ended in early 1169 the apparent fragility of Saladin's government meant the planned invasion still went ahead.

The Greeks made a substantial commitment: Manuel sent around 200 ships, intending to rendezvous with Amalric's land-based force from Jerusalem with a first target of the city of Damietta at the top of the most easterly navigable branch of the Nile.[35]

In September 1169, Egyptian patrol vessels encountered the Byzantine fleet off Cyprus. On receiving this warning Saladin wrote to Nur al-Din explaining his dilemma – if he did not go to Damietta, the Franks could take it but if he left Cairo then the Egyptians would foment trouble in his absence. Nur al-Din saw that his protégé needed help, and he appreciated that Byzantine–Frankish power in Cairo could potentially be lethal to his own position in Syria; he duly dispatched several squadrons of men to Egypt. Similarly energised by the prospect of this latest Christian invasion, Caliph al-Adid offered his vizier massive financial help in raising troops to defend the city.[36]

The city of Damietta stands on the west bank of this branch of the Nile. On the other side of the river stood a massive tower and slung across the water lay a great chain that prevented the Christian fleet from heading upstream and also stopped it getting alongside the river walls. Of equal importance, the protective chain enabled the Egyptians to keep bringing in troops and supplies by water. After fifty days' stern resistance, Christian determination crumbled. Amalric announced a truce and it was agreed that the siege would end in return for payments of tribute. With the fighting over, for three days the Christian and Muslim troops traded and mingled with one another, just as at Alexandria in 1167. For all on the Muslim side, Damietta's survival was a noteworthy moment. As Ibn al-Athir wrote of the Franks: 'the ostrich went forth seeking horns and returned without ears'.[37] It was the longest siege mounted by a Christian army in the Levant since the capture of Ascalon in 1153. For Saladin to co-ordinate successful resistance to such an invasion was a significant achievement that helped to solidify his authority. The Egyptians duly sent money and gifts to Constantinople to confirm the treaty.

The new vizier had, in this instance, acted in conjunction with Nur al-Din to the benefit of them both. At this point it seems that Nur al-Din was reasonably content with the situation. In the broadest sense, his power over Egypt was starting to take root and he could anticipate ever greater strategic and economic benefits from pincering the Franks by land, and potentially, by sea. That Saladin was now in a position of immense influence yet under the notional authority of a Shi'ite caliph remained, of course, problematic. In the short term, however, the advantages seemed to make tolerating this worthwhile. In fact, Nur al-Din agreed that Saladin's father, Ayyub, could join him in Egypt in early 1170. Ayyub had proven a loyal backer of the Syrian ruler and his presence may have been designed to reinforce such a view. Soldiers, merchants and other supporters of the new vizier accompanied him.

Ayyub reached Cairo on 16 April 1170. Aside from the strong bonds between Saladin and his father this must have been a curious meeting because the former had unexpectedly inverted the conventional family hierarchy. Caliph al-Adid recognised the significance of Ayyub's arrival and amidst great festivities (that lasted seven days) came out to welcome him formally into Cairo. Saladin himself received his father with all due deference and offered to submit to his authority, but Ayyub declined, observing that God had selected Saladin for the task and that it was improper to change this.[38]

Ayyub was soon awarded a powerful administrative role in charge of the treasuries, thereby overseeing the continued distribution of money and gifts. He also did much to develop the standing of the Sunni establishment. Al-Wahrani lavished considerable praise on Ayyub as a figure who did much to challenge and then 'to extinguish the heretical innovations, making them disappear until Islam was perfected and the religion of the Prophet, peace be upon him, completed'.[39] Saladin demolished the ironically named House of Assistance, formerly a place where the police questioned prisoners, and in September 1170 he rebuilt it as a Shafi madrasa. He thus removed a symbol of tyranny and replaced it with a religious foundation of his own leaning. Likewise, the Hall of Justice was reconstructed as a Shafi madrasa. The reach of the Sunni establishment extended further with the removal of Cairo's Shi'ite *qadi*; once again, a Sunni candidate was installed and, across the land, deputies were appointed too.[40] This sense of a heightened morality can be seen in the purchase by Taqi al-Din, Saladin's nephew, of the Fatimid pleasure palace the Abodes of Glory in Old Cairo, and the conversion of the establishment into another madrasa. A new elite was slowly beginning to put its stamp on the city.[41] Saladin continued to build his networks of patronage, as well as looking to acquire more revenue. A surviving letter from 1170 reports that a Damascene merchant who accompanied Ayyub to Cairo managed to gain the latter's recommendation and get access to Saladin. Over several days the merchant petitioned to be allowed to collect taxes, including that on cheese sold in Fustat and Cairo, in return for a salary. Once this was agreed the man was given robes of honour and gold coins, and duly became a loyal official delivering good revenue to the state treasury.[42]

Recent events in Alexandria and Amalric's assaults on Cairo a couple of years earlier showed the danger posed by the Franks; further insurrections from the remnants of the Fatimids' Nubian and Armenian groups also remained possible. Such a situation evidently prompted a strategic review. Saladin felt vulnerable in Cairo and in 1170–1 he ordered the renewal of parts of the walls. These dated from the late eleventh century and demarcated Cairo (al-Qahira) as it stood at the time, including the imposing gates at Bab al-Futuh and Bab al-Nasr.[43] While the gates were constructed in stone the rest of the walls were hard-baked mud. The campaign at Alexandria had shown the Franks possessed formidable siege machinery and Cairo's walls seemed outdated; military technology had moved on – it was time to modernise. The Ayyubids were effecting, therefore, a physical as well as a political and religious change on Cairo.

Control of Egypt generated strategic opportunities, as well as challenges. The eastern border with the Franks was smothered by the harsh terrain of the Sinai peninsula, leaving only a couple of land routes. One ran along the north coast of Egypt to Gaza, while to the south the other went from Cairo to Suez, then across the Sinai peninsula to the Frankish-held town of Ayla (modern Aqaba) at the top of the Red Sea. Saladin had traversed each of these during the wars of the 1160s but now he wanted both to increase Egypt's security and to put active pressure on the Christians. Around this time he ordered the construction of the small fortress of Sadr high above the second of these roads and at the western edge of the Sinai.[44]

Keen to show Nur al-Din his continued commitment to the jihad, Saladin attacked the Templar fortress of Darum on the south-western extremity of the kingdom of Jerusalem in December 1170. He then raided the nearby town of Gaza but avoided battle.[45] Soon afterwards

Saladin launched a bold assault on the Frankish castle at Ayla, located on an island just offshore. Clever use of prefabricated boats, transported over the Sinai by camel, meant that he could besiege Ayla on land and sea, and he duly seized the island castle and refortified it.[46]

Back in Syria, by early 1171 Nur al-Din had become the overlord of Mosul, and the underlying tension between his growing strength as the champion of Sunni orthodoxy and the continued existence of the Shi'ite caliph in Cairo started to break to the surface more frequently. The Syrian ruler had strongly encouraged the religious classes to tackle unbelief in all its forms, especially what they regarded as the heretical stain of the Shi'ites. Ibn Asakir's *Forty Hadith for Inciting Jihad* contained texts that emphasised the need to be an authentic Sunni Muslim, in other words to remove the Isma'ili Shi'ite Fatimid caliphate.

From Baghdad, the Sunni caliph al-Mustadi transmitted frustrations of his own. From Syria, Nur al-Din urged Saladin to cease using al-Adid's name in the *khutba*, but his lieutenant demurred, fearing the response from the local population. To change public allegiance from one line of Islam to another, not to mention the removal of a dynasty of almost 200 years' duration, did not feel as if it could be rushed. One source suggests that Saladin asked a jurist from his favoured Shafi law school for an opinion, and when this was duly provided it gave the necessary affirmation to act.[47]

By coincidence – and in one of the many turns of good fortune that Saladin seemed to accumulate or attract – al-Adid became seriously unwell. By this stage, his ability to exercise any real power was extremely limited and the near-extinction of the Fatimid army only emphasised his impotence. The relentless erosion of political, military, economic and now religious power (as the Ayyubids bolstered the Sunni hierarchy in Cairo) had all but broken the dynasty. Yet, set against all of that, he held what was regarded by many as a divinely appointed office as the rightly guided Imam.

The arrival of a Sunni preacher from Persia provided the real catalyst for change. Against the backdrop of pressure from Nur al-Din, coupled with the incapacity of al-Adid, the visitor decided to make his move. On 3 September 1171 he mounted the pulpit in the mosque of Amr and said a prayer for the Sunni caliph of Baghdad. No one objected.

Encouraged by this, Saladin ordered that the following Friday, preachers in all mosques across Fustat and Cairo should drop al-Adid's name from the *khutba* and replace it with that of his Sunni counterpart in Baghdad. Again, there was little reaction. This lack of response seems extraordinary, and quite the opposite of what Saladin and his advisors had feared. Such an apparently passive acceptance of this basic aspect of the Islamic faith seems, on the face of it, bewildering. At times, present-day relations between the Sunnis and Shi'ites can be tremendously charged. In more recent decades some Shi'ite scholars have moved away from the customary veneration of Saladin as a hero of the Muslim world and vilified him as a murderer and heretic for his removal of their caliph; they characterise him as a man 'who tolerated the crusaders and oppressed Muslims'. Noticeably, however, this sectarian divide was not expressed by many contemporaries. An exception might be the Shi'ite jurist Abu Turab, living, confusingly, in Baghdad, the seat of the Sunni caliphate. He lamented what had happened and cried 'may God not be pleased with Saladin. He is *Fasad al-Din* – Destruction of the Faith'. By contrast, one of Saladin's most important contemporary biographers was Ibn Abi Tayy, a Shi'ite, who admired him greatly, yet disliked Nur al-Din who had sent the author's father into exile.[48]

We are still left with no obvious explanation for the immediate situation in Cairo; a sense that the population had become weary and disillusioned with a rather substandard dynasty no longer worthy to be their spiritual leaders may be significant; in other words the Fatimids were simply a figurehead of the state religion alone. Certainly there was no mass uprising or protest which might indicate deep-held allegiance to al-Adid and his forefathers. Some may have seen the strength of the Ayyubids and feared confrontation with a superior force. The timing of a 15,000-man military parade on 11 September, in the presence of Byzantine and Frankish envoys, was not the most subtle way to make this point.[49] Finally, not all would have been unhappy at what had happened: a significant proportion, if not a majority, of Egypt's population was Sunni anyway, and as we saw in Alexandria, where Sunni madrasas had existed for decades, the regime lacked universal support. Fustat was largely Sunni, with communities of Jews and Copts, Maghrebis, Sudanese and foreign traders. Cairo itself had Armenian and Turkish slave troops, while at times the Fatimids themselves had relied upon North African Berbers.[50]

In such a complicated environment the Fatimids had blurred the lines between Isma'ili Shi'ites (the branch adhered to by the Fatimids) and the Sunni; 'ritual unity had to be in a broadly Islamic and not specifically Isma'ili or even Shi'ite context'.[51] One example of this was the Festival of Breaking the Fast (the Eid festival) at the end of Ramadan. The Isma'ilis believe the fast cannot be broken until the last rays of light disappear from the sky, while the Sunni can do so once the *maghrib* prayer begins, which is when the sun is no longer visible on the horizon (although it can still be light, of course). Banquets were staged that allowed the caliph to present food, symbolically kiss it, place it on the arm but not eat it and thereby break the fast. Thus the many non-Ismai'ili officials could be involved in the celebrations. The caliphs also engaged with popular religious practices; they gave gifts to the wider population, often in the form of clothing; they made important Isma'ili festivals such as Ghadir Khumm (the Prophet's designation of Ali as his heir apparent) less ideological.[52] Thus, in responding to the cosmopolitan nature of Cairo, and recognising the limitations of their own political power, the Fatimid elite ultimately made it easier for themselves to be removed. Compounding this complexity, as we have already seen, Saladin had also started to sow the seeds for a growing Sunni intellectual influence in Cairo and beyond.

Back in the royal palace, al-Adid's health was so poor that no one was willing to tell him of the change in the *khutba* for fear of making him worse. On 13 September he died, never knowing what had taken place. In his final days he had sent for Saladin but the latter suspected a trap and declined to visit. Afterwards, Saladin expressed regret at not talking to a figure whom he described as a gentle and generous man.[53] This marked the end of the line for the Fatimids. After the change in the *khutba* the previous week, al-Adid's death confirmed the demise of Ismai'ili Shi'ism as the state religion of Egypt: Saladin and Sunni Islam were now the leading players in the land. There remained the formality of al-Adid's funeral, and the Kurdish vizier was careful to pay his last respects to the man who had appointed him. He spoke to the late caliph's young son: 'I am the agent of your father in the matter of the caliphate and he has not made a bequest that recognises you as his successor'; thus the child could not inherit.[54]

Just a few years before, such seismic changes could not have been envisaged, but the way now lay open for Saladin to establish his own position, that of his family and the Sunnis, ever more firmly. Coins were struck in the name of the caliph of Baghdad and of Nur al-Din, and the silver plaques that proclaimed the names of the Fatimid caliphs were stripped from the *mihrabs* of Cairo. Messengers announcing this momentous turn of events rushed to Baghdad where the news was greeted with predictable delight. The city markets were decorated with banners and resounded to the pounding of celebratory drums. The Sunni caliphate could feel empowered and confident; its main rival was gone. Entirely appropriately, robes of honour were dispatched to both Nur al-Din and Saladin.[55] Poets congratulated the two men. Saladin's secretary Imad al-Din wrote of the Egyptian ruler's death: 'The era of its pharaoh has come to an end and tomorrow Yusuf would be the ruler.' This neat play on Pharaoh and the Quranic figure of Yusuf (Joseph) as against the Fatimid 'pharaoh' and Saladin (the new Yusuf/Joseph) is image-making that put Saladin in the position, by association, of a pious ruler, thereby emphasising the legitimacy of his rapid (if potentially questionable) ascent to power.[56] Yet he had shown both strength and subtlety in his new role as vizier. His harsh suppression of the 1169 revolt demonstrated a ruthless side to his character while his willingness to engage with the detailed administration of the Nile flood indicated his need and determination to understand and exploit the resources of Egypt to the maximum. Coupled with an important military victory at Alexandria and the surprisingly smooth removal of the Fatimids, the Ayyubids had made a highly effective start in their bid to grasp power.

6

Steps Towards Independence: The Break with Nur al-Din

'By God, if Nur al-Din wanted even a piece of sugar cane I myself would fight him to stop it or be killed in the attempt'

This was uncharted territory for Saladin. Etiquette required officials and senior figures to come to him as vizier and to offer formal expressions of condolence, a dynamic that placed the Ayyubid squarely as the sole figure of authority. Such a position would cast his relationship with Nur al-Din under an increasingly harsh spotlight. How far, and how quickly, did Saladin want to use this extraordinary power base to establish his independence?

In the short term, his hold on the administration of government enabled him to take control of the palaces, royal possessions and the remaining members of al-Adid's family. Concubines and children were removed and kept under close guard. Surplus members of a deposed dynasty tend to meet an abrupt fate, but in this instance Saladin displayed caution in keeping them alive. Other relatives, especially the men, were kept in very close confinement, living off alms alone. His successors maintained this practice and we know that over sixty Fatimids were still alive in the 1210s, a number partly explained by the fact that al-Adid had fathered seventeen or eighteen boys before his death at the age of twenty-one.[1]

In the space of a month Saladin had effected the end of both Shi'ite religious leadership and the Fatimid dynasty. Moving forwards, he now had the fabulous treasures of the Fatimid palace at his complete disposal; Qaraqush brought out a few particular highlights. One such marvel was the 'ruby mountain', a stone weighing over sixty grams.

Another was an emerald sceptre, about ten centimetres long that Saladin is said to have broken into three pieces and given to his favourite women. Less alluring perhaps was a drum used to treat the caliph's colic, an instrument notorious for triggering an immediate fart from anyone who beat it. Ambushed by this percussive experience a Kurdish warrior smashed the drum, not realising its potentially restorative powers.[2] Numerous slaves were a further category of disposable property, with some being sold, others given as gifts and a lucky few set free.

Qaraqush also began to disperse the royal library, one of the greatest collections of books and manuscripts in the medieval age. The library was huge; some sources suggest over a million volumes. Ibn Abi Tayy described it as 'one of the marvels of the world ... it is said that there was not, in all the lands of Islam, a library larger', and among its wonders were 1,200 volumes of al-Tabari's famous early tenth-century history of Islam. Although this was not a systematic or sectarian destruction of the Fatimids' literary heritage, or of the specifically Shi'ite texts therein, it was nevertheless a slow dispersal of the books, driven largely by the wish to keep raising cash. Selling off these precious items took years. Imad al-Din later reported that book sales happened twice weekly in the Fatimid palace. As a writer and bibliophile he was only too pleased to purchase many precious books at low prices: 'I, like everyone else took advantage of the situation.' On one occasion Saladin learned of this and allowed him to take several tomes as a gift, and then supplemented this selection with even more folios, a gesture that naturally delighted the recipient. Many thousands of volumes also found their way to Qadi al-Fadil's own madrasa in Cairo, which opened in 1184–5.[3]

The caliphal palaces were subject to dramatic change. Some areas were turned over to living quarters for Saladin's followers, a few were simply boarded up, others were opened out and had roads run through them. His father was given the splendidly named Pearl Pavilion, overlooking fine gardens on the main canal in north-west Cairo.[4] Saladin chose to stay in the 'Seat of the Vizierate', his existing home and the traditional vizier's residence close to the section of wall he had recently refortified in north-east Cairo. The grandeur of many of these palaces later declined and almost nothing of them survives today, but the emergence of new religious schools and markets created by the presence of the Kurdish and Turkish emirs meant that Cairo itself would not fall into disrepair – far from it, in fact.[5]

His most important political relationship remained that with Nur al-Din, and the first big cracks appeared in the autumn of 1171. Ibn al-Athir tells us that the ruler of Syria ordered his protégé to gather the troops of Egypt and blockade the huge castle of Kerak. This controlled the Transjordan region and hence threatened one of the principal roads to the holy cities of Mecca and Medina, as well as stifling trade between Syria and Egypt.[6] Nur al-Din planned to march south from Damascus and together they could bring maximum pressure to bear upon this important target. Saladin departed from Cairo and informed Nur al-Din that he was en route. He headed out towards Shaubak (known as Montreal to the crusaders), another big fortress and a day's march south of the rendezvous. In the interim, Nur al-Din reached Kerak, only to learn the shocking news that Saladin had decided to withdraw back to Egypt with immediate effect. Ibn al-Athir relates that Saladin's 'companions and close friends' had counselled him against the meeting. They warned him that if he were at Kerak, then Nur al-Din could invade the kingdom of Jerusalem and capture King Amalric, giving the Syrian ruler a dominant position in the Near East. Should Nur al-Din come face to face with his lieutenant he might confirm his authority – or he might dismiss him. If intending the latter, he would presumably fill the room with his own followers and Saladin would be powerless to resist. This narrative does, of course, helpfully remove the direct initiative for turning back from Saladin himself, although his acceptance of the arguments hardly absolves him from this apparent disloyalty.[7]

The sultan sent messengers to Nur al-Din claiming news of disturbances in Egypt and plots by the Shi'ites. His absence, he argued, made such a coup more likely, something that had been patently obvious before he set out. However unconvincing this explanation seemed, Nur al-Din would not wish the Sunnis to lose control of Egypt so quickly. Likewise, he could hardly order Saladin to ignore such rumours because in many respects this was plausible; the caliph had only just died and there were some signs of unrest in Cairo. Nur al-Din was in a real quandary; his former lieutenant now ruled lands that were wealthier than his, and while he remained Saladin's nominal overlord he could rely only on those theoretical bonds to sustain and perpetuate that position. Equally, however, it was Saladin (and his family) who had removed the Shi'ite caliph and enormously enhanced the authority and status of the Sunni caliph of Baghdad, an achievement that reflected well on Nur al-Din too. Egypt could provide immense funding for the jihad, and if campaigns against the Christians were co-ordinated between Syria and Egypt, then the Franks might well be defeated more quickly. With al-Adid alive it was hardly in Nur al-Din's interests to destabilise Saladin, but in the new situation Saladin's reluctance to obey, or at least to show willing, gave Nur al-Din grounds to doubt his associate's motives. We saw earlier that Shirkuh had been open in his ambitions to conquer Egypt and that Nur al-Din had seemed reasonably content to go along with this, given all the strategic and religious advantages it held. Shirkuh's unexpected death meant their relationship was never tested, but Saladin's behaviour was starting to appear provocative.

Ibn al-Athir wrote that Nur al-Din's 'attitude towards [Saladin] changed and he resolved to enter Egypt and expel him'.[8] The rift became highly public. The loyalty of the Ayyubid family was now openly questioned and challenged, a situation that potentially undermined their position within Egypt because opponents saw they were no longer assured of support from Syria; a perturbed Saladin called a family meeting. Ibn al-Athir's vivid account may benefit from a strong infusion of literary imagination, but it does give a sense of the conflicting sentiments swirling around such a discussion.

Also present were Saladin's father and maternal uncle, his nephew Taqi al-Din, and many other senior emirs. The unfolding scene delivers an intriguing portrayal of the political influence and razor-sharp pragmatism of the senior member of the clan. Saladin outlined the crisis and the prospect of an invasion by Nur al-Din. At first, no one replied until Taqi-al-Din exclaimed: 'If he comes to us, we shall fight him and keep him out of the country'; various other emirs concurred; a sense of resolve and resistance spread through the group. But Ayyub was deeply angered. He reprimanded the young man and ordered him to sit. Turning to his own son, he invoked his seniority to give Saladin a clear and salutary perspective:

We love you more than all those you see here. By God, if your uncle and I were to set eyes on Nur al-Din, we could do nothing but kiss the ground before him. If he ordered us to strike off your head with a sword, we would do so … This country is Nur al-Din's. We are his Mamluks and lieutenants in it. If he wishes to dismiss you, we shall hear and obey. Your best course is to write a letter saying 'I have heard that you intend an expedition to secure the country. What need is there for that? Let my lord send a courier here by dromedary with orders to put a turban-sash around my neck and lead me to you. No one will resist your will.'[9]

Such a powerful and direct speech shocked the room. Ayyub dismissed the emirs, but he had not yet finished with his son. Alone with Saladin he continued to upbraid him for his actions. Perhaps the decision to avoid meeting Nur al-Din at Kerak was taken in the course of the campaign, without Ayyub being present, and it was only now that the consequences were being fully understood. The older man asked his son what on earth he thought he was doing, surely such conduct would only make Saladin the Syrian ruler's top priority? Had his son considered the danger posed by being cast as an upstart and a traitor? Ayyub's message was not wholly hostile, though. As he pointed out, given the way that he had so openly chastised Taqi al-Din for suggesting resistance to Nur al-Din, messengers to Syria would certainly report that Saladin had been brought to heel – by his own father, no less – and that his loyalty was now assured.

While there is little doubt that Ayyub was genuinely alarmed at this sequence of events, his next comment left little doubt as to his ultimate position. Notwithstanding his earlier, very explicit, professions of loyalty to the Syrian regime, he now revealed an entirely different stance: 'By God, if Nur al-Din wanted even a piece of sugar cane I myself would fight him to stop it or be killed in the attempt.'[10] In other words, the denunciation of Taqi al-Din was purely for public, political consumption, the behaviour of a shrewd politician who knew where and when to pick a fight. The performance worked perfectly – and there was no invasion from Syria. As Ibn al-Athir confirmed, 'This was an example of really good and excellent advice.'[11] Al-Maqrizi, a later writer, expressed the matter more concisely: 'So Saladin did as his father counselled him and Nur al-Din was deceived and turned aside from his invasion.'[12] It also reveals the true agenda of the Ayyubids, or at least what it was perceived to be. They seemed, as a family, intent upon carving out a dynastic power base centred on Egypt, and no longer unquestioningly obeyed Nur al-Din; Shirkuh's original desire remained well in play. That said, they still shared with Nur al-Din common enemies such as the Franks and the Shi'ites, and acknowledged the same religious leader, the caliph of Baghdad. In the short term, the public assurances that emerged seem to have placated Nur al-Din. He chose to forward on to Saladin the robes of honour dispatched by the caliph. In essence, as the Ayyubid clan well knew, Nur al-Din was trapped by the need to prevent his feud with Saladin from destroying Sunni authority in Egypt.

In early March 1172, the bearer of these robes, an acquaintance of Ayyub himself, arrived just outside Cairo. The symbolic importance of such events was considerable. The Fatimids had been masters of the ceremonial and it was vital for Saladin to maximise opportunities to demonstrate his authority. Senior religious figures, such as preachers and Quran readers, came out to greet the envoy while the city was decorated with banners; the sultan's band played three times during the day at the Nasiri Gate on the northern side of Cairo. After the formal reception ceremony, Saladin donned the robe, a splendid black fur mantle with a collar of gold. He then rode through the streets of Cairo allowing everyone to see him, showing the people that his power had been acknowledged by the caliph, and the dominance of the Sunni creed. Such points duly made, on reaching the gate of Bab Zuwayla at the southern end of the main street, he took off the robe and had it sent back to his palace. Then, keeping what we might now call a work-life balance, he let off steam by riding out of the city to play polo with his friends.[13]

Given that in the short term the Ayyubids had seemingly fixed upon establishing a semi-independent status, Saladin's subsequent moves come into a clearer light. While active co-operation with Nur al-Din did not appear the aim, sparking open conflict was not part of the plan either. The requirement to render annual accounts to Syria was something that had to continue in order to preserve at least a facade of loyalty. In February 1172 Qaraqush conducted an inventory of a private palace treasury listing dozens of coffers filled with gold, silver, jewelled garments, necklaces and other valuables.

Saladin had to chart a cautious but clear path. Within that his need to generate money was plain. Aside from the essential requirement to reward followers and run the country, the sultan had ambitious building plans that encompassed social, political and spiritual issues. Blending religious aspiration and public finance was an uncomfortable task. Taxes and *iqtas* obviously yielded cash too, but Saladin's scale of outlay was vast. The dead caliph's support for the struggle against the crusaders at Damietta in 1169 was said to have cost a million dinars. More notably, aspects of Saladin's religious policy had a significant impact upon government finances because implementing a conservative Sunni agenda meant the abolition of taxes that were illegal under Islamic Sharia law. Part of al-Makhzumi's 1169–70 report had attempted to find a grounding for each tax in Sharia. Conforming correctly meant losing various sales and land taxes which totalled over a million dinars per year in revenue. They were replaced by a Quranic (9:60) alms tax (*zakat*) collected on merchandise, livestock, palm dates and vegetables, some of which was then distributed as social benefits for the poor, to travellers, and to those who fought in the holy war.[14] This all added to the feeling of change from the Fatimid Shi'ite line to the new Ayyubid Sunni regime. It also helped to promote Saladin as a good ruler just as the Quran (4:58) and sundry advice books suggested, and likely as Nur al-Din would have wished too. With a sharp eye on the need to keep the people of Cairo happy, Saladin also abolished customs duties at the city's two ports.[15]

But the cost of distributing land rights, and of bringing taxes into line with Islamic law, was immense. Saladin's habitual gift-giving, along with the multiple building projects in train, conflicts in the Upper Nile and crusader Transjordan, as well as Nur al-Din's ongoing financial demands, cumulatively created a damaging outflow of funds which hit the Egyptian economy hard. There was a dramatic decline in the gold and silver coinage available. Coins were a vital way of conveying authority, with minting a royal prerogative, and having coins struck in the name of a ruler (*sikka*) was one of the prime markers of power in Islamic lands. As we saw above, with the demise of al-Adid money had to be restruck in the names of the caliph in Baghdad and Nur al-Din. Yet the gold coins produced under Saladin were of a markedly weaker quality than those of the Fatimids, being both lighter in weight and with an inconsistent and lower percentage of gold.[16] Action was needed. In April 1172, in the company of the inner circle of his father, maternal uncle and nephew, Saladin went to Alexandria where he hoped to secure more resources. His nephew Taqi al-Din was dispatched at the head of 500 horsemen towards Libya, where he seized crops and booty. This would be the first of a series of campaigns westwards as the Ayyubids repeatedly sought to extend their hold on the region, possibly fearing an invasion from the powerful Almohads of the Maghrib. This was also a way of trying to take control of some of the Trans-Saharan gold trade, thus compensating for a decline in output from the southern Egyptian mines of Wadi al-Allaqi, south-east of Aswan, a region now hostile to the Ayyubids.[17]

Internally, some governmental decisions proved better conceived than others. A fear of disloyalty from Coptic Christians and Jews in administrative positions caused Saladin to order their dismissal from all offices, with their property being taken as well. A few did leave, while others converted to Islam to keep their posts. In some departments the officials in charge simply refused to implement the order because the office-holders were deemed too well versed in their roles to be sackable. In this instance, the Cairene civil service triumphed and the need for efficiency trumped any political or religious agendas.[18]

Saladin's rise to power had begun to draw attention on the wider international stage as well. In 1172, within the context of ongoing tensions between Emperor Frederick Barbarossa of Germany, the papacy, the rulers of Norman Sicily and the Byzantine Empire, the Germans sent envoys to Cairo offering friendship. The sultan responded, and in the autumn of 1173 his embassy brought a series of splendid gifts to the imperial court; in this cordial environment rumours circulated of a possible marriage between Frederick's daughter and one of the sultan's sons. It is striking that the Germans appear to have treated Saladin as a separate and independent power with little reference to Nur al-Din. A visit by the German cleric Burchard of Strasbourg marked the next step in this diplomatic exchange. He made a remarkable journey to Egypt and Syria, visiting shrines shared by Christians and Muslims, notably those with a focus on the Virgin Mary, hence a trip to the Matariyya near Cairo and the monastery of Saidnaya, north-west of Damascus, where to this day an image of the Virgin lactates holy oil and is regarded by both faiths as having miraculous properties. Burchard engaged in debate with Muslim holy men and depicted very positive relations between

Egyptian Copts, Syrian Christians and their Muslim overlords. The result of this was an agreement with Saladin strong enough to endure until 1188 when, once he had taken the Cross for the Third Crusade, Frederick formally communicated the end of the relationship.[19] In its entirety this series of exchanges again challenges the simple image of unbending and interminable Christian–Muslim hostility in the age of the crusades. Of course, both parties were looking for advantage within the wider spectrum of international affairs, but the fact that the two sides engaged with one another so closely was significant. Likewise, for a senior churchman to make a pilgrimage into Muslim lands and to debate with their holy men was a (relatively rare) inter-action at a more theological level, and seemingly far more cordial in tone than the crude stereotypes both groups often affirmed.

While Saladin had managed to evade a direct military confrontation with Nur al-Din, the Syrian ruler remained highly suspicious of the Ayyubids. The continued dispatch of annual tribute was part of Saladin's demonstration of loyalty; in the summer of 1173 this included gold, silver, jade, crystal, pearls, rubies, an elephant and 60,000 dinars. Such actions barely mollified Nur al-Din who sent his vizier Ibn al-Qaysarani to check the correct amount of money was actually being paid and to try to establish a clearer understanding of obedience between the two parties. Ibn al-Qaysarani demanded full account of all the treasures of the caliphal palaces and the revenues collected. Saladin protested his honesty but in reality he cannot have been surprised at such a move. He explained why he had spent so much money, indicating that officers of state expected a high living and that they had either disposed of existing resources themselves or would not tolerate a decrease in revenues. He argued that keeping the wheels of state moving needed a serious degree of financial lubrication. For all that, al-Qaysarani's presence was a constant reminder that the ruler of Syria still cast a shadow over his former associate.[20]

Lands to the south continued to pose a threat to the fledgling Ayyubid regime in Cairo. With the tension between Egypt and Syria at such a height, not to mention threats from internal revolt and the ongoing battles with the Franks, it is easy to ignore the danger posed by the Nubians. They had been closely linked to the Fatimids and remained keen to derail the newcomers. They invaded Aswan in 1172–3 and in response Saladin sent a contingent to bring them to battle and drive them back.[21] Later in the year no less a figure than Turanshah marched down into Nubia and captured men, booty and the fortress of Ibrim, which he entrusted to a Kurdish noble and his followers. Once again we see Saladin's inner core of associates working closely with a group of trusted companions, all outsiders to the area, but tough warriors capable of this frontier warfare. The Nubians dispatched envoys to Turanshah who was based at Qus, on the Nile north of Aswan. This was meant as a conciliatory move by the Nubians, but in return the Ayyubid sent the herald two pairs of arrows with the ominous message: 'Tell the king I have no answer for him save this.' Evidently the Kurds were not prepared to compromise and Turanshah directed his own envoy to scout out the lands as a possible prelude to an invasion. The report was not, however, encouraging. The envoy dismissed the land as miserable and unproductive, claiming it yielded only maize and small date-palms. The contrast with the splendour and ceremonial of Cairo was marked; the king of Nubia was said to ride bareback, wrapped only in a shabby mantle and with no crown on his bald head. The city of Dongola was derided as a bunch of reed huts huddled around the sole building of the royal palace. While the Nubians derived considerable income from the important Red Sea port of Aydhab their lands were clearly not attractive to Turanshah.[22]

While there remained a theoretical prospect of Nur al-Din removing the Ayyubids from power in Egypt, internal revolt was another means by which the Kurds could fall. Should this happen the clan would face ruin, and even if they survived, it would be difficult to return to their former lands in Syria. Yet they had plainly acquired a taste for power and were proving tough and resourceful rulers. Within this promising environment the loss of the family figurehead was a heavy blow. On 31 July 1173 Saladin's father, Ayyub, died. Riding out of the Victory Gate in Cairo, he was thrown from his horse and succumbed to his injuries several days later. Ayyub was known as a fanatical horseman and an obsessive polo player, so much so that people had joked that he would certainly die falling from a horse. Saladin himself was absent on campaign in Transjordan and was distraught at not being present. Aside from the grief of a son losing his father the passing of Ayyub meant much more. He had been a hugely influential character in the family's transition from loyal, regional governors to an ambitious international dynasty. Ayyub's political skills had helped to steer Saladin through his first crisis with Nur al-Din and his careful, calculating approach clearly rubbed off on his son. Ayyub was buried next to his own brother Shirkuh in the royal palace, although a decade or so later, both were moved to Medina as a mark of respect.[23]

If Nubia had been deemed an unsuitable regional power base for Turanshah, Yemen emerged as an alternative. The Fatimid court poet Umara was of Yemeni origins and he told Turanshah of its wealth and the weakness of its rulers, encouraging the Ayyubid to act, although as we will see shortly, he had other agendas as well.[24]

Turanshah chose a more collegiate path and asked his brother to endorse an invasion of Yemen. Saladin in turn asked Nur al-Din for permission to do this on the grounds that the Yemeni ruler was a Khariji (a further splinter of the Islamic faith, founded in the seventh century and existing on the margins of Islam), who was suppressing the Abbasid *khutba*.[25] In its narrowest terms this seems logical enough; as champion of the cause of Sunni Islam, Nur al-Din would have wished for the Abbasid caliphate to extend its reach into a recalcitrant area. Thus he agreed, although the wider political dimensions of such a move cannot have been lost on him. If taking Yemen was conceived as founding an Ayyubid refuge in case of the loss of Egypt, while the latter remained under their authority as well this new land was a significant addition to their political and economic standing.

Turanshah gathered his troops and set out in February 1174, taking the opportunity to perform the pilgrimage to Mecca en route. In May he captured the prime city of Zabid and soon he held sway over the remainder of the land, seizing the profitable trading port of Aden on the southern coast, and extracting considerable sums of money from the populace. As was customary, the *khutba* was recited in the name of the caliph of Baghdad and followed by that of the new ruler, Turanshah himself.[26] The good news was sent back to Saladin in Cairo, who in turn despatched a messenger to Nur al-Din and then to Baghdad.

The project to acquire Yemen as a place of refuge took added relevance given continued threats from pro-Fatimid factions within Egypt. The spring of 1174 saw a particularly serious bid to unseat the Ayyubids, an effort compounded by the plotters' efforts to link up with external allies, the Franks of Jerusalem and, unusually, the king of Sicily, a monarch whose people had taken little part in recent crusading expeditions.

This plot began to ferment in late 1173, driven largely by groups of Sh'ites determined to restore the survivors of the Fatimid dynasty. The poet Umara was alleged to be one of the ringleaders and his encouragement to Turanshah to head for Yemen can be seen as a way to deprive Saladin of one of his most important associates. Coming relatively soon after the death of his father Ayyub, the absence of his elder brother could expose Saladin further; Turanshah might have been a potential successor to Saladin and so he was worth sidelining for that reason as well. Other plotters included a number of senior court officials and, emphasising the sectarian nature of this revolt, the chief propagandist of the Nizari (Assassins) Shi'ite sect (see Chapter 7). Compounding this, senior figures from the former Fatimid army, large numbers of Nubian infantrymen, as well as some disaffected men of Saladin's, contrived to entice the Franks and the Sicilians to join the plan.[27]

The scheme was pretty simple. Once the Christians landed at Alexandria, Saladin would have two choices (just as in 1169): either to go north and face them in person or to remain in Cairo and send his troops out to confront the invaders. In the former instance, the rebels would seize power in Cairo and those troops hostile to him would abandon him to be defeated by the Franks. In the other scenario, those in Cairo would take advantage of the absence of the army to the north and capture Saladin in person. The Franks were apparently all ready to go when, as Ibn al-Athir commented, 'by God's grace to the Muslims', the conspiracy was rumbled.[28]

In anticipation of success the plotters had carefully divided out the offices of state, but a squabble over the prized position of vizier brought a preacher, Ibn Nujiyya, into the group. For reasons of personal advantage, he chose to tell the Ayyubids what was afoot. As with an earlier plot, Saladin did not rush to expose the conspirators but told Ibn Nujiyya to continue to pass on intelligence and to keep him appraised of the situation. King Amalric meanwhile sent an envoy to Saladin, on the surface part of conventional diplomatic exchanges, but in reality, a man briefed to contact the plotters via a local Coptic Christian and to move the coup onwards. Saladin enrolled his own Christian agent to befriend this man and inveigle the truth from him; the full extent of the plan, which included a further cell in Alexandria, was duly revealed. Saladin ordered the traitors to be arrested, interrogated and then strangled and hung crucified in various public places to ensure that as wide a section of the populace could learn of their fate. However brutal this seems, the sultan had to be very clear that traitors could expect no mercy whatsoever. The land and money of the traitors was seized and their families disinherited as well.[29] Any remaining Fatimid troops, including Sudanese contingents, were given an amnesty to leave Cairo immediately and to depart for Upper Egypt. Here we have a carefully calibrated action – in some respects, these men deserved execution too; but to do so might have provoked a revolt in its own right. While this potentially left the problem open to trouble in future, it was probably a wise move. The remaining members of the Fatimid dynasty were placed under tighter surveillance as well.[30]

One further prominent figure was also executed, and this was more controversial. As we saw above, Umara was a high-profile poet and, notwithstanding his dubious political choices, it is not hard to detect a whiff of regret – on artistic grounds at least – at his demise. Indeed, Qadi al-Fadil, although a rival during their earlier time at the Fatimid court of Caliph al-Adid, is said in some accounts to have tried to intercede on Umara's behalf. In a final gesture Umara asked to be taken past al-Fadil's literary salon en route to his death, but the patron locked his door and declined to meet him.

Another version of his death claims the (ultimately) false attribution of this heretical verse as the reason for Saladin's fury:

The origins of this religion spring from a man [Saladin]
Who strove so much that they addressed him as 'Lord of Nations!'[31]

The two explanations of a plot and the poem can, of course, overlap, but at the very least they demonstrate the persuasive influence a court poet could have. They also indicate that even by the quicksilver standards of contemporary allegiance, danger could strike if a poet chose unwisely in their patron or outlook.

The prominence of poetry in this episode signals the importance of the genre in public life. Just as Saladin understood the significance of display, he could see that poetry was integral to the culture of Egypt. It was an art form and a means of entertainment, but also had a strong role as an authoritative form of discourse. In other words, it was a way to transmit messages and influence opinion. Poetry had held such a position in Arab culture before the emergence of Islam and offered a culturally acceptable genre to deliver powerful emotions and arguments. The prominence and popularity of poetry in the Near East is perhaps hard for a modern western audience to comprehend. A messy blend of social media, protest songs and flashes of low-end journalism, set alongside complex theology and powerful religious polemic, gives a suitably confusing sense of the scale and scope of the genre. Poetry was an essential element of *adab*, the prized cultural attributes of a great man, and was thus vital for leaders, courtiers and men of, or seeking, standing from many walks of life.[32] It was a basic means of communication that could be an ideological or political vehicle for holy war, or it might be a way of denigrating, in artfully obscene and savage terms, a rival or an opponent.[33]

Leaders could use poetry as a way to create an image; in the case of Saladin, as a rightful ruler and as a holy warrior intent upon recovering Jerusalem. Verse could reinforce prevailing sentiments, and may help to reflect how ideas and images evolved in this highly literate society; it could also form part of a response to events. It is interesting to note that the language of poetry was classical Arabic, yet the main recipients and patrons in Syria at least, were Kurdish and Turkic nobles, which must say something about the range and depth of linguistic skills amongst these groups. Saladin himself was known to be very fond of poetry and a considerable quantity of verse was produced by members of his household. He was said to have memorised the anthology of the ninth-century Arab poet Abu Tammam, and to carry around a copy of the collection produced by the courtier, diplomat and poet Usama ibn Munqidh.[34] Ibn Jubayr reports Saladin hosting poetry symposia in Damascus.[35] Similarly, Imad al-Din organised a poetry competition to entertain the court during a campaign in the Jazira, a chance for the local poets to parade their talents in front of the sultan. In the event, they were, in the judgement of the sophisticated secretary, pretty mediocre, although typically Saladin rewarded them well nonetheless.[36] Numerous poems were dedicated to the sultan and verses often feature within the narrative accounts of his life as well.[37] Much of the poetry connected with him is celebratory in nature, rejoicing in his victories, from Jacob's Ford to Hattin,

Jerusalem and beyond. Some of it was anticipatory as well, predicting success and urging people to support his cause.

Yet moving outside material composed by the sultan's immediate entourage reveals a much broader range of contemporary poetic discourse and can also illuminate how the regime, or those within it, were perceived by others. Verse could communicate something quite mundane. A Kurdish soldier wrote a poem to Saladin to grumble that he had been assigned an *iqta* at Qus in Upper Egypt yet he served hundreds of miles away in Mosul. His petition succeeded and he was awarded a different form of remuneration.[38]

A significant proportion of the poetry that survives was satirical in tone and the level of innuendo and the willingness to make what seem to be immensely damaging claims suggest a high, but not infinite, level of tolerance for this subgenre. In other words, viewed through the lens of poetry, court life around the Ayyubids was not wholly as upstanding as the emphasis on holy war conveyed by the narrative texts. That said, satire and scandal can encourage exaggeration and so some degree of caution may be appropriate.

At a relatively mild level, al-Arqala was scathing about a physician who fancied himself as a poet, but had also fallen down drunk and managed to scar his own face:

We have a doctor, a poet, with an inverted eyelid. May God relieve us of him!
Whenever he visits a patient in the morning he composes an elegy for him the same day.[39]

More pointed was the output of Al-Wahrani, who attacked Saladin's nephew, Taqi al-Din, for his supposedly immoral behaviour and suggested that rather than fight the holy war he should consort with the courtesans of Damascus, Mosul and Aleppo and leave his fate to God. He scathingly observed that the Ayyubid's words were 'sweeter than a beating with a prostitute's slipper'. The poet also criticised the appointment of, as he argued, rustic Kurds, as *qadis* in areas of Egypt. He claimed that the *qadi* of Damascus appointed deputies of dubious quality: 'whoever uses wolves as sheepdogs is a wrongdoer'. Imad al-Din came into his sights for his close friendship with a male singer, while such was his attitude to religion that Saladin himself accused the poet of heresy. Notwithstanding the fact that his output clearly contained some fairly provocative material, his posthumous reputation was positive with Ibn Khallikan praising his 'buoyant humour, acute mind and accomplished wit'.[40]

Sometimes people went too far. Ibn Unayn published a stream of invective against several of Saladin's physicians, writing of Ibn Mutran that 'His existence itself is a satire of existence.' The nephew of the Damascene historian Ibn Asakir was given the nickname 'khara bi-dibs', meaning 'shit with dibs' – the latter term being a syrup from grape or date juice that the poet explained was being used to decorate the excrement. Even as senior a figure as Qadi al-Fadil was attacked, caricatured for his hunched back and for allegedly having sex with his black slaves and with dogs. Ibn Unayn also described Saladin himself as being crippled. This overstepped the mark and he was exiled from Damascus, although decades later he returned to the city and achieved high office under one of Saladin's sons.[41]

The format of poetry varied widely. Some verses were highly ornate, complex compositions, designed to dazzle and impress an educated literary elite with their wordplay and elaborate multilayered meanings. Others were simple pieces, either relaying a basic message, or else deliberately formulated in a way that would be easy to understand for a large audience, perhaps resonating with well-known verses from the Quran:

> The victory of God and the conquest have come – which the Messenger promised, so glorify God and seek his forgiveness.
> Syria has been conquered and Jerusalem, which is the gathering place for creation at the resurrection, is purified.[42]

One genre of poetry had a highly distinctive format. The Spanish physician al-Jilyani composed stunningly decorative texts, picture poems, or 'brocaded' pieces as he himself called them. They described Saladin's successes in the holy war and contained images with poetry therein, as well as one or more secondary texts, colour-coded. These poems could be of a length that required scrolls of paper three metres long. As well as glorifying Saladin in the content, the presentation of such poems was a performance in itself as the scrolls were unrolled and deciphered by the audience; for example the figure of a tree included detailed instructions as to how to add syllables to the stem *mawa*, in order to produce a piece on Saladin's immense generosity and also linking him as a ruler to God. Other shapes al-Jilyani filled with words were a variety of geometrical patterns, such as stars, circles and chequerboards, a bravado display of technical skill and devotion.[43]

During his years in Cairo, Saladin came to develop a strong court life around himself, and his time in Egypt exposed him to a wider cultural scene. A circus of peripatetic poets needed patronage to earn a living, and in the turbulence of contemporary Egypt that meant coping with a carousel of leaders and catering for frequent changes in religious and political allegiance. A track record of consistency was very difficult to achieve, which meant that being a poet of laudations was a hard, and potentially dangerous task; al-Wahrani puts the realities very plainly:

One day ... I gave myself a free rein and made gilded poems my wares, sucking on the teats of erudition. I did not pass by a prince without alighting at his courtyard and invoking the rain of his palm [i.e. his munificence], or a vizier without knocking at his door and asking for a reward or a *qadi* without taking the flow of his gifts, emptying his pockets.[44]

The executed high-profile poet Umara had been a merchant, a scholar and a diplomat before starting his career at court under the previous regime. Showing the kaleidoscopic nature of the Fatimid era, Umara was himself a Sunni although at times he came under pressure to profess the Shi'a doctrine of the ruling class.

When Saladin rose to power Umara fell under the reverse suspicion because his apparent admiration for the Fatimids meant he was accused of being an adherent of the Shi'a. His composition of an elegiac ode for the fallen dynasty was widely admired in artistic terms yet it was a politically questionable move. Of course, its success may represent a measure of wider sympathy for the Fatimids. Umara wrote:

O Fate, you have stricken the hand of glory with paralysis,
And its neck, once so beautifully adorned, you have stripped bare.[45]

Attempts to praise Saladin and his colleagues formed further examples of his oeuvre, although as we have just seen, their presumed lack of integrity came to play a part in his ultimate demise.

Saladin wrote a report on the whole episode which he dispatched to Nur al-Din along with the annual submission of tribute. An inventory of items submitted has survived, and bearing in mind the volume of money that Saladin had already expended, it is worth quoting just to contemplate one part of the staggering wealth amassed by the Fatimids over the centuries, and to register the continued exodus of such funds:

Five copies of the Quran, one being thirty parts with covers of blue satin and held together by golden clasps with gold locks bearing gold inscriptions, another of ten parts and covered with pistachio-coloured brocade, and a third of leather with a gold lock and written in the hand of Ibn al-Bawwab [a famous calligrapher]. Three Balas rubies [from near Samarkand], one weighing 22 mithqals [a mithqal weighs 4.25g], another 12, and a third, 10.5; six emeralds, one weighing 3 mithqals, one red ruby weighing 7 mithqals, one sapphire weighing 6 mithqals, one hundred jewelled necklaces weighing 857 mithqals, 50 vessels of balm ointment, 20 pieces of crystal, 14 chequered earthenware drinking bowls and dishes, an ewer and basin of jade, a gilt wine cup with a handle containing two pearls and in the centre a sapphire ... two large blocks of aloe-wood, amber including one piece weighing 30 ratls [a ratl weighs 437.5g] and another 20; one hundred satin garments, 24 gold-embroidered black carpets, 24 garments of white figured silk; a gold-embroidered pepper-coloured set of clothes; another splendid set, yellow-coloured and gold-embroidered; a magnificent blue set ... and many clothes as well, the value of it all amounting to 225,000 dinars.[46]

By this time, however, the relationship between Nur al-Din and Saladin was past the point at which financial payments could hold it together. The ruler of Syria had finally lost patience with Saladin's failure to pull his weight in the conflict against the Franks. He had consistently ducked making a co-ordinated attack on the kingdom of Jerusalem. Given the Franks' limited resources, applying pressure from two sides – the golden strategic benefit of holding Egypt and Syria – would surely break them in the end. Saladin could argue that he was simply consolidating the Sunni position in Egypt – which was true. But at the same time it seemed ever clearer that he was doing so for the advantage of the Ayyubids, rather than Nur al-Din. In not trying to defeat the Franks, Saladin also used them as a counterweight to his former master because to some extent they demanded the Syrian ruler's attention. The ongoing (as it was then) conquest of Yemen by Turanshah made plain the dynastic ambitions of the Kurdish clan too.

In the spring of 1174 Nur al-Din cast aside any reservations he may have had about triggering a civil war and summoned men from Mosul, the Jazira and Diyar Bakr to invade Egypt. He could claim that the Ayyubids were no longer fighting the true jihad and they needed to be removed in order for the struggle to advance more effectively. To the Franks, a Sunni civil war must have seemed an astonishing opportunity, one that the imminent Sicilian invasion of Egypt looked, by coincidence, poised to exploit.

But in mid-May 1174 as he brought his preparations to a close, Nur al-Din fell seriously ill in his quarters in the citadel of Damascus. Sources write of quinsy, an illness whereby pus-filled abscesses in the throat can swell, cause breathing difficulties and spread a bacterial infection throughout the body. His physician advised bloodletting but the patient refused saying that 'a sixty-year-old should not be bled'. He died a few days later on 15 May 1174. He was buried in the citadel, but soon moved to a mausoleum in the madrasa he had founded himself, deep in the heart of the old city, near the Bazaar of the Palm-Leaf Workers. The madrasa still functions today.[47]

Nur al-Din's piety, personal bravery and consistent support for Sunni religious scholars across his dominions brought about a sea change in the approach to and support for holy war. Beforehand it was sporadic and patchy; under him, a man who drew together lands and cities across Syria and the Jazira, emerged the intellectual building blocks to justify and to propagate jihad against the Franks. He also brought an end to what he saw as the heresy of the Shi'a in Aleppo and oversaw the capture of Egypt from the Fatimid Shi'ite caliphate. The Sunni religious classes received a level of patronage and personal engagement not yet seen from a Syrian ruler. He was a man who, in his duty as a good Islamic monarch, did much to administer justice to his people, regardless of their social position. He sponsored hospitals, orphanages, bathhouses and fortified many cities in the region. In his personal piety he engaged mightily in the internal, and greater, jihad.[48] His success in ruling both Syria and the Jazira, and his support for the external jihad, created the climate in which Saladin and the Ayyubids emerged. It is no exaggeration to suggest that in this respect Nur al-Din did much of the vital groundwork without which Saladin could not have come to the fore, nor been in a position to deploy his own formidable gifts to such great effect.

While Nur al-Din was a vigorous and splendid warrior in his own right, the practicalities of power in medieval times meant that he had to delegate to others. Shirkuh and the Ayyubids were, in military terms, an excellent choice, but as we have seen, the array of riches and opportunities on offer in Egypt drew them away from him. The fact that he was on the verge of outright conflict with Saladin shows just how badly fractured his relationship with the Kurdish clan had become.

His death brought an admiring but no doubt relieved tribute from William of Tyre in the kingdom of Jerusalem. He wrote of 'a mighty persecutor of the Christian faith ... a just prince, valiant and wise, and according to the traditions of his race, a religious man'.[49] Notwithstanding the predictably waspish tone in commenting on Islam, this brief sketch is consistent with that drawn with greater warmth and colour by the Muslim authors.

On the other hand, the picture was not entirely flawless.[50] Along with the problems he faced with Saladin there were a few military defeats – his absence from the siege of Ascalon in 1153, and the loss near Hisn al-Akrad in 1163. We might also note that he was frequently in conflict with his fellow Muslims. Most notably, he intimidated and then dislodged the Burid dynasty from Damascus, justifying his own act of usurpation on the grounds that it would advance the cause of the jihad. He also experienced difficulties with his brother Nusrat al-Din in the late 1150s, periodically clashed with the Seljuks of Konya as well, and in 1171 he annexed Mosul to his lands. In other words, as with any contemporary, he was not above, or disinclined to avoid, fighting or displacing his co-religionists in order to establish and extend his own power base.

A contemporary pilgrimage guide stated that Nur al-Din was among the saints, while a biographer mentioned that the tomb 'is visited and its grills are sprinkled with fragrance and perfumed and every passer-by seeks blessings from it'. Ibn Khallikan reported that 'I heard a number of the Damascene people say that prayers offered up at his tomb were answered and, having wished to prove the fact, I found it to be true.' In the fifteenth century his powers were still being successfully invoked by locals in disputes. Today, a small, barred window of the mausoleum opens to the outside alleyway and, peering inside, one can see the modest cenotaph of this central figure in the counter-crusade movement.[51]

7

Saladin's Takeover of Damascus: Open Ambitions

'This wicked man, who repudiates my father's goodness to him, has come to take my lands'

The sudden death of Nur al-Din fractured the political landscape of the Muslim Near East. Most immediately it removed the threat of civil war between Egypt and Syria, and for Saladin it created a whole host of opportunities to increase his power. Nur al-Din's demise did not open the door for him alone, though. Other members of the Zengid family shared an acute distrust of Saladin and, at the very least, were determined to take over Nur al-Din's Syrian possessions for themselves. The pawn in all of this was the eleven-year-old Prince al-Salih, Nur al-Din's son and designated successor; guardianship of his person would be a significant advantage to anyone looking to advance their standing. For all the potential of this unexpected new vista, Saladin was in no position to rush over to Syria, not least because Alexandria faced imminent assault from the Sicilians and Franks.

Nur al-Din's death presented the Sicilians with a rare prospect too. They were the nearest western European power to the Holy Land, but aside from the substantial Norman–Sicilian contingent on the First Crusade their involvement in subsequent expeditions and the settlement of the Levant was limited. The Normans had conquered Sicily from its Islamic rulers by 1091, although a substantial Muslim population remained on the island. Relations with Fatimid Egypt had generally been positive (aside from a raid on Alexandria in 1154), in large part because of trade, while from the 1130s strong cultural ties with Egypt became apparent as well.[1] When Saladin took power in Cairo this equilibrium was disturbed, a change accentuated by the kingdom of Jerusalem actively looking for help from Sicily in its conflict against the Muslims of the Near East.

Latin and Arabic sources indicate that the Sicilians assembled around 200 vessels, with perhaps forty horse transports and over 1,000 knights. By any contemporary standards this was a formidable force, a fact which makes its utter lack of progress all the more dismal. Whether the Sicilians already knew that Saladin had exposed the Fatimid plot (back in late April) is not clear; they sailed in early July, which makes it improbable the news had not reached them. To journey from Sicily to Alexandria takes around eight to ten days, slightly longer for a large fleet. More likely, however, was their ignorance of another seismic shift in the political landscape of the Eastern Mediterranean. On 11 July 1174 King Amalric died of dysentery, aged only thirty-eight. The throne fell to Baldwin (IV) his eldest son, who was thirteen years old. Even more serious than having a juvenile heir was this young man's chronic ill health. As the parallel with Prince al-Salih emphasises, minorities were a period ripe for political turmoil, but compounding this many times over was that Baldwin was suspected of suffering from leprosy.[2] In harsh dynastic terms it meant that he could not have children, and with his siblings being two younger sisters, the situation in Jerusalem was potentially very complex. For Saladin, this was a second stroke of good fortune within weeks.

Ever the diplomat, the sultan sent the young king a letter expressing his condolences on learning of the death of Amalric. He wrote of his own 'devastation of the passing away of a friend and of the void left in his stead ... Let him [Baldwin] know that, like his father, he has from us a pure love, a true faith, an affection that is strong in life and death, and a heart that has been strengthened in this life by loyalty despite the religious differences. Let him rely on us as the son who carries the burden which his father carried before him. May God perpetuate his longevity, look over his emirate, make him attain success and inspire him to trust the intentions of a friend.'[3]

To some extent this feels like simple convention (Qadi al-Fadil wrote a similar letter to a northern Syrian emir after Nur al-Din's death only two months previously), but as we saw earlier, Saladin and Amalric had met each other in 1167 and seemingly formed a positive relationship. They shared a fear of Nur al-Din, and Saladin had, to the benefit of Amalric too, evaded supporting his overlord in fighting the Christians.[4] This letter might also have been a way to suggest that the Franks not join the attack on Alexandria; the sense of wishing for peaceful relations, in the short term at least, certainly suited both parties.

The most immediate effect of Amalric's death was that the Franks of Jerusalem missed their rendezvous with the Sicilians outside Alexandria. Preoccupied by their own political affairs, they did not set out at all and lost a real chance to topple Saladin. What had looked like a triple-pronged assault on the sultan was reduced from Fatimid plotters, Franks and Sicilians, to a single spike, albeit one of significant strength.

On 28 July the Sicilian fleet disembarked easily and set up siege towers and trebuchets, evidence of well-funded preparations and a measure of their intent. The Alexandrians sent news of the invasion to Saladin in Cairo while local troops were urgently summoned to the defence of the city. The initial momentum of the attack took the Sicilian ships inside the inner port, and during the ensuing panic the Egyptians burnt all their warships and commercial vessels – a further blow (after the fire at Fustat in 1168) to the country's collapsing naval power. The second day, the Sicilians managed to bring their siege towers close to the walls, poised to launch a full assault. The arrival overnight of reinforcements boosted the defenders' resolve and the Alexandrians exploited woeful enemy discipline to burst out of the gates and cause havoc. They knew how best to hit Sicilian morale, and on reaching the siege towers quickly set fire to these expensive, complicated constructions. Fighting continued all day with the Muslims inflicting serious casualties on the Christian troops. As Saladin drew near he wisely sent ahead a messenger. News of the sultan's approach greatly encouraged the defenders and, even though it was now late afternoon, they were inspired to launch a further thrust into the Sicilian camp, tearing through the tents, slaughtering the foot soldiers and taking large amounts of weapons and booty. The siege was duly lifted. Passive Sicilian leadership brought what could have been a major threat to Saladin to a swift and, from his perspective, successful conclusion.[5]

The turmoil of Nur al-Din's death and the Sicilian invasion provided a cue for others to challenge Saladin's authority. In Upper Egypt the ruler of Aswan killed one of the sultan's emirs and sparked a wider rebellion that sought to restore the Fatimids and to bring the troops from southern lands back to prominence. A swift response from the murdered emir's brother, the Kurdish warrior Abu'l Hayja al-Samin, 'the Obese', and Saladin's own brother Saphadin (as he became known in the West), brought the situation under control. Beha al-Din, later Saladin's army judge and close associate, observed that the soldiers sent to put down the revolt 'had tasted the sweetness of ruling the land of Egypt and feared to lose it', a pithy assessment of the motives of the Syrian and Kurdish troops and their wish to keep hold of the lands so recently given to them by Saladin. Incidentally, such was the fame of Abu'l Hayja's weight that pottery-makers in Baghdad named extra-large sized bowls 'Abu'l Hayja' in honour of this man's magnificent frame.[6]

Faced with these various threats Saladin was unable to advance his position in Syria – others, however, were not so compromised. Almost immediately, Sayf al-Din Ghazi, one of Nur al-Din's nephews and now the ruler of Mosul, moved to establish his ascendancy in the family. He swooped through the lands of the Jazira, taking the cities of Harran, Edessa, al-Raqqa and Saruj to create a regional power base across the north-east of Muslim Syria.

Prince al-Salih (Nur al-Din's son), meanwhile, was living in Damascus under the guardianship of Ibn al-Muqaddam, a senior local emir. Saladin chose to take a careful approach, recognising that some in the city worried about his intentions. He wrote to the prince to offer his condolences and sent dinars struck in the youth's name, saying that the *khutba* and allegiance were his. When he heard of Sayf al-Din's successes, however, he castigated the young man for not turning to him (Saladin) to prevent this while also making the potentially spurious claim that Nur al-Din would have assigned him the regency had he not died so suddenly. Given the recent history between the two men this was highly unlikely, but the emergence of a new power in northern Syria had obviously alarmed the sultan.[7]

Both Aleppo and Damascus feared Sayf al-Din's ambitions, and to halt his progress it was decided to send Prince al-Salih north with an army. Soon after the prince arrived in Aleppo, however, the pieces on the political chessboard moved again when officials there, led by the eunuch emir Kumushtakin, chose not to fight Sayf al-Din and instead recognised his authority.[8] In other words, just at the wrong moment, the Damascenes had made the ghastly error of handing over their trump card, Prince al-Salih, to a new northern Syrian elite. Given the Damascenes' desire to avoid falling under the control of Sayf al-Din, only one option remained open to them – Saladin. Thus in October 1174, Ibn al-Muqaddam, along with several other important figures, invited the sultan to come to the city and take power.

Saladin's dynamic reaction indicated just how critical a moment this was. Gathering 700 horsemen he rushed across the southern Sinai, bypassing the Frankish strongholds of Kerak and Shaubak to reach Bosra, the southernmost settlement of Damascene lands. A huge Roman theatre formed the centrepiece of the city and, over the centuries, it had become heavily fortified.[9] The local governor, one of those who had asked him to travel to Syria, saw how few men Saladin had with him and pessimistically observed that if the locals resisted him for an hour the Bedouin would pick over the survivors. Money, he suggested, was one way to procure loyalty, at least in the short term. How much, the emir asked, did Saladin have with him? 'It could be 50,000 dinars' was Qadi al-Fadil's gnomic reply. 'Hopeless', came the response: 'we're done for'. In fact, the sultan had only 10,000 dinars, but nonetheless, he pressed on northwards.[10]

By 25 October he had arrived at Damascus. Saladin held the advantages of an invitation from the ruling elite and the credibility of his recent victory at Alexandria. He was also, of course, deeply familiar with the place from his youth. The sultan laid great emphasis on his allegiance to the absent Prince al-Salih, and claimed that he had come to educate and support him and that he would keep the *khutba* in his name. Saladin did, however, assume control of the citadel to give himself a secure location and, more importantly, to seize all the money therein. As one writer noted, 'It made him rich, established his position and strengthened his resolve.'[11] Exactly what this resolve might lead to was not wholly clear. Had the prince been in Damascus, would Saladin have acted as his loyal protector? In the first instance almost certainly so, given the city's residual loyalty to Nur al-Din.

Saladin soon took measures to bolster both his own standing and that of Damascus relative to the northern Syrians. In some respects this took the form of diplomatic moves, such as the lengthy letters Qadi al-Fadil wrote to the caliph of Baghdad.[12] These letters were basically a manifesto that rehearsed his achievements to date and made the case as to why he was the right man to take forwards the cause of Sunni Islam and the inheritance of Nur al-Din. He described his conquests in Egypt, Yemen and the Maghreb and, of course, the establishment of Sunni orthodoxy at the head of the state in Cairo and in Yemen too. He restated the role that he, his father and his uncle Shirkuh had played in advancing the cause of Islam against the heresy of the Shi'ites. He noted his resistance against the Greek emperor, the strength of this 'proud tyrant', whom he characterised as 'a Goliath of unfaithfulness', but who now wished for peace. Saladin boasted of his defeat of the mighty Sicilian fleet and also asserted that he had made deals with the Italian commercial cities of Genoa, Pisa and Venice to trade in materials of war (metal and wood) which would enhance his military abilities. He argued that it was difficult to conduct jihad from Egypt because of the distance and harsh terrain; better provisions and fresh horses would be available in Syria. False beliefs would be challenged and discord ended. Saladin represented himself as the best and most worthy protector of al-Salih and stated that he wanted to guard his dynasty, all in the ultimate name of the Abbasid caliphate. The sultan asked to be invested with the rule of Egypt, Yemen, the Maghreb and Syria. and everything from the lands of Nur al-Din along with all else that he conquered with his own sword on behalf of the Abbasid caliphate. Such a commission was suggested to extend to his sons and his brother, signposting his long-term dynastic aims. But there was a further forward-looking aspect too: he forcefully argued that no one else in Syria was capable of conquering the holy city of Jerusalem – only he could do this and he promised to recover the Dome of the Rock. A second letter placed his efforts in Syria into a continuum with Nur al-Din's. It also noted the threat of the Shi'ite Assassins and the losses of lands and frontier towns. Saladin claimed that his presence in Syria had provoked great anxiety amongst the Franks and prompted them to appeal for outside support, to hold prayers in the Holy Sepulchre and to process the relic of the True Cross. Holy men had threatened their leaders with terrible punishment on the Day of Judgement and carried banners with messages and images of saints to reinforce the point. He concluded by warning that many powerful figures in the West were making preparations to come and assist their beleaguered brethren in the Holy Land.

Underpinning all of this was Saladin's desire for legitimacy and an unreserved endorsement from the spiritual head of Sunni Islam. He had certainly achieved much in Egypt but now he wanted power in Syria too. And herein lies the eternal dilemma with Saladin – was this simply dynastic empire-building? Or was he now leading a selfless holy war on behalf of his faith? Both positions are too simplistic and in a less extreme form need not be mutually exclusive, although as his behaviour in Egypt had unambiguously demonstrated, an Ayyubid family power base was clearly important. His claim to be acting as guardian of al-Salih was the easiest way to increase his strength in Syria, but how that relationship might play out was open to question. Plainly many Zengids bitterly resented Saladin's rise and did not wish to lose their authority to another clan. On the other hand, Saladin had a record of successfully fighting Christians and extending the reach of Sunni Islam; Jerusalem was stated as his ultimate goal and represented a tangible, plausible and highly desirable target. With the letters and envoys dispatched to Baghdad, the sultan had now to wait to see what the response might be.

In the interim, we can glimpse a couple of further instances of the personal style of government operated by Saladin. Writers note that when in Damascus he held audiences every Monday and Thursday to give people a chance to petition him with grievances, or on occasion, to appeal for work. A letter preserving the request of a eunuch named Iqbal survives. This man, originally from eastern Uzbekistan, was previously in the entourage of Nur al-Din, no less, but now he needed work and so humbly approached Saladin. We have seen the sultan engage former Fatimid officials in Egypt and here he did the same. Saladin evidently chose his employees with care, and aside from the qualities of a particular individual, the idea of continuity and knowledge of the previous regime – yet loyalty to their new master – appealed to him. Iqbal was taken on and enjoyed a distinguished career as a diplomat and an advisor.[13]

Around the same time, a Kurdish emir named Mankalan 'knowing of the generosity of our master' also petitioned Saladin. He complained the lands given to him by relatives were insufficient and asked to hold an *iqta* directly from the sultan himself to improve his situation and status. Part of Mankalan's approach was to play upon a distant relationship with one of the sultan's cousins, an important army commander in Egypt. Saladin responded positively to the Kurd and with a blend of patronage and personal judgement employed Mankalan in his bodyguard – a role in which we will encounter him again soon.[14]

Saladin's ability to improve his position was enhanced by a series of political convulsions amongst the Franks of Jerusalem that culminated in the murder of Baldwin IV's regent, Miles of Plancy, in Acre in October.[15] Saladin meanwhile took the Syrian town of Homs in early December, but the citadel resisted. He moved on to Hama where once again the citadel held out. Emirs loyal to Nur al-Din were sceptical of Saladin's professions of allegiance to Prince al-Salih. The sultan had to swear that he would preserve the prince's lands for him, which he duly did. Finally, on 30 December 1174 he reached Aleppo, hoping to work with the young man.[16]

Such a wish would prove ill-founded. The prince – influenced by his hosts' traditional antagonism towards Damascus, coupled with his own father's recent hostility to Saladin – is said to have addressed the people in these emotive terms: 'You know well my father's kindness to you, his love for you and his good rule over you. I am his orphan. This wicked man, who repudiates my father's goodness to him, has come to take my lands.'[17] Doubtless many others saw Saladin in this negative light and his audience were stirred to resist. Sorties and raids prevented the sultan from bringing Aleppo under tight siege; activity from the Franks of Antioch further distracted him.

Saladin soon had to face a more subtle enemy than warriors charging at him on horseback. Kumushtakin, the eunuch emir of Aleppo, adopted another tack. He wrote to Sinan, leader of the Shi'ite Nizari sect, offering to pay them to murder Saladin.[18] The group had split from the Fatimid Isma'ilis in 1094 over a dispute as to who was the true successor to the caliphate in Cairo. They had favoured the dead caliph's eldest son Nizar, believing that when he was passed over by the vizier and then killed, Nizar's son, whom they regarded as the rightful caliph and Imam, had been brought to their castle at Alamut, south-west of the Caspian Sea, where he remained hidden. The Nizaris claimed to rule on his behalf.[19] Along with assertions of theological correctness they lived an austere lifestyle, an overt contrast with some of the luxurious Seljuk and Fatimid courts. They had two areas of authority, one in Persia, the other centred upon the powerful castle of Masyaf in the Jebel Ansariye, the dense mountainous district of

Syria that lies between, on one side, the fertile Orontes valley and the Muslim-held towns of Hama and Shaizar, and on the other (towards the coast), the Frankish principality of Antioch and the castles of Safita and Hisn al-Akrad. Persecuted by the rulers of both Aleppo and Damascus during the early decades of the twelfth century, they established what was, de facto, an independent lordship in this tough terrain.[20]

They became known as al-hashishiyya, meaning hash-smokers, a derogatory term of abuse coined in the 1120s by their opponents as a metaphor for low social and moral status. By the 1170s western writers had morphed this word to 'Heysessini' and soon to 'Assissini', which became a byword for political murder. From their early days, a record of political violence made them a dangerous target for those who sought to eliminate them. In 1094 the Seljuk vizier had made a call 'to stem the pus of sedition and excise the taint of inaction' only to fall victim to Assassins disguised as Muslim holy men. In the early decades of the twelfth century rulers in Mosul, Damascus and Homs all perished at their hands, as did the Fatimid caliph of Cairo. Christians were not exempt either, and Count Raymond II of Tripoli was stabbed to death in 1152, although in the face of persecution by Nur al-Din the Nizaris came to pay the Franks what amounted to protection money to ensure they were not disturbed from at least one quarter.[21]

Because the Nizaris were such a secretive body, writers of all persuasions had the scope to compose ever-more lurid stories about them. The Spanish pilgrim of the 1180s, Ibn Jubayr, utterly loathed the group whom he regarded as heretics and claimed that their leader Sinan was 'a devil in a man's disguise ... [who] bewitched them with black arts, so they took him for a god and worshipped him ... reaching such a state of obedience and subjection that did he order one of them to fall from the mountaintop he would do so'.[22] Western visitors such as Burchard of Strasbourg wrote of brainwashing childhood recruits and described their lands as gardens of delight.[23] William of Tyre reported that their leader was known as the 'Old Man', disdaining a more dignified title, and he praised Sinan for his eloquence and intelligence.[24] Operatives usually acted in pairs or as lone killers armed with a dagger. The use of such a weapon gave a ritualistic element to the deed which was, almost inevitably, a suicide mission; eternal pleasure was promised to those handed a dagger.

Saladin had already shown himself to be a determined and dangerous opponent of the Shi'a, and given his ongoing claim to be the champion of Sunni orthodoxy, he posed a serious threat to the group. Against this background, accepting a commission to kill the sultan seemed a sensible move; rendering such a service to Kumushtakin, their powerful new neighbour in Aleppo, would presumably ensure that he then left the group alone.[25]

In early January 1175 the Assassins entered Saladin's camp outside Aleppo and started to mingle in his presence. By good fortune, a local emir who had just joined the sultan's troops recognised the newcomers from years of fighting them. He challenged the infiltrators but was immediately slaughtered; realising their cover was blown, one of the assailants rushed towards Saladin only to be downed before he could strike. The rest of the group was quickly dispatched and the danger averted.[26]

Kumushtakin was a resourceful character and soon lighted upon another way to drive Saladin away from Aleppo. Back in 1164, Nur al-Din had captured Count Raymond III of Tripoli, one of the Franks' most senior nobles ('a leading devil' according to Ibn al-Athir) and a close relative of the ruling house of Jerusalem. In late 1173 or early 1174, a huge ransom of 80,000 bezants and a handover of prisoners secured Raymond's release; by late October 1174 he was the regent for the young leper-king of Jerusalem. The count fully appreciated the need to try to break Saladin's momentum, and when asked by Kumushtakin to attack the sultan's lands to the south, he did so. The scheme worked and, duly distracted, Saladin lifted the siege of Aleppo.[27]

William of Tyre described these events and, as well as giving a narrative, offered his thoughts on Saladin's progress and the nature of the threat that he posed. He admits a slight element of hindsight (because he wrote in the early 1180s, although still years before the loss of Jerusalem). Concerning the situation in 1174 he stated the Franks could see that 'whatever augmented his [Saladin's] authority seemed wholly injurious to the good of the kingdom. He was a man wise in counsel, valiant in war, and generous beyond measure. All the more, for this very reason he was distrusted by those nobles who had keener foresight ... there is no better means by which princes can win the hearts of their subjects, or for that matter, others than by showing lavish bounty toward them.'[28] This is a fascinating evaluation of Saladin's character and abilities from someone who had every reason to fear him. While military prowess is noted, William also recognised the sultan's intelligence and gave an implicit nod to the quality of his advisors and officials, as well as his willingness to listen to them. Yet singled out as his most dangerous characteristic was his generosity. Time and again, Christian and Muslim sources mention this.[29]

The giving of gifts is a basic facet of human interaction and can establish, maintain and reinforce personal and communal relations. It was a behaviour prominent amongst the pre-Islamic Arabs and then emphasised further in Islamic society, not least in one particular context: acts of charity to the poor, zakat (almsgiving), the third Pillar of Islam.[30] Generosity, often symbolised as the giving of gifts, perhaps on a scale above the norm, was a widely admired virtue. It also figures as an aspect of successful leadership in advice books for rulers in the Muslim world, and even formed a literary subgenre in its own right; it was expressly noted as an attribute for rulers in the West too.[31] In many respects it is a typical quality for those in power, although not everyone in such a role displays or deploys it; Nur al-Din, for example, was described as conventionally generous, but anecdotes indicate that some saw him as rather tight-fisted.[32] Most crucially of all the giving of gifts has an understood element of reciprocity: acceptance implies the recipient gives the donor something in return. The tenth-century Abbasid caliph al-Muqtadir was blunt in his evaluation: 'I claim gratitude for benefits and favours; you enjoy benefits and gifts from me which I hope you will acknowledge and consider binding.'[33]

Gifts were, in effect, a lever of government that spread across almost every aspect of political, religious and cultural life, including relations with other powers (of whatever background) where the presentation and exchange of objects was an integral element of diplomacy; again, something we will observe throughout Saladin's career in a variety of settings. The giving of land or iqtas, as Saladin did on taking power in Egypt, had an overtly political aspect and was a way of providing payment for service and loyalty in the past, present and future. That said, such an act can also be characterised as one of generosity and a gift as well. Saladin took the practice of gift-giving to a particularly refined and rarefied extent.[34] In part this may have been an issue of character; we have read of the generosity of his father and uncle. But in the main it was a matter of rapid adaptability and political judgement. As an outsider in a minority group taking power in a potentially very hostile environment, the giving of gifts on a large scale was a vital way to reward and attract supporters. What fused these points together was the opportunity presented by the huge wealth of the Fatimids. We have already seen Saladin's interest in state finances and this, coupled with the removal of the caliphal family and their military elite, gave the sultan the opening to dispense rewards on a colossal scale, both to his own kin and to his allies.[35] Saladin also gave generously to poets, who could then laud their great patron, and to religious institutions in Cairo and now Damascus which meant prayers would be offered for the Ayyubids. In light of the prominent role of the religious classes, the patronage of holy men, lawyers and judges had the capability to deliver the loyalty of such people and also confer upon Saladin and his clan (many of whom were generous donors too) a much-needed aura of legitimation.[36] The one person whom he did not visibly enrich was himself; again perhaps a matter of character but in terms of his image, a huge bonus because he sidestepped accusations of greed and duly amplified his own reputation for generosity. Of course, Saladin possessed considerable lands of his own but he was not given to ostentatious personal display and shunned excessive luxury.

Gift-giving was not free from snares, however. Declining or omitting to give a gift could cause grave offence, as could returning one. And while a reputation for generosity undoubtedly attracted supporters it might lead people of all ranks, from courtiers to foot soldiers, to a dangerous sense of expectation or entitlement that could not always be satisfied. One way to alleviate this was to keep acquiring new streams of income, and in Saladin's case, expansion into the Sudan, Yemen and the Maghreb addressed the issue. That said, a period without major successes, or years affected by bad weather, a failure or a surfeit of the Nile floods, might seriously hamper the ability to dispense rewards and, as we will see later, create problems of loyalty and support. In essence, though, the generous giving of gifts was, from his earliest days in power in Egypt to the time of his death, one of the most prominent characteristics of Saladin's career and, as William of Tyre recognised, a significant reason for his success.

Looking back at the first few months free from the shadow of Nur al-Din, the balance sheet was mixed. The sultan had consolidated his hold on central Syria, but the prize of Aleppo still eluded him. The two major powers in Syria now stood as Saladin and Sayf al-Din. The latter strengthened his hand further by integrating large contingents from the Jazira along with those of Aleppo. Saladin responded by offering to hand over the important towns of Hama and Homs in return for an acknowledgement that he was the legitimate guardian of Damascus on behalf of Prince al-Salih. Sayf al-Din was unmoved: 'It is imperative that you surrender all the Syrian territory that you have taken and return to Egypt.'[37] The ambitious Saladin would not be cowed and took to the offensive.

8

Progress Stalls

*'This magnificent citadel ... combines utility
and embellishment, and comfort and shield
to whosoever seeks refuge in the shadow
of his kingdom'*

The next few years brought home to Saladin the scale and complexity of the challenges he faced in extending his authority into northern Syria. Issues of faith and family emerged alongside more obvious political rivalries to deal him some very harsh lessons. Egypt, meanwhile, remained the fulcrum of his economic and political strength and the Ayyubids continued to build up the administrative and diplomatic expertise that enabled them to survive.

Matters with Sayf al-Din quickly came to a head. This had become a straightforward territorial and political conflict over the future direction of the Muslim Near East. The armies met near Hama on 13 April 1175. Sayf al-Din's forces were poorly led with one wing collapsing almost immediately and the other shortly afterwards; it became a rout and Saladin's army took much in the way of booty, weapons and war horses. The sultan's proactive approach had paid off and the Zengid soon made a peace agreement conceding that Saladin could keep his Syrian territories but that he, Sayf al-Din, would remain in Aleppo. There was, however, one crucial development because, in late April, Saladin ordered that Prince al-Salih's name should no longer be on the coinage issued in his lands and that he should be omitted from the *khutba*.[1] This marked a decisive shift. With al-Salih firmly based in northern Syria, Saladin was no longer portraying himself as the faithful guardian of his former lord's young son. The struggle with Sayf al-Din had compelled him to make his position clear: any pretence that he still acted as a prop to the Zengid dynasty was now removed. The strength accorded to him through his new role as protector of Damascus sharpened the rift, but the prince's (understandable) lean-ings towards his own family and their clear antipathy towards the Kurdish upstart compounded the matter. The Ayyubids had managed to establish themselves firmly in Egypt; given Saladin's current progress, why should they not aspire to do the same across all of Syria?

After placing family members in control of Hama and Homs, the sultan returned to Damascus in mid-May 1175. Envoys arrived from Baghdad to deliver a response to Saladin's request that the caliph endorse his efforts in Syria. The diplomats carried robes of investiture, the black banners of the Abbasids and a signed patent for rule, which disappointingly extended only to the lands he already held in Egypt, Yemen and Syria. While this included Damascus and was in that respect a step forwards, other robes were to be sent on to al-Salih in Aleppo. As yet, therefore, the caliph was not prepared to give Saladin complete authority in the Near East; the Zengid lineage of al-Salih and the wishes of the Aleppans were to be respected. The sultan should concentrate on the recovery of Jerusalem, although in response he claimed that the northern Syrians prevented him from focusing on this.[2]

In the summer of 1175 the sultan made peace with the Franks, evidently looking for a pause after the long series of campaigns in the north; a bad drought made for a difficult situation as well.[3] It was around this time that another great administrator joined Saladin's entourage. Imad al-Din al-Isfahani had been a chancery official and secretary under Nur al-Din from the mid-1160s. When his master died Imad al-Din feared that the counter-crusade might fail, although he regarded Saladin as the best man to unify the Muslims, an interesting view for someone who had formerly worked with Nur al-Din. When the group coalescing around Prince al-Salih expressed opposition to Saladin, the secretary fled to Baghdad. On hearing that Saladin was now active in Syria he came back to the area to try to secure a posi-tion with him. He wrote various eulogies of the sultan and joined his army but it took the patronage of Qadi al-Fadil to get him a proper secretarial role. Imad al-Din was with the sultan for much of the remainder of the Ayyubid's life and, along with his patron, steered

Saladin towards the ideology of jihad. Imad al-Din's key historical works, in which he is always sure to remind readers of both his own literary skill and proximity to the heart of matters, are *The Syrian Lightning* and *The Eloquent Exposition of the Conquest of Jerusalem*, narratives based around poems, diplomas, letters, reflections and opinions from his time in service to his great hero. Thus, through the author's privileged position, and refracted through his literary virtuosity, we gain a sliver of access to the sultan's thoughts and reflections.[4]

By early 1176, however, rumours that Sayf al-Din was looking to cause trouble prompted Saladin to gather his forces and head northwards. His troops were shattered by the time they reached Tell al-Sultan, some thirty-seven kilometres south of Aleppo, but more poor generalship – in this instance sheer complacency – from Sayf al-Din allowed them time to recover. His error was compounded the following day (22 April) when one of the senior northern commanders positioned troops carrying his personal banners in a dip in the ground, which meant that large numbers of his men could not see them. Understanding this to mean that their commander had abandoned the field of battle, they fled back to Aleppo. Another group of Sayf al-Din's troops failed to keep formation when they charged, leaving them to be turned and driven back with ease. Saladin achieved an almost bloodless victory and took rich rewards from the baggage train. It seems that Sayf al-Din travelled in some style and Imad al-Din smugly reported that the haul contained morally dubious possessions such as wine, musical instruments and singing girls, a contrast to the more upright household of his own master. The captives also included a collection of birds such as doves, nightingales and parrots. Saladin returned the birds to their master with the patronising instruction to the courier: 'Tell him to go back to playing with these birds for they are safe and will not bring him into dangerous situations.'[5]

It is noticeable that Saladin made little attempt to follow up his military successes and to kill or imprison his opponents. He was well aware of the inherent tension within his position as the self-proclaimed leader of the Sunni holy war and de facto ruler of Syria, as against the preference of Nur al-Din's family and associates to remain independent and to resist and reject a man whom they regarded as a usurper. If diplomacy fell short then Saladin needed to achieve military victories, but they did not have to be tainted by excessive violence and punitive slaughter, a strategy that would only make it harder to acquire and to hold a population's loyalty. The dictates of Islamic law also required that after a battle he should not kill, but release fellow Muslims.[6]

The sultan moved into northern Syria taking towns such as Manbij near the Euphrates. The defence was led by a man known to loathe Saladin, but in line with the latter's moderate approach, rather than inflaming the situation by killing the individual he was dispatched back to his allies in Mosul. As well as acquiring substantial quantities of cash and weapons which, with his customary generosity, Saladin distributed to his men, he found a number of vessels marked 'Yusuf', his own given name. He enquired why these objects were thus inscribed and heard that the castellan had a favourite son bearing the name. Saladin was amused by the coincidence and in this rare instance kept the spoils for himself.[7]

Nearer to Aleppo stood the castle of A'zaz; another formidable site that required the full array of siege weapons and mining skills. It was here, in May 1176, that the Assassins launched a second and more serious attempt on his life. Saladin was talking in the tent of one of his emirs when a man leapt at him and struck at his head with a dagger. Being on campaign the sultan was prudent enough to be wearing a chain-mail hood under his cap and this deflected the first blow, but the blade still cut his cheek. Saladin grabbed the man's knife hand and they twisted and grappled, the would-be murderer trying desperately to strike his victim's neck, but the sultan just managed to take the power out of these potentially lethal thrusts. The collar of his body armour, probably made from leather plates, was pierced but the chain-mail hood did its job again and protected his neck. As the two men wrestled, an emir (one of Shirkuh's old retainers) boldly seized the knife itself. By this time the assailant himself had also been struck, and he died. A second and then a third Assassin rushed at the sultan but at this point his bodyguards were sufficiently alert to down them. Saladin was profoundly shaken. These men had penetrated the heart of his encampment and come within millimetres of killing him. He took immediate measures to prevent a repeat, ordering a review of his closest troops. Those whom he did not recognise were sent away. He also built a stockade around his personal tents and raised the sleeping area on stilts.[8] One sad coda to this episode was the death a few days later of Saladin's bodyguard, the emir Mankalan, wounded in the struggle to deal with the second and third attackers. We saw how the emir had recently petitioned the sultan to secure a better grant of land for himself. In consenting to this, Saladin took to Mankalan sufficiently to appoint him to his royal guard, only for the Assassins to cut short the emir's new career.[9]

In his biography of the Assassins' leader Sinan, Kemal al-Din, an author from the first half of the thirteenth century, provides an engaging story about their ability to get to Saladin:

> My brother (God have mercy on him) told me that Sinan sent a messenger to Saladin (God have mercy on him) and ordered him to deliver his message only in private. Saladin had him searched, and when they found nothing dangerous on him he dismissed the assembly for him, leaving only a few people, and asked him to deliver his message. But he said: 'My master ordered me not to deliver the message [except in private].' Saladin then emptied the assembly of all save two Mamluks, and then said: 'Give your message.' He replied: 'I have been ordered only to deliver it in private.' Saladin said: 'These two do not leave me. If you wish, deliver your message, and if not, return.' He said: 'Why do you not send away these two as you sent away the others?' Saladin replied: 'I regard these as my own sons, and they and I are as one.' Then the messenger turned to the two Mamluks and said: 'If I ordered you in the name of my master to kill this sultan, would you do so?' They answered yes, and drew their swords, saying: 'Command us as you wish.' Sultan Saladin (God have mercy on him) was astounded, and the messenger left, taking them with him. And thereupon Saladin (God have mercy on him) inclined to make peace with him and enter into friendly relations with him. And God knows best.[10]

Whether such a story is true or not matters less in this instance than the point it underscores. Namely, by this time the Assassins' list of victims was so lengthy that, as events at A'zaz showed, the episode described above was plausible.

After over a month, A'zaz fell; Aleppo itself still stood firm and so Saladin made a truce in which he renounced his claim to be the proxy guardian of al-Salih, in part an acknowledgement of his recent rebuff by the caliph of Baghdad. Now, of course, the sultan also had a score to settle with the Assassins. In early August he marched down towards Masyaf, ravaged its lands and laid siege to the castle with Sinan himself inside it. Masyaf was a tough defensive site and the Assassins resisted fiercely, inflicting significant casualties on the sultan's troops. After a month or so of stalemate, both sides looked to make peace and concluded terms.[11] With hindsight, this was a settlement that each side adhered to for the remainder of Saladin's and Sinan's lives; in fact both died within a year of one another. For all his anger and shock at the attempts on his life, as well as his repeated assaults on the heretical nature of Nizari belief, the sultan had made a well-calibrated choice. In the immediate term Masyaf might be extremely hard to break and a long drawn-out siege would leave both the Franks and the Aleppans (possibly working together) free to exploit the situation. While it was patently essential to end the threats to Saladin's life and to stop suggestions that others in his family might join the roster of possible targets, if such a danger could be neutralised by treaty this was one less enemy to worry about, and it freed him up to address greater priorities.[12]

By the autumn of 1176 the situation in Syria was stable enough to enable Saladin to go back to Cairo. Before departing he attended to one further formality in Damascus, a gesture intended to build and enhance the permanence of his links with the city. Ismat al-Din Khatun was the daughter of Unur, the man who, as we saw earlier, had ruled Damascus in the 1140s. When Nur al-Din took power there in 1154 he chose to marry Ismat as a way of forging a sense of continuity with the ruling house. Ismat had joined with Saladin when he reached Damascus in 1174 and now, as he left for Egypt, he married her.[13] We know dispiritingly little about the women who bore him children, some of whom did so over several years. His eldest son, al-Afdal, was born in Cairo in 1170 and the same mother gave birth to another boy seven years later. In 1172, Shamsa produced al-Aziz Uthman and then in 1176, Ya'qub; another woman had al-Zahir Ghazi in 1173 and Da'ud in 1178. Sometimes the concubine who mothered his children would be married off to an emir and given an allowance and properties to generate income, presumably as a way for the sultan to reward an associate and, as he himself had married Ismat, to form a bond. Exact numbers of Saladin's progeny are hard to ascertain – one source suggests that he had fathered twelve sons by 1178, with a possible total being seventeen boys and one recorded daughter.[14] Notwithstanding the number of women with whom he coupled, such impressive dynastic safeguarding would have been the envy of many a contemporary ruler. Louis VII of France produced one son across three marriages; Richard the Lionheart had only one, illegitimate, son. Of all those who bore Saladin children, from what little evidence we have, it was his wife Ismat who seems to have been the most important to him because when, as we will see later, Saladin fell gravely ill in 1186 he insisted on writing to her on an almost daily basis. When, by a terrible coincidence, she died during this period the sultan had to be protected from news of her death for several weeks for fear of the effect it might have on his own recovery.[15]

It had been two years since Saladin had left Egypt and on his return a brief window of calm allows us to see his mind – and those of some of his associates – turning to other matters. The political narrative often preoccupies many of the chroniclers and it is not often we get a sense of everyday life for Saladin's inner circle.

When the sultan and his entourage reached Cairo in late September 1176, he assigned Imad al-Din the task of editing his letters to Syria. While this was obviously his secretary's top priority it also gave him an opportunity to immerse himself in the lively intellectual life of Cairo. We have seen the centrality of poetry in the cultural milieu of the Near East and Imad al-Din attended readings over at Giza and Roda Island, the site of the Nilometer. Some evenings, Saladin himself would engage in discussions about literature and listened to readings by ascetics. At other moments there was a need to work and the sultan would dictate particularly sensitive letters in draft, leaving his administrator to produce the text overnight for checking the following morning.

For Imad al-Din, at least, there was some time for leisure and, like most visitors to Cairo, he expressed a wish to visit the pyramids. A wealthy judge, clearly keen to impress a man so close to the heart of power, organised a very agreeable outing, something that sounds rather like a corporate entertainment event. He held a party at his island on the Nile en route to the pyramids before he hosted a reception in tents put up by his servants out at the great monuments. Imad al-Din was suitably awestruck by the size of the pyramids and 'dazzled by the Sphinx'; the group spent the evening talking about the grandeur of the structures and the skills of their builders. En route, however, he had seen a less salubrious side to Cairene life, observing a circle of men dressed in mantles as Syrian and Iraqi jurists were accustomed to do. Curiously, they fled when approached. Imad al-Din expressed surprise that such people would run away, only for his host to gently inform him that they were not religious men but beer-drinkers! Their cloaks were to hide their alcohol consumption from the religious authorities.[16]

It was during this stay that Saladin ordered his most lasting change to the city. Six years previously an existing section of the walls had been refortified, but now the sultan initiated something far more ambitious, a blend of guarding against particular threats, but also a visible demonstration of his authority. He launched a massive building programme intended to enclose both Fustat and Cairo behind one defensive wall. He also decided to fortify the seventy-five-metres high spur of the Muqattam hills adjacent and above the main inhabited areas (the site acting as a pivot for the Cairo–Fustat wall) to create a citadel.[17] A later writer recorded the reasoning behind this, namely that Saladin had divided the Fatimid palaces amongst his followers but, still fearing partisans of the previous regime, he thought it best to establish a secure new site. An anecdote from al-Maqrizi tells of the sultan hanging meat in Cairo only for it to go bad after a day and a night. He then hung more meat on the citadel and it lasted two days and two nights; in other words, the hill provided a more hygienic location.[18] These prestigious projects came at a colossal cost and their implementation may suggest that Saladin's income from various campaigns in North Africa and Nubia, as well as the basic running of the state, was reasonably good. In charge of the enterprise was his trusted associate Qaraqush, a man described by a contemporary in this context as 'a man of genius'.[19] Aside from the obvious need to enhance security, Saladin's recent campaigns in Syria brought home to him the advantages created by fortified cities and citadels. He had besieged numerous settlements, many of which had been walled by Nur al-Din, such as Baalbek, Hama and Homs. Damascus itself had walls and a fortress just about strong enough to hold off the Second Crusade (1148) during Saladin's own youth, while the formidable citadel of Aleppo on its steep natural (albeit much enhanced over the years) mound overlooked walls that he had yet to penetrate.[20] In other words, while Cairo already had some defensive structures, in comparison to those of Muslim Syria they were fairly rudimentary and old-fashioned.

The citadel still stands today, much modified down the centuries, but in surveying the city below it immediately reveals itself as an ideal vantage point. Prior to Saladin it housed only mosques and tombs but these were demolished by Qaraqush. Some of the stone was taken from the small pyramids at Giza, although their larger brethren were ignored, presumably partly out of admiration of the sort expressed by Imad al-Din and partly through the convenience of using materials from closer by (it was about fifteen kilometres to Giza), in this case the ditch around the citadel. Being above the main settlement gave excellent security from any unrest in the city and, as had happened in the 1160s, should the Franks, or indeed any other hostile force, get close to Cairo it offered a formidable defensive site. A visitor in 1183 marvelled at the construction of 'an impregnable fortress' and noted with pleasure that thousands of Frankish prisoners were digging out the huge ditch, as well as cutting the stones and sawing marble, thus relieving Muslims of such labour. It was through the use of such a substantial workforce that the building was completed so rapidly.[21]

Within the citadel Qaraqush enlarged a water source known as Joseph's Well, a reference to events in the life of the Quranic Yusuf when his brothers cast him into a well. This was a shaft ninety metres deep circled by spiral paths that allowed cattle to draw the water up from deep into the hillside and giving a safe supply to the fort's inhabitants.[22] The stone from Giza was likely utilised on a further ambitious structure: a causeway that ran nine kilometres from the Nile shore at Giza and ended in a spectacular series of bridges with about forty arches that stretched into the desert. The reason to build what seemed like a road to nowhere was to enable troops to leave Cairo and confront an invasion from the north at the time of the Nile Flood. Normally the inundation would prevent any large force from leaving the city, but this clever creation permitted an army to move out regardless of the season. Aside from the engineering skill involved here this showed Saladin's and Qaraqush's strategic grasp and again highlights their fear of Frankish, Byzantine, and possibly even North African Almohad attacks.[23]

Work on the military heart of the citadel was, according to an inscription on the main gate, the Bab al-Mudarraj, finished by 1183–4.

This highly prominent text survives today and is effectively a manifesto for the project:

> In the name of God the Merciful, the Compassionate. Lo, we have given you (O Muhammad) a signal victory ... And that God may help you with strong help [Quran 48:1–3], ordered the construction of this magnificent citadel, near the God-protected city of Cairo, on the strong mound which [the citadel] combines utility and embellishment, and comfort and shield to whosoever seeks refuge in the shadow of his kingdom, our lord [Saladin], the reviver of the dominion of the prince of the believers, under the guidance of his brother and heir apparent [Saphadin] ... and under the supervision of the emir of his kingdom and the assistant to his rule, Qaraqush, in the year 1183–4.[24]

It alludes, through the Quranic quotation, to Saladin's rise to power in Egypt and thus suggests divine approval. The honorific 'reviver of the dominion of the prince of the believers' was not one found elsewhere and is a confident assertion of his role in removing the Fatimids. It may also have been a message to the caliph of Baghdad to emphasise Saladin's credentials in both military and religious terms because, bearing in mind the recent and ongoing tensions with Nur al-Din and his successors, the ruler of Egypt was seeking the warmest possible endorsements from the spiritual head of Sunni Islam as he took his fight to the Franks during the early 1180s. Thus the reasons given for building the citadel form a blend of the practical coupled with a reminder that it is 'his [i.e. Saladin's] kingdom'. While the full extent of the walls as originally conceived was never completed, the substantial sections that were finished, along with the drawing together of Fustat and Cairo and the obvious arrival of the citadel on the skyline, provided a definitive stamp of Ayyubid power.

But to answer the challenge that he was only interested in dynastic advance, the sultan really needed to make progress against the Franks and start living up to his claim that he wanted to recover Jerusalem.

In early December 1177 riders appeared at the mighty gates of Cairo bearing good news. God had given victory to the Muslims over the accursed Franks! Saladin had achieved a great triumph and was on his way back to the city bearing the spoils of war; the sultan and his clan were entirely safe and would arrive back soon; a cause for celebration, processions and music.

The messengers were lying. Saladin and his army had been thrashed at the Battle of Montgisard and the sultan was lucky to escape alive. In the chaotic aftermath they had become horribly dispersed with some of the men falling captive and others, including Saladin himself, scattering into the bare and rocky lands of south-western Palestine and needing to be rescued by local guides. Imad al-Din was in Cairo at the time and heard the victory announcement. Well versed in official language, he immediately 'translated' the overly effusive assurances of the sultan's well-being as meaning his narrow survival after a heavy defeat.[25]

The campaign that culminated in Montgisard had been, in theory, a sound enough idea. Given that Saladin had recently spent so much time fighting his fellow Sunni Muslims, he had to be seen to take the counter-crusade to the Franks and a large-scale incursion would deliver just such a signal. Skirmishing aside this was the first proper offensive that Saladin had mounted against the Franks for three years. The sultan also hoped to distract the settlers, boosted by the presence of the powerful crusader, Count Philip of Flanders, from activities in northern and central Syria.[26]

Initially the omens seemed good. This was a carefully organised expedition that comprised both standing troops and a draft of extra levies, totalling several thousand men. The purpose seems to have been a major raid; it was not a serious attempt at permanent conquest, something Saladin was not yet in a position to contemplate. Raiding was the basic staple of medieval warfare in both western Europe and the Near East. The intention was to seize prisoners and booty and to shatter morale amongst the native population, to breed fear and discontent, and to encourage political instability and insurrection.

The sultan rode out of Cairo on 28 October 1177. He left his baggage train at al-Arish, a small coastal settlement at the northernmost edge of his Egyptian lands, and advanced quickly past the Frankish fortresses of Darum and Gaza, the latter garrisoned by a strong contingent of Templars. By 18 November he reached Ascalon, the first big Christian settlement, lying towards the southern edge of what land could reasonably be cultivated before scrub and desert took over. Ascalon had been a huge city in Roman times, girdled by an impressive circuit of walls and towers. Today the site is a national park with a modern town sitting adjacent to the ancient and medieval ruins. The stone defences are very largely destroyed, but their remains rest on a surviving ridge of earthwork defences (themselves seven to ten metres high) and still give a feeling of real strength. Walking around their landward perimeter of about 1.5 kilometres you look across at an enclosed area bigger in size than the walled cities of Jerusalem and Acre. Ascalon was also a port, albeit a rather mediocre one, more useful as a water-supply point than as a trading centre.[27] Its formidable nature meant that it was the last coastal city to fall to the Franks, resisting until 1153.

Once into Christian territory Saladin's forces tore around the fertile farmlands, seizing cattle, killing those peasants too slow to flee and destroying property; with little active opposition it all seemed very easy. In fact, King Baldwin, with his leprosy in a relatively stable phase, had chosen to take a personal lead in confronting this assault. He mustered all the available troops, although many of the Hospitallers were in northern Syria and the royal constable, the nominal head of the army, lay sick. Baldwin had to demonstrate that he could defend his people, rather than simply watch his lands be savaged. The king issued the call for the *arrière ban*, the summons for all able-bodied men to serve, a clear sign as to how dangerous a situation this was. He was joined by important members of the nobility including the Ibelin brothers, Baldwin and Balian, members of the powerful clan whose lands lay under attack. Also present was Reynald of Sidon and the royal marshal, Joscelin of Courtenay; arguably the most senior of all those present was Prince Reynald of Châtillon. This is a man who would cross paths with Saladin on many, many occasions over the next decade or so and their relationship evolved into a bitter, and ultimately lethal, personal duel. Reynald had only recently been released by the Zengids after almost sixteen years of captivity in the dungeons under the citadel of Aleppo. While conditions must have been tough they were not seemingly so bad as to break his health.[28] Back in the saddle, he constituted a truly formidable opponent, as Saladin was about to discover.

News of the invasion's progress deep into Frankish lands provoked, as intended, near panic in the settlers. One group of Muslims thrust northwards to Ramla, a barely fortified town governed by the Ibelin family. Nearby was Lydda, the place associated with the third-century soldier saint, George, and the traditional location of his tomb. During the siege of Antioch back in 1098 a vision of George had inspired the armies of the First Crusade and when they reached Lydda a year later they reconstructed the church where he was buried.[29] In the face of Saladin's attack people sheltered on the roof of this church waiting for the danger to pass. Jerusalem itself lay only twenty-three miles from Ramla. Such a powerful incursion terrified the inhabitants of the holy city. At one point the population were reported as planning to flee having lost confidence in the strength of its fortifications. The walls were not in the most robust condition because they had not been under direct threat since the crusader siege of 1099 and hence had fallen into disrepair. The early decades of conquest saw intensive warfare in the coastal regions as the crusaders took hold of the Holy Land but since the early 1130s, aside from brief forays into the southern borderlands, the heart of the kingdom had been remarkably secure. People in Jerusalem prepared to take refuge in the Tower of David, the massive fortification that still stands (in modified form) at the Jaffa Gate. Patriarch Amalric of Nesle remained in charge of the city and with so many knights either absent in the north or on campaign with the king he co-opted women to help defend the walls and urged patients in the Hospital of St John to contribute to the situation by praying for deliverance.

Baldwin decided to base himself at Ascalon, a prudent move given the huge numerical advantage enjoyed by the Muslims. Scouts kept a close eye on Saladin's troops. They observed a lack of discipline as the invaders spread out looking for both booty and pasturage, a fault compounded by their failure to keep proper lookouts.[30] Baldwin and his nobles sensed an opportunity. The king was joined by the eighty Templar knights stationed in Gaza and he led the Christian forces out of Ascalon. The True Cross had been brought along to accompany the Frankish army as well. This was to be the first time that Saladin himself led an army in battle against the Christians' great talisman, the relic discovered in the aftermath of the First Crusade and believed to represent a part of the wood of the cross upon which Christ was crucified. It was housed in its own chapel in the Church of the Holy Sepulchre and taken on campaign when the kingdom was in danger. Almost invariably the Christian army carrying this relic proved victorious, or at the least avoided defeat.[31]

With perhaps 375 knights at his disposal King Baldwin sought to attack the sultan's camp. Belatedly, Saladin realised the danger and put out an urgent command for his scattered troops to gather; any thoughts of an appearance outside the walls of Jerusalem had certainly vanished. Near the hill of Montgisard (today Tel Gezer, close to the village of Abu Shusha), the sultan tried to pull his forces together.[32] Early in the afternoon of 25 November the Franks pounced. Saladin himself later said that his men, hampered by the arrival of the baggage train, were at a small river crossing, obviously a particularly vulnerable and awkward position, and at that exact moment the Franks charged. Some Muslim writers claimed that their troops were attempting a complex reorganisation of their battle lines but before this could be completed the enemy smashed into them, the Templars 'nimble as wolves, barking like hounds they attacked en masse, ablaze with fervour'.[33] In either event, the result was the same. A powerfully delivered charge by a relatively small group of heavily armed knights created havoc amongst the Muslims. Many fled, leaving the elite Mamluks to defend their leader. Saladin's yellow-clad bodyguards fought fiercely but three Frankish knights shouldered their way through the melee. Standing directly in front of the sultan, they were a couple of blows from plunging the Muslim Near East into chaos. Saladin described how the first knight ran at him, pointing a lance at his chest but, at the last moment, three of his officers hurled themselves in the way, absorbing the shock of the attack and saving their leader.[34]

The battle raged on through the afternoon – the Muslims made at least two cavalry charges in their efforts to break through the Frankish lines. We get a measure of the ferocity of this exchange from an eyewitness report of 1,100 Christians dead on the battlefield. This was actually the first recorded engagement with a mobile field hospital present – the medical expertise of the Knights of St John (the Hospitallers), still in attendance at so many sporting events in Britain today, was in evidence at Montgisard. The flood of injured and dying was overwhelming, and in the end no less than 750 were brought safely back to Jerusalem to be housed in the main hospital. With up to 900 patients already in situ, this stretched capacity to uncomfortable levels; but the point was made and a direct, pre-planned link between battlefield and hospital was established.[35]

With his lines broken, Saladin had little option but to flee; even his personal tent was lost – a terrible humiliation. The Franks surged after the Muslims who shed booty and armour as fast as they could in their attempts to shake off the pursuers. Christian captives in the Muslim baggage train broke free from their bonds and escaped. In such a chaotic situation there was no chance for Saladin's men to re-form and try to make a stand; the rout was complete and thousands of his men perished.[36]

Those raiders who had strayed far from the main force now found themselves totally isolated and they were swiftly rounded up and captured, including Saladin's loyal advisor, the jurist Isa al-Hakkari.[37] Ten days of rain compounded the Muslims' misery, and to make matters even worse some local Bedouin, sensing a wounded creature, descended on the sultan's base camp at al-Arish and duly sacked the place. With deep satisfaction, William of Tyre quoted the Book of Joel: 'that which the locust has left, the canker-worm has eaten'. Saladin and the remnants of his forces straggled back across the northern desert of the Sinai with barely any supplies or horses.[38] The sultan was only too aware of the implications of his defeat and how it might be interpreted by both his allies and enemies. As we saw above, he tried to spin the story by reporting a victory and emphasising his own well-being. He sent further letters to various emirs and to the caliph's vizier trying to put on a brave face and stressing the number of enemy dead. By any standards, however, this was a serious setback. Furious, and no doubt deeply embarrassed, he also ordered several Kurdish officers to be deprived of their iqtas; clearly it was imperative to transfer the blame for this fiasco to someone else.[39]

For the Christians, however, this was a major boost. It seemed the new ruler of Egypt and Damascus was not a particularly great warrior – certainly in comparison to his predecessor Nur al-Din, or his own uncle, Shirkuh. Saladin's tent was paraded before the walls of Harim to symbolise his defeat. Once again, the True Cross had proven its value as a protective talisman and it was welcomed back into Jerusalem with the proper blend of reverence and celebration. St George himself was said to have been sighted on the battlefield, a phenomenon barely seen since the heady days of the First Crusade, and messengers carried news of this triumph over to western Europe. In the medium term, however, this may not have been quite such a helpful move. Many northern European chroniclers recorded the victory but the effect proved counterproductive because subsequent pleas for support from the Franks, notably in 1181 and 1184–5, elicited little response. While political rivalries in the West help to explain this, surely, some people reasoned, if the Franks could defeat the Muslims as heavily as had happened at Montgisard, they really did not need much help.[40]

One Muslim writer claimed that Saladin only made up for this loss with his victory at Hattin ten years later – an interesting comparison and, given how comprehensive a victory that proved to be, a telling indication of the weight of the punch delivered by the Franks at Montgisard. There is little doubt Saladin came to act upon the many hard lessons he learned on that late November day.[41]

At this particular moment, Ayyubid lands in Syria were under extreme pressure. Alongside the disaster of Montgisard, Count Philip of Flanders had led a combined Flemish and Frankish army in the siege of Hama, on the River Orontes in central Syria. Saladin's maternal uncle ruled the place but he was seriously ill, meaning he required the help of the Kurdish emir al-Mashtub to resist. The Franks briefly forced their way into part of the city. Had they kept hold of Hama this would have marked another major achievement because it was an important strategic and economic site; the defenders, however, rallied and drove the attackers back.[42] A request from Bohemond III of Antioch to besiege Harim, close to Antioch, drew the Franks away and Hama was saved. From Saladin's perspective the tension eased. Harim was held by his Zengid opponents and the start of an unsuccessful four-month siege meant the crusaders were tied up fighting his rivals.[43]

After the fiasco of Montgisard, Saladin spent a couple of months lying low in Cairo. His grand rebuilding of the citadel began to take shape with new walls appearing above the ground and other building projects well underway.[44] Once he had re-equipped his troops and gathered some energy there was a need to fight back and to re-establish some momentum. In this instance, trouble came from an unexpected quarter and one much closer to home.

By February 1178 Saladin had decided to return to Syria and in April he was camped outside Homs. A letter to the caliph of Baghdad expressed great optimism, making the strikingly ambitious claim that he could take Jerusalem the following spring![45] In the short term, however, domestic politics intervened as a rare rebellion broke out within the Ayyubid ranks. It was tricky to balance out the expectation of due rewards with the demands of family ties, although it has to be said that Saladin usually succeeded in this respect. The sultan's elder brother Turanshah was in Damascus, apparently taking a more relaxed attitude to holy war and being described as 'devoted to his pleasures and inclined to take things easy'.[46] He had run up large debts, a situation compounded by his personal generosity and wider conditions of drought and poor harvests. Saladin needed to move him aside. Turanshah duly consented to the idea – but only if given appropriate compensation. His choice settled upon Baalbek, the place he had grown up in; he thus professed a special affinity for it. Baalbek was an important town, based around the spectacular Roman temple of Baal. Powerful ruins catch the eye of modern visitors while the place is also known for the incarceration of the Beirut hostages that included Brian Keenan, John McCarthy and Terry Anderson in the 1980s, and as a stronghold of the Hezbollah organisation. Back in the medieval period the classical site was developed to feature walls and fortifications. Indeed, once a tourist takes his or her eyes away from the towering classical columns, hefty stretches of medieval construction come into focus.[47] Baalbek also dominates the highly fertile Beqaa valley, thus presenting its ruler an ideal source of income, as well as controlling routes from Damascus to the Mediterranean coast. Turanshah's proposal was, however, problematic, largely because Saladin had already awarded the town to Nur al-Din's former emir, Ibn al-Muqaddam, one of the men so instrumental in the surrender of Damascus to him not four years previously. Simply to strip an individual of a gift would send out an extremely bad signal to all and sundry, yet Turanshah needed to be dealt with in a way appropriate to his seniority. Saladin tried offers of compensation but Ibn al-Muqaddam declined and reminded the sultan that he had been promised the town.[48]

Saladin set up camp near Homs, hoping the emir might give way; he later moved close to Baalbek itself. He tried intimidation, flattery and a fairly unsubtle smear campaign, going as far as to suggest that his opponent harboured heretics and thieves or was in contact with the Franks, but to no avail. Saladin was desperate to avoid open conflict, not least because, if rumours were to be believed, the Aleppans and the Assassins were both looking on with interest. Ibn al-Muqaddam's conduct also put a highly effective brake on any wider ambitions. For all the talk of advancing the holy war and being at Jerusalem by 1179, Saladin had not achieved anything of note in the six months since his return from Egypt in the spring of 1178.

A sign of the tension he felt may be gauged in the harsh treatment of Frankish prisoners captured in a raid near Hama around October 1178. We associate Saladin with his merciful behaviour after the fall of Jerusalem in 1187, but he was not universally forgiving and in this instance, perhaps in part because he was looking to bolster his credentials as a holy warrior, he ordered a number of captives killed. The execution of these 'enemies of God' was to be carried out not by military men, however, but by men of religion. Imad al-Din was summoned to the sultan – 'I thought that I was needed for something important that could not be carried out by anyone else', he wrote. Instead, to his apparent unease, he was told to draw his sword and kill an infidel. 'I am a man of the pen and do not compete with swords. I announce victories but do not cause deaths.' Saladin laughed and exchanged the prisoner with the Franks instead, rewarding his secretary's response with the gift of a slave. Vanity, as well as squeamishness, may also have played a part in his actions. As Imad al-Din commented afterwards: 'I did not lose anything by my decision not to spill blood. I had turned from that deed for fear the company would laugh at me as they had the others.' Presumably, the amateur executioners were less than efficient in their labours.[49]

In October 1178 Saladin's focus remained on Baalbek. The Franks exploited this with a sharp and very cleverly thought-out move. We tend to think of castles as defensive structures, a place of refuge; but castles could also be offensive in nature. The fortress of Jacob's Ford (Vadim Jacob) would be just such a site, and to Saladin, it posed a really active threat.

9

Victory at Jacob's Ford

'I give you good advice ... Leave the
House of Jacob, for Joseph has come!'

Towards the bottom of a gradually sloping valley lies an unassuming, grassy mound, perhaps three or four metres high. Running along one section of it the vegetation and soil have been stripped away to reveal a stretch of pale limestone wall, each stone still fitting snugly together more than 800 years after they were laid. Walk about a hundred metres south and another length of wall, a broken gateway and the lower level of a tower also stand proud of the earth with some features embellished by shelves or lintels made of black basalt. What at first glance may seem slightly unpromising ruins comprise the remains of the crusader castle that constituted one of the most serious challenges Saladin had faced to date. It is also the most remarkable archaeological site associated with crusader warfare and can starkly illuminate the realities of medieval conflict.[1]

The reason why this place was so central to the struggle between Saladin and the Franks is because of its location. Most seriously from Saladin's perspective is the fact that it lies only around eighty kilometres from Damascus, or to put it another way, only a couple of days' ride. The castle itself stands about thirty metres above the River Jordan in what was described by various authors as being (just) inside Muslim territory. The river is not especially wide at this point, and apart from a seasonal rise from the winter rains (when it certainly does flow very briskly) it winds its way sluggishly through the valley before easing southwards towards the Sea of Galilee (Lake Tiberias) twelve kilometres downstream. That said, the water does form a natural barrier of sorts and Jacob's Ford is, as the name suggests, a convenient crossing point.

Reminders of the modern sensitivity of this area are present too. As you look around the site, close by are fenced-off areas with mine-fields; check further and one can see decades-old abandoned tanks, a sign that this has been the stage for many conflicts down the centuries; over forty kilometres to the north are visible the Golan Heights. Heading north-eastwards, the Golan Heights form a very obvious barrier between Ayyubid Syria and the kingdom of Jerusalem, or now between Syria and Israel. Control over this knuckle of land to the south-east of the mountains has the scope to make either side feel threatened or exposed.

King Baldwin and his advisors had made a brilliantly aggressive move. They saw that Saladin was vulnerable after the defeat of Montgisard; the crusade of Philip of Flanders could still descend from northern Syria and the rebellion of Ibn al-Muqaddam constituted a frustrating distraction. We do not know when the idea was first mooted but the concept was executed with full commitment. To construct a castle closer to Damascus than any previous Frankish fortification was a razor-sharp way to ratchet up the pressure on the sultan. The fact that the crossing was also a Muslim holy site made it even more provocative. Nur al-Din had built a small shrine there after his 1157 victory, and it was described by Imad al-Din as a place of pilgrimage, traditionally identified as the location of the dwelling of the patriarch Jacob and the spot where he learned of the death of his son Joseph (Yusuf). Saladin vowed to liberate the place and to enable the faithful to visit it as they had in the past.[2]

The Franks poured vast resources into the project. King Baldwin himself, now aged seventeen, spent several months living there and supervised the work. The site's isolation and almost complete aban-donment after the siege means that until recent years the remains of the castle have stood largely undisturbed. On the western hillside of the valley archaeologists from the Hebrew University of Jerusalem have uncovered the quarries from which the stone was taken, only a couple of hundred metres uphill from the actual fortress. Dozens of oxen (we can still see their drinking troughs and the stone holes for their tethers) hauled materials to the construction site while workmen, including Muslim prisoners, laboured to dig the foundations, to create a drainage system, to make a cistern and an oven, and to lay the inner walls. There was such a push to complete this vital first ring – to form some kind of viable defensive structure to resist attack – that the royal treasury ran out of cash to pay the workers and had to resort to giving them lead tokens.[3] A whole village of artisans established themselves outside the walls: stonemasons, architects, blacksmiths, carpenters, armourers, plus cooks and washerwomen. Such people also needed to be guarded, adding a further group to the community and a substantial extra expense. The blocks of stone we see today are neatly faced around the edges and produced to a very high standard; this was not going to be a simple tower but a substantial and formidable castle. To give an even more threatening aspect the king decided that it should be entrusted to the Knights Templar, the warrior monks who formed the elite troops of the Latin East and, thanks to their huge network of properties in western Europe, an organisation wealthy enough to maintain it in the future. It is thought that the Templars may have been behind the project in the first instance, especially given the relative proximity of their castle at Safad, about twelve kilometres to the west. Through the late autumn and winter of 1178 and then into the early months of the new year, the Franks laboured away, slowly raising their castle.

In April 1179 Saladin ordered one of his nephews, Farrukhshah, to lead the main army from Damascus and to move into enemy lands. Once again it seems the Muslims were not especially vigilant and they were surprised in battle near Banyas, although on this occasion they triumphed. In the ferocity of the exchange King Baldwin's horse bolted towards the enemy troops. The royal constable, Humphrey of Toron, saw the danger and hurled himself forwards to protect his lord, suffering terrible injuries in the process. One arrow penetrated his nose, smashed through some of his teeth and exited from his chin, another arrow tore through his foot, exiting from the sole, a third hit him in the knee. As if that was not enough, he received three further wounds in his side, as well as two broken ribs.[4] This may begin to sound slightly ridiculous – a touch of *Monty Python and the Holy Grail*'s 'It's only a flesh wound' – but as some of the grisly discoveries at Jacob's Ford show, the list is all too realistic a manifestation of medieval warfare. The blend of arrow wounds and sword injuries also reveals the methods of fighting employed by the mounted horsemen in the armies of Muslim Syria.[5] Humphrey, unsurprisingly, died of his injuries a few days later, almost certainly an agonising death caused by infection.

Farrukshah dispatched carrier pigeons bearing the good news of this victory to Damascus, and that same day Saladin advanced out to receive the heads of the slain and to bring the captives in. This was a welcome success for the sultan, the first triumph against the Franks for several years and, with the death of the fearsome Humphrey, a useful boost to morale. 'He was a tribulation that God inflicted on the Muslims and God gave relief from his wickedness.'[6]

In the spring of 1179 the situation with Ibn al-Muqaddam at Baalbek was finally resolved. Saladin's blockade meant the emir had to capitulate sooner or later and he agreed to accept other lands as compensation. While it was a relief to see the end of this distraction, along with the legacy of Montgisard it had been a damaging episode that encouraged Aleppo and Mosul in their opposition to the Ayyubids. Most pressingly, however, Jacob's Ford continued to take shape. Just to make things worse, Muslim Syria was struggling with a drought causing serious crop failure and real economic hardship. Saladin dispatched Turanshah to Egypt with instructions to get more troops and money. One further source of income was North Africa, and Ayyubid troops mounted an expedition to the Maghreb where they seized three important towns while another force went south to campaign in the Sudan.[7]

Saladin briefly took a different approach to the problem of Jacob's Ford: in May 1179 he tried to buy off the Franks and offered them 60,000 dinars in lieu of their construction costs. When this was rejected he increased the bid to 100,000 dinars, but again this was declined. The Christians realised they had a strong hand here and even the act of building the castle, let alone what might be accomplished from it afterwards, was destabilising to Saladin. As an aside, a letter from Qadi al-Fadil mentioned the castle was formed of 20,000 stones at four dinars apiece; to this, the costs of wood, cement and the labour force would add considerably more, all of which explains why the sultan made such large offers.[8]

Saladin directed a series of raids in the northern Galilee region, loosely threatening the building site and testing Frankish strength. He based himself around Banyas (now just inside the modern Israeli border with Lebanon) and then sent his troops deeper into Frankish lands, towards even the coastal cities of Sidon and Beirut; he also seized the harvest wherever possible, vital given the shortages in his own territories. His camels returned laden with sheaves of wheat while his men destroyed the remaining crops. The forward momentum of the victory near Banyas continued through the early summer. On 10 June another battle took place, this time at Marj Ayyun, again close to Banyas.[9] Saladin himself led the army, his first engagement since the humiliation of Montgisard a little over eighteen months previously, and on this occasion, he prevailed, The Franks lost many distinguished figures, some killed and others taken prisoner. Amongst the latter were the Masters of the Templars and the Hospitallers – a real coup to capture these figureheads of the crusader states. As custom dictated, noblemen were made prisoner where possible in order to be ransomed. At a time of economic hardship and increased military expenditure, such a convention could prove both profitable and expedient for both sides. In the case of the jurist Isa al-Hakkari, taken prisoner at Montgisard in 1177, a partial exchange for Balian of Ibelin helped to engineer his release.[10]

This victory encouraged Saladin to try to break Jacob's Ford once and for all. The commander of the Asadiyya troops (Shirkuh's crack Kurdish regiment) suggested a simple, direct assault. This was a sensible enough move and if successful, it would save the trouble of a full siege. Saladin agreed and the assault was made. The fortress was still unfinished in the sense that its walls and towers were not nearly at their full height, but they were complete enough to form a protective ring that constituted a formidable obstacle in its own right. Various outworks (housing a workers' village and a mill) also existed, and these were swiftly taken by the Muslim troops, bringing them up to the main walls and enabling a proper investment to begin. Saladin distributed his emirs around the castle, although the eastern side that drops down to the river is beguilingly steep and formed an effective defensive feature. Once more the tight Ayyubid core lay at the heart of the action. Present were Farrukshah, Nasr al-Din ibn Shirkuh (a cousin of Saladin's) and Taqi al-Din.

This was now a race against time. It would take King Baldwin five or six days to bring a relief force to the site. To capture the outworks took one precious day; behind them the half-raised walls were 4.3 metres thick and it was in these huge stones that the Franks placed their trust. Even though night had fallen on 24 August, the sultan ordered his men to start digging a mine. This was difficult, dangerous work with the Franks fully aware that a properly executed mine was extremely hard to resist. Specialist engineers were a feature of medieval armies and with protective screens in operation they started to burrow under the fortifications in at least two places. Such obvious activity made this a particular focus for a bombardment of arrows and missiles. For two days they laboured, hoping to excavate far underneath the walls. Wooden beams supported the tunnel roof and once complete the shaft was filled with flammable materials. The contents were set light with the intention that burning the timbers would bring the passage and the wall above crashing down. On the morning of Tuesday 27 August the order was given to fire the tunnel, smoke poured out of the opening and the Muslims waited for the fracturing and splintering sounds to signal the wall was about to buckle and fall – but nothing happened: it remained intact. With every passing hour the possibility of holding on for King Baldwin's relief force gave the defenders hope, and by the same token, inspired the attackers to redouble their efforts. The wall was seemingly just too strong. There was only one option – the fire had to be doused and the shaft extended. Tunnelling was patently dangerous, but to be tasked with extinguishing the smouldering flames and then to go into a precariously weakened mine was at the high end of the risk register. Saladin offered a dinar to anyone prepared to take a goatskin of water into the dark, scorched opening to accomplish this task. The sappers returned and duly completed their labours at sunrise of 29 August. This time, the fire did its work. To a huge cheer from Saladin's men the wall cracked, shuddered and tumbled downwards, collapsing in a great cloud of dust.[11] A tremendous blast of flame belched out of the breach, killing some of the defenders and setting alight piles of wood stacked up by the Franks to form a makeshift barrier. Muslim sources gleefully report the garrison's commander plunging into the flames to meet his fate.

This fractured section of wall became the focus of a desperate struggle as the Franks tried to stem the flood of attackers scrambling across the breach. The ringing clash of weapons and the screams of the wounded all played out against the hellish backdrop of a great pall of smoke. Saladin's men hacked their way through and once inside the fortress it was only a matter of time before the remaining defenders were either killed or captured. This was desperate hand-to-hand fighting and the surviving archaeological evidence allows a vivid reconstruction of this terrible scene. Over 800 years later we can see how a few of the defenders met their deaths.[12] Saladin's archers evidently chose their ammunition with care, selecting chain-mail-piercing arrowheads (without barbs) when they engaged personnel. We know that several individuals sustained such wounds in their neck, shoulder or pelvis. In the remains of horses are found different arrowheads, this time with a flatter, broader head that penetrates flesh alone. Once into the castle itself, it was a matter of using swords. One skeleton lacks a lower arm, presumably having received a blow just below the elbow-length chain-mail hauberk popular at the time. The same man has wounds to the head as well, including three arrow wounds to his neck, a glancing cut to his cheekbone and a fatal blow that cleft his skull apart. Another took a savage blow to the shoulder with a deep cut visible in the bone. A third had an arrow pass through his pelvis which may have punctured the large blood vessels nearby and caused him to bleed to death. Belatedly, the Frankish relief army had reached the vicinity but seeing the tower of smoke they decided not to approach further. With no prospect of escape, surrender was inevitable.

Once more Saladin acted harshly. Perhaps 700 prisoners were gathered up; many were executed on the spot, particularly those described as apostates of Islam, in other words, turcopoles.[13] One skeleton found lacks a head, suggesting that he was one of these unfortunates. The archers were also killed, a bitter compliment to their military effectiveness as well as a reflection of their lack of individual wealth; those few surviving men of greater value were sent as prisoners to Damascus. One group of Saladin's troops set to the reconstruction of the shrine to Jacob, others started to pull down the castle walls to ensure the remainder of the place was not used as a fortress again. A further task was to cast the dead into the cistern – a grave mistake, if you will pardon the phrase, because in the immense heat of late August, the bodies rapidly putrefied. In the few days the sultan's men spent destroying the castle an outbreak of plague occurred and killed many soldiers, including ten emirs. The Muslims swiftly withdrew, leaving the site abandoned. As mentioned earlier, it is not the most defensible of locations anyway and no one down the centuries chose to refortify it. Pilgrims returned; there was some minimal habitation during the Ottoman period, but the ruins swiftly became overgrown. Nature absorbed the mound back into the landscape to seal these extraordinary secrets until modern times.

For Saladin this was a major achievement. Eight months previously he had looked in serious trouble with the defeat of Montgisard still lingering, the rebellion of Ibn al-Muqaddam at Baalbek and the presence of Philip of Flanders' crusade. Compounding all of this was the blatant challenge of a castle being planted within a couple of days' ride of Damascus. Yet by the late autumn of 1179 he had seen off all of these dangers and managed three impressive victories in a row. His poets produced outpourings of praise for the sultan whose credentials as the leader of the holy war suddenly looked far more convincing:

The destruction of the Franks came speedily.
Now is the time to smash their crosses.
Had the time of their death not been near,
They would not have built their House of Lamentations.

Making a nice play on Saladin's given name, a Damascene poet wrote:

I give you good advice (and advice is a duty of religion):
Leave the House of Jacob, for Joseph has come![14]

Just to capitalise on this success, and to show that he was developing a broader strategic approach, Saladin's reconstituted Egyptian navy began to come into play. Numbers of vessels had risen from forty to twice that number, and in mid-October his ships mounted a determined assault on Acre, or the 'Constantinople of the Franks' as the Muslims described it. They destroyed a tower and entered the outer harbour, attacking several ships. A couple more days of ravaging the coastline and they returned to base having achieved the first big naval success for an Egyptian force in decades, 'a blow which was heard on Mount Thabir [near Mecca]', as Qadi al-Fadil proudly exclaimed.[15]

Momentum had swung dramatically towards Saladin. The Franks had lost several leading warriors, they had needed to pay a number of big ransoms and, most seriously of all, had seen the utter destruction of all the men and money poured into Jacob's Ford. Their estimation of Saladin had been forcibly revised.

The sultan's victory at Jacob's Ford did much to boost his credibility. Having finally landed a heavy blow on the Franks, he could once more turn to establishing his ascendancy over the Muslim Near East. But this continued to be a problematic and sensitive matter, and an episode from the summer of 1180 illuminates his potential vulnerability on this issue. The story is wrapped up in a curious tale of sex, honour and power. Nur al-Din Muhammad, the Artuqid lord of Hisn Kayfa (up on the River Tigris, north of Mosul) had married the daughter of Qilij Arslan, the Seljuk sultan of Iconium. The Artuqid, however, had fallen in love with, and then wed, a singing girl. Qilij Arslan was furious at this affront to his daughter's name, and threatened to attack his son-in-law who appealed to Saladin for help. Implicit in him doing so was a recognition of the sultan's growing authority, something Saladin naturally wished to affirm, not least because the Artuqids could be useful allies. He made a truce with the Franks and headed north to deal with the dispute. In the meantime messengers from the Seljuks tried to convince Saladin of Nur al-Din Muhammad's immorality, only for the sultan to react angrily and threaten to respond with force.

The Seljuk ambassador tried a different tack, speaking on his own initiative and not as an official envoy. He talked frankly and asked whether it was a good thing 'that people should hear it said of you that you have made peace with the Franks, abandoned the holy war and the interests of the kingdom, turned away from everything in which lies salvation for you, your subjects and the Muslims at large [to gather, at great expense, a huge army] for the sake of a harlot? What will be your excuse before God Almighty?'[16] He then challenged Saladin's sense of honour, questioning how the sultan would have reacted to a direct plea from the spurned Seljuk princess: 'If she did so, the expectation is that you would not reject her.'

This clear criticism for prioritising conflict with Muslims ahead of the Franks, coupled with the dubious morality of the cause that he had chosen to back, shows the lurking pitfalls of the sultan's broader actions. Saladin was now trapped – he had promised (and wanted) to help Nur al-Din Muhammad, although he could see the wrong that had been done to the Seljuk bride. In the end a reasonably pragmatic solution emerged: Nur al-Din Muhammad was to promise to dismiss the singing girl within a year, and if he failed to do so Saladin would turn against him. The condition was duly met and the campaign ended with a treaty.

Ever-mindful of the need to gather strong fighting men to his side, Saladin also moved to punish an Armenian prince who had tricked a body of nomad Turkmen into using his pastureland, only to seize their flocks and imprison their men and women. Saladin's forces raided Armenian lands and compelled the prince to release his captives.[17] These two episodes took place between May and October 1180 and give a glimpse of geopolitical life in northern Syria, the Jazira and beyond. The need to engage with the Artuqid Turks, the Seljuks of Iconium and the Armenians may add even more names to this story, but they show once more the spectrum of potential allies and opponents that Saladin had to deal with. This reinforces the point that the Franks were far from the sultan's only concern.

Events elsewhere prompted further political recalculations. In late March 1180 the Abbasid caliph died, giving Saladin the hope of persuading his young successor (the twenty-one-year-old al-Nasir) to consolidate, or even to extend further, caliphal recognition of the lands he ruled over; envoys were duly dispatched to Baghdad.[18] Closer to home, almost farcically, Saladin's older brother Turanshah had decided that he no longer wished to hold Baalbek. Continued poor harvests in Syria meant the town seemed a less attractive proposition than before, and he now asked for Alexandria instead. Given the colossal fuss needed to acquire Baalbek on his behalf, his actions may have provoked a measure of exasperation, but Saladin could see a silver lining here. Turanshah had not been the most vigorous holy warrior and the sultan was able to put a nephew, the more dynamic Farrukshah, in control of Baalbek and to send his brother to a position of suitable status in Egypt. Turanshah did not live long in his new home and died in the summer of 1180. He had been invaluable as the conqueror of Yemen in 1174, but he took the family trait of generosity too far and left large debts (over 200,000 dinars) that his brother duly paid off.[19]

In the aftermath of their defeat at Jacob's Ford the Franks were quiescent, neutralised by a combination of their own internal political ructions and the ongoing bad harvests; the winter wheat and barley crop had failed, extending a miserable period of hardship. King Baldwin IV's leprosy worsened, and after his sister Sibylla's husband had died within months of reaching the Holy Land (October 1178), her marital status again became a focus of debate. Fearing the influence of Count Raymond of Tripoli, the king had allowed Sibylla to marry her young sweetheart, the Frenchman Guy of Lusignan, rather than see her wed to a powerful nobleman from the kingdom of Jerusalem.[20] With these sundry distractions it had suited both Saladin and the Franks to make an agreement. William of Tyre wrote: 'A truce on both land and sea, for foreigners and natives alike, was accordingly arranged and confirmed by an exchange of oaths between the two parties. The conditions were somewhat humiliating for us, for the truce was concluded on equal terms, with no reservations of importance on our part, a thing which is never said to have happened before.'[21]

His rueful closing comment is an interesting marker as to how the Franks acknowledged Saladin's progress. The combination of his growing power in the Muslim Near East, coupled with his recent military victories over the Franks and the rising strength of the Egyptian navy, not to mention the succession troubles in Jerusalem, were forcing the Christians to recalibrate in a way that deeply worried them.

10

Saladin, Cairo and the River Nile

*'Among the rivers of the world, there is none
referred to as "a sea" apart from
the Nile of Egypt, given its size and
inundation'*[1]

In these circumstances the sultan could head back to Cairo and he reached the city on 2 January 1181. Over the next sixteen months he initiated several long-term projects clearly intended to consolidate his position in Egypt and to give a secure starting point for further major campaigns in Syria and Palestine. There was also the normal routine of the country, focused largely on the River Nile.

Rains from the Ethiopian highlands and the African Lakes Plateau generate the Nile flood, a phenomenon that transforms cultivated areas into a broad freshwater expanse. The inundation first appears in mid-June and water levels continue to rise until they peak in late August or early September before falling away in October and November. This flooding is, in essence, the heartbeat of Egypt, and dictated the basic survival and sustenance of the country especially before the age of modern controls, such as the irrigation network of Muhammad Ali in 1820 and the Aswan Dam from 1964. A formal record of the progress of the water was essential. Thus came into existence the Nilometers, the most famous being on the island of Roda, located in the river between Fustat and Giza. Housed in a specially constructed building this is, in effect, a very large measuring stick. Its main purpose was to indicate that a certain height of water, or plenitude, had been reached. This level would more or less guarantee the harvest and, in turn, it permitted the government to levy the *kharaj* tax so closely detailed in the contemporary writings of al-Makhzumi in 1169–70.² It was also the cue to open, in carefully ordered sequence, the numerous irrigation canals that flooded the fields. Given the importance of this moment, rituals associated with the flood can be traced back to pharaonic times. True to form, the Fatimids turned these into astonishingly elaborate events focusing on two major ceremonies, namely the Perfuming of the Nile, and the Cutting (i.e. opening) of the Canal.

Under the Fatimids many aspects of power had evolved into complex and spectacular public performances. As he had done with other facets of government, Saladin wisely chose to show continuity with these practices, rather than discarding them simply because they were a manifestation of a previous regime. Those that reflected overtly Shi'ite tendencies were obviously problematic. In contrast, rituals connected with the seasonal flooding of the River Nile were utterly intrinsic to life in Cairo and Egypt.³ The sultan and his successors continued such practices and, in modified form, they were still witnessed by travellers well into the eighteenth century.⁴

Saladin's own interest in the Nile can be understood by Imad al-Din's mention of the death of the officer of the Nilometer in his account of the sultan's life. Had this been some nondescript administrative role it would hardly have merited inclusion in such a work, but he wrote:

> The site of this meter was established from the time of the Abbasid caliphs [it dated from the year 861], so as to know the rise and decrease of water with the meter. And there is a division in the water apportioned with increases per year, measured by fingers ... he (Abd al-Salam ibn Abi al-Raddad) was known for his honesty and knowledge ... he was gifted with the wearing of noble clothing (reflective of his status) in the seasons and when he died in Sha'ban [beginning of 1179], the sultan appointed his brother to his position.⁵

In August 1181, Saladin accompanied this man to take the measure of the Nilometer. While people could guess at the height of the water, it was the official who made the definitive ruling on the matter. A contemporary writer noted of the measurement: 'it would remain protected and hidden; no one would know of it before the ... vizier.' The level of sixteen cubits, the 'Fulfilment Cubit', was seen to be a good marker; on the other hand, anything towards twenty cubits could bring terrible flooding, while conversely as recently as 1179 the Nile had failed to rise sufficiently, which caused serious problems with the harvest and also meant trading vessels struggled to reach Cairo.[6]

During the Fatimid era, the caliph led the festivities and we have vivid descriptions of this from earlier in the twelfth century. Saladin almost certainly saw the event when he was vizier, and in the same way that he had taken an interest in financial affairs, he had asked for a written guide to processions and festivals too.[7] Once the ceremony was announced the entire population of Cairo celebrated, decorating the place with candles and sweets. The same text also noted that 'this was the opportunity for the caliph to attach importance to his commands more than any other season'. In other words, this was not an occasion to be missed.[8]

Al-Maqrizi records that in 1181 Saladin rode to the Nilometer and after it was measured he invested the man with robes of honour, just as the Fatimids did.[9] In performing this himself Saladin demonstrated that his government was maintaining good order. The official in charge certainly bore the same title under Saladin and in fact this one family held the position from the ninth century until the Ottoman age. By tradition, the night before the river reached the Fulfilment Cubit, the presiders of the congregational mosques of Cairo and Misr spent the hours of darkness in the mosque at the Nilometer reciting the entire Quran. Saladin's personal concern for the Misr mosque can be discerned in his payment for restoration work on the building, a place thought to help encourage God's protection for the river.[10] A couple of years previously the particularly low level of the Nile meant the water drained from the foot of the Nilometer and the sand fell away to reveal what was said to be the tomb and coffin of Joseph the Faithful, hidden since Moses himself moved it there. Thus emerged another Joseph/Yusuf connection for Saladin to enjoy, and which was perhaps a prompt for him to fund the buildings there.[11]

The main procession for the Perfuming of the Nile followed a carefully planned route, moving from the royal palace in Cairo, passing out of the southern gate of Bab Zuwayla and heading down towards Ibn Tulun's great mosque. Vast crowds gathered to participate in a date that was vital for Cairo and for the country as a whole. The grand cavalcade snaked past the shipyards to the market hall of the goldsmiths and then the customs house before it reached a small pavilion or belvedere, the Dar al-Mulk (the Seat of the Kingdom) on the banks of the Nile. This appearance in the commercial district helpfully coincided with the presence of most of the foreign merchants in Cairo, and was a useful opportunity for the ruler to show himself to the visitors and to impress with the regime's pomp and ceremony. Accompanied by a select few officials he embarked upon a private boat bearing an ebony pavilion inlaid with ivory and covered with sheets of gold and silver. Spectators eager to watch this spectacle filled hundreds of small boats. The royal party then crossed to the island of Roda and the location of the Nilometer itself. The sultan went to the well where the column stood. Prayers were said and by tradition he mixed a perfume of saffron and musk in a bowl. Next came the central moment of the ritual, a process hard to envisage. As reciters intoned verses of the Quran, the official had to throw himself into the well wearing only his undershirt and turban. He hung from the column by his legs and left hand while with his right hand he sprinkled the perfume onto the column. Once this man was safely restored to good order the ceremony was complete and the party crossed over the river to process back to the royal palace in Cairo. The official was duly rewarded for his acrobatics with a fine robe of honour, horses and a feast.[12]

Around the same time another major ceremony took place to mark the annual Cutting of the Canal to allow the water into the irrigation channels upon which the country relied. The first to be 'cut' was the central channel in Cairo, known as the Canal of the Commander of the Faithful, and then the important canal of Abu l'Munajja; hundreds of others were breached across the country through September.[13] This involved removing dams made of mud and esparto grass (particularly tough vegetation) that were put up when the water was at its lowest, probably around February, buttressed with poles and culverts. The main dam was cut at Fustat and during the inundation its rise created an aquatic roadway past the heart of Cairo itself.

On 12 September 1181 it is recorded that Saladin himself opened the Cairene canal of Abu l'Munajja. Once again we have descriptions of extraordinarily lavish ceremonies from the Fatimid age. These involved special costumes of brocade and linen, Quran-reciters, huge numbers of officials, attendants and soldiers, as well as a complex series of greetings and submissions, the latter stages taking place in vast tents erected annually for this very purpose. Such an overwhelmingly opulent display – followed by multiple banquets – may not seem Saladin's style, although it should be noted that he was not at all averse to large-scale festivities, such as attending the circumcision of a cousin's sons, an event that required the slaughter of 700 sheep and the preparation of eighty *qintars* of sweets.[14] Workmen stood on the dam and at the sultan's orders took their pickaxes to it, Quranic-reciters intoned 'God is most great' on one side of the canal, while trumpeters played a fanfare on the other. As the labourers pulled away some of the supporting wall, the water poured into the canal.[15]

In late December news from Aleppo jolted the sultan from his cycle of Cairene life: Nur al-Din's son, Prince al-Salih, had died aged only eighteen. He was mourned as a young man of constancy and moderation and as a good and just ruler. From Saladin's point of view this was a potentially transformative moment. With the prince gone, there was a chance for the sultan to take power in Aleppo and to bring the second of Syria's great cities under his authority. Prince al-Salih had been the figurehead of the Zengid clan that so opposed the sultan and who wished to preserve the power of Nur al-Din's line. While Saladin initially worked hard to claim that he represented the best interests of the young man by now such a facade had evaporated. He wrote to Baghdad asserting (tendentiously) that Aleppo had been granted to him by the previous caliph. He stressed that the new regime in the city was in contact with the Franks and the Assassins; he also put forward the need to protect pilgrims and stressed his role as protector of the holy city of Medina. The sultan argued that he was the proper upholder of orthodoxy and he restated his desire to purify Jerusalem from the filth of the unbelievers. The greatest obstacle to this goal was that 'if the sharing of Syria continues it will lead to a weakening of unity', an argument repeated many times down the years. In essence, Saladin's case amounted to a plea for Aleppo, to which he had no real claim, on the basis that he was the champion of Sunni Islam and looked best placed to recover Jerusalem.[16]

Of course, after Prince al-Salih died, other members of the Zengid clan looked to step in. Following a few months of political horse-trading, Imad al-Din Zengi, the late prince's cousin and brother-in-law, assumed control of Aleppo. Had Saladin been in Syria rather than

Egypt he may well have tried to intervene immediately, but this shuf-
fling of the pack instead triggered a decision to return to Damascus.
It also prompted the sultan to consolidate the Ayyubid family hold
on Egypt, further embedding the Sunni religious hierarchy and making
a range of practical measures to enable him to finance war against
both the Franks and his co-religionists in the north.

Saladin had already moved to bolster the boundaries of Egypt,
possibly as a fallback position in case of defeat in the Holy Land but
also as a response to Frankish raids by land and sea. Damietta was
given new walls while the great chain over the river was placed across
a series of ships in order to block any attempt to penetrate upstream.
It seems that Saladin continued to give considerable attention to
maritime affairs. A new Ministry of the Fleet was set up and the
financial basis of the navy was reassessed with the profits from
particular regions and commodity taxes providing some clarity of
resource. No less than fifty vessels were now harboured at Damietta
and crews were levied to act as raiding parties. Further east the
sultan also ordered the construction of a small fortress on the island
of Tinnis (which stands in a large lagoon that contains water from
both the Mediterranean and the Nile) and the restoration of its
city walls.[17]

It was not just the northern coastline that was vulnerable. A fortress
was constructed at Suez on the Red Sea to protect the valuable trade
in alum to the Christian lands. Shipyards in Cairo also created prefabricated vessels to move troops to Yemen, either from Aydhab on the
Red Sea coast or Ayla in the Gulf of Aqaba. The latter was beginning
to come under pressure from Reynald of Châtillon, the man who had
engineered Saladin's defeat at Montgisard and who, earlier in the year,
had married the widowed heiress of Transjordan, centred upon the
powerful castles of Kerak and Shaubak. In the summer of 1181
worrying rumours started to emerge that he intended to strike south-
east from there along the haj route from Damascus to Medina and
then to head towards Medina itself, the city of the Prophet's tomb.[18]

Saladin was attentive to more than just military matters alone. Ibn
Mammati was a third-generation administrator of Coptic descent,
although he converted to Islam during the brief period of Shirkuh's
vizierate. His close friend, Qadi al-Fadil, described him as 'the night-
ingale of the council' because of his eloquence. Ibn Mammati was

first in charge of the army ministry and then added the finance ministry to his portfolio; he was also the author of multiple works, including a (now lost) biography of Saladin, and several poems. In 1182/3, specifically for the sultan, he produced a huge overview of the administrative departments of the government, their practices and principles, as well as a complete recording of property boundaries in Egypt, listing 4,000 estates, their acreage and yields. This incredibly detailed piece of research also included information on waterways, taxes on all sorts of trade and produce as well as minutiae such as when to give out different types of seeds. Through the efforts of Ibn Mammati we can see once again Saladin's ongoing interest in financial matters, seeking to understand how Egypt's economy functioned and how best to use it as he wished or needed.[19]

The sultan's continued drive for a better religious observance was pursued through the closure of over 120 beer houses in Alexandria, while a couple of years earlier, Saphadin had attempted to shut down brothels in Egypt. Far to the south, unpopular taxes on pilgrims to Qus in Upper Egypt (en route to the Arabian peninsula via the Red Sea) were ordered to cease, although a few years later the angry complaints of the Iberian pilgrim Ibn Jubayr suggest the measure was not fully implemented. Reflecting more worldly concerns, orders were sent out across the land for proper maintenance of the canals; fiefs were confiscated from the nomadic Arabs of Egypt, a group whom Saladin had evidently decided to exclude. Their territories were redistributed as he reorganised the financial affairs of his lands, largely to provide for the army. Qadi al-Fadil recorded the financing of over 8,500 troops, as well as eleven regimental commanders (who each had a hundred men), almost 7,000 junior officers, and Mamluks who had a baggage train of less than ten animals. In addition to these more heavily armed men were around 1,500 non-Mamluk horsemen, who acted as military policemen. Any troops from the previous regime were recorded separately, as well as men without fiefs, plus the entourage of jurists, Sufis and other officials. Around half of these forces were to accompany Saladin to Syria, while the others were needed to maintain good order in Egypt. The demise of much of the extraordinarily opulent Fatimid court must have made a considerable financial saving as well, again, enabling money to be diverted to military affairs.[20]

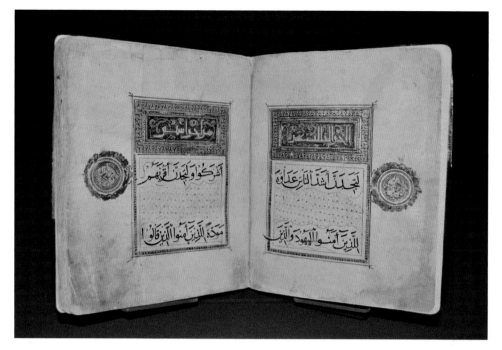

This beautifully decorated Quran (now in the Keir Collection, Dallas Museum of Art) was dedicated by Nur al-Din to a teaching college in Damascus in September 1167. It demonstrates his own piety and his support for the advance of Sunni Islam.

The Great Umayyad Mosque in Damascus, a magnificent building at the heart of the city that was the intellectual driving force of the twelfth-century jihad.

The Nilometer on Roda Island, Cairo. The measurement of the flood waters was a major event in Egypt for thousands of years and it was a ceremony that Saladin himself embraced when he became ruler of Egypt.

Fragment of a battle scene from the Ayyubid period showing archers and mounted warriors outside a city; Egypt, thirteenth century.

The formidable Frankish castle of Kerak in Transjordan was twice unsuccessfully attacked by Saladin in 1183 and 1184, but it eventually fell in 1188 after a siege of nine months.

Saladin was an enthusiastic polo player and this image on a silver and brass basin from thirteenth-century Syria shows near-contemporaries enjoying the sport.

Nur al-Din's wooden pulpit, completed in 1174 in Aleppo and intended for the al-Aqsa Mosque in Jerusalem; it was installed there by Saladin after his capture of the holy city in 1187. This masterpiece was destroyed in 1969, although a fine replica is now in place.

An ingenious archery device – a crossbow mounted within a shield – taken from a treatise on weaponry and warfare, written for Saladin by al-Tarsusi prior to 1187.

The Dome of the Rock, Jerusalem, of immense importance to Muslims as the site of the Prophet's ascent to heaven; behind is the Mount of Olives.

A modern image representing Saladin receiving ransom payments from the citizens of Jerusalem in October 1187, on display in the museum of the Tower of David, Jerusalem.

In the immediate aftermath of his capture of Jerusalem, Saladin was the object of great fear and vilification in the West. This illustrated text by the contemporary mystic, Joachim of Fiore, warned of the imminent Advent of Antichrist. Saladin is the sixth head, wearing a crown, the immediate forerunner of the Antichrist, the dragon's seventh head.

The city of Acre, besieged by the Franks in August 1189 and taken by the armies of the Third Crusade in July 1191, a huge blow to Saladin.

Saladin's mausoleum in Damascus contains his wooden medieval tomb and a marble cenotaph installed by the Ottoman Sultan Abdul Hamid II in the late 1870s in admiration of the Ayyubid ruler.

A scene from David Eldridge's play *Holy Warriors*, staged at the Globe Theatre, London in 2013. In the aftermath of the Battle of Hattin, Saladin ponders the fate of (left) Reynald of Châtillon and (right) Guy of Lusignan.

A statue of Saladin outside the citadel of Damascus shows the sultan riding to victory, flanked by his warriors, as defeated Franks slump behind him; a powerful symbol for the Asad regime of victory over the West.

A poster for Youssef Chahine's 1963 movie *Saladin the Victorious*, an epic depiction of Saladin's conflicts with the crusaders and a clear expression of the ideals and aspirations of Arab Nationalism at the time.

Before he set off for Damascus he conducted a quick tour of the northern Egyptian lands. In Alexandria the sultan caused a hospital and a hospice to be built for travellers from the Maghreb. A school was endowed beside the tomb of his late brother, Turanshah, and he also took the time to visit and listen to a famed jurisprudent lecturing on the life of the Prophet. Back in Cairo he opened a much-admired hospital well supported by generous benefactions. The complex was fully staffed by doctors, scientists, surgeons, attendants, servants and administrators, with another establishment for women and a further one for the insane, again well provided for in terms of staff and money. In total, Saladin was personally responsible for the commission of fourteen buildings in Cairo, including the walls, the citadel, four madrasas, two hospitals and a *khanqah*, a significant and lasting contribution to the life of the city.[21]

Although it is the high-level political narrative which drives much of this story forwards, it is as well to remember – and interesting to search out – other aspects of the sultan's life. As a young man Saladin was an enthusiastic polo player and his involvement in high politics and holy war did not extinguish this passion. About fifteen miles north of Cairo lay the Birkat al-Jubb (Pond of the Pit), a favourite hunting ground of the Fatimids. Saladin had used the place as a muster station en route to and from Syria. Sometimes, however, he went there for recreation, to hunt and to play polo. Several times he chose to base himself there, blending work, such as a review of the troops heading to Syria, with leisure.[22]

Meanwhile, from March 1182 onwards, forces gathered outside Cairo at Birkat al-Jubb, preparing for the journey to Syria. Saladin waited for the Muslim New Year on 7 May 1182 to depart, and he received a fine send-off as he left for the north. Reciters and poets performed the customary farewell verses, although when a tutor of one of Saladin's sons declaimed 'Enjoy the scent of the chamomiles of Najd, for after the evening they are no more', it was widely interpreted as a bad omen.[23]

This was claimed, perhaps with the benefit of hindsight, as a forewarning that the sultan would never again return to Cairo, even though he lived for over a decade more. Given that Egypt was the original springboard for his emergence as a figure of power, and because its resources would remain central to his actions in future, this is an intriguing point; at the least it shows that he had left the region in good administrative hands. More pertinently, it reveals that his ultimate priorities lay in Syria and the Holy Land; achieving and consolidating his aims there would prove an immensely arduous and time-consuming process, requiring first of all the submission of Aleppo.

II

Progress in Syria and Reynald's Red Sea Raid

'Saladin was a man of tireless energy who always
acted the role of a vigorous leader in everything ...
a man inspired by the greatness
of soul natural to him'

Thus wrote William of Tyre in his typically generous assessment of the sultan. As Saladin rode up to Damascus in the early summer of 1182 he began a phase of near-relentless movement almost exhausting just to contemplate in its scale and duration. Over the next few years he would campaign in Transjordan, the county of Tripoli, up to northern Syria around Aleppo, as well as Mosul over 600 kilometres away in the far east of the Jazira. The need to consolidate and expand his position in Muslim lands was interwoven with his efforts to take the counter-crusade to the Franks. Without the former he could not engage in the latter, yet fighting his fellow Muslims continued to compromise Saladin's credentials as a holy warrior.

The prospect of taking power in Aleppo had drawn him to Syria, although the longer-term struggle against the Franks could not be ignored, not least because of the ongoing threat from Reynald of Châtillon. Disregarding a truce between the Franks and the Muslims, the prince had captured a number of travellers and refused to release them. Thus Saladin determined to punish him, and in July 1182 a series of skirmishes took place south of the Sea of Galilee (Lake Tiberias) and on the western edge of the River Jordan, close to the recently constructed castle of Belvoir, perched on the escarpment edge above the valley. At the nearby village of Forbelet a group of 700 Frankish horsemen faced a far larger Muslim force. According to William of Tyre they stood fast and their defiance eventually drove the enemy from the field. He also noted that so great was the heat that as many men died of heatstroke as by the sword, graphic testimony to the sun's destructive power at the height of summer. This was the first of three battles in this area over the next six years, opportunities for Saladin to learn more about the local landscape and his opponents' specific weaknesses.[1]

Discomfited, Saladin returned to Damascus while the Franks dropped back to their customary muster point, the Springs of Saffuriya in Lower Galilee. The Christians knew that the sultan was preoccupied with Aleppo and Mosul, but his immediate target turned out to be the coastal city of Beirut. Having made a serious effort to build up the Egyptian navy it was now time to put it to use. Messengers instructed Saladin's brother Saphadin to send ships from Alexandria and to rendez-vous at Beirut on 1 August, the intention being to blockade it by land and sea.[2] With the ships dispatched Saphadin himself headed out to raid the kingdom of Jerusalem's southern borders near Gaza. This was, therefore, a three-pronged assault showing that control over southern Syria and Egypt offered a potentially lethal strategic advantage. But for all the promise of such a plan, stern resistance from the defenders of Beirut prompted the Egyptians to withdraw.[3]

For Saladin the real priority was Aleppo. Even though Imad al-Din Zengi had assumed power there in May 1182, the extended Zengid families continued to be at odds with one another, while the loyalties of the various emirs in northern Syria were fluid.[4] Such an environ-ment created real possibilities for Saladin, and alongside seeking to exploit local political issues he continued to emphasise the jihad. While the rhetoric of holy war helped to draw many towards Saladin, espe-cially when fighting the Franks, for others who entered his service, financial matters were important too.

The Turkmen ruler of Harran, Muzaffar al-Din Keukburi ('Keukburi' is a Turkish name meaning 'Blue Wolf'), approached Saladin offering to support his plans. Partly this was because he had fallen out with some of the Zengids and presumably he hoped to back the right horse in the broader regional power struggle. In this instance, Keukburi's personal piety may also have contributed to his motives in working for a man so publicly determined to recover Jerusalem. A thirteenth-century writer knew Keukburi extremely well and described his activities in detail.

Keukburi became famous for his generous almsgiving and charitable foundations, as well as his military deeds. While the events related here date to the early 1190s and could, therefore, represent a sudden transformation, his behaviour broadly indicates a man of strong piety and interest in the holy war, as well as a love of ceremony. In Irbil (west of the River Tigris relatively near Mosul) he built multiple institutions for the blind and the chronically ill, choosing to visit the patients and converse with them. He endowed houses for orphans, widows and foundlings. Institutions for visiting scholars, *khanqahs* for Sufis and a madrasa were other new foundations, the last of these a particular favourite because of the patron's love of spiritual music. In line with his religious duty he always gave generously for the recovery of captive Muslims. Pilgrims received munificence from Keukburi, and when he made the haj himself he paid for the construction of an aqueduct and fountains to aid those making this arduous journey.

Most famous of all was his celebration of the Prophet's birthday when swarms of jurists, Sufis, preachers, Quran-readers and poets from across the Jazira and Persian Iraq came to Irbil. Twenty splendidly decorated pavilions lined the street between the gate of the citadel and the Sufi *khanqah* that stood adjacent to the old hippodrome. Each of the pavilions had a musical band and a troop of Chinese-style shadow-players, a form of entertainment highly popular in the Near East. Keukburi visited each of these pavilions, listened to music there, and then went to the *khanqah* where he prayed and stayed the night. The following morning he would go out to hunt and then the cycle would repeat. Two days prior to the eve of the anniversary – either the 8th or 12th of the month of first Rabi (Keukburi alternated these annually because of a dispute concerning the correct date), he ordered the preparation of a huge feast. Camels, oxen and sheep were driven into the hippodrome to be ritually slaughtered and then cooked. On the day itself, Keukburi occupied a special wooden tower where he received a preacher and heard his sermon and prayers, and from where he could also see his troops, formed up in the hippodrome and whom he then reviewed as they marched past; ceremonies that displayed a neat blend of both power and piety. After this a great feast was given to the poor. The visitors of status who had listened to the sermon were each given a special cloak by Keukburi himself before they too received a meal.[5] All of this shows that acts of piety and generosity were not solely the purview of Saladin (or Nur al-Din previously) and that Turkmen in the towns and cities away from Aleppo, Damascus and Mosul could and did demonstrate considerable religiosity.

Setting aside Keukburi's character, he joined Saladin at an auspicious moment because the sultan was making real gains in northern Syria. Saladin wrote to the local lords to ask for their allegiance. 'All who obeyed were allowed to preserve their estates on condition of serving in the sultan's army and following him in his warfare against the infidels.'[6] In this way he brought a number of important towns and castles under his control, creating a further layer of military and political muscle and, crucial as ever, a source of patronage to bind people to him. Thus, al-Bira, Hisn Kayfa and al-Raqqa were acquired; he also took Edessa and handed it over to Keukburi, as well as confirming his possession of Harran. Further places were given in reward to loyal followers, for example, Nisbis was granted to Abu'l Hayja, 'the Obese'.[7]

By late September Saladin was near Aleppo, but he then chose to head further east and made an ambitious and aggressive statement of intent by laying siege to Mosul itself. His recent successes had provoked lively debate from both Christian and Muslim writers. William of Tyre reported deep anxiety amongst the Franks who could sense the wider threat posed by the sultan's growing power. William again complained that it was Saladin's near-legendary giving of money that underlay his success: 'by his great liberality he corrupted the magnates of his land'.[8] While the Ayyubid patently understood the positive effect of dispensing riches in exchange for promises of support and submission, his presence at the head of a large army could have a persuasive effect too. Giving out largesse had a negative side as well. Imad al-Din al-Isfahani, Saladin's secretary, was present on campaign and he observed that some of the local Kurdish and Turkish troops who decided to join Saladin only as he approached Mosul began to fear for their own lands if he made peace with the city rather than, as had first appeared, conquering it. They accepted offers of a pardon from the Mosulis in return for leaving his armies and being allowed to keep their own lands, a counter-play of gifts and honours that even lured away some of Saladin's troops too.[9]

To have two of the senior figures in the Sunni world – Imad al-Din Zengi and Saladin – at war over this great city, located around 350 kilometres from the seat of the caliphate in Baghdad, was a stark illustration of the many fissures within the Muslim Near East. Warfare alternated with negotiation, but in the end Saladin saw that at this point, Mosul was simply too strong for him to defeat.[10] Instead he chose to isolate it by taking nearby Sinjar (December 1182) and then in the spring of 1183, Amid, a famously formidable site. The former he gave to his nephew, Taqi al-Din, the latter, after showing suitably generous behaviour to the defeated governor, he presented to his Turkish Artuqid ally, Nur al-Din Muhammad.[11]

In late 1182 and in the spring of 1183 the Franks chose to exploit Saladin's presence in the north with some heavy raids into Egypt. In February Reynald of Châtillon struck a startling blow on behalf of the Christians, but unaware of this, Saladin laboured to complete his work in Syria. On 21 May 1183 he besieged Aleppo. Within a month, Imad al-Din Zengi realised the investment would not break and this, coupled with tensions between himself and the local Aleppan emirs, led him to seek terms. Saladin gave the emirs robes of honour and promises of good treatment as well. Imad al-Din Zengi himself was presented with splendid gifts, including horses and further robes of honour for his entourage. The locals, however, were deeply unimpressed with his lack of resilience and brought out a tub of water, shouting at him 'You are not fit to rule. You are only fit to wash clothes!'

On 20 June 1183 Saladin entered Aleppo and his yellow banners were raised over the citadel. A feast marked this triumph, although the sense of breakthrough was marred by the awful news of the death of his brother, the twenty-two-year-old Taj al-Mulk Buri. The young man had been wounded in the knee during exchanges outside the city and presumably the injury became poisoned and caused his death. Saladin concealed his grief at the dinner, not wanting to show weakness to Imad al-Din Zengi nor to spoil this momentous event for others.[12]

Personal feelings aside, this represented another major advance. To have both Aleppo and Damascus under his control replicated the achievement of Nur al-Din but, unlike his former master, Saladin could also boast of having direct rule over the enormous resources of Egypt too. William of Tyre grimly observed that the Franks' position had declined to a new low: 'From the first it had been apparent to the Christians that if Saladin should succeed in adding Aleppo to his principality our territory would be as completely encompassed by his power as if it were in a state of siege.'[13] The chronicler Ibn al-Athir reflected a similar appreciation of transition: 'With this gain Saladin's power became established, although it had been shaky: through the surrender of this place his foot became firmly fixed, although it had been on the brink of an overhanging precipice. When God wills a matter there is no turning away.'[14]

A week later the sultan stood down much of his army. With the harvest approaching the timing was helpful; it was apparent to all that this had been a long campaigning season and the men needed a rest. Creating a break from incessant warfare helped both morale and the wider health and well-being of the troops, matters that could only be of benefit in the longer run.[15]

While in Aleppo, Saladin would have been given a sharp reminder of his duty to wage jihad, and indeed of his earlier fractured relationship with Nur al-Din, by the presence of the beautiful wooden pulpit commissioned by the Zengid. In particular the work of two jurists would have focused his mind on Jerusalem as a primary objective. Ibn Jahbal, a local Aleppan, wrote to Saladin prophesying that the holy city would fall in October 1187 (Rajab 583 AH). The jurist gave the letter to one of the sultan's inner circle, Isa al-Hakkari. He regarded the idea with suspicion, but when one of Saladin's religious men heard of it, he composed his own poem which he presented to Saladin directly: 'Your conquest of Aleppo with the sword in Safar is a sign of your conquering Jerusalem in Rajab.' This man, Muhyi al-Din ibn al-Zaki, would come to the fore in the aftermath of the capture of Jerusalem, although Ibn Jahbal received some recognition as well. The image of Saladin as a potential liberator of the holy places was taking root in the collective imagination of the population.[16]

With his hold on Aleppo as secure as it could reasonably be, Saladin needed to return his attention onto the Franks. Beha al-Din wrote that 'his purpose [in the northern campaign] was to gain aid from those territories for the holy war'.[17] In fact, there had been much to distract him but such was the importance of the northern campaign that he could not afford to turn aside from it, even in the face of profound provocation. The Franks' decision to mount a series of raids around Damascus was hardly unexpected given Saladin's absence, and they damaged crops and destroyed farms.[18] Far more dangerous was an episode that posed a stark challenge to Saladin's recent claim to the caliph to be the defender and champion of Sunni Islam, namely a Frankish raid on the Arabian peninsula that threatened the holy city of Medina and, according to some reports, included a plan to dig up and steal the Prophet's body. For a Christian force to even contemplate such an act was quite staggering, both in its apparent implausibility and its sheer effrontery. As a way to destabilise Saladin, it was potentially devastating.[19]

The individual behind this move was Reynald of Châtillon, the nobleman who had been imprisoned in Aleppo, probably in one of the rock-cut chambers underneath the citadel, for almost sixteen years – longer than any identifiable contemporary in the twelfth century. During this time he may well have learned Arabic and gained some insight, if little sympathy, into his captors' faith, hence the careful targeting of a raid that was calculated to hurt, and to hurt hard, the people of Islam.[20] He is often characterised by contemporary Muslim sources as having conceived a deep hatred of their faith during his incarceration, and while this may well be true, his frequently appalling behaviour towards fellow Christians marks him out as a man of intrinsically vicious temperament. When, for example, the aged patriarch of Antioch refused to endorse his marriage to Princess Constance of Antioch in 1153, Reynald had the old man tied up naked, whipped, forced to sit in the open sun with his head smeared with honey while a bees' nest was released onto him. Likewise, when raiding Christian Cyprus a few years later, he ordered his troops to rape and murder the civilian population as an act of revenge for some perceived slight.[21] A pithy assessment from William of Tyre noted that 'he was a man of violent impulses, both in sinning and repenting'.[22]

The tomb of the Prophet at Medina lay hundreds of kilometres south of Frankish lands, deep in the inhospitable terrain of the Arabian peninsula. Back in 1181 Reynald's threatened raid towards the haj pilgrimage road had given some warning of his intentions. But Muslim control over the limited access routes meant it would be impossible to fight to Medina by land. Frustrated in this respect, Reynald showed great ingenuity by formulating an alternative plan – to go by water. Medina lies relatively close to the coast of the Red Sea. If, therefore, the Franks sailed down to the port of Rabigh, they could strike inland. The catch was that since Saladin had taken Ayla at the top of the Red Sea in 1171, they had no access to the sea. This proved little obstacle to Reynald. He instructed his engineers at Kerak to make eight small ships in kit form and then, probably in late December 1182, had them transported by camel down to the shore near Ayla. The vessels were rapidly reassembled and launched – the first Frankish ships in the Red Sea for over a decade.[23]

Two of them engaged the garrison at Ayla while the others disappeared off into the open sea, moving southwards past the barren, rocky coastline of the Arabian peninsula towards Aydhab, the main port of eastern Egypt for transportation across the Red Sea. The Franks quickly caused havoc, disrupting commercial and pilgrim shipping and raiding the local towns. The psychological effect of their attack was immense: Imad al-Din wrote: 'The presence of the Franks in that sea had never been known and such extreme wickedness had never confronted a pilgrim.' They constituted a fast-moving threat that appeared poised to hit at the very heart of Islam. News of the raid must have reached Cairo soon after the ships left Ayla, and Saphadin rapidly dispatched Husam al-Din Lu'lu, an Armenian formerly in the service of the Fatimids and their leading naval commander, to pursue the Christians ('Lu'lu' means 'Pearl', a name often given to slaves).[24]

Lu'lu soon reached Ayla and captured the Franks there; he then set sail southwards to try to find the main raiding party. The Franks had continued to roam around the region and were believed to be near the port of Rabigh, some 140 kilometres north of Jeddah. Quite how the Christians expected the campaign to end is not obvious. Whether they truly intended to snatch the Prophet's body or whether their purpose was simply to sow fear and to take booty is not evident; one writer suggested they planned to head down to Yemen. In any event they did not seem to have a discernible exit strategy. Lu'lu tracked them down to the Hawra region. Panicked, the Franks left their ships and fled inland. Lu'lu commandeered horses from the local Bedouin and pursued the Christians; he cornered 170 of them in a ravine and after a fierce struggle, they asked for quarter, an assurance that their lives would be spared if they stopped fighting. This was duly agreed and they surrendered. Given the affront that they had caused to Islam the fate of these men was never going to be easy; in fact, it became a matter of some controversy.

The nub of the problem was that the promise of quarter was a principle enshrined in Islamic law. Yet Saladin thought differently. This was not the merciful figure so familiar to us, but an angry and embarrassed ruler, determined to exact public retribution. He argued that 'if in these circumstances faith is kept with the unbelievers it will cause a rent that can never be mended'. A series of letters passed between the sultan and his brother in which they argued over whether Lu'lu's agreement should be honoured or not. Saphadin suggested that they should seek the advice of scholars but his brother brushed this aside: 'there is no need to refer back to the question of killing the prisoners ... There is no good to be got out of preserving any one of them, not any excuse that God will find acceptable for closing our eyes to them. The judgement of God on men like this is not a problem for scholars ... Let the decision to kill them be carried out ... Their attack was an unparalleled enormity in the history of Islam.'[25]

A number were sent to Mina, just five kilometres from Mecca and the place of animal sacrifice on the haj. There they were killed as an exemplary punishment 'for those who desire to cause terror at God's sanctuary and the sanctuary of the Prophet (may God bless him and give him peace)'.[26] The remainder were dispatched back to Cairo where many were slaughtered by Sufis, jurists and religious officials; others were sent to towns and cities across Egypt where they met a similar end. The Iberian pilgrim Ibn Jubayr arrived in Alexandria and witnessed the executions in March 1183. Amidst a cacophony of horns and kettledrums the men were brought into the city on camels, bound and facing the tail as a sign of humiliation. The author expressed his horror at their reputed plans: 'The worst, which shocks the ears for its impiousness and profanity, was their aim to enter the City of the Prophet – may God bless and preserve him – and remove him from the sacred tomb.'[27] Lu'lu was congratulated by the poet Ibn al-Dharawi on his success: 'You were sufficient [protection] for the people of the Haramayn [the two sanctuaries of Mecca and Medina] from their enemies and you protected the Prophet and the Ka'ba' [the sacred Black Stone towards which prayer is directed].[28] Saladin needed to make crystal clear this threat was over and that it had been dealt with in the most severe manner possible.

Whatever the Franks' real aims were, their actions certainly had aroused profound anxiety. Qadi al-Fadil reported:

> The fear of the people of those areas grew ... especially when the consequences flashed before them. The Muslims were sure that it was the Day of Judgement and that its portents were clear, and that the world would be laid out and spread [for the judgement]. They waited for the anger of God to end [the danger to] his sanctified house, and the station of his noble friend [Abraham] ... they hoped that a miracle of this house would sharpen their eyes like when the companions of the elephant intended to take it.[29]

This reference to the elephant echoes a chapter from the Quran referring to the Christian king of Ethiopia attacking Mecca, but in the context of the twelfth century it fitted Reynald of Châtillon.[30]

Qadi al-Fadil wrote two letters to the caliph of Baghdad to explain the situation and to reassure him that all was well.[31] Given that Saladin ruled Egypt, southern Syria and Yemen, it was his power and leadership that had been so blatantly challenged. The fact that he had provided Reynald with the opening to try this audacious act through his focus on fighting his fellow Sunni Muslims in northern Syria obviously raised the question of the sultan's priorities.

Saladin returned to Damascus on 24 August 1183. By early September he had summoned his forces and headed south-west below the Golan Heights towards the Sea of Galilee. The Franks meanwhile learned that the sultan was back in Damascus and they reacted in turn. The call went out to all the troops across the kingdom, to the Military Orders, to the northern states of Antioch and Tripoli, and to those western pilgrims present in the Holy Land, to gather at the Springs of Saffuriya in Lower Galilee.

By this time the leper-king Baldwin IV was in steep decline; he had lost feeling in his hands and feet and had gone blind. In the face of some strident opposition he turned to his brother-in-law, Guy of Lusignan, to act as regent; this campaign would be the newcomer's first major test. The initial thrust came at Bethsan, a small fortress just west of the Jordan. The inhabitants fled as the Muslim troops approached and the lands were duly ravaged and the animals taken.

From there the sultan went east to Goliath's Spring; like the Franks, he chose to base himself at a safe water supply.

Saladin's hope was to draw his opponents into a pitched battle and what followed was, from the Christian viewpoint, a carefully choreographed shadow dance. At one point the vanguard of 500 horsemen managed to engage the Franks but their footmen protected the cavalry and beat off the attack. The Muslim troops roamed around the area, pillaging the land and local villages, ranging up to the monastery on Mount Tabor and across to Nazareth. All of this created distress and hardship for the local population as they watched or learned of the ruin of their houses and livelihoods. It also generated massive pressure on the Franks, especially Guy, to defend his people and lands. Yet, for entirely pragmatic military reasons, the Christians simply moved around, keeping very strict formation, and even when camped within a mile from the sultan did not engage. Saladin repeatedly tried to draw out the Franks, but they would not uncoil.[32]

By early October the situation was at a stalemate. Saladin's leaders advised him to end the campaign; while there had been no great battle, enough had been achieved in terms of devastating Christian lands to judge the expedition as a guarded success. From the Franks' perspective, there was the immediate pain of the loss of crops and livestock, but they had suffered few casualties and managed to preserve their discipline with impressive fortitude. As we will see, however, the intensive political manoeuvring within the Frankish nobility, at root caused by King Baldwin IV's leprosy and questions over the regency and succession, meant the conduct of this campaign came to have profound long-term consequences for the Christians.

Back in Damascus on 13 October, Saladin was far from finished for the season. The energy he showed here was remarkable because just nine days later, he headed south to besiege the mighty fortress of Kerak, the castle that had been the subject of his and Nur al-Din's interest a decade previously. Along with its patent importance as a block on the route between Egypt and Damascus it was the base of Reynald of Châtillon, a factor that gave the siege an extra edge. Saladin had clearly planned ahead for this campaign, not least because of the strength of the castle, and he arranged for his brother Saphadin to bring up a substantial Egyptian contingent as well. Once the Muslim troops assembled, eight siege engines started to pound the fortress.

By disastrous coincidence for those involved, the attacking forces arrived just as the nuptials of Humphrey IV of Toron (Reynald's stepson) and Isabella, the younger sister of King Baldwin IV, were scheduled to take place. An unhappy blend of refugees from the town of Kerak now huddled inside the castle and mingled with wedding guests, performers and musicians. A Frankish source records that Saladin learned of this unfortunate timing when the bridegroom's mother sent the sultan food from the wedding banquet. As an act of courtesy he ordered his cata-pults not to fire during the wedding feast and to spare the tower where the happy couple were to spend their first night together.[33] In the days afterwards, however, the siege was pursued with increasing ferocity. A relentless bombardment of stones and missiles smashed and splintered on the castle's defences causing terror to those inside. Such was the intensity of the attack that people feared to show themselves on the walls, which allowed the Muslims to steal the animals herded into the moat in front of the citadel. Yet Kerak is a very strong site, located at the end of a finger of land with steep drops on the other three sides. While the landward flank was obviously the most vulnerable it was correspondingly the best fortified and managed to hold firm.[34]

In early December news arrived of the impending approach of the valiant King Baldwin, Count Raymond of Tripoli (who had replaced Guy as regent), and a large relieving force accompanied by the True Cross.[35] Unwilling to be trapped outside the castle Saladin decided to abandon the siege and moved back to Damascus. He asked Saphadin to come with him, rather than return to Egypt, having in mind a serious new responsibility for his brother.

When Saladin left Aleppo back in August he had placed it under the nominal control of al-Zahir Ghazi, his third son, a youth known for his bravery, intelligence and respect for his father. Given how crucial Aleppo was and because, for example, his enemies still controlled Mosul, Saladin decided that he needed someone more senior in command there and he gave Aleppo to Saphadin. Al-Zahir Ghazi was said to be – naturally enough – disappointed by this, but behaved with proper dignity for which he was duly praised. The use of a close and trusted core was once again the trademark of the sultan's strategy.[36]

In early 1184, as an unexpected side effect of this wider diplomatic activity, there emerged another individual who would eventually become a central member of Saladin's inner cadre. Because the situation in the Jazira remained unresolved the Mosulis decided to send a diplomatic mission to Damascus. Amongst the party was Beha al-Din Ibn Shaddad, a jurist and secretary who had trained and worked in Mosul and Baghdad.[37] While the mission stayed in Damascus he evidently caught Saladin's eye and prompted the sultan to make an opportunistic pitch to switch loyalties, gilded with the lure of a senior administrative position in Egypt. The career of Saladin's other close household members, such as the former Fatimid chancery director and now the sultan's trusted advisor, Qadi al-Fadil, make plain that such a fluid path was far from unusual. For the time being, Beha al-Din declined, although he would soon change his mind. Saladin's actions show him as a sharp judge of character who had calculated that his administration could only benefit from the presence of such a variety of talented people, regardless of their prior employer.[38]

With pressure building on the Franks, we must remember that it was also rising for Saladin. He had made his pitch as the defender of Islam, his propaganda relentlessly emphasised the sanctity of Jerusalem, and he explained his fighting against fellow Muslims in terms of a grander vision of recovering the holy city. In more practical terms, although not in contradiction to the last of these points, he also needed to reward his troops with booty and, in the case of senior figures, with land. To achieve such aims it was imperative to make further military progress, and with that in mind, in the summer of 1184 he once again headed south to Kerak.

12

Final Preparations: The Sieges
of Kerak and Mosul

'The soldiers engage themselves in war,
while the people are at peace and the world
goes to him who conquers'

Saladin's immediate priority in his conflict with the Franks remained the castle of Kerak. With the buccaneering Reynald of Châtillon in charge it posed a constant threat to the arterial link between Damascus and Egypt and was the base for repeated raids on Muslim lands. Qadi al-Fadil conveyed the danger in his typically expressive fashion: Kerak 'is the anguish which grips the throat, the dust which obscures the view, the obstacle which strangles hopes and lies in wait to ambush courageous resolutions; it is the wolf that fortune has stationed in this valley and the excuse of those who abandon the duty of pilgrimage prescribed by God'.[1]

The sultan knew Kerak well – he had, after all, made an unsuccessful attempt to take it the previous year. The scale of the challenge is shown by Saladin's summons to several key allies and senior family members from northern Syria and Egypt. The sultan's health was reported to be causing some concern but he recovered sufficiently to give both his ally, the Turkish lord Nur al-Din Muhammad, and his brother Saphadin, a warm welcome. The particular illness is unknown but it was serious enough to warrant recording by Beha al-Din. This was the first of a series of chronic health issues to afflict the sultan over the remainder of his life, and these recurrent illnesses show the enormous physical and mental strain that he needed to endure.[2]

Potentially the most vulnerable side of Kerak was the ditch facing the town. This was no shallow trough, but a ravine, perhaps as much as thirty metres deep and over twenty metres wide, and an impressive defensive feature in its own right. With the failure of 1183 in mind Saladin and his siege engineers had evidently thought carefully as to how to achieve a breakthrough. A tunnel or a straightforward assault via siege towers and ladders were theoretical options, but both needed direct access to the walls, something prevented by the immense sloping glacis (a steep sheath of smooth stone over the natural contours of a hill) and the deep ditches. A further possible solution was – ambitiously – to fill in part of the ditch to get up to the wall. Obviously the defenders could see this happening, and as Saladin's troops brought up stones and debris to pitch into the fosse, the Franks launched a barrage of missiles that made it almost impossible to approach the edge. Undeterred, the sultan's ingenious engineers ordered the immediate construction of three brick tunnels to run up to the lip of the ditch. Using bricks made on the spot from kilns within the town, this was a canny solution that enabled labourers to try to fill the chasm without running the risk of being hit by arrows.[3]

Such inventive thinking was rewarded with good progress as, coupled with the damage caused by the sheer volume of bombardment, one section of the ravine slowly began to fill up. Qadi al-Fadil wrote that morale was high with 'not a word of weariness nor of complaint' amongst the besiegers. But Kerak was a formidable site and after several weeks still stood firm. More worryingly, the Franks had gathered substantial relief forces which were heading to the area. It was vital not to get trapped between an attacking army and the new arrivals, so the Muslims decided to break the siege. In one sense this feels like a convenient excuse to disengage, although it did create the possibility of bringing the Christians to battle. Just like the previous year, though, the Franks deliberately eluded them. Seeking to gain at least some benefit from the campaign, Saladin's forces once more pushed into the central Galilee area. His men seized cattle and movables and ravaged the towns of Nablus, Samaria and Janin. Laden with plunder and prisoners the army headed back to Damascus without the victory they had wished for but having dealt another bludgeoning blow to the settlers' sense of safety.[4]

Ibn Jubayr, our trusty Iberian pilgrim, reported that Saladin allowed 'each hand to hold what it had gained, and became rich and prosperous', as ever, keeping his supporters well rewarded. The author saw some of the returning troops enter Damascus, and noted thousands of prisoners. Ibn Jubayr's presence, as a pilgrim, in the midst of what was patently a war zone reminds us that for all the horrors of armed conflict, many aspects of everyday life still carried on. The traveller did register surprise at this:

> One of the astonishing things that is talked of is that though the fires of discord burn between the two parties, Muslim and Christian, two armies of them may meet and dispose themselves in battle array, and yet Christian and Muslim travellers will come and go between them without interference ... The soldiers engage themselves in war, while the people are at peace and the world goes to him who conquers ... The state of these countries in this regard is truly more astonishing than our story can relay.[5]

He commented that he moved into Christian territory at a time when Frankish prisoners were entering Muslim lands. He noted border areas where crops and livestock were shared between Christian and Muslim neighbours, and he expressed disgust at the apparent contentment of the many Muslim farmers living under Frankish overlordship, a situation he put down to the low taxes they paid and being left largely to their own devices.[6] Trade continued as well. Records from Italian mercantile cities such as Genoa attest to a vigorous commercial environment across the entire Mediterranean almost regardless of religious allegiance, an assertion given life by Ibn Jubayr's engaging description of his arrival in Acre in the warm September sun. Christian clerks sat on carpet-covered benches outside the customs houses, talking and writing in Arabic, and recording the taxes charged on those who passed through. 'All this was done with civility and respect, and without harshness and unfairness. We lodged beside the sea in a house which we rented from a Christian woman.' He regarded Acre as 'a meeting place of Muslim and Christian merchants from all regions', although he described it as a city where unbelief burned fiercely and as being both morally degenerate and physically filthy. It did, however, have a small mosque within the precincts of the Cathedral of the Holy Cross, set aside for the offering of the obligatory prayers.[7]

One marker of the pressure being applied to the Franks was a decision by the High Court, in the summer of 1184, to send to the West yet another appeal for help. Similar embassies had set out over the years and sometimes these missions induced nobles of standing to travel to the Holy Land, but they had not yielded the large-scale crusade the Franks felt they so desperately required. By 1184 they judged – rightly – that the situation had escalated to an unprecedented level of urgency. Previous messengers had been officers of the Military Orders or senior churchmen. This time they chose the most elite group possible, consisting of the patriarch of Jerusalem himself, Heraclius, along with the master of the Templars and the master of the Hospitallers. Alongside the fact that King Baldwin was in such terrible health, it was probably unwise for a reigning monarch to risk the lengthy sea voyage to the West.[8]

It would be a mistake, however, to regard the Franks as entirely cowed, or simply waiting for an inevitable defeat unless they were sent help. Saladin's vigorous efforts to bring northern Syria under his control testify to the scale of the resources that he felt would be needed to break the Christian hold on Jerusalem. Twice in six months the Franks raided into Egypt. The first thrust troubled Ayla and Sadr in the Sinai peninsula. The second, in September 1184, pushed northwards and drove much deeper into Egypt, hitting the town of Faqus on the eastern edge of the Nile Delta. The instigator of these raids was almost inevitably Prince Reynald, again demonstrating what a menace he posed. News of this latest incursion caused terror in the town of Bilbais, the place so badly savaged by King Amalric's forces back in the 1160s. The inhabitants fled and transmitted panic as far as Cairo and Misr. Taqi al-Din headed out from Cairo to deal with the threat, but with their mission accomplished the raiders simply faded away, taking with them over 200 prisoners.[9]

From Saladin's perspective, the Muslim Near East also required attention, as ever. His desperation to acquire Mosul was a clear sign of his wish to consolidate the Ayyubid hold on the Jazira and to remove powerful enemies from his borders. But it also indicated his need to control the military and material resources of this region, not least to provide him with the large numbers of experienced cavalrymen he required.[10] So while the Franks were manifestly alarmed at the steady, if not always linear, rise of the sultan, he in turn still had to increase his own strength in order to defeat them.

The Mosulis were not at all ready to submit to Saladin's authority and the caliph of Baghdad continued to seek a diplomatic solution to the simmering tension between the two parties. Yet another mission from Baghdad reached Damascus in September 1184 but it made no progress. The embassy was not wholly without advantage to the sultan because it brought robes of honour for both Saladin and Saphadin. It is interesting to see the status accorded to Saphadin, showing his centrality to the Ayyubid cause and his strength and competence.[11] The men donned their robes with due ceremony; Saladin then awarded his to Nur al-Din Muhammad to show gratitude for his help at Kerak and afterwards. A less happy note was the death (through disease) of the two envoys from Baghdad, a bad omen for the chances of peace with Mosul.[12]

As the winter of 1184 approached it was too late to begin any further campaigns and the sultan released his troops back to their homes and families. Those who accompanied Taqi al-Din to Egypt faced difficult times because the Nile had flooded to an unusually high level causing damage to houses, orchards, sugar plantations and the irrigation canals.[13]

The following year started with relative calm. The Franks could see that King Baldwin's health was in terminal decline and this tragic young monarch died, aged only twenty-three, in March 1185. His determination to remain on the throne generated a bitter struggle to succeed him, playing out between the supporters of his uncle, Raymond of Tripoli, and his brother-in-law, Guy of Lusignan. There is an argument to be made that he clung on to power too long, in part fomenting some of these troubles, yet Baldwin's own bravery in appearing on campaign whenever his health permitted won wide-spread admiration. The dying king had made careful provision for his succession and his seven-year-old nephew was crowned Baldwin V with Raymond of Tripoli as regent. The importance of preserving the royal bloodline was paramount in most western societies at the time, although the coronation of a seemingly sickly child was, on the part of the Franks, the continuation of a desperately unhappy run of dynastic ill fortune that could only assist Saladin's cause.

In February 1185, the imminent passing of Baldwin IV, coupled with months of no rainfall, had prompted Raymond of Tripoli to make a truce with Saladin.[14] While this plainly suited the Franks it was very much to Saladin's advantage too. Efforts to set up truces with the Greeks and the Armenians show just how hard the sultan was working to clear the decks in order to focus on Mosul.[15]

The situation with Mosul slowly came to a head. In April 1185 Saladin moved to Hama where his Syrian subjects brought him men and money for the forthcoming campaign. An invitation from Keukburi, the lord of Harran, looked like providing a big step forwards. The Turkmen emir is said to have offered huge financial help to persuade the sultan to join forces with him against Mosul, only for Saladin to discover the promises to be false. As was so often the case, the sultan dealt with a difficult situation with a blend of firmness and pragmatism. Keukburi had remained in Saladin's camp still hoping to convince the sultan to help him, but he had been rumbled and as they finished playing polo, he was arrested and imprisoned. Saladin understood, however, that this was an influential regional figure who had helped him in earlier campaigns. Thus, after four days, the sultan released him – having shown very clearly who was in control.[16] Keukburi proved an important character over the next few years and, as we will see, Saladin devoted considerable attention to keeping him onside.

The broader geopolitical scene of the Muslim Near East again came into view. While we have focused on Saladin and his labours in Egypt, Syria, Iraq and the Holy Land, there was a wider circle of Islamic lands to remember as well. Saladin's emirs had moved into North Africa over previous years and by this stage were at the peak of their power, ruling the fertile lands of Ifriqa (roughly the equivalent of modern Tunisia) except for the cities of Tunis and Mahdia. To the west lay the Almohads, a powerful dynasty based in the Atlas Mountains; periodically Taqi al-Din wanted to attack them, but given other priorities closer to home the sultan discouraged such a plan.[17] Over to the east lay Baghdad, the heart of the Sunni caliphate, itself often under the influence of the Seljuk sultans of Iraq (centred even further east on the cities of Hamadan and Isfahan, but also stretching north to Azerbaijan). By the mid-1160s the caliph and his viziers had begun to reassert their independence and had become sworn enemies of the over-mighty Seljuk *atabeg*, Jahan Pahlawan, a man with a major interest in Mosul too. Regardless of their own rivalries, these powers looked upon the rise of the Ayyubid dynasty with a blend of irritation and concern.[18]

Likewise, envoys from the powerful sultan of Iconium (modern Konya) in central Turkey reached Saladin in June 1185, and told him quite unambiguously that if he did not leave Mosul alone, then he would be attacked by 'all the princes of the East'. By this point, however,

Saladin was committed to a course of action and moved towards Mosul in June. Ever aware of the need to try to woo the caliph of Baghdad, he sent a formal notification of his plans. He sought, as before, a diploma of investiture for the city and he argued that he wanted 'to bring Mosulis back to obedience to the caliph and to make them aid Islam'.[19] Ibn al-Athir, who was actually in Mosul at the time, suggests that on this occasion Saladin's usually strong diplomatic skills deserted him at this point, resulting in a missed opportunity.

The leadership of Mosul sent out envoys who included the mother of Izz al-Din Zengi, the ruler of the city, along with one of Nur al-Din's daughters, and other distinguished ladies, all a carefully calculated means of applying pressure to the sultan. They offered to provide troops whenever requested if he would depart. Many of Saladin's advisors favoured an agreement, but two of his closest Kurdish associates, Isa the jurist and al-Mashtub, men from the Mosul region, dismissed the plan, arguing that it was a sign the city was weak. Ibn al-Athir wrote that this rejection of the women aroused great anger inside Mosul and prompted a renewed will to resist. Saladin was said to have regretted this loss of reputation, an interesting sign of his sensitivity to such issues, and to have blamed his advisors.[20]

The extreme summer heat limited military activity, but the siege still got underway. As we saw with the construction of the brick protective tunnels at Kerak, Saladin was prepared to think flexibly in these situations. Here he considered something much more ambitious, namely diverting the River Tigris to cut off or reduce Mosul's water supply, although in the end the idea was rejected.[21] Meanwhile the distribution of Mosuli *iqtas*, notably to the Kurdish troops of al-Mashtub, was one way Saladin rewarded his men and showed he was taking charge.

After a brief foray north, he set up camp outside Mosul once more in November 1185. Given the tough winter weather conditions the Ayyubid strategy encompassed a combination of overt military presence, hoping to squeeze the city into surrender after a lengthy period of confinement, blended with the background diplomatic pressure of Saladin's holy-war propaganda.[22] This resembled Nur al-Din's approach to the subjugation of Damascus three decades previously, with a mixture of blockade, propaganda and threat, although at Mosul the last of these was much more overt.

But during the holy month of Ramadan (December 1185) any momentum was forcefully checked when Saladin fell seriously ill. He was reportedly suffering from a quartan fever (a form of malaria), doubtless exacerbated by the tough climate of northern Iraq in December. In spite of his condition Saladin managed to ride to the castle of Harran, over 400 kilometres west, where he chose to remain for the next three months. For several weeks his position was dire; at times he would seem to recover but then suffered a relapse and be so weak he could not even sit up. Concern for him spread from the Ayyubid camp to their wider territories. The political scene in Damascus became restive and there were fears of Frankish attacks. Some were unhappy that he was based at Harran, still outside his own lands, and wanted him back in Aleppo, but his health was too feeble. Instead, family members came to him. Saphadin rode over from Aleppo bringing with him his own doctors, while three of his sons also arrived.[23]

Such a state of affairs naturally encouraged the Mosulis. Beha al-Din was again dispatched to the caliph while he also sought the backing of other Persian princes. Yet no such help was offered, not least because Caliph al-Nasir did not want Mosul and *atabeg* Pahlawan working together and, in his eyes, becoming a greater threat to him than Saladin. By this point, even with Saladin so ill, the Mosulis felt that their chances of preserving independence had gone. They sent Beha al-Din instructions to negotiate a settlement and this he duly did, with Saphadin also taking the oath on account of his brother's obvious weakness.[24]

Finally on 3 March 1186 a peace agreement was reached. Izz al-Din Zengi would swear obedience and supply troops to the holy war. At last Saladin had asserted himself over the remaining great metropolis of the region and ended the remnants of large-scale Zengid power. The crucial symbols of authority, the striking of coins and the recitation of the *khutba* in his name, rather than that of the Seljuk Turkish rival, *atabeg* Pahlawan, signified his victory. His control over places such as Jazirat Ibn Umar, Irbil and Takrit was also confirmed.

This was the breakthrough he had so long desired, and now he could contemplate his ultimate goal of Jerusalem. In the short term, however, his illness inevitably generated real instability. Rumours of his death had circulated in northern Syria. Unwisely, a cousin prematurely announced that he would succeed the sultan in Damascus. Such a blatant challenge to the planned succession had to be dealt with. At a dinner the man was plied with copious amounts of wine and found dead, poisoned, the following morning. Some accused the sultan himself of ordering this murder, although this was not Saladin's usual style and his direct involvement can be seriously questioned. By this same version the man's money, horses and equipment were seized but, given that the putative usurper's widow was one of Saladin's sisters, he is unlikely to have rendered her destitute. By late May the sultan had recovered and was back in Damascus where he received the welcome news that *atabeg* Pahlawan had died and his successors were embroiled in a dispute. In other words, he need not worry about a threat from this direction for a good while.[25]

It seems that his own brush with death had destabilised the usually steady higher echelons of the Ayyubid clan. In the summer of 1186 a quarrel broke out in Egypt between Saladin's nephew, Taqi al-Din, and the sultan's eldest son, al-Afdal. The former claimed that al-Afdal was too mild and generous a person to permit him to collect taxes and to punish those who refused to pay. The sultan seems to have suspected that if he was to die Taqi al-Din might remove al-Afdal and take over Egypt in his own right, and so he dismissed him from his role as the sultan's representative there. Taqi al-Din was livid and according to rumour was said to be heading off to campaign in North Africa. Saladin sent Isa the jurist down to Cairo to reason with his nephew who, it should be said, had been a formidable warrior and an important political figure in the Ayyubid clan for almost two decades by this time. That said, Imad al-Din characterised him as an individual 'with the potential for violence'.[26] Isa placated the irate man and convinced him to go and make peace with Saladin in person. This he duly did, and in spite of his concerns the sultan chose to forgive him this outburst, to let him keep his northern Syrian possessions and to offer compensation in the form of the fine town of Hama. As usual, Saladin had assessed that, if at all possible, it was best not to set up a powerful rival.[27] Al-Afdal, meanwhile was assigned Damascus, obviously an immensely prestigious fief in its own right.

Another territorial reshuffle involved Saphadin, although this seems to have been managed more effectively. The prompt for this is given an intriguing literary vehicle via a story describing the advice of an old friend of Saladin's, a man said to have been his loyal companion from the time before he came to power in Egypt. This man reeled off the rulers of the sultan's various territories and noted that they were largely held by his close relatives, rather than his sons. This may well have been an accident of age – the sultan's oldest son was around sixteen and simply not yet capable of ruling in his own right. But, the point underlying this entertainingly imagined conversation was made – he needed to draw the circle of power inwards. Thus Saladin decided to remove Saphadin from Aleppo and make him *atabeg* for the now vacant land of Egypt, overseeing the rule of the sultan's second son, al-Aziz Uthman, until the latter proved himself competent. The fact that Saphadin had expressed a real preference for living in Egypt meant this all fitted very neatly.[28] A third son, al-Zahir Ghazi, was restored to Aleppo having been demoted from the (largely nominal) post by his father in early 1184 – perhaps it was now deemed appropriate for him to hold a city described by Beha al-Din as 'the very root, foundation and source of power'.[29]

If this period could be characterised as one of some friction within the Ayyubid camp then it was dwarfed by the political soap opera taking place in the Latin kingdom of Jerusalem. Heraclius' mission to the West did not prompt the huge crusade he hoped for, although it had convinced a few knights to make the journey to the Holy Land. There was a catch, however; during the patriarch's absence, as we saw above, the Franks had arranged a truce with Saladin. In other words, the men who had just spent months flogging all the way to Jerusalem were politely told that there was no fighting for them to do. While the truce was, of course, a good thing for the settlers, its timing hardly enhanced the effectiveness of their pleas for help.

The child king Baldwin V died in the summer of 1186. This ended the regency of Raymond of Tripoli and meant the nearest blood relative in the royal line was now the dead boy's mother, Sibylla. Her husband, the Poitevin Guy of Lusignan, was regarded by Count Raymond as an incompetent outsider, although Guy was from a family with a noteworthy crusading heritage.[30] Count Raymond was patently determined to try to take the crown for himself, and a number of writers regarded him as by far the best prospect. Even Ibn Jubayr was impressed and recalled him thus: 'The most considerable amongst the accursed Franks is the accursed count ... he has authority and position among them. He is qualified to be king and indeed is a candidate for the office. He is described as being shrewd and crafty.'[31] The chasm between the two Frankish factions was vast. Raymond refused point-blank to perform homage to Guy and returned to his lordship in Galilee. The king and many of the other nobles marched on Tiberias on the west shore of the Sea of Galilee, which prompted Raymond to take drastic action. In what looks like nothing other than an act of total self-interest he turned to Saladin for help. The sultan appreciated this golden opportunity and acted rapidly to draw Raymond towards him, releasing various of his knights whom he held prisoner and promising to 'make him an independent ruler of the Franks'.[32] Raymond garrisoned Muslim troops to bolster his forces and swore the sultan's men could pass freely through his lands if Saladin would make him king. This proposal relied upon Saladin actually wanting to preserve a Christian king – although presumably not one based in Jerusalem, a notion far out of tune with his stated aims over the previous decade and in contradiction to the very basis of his efforts to bring the Muslim Near East under his authority. Raymond must have understood this, so sheer personal ambition and short-term expediency surely underpinned his actions; indeed, Qadi al-Fadil described his behaviour as being inspired by greed alone.[33] Ibn al-Athir captured just how profound this move was: 'Thus their unity was disrupted and their cohesion broken. This was one of the most important factors that brought about the conquest of their territories and the liberation of Jerusalem.'[34]

The rapidly accelerating sense of dysfunction within the kingdom of Jerusalem soon took another dramatic leap. Spies informed Prince Reynald that a large trading caravan was moving from Cairo to Damascus, 'accompanied by good number of troops'. A generous reading of this offers it as a breach of the truce, but in any case, Reynald could not let pass an opportunity to inflict damage on the sultan's people. He immediately gathered his men and intercepted the caravan, seizing the travellers and their goods. Some western sources said that Saladin's sister was in the party, adding a deeply personal edge to the episode, although Muslim writers place her in a later, safe, caravan. Had she been taken captive, the level of contemporary outrage would surely have been deafening.[35]

Saladin was furious and demanded the return of the prisoners, citing the existence of the truce that dated to the time of Baldwin V.

King Guy instructed Reynald to release the caravan but the prince refused, saying that he was the lord of his own lands (Transjordan) and had no truce with the Muslims. This was a hugely destructive and provocative stance. It was a savage blow to Guy's already shaky authority and it added further fuel to the crackling rivalry between Reynald and Saladin. The latter swore that 'when God gave him into his hands, he would personally slay him', a prescient statement indeed.[36]

Reynald's actions, coupled with Count Raymond's apparent treachery towards the king, presented Saladin with an unprecedented opportunity to strike. Patently the Franks were more interested in their own political situation than anything else. While internal squabbling may have been an option when the truce was in operation, for Reynald to engage in an aggressive external act, to break the agreement, or to pretend that it did not exist created a different picture. For Saladin, now that he had finally drawn Mosul into his own orbit, this was an ideal moment to move. After his own brush with death at Harran he had sworn to devote himself solely to the capture of Jerusalem. One writer commented 'that sickness was sent by God to turn away sins ... and to wake him from the sleep of forgetfulness'.[37] There is here an implicit rebuke for his years of fighting fellow Muslims, albeit working behind the premise that removing the Franks from Jerusalem was his ultimate goal. As we have seen, this had often been difficult for others to accept, but through his persistence and political skill he had pulled together a broad, albeit potentially fragile, coalition that stretched from Egypt to the Euphrates. This was a phenomenal achievement, but it generated immense pressure to deliver tangible progress or victory. Reynald's inflammatory actions offered a legitimate casus belli, meaning that Saladin could now bring this grand array of forces fully to bear on the Franks.

Saladin's first move was, almost inevitably, against Prince Reynald, aiming to pin him down in Kerak and to enable the Egyptian army to move up to join him in Syria. In April 1187 Saladin's son al-Afdal, working in conjunction with Keukburi, was commanded to make a raid on Reynald's territory, although to do so required him to pass through lands controlled by Count Raymond. Given the existence of a treaty between Raymond and Saladin, Keukburi politely asked permission to do this. Such a request brought Raymond's position into stark focus: he could alienate his new Muslim ally by refusing to agree, or he could consent, but risk bringing shame upon himself by effectively aiding and abetting a raid against his co-religionists.

Raymond settled upon what seemed to be a clever solution, telling Keukburi that the Muslims had to be off his territory by sunset and that he must promise not to take or damage anything, and if the population remained inside their homes they were to be assured of their safety. By unhappy coincidence, however, a diplomatic effort to try to draw Raymond back into the broader political fold was underway, led by the masters of the Hospitallers, Roger of Moulins, and the Templars, the bellicose Gerard of Ridefort.

Notwithstanding Raymond's warnings about the presence of Keukburi's men, Gerard and a large troop of his knights based themselves at the Templar fortress of La Fève, south of Nazareth. Once again, a Christian group was acting of its own initiative. Caring little for Raymond's arrangement with Keukburi, Gerard and his men went out from La Fève. The Muslims were actually heading back to their lands when the Franks came upon them at the Springs of Cresson (near Kafr Sabt, close to the road from Saffuriya to Tiberias).[38] The Christians numbered around 140 knights, plus squires; the Muslim forces are estimated to total perhaps 6,000. What followed was a calamitous error, one fuelled by the periodically suffocating notions of honour and pride that could trigger acts of either great heroism, or in other circumstances, such as this one, foolishness. The warrior classes of Christendom were raised on tales of bravery, elaborately garlanded in the epic stories of the *chansons de geste* sung in the halls and camps of men-at-arms. These tales emphasised unswerving bravery and condemned cowardice; they would have been familiar to all the men at Cresson. Given that the majority of the Christian army were members of the Military Orders, warrior monks sworn to defend Christians, this added an especially emotive spiritual layer to their sense of honour. The Military Orders were not blindly aggressive, however. Their regulations mandated strict discipline and warned against displays of vanity. As a religious Order, however, obedience to one's superior was also part of an individual's vow.

Roger of Moulins and even James of Mailly, marshal of the Templars, advocated caution. Yet Gerard, described by a contemporary as physically strong but presumptuous in temperament, scoffed and accused his colleagues of cowardice. A predictable tit-for-tat exchange ensued, with an escalating level of insult. Finally the Franks charged – the Hospitallers could hardly stand by and watch their great rivals the Templars take all the glory – and, as a western writer stated, 'the Saracens withstood them joyously and closed in on them so that the Christians could not pass through'. In the inevitable massacre, Roger and James were both killed and then beheaded, all the other Hospitallers died and only four of the Templars escaped; the squires saw what was happening and prudently fled. By grim irony, Gerard, the architect of the disaster, was one of the Templars to survive. As Ibn al-Athir commented, 'this was a battle fit to turn black hair to grey'.[39]

Keukburi's men paraded the heads of the slain and their prisoners (a relief force was captured almost to a man as well) past the walls of Tiberias, provoking horror and grief as intended. As news of the disaster filtered through to the Franks, they dispatched packhorses to the battlefield for the grim task of collecting the bodies for burial. For the Muslims this was a big step forwards. The slaughter of over a hundred knights, men of the Military Orders, dealt a heavy blow to the Franks – the warrior monks were their elite troops, highly trained and perfectly equipped; this was a 'great triumph [for Saladin] for the Templars and the Hospitallers are the Franks' firebrands'.[40] Perhaps one-seventh of the front-line fighting strength of the crusader states had been needlessly wasted in a bragging match. As a springboard to greater things this could hardly have been a more auspicious start for Saladin and he wasted no time in broadcasting this success, sending out victorious communiqués across his lands.[41]

13

The Battle of Hattin

*'The Devil and his crew
were taken'*

By the early summer of 1187 Saladin had spent well over a decade proclaiming his desire to liberate Jerusalem. He now had the men and the resources of Egypt, Syria and much of the Jazira at his disposal and an array of diplomatic arrangements in place to prevent unwanted distractions. But, as he was well aware, this was not a balancing act that could be sustained indefinitely. Reynald's attack on the trade caravan violated the truce and provided Saladin with a cause for war. The prince's refusal to return the captives demanded a response.[1]

An immediate consequence of the Frankish defeat at Cresson was a reconciliation between Raymond and King Guy. The count belatedly recognised that the Christians had to pull together. He expressed bitter regret for the disaster and finally performed homage to Guy and the queen, Sibylla. Guy likewise acknowledged the need for peace and the two men embraced one another.[2] Such developments can hardly have surprised the Muslims but Saladin's officials still excoriated Raymond for this latest change of allegiance, writing that 'his hypocrisy and breaking of covenants became clear', or as a later author suggested, 'the devil only promises to deceive'.[3]

By late June Saladin had mustered the largest army yet assembled during his rule, consisting of contingents from Harran and Edessa, from Aleppo, Mosul, Irbil and Mardin. Total troop numbers are hard to establish but a reasonable consensus would be just over 30,000.[4] As the yellow banners of the Ayyubids fluttered above this vast array of men and horses, Imad al-Din rhapsodised: 'The earth adorned itself in new clothes, heaven opened so that the angels could descend from its gates, the ship-like tents rode at anchor in this expanse and the battalions flooded in wave upon wave ... Swords and iron-tipped lances rose like stars, crescent swords like arches of myrtle ... coats of mail glittering like pools.'[5] Saladin came forward to inspire his men and to remind them what was required, reinforcing 'the debt owed to the Faith'; in other words, their obligation to wage jihad. Prayers and pious works were complemented by more earthly actions too. The sultan had conserved a store of treasure specifically for the occasion, and he duly distributed this largesse while moving amongst the army making sure to raise morale to a peak of readiness and expectation.[6]

Four years previously Saladin had thrust deep into Frankish lands around Bethsan, Mount Tabor and Nazareth. While the incursion had created panic in the local population and generated a corrosive political discord amongst the Frankish nobility, his opponents had made sure to avoid pitched battle. Some Muslim emirs favoured a continuation of this approach, a slow grinding down of the enemy. But for Saladin such limited achievements were not an option. After years of propaganda the sultan needed to land a decisive blow. An emir made this abundantly clear: 'If any Frankish force stands against us we should meet it. People in the east curse us and say, "He has given up fighting the infidels and has turned his attention to fighting Muslims." In my opinion our best plan is to take a course of action that will vindicate us and stop people's tongues.'[7] Saladin agreed: 'It is the day I have been waiting for and God has gathered the troops for us and I am a man who has aged and I do not know my time of death, so make use of this day. And so fight for God, not for my sake.'[8] This was the moment to act.

On 27 June the Muslim advance guard marched across the Jordan and camped at the southern end of the Sea of Galilee (Lake Tiberias).[9] The Franks knew the invasion was imminent and, as the *Libellus* (a text based on the eyewitness account of a soldier who was in the Holy Land at the time) tells us, the Christians assembled all possible troops. Such was the gravity of the situation that Gerard of Ridefort broke open the great money chests that contained the cash donated to the Holy Land by King Henry II of England as part of his penance for the murder of Thomas Becket seventeen years earlier. While spending this money theoretically required Henry's permission, in such desperate circumstances Guy ignored the stipulation. The Templars and the Hospitallers, drained by the losses at Cresson the previous month, still managed to send a total of around 600 knights, along with contingents of mounted sergeants; Count Raymond gathered his men from Tripoli and Galilee, Prince Reynald brought his contingents from Kerak and Shaubak, and the lords of Ibelin, Sidon and Caesarea assembled their forces as well. 'There did not remain a man in the cities, or towns, or castles who was able to advance to war that was not urged to leave by the order of the king.'[10] The True Cross, the Franks' great protective talisman, was brought up from Jerusalem, although the worldly patriarch Heraclius remained with his mistress in the holy city, passing responsibility for the relic to the bishops of Lydda and Acre. The total army numbered perhaps 20,000, with up to 1,200 knights and a few thousand turcopoles, the remainder being infantrymen.[11] A contemporary Muslim source gives a loosely comparable figure for the Franks too; in other words, in overall terms the Muslims likely had an advantage greater than 3:2.

The Franks gathered first at Acre, vigorously debating whether they should confront or shadow the invaders. They then moved east to the Springs of Saffuriya in Lower Galilee.[12] Saffuriya was ideally located to face an invasion from Damascus, although Saphadin lurked in Egypt adding another layer of threat and uncertainty. The Franks needed almost all of their men to face Saladin, even though this meant ignoring his brother and leaving their southern borders practically wide open.

On 30 June, Saladin's full army moved north-west, advancing up from the Jordan valley floor (210 metres below sea level), along the Wadi Fedjas to the village of Kafr Sabt (160 metres above sea level) on the road from Acre to the Jordan valley. This was a vital opening move by the sultan, especially given the size of his forces, because Kafr Sabt has a good water supply from the valley. There are six springs within four kilometres, and it is only about fifteen kilometres from the River Jordan; it also controls or threatens the two roads that run from Saffuriya to Tiberias. Back in 1182, before Guy was regent, Frankish troops had moved into this area and in holding the higher ground, they had parried Saladin's initial thrust. This time, in remaining at Saffuriya they passed up this advantage and handed the Muslims a useful initiative.[13]

Provocation was now the order of the day. Muslim troops raided the monastery on Mount Tabor (the scene of the Transfiguration of Jesus) and then sped west to the town of Nazareth, two places of manifest importance to the Christians. This was all by way of preliminaries intended to generate pressure on the Franks but, as before, it did not draw them out. The sultan remained optimistic and he conducted a reconnaissance mission, looking over different options for battlefields. The recent victory at Cresson, only seven kilometres west of his camp, plus the campaigns of 1182 and 1183 had given some of his warriors a familiarity with the local landscape, and information from traders and pilgrims added further layers of strategic intelligence.[14] Having assembled such a colossal army the sultan was determined to make the best possible use of it – and not to be caught unawares as happened at Montgisard ten years earlier. Yet he had to find a trigger, something to prompt a reaction. Reflecting a concern of the Muslim leadership, Ibn al-Athir imagined the Franks suggesting that the sultan's men 'will be unable to endure the long time away from their homes and families, so he [Saladin] will be compelled to leave'.[15]

On the morning of 2 July the sultan revealed that he had just such a ploy when a group of his men laid siege to the small town of Tiberias on the western shore of the Sea of Galilee. The lord of Tiberias was, of all people, Count Raymond, but at this time he was with the main Christian forces at Saffuriya. Defence of the town rested with a small garrison led by his wife, Eschiva. When Raymond departed he had told Eschiva that in the event of a Muslim attack she should take to the boats and seek refuge on the lake until he was able to come and save her. It seems that his advice was not, or could not, be followed. By midday Saladin's men had broken into the town leaving Eschiva to take refuge in the citadel. A messenger escaped and rushed over to Saffuriya to tell her husband and King Guy this terrible news.[16]

Saladin had presented the Franks with a fiendish challenge. Should they do the honourable thing and go to rescue Eschiva, even if this meant leaving the security of the Springs of Saffuriya? What would Raymond, her husband, advise? He had, after all, been a leading advocate of the non-engagement policy back in 1183. What about Guy?

Could he leave the wife of his most senior noble, a man only just reconciled to him, to her fate? Lurking in the background was a memory that the last time he chose not to fight it prompted his removal from the regency. As a man whose kingly qualities were patently open to question – something that Saladin was very much aware of – this was a mighty test. From the sultan's perspective he had played a strong opening hand: how would the Franks react?

On the evening of 2 July, King Guy summoned the nobles and the masters of the Military Orders to hear their advice. Accounts of the meeting vary, but it seems that at first the consensus was to fight. A powerful intervention from Count Raymond changed the mood. As he pointed out, 'none of you stand to lose as much as I do' from the fall of Tiberias, but he remained adamant that the greater good of the Latin kingdom was at stake. The route to Tiberias lay across lands without food and water and the scorching summer heat would surely prove lethal to men and horses alike. He advocated bringing the Muslims to battle, but only from a position of strength; that is, with the water of Saffuriya nearby. Such sound counsel looked to have settled the matter; if Raymond was prepared to lose his lands and his wife, then the nobles' anxiety at leaving a lady in distress was partially assuaged. In purely tactical terms, his diagnosis made perfect sense. With agreement seemingly reached, all retired to their beds. Saladin's bold pitch looked to have fallen short. But late at night King Guy had one more visitor to his tent, a man bearing multiple grudges and with a most aggressive track record.

Gerard of Ridefort clearly thought Raymond was wrong. To him the count had demonstrated total unreliability in his recent alliance with Saladin. Gerard reminded Guy of the price he had paid for inaction in 1183; surely he would not want to make the same mistake again. 'Sire, do not trust the advice of the count for he is a traitor and you well know that he has no love for you and wants you to be put to shame and lose the kingdom ... move immediately and let us go and defeat Saladin ... if you withdraw at his attack the shame and reproach will be all the greater for you.' At the Battle of Cresson Gerard had taken a highly bellicose attitude towards fighting the Muslims, and the humiliation he suffered there further inflamed his feelings. He wished 'to avenge the shame and loss the Saracens had inflicted on him and on Christendom'. Compounding this, he also bore a deep personal grudge against the count. Years before, Gerard had been engaged to a young Frankish heiress, only for a Pisan merchant to offer her weight in gold in return for her hand in marriage. To Gerard's rage and dismay Raymond, acting as the girl's overlord, had accepted the proposal, taking the money for himself and triggering a lifelong enmity.[17]

Gerard's arguments were highly persuasive and the king, again, was swayed. The siren call of the challenge to a man's honour, coupled with the desperate wish to affirm his own power as monarch, took effect. The following morning (3 July) the camp awoke to the order to march. The troops were amazed and asked why the king had changed his mind. His response was brusque: 'You have no right to ask by whose counsel I am doing this. I want you to get on your horses and head towards Tiberias!'[18] As he performed his prayers, down at Tiberias scouts brought Saladin news of the Frankish decision to march.[19] From the sultan's perspective, the trap, at last, was sprung. As Ibn al-Athir wrote, 'his purpose in besieging Tiberias had only been that the Franks should leave their position so that he could engage them'.[20]

The Christian force set out in clear formation, led by Count Raymond because it was in his lands they were fighting. In the middle rode King Guy, accompanied by the True Cross, with the Templars and the Hospitallers at the rear. Infantrymen and archers protected the cavalry from Muslim horse-archers, while the heavy cavalry was there to take action if the Frankish footmen came under direct assault. While we have a number of (sometimes confused) accounts of the ensuing struggle, emerging battlefield archaeology offers a tremendous insight into the physical conditions during this unfolding conflict, an event that took place, of course, during the height of summer.[21] In essence, the Franks had about fourteen hours of daylight to cover the thirty kilometres from Saffuriya to Tiberias; just over two kilometres an hour, therefore. This may seem an undemanding rate, but in practice there were serious issues to contend with: water supply, the irritation of marching into the sun for the first part of the day, not to mention the minor matter of the huge Muslim army ranged against them. In fact, the initial stages of the march went well for the Franks.

It is sometimes too easy to be guided by our knowledge of the sultan's eventual triumph, but even with his careful preparations and numerical advantage this was by no means a foregone conclusion. Most of the mounted Frankish knights were hardened warriors, heavily armed and highly skilled. Their cavalry charge was famed for its lethal potential and avoiding the circumstances in which this could be unleashed was part of Saladin's plan. However, with the unprecedented scale of the summons to arms, many thousands of the Frankish foot soldiers were untrained and their discipline and fortitude remained open to question. And it was these men who dictated the pace of the march. An army of this size probably stretched out over a kilometre in length, giving a sense of scale to the Frankish force.[22] As Imad al-Din wrote with characteristic aplomb: 'they looked like mountains on the march, like seas boiling over, as the waves clash'.[23]

The sultan's men were also arranged in three groups, with Saladin himself in the centre, his nephew Taqi al-Din commanding the right wing, and the left under the experienced warrior Keukburi, lord of Harran.[24] The sultan's logistical preparations were admirable and immense: 400 wagonloads of arrows, along with a further seventy camel-loads ready to be brought onto the battlefield when needed.

While the Muslims made brief feints towards the Christians it took them until early afternoon to come up from their camp at the springs of Kafr Sabt, about six kilometres to the south. Once the two sides made contact, wave upon wave of Muslim light archers poured arrow-fire onto the Christian forces and dramatically retarded their progress. By mid-afternoon the air temperature was up to around 35 degrees and by this point on the road the landscape was without trees or vegetation. It was imperative to keep helmets on when under attack; chain mail and protective padding were essential too; weapons had to be carried and wielded or fired as appropriate, all of which expended energy and generated thirst. Such basic factors applied to both sides – and indeed, to all such encounters – although in this case the knowledge of numerical superiority and, most importantly for the Muslims, ample supplies of water created a stark contrast in psychological outlook.

The Christians' route ran along a reasonably wide valley with the steep slopes of Mount Turan to the north. Further north from the road again was the village of Turan itself where there was a minor spring, potentially a source of some refreshment for the Franks, although it was far smaller than the Springs of Saffuriya or, further ahead, Hattin; it was also located in an awkward spot between two spurs of a hillside. This was not a good place to halt an army of such numbers, although it seems the Franks discussed the possibility before deciding to carry on. Regardless of the size of the spring, Saladin moved rapidly to secure it once the Franks had departed, sending Taqi al-Din and Keukburi around behind the Christians. The sultan believed the decision to continue the march was a serious error and wrote that 'the Devil seduced him [Guy] into doing the opposite of what he had in mind and made to seem good to him what was not his real wish and intention. So he left the water and set out towards Tiberias.'[25]

A horse requires about twenty-seven litres of water a day; an adult male two and a half litres a day, an impossible volume and weight (at one kilogram per litre) for an army of this size to carry when under direct attack. The need to keep men and mounts going forwards became ever harder for the Franks. Above them, 'the dog star (the meridian), burned with unrelenting heat. The troops drank the contents of their flasks, but this could not slake their thirst.'[26] With Muslim troops now behind and ahead of the Franks, with infantrymen along the hills to the north and Saladin's main forces to the south, the Christians were loosely surrounded, in effect being shepherded eastwards. Beha al-Din summarised the situation, gilding his narrative with the imagined thoughts of the Frankish warriors. 'They were closely beset as in a noose, while still marching on as though being driven to a death that they could see before them, convinced of their doom and destruction and themselves aware that they would be visiting their graves.'[27]

As night fell, the Franks stopped, probably at the village of Maskana, about five kilometres past Turan, meaning they had managed around seventeen kilometres in the day. Maskana has a large pool, sometimes containing a good amount of water; perhaps this was why the Franks had pressed on.[28] If this was their hope then it seems to have been misplaced; the narratives do not mention finding such a supply. Saladin had suffered enough defeats to know how dangerous the Franks could be, but now he could witness the series of tactical errors that he had forced upon them. As the pace of the Christian advance slowed it became ever more plain just how badly they were struggling with the heat, the lack of water, and the relentless bombardment of the Muslim archers.

Night-time brought the hope of a little respite. Temperatures drop to around 20 to 23 degrees but humidity can be over 80%. Faced with sporadic assaults the Franks could not take off their clothing to allow their sweat to evaporate, meaning they continued to dehydrate. A cooling west wind may have offered some brief relief for them, but in fact, it would do the opposite.[29] Saladin commanded that fires should be lit. In summer this is a landscape of parched grass and scrub, bleached to the colour and texture of brittle bone. Overnight, as the Franks huddled grimly in their camp, the Muslims took advantage of the breeze to set fire to the tinder dry vegetation, delivering choking smoke towards their enemy, compounding their misery, exacerbating their thirst and dragging down morale a further notch or two.

Playing oppressively loud music is an occasional part of modern warfare; Saladin's troops did something similar, periodically drumming and blowing horns to disturb the Franks' rest. Most crucially of all for the Muslims, camels brought up fresh supplies of water from Lake Tiberias. They were also in the position to choose the moment to unleash another blast of noise or to structure at least some periods of calm for themselves; anticipation of success coupled with proper hydration were powerful restoratives. Cries of 'God is great' and 'There is no god but God' emphasised their conviction and shared endeavour, while the presence of holy men added to the sense of expectation and fervour. Saladin himself went amongst his troops, encouraging the ranks and urging them to the victory signalled by God's blessings.

The sun rose at 4.37 a.m. on Saturday 4 July. The Franks had only thirteen kilometres to reach Lake Tiberias and relief, but the first section of the march was across an arid and largely waterless plateau. A few open cisterns lay near the village of Lubiya, but these were too small to be of much use and may well have dried out already or been contaminated by Saladin's men. Muslim troops held several more cisterns on the stony hillsides to the north, while to the south and east they had easy access to supplies from their camp.[30]

Saladin missed little chance to ratchet up the psychological pressure. Further fires choked the parched mouths of the Christians; to ram home their superiority Muslim troops poured water onto the ground, an excruciating sight for the Franks. 'The people of the Trinity were consumed by a worldly fire of three types, each invincible and obliterating: the fire of flames, the fire of thirst and the fire of arrows.'

As the morning wore on, more Muslim forces committed to the fray, driving in repeated charges, releasing volley after volley of arrows and slowing the Frankish advance to a pitiful crawl. In every direction they were surrounded 'tormented by the heat of war ... and tortured by thirst ... Not even an ant among them could have advanced, nor could it have escaped to safety ... the arrows stuck in them transformed those who had seemed like lions into hedgehogs.'[31]

Still there was the fear of a heavy Frankish charge – if one could be organised. Count Raymond gathered a group of the senior nobles and together they plunged towards Taqi al-Din's squadron. Immediately appreciating the threat, the sultan's nephew reacted with brilliant tactical awareness. The Christians tore downhill, gathering a deadly momentum to smash into the Muslim troops, providing the latter waited to be hit. Just as the Franks prepared to strike, Taqi al-Din's men simply drifted aside, allowing the knights to pass through their position; they then closed ranks. By the time the Christians had come to a halt, the advantage of the slope had completely gone, which left them only two real options. They could charge back uphill, their mounts tired and thirsty, and then take on Taqi al-Din's well-watered heavy cavalry. Alternatively, they could depart the field of battle entirely, arguing that they had not supported the decision to march anyway and that to return to the fray was to face certain death or capture. They chose the latter, inevitably provoking accusations of collusion between the sultan and his former ally, although these are not sustainable. Of more immediate significance, Taqi al-Din's deft leadership had neatly peeled away a thick layer of the Franks' strongest troops at no cost to his own side.

Back with the bulk of the Christian army, the combination of cease-less volleys of arrow-fire, coupled with the dire lack of water had obliterated morale, especially amongst the infantry. By 8 a.m. the temperature was probably around 27 degrees and by midday and the early afternoon it was up into the mid-30s; as before, nothing in the landscape offered shade or shelter.[32] The foot soldiers suffered particu-larly and were on the verge of surrender. Desperate to keep a vestige of hope alive, and needing the different components of the army to work together properly, the king and his knights urged all of the troops to hold firm. This state of near total disarray was, in part, the conse-quence of poor discipline, untrained troops and weak leadership, sparked by the decision to leave the security of Saffuriya in the first instance. But Saladin and his generals must take credit for creating the situation, for their careful preparations in identifying the battlefield, in moving quickly to take control of the water sources, and then having the organisation to keep their own people properly hydrated and immaculately supplied with arrows. The Frankish advance ground to a terminal halt. As Ibn al-Athir wrote, the Muslim vanguard shot arrows like swarms of locusts; inevitably gaps in the Christian ranks began to appear. Saladin himself continued to ride back and forwards, encouraging his men and instilling in them the need to keep their discipline. Muslim cavalrymen charged too, their swords taking a heavy toll on the enfeebled Frankish footmen.[33]

By this point the Franks had reached the geographical feature that gives its name to the battle – the Horns of Hattin. This is a pair of extinct volcanoes with the larger, southern one, having a broken rim on its western side that provides access to the plain below. Iron Age settlers had fortified this strategic location, and in 1187 the infantry saw the shallow main crater, about 215 metres by 160 metres, and the colossal basalt stones on its edge, as the best place to make a last stand. The Franks pitched camp in this natural bowl with the red tent of King Guy and the True Cross at its centre.[34]

Twice the knights urged their few remaining horses down the slope in a desperate attempt to kill Saladin himself. This was a smart decision; the death of a leader almost inevitably meant the disintegration of his army (as the loss of King Harold at the Battle of Hastings so plainly demonstrated), although by this stage the Franks at Hattin were almost beyond hope. Yet charge they did, the second such foray surging dangerously close to the sultan. Each time this happened, though, more knights and horses were killed and the levels of exhaustion grew and grew.

With the Franks pinned up in the crater of Hattin, the moment of triumph was at hand. Saladin's eldest son al-Afdal stood alongside him, assessing the scene. Some years later, in conversation with the chronicler Ibn al-Athir, al-Afdal recalled what happened over the next few minutes:

> I looked towards him [Saladin] and he was overcome by grief and his
> complexion pale. He took hold of his beard and advanced, crying out

'Give lie to the Devil!' The Muslims rallied and climbed the hill. When I saw the Franks withdraw, pursued by the Muslims, I shouted for joy 'We have beaten them!' But the Franks rallied and charged again like the first time and drove the Muslims back to my father. He acted as he had on the first occasion and the Muslims again turned upon the Franks and drove them back to the hill. Again I shouted, 'We have beaten them!' but my father rounded on me and said 'Be quiet! We have not beaten them until that tent [Guy's tent] falls.' As he was speaking to me the tent fell. The sultan dismounted, prostrated himself in thanks to God and wept for joy.[35]

This was it, victory at last! The demoralised Franks laid down their arms, sat on the ground and surrendered; thus, as Imad al-Din wrote, 'the Devil and his crew were taken.'[36] A contemporary letter names a Kurdish warrior, Dirbas, as the man who captured Guy, while the emir Ibrahim al-Mihrani took Reynald. Just as in western society the prestige accorded to those individuals responsible for such key moments meant their names were recorded and quickly became widely known.[37] Saladin's troops started to round up the shattered and dejected Franks, claiming prisoners for themselves and hoping to secure ransom money from a knight or noble, or to sell lesser men as slaves. Men were roped and then chained together, stumbling around like drunks; a market of human despair. For the Franks, there was the fear and confusion of defeat. Who had died? Who would succumb to their wounds? What was their fate to be? For Saladin came the realisation of the scale of his victory – that he had made prisoners of King Guy and his brother Aimery, Gerard of Ridefort and Prince Reynald, that he had captured the True Cross and that the vast majority of the Frankish troops were either dead or in captivity.

The sultan prepared to take stock. King Guy's tent had fallen, now Saladin's household brought up his own tent to allow him to decide his next move. He ordered the most important prisoners presented before him. To Guy, he gave a drink of iced julep and the parched king downed most of it before he passed the cup to Reynald. In a flash, Saladin intervened. This was not permitted. He said to the interpreter: 'Tell the king, "You are the one who gave him a drink. I gave him no drink, nor any of my food."' In Near Eastern culture, as

Beha al-Din recounts, if a prisoner took food or drink from his captor he was safe, but Reynald had patently transgressed the limits of accept-able behaviour so frequently and so drastically, that he would not be accorded such a courtesy. Saladin berated Reynald for his raid towards Mecca and Medina and the attack on the trading caravan at a time of truce. Then, according to our closest sources, he sent the prisoners away. The sultan wanted to reflect on what to do next and so he went for a ride to clear his mind. Reynald, meanwhile, was left 'to roast at the fire of his fear'. When Saladin returned he once more summoned Guy and the prince to his presence. In front of his own senior nobles and entourage, he offered Reynald a deal – he could convert to Islam in return for his life. The man described as being 'more hostile to the Muslims' than any other was hardly likely to accept such a proposal and he declined. Now, having made at least a token gesture, the sultan finally exacted full revenge for Reynald's serial insults. He drew his scimitar and slashed the prince's shoulder, dropping the Frank to his knees before his bodyguards rushed forwards to finish the job; thus 'his soul was sent to hell'. Seeing his fellow Christian butchered, King Guy trembled with fear, expecting to be next, but Saladin calmed the terrified man and assured him of his safety.[38]

Prestigious prisoners were sent to Damascus. For the lesser men the slave emporia of Syria awaited them, with reports of multiples of prisoners, thirty to forty on a rope, being led away by a single man. One group who did not join them was Raymond's wife Eschiva of Tiberias, her children and household. Trapped in the citadel and plainly without hope, they quickly surrendered and Saladin courteously allowed them to leave for Tripoli.[39]

For some Franks, captivity was not to last. Having incited jihad amongst his people for so long, Saladin had, in part, created a hunger for vengeance. This was not an urge to inflict indiscriminate violence on all Christians, but just one particular group. The knights of the Military Orders, men 'devoted to slaughter' as one western source described them, were the sworn enemies of Islam and, as Beha al-Din commented, 'the fiercest fighters of all the Franks'.[40] As warrior-monks these men were not going to apostasise, and there was little attraction in simply keeping them prisoner, perhaps only to release highly trained men to fight again. 'I shall purify the land of these two impure orders', the sultan pronounced. The call went out to round up any captured

Templars and Hospitallers with a reward of fifty Egyptian dinars for each one. This was to be a public execution, symbolically performed by his own holy men, a practice seen before in 1178 and after the Red Sea raid in 1183. The knights were herded together and then, amateurishly, slaughtered by the clerics. Some could not bring themselves to kill; others, unused to wielding weapons, botched it horribly, dragging out this macabre exercise and requiring the sultan's guards to complete the task. As Imad al-Din grimly affirmed, the 'faces of the infernal Templars were ground into the dust'.[41] Incredibly though, as at the Battle of Cresson, Gerard of Ridefort survived. Given his culpability for the march on Hattin this seems rough justice for the thousands who died, but his status as master of the Templars meant he was a valuable bargaining chip and so he alone was spared.

The Franks were so pulverised by what happened that no one was left to bury the dead. Saladin's men stripped the shattered bodies of their armour and valuables and in the summer heat the corpses rapidly putrefied. This hideous landscape was quickly abandoned to the forces of nature. A couple of years later Ibn al-Athir wrote: 'I passed by the site of the battle and saw the ground covered with their bones, visible from afar, some of them heaped up and others scattered.'[42]

It was not just in terms of manpower that Saladin had obliterated the Franks. As crushing a blow as this was, the capture of the True Cross was a major feat. Imad al-Din was well aware of this: 'in their eyes its loss was more important than that of the king ... the cross that was taken was irreplaceable'.[43] On perhaps thirty previous occasions this most holy of relics had afforded protection to the Franks, but now it was held by the Muslims and its return, or not, would be a central feature of relations between the two parties for decades to come.[44]

Saladin and his forces spent a day or so recovering. Notwithstanding the elation of victory, they needed to recuperate from the immense physical effort of a two-day battle at the height of summer. The Franks had hardly been entirely passive in their resistance; the Muslims suffered casualties too, and it took time to assess their own dead and injured.

By any measure, however, this was a phenomenal victory, celebrated as such by Saladin's admirers and recognised as opening the door to his ultimate aim of Jerusalem. Perhaps at this point Saladin commissioned the Dome of Victory that marked the site of the battle. Imad al-Din wrote:

> Glorious and all-powerful God, may he be glorified and honoured, gave the sultan the power to achieve what others had not been able to accomplish. He reserved for him the most illustrious day, the purest triumph ... the most dazzling glory. Was there no other merit of his than this day the sultan would be singled out from the kings of old, and even more so those of the present, by this illustrious deed ... But this famous feat of arms was not only the prelude to the conquest of Jerusalem, it strengthened and consolidated the way to ultimate victory.[45]

14

The Capture of Jerusalem

*'The World of Islam was ready and
adorned for a festival to celebrate the
fall of Jerusalem'*

Saladin's victory at Hattin and his destruction of the Frankish forces
upended the balance of power in the Near East. As the sultan and his
advisors considered their next move it is interesting to wonder how
far ahead they had planned and whether the scale of their success
exceeded anything they had imagined. Jerusalem, of course, remained
the primary goal, but to be in a position to besiege and capture it still
required some substantial preliminary moves.

To capitalise fully on the psychological and strategic blow of Hattin
meant acting rapidly to isolate the holy city. As the entry point for
troop reinforcements from, conceivably, Antioch or Tripoli – and,
eventually, western Europe – the coastal cities had to be a priority.
The ports were also a source of great wealth; if Saladin intended to
rule these lands, he needed to control the economy. Over the next
seven weeks he orchestrated a series of dynamic campaigns across
the kingdom of Jerusalem, many led in person.

In terms of strategic and financial importance, Acre was by far the
most desirable target. Two days' march from Tiberias saw the Muslim
forces arrive at the Mediterranean coast on 8 July. With no fighting
men to defend its walls the city capitulated almost immediately. Imad
al-Din gleefully claimed that the Frankish banners hung from the
battlements transmitting their owners' fear by wobbling like tongues;
Saladin took pity on the inhabitants and promised them their lives.
Most of the merchants had fled, which left the sultan free to distribute

the wealth he found inside, greatly enriching the poor in his army; here were some of the more earthly rewards promised to the soldiers of the jihad. He gave control of the city to his son al-Afdal, who followed paternal practice and distributed considerable largesse and earned widespread praise for his generosity. Many other senior figures were beneficiaries, including the sultan's long-time supporter Isa al-Hakkari, to whom was given the houses, farms and lands of the Templars. Most powerful of Saladin's actions at Acre, and a clear manifestation of his religious agenda, was to install (or reinstall) a *minbar* (pulpit) and *mihrab*, basic symbols of the Islamic faith, in the main places of worship. When the crusaders had captured Acre in 1104 they took the principal mosque as their cathedral but now Saladin gathered a group of Frankish prisoners and ordered them to whitewash the walls, effacing Christian pictures and inscriptions. With the building duly cleansed, the first Sunni-led Friday prayer on the Syrian coast for decades took place on 10 July 1187.[1]

Sidon and Beirut soon fell too. Meanwhile Saphadin had moved up from Egypt and ravaged the southern lands of Jerusalem, taking Jaffa and the castle of Mirabel, in the latter case giving the defenders safe conduct back to Christian territory. He and Saladin met at Ascalon. Back in 1153 the city had resisted the Franks for several months and now, even with just a skeleton garrison it required the use of sappers, catapults and a siege of two weeks to bring it to surrender. Here, as with almost everywhere else, Saladin granted the defenders terms. He did not wish to perpetrate a series of massacres and wanted places to submit swiftly; some of these towns had considerable Muslim populations nearby, and in any case, as the incoming ruler of such settlements it would be better if they were taken over in good condition, rather than requiring a rebuild. The capture of Ascalon also enabled free movement between Egypt and southern Palestine, an important strategic step; in fact one of sufficient value that the defenders negotiated the release of some important prisoners including the bishop of Lydda and King Guy's brother Aimery, as well as a promise of freedom for the king a few months later. The inhabitants of Ascalon were permitted to leave for Jerusalem where they joined thousands more refugees who had flooded to the holy city in the hope of making a defiant stand for their faith.[2]

Gaza, Hebron, Nazareth, Sebastea, Nablus, Bethlehem and Ramla fell in swift succession, leaving almost the entire kingdom of Jerusalem in Muslim hands. Only the castles of Transjordan, including the indomitable Kerak, held out along with the two big northern fortresses at Belvoir and Safad, and one coastal town, Tyre.

Saladin's good fortune has been remarked upon several times already, but his efforts to take Tyre were a rare occasion when fate turned against him. As with most of the other Frankish settlements it was capable of only limited resistance after Hattin. Just as it was about to capitulate, a northern Italian nobleman and adventurer, Marquis Conrad of Montferrat, arrived by sea. Conrad was the uncle of the late King Baldwin V, and his own father, William the Old, was one of the important nobles captured at Hattin. Conrad himself had led a colourful existence, marrying the sister of the Byzantine emperor Isaac II Angelos in early 1187 and taking command of the imperial army. Political machinations in Constantinople meant that westerners fell out of favour and Conrad had to flee the city. Years before he had taken a crusade vow and now he chose to fulfil it, hence his appearance in the Holy Land. Given the chronology there is no possibility that he knew what had happened at Hattin. Thus, in complete ignorance, he attempted to dock at Acre only to realise that the quayside was full of Muslims rather than Franks. He managed to scurry northwards to Tyre where Reynald of Sidon had started to negotiate the surrender.[3]

Conrad was not going to give up so easily. He was a highly skilled warrior and rapidly organised the proper defence of what was a well-fortified city. Sensing that it would take time to break down this resistance Saladin had opted to head south to besiege and take Ascalon. Some historians have, wholly with the benefit of hindsight, viewed the failure to take Tyre as a terrible error, principally because over the coming months and years it became a focus for Frankish resistance and provided a bridgehead for western crusaders.[4] But this is harsh. Jerusalem had been the sultan's stated target for almost twenty years by now, and its recovery was intended as the crowning achievement of his life. To be sidetracked by the resistance of one port, remembering that the Franks still held coastal cities further north in Tripoli and Antioch as well, was not a logical course of action. Given the Muslims' apparent military superiority there was no reason to believe that it could not be taken soon after the capture of Jerusalem. Saphadin later recalled a rather more personal prompt to his brother: 'I pointed out to him that he was liable to attacks of colic and I said "If you die of an attack tonight, Jerusalem will stay in the hands of the Franks" ... He said: "I shall do what you order and advise."'[5]

While some of his troops garrisoned their new conquests, the bulk of those present at Hattin were joined at Jerusalem by Saphadin's Egyptian troops as well as large numbers of religious men, many from Damascus, who flocked to the army in anticipation of the momentous victory to come. Not that they were overconfident; the Muslims were well aware of the Christians' determination to defend their own holy city and recognised that both parties had a binding duty to try to prevail.

Saladin reached Jerusalem on 20 September 1187. Here was his ultimate goal, the city that contained the Dome of the Rock and the al-Aqsa Mosque. The Muslim troops set up camp around the Jaffa Gate on the western flank, running along and around the north-west corner of the city towards the Damascus Gate. A blast of trumpets accompanied by pounding drums and fierce chanting generated an ominous atmosphere intended to intimidate the Christians. Arrow-fire rained towards the walls, taking a heavy toll on the defenders; even the vast Hospital of St John, arguably the greatest hospital in Latin Christendom, could barely cope with the numbers of wounded. The author of a Latin eyewitness account told of an arrow striking the bridge of his nose and while doctors were able to remove the wooden shaft, the metal tip remained with him for life. For all the Franks' claims about a lack of troops the Christians would not capitulate so easily and they had gathered a force strong enough to make a series of fierce sallies, one of which killed a senior emir.[6]

Fortifications near the Tower of David and the Jaffa Gate provided stubborn resistance. Progress was insufficient and so Saladin circled the walls to assess his options. In doing so he ascended the Mount of Olives, overlooking Jerusalem from the eastern side. The morning sun rises behind here to illuminate a panorama of this inspiring city and, disregarding the high-rise buildings in the background, offered the sultan comparably the same absorbing view as we see today. Jerusalem stands on a slope that runs west-east; once outside the eastern walls, it falls steeply into the valley of Jehoshaphat. Dropping down in front of him, at the foot of the valley Saladin saw the great abbey of St Mary, built at vast expense by Queen Melisende (d.1161) and containing the richly decorated tomb of the Virgin Mary.[7] The building itself would be destroyed by the Ayyubids, but given Mary's prominence in the Quran and as the mother of the prophet Jesus, the tomb and its Frankish entrance structure were spared and still survive. Ascending up the other side of the valley stood the city walls, although the fortifications that exist today are largely Ottoman, dating from the reconstruction ordered by Suleiman the Magnificent between 1537 and 1541.[8] Gates stud the walls: on this side of the city, the Golden Gate, which provided direct access to the Muslim holy sites and the smaller Jehoshaphat Gate (today the Lion Gate) at the north-eastern end.

Above the walls Saladin laid eyes on the two sacred buildings he so desired. They stand on the huge platform called the *Haram al-Sharif* (the Sacred Precinct, also known by the Christians and the Jews as the Temple Mount). As if to flaunt Christian possession of these places a huge golden cross stood on top of the Dome of the Rock, symbolising its use as a church, the *Templum Domini* (Temple of the Lord). To the left was a complex of structures centred on the al-Aqsa Mosque; although under Frankish rule, they were the headquarters of the Knights Templar. Both behind and to the north of these buildings, still looking gently uphill, he would have seen dozens of church towers, advertising the polyglot population of crusader-era Jerusalem with churchmen, pilgrims and traders from across Christendom, representing Greek Orthodox, Maronites, Jacobites, Nestorians, Melkites, Armenians and Georgians, as well as the Franks. Reasonably easy to pick out was the domed roof of the Church of the Holy Sepulchre and, just opposite, the bell tower of the vast Hospital of St John. The latter has now gone, with the early twentieth-century tower of the Church of the Redeemer, commissioned by Kaiser Wilhelm II, rising powerfully upwards from this site. To the left of this, a couple of hundred metres further west and near enough out of this line of sight, stood the formidable Tower of David, the city's main fortress and the royal palace.[9]

With King Guy in captivity the defence of Jerusalem fell to Balian of Ibelin (who had escaped from Hattin) and Patriarch Heraclius. Thousands of refugees gathered in Jerusalem, trusting in its walls and its sanctity. Dealing with such a tide of extra inhabitants would have been difficult at the best of times, but to compound the defenders' troubles the ongoing fighting also meant the annual harvest had not been properly gathered in. The Hattin campaign had absorbed the vast majority of the Frankish troops and one writer suggests that only a handful of able-bodied men remained, requiring the patriarch to knight youths and old men. Given the levels of resistance shown this may not be quite accurate, bearing in mind that many had fled to Jerusalem from the other Frankish cities, but the basic shortage of well-trained knights was true enough.[10]

The sultan spent five days surveying the city. Imad al-Din reports a speech (at which he was not present) that, in essence, made a powerful case to affirm divine approval for the Ayyubid family's actions over recent years. We have seen criticism of the Kurdish clan from Nur al-Din, from his successors in Syria and from the caliph. But Saladin's triumph at Hattin and now this chance to recover the holy city were, the sultan asserted, clear examples of God's blessing and unequivocal evidence that his behaviour was right. He argued that 'Jerusalem has been in enemy hands for [eighty-eight] years, during which time God has received nothing from us here in the way of adoration, while the zeal of [Muslim] sovereigns languished and the generations followed one another and the Franks were settled here in power.' In other words, before now, until this particular family emerged, others had lacked the focus, the determination and the moral purpose to act and to succeed. Thus, 'God has reserved the merit of conquest for a single house – the sons of Ayyub – to unite all hearts in appreciation of its members.'[11] The notion of victory being a sign of God's favour was familiar to contemporary Muslims (and Christians too). At the end of the oration Saladin swore not to leave Jerusalem until the Dome of the Rock was in his hands.

After Saladin's reconnaissance the Muslims decided to move away from the strongly fortified area around the Tower of David and the Jaffa Gate to set up camp to the east and north-eastern side of the city. For a tantalising moment, as the defenders saw their enemy breaking their tents, they thought the Muslims had given up, only to realise that this was a strategic move, rather than a retreat. From this point onwards the focus of the siege would run from the Damascus Gate to the Jehoshaphat Gate and it was from this direction that Saladin intensified his attack on 25 September.[12] As well as military pressure the sultan exploited the doctrinal differences between the Christian inhabitants. A Melkite Christian (Melkites were often Greek émigrés, who believe in the two natures of Christ, divine and human) from, originally Jerusalem, had long served Saladin and Saphadin. He had been used as a diplomat before and now the sultan engaged him to try to entice his co-religionists inside Jerusalem to surrender in return for a large financial payment. The Melkites were a sizeable group, and when Balian of Ibelin heard they might cause trouble he was forced to think hard about his options.[13]

Meanwhile, relentless bombardment from Saladin's trebuchets drove the defenders from the walls. Extra cavalry forces lurked to prevent sorties by the Franks, and this allowed sappers to fill in the ditch and then to bring a section of the fortifications to the verge of collapse. The scale of the defeat at Hattin meant there was no prospect of a relief army coming to the rescue, leaving the besiegers free to concentrate on their prey. Trebuchets and archers, plus the lethal naphtha-based incendiary known as Greek Fire kept up the tempo. A sally from the Jehoshaphat Gate failed and morale inside crumpled. Not even offers of lavish payments to guard that area of wall could induce people to act. The Franks realised the game was up; it was time to start surrender negotiations.[14]

Balian of Ibelin asked for a truce but Saladin took a tough line and flatly rejected him. According to Imad al-Din, he said: 'I wish to deal with Jerusalem in the same way that the Christians treated it when they took it from the Muslims ... they inundated it with blood and did not permit it a moment's peace. I will cut the throats of their men and enslave their women.'[15] It is hard to tell whether this was a negotiating tactic – in the circumstances, an entirely plausible one – or whether he was really prepared to act in this way. This latter approach seems very much counter to Saladin's later reputation for mercy, and as we have seen there are several examples of him killing captives. The recovery of Jerusalem reversed the loss of 1099 and a slaughter of the Franks would have been in tune with some of the remorselessly confrontational contemporary rhetoric. It is also true that most of the defenders of Jerusalem in 1099 had been Shi'ite warriors of the Fatimid rulers of Egypt, and that many Jews were also killed there too. With Jerusalem in their grasp at last there was a tangible sense of anticipation amongst the Muslim forces. It was over thirty years since Nur al-Din had provided real energy to the idea of recovering Jerusalem and the work of his preachers and teachers, fulsomely perpetuated under Saladin, was now poised to bear fruit. Examples of jihad material, such as the *Forty Hadith for Inciting Jihad* produced by Ibn Asakir in the mid-1170s, are pitched in very aggressive terms. A sermon given in the days after the city fell (see below) spoke in broad terms of vengeance too.[16] For all that, recent research argues that it was not until the thirteenth century that Muslim accounts of the 1099 capture became especially graphic, and looking at the spectrum of contemporary sources it is apparent that the overwhelming impetus behind both Nur al-Din's and Saladin's jihad was the recovery of the holy sites rather than pure revenge.[17]

Balian's response was bold, falling just short of entirely calling Saladin's bluff yet playing the limited cards that he had to tremendous effect. In essence, he told the sultan that if Saladin declined to offer the defenders protection, he would pay such a terrible price for his victory that it would be horribly tarnished. With knowledge of their imminent fate he claimed that the Franks would fight with utter abandon, killing many thousands of Muslims as they went down; they would also execute the 5,000 prisoners in their custody; they would destroy their own houses and kill their own children rather than let them become slaves. Finally, they would demolish the Dome of the Rock and smash the rock itself.

Saladin consulted with his senior emirs and advisors; patently he had to get emphatic support for whatever course of action he chose. Most immediately, the fate of the Muslim prisoners weighed heavily for all; effectively just to sentence them to death would cast an irredeemably dark shadow. Likewise, given the decades-long focus on regaining the Dome of the Rock and the al-Aqsa, the destruction of the Muslim holy places in Jerusalem was not remotely desirable either.[18]

Inside the city, of course, fear as to what the besiegers might do fomented constant anxiety; might the Franks have to enact Balian's desperate strategy? In such circumstances, no one could, or would, expect mercy. Women cut their hair off to make themselves unattractive; the Syrian Orthodox brought out their piece of the True Cross and people venerated it and prayed for divine intercession.

Over the course of a few days, the sultan – enjoying the luxury of not having to worry about a Frankish relief army – moved towards a negotiated settlement. The advantages of avoiding a bloody conflict were self-evident, in terms of the saving of Muslim lives and holy places, but also in the opportunity for financial gain; slaves and ransoms would enrich and continue to reward the troops in a way that corpses could not. At a more practical level the conditions of the surrender were formulated: ten dinars for every male, rich or poor, over ten years old; five dinars for women; one dinar for a child, whether a boy or a girl; and for people to be allowed to take whatever they could carry. The Franks were given forty days to raise the money; those who could not do so would be enslaved. The treaty was announced on the streets of Jerusalem. The terms evoked widespread lamentation from the poor; the loss of the holy city had been understood for days, but the need to gather this much money or else lose one's liberty was a new cause for alarm.[19]

The date of the surrender was fixed for Friday 2 October, an extraordinarily auspicious day in the Muslim hijri calendar that year because in 1187 it coincided with the anniversary of the Prophet's Night Journey and subsequent ascent to heaven from the rock housed in the shrine building that was the focus of so much concern, the Dome of the Rock. As well as providing an opportunity to fulfil their pious needs, Saladin and his entourage were excellent propagandists; they realised that a crucial aspect of their success was to ensure their aims and achievements were broadcast as widely and as positively as possible. With all the variables of a military campaign such a coincidence cannot have been foreseen at too great a distance (before Hattin, for example), but once the surrender negotiations were underway then extending them by a few days to synchronise with this date of huge spiritual resonance was a perfect opportunity to hammer home divine approval for Saladin's campaign.[20]

By this time dozens of Sufi mystics and holy men had arrived to witness the liberation of Jerusalem, and the implicit connection between this event and God's endorsement of Saladin was plain. What a moment! Witnessed by his family, his household (although not Imad al-Din, who was still travelling from Damascus, having recovered from an illness), and the armies that he had inspired, cajoled and incentivised, the sultan finally took possession of Jerusalem. After just over eighty-eight years, the Christian hold on the city was at an end.

The Muslim troops swarmed in, raising their banners on the walls and closing the gates to prevent anyone from escaping. Important Frankish nobles such as Balian, Patriarch Heraclius, Queen Sibylla and Maria Komnene (King Amalric's widow) were identified and held. With the tenor of the capture clearly established Saladin duly displayed the mercy – especially towards women – for which he is so well known. It is interesting to speculate as to his motives; was he genuinely sympathetic to the plight of these women? It would seem so; he could have killed, sold or turned them over to his troops; it is not hard to imagine someone like Zengi behaving harshly. It is certainly true that their status was of note: in most cases in medieval warfare, both across and within faiths, high social standing helped to ensure safety. Saladin's behaviour here was widely admired and, as we will see later, other similar examples were reported by Christian authors. His actions also fitted with the virtues advocated by the 'Mirrors for Princes' genre. The late eleventh-century text of Nizam al-Mulk told of the kindness and mercy of the Caliph Umar to a poor woman and her two children.[21] Likewise *The Sea of Precious Virtues* from the early 1160s said: 'The king must be inclined to mercy in his rule, for he has the power to do whatever he wishes. No one earns fame and good repute in the world for injustice and evil, but rather for right conduct and mercy. He who is dominated by anger is like the demons but he who is merciful and shows forbearance resembles the prophets.'[22] Another contemporary text, albeit a few years after the events at Jerusalem, is al-Harawi's *Discussion on the Stratagems of War* commissioned either by Saladin or his son al-Zahir Ghazi. Here, in a more explicitly military setting than the broader governmental contexts of the writings noted above, we get a strong steer towards merciful treatment of the defeated. There is an encouragement to use self-control, to be aware of the reputational boost that acts of mercy can generate, and to indicate that guaranteeing the security of peasants and the poor will help encourage a place to surrender.[23] Ultimately, mercy is a sign of authority, strength and power.

In any case, the sultan's behaviour towards the majority of Frankish women seems generous and consistent. Sibylla was sent to visit King Guy, imprisoned in Nablus (although another source suggests this had happened before the siege) while Maria Komnene and her retinue and their valuables were also set free, as was Prince Reynald's widow.[24]

Those able to raise the ransom prepared to depart. Clerks were stationed at the gates to collect payment, a process that generated a few tensions over the next few days and weeks. One source claimed that a 'reliable count' indicated the presence of 60,000 men in the city, plus women and children. Balian co-ordinated the raising of funds from the patriarch, the Templars, the Hospitallers and the wealthier citizens, and he negotiated a lump-sum payment of 30,000 dinars on behalf of 18,000 of the poor. Over the next few weeks people desperately sought to liquidate goods and chattels in order to raise the money and to receive the precious receipt that confirmed their freedom. Merchants following the Muslim army swooped in to buy up such bargains, as did the local Eastern Christians who negotiated the right to remain in Jerusalem for the customary Islamic payment of the *jizya*, a poll tax on non-Muslims. Several thousand Franks managed to scrape together the ransom and they formed a steady exodus of dispirited refugees streaming from the Jaffa Gate to camps outside the city where, once assembled, they trudged in groups towards Tyre and the northern states. A few refugees were claimed by the emirs from where they originated, such as Keukburi's call on 1,000 Armenians from Edessa. Stories were rife of unscrupulous emirs disguising Franks as Muslim soldiers, presumably a reasonably easy task for mixed-race turcopoles, and then taking the ransom payment for themselves. In some instances, Saladin chose to reward troops by giving them prisoners to then sell on for profit. His strict adherence to the ten-dinars price caused a few eyebrows to raise, especially in cases such as the patriarch of Jerusalem. Here was a man of immense wealth, who overtly carried with him objects of high value. Some called for these to be seized, but Saladin said 'I will not act treacherously towards him', and even provided Heraclius with an escort to Tyre. Other sources indicate further acts of integrity and mercy. A western writer described Saphadin asking for 1,000 prisoners and then freeing them; Saladin himself responded to pleas from Balian and the patriarch to hand over some of the poor and he duly released several thousand without payment. Many were not so fortunate, and in the end, perhaps 16,000 penniless people were led away to the slave markets of Egypt and Syria.[25]

One family to receive special treatment called in an old promise. Ibn Abi Usaybi'ah wrote *The Best Accounts of the Classes of Physicians* in the middle of the thirteenth century. This remarkable text contains numerous biographies of medical practitioners in the Near East including the Eastern Christian Abu Sulayman, a man born in Jerusalem but who ended up in the pay of the Fatimid caliphate. During Amalric's invasions of the 1160s Abu Sulayman met the king, who asked to take him into his service and thus he moved back to Jerusalem. At one point it seems his family cared for, and gave money to, 'the famous jurist Isa' who was imprisoned after the Battle of Montgisard but then freed. Years later Abu Sulayman learned through astrological readings that Saladin would become ruler of Jerusalem on a certain date. He sent one of his sons to Saladin (who was in Damascus at the time, 14 April 1184) to tell him this. The young man met Isa, who was naturally delighted to see a member of the family who had assisted him so much. The jurist took him to Saladin who listened to the prediction. 'The sultan was very pleased indeed and bestowed upon him a splendid reward and gave him a yellow banner and arrow of that colour, saying to him, "When God enables me to do what you have said, put this yellow banner and arrow above your house and the quarter in which you live will be completely safe because of the protection given your house."' The prediction was duly realised, and when the Muslims entered Jerusalem in October 1187 Isa went to the house in which Abu Sulayman lived in order to protect it. The writer reports that 'No one in Jerusalem was spared from imprisonment, killing or levying of taxes, except the house of the said *hakim* Abu Sulayman.' The sultan also gave Abu Sulayman's sons (four were doctors and one a warrior) gifts, tax exemptions and a place in his retinue. We have already seen that predictions of success were part of the culture, and while there is little evidence to corroborate this tale it has a pleasing ring to it with an act of kindness towards one of the sultan's inner circle being amply rewarded.[26]

Whatever his motives, the legacy of Saladin's actions at Jerusalem have echoed down the centuries; the contrast between the stories of a bloodbath of 1099 and the sparing of thousands of Christian lives in 1187 stand to his eternal credit. Muslim writers used this to demonstrate the qualities of their ruler, while for Christians it became a matter of admiration and, as we will see, is certainly part of the reason why the sultan has come to enjoy such a positive reputation across their faith too. Paradoxically, stories of the slaughter of the defenders of Jerusalem in 1099 seem to have circulated sooner and with far greater intensity in the West, perhaps because the First Crusaders sought to amplify and emphasise their victory, best personified by the infamous tale of the Christian warriors wading in blood up to their ankles or calves, an image from the apocalyptic book of Revelation 14:20.[27]

As we saw, the surrender of Jerusalem occurred on a Friday, but Imad al-Din, who arrived in the city the following day, tells us that proper observance of the obligatory prayers was impossible. This was not simply a case of restoring ownership, but also the requirement to physically cleanse, purge and purify. Decades of crusader rule had seen the Franks modify and decorate buildings to suit their own religious iconography and practical needs, affecting most especially the Dome of the Rock and the al-Aqsa Mosque; everything offensive to Islamic sensibilities had to go.

Acts of liberation often have a symbolic moment; in recent times the breaking of the Berlin Wall or the toppling of the colossal statue of Saddam Hussein come to mind. Back in 1187 the most visible manifestation of Christianity was the great golden cross on top of the Dome of the Rock (the Christian *Templum Domini*). With the city secure a small group of Saladin's men scrambled up to the top of the dome and broke the crucifix away. To the delight of the Muslim troops and the distress of the Franks, it plummeted to the ground and was then dragged through the streets to David's Gate where it was smashed into pieces. Other crosses from around the city were gathered up and tied together with ropes and hurled from the walls.[28] A further priority was the safe release of the Muslim prisoners and this too was duly achieved.

Saladin instructed the Sacred Precinct that encompassed the al-Aqsa Mosque and the Dome of the Rock to be cleared of extraneous crusader buildings and structures in order to accommodate the crowds who would attend the first Friday prayer the following week. Thus, for this one grand event it would form an extended congregational courtyard. The al-Aqsa Mosque had become the headquarters of the Knights Templar and internal walls were swiftly removed, a covering over the *mihrab* was brought down; Qurans arrived, floors covered in matting were replaced with carpets and prayer mats laid out.

Because it had been used as a place of Christian worship since 1099, the interior of the Dome of the Rock was covered with mosaics of religious scenes, figurative statues, while the actual rock with the imprint of the Prophet's foot had been cased with marble.[29] All of these were quickly stripped back because Saladin wanted 'the pearl extracted from its shell', illuminated by new candelabra and protected by a fine wrought-iron grille. The building was washed and purified with rose water (consciously following the practice of the Prophet) by Saladin's nephew, while one of his sons brought in fine, deep carpets and made many other gifts. Subsequent restoration of this building was the responsibility of Isa al-Hakkari and he was also appointed the first *wali* (governor) of Jerusalem.[30]

With the city in his hands, the sultan and his advisors staged a formal ceremony to allow his emirs, holy men, Quran-reciters and poets to acknowledge his success. Again we see the importance of a public event to reinforce Saladin's leadership and standing. The sultan's 'face glowed . . . his person emanated sweetness, his hand was employed in pouring out the waters of liberality and opening the lips of gifts; the back of his hand was the *qibla* of kisses and the palm of his hand the *ka'ba* of hope . . . the World of Islam was ready and adorned for a festival to celebrate the fall of Jerusalem.'[31]

The ninth of October was the first Friday with Jerusalem back in Muslim hands, and the celebration of the midday prayer was the pivotal event. To be chosen to present this sermon would be hugely prestigious, and a further chance to assimilate the spiritual importance of what had happened and, of course, to reflect upon the achievements of Saladin. The man organising this process was Imad al-Din, and he became the subject of some serious lobbying by those who sought such an honour, a position of patronage that one senses he thoroughly enjoyed. A number of candidates sent in texts of their proposals but in the end, Saladin chose Muhyi al-Din, the eminent Damascene jurist, poet and sermoniser who had prophesied the fall of Jerusalem back in 1183 just after the sultan took Aleppo.

The sermon itself was delivered in al-Aqsa in the presence of Saladin and all his leading men, probably from a temporary *minbar* (pulpit). This was a compelling and powerful piece of oratory that took as its themes the place of Jerusalem and then of Saladin in the history of Islam. The sultan had undoubtedly achieved a landmark victory for his faith, and one remembered, celebrated and admired down to the present day. This set-piece event, the first Muslim sermon in the holy city for eighty-eight years, was going to be another moment for Saladin and his entourage to make the case that they had been proven right in their actions and, as the sermon pointedly emphasised, had received God's favour.

Imad al-Din handed the preacher a black robe of honour from the caliph and Muhyi al-Din ascended the *minbar* to address his audience. Many others listened or were in attendance in the large open space outside, stretching as far back as the Dome of the Rock itself (a distance of over 150 metres). Muhyi al-Din praised God and then lauded his power in defeating the Franks and the 'cleansing of his holy house from the filth of polytheism and its pollutions'.[32] He described how 'this strayed camel' (Jerusalem) had been recovered from the infidels. He outlined the place of Jerusalem in the history of Islam and its role as the place of the Prophet's Night Journey and the location of the Day of Judgement. He also restated Christ's position as a prophet in Islam, although naturally rejected his divinity.

The preacher praised the success of the Muslim army and spoke of the great conflicts of Islamic history, such as the battles of Badr (624), Yarmuk and Qadisiyya (636). He compared the events of 1187 to the conquest of Jerusalem by Umar in 638 and then joined to this most rarefied of lines Saladin, the new hero of Islam.[33] This sense of continuity is a central part of Muslim understanding and memory, and these themes are repeated again and again down the centuries with Saladin assuming a prominent and revered position in the sequence.

Muhyi al-Din also spoke of the need to recognise God's blessing in delivering Jerusalem: 'How great a favour was that which rendered you the army by whose hands the Sacred City was recaptured.' He warned against slipping into sin: 'maintain this holy war ... protect His religion and He will protect you'. Almost inevitably the final section of the sermon was a magnificent tribute to Saladin himself, piling title upon title on the sultan at this moment of triumph: 'thy trenchant sword ... him who gave might to the declaration of the true faith, who vanquished adorers of the Cross, the well-being of the world and of religion, the sultan of Islamism and of the Muslims, the purifier of the Holy Temple ... the giver of life to the empire and the commander of the true believers'. He could not resist pointing out that 'some men had begun to doubt your intentions' but 'you have enabled his hand to take Jerusalem'. He concluded by praying for Saladin's continued success, for his longevity and for the ongoing achievements of his successors.[34] On the same day Saladin 'prayed in the Dome of the Rock amid throngs of believers', marking another milestone moment in the counter-crusade when the self-appointed leader of the jihad performed his spiritual obligations in the third most important shrine to his faith.[35]

Such tremendous news needed to be broadcast as widely as possible; it was the ideal moment for Saladin's secretariat to display their considerable talents. Imad al-Din had arrived in Jerusalem on 3 October and claimed to have written seventy letters that very day, 'each more intricate and ornate than the last. Then I followed that night with a number of letters in which I included all the details of the conquest and I prefaced each with great praise for the conquest and the conqueror.'[36] Likewise, Qadi al-Fadil wrote letter after letter extolling the achievements of his master and sent them as far afield as Samarkand and Rayy, in Persia, as well as addressing the caliph of Baghdad, an individual who had been unsupportive and critical of Saladin. A man of Qadi al-Fadil's literary prowess was not going to miss the opportunity to announce the destruction of the infidels and 'the triumph of God's religion ... the Holy Land has become the pure one after being in a state of impurity'. He praised Saladin's patience and endurance in the face of stubborn opposition from amongst Muslims, and the ferocity and numbers of the Franks. 'He mowed away infidelity and sowed Islamism.' He told of the Battle of Hattin and the siege of Jerusalem, the latter in some detail, explaining the negotiations and terms of surrender. He also described the celebratory first Friday prayer in the al-Aqsa: 'The name of the Commander of the Faithful was announced from the pulpit.' Al-Fadil concluded with a warning to the caliph that the Franks would not give up and that Saladin had already started to repair castles and to arm his men.[37]

The sultan chose to remain in Jerusalem until the end of October. By this point one source records that 220,000 dinars had been raised from ransoms, all of which Saladin distributed to the religious men and his emirs, and they in turn gave it to their troops. Once again, his generosity was extraordinary and the conquest of Jerusalem gave him the chance to exercise patronage on an immense scale. Unlike taking power in Damascus or Cairo, where he had to work within the parameters of the existing regime, here he had almost carte blanche to anchor the Islamic faith and to enrich his supporters. Holy-war rhetoric undoubtedly attracted many to his cause, but this encompassed earthly as well as heavenly rewards and, after the capture of Acre in early July, followed by the taking of Jerusalem, the former benefits certainly arrived in abundance.

With Jerusalem back in Muslim hands the sultan acted rapidly to reward the religious classes amongst his followers and to re-establish an Islamic presence there. The holy sites needed to be staffed, and clerics and readers arrived in Jerusalem to take over important positions. The longer-term spiritual care of the city was important too; a madrasa would help to sustain this. Saladin discussed the matter with his inner circle and they recommended the creation of colleges and hostels. One early decision was to establish a madrasa for Shafi lawyers, probably reviving an institution that had existed in the city before the crusader period. The site chosen was the beautiful Romanesque church of St Anne's, just inside the Jehoshaphat Gate, an archetype of elegant, rounded arches and clean lines. Out of sheer practicality, Christian buildings were repurposed in the way that the Dome of the Rock had been given a Christian identity during the crusader period.[38] Today it is part of a complex run by the White Fathers, a Christian French monastic and missionary organisation. Above the doorway to the church, however, remains an Arabic inscription dating from 25 July 1192 confirming that the 1187 decision had been put into practice. It includes the Quranic lines: 'In the name of God the Compassionate, the Merciful. And whatever blessing you have received it is certainly from God [Sura 16:53]. This blessed madrasa was founded as a *waqf* [endowment] by our master [Saladin].' Once again, the point of Saladin's divine blessing was made, although this time not through the spoken word, but in a permanent and visible text at the entrance to the building. In this case, and many others, Saladin also provided lavish endowments of cash, land and rights to ensure they were properly funded.[39]

An inscription inside the al-Aqsa Mosque reveals that the restoration took only five months, an indication of how high a priority this was for Saladin and the vast resources and manpower that he directed towards the work here and at the Dome of the Rock. The first Friday sermon had used a rather precarious temporary pulpit, and there was a need for a proper replacement. Saladin first thought to commission one, but he was then reminded of, or remembered, the magnificent structure created at the order of Nur al-Din especially for the purpose of standing in the al-Aqsa. Given the fracture with Nur al-Din's family this may have seemed awkward. Equally though, to leave the pulpit in Aleppo was an overt snub to his predecessor; neglecting the message carried on it, not to mention the beauty and craftsmanship of the piece itself, would not seem appropriate either. The precious item was duly brought down to Jerusalem where it stood until 1969 when a madman set fire to it. Only fragments survived, although the large numbers of photographs taken prior to this disaster have enabled a very fine replica to be created and installed.[40]

The *mihrab*, or prayer niche facing in the direction of Mecca, was manifestly important and the style and content of this splendid and richly coloured creation were almost certainly established while the sultan was in Jerusalem. One feature is the beautiful range of coloured marble panels: dark green, sea green, purple, orange, pink, salmon pink, black, white and grey.[41] The mosaic decoration on and around the *mihrab* was, according to Ibn al-Athir, 'in the manner of Constantinople', a nod to the artistic fluidity of the age that moved across the religious and cultural boundaries of the southern Mediterranean. It also features an intriguing inscription: 'In the name of God, the merciful, the compassionate. The renovation of this hallowed *mihrab* and the restoration of the Aqsa Mosque, founded on the fear of God, has ordered the slave and friend of God, Yusuf, son of Ayyub, al-Malik al-Nasir, Salah al-Din, at a time when God conquered it through his hands in the months of the year 583.'[42] The vast majority of Saladin's inscriptions – and those of contemporary rulers – contain ornate titles that reflect his status as a holy warrior and a leader of Sunni orthodoxy. To this is added the formula 'slave and friend of God', indicating his deep personal piety, a point underscored by an unusual sequence that starts with his personal name, Yusuf, prior to his throne name. Coupled with the prayer for gratitude and blessing, the conquest of Jerusalem becomes very much Saladin's personal achievement – and one publicly memorialised above the prayer niche of one of Islam's most important sites.

The fate of the Holy Sepulchre itself provoked animated discussion. Saladin had anticipated as such and kept the building closed in the first few days after the conquest to prevent any random acts of violence against it. As the very heart of Christianity, some urged that the church should be destroyed. Saladin was not convinced, arguing that even if the building was erased Christians would seek to worship and recover the place of crucifixion; he also chose not to convert it into a mosque. More significantly, he noted that the caliph Umar had confirmed Christian possession of the building back in the seventh century, a precedent and a memory that seemed fully appropriate to follow. Just opposite the Holy Sepulchre stood the great Hospital of St John and the sultan also gave permission for ten brothers to stay on there to care for the sick, once again showing a measure of practicality and mercy.[43]

By late October Jerusalem was settling down to Muslim rule again. Most of the Franks had departed, leaving only the communities of Eastern Christians and those in the hospital. With his primary task now accomplished Saladin knew full well that he would have to confront a new crusade from the West. The best way to make this as difficult as possible, and to further consolidate his hold on the Near East, was to conquer the remaining Frankish lands. For the next couple of months, before the winter took hold, he was back in the saddle and campaigning hard. Saladin's next priority was the port of Tyre.

15

The Siege of Tyre

*'The only arrow left in the quiver of
the infidels'*

Today just inside southern Lebanon, Tyre's ancient port had seen Phoenician, Assyrian, Persian, Greek, Seleucid, Roman, Byzantine, Umayyad and Fatimid rule before it fell to the crusaders in 1124. The medieval city lay upon what was formerly an island that had, centuries before, been joined to the mainland by a low, broad isthmus. Needless to say, while the sultan was making his mark on Jerusalem, Conrad of Montferrat had not only continued to send out urgent appeals to Europe but worked hard to strengthen the coastal city's fortifications.[1] Any attacker would need to overcome a formidable series of obstacles: a double wall on the seaward sides, and on the landward face, a triple-layered wall, complete with towers and a sea-level moat that could be flooded if required. The inner harbour was also well fortified with large sea-towers and a protective chain slung between them to control entry and exit.[2] Having chosen to bypass the place before he besieged Jerusalem, Saladin now heeded the advice of his Kurdish general, al-Mashtub, who urged him to finish off the Franks as fast as he could. Tyre was, he opined, 'the only arrow left in the quiver of the infidels; every day there is an opportunity which cannot be grasped once it has gone'.[3]

Saladin summoned the forces of Aleppo and the Egyptian fleet to try to blockade the city by land and sea, starting the engagement in mid-November 1187. Frankish ships bearing contingents of crossbowmen niggled at the Muslim troops along the isthmus and this, coupled with aggressive defensive tactics, frustrated the sultan's progress. The presence of the Egyptian fleet helped increase pressure for a while, but a combination of Frankish naval skill and a woeful lack of caution by the Muslim commander exposed the latter's vessels to attack. Five of the ten ships fell captive on the spot and the remainder fled the scene to be abandoned and broken up, a significant loss to the Fatimid navy. Saladin had tried hard to bolster the Egyptian fleet because he realised the importance of being able to compete with the Christians in this arena of war. With the imminent prospect of multiple seaborne crusaders arriving in the Levant, the need to hamper these fleets, and to besiege places such as Tyre by sea as well as land, meant a naval capability would be even more crucial. But given the enduringly low status of seafaring amongst the Muslims – it was regarded as the occupation of criminals – there was a lack of residual knowledge and experience, a shortcoming sharply demonstrated in this dismal defeat.[4]

Saladin, Saphadin and al-Zahir Ghazi made a concerted effort to break into Tyre, deploying an impressive array of siege engines and towers, but to no avail. They tried another tactic – bringing along a high-value prisoner to use as a bargaining tool. With Conrad of Montferrat inside, who could be a better candidate for such a role than his father, William the Old? Saladin suggested that if Conrad surrendered, his father would be freed. Feelings of filial affection looked in short supply as the marquis mocked the idea, jeered at threats to his father and when the latter was paraded in chains in front of the walls, fired a crossbow at him. Conrad shouted that he actually wished for his father to be killed because such a wicked man would have a good end as a martyr. Clearly the sultan had to find another way into the city.[5]

A jarring intrusion on the siege arrived in December in the form of a horseman bearing a letter from Caliph al-Nasir of Baghdad. Given his remarkable achievements, Saladin had every expectation that he would be in receipt of a message of congratulation. In fact the caliph's reaction was utterly underwhelming. While the liberation of Jerusalem was obviously a great success for Islam, the caliph seemed more concerned about the political consequences of this for his dealings with Saladin. The prickly nature of the relationship was exposed by a seemingly trivial matter. In his enthusiasm to inform Baghdad of the recovery of Jerusalem Saladin had sent a young and inexperienced envoy. Imad al-Din had cautioned against this, arguing that the man was of insufficient skill and standing to convey the news in its full glory. Saladin had ignored him, but Imad al-Din was correct; this had, it seems, been interpreted as a slight on the caliph's dignity, hence, in part, the frosty response.[6] The caliph then set out a series of minor niggles such as continued criticism of Saladin for using (or rather, usurping as he saw it) the title 'al-Malik al-Nasir' ('the king who supports'), one borne by Caliph al-Nasir himself. Saladin was also accused of encouraging Turkmen and Kurds on the borders of the caliph's lands to slip away from his authority. In diplomatic terms what this really meant was a concern that the Ayyubid Empire was starting to look too formidable for Baghdad's liking. Al-Nasir was determined to assert the power and independence of the caliph, but if the Franks were either expelled or fully brought to heel then the Ayyubids could turn their attention eastwards and potentially impose their influence on him. Al-Nasir was also deeply engaged with other matters. The Great Seljuk sultan Tughril III had announced his intention of taking up residence in Baghdad, but the caliph had shown his absolute opposition to this and responded by razing the sultanic palace to the ground. The result was a confrontation between the two parties and the Seljuks won a convincing military victory in April 1188.[7]

There was an attempt to soften the harsh tone of the letter from Baghdad by blaming poor phrasing, an explanation Saladin brushed aside with the sarcastic comment that 'the caliph is too great to have ordered these coarse expressions, and these blunt rhymes; he would certainly have instructed that his thoughts would be phrased more delicately, more softly, more correctly and more suitably'. The aggrieved sultan cited his actions in Egypt and Yemen on behalf of Sunni Islam. Most pertinently of all: 'Did I not recover Jerusalem and unite it with Mecca? ... Indeed, I have returned to the native land a part that had been missing from it ... Have I not frightened the West with the vigour of my actions?' A number of Saladin's family and advisors encouraged a crisp response, and while he was both angered and disappointed at the caliph's letter, with the Third Crusade on the horizon he simply could not alienate the spiritual leader of Sunni Islam when trying to drum up support for a holy war. Thus, in conjunction with Imad al-Din, he managed to formulate a reasonably civil reply that politely indicated that Saladin had used the title 'al-Malik al-Nasir' for years. More importantly, he affirmed his obedience to Baghdad and stated that he was a true servant of the faith.[8]

For the moment, nothing further could be done, and in any case the situation at Tyre had come to a head. After six weeks, the attack had stalled badly and the leadership debated its next move; heavy winter rains and the lack of progress had wrecked morale. According to Beha al-Din many of the troops simply refused to fight. It seems that the emirs were divided, with some no longer committed to the campaign. Isa the jurist advised persistence but the majority decided to withdraw and the siege was lifted on 3 January 1188. After six months of near-universal success, this failure was a definite bruise to the Muslims' confidence.[9]

With the benefit of hindsight, Saladin's inability to capture Tyre proved fundamental to the very survival of the Frankish East and the achievements of the Third Crusade. This is not to say that Saladin could not, or should not, have foreseen the potential consequences of this withdrawal. Returning at a later point with a bigger and well-rested force might well have been expected to yield victory. Certainly the men at his disposal seemed insufficient to take the city and did not regard themselves as capable of doing so. The Franks' determination to preserve this vital strategic and economic centre, along with Conrad of Montferrat's evident military and political skills, should not be underestimated either. Ibn al-Athir, writing in the early 1230s and admittedly a partisan of the Zengid house, delivered a coruscating evaluation of Saladin's leadership here. He stated:

> No one was to blame for this but Saladin, for he was the person who had sent Frankish troops there ... from the populations of Acre, Ascalon and Jerusalem and elsewhere ... thus the surviving Frankish knights on the coast came to be there with their money and the money of merchants and others. They held the city and wrote to the Franks beyond the sea asking for their aid ... They replied and bade them hold Tyre so that it could be a rallying point and a base ... this increased their eagerness to hold and defend the place. God willing, we shall mention this sequence of events to make it known that a ruler ought not to give up resoluteness, even if fates are aiding him.[10]

The sultan moved back to Acre, an obvious target for future crusading expeditions. It would be prudent to repair and enhance the fortifications and so Saladin summoned his master builder, Qaraqush, the man responsible for heading so many of the Ayyubid's great construction projects in Cairo. He was duly instructed to rebuild and heighten the towers of Acre, making use of the large supply of Frankish slave labour available.[11] The sultan's activities were not entirely focused on military matters, though. Acre had been in Christian hands for over eighty years and Saladin continued to restore its Islamic character. The Hospitaller property was divided between a hostel for Sufis and a college for jurists, while he turned over the Latin patriarch's palace to a Muslim hospital.[12]

After a few weeks in Acre Saladin set his sights on a couple of the Franks' strongest fortifications, the Hospitaller castle of Belvoir, over-looking the Jordan valley and the Templar castle of Safad, nestling high in the hills of Upper Galilee. These powerful and well-provisioned castles were held by tough, seasoned warriors of the Military Orders and proved immensely difficult to take. Saladin spent a few weeks at Belvoir in April 1188 but there, and at Safad, he realised these would be lengthy engagements and he had to leave senior emirs and around 500 horsemen in front of each, a tangible drain on resources for many months.

At this point, however, the gloss of Saladin's victory at Jerusalem was still far from fading and envoys across the Muslim Near East arrived to congratulate him on his achievements. Ambassadors came from Rayy, well to the east of Baghdad (near Teheran in today's Iran); from the ruler of Hamadan and Azerbaijan; from the Seljuk sultan of Iconium (Anatolia), and from the lord of Diyr-Bakr, all keen to pay their respects to the sultan, and in the case of the last of these, to seek a marriage alliance with the Ayyubids. Such recognition was all very welcome, but what really concerned Saladin was the need for support and loyalty in the future.[13]

From Belvoir he decided to return to Damascus. It was over sixteen months since Saladin had visited the city that lay at the heart of his power in Syria. Now, as the hero of Sunni Islam he entered in triumph, bathing in the pride and admiration of the inhabitants. The religious and cultural figures of this great metropolis embraced their leader, and in accordance with the sultan's customary practice he dispensed justice and held audiences with senior officials. He also heard from intellectuals and poets; in all cases – as ever – his liberality brought delight and allegiance from the people.[14]

His stay in Damascus was brief. By May 1188, the campaigning season was underway again and the reported presence at Aleppo of powerful armies from the east looking 'to serve in the jihad' prompted the sultan to move. News of a Frankish attack on the recently conquered port of Jubayl also required a response and so, looking to deal with this and to link up with the new arrivals, he suggested a rendezvous at Qadas on the River Orontes, south of Homs. There Saladin met his allies, and from the lavish show that he put on for them, lovingly described by one of his entourage, we can ascertain just how essential this outside help was gauged to be.[15]

The leader of this army was Imad al-Din Zengi, lord of Sinjar, a nephew of Nur al-Din himself and husband to one of his daughters. The last time he had encountered Saladin was back in June 1183 when he surrendered Aleppo to the sultan in exchange for Sinjar and several other cities.[16] Now, the two men met, accompanied by their troops but also by the full entourage of poets, Quran-readers, and men of science and literature. Visits to each camp and shows of honour were the order of the day, with Imad al-Din Zengi's chief poet declaiming a panegyric to mark the occasion. A wonderful feast followed, with sweetly flavoured meats, sharp and spicy soups, roast dishes and fried food. The presentation of gifts was next: horses, clothing decorated with gold braid and many other fine objects. Then, in turn, Saladin and his court hosted Imad al-Din Zengi, inviting the new arrivals into their own tents, especially fragranced with jasmines and roses. The sultan placed his guest on a sofa next to him, a magnificent gathering of the elites from both parties. It was also the apricot season, grown and nurtured in the great orchards that girdled Damascus. Saladin's cooks dispensed vast quantities of this delicate fruit and, in a touch that a modern communications department would appreciate, carefully and deliberately matched their yellow colour to the Ayyubid's own yellow banners. Fine food and drink followed with, at the end of the meal, gifts of particularly valuable and beautiful racehorses, along with finely produced mail coats, helmets and lances, as well as clothes from Egypt and material from the Maghreb, Iraq and Tunisia. Such luxury and harmony contrasted sharply with the realities of warfare, but this was a time to demonstrate Saladin's status and honour and to build what would turn out to be an important, if periodically tense, relationship.[17] With Jerusalem taken it was essential for the sultan to reach out beyond his own Ayyubid clan and the wider Kurdish group and to draw in some members of Nur al-Din's family; in other words, to include Turks as well. Imad al-Din Zengi was someone with substantial resources at his disposal and who seemed positively disposed towards the jihad against the Franks. The presence here of Keukburi, an important figure in the Hattin campaign, was also of note.[18]

This lavish event was the prelude to a three-month campaign across northern Syria, an episode characterised by considerable success not least in the acquisition of booty, something which helped to oil the wheels of holy war.[19] The unprotected port of Latakia was notably bounteous, with the merchant community offering rich pickings to the attackers. The Muslims had a formidable array of siege machinery at their disposal. To capture sites such as the spectacular fortress of Saone (renamed 'Saladin's Castle' in 1957), perched on a ridge three-quarters of a kilometre long and boasting a phenomenal rock-cut ditch twenty-eight metres deep, was an impressive achievement.[20] Places including Latakia and Darbsak surrendered in the face of complex mining operations. The fortress of Bourzey, perched on top of a hill 320 metres high, required the deployment of three shifts of men to break it.[21] In character with his campaigns in the kingdom of Jerusalem the previous year, the offer of generous terms was frequently employed to prompt a surrender. In one or two cases, it was judged too difficult to proceed: for example, the Hospitaller castle of Marqab close to the coast was a formidable challenge in itself. The lurking presence of a sixty-strong fleet of Sicilian ships, marking a relatively swift response to the calls for a new crusade that echoed around Europe, meant this castle was left well alone.[22]

One episode that stands apart from the usual mild treatment of a town that capitulated was at Tortosa (Tartus), a walled port on the Syrian coast controlled by the Templars and home to the cathedral of Our Lady of Tortosa. Initial progress was fast, so much so that the city walls were penetrated before Saladin's tent was put up. Resistance soon stiffened and centred upon a massively walled tower overlooking a moat in the north-eastern corner. A combination of this stern defence, coupled with the fact that the city was held by the Templars, led by the exasperatingly durable figure of Gerard of Ridefort, sparked unusual ferocity. Another factor was the release of King Guy. This had been promised as part of the terms of surrender at Ascalon in the summer of 1187, and Queen Sibylla wrote to Saladin to remind him of the arrangement. The sultan ordered the king and other prisoners of status, such as William the Old of Montferrat, to be liberated on the promise that they would go overseas and never bear arms against him again. The king duly boarded a vessel – and sailed half a kilometre to the little island of Ruad that lies off Tortosa. He told Saladin's messengers that he had now been overseas and was released from his vow; he then sailed down to Tripoli where he was reunited with his wife.[23] Doubtless infuriated by this, unwilling to be further delayed at Tortosa, yet determined to make some demonstration of strength, the sultan ordered the city, including the church (which lay just outside the walls), to be demolished and put to the torch. Outright destruction of religious buildings was not a habit of Saladin's and the important role of the Virgin Mary in Islam clouds the matter further. (A sign that damage to the church may have been limited is through evidence of Muslim and Christian pilgrims visiting the shrine over subsequent decades.[24])

By late September 1188 the campaign was drawing to a close. Saladin had taken large swathes of territory from the county of Tripoli and the principality of Antioch, although this was by no means a systematic conquest. Its effect was to bear down heavily upon the surviving Franks in the north with Antioch in particular reduced to a handful of castles beyond the great city itself. After the death of Count Raymond of Tripoli in September 1187, Prince Bohemond III now ruled both Antioch and Tripoli, and given recent events he was relieved to make a truce with Saladin and to hand over prisoners. At this stage the Muslim forces were exhausted and in need of a break. Imad al-Din Zengi was anxious to head back to his own lands. Prior to leaving, however, he was given a splendid send-off by the sultan, setting the seal on a successful joint enterprise with the promise of more co-operation to come.[25] Saladin distributed some of the captured towns and castles to his long-term supporters, including a veteran ally of Shirkuh, but a greater proportion of the rewards went to recent adherents of the Ayyubids, men of mid-level power whom he hoped would extend the roots of his authority and provide resources and loyalty in the future.[26]

For Saladin there was a triumphant reception in Aleppo before he moved south through a recently refortified Hama, and then to Damascus by around 10 October where he enjoyed a brief period of rest. We can understand the need for his men to take a break, not least to bring in the harvest; contingents from other parts of his lands could also take part in some of these smaller campaigns. But it is noticeable that the sultan himself – and presumably his immediate entourage of secretaries, advisors, holy men and household – very rarely stopped. His secretary, rightly, made a virtue of this unyielding commitment to the jihad, commenting on his preparedness to set out even in the holy month of Ramadan and to leave his 'household, his children and his home town in this month when people, wherever they may be, travel to be united with their families'. Admirable as this was, as we will see, it eventually and inevitably started to take a heavy physical and mental toll on Saladin and his close associates.[27]

Aside from Tyre, Saladin had left three major castles still in Frankish hands. This represented an irritating drain on manpower. It required valuable troops to keep them under siege and also denied further sources of reward and income to his own men. He knew that they needed to be dealt with and so, after only a couple of weeks in Damascus, he set out once more on what proved to be a very fruitful campaign.[28]

First in his sights was the Templar castle of Safad. Very little remains of this fortress now, but the surviving foundations and underground rooms, coupled with its location nestling in the steep northern reaches of the hills of Galilee, indicate that it was a sturdy and difficult target. The arrival of Saphadin greatly encouraged the sultan. We have already seen the close political relationship between the two men and his presence here plainly energised Saladin and gave him the conviction to finish these tasks. Neither a huge array of trebuchets, or even efforts to mine the place had succeeded but finally, after several weeks' resistance, imminent starvation compelled the fortress to surrender on terms on 6 December. The Templar garrison was allowed to leave for Tyre, perhaps a reflection of just how pleased Saladin was to negotiate the capture of this powerful site.[29]

Just before then, a curious incident took place involving two Hospitaller captains. The Franks had sent a relief force to try to dislodge the sultan only for this to be discovered and routed. Amongst the captives were two Hospitallers brought before Saladin in the expectation that he would, as usual, command their execution on account of the Order's known hatred of the Muslims. He duly pronounced the death sentence, only for one of the knights to try his luck with the sultan: 'I was not expecting any harm to befall us once we had seen your blessed person and your handsome face.' Flattery might not seem the obvious tactic to work on the leader of a holy war, but in this instance it did the trick and this 'winning entreaty' prompted Saladin to spare the lives of these charming and lucky men and to imprison them instead.[30]

News of major importance arrived at the end of the siege of Safad with, at last, the surrender of Kerak. The fulcrum of Transjordan had resisted both Nur al-Din and Saladin on numerous occasions and had been the subject of a blockade by Saphadin's troops for nine months. Finally, having run out of weapons and supplies, the garrison asked for terms and this long-term irritant to Ayyubid power was brought to heel in November 1188. The pilgrimage route to Mecca and Medina was safe, and after the other Frankish castles in the area such as Shaubak (where the defenders reportedly suffered blindness after running out of salt) and Petra capitulated as well, then the road linking Damascus to Egypt was fully under their control too.[31]

Last on the list was Hospitaller Belvoir, the Order's 'shining star', perched on the edge of the Jordan valley and hoping to survive until the arrival of the crusading armies from the West. By now winter weather had well and truly set in, with strong winds and relentless rains turning the Muslim camp on the plateau to a quagmire. Saladin led from the front here, directing operations from a stone shelter, well within arrow-range of the castle. Threats to slaughter the garrison had little effect, but a ferocious series of assaults, again using a shift system to maintain momentum, took their toll. By early January 1189, with the walls looking pretty ragged and a mine well advanced, the garrison bowed to the inevitable and asked for terms, successfully negotiating their safe passage to Tyre. Once more, Ibn al-Athir criticised Saladin for this because 'every valiant, devilish champion of the Franks gathered there [Tyre] ... this was due to Saladin being remiss in releasing all whom he besieged so that he ended up biting his thumb in regret and chagrin when that was of no use'.[32]

A satisfying campaign completed, the troops were dismissed in mid-January 1189. In little over eight weeks, three of the Franks' most formidable castles had been taken, doing much to increase the security of the Ayyubid lands. Saladin and Saphadin went to Jerusalem before the latter headed back to Cairo. The sultan passed through Acre, checking on Qaraqush's progress in the refortification work before he went to Damascus in March. Alongside the customary rendering of justice, the gifts to the poor and the usual cultural gatherings, the arrival of another ambassador from the caliph of Baghdad merited particular attention. He expressed the caliph's desire to have *khutba* recited in the name of his son and heir, a request duly agreed upon. Saladin took the opportunity afforded by this ceremonial event to reinforce once more his credentials as the defender of Sunni Islam. He dispatched ambassadors back to Baghdad bearing gifts of captured Frankish knights in full armour, the crown of King Guy of Jerusalem and the great golden cross which had stood on top of the Dome of the Rock. The last of these objects was then buried beneath the threshold of the Nubian Gate in Baghdad, meaning that every day thousands of people trod upon it to render shame on this formerly ostentatious symbol of Christian rule in Jerusalem.[33]

With the spring sailing season on hand, there was a need to prepare for the arrival of the first real wave of crusaders in the early summer. Since the loss of Hattin and the subsequent fall of Jerusalem, messengers from the surviving Frankish lords, the Italian trading cities, the Military Orders, Conrad of Montferrat and now the recently liberated King Guy had flowed to the West. Archbishop Joscius of Tyre left the Holy Land to tour Europe and to act as a compelling narrator describing how Christ's people had been driven from his patrimony. The crusade was preached with enormous fervour and sermons related the terrible slaughter of Christians. Saladin himself was said to be thirsting after Christian blood while the Muslims defamed the holy places.[34] An eyewitness account of the fall of Jerusalem portrayed the Muslims as servants of evil; Saladin himself was a cruel tyrant and said to be the son of Satan.[35] Peter of Blois' *Passio Reginaldi*, an incendiary western text, imagined Reynald of Châtillon vainly defying the sultan after the Battle of Hattin and describing Saladin as the 'profane, impious and cruel Antichrist', 'the dog of Babylon, the son of perdition' and a man who wanted to terminate the Christian religion.[36] The loss of Jerusalem was a truly cataclysmic event of a nature not previously experienced in the Latin world and, as the architect of this,

Saladin stood centre-stage as the very worst of creatures. Part of this response was shock, part of it was motivational rhetoric designed to transform outrage into real action. It is, nonetheless, intriguing to register just how demonised a figure Saladin was and then to see how this matched up with reactions during and after the Third Crusade itself.

In practical terms, by this point many senior figures in Europe had taken the Cross, including Duke Richard of Aquitaine, his father King Henry II of England, King Philip Augustus of France, Count Philip of Flanders and Emperor Frederick Barbarossa of Germany. The time needed to preach the crusade, to recruit and to equip forces, to make regency arrangements and to establish a means of travel to the Levant often took well over a year, if not longer, given the intended scale of operations. Smaller expeditions had set out the previous year and more were en route, with Tyre their first place of arrival. Most seriously for Saladin, Frederick Barbarossa had been particularly efficient in getting organised and in May 1189, having decided to take the landward route, he started the long march east.

The need to crack Tyre was now paramount, and the nearby castle of Beaufort seventeen miles to the north-east (today just inside the southern border of Lebanon) was a likely preliminary. In mid-May 1189 the sultan began to apply pressure on the fortress. As a way to try to prolong matters, the owner, Count Reynald of Sidon, opened diplomatic contacts. Beha al-Din writes that Reynald was received with honour and respect and permitted to enter the sultan's tent. Reynald was a prominent figure, one of the Frankish 'wise heads who knew Arabic and had some familiarity with histories and hadith collections. I heard that he kept a Muslim who read to him and explained things. He was a man of cautious deliberation.'[37] Reynald was partly attempting to play for time and he proposed that if he surrendered the castle he might need to live in Damascus for his own security. He wanted land, the opportunity to gather the remainder of his family and household from Tyre, as well as to collect the annual revenue from the harvest – and Saladin consented, presumably making the assessment that Beaufort was a difficult target and worth waiting for. Most interesting of all was Beha al-Din's comment that 'all the time he [Reynald] continued to frequent the sultan's presence, disputing with us about his religion while we argued for its falsity. He was an excellent conversationalist and cultured in his talk.'[38] The author seems to have been an eyewitness to these events, which took place over a series of weeks – and he lauded Reynald as a man of words, presumably acknowledging in him some of the virtues of an *adib*, or cultivated man, so esteemed in the courts of the Near East.[39] The willingness of a contemporary Latin Christian, particularly from a secular background, to lock horns in an intellectual debate on matters of religion is not often seen. Reynald himself seems to have been well educated; aside from being fluent in Arabic, his familiarity with histories and hadith collections identify him as someone with a manifest curiosity about Islam.[40]

To put this into context, there was some interest in the Muslim Near East in the 'errors' of Christianity. Ibn al-Jawzi, a prolific Hanbali scholar in Baghdad from the 1160s to c.1180, produced *The Devil's Deception*, which showed how people, including the Shi'a, Sufis and Christians, could be led astray. In the case of the Christians this was because they are deluded to think that God is a person, that Christ is God, or the Son of God, and that Satan blinds them to the prophecies about Muhammad by making them claim that he was sent only to the Arabs.[41] Inevitably, perhaps, the picture is not entirely consistent. A writer in Baghdad produced, in Arabic, an apologetic commentary on the Nicene Creed that drew upon a range of literature to address Muslim objections to Christian belief.[42] In general, contemporary Muslims had a much clearer understanding of Christianity than western Europeans did of Islam.[43] That said, the debate between Reynald and Saladin was a step above the customary level of discussion.

Activity around Beaufort was given greater impetus by fears that the Franks were gathering in strength and might start to work together, rather than pursuing their customary political rivalries. Following his liberation in June 1188 Guy went to Antioch where he had been joined by his brother Geoffrey and a strong contingent of French crusaders as well as a force of Templars and other local knights. Yet Guy was a king without a kingdom. Conrad of Montferrat was adamant that his successful actions at Tyre made him the legitimate ruler and he acted as such in granting privileges to, for example, Pisan and southern French traders.[44] Guy, however, remained the crowned and anointed monarch, albeit one whose credibility had been shredded by the disaster of Hattin.

Saladin was back in Acre by mid-July 1189, once more checking that its fortifications were properly prepared. For all his victories, from the day that Jerusalem fell he understood that western Europe would eventually launch a massive effort to recover the holy city, and by the summer of 1189 a few contingents of crusaders had reached the Near East. In the meantime, Reynald of Sidon continued to play for time as he asked for further extensions of their agreement. The Frankish lord is described as spending a number of days with Saladin and being well treated, although by now he was plainly stringing the sultan along. The Muslim chroniclers depict their hero as being honest and trusting, although it is hard not to see him as just a little gullible here.[45] In the end his patience broke and Reynald was sent to Damascus, where his jailers 'inflicted pain and distress' upon him.[46]

By the middle of August Saladin's health was causing troubles, a sign perhaps of increasing tension. He was worried by the Franks' growing assertiveness, raiding and feinting further and further from Acre. While he had troops from Damascus and the Hawran with him, volunteers 'inspired to take part in the holy war', he needed much more substantial forces at his disposal, thus he summoned 'all the rulers under his dominion' to send him support.[47]

In the early summer, King Guy and his army had marched down to Tyre where he and Sibylla hoped to be recognised as the true rulers of the city. Conrad refused to let them enter; some of the Franks joined Guy, others stayed inside. A few advised Guy to attack the city, but this would play into Saladin's hands far too easily. Guy knew the major Christian monarchs were coming to the Levant eventually and, as his brother Aimery pointed out, 'it is much better that they should find that you have besieged a city rather than you have been idle'. In other words, he had a greater chance of holding on to his crown if he acted in a decisive and kingly manner. He was also aware that smaller contingents were en route to the Holy Land and could offer further momentum to his plans.

Duly emboldened, Guy made a stunning tactical move. Disregarding the limited size of his army, probably 9,000 strong, he resolved to lay siege to Acre. It was, of course, held by the Muslims who would presumably engage him from both inside the city and from behind, with a relief force. As a contemporary wrote, 'They placed themselves between the hammer and the anvil. If the men of the city so desired they could have devoured the Christians and taken them just as a sparrowhawk takes a small bird.' Saladin would come to wish with all his heart that it proved so easy.

In late August Guy set out south from Tyre. This was a seemingly high-odds gamble but for the first time in over two years, it gave the Franks a sense of optimism. They marched along the coast with their land-based troops being supplied by a Pisan fleet, foreshadowing the same co-ordination and skill made famous by Richard the Lionheart two years later. The Muslims were in a dilemma here – should they try to intercept this army on the move, or wait to confront them when they reached their goal? Saladin reportedly favoured the former option which, had it succeeded, could well have prevented the ensuing siege. In the event, his emirs argued that the Franks could be more easily defeated once they were at the city, and the army was allowed to continue. By 29 August the Franks had reached their goal and Guy set up his headquarters on the low hill which they called Toron.[48] While it is only around thirty-five metres high, the flat coastal plain meant it offered a good view of the city a few hundred metres to the west, and also inland where Saladin and his men began to arrive. The Pisans created a beachhead and this hold on the shoreline proved essential in enabling the Franks to receive supplies by sea, a consideration that would be vital over the coming months and years.

In essence the various armies were arranged like the skin of an onion with the Muslims inside the city of Acre at the centre; next out came the Franks, while they in turn were largely surrounded by Saladin's men. The sultan had, for the moment at least, taken up a more distant position with his base about eight kilometres south-east of Acre on Tell Keisan, with his troops stretching about four kilometres north to Tell al-Ayadiyya and about the same distance west to the River Belus.

Saladin acted to bolster Acre, sending in men and supplies and soon reinforcements began to appear, notably 'the intrepid lion' Keukburi of Harran, and Taqi al-Din, the lord of Edessa and Hama. But the Franks were boosted by new arrivals too, including the formidable James of Avesnes and a fleet of Frisian and Danish crusaders. With Guy's ambitious scheme now in play, and with the Franks settling in around Acre, the onus was firmly on Saladin to bring this to a head.[49]

16

The Siege of Acre, Part I: 1189–90

*'A letter from Baghdad is an insipid,
dry, lifeless letter'*

The struggle for Acre was one of the longest, and certainly the largest, sieges in the medieval period, stretching out for almost two years. Whoever prevailed would secure a potentially decisive advantage in the subsequent fight for Jerusalem. So strong was each side's desire to succeed that tens of thousands of men and women converged on the port from across the Christian West and wide areas of the Muslim world. As one western author wrote, 'if the ten-year war made Troy famous ... then Acre will certainly win fame, for the whole globe assembled to fight for her'.[1] Perhaps more precisely, we can see crusaders from England, France, Wales, Denmark, Flanders and the Low Countries, the German Empire (including northern Italy, most notably a big contingent from Bologna), Poland, Hungary, southern Italy and Sicily, Iberia, and the Italian trading cities of Genoa, Venice and Pisa. They fought against warriors from Egypt, Syria, Yemen, Asia Minor, Azerbaijan and Khurasan, polyglot forces that contained men of many ethnicities: Turks, Kurds, Arabs, Nubians, Armenians and Bedouin.

If Saladin won he would stall the crusader assault, knowing that ultimately the westerners had to return home. If the Christians triumphed they would gain a tremendous bridgehead in their efforts to recover the Holy Land and deliver a heavy blow to Saladin's attempts to keep the Muslim Near East working with him. The most famous episodes in the siege took place when the armies of Philip Augustus of France and Richard the Lionheart of England reached Acre in the summer of 1191, but for almost twenty months beforehand the city was the scene of an unfolding epic.

While periods of warfare tend to attract the headlines, in a conflict of such duration it was physically and mentally impossible to fight all day, every day, throughout the year. Thus emerged phases of diplomacy; times when the participants sought to rest, recover or wait for reinforcements; weeks when bad weather halted the fighting; boredom is a well-documented aspect of warfare too. Finally, and of very considerable influence here, was the matter of disease. Physical and mental deprivation, lack of food and shelter, new climes and conditions all played a part in generating the vast levels of illness and mortality experienced in both camps, afflicting the humblest foot soldier to the highest noble. Far more than swords, arrows and missiles, it was illness that killed the greatest numbers and did much to shape the fortunes and the decision-making of the leaders across the religious divide.

For all the participants, motives in this holy war went beyond simply the matter of faith. The Franks of the Near East wanted to return to their towns, farms, churches and castles; in doing so, they would also safeguard Christian possession of the holy places. Merchants wished to reopen trading centres lost in Saladin's invasions. Crusaders had multiple motives too, and while the religious aspect certainly triggered the expedition, status and honour were central to the lives of kings, nobles and knights; being seen to lead and to participate in brave acts of holy warfare were strong attractions. Other warriors were mercenaries, Christian men who had signed up to the campaign primarily to earn a living; sailors likewise. Many took part because their master told them to. Indeed, the whole gamut of households, religious men, administrators, cooks, blacksmiths, servants, armourers and washerwomen, as well as camp-followers such as traders and prostitutes, came with or accreted around the crusading forces.

In Saladin's case, wholly interlocked with his devotion to the jihad was the sultan's deep commitment to the pre-eminence of the Ayyubid dynasty which required not only the loyalty of his family but also the active backing, or at least the neutrality, of other powers in the Near East. That said, just as many of the crusaders were motivated by faith, so too was basic religious appeal vital to Saladin's support. The ongoing influence of decades of jihad preaching and teaching, crowned with the glittering achievement of October 1187, remained crucial. The sultan had to juggle the delight of the religious classes and the pious enthusiasm of militia volunteers from Syrian cities, against the sometimes overtly mercenary concerns of Turkmen warriors of the Jazira and Azerbaijan. Many lands and cities owed Saladin allegiance, and so a sense of obligation, again, potentially suffused with religiosity, was important. The sultan and his nobles had households too of course, although proximity to their homelands enabled a large cultural and administrative element to attend on them, certainly at the various camps and bases removed from the front-line. For all the emphasis on religious differences and on conflict it is easy to draw lines that are too stark and simple. Aside from sharing the suffering of war in all its forms, by the end, and certainly in the aftermath of the Third Crusade, there emerged amongst the participants some sense of common values, experiences and boundaries.

Acre is perched on a promontory that marks the northern edge of the Bay of Acre (today called the Bay of Haifa), a feature that curves gently southwards for about twenty kilometres before it encounters the abrupt barrier of Mount Carmel and the town of Haifa. The city itself was shaped a little like a lopsided rectangle with northern walls running inland from the Mediterranean Sea for about 1,100 metres before turning at their north-eastern corner to head southwards for another 350 metres where they met the waters of the bay.[2] Outside of these walls was a ditch and some small outer defences or forewall. Nestling on the south-east of the city was one of the best ports of the Levantine coast with a well-protected inner harbour fringed by large ashlar breakwaters, sometimes known as moles. At the end of the eastern breakwater stood the Tower of Flies, a robust defensive structure and lighthouse that attracted a lot of attention during the siege. As with all medieval harbours, the entrance was protected by a chain, lowered to allow ships to enter or leave and slung between the Tower of Flies and a smaller tower at the end of the southern breakwater. The gap was only eighty-five metres wide and the shallow harbour itself a mere 400 metres from front to back, which meant that in peacetime bigger ships tended to moor outside and have their goods brought to shore by tender. Today Acre is a bustling tourist destination and fishing port, with the superbly excavated Hospitaller headquarters at its centre. Fine walls, coupled with narrow, shadowy streets and lively markets give the visitor, in spirit at least, a tantalising taste of the size and physicality of the twelfth-century city.

Acre stands on the edge of a broad coastal plain that spreads around five to eleven kilometres inland before giving way to the north–south run of the Hills of Galilee. This modestly steep barrier is penetrated by roads east towards Safad and to the south-east towards Saffuriya and the Sea of Galilee (Lake Tiberias). The actual plain is a rich, arable landscape that in times of peace was a fertile and productive region that yielded wheat, fruit, vegetables and sugar, as well as grazing land. Nearer the coast the River Belus wearily winds southwards to the Bay of Acre, encouraging an area of marshland before the beach takes over. Interrupting the plain itself are a few natural geological features, some enhanced by builders from the ancient past.

Closest to Acre, only a few hundred metres from the city walls, is the hill the Franks called Toron, today on the eastern edge of the modern city and adorned with a metal silhouette of Napoleon and his horse, symbolising his failure to take the port in 1799. It was upon this hill that Guy had camped in August 1189 and it would be his home for the next couple of years. As a Frankish writer noted, 'from it a clear view spreads out all around before the roving eye, far and wide across the plains'.[3]

Saladin and his allies based themselves on a series of similar features, moving to those closer or further away from Acre according to the intensity of the fighting and the season. Taken together they formed a loose screen that pinned, by land at least, the Christians between themselves and the city. Due east of Acre by about seven kilometres was one of the more forward positions, Tell al-Ayadiyya, frequently the launching site for major engagements. About eight kilometres south-east of Acre stands Tell Keisan, meaning Place of Betrayal.

Tell Keisan is an oval-shaped mound twenty-five metres high covering fifteen acres, a site periodically inhabited since the Bronze Age. By the crusader era it had been abandoned, although the ruins of a Byzantine-era church gave some shelter; this would be a place used by Saladin on a number of occasions because it stands as a natural vantage point over the flat plain below.[4] Another of his bases was at Shafar'am, slightly further back.

On a clear day, Tell Keisan affords a panoramic view towards Acre and it might appear easy enough for either side to see what their opponent was up to. That said, vagaries of weather and light might interfere, plus the fact that while the area is reasonably flat, it is in total quite large. Thus, while at a glance it might look simple to move around on, the distance from Tell Keisan to Acre, for example, would require roughly forty minutes to cover by horse. In other words, it could take some time to react to an opponent's move. On top of this, heavy rains can render the ground difficult to traverse, potentially slowing up movement even more.

The first few weeks saw a number of sharp exchanges and missed opportunities for both sides. Saladin's initial aim was to bolster the garrison of Acre. Taking his cue from the encouragement of the Friday preachers, the sultan ordered a major offensive. After two days' fighting, his nephew Taqi al-Din led a thrust into the city from the north, creating a corridor along the coastline to allow the Muslims to move in and out of the port by land. Traders could enter as well, and Saladin boosted morale by appearing on the streets in person. He appointed the famously well-fed Kurdish warrior Abu'l Hayja, the Obese, as commander of the city.[5] Days of skirmishing, attack and counter-attack followed with Saladin well to the fore, although his secretary worried that in contrast to his associate inside Acre, the sultan was barely eating. The Franks seemed to have learned well from their earlier defeats and kept tight co-ordination between their cavalry and footmen, periodically inflicting notable casualties on their opponents.[6]

The presence of the dynamic James of Avesnes, an 'Achilles in arms' according to a western admirer, prompted the Christians to strike.[7] They could see that the Muslim forces at Acre represented only a relatively small proportion of their potential army. Various contingents were away to the north, preparing for the end of the truce with Bohemond III of Antioch and Tripoli; another group was in front of Tyre, some formed the port garrisons of Egypt; most notably of all, Saphadin had yet to arrive with the main Egyptian army. In other words, now was a good time to act.

The fourth of October 1189 saw one of the biggest battles of the siege of Acre.[8] The Christians organised themselves into their usual three contingents with King Guy at the centre. Lacking the True Cross the Franks had a beautiful copy of the Bible carried before them, borne by four men and covered in a satin cloth. 'Like a plague of locusts creeping across the face of the earth,' wrote one Muslim chronicler, 'their lions advanced in a forest of lances ... zealous to give victory to the cause of the Cross.'[9] Detailed descriptions of the battle allow an unusually precise insight into the constitution of the Muslim army. Some familiar faces included Isa the jurist, the sultan's nephew Taqi al-Din, and his sons al-Afdal and al-Zahir Ghazi. Turkish contingents from north-eastern Syria and the Jazira were also prominent, including Keukburi. Saladin himself was located in the centre around Tell al-Ayadiyya, although he moved freely around the lines to inspire the men. From a total of fourteen contingents, we have three royal princes and three Kurdish commanders showing the importance of this ethnic group in positions of authority. An anonymous western survey of Saladin's forces at Acre mentioned the Kurds – not a group that had attracted much attention from Latin authors hitherto – and stated they were the Muslims' best warriors.[10]

Taqi al-Din was one of Saladin's most experienced commanders, and so when he saw a substantial crusader force pushing hard against his men he dropped back, hoping to draw them out and cause the Christians to lose formation, thereby giving him the chance to counter-strike. What followed illustrates the practical difficulties of communication on a battlefield. Saladin saw his nephew retiring and assumed that he was in trouble, rather than making a calculated manoeuvre. Worried by this apparent setback, the sultan sent men across from his own central division, and when the Franks saw this group weaken they reacted extremely quickly. Preserving the unity of their horsemen and footmen they punched into the contingent from Diyar Bakr, a volunteer militia and one of the less effective elements of the Muslim army. Almost immediately it folded and the crusaders flooded after the panicked Muslims, soon reaching their base camp where Saladin's own household was located. Crusaders began to move through his tents, killing members of his staff, including one of his religious scholars, while another group of Christians penetrated the market area where they inflicted further casualties. The Muslim left wing held firm while Saladin himself, with only five associates, hurried around the remaining divisions, 'making them fair promises and encouraging them to wage the jihad'. The crusaders inside his camp could see continued Muslim resistance over to the left and began to fall back. Interestingly, one Muslim commentator claimed that had they thrown down the sultan's tents then the breaking of such a prominent symbol of authority would have provoked utter panic in the ranks and led to a rout.[11]

Saladin had anticipated the crusaders' retreat and ordered a well-timed charge, a move that turned the tide. With the Muslim right wing reforming it was now the fate of the Christians to be thrown back into their camp. By this time, exhaustion had set in and the battle ended. This had been a brutal exchange for both sides with, according to the eyewitness, the Muslims 'wading through the blood of the [Frankish] dead back to their tents, happy and delighted'.[12] Two notable casualties were the Kurds, Emir Mujalli, and also Isa's brother; the jurist himself had been unhorsed and almost killed. Frankish casualties probably numbered a few thousand. They included – and, one is tempted to say, at last – the master of the Templars, Gerard of Ridefort, one of Saladin's most steadfast and bitter opponents, who was captured and executed.[13]

Almost more problematic to Saladin was the complete disintegration of discipline amongst the camp followers and grooms. Early on in the battle they had judged their own cause to be lost. They panicked and decided to ransack their own camp, load up the pack animals and flee eastwards. Even Imad al-Din admitted that he had scurried back to Tiberias, although his colleague Qadi al-Fadil wrote to reassure him that 'congratulations on safety are better than felicitations on martyrdom'.[14] Huge quantities of saddlebags, clothing and weapons had been grabbed and moved, yet now had to be found, brought back to the camp and restored to their rightful owners. To make this happen Saladin needed to issue proclamations (accompanied by threats) and then to oversee the proper redistribution of goods; 'I saw a market for justice in action of unsurpassed size', commented Beha al-Din.[15] Imad al-Din wrote a triumphant letter to broadcast the victory and to delight in the zeal of the Muslims, the people of the true faith who, he claimed, had brought misery upon the shattered polytheists. In fact, given how deeply the Franks penetrated the Muslim lines this was a lucky escape, although the recovery was impressive. The message ended on a cautionary note, describing the religious zeal of the Christians from overseas and stating that they would not rest until they had sent aid to the battle for the coast. He urged his readers to act in the face of this danger.[16] One side effect of the episode involving goods and weapons was, as Saladin himself recognised, to totally

absorb his troops' attention the day after the battle. Ibn al-Athir postu-
lated that had they followed up on the sultan's wish to capitalise on
the momentum of the previous day, they could have damaged the
Franks quite badly.

The Muslims wisely decided to move away from the smell and
dangers of so many putrefying corpses. Yet Saladin himself fell ill,
suffering from what Ibn al-Athir names as 'a recurring painful colic'
and what the eyewitness Beha al-Din suggests was extreme mental,
as well as physical, exhaustion. It was not just the sultan who was
struggling. His men and horses had been under arms for fifty days
and everyone was shattered. Saladin was said to favour a final push
against the Christians, fearing the reinforcements that would arrive
on the spring sailings from Europe, but in the end his counsellors
advised that he drop back to the hill of al-Kharruba (about twelve
kilometres south-east of the city) and await the presence of Saphadin
and the army of Egypt.[17]

While this may have been a logical course of action, it had a
profoundly negative consequence in the long term because it allowed
the crusaders to dig in. With almost manic intensity the Christians
started a phenomenal construction project – the building of huge
ditches on either side of their camp, running from the south of the
city and the Bay of Acre around to the Mediterranean coast to the
north.[18] The dislodged material was used to build up great earthen
ramparts, some topped with palisades, while the ditch itself was littered
with discarded wood and metal to discourage any trespassers. With
most new castles being made of stone this sounds like an old-fashioned
style of defence from the Viking or Norman eras, but in this instance
it was simply the most practical form available and acted as a superb
protective screen from the attentions of Saladin's men. Older earthworks survived on Scandinavian sites and many contemporary castles
in the West still had earthen mottes at their heart, such as Cardiff or
Windsor. On the scale here, a relatively recent precedent for such a
structure existed in northern Italy where in 1158 the citizens of Milan
created a three-mile earthen rampart, complete with water-filled moat
to try to protect themselves against Frederick Barbarossa. Because the
Acre earthwork extended from shore to shore it acted as a bulwark
and a serious defensive position; Imad al-Din asserted that not even
a bird could penetrate the parapets.[19] The effect was also to prevent

direct entry to the Christian camp and it enabled the crusaders to focus more fully on the walls of the city itself. For those struggling inside Acre, a further piece of clever engineering, the diversion of the River Belus, meant a reduction in fresh water supplies as well; one source suggests this also passed into one of the crusaders' moats too. For the defenders of Acre the earthwork cut off a land route into the city; simultaneously, the crusaders' maritime supremacy did much to throttle the defenders' food supply while at the same time providing provisions and reinforcements to themselves.[20]

Naturally the Muslims made several attempts to disrupt this project and launched sorties from inside Acre, as well as the external camps, but to little effect. Aside from these raids this was a relatively calm period compared to recent months. Boredom set in and as Beha al-Din reported, from time to time troops from the two sides would leave off fighting and start to talk, sometimes even singing and dancing together, a curious scene in a holy war.[21]

Such a waiting game must have been intensely stressful for the sultan, who was well aware that the foremost crowned heads of the Latin West were preparing to lead armies to the Near East. In mid-October 1189 ominous news reached Acre as al-Zahir Ghazi reported from Aleppo that Frederick Barbarossa had set out for Constantinople with an army said to be 200,000 or 260,000 strong, a gross overestimate but a marker of the trepidation caused by his expedition. In reality the force was perhaps 15,000, although this included up to 3,000 mounted knights. When recalling that the Franks had mustered about 1,300 knights at Hattin, the potency of this army becomes apparent. Progress was not smooth, however. Relations between Frederick and the Greeks were poor, with issues of rival imperial status and mutual suspicion generating much tension.[22]

By the time Saladin learned of Frederick's progress the Germans were deep into the Byzantine Empire where they would remain over the winter of 1189-90, periodically fighting and raiding the lands of the Greeks. Aside from the formidable size of this army, by reason that it travelled overland it posed Saladin a difficult strategic conundrum. The majority of crusaders arrived by sea, which in itself limited the numbers involved and meant that most were funnelled through the ports of Tyre, Beirut and Latakia. The prospect of a huge land force crossing Asia Minor, potentially linking up with the Franks of

Antioch, and then either threatening Aleppo or forcing its way down to Tyre and Acre, was a far larger challenge. Preventing the latter was particularly desirable and it meant that Saladin had to keep a strong contingent of men up in northern Syria to confront the invaders. This in turn compromised his efforts at Acre because it reduced the troops available to fight there.

With this first main wave of the crusade poised to arrive the following spring, Saladin needed to look across the Muslim Near East for help. Given Beha al-Din's earlier career as a diplomat, in late October 1189 he was commissioned to visit the lords of Sinjar, the Jazira, Mosul and Irbil and urge them to join the jihad. He was then to go on to the caliph of Baghdad and to convince him to help; a journey that would take around six months.[23] Imad al-Din wrote further letters to the caliph arguing the case for supporting Saladin and emphasising the total focus of the West: 'all the inhabitants of the lands of impiety, not any province, town, island, or region, large or small' failed to send men and armaments 'to try to recover the True Cross and to make war on the people of Islam'. Saladin was the man who, with the blessing of the caliph and the favour of the Prophet, could make 'the land a sea of blood, the blood of those who came by land and sea' and destroy the race of impious people.[24]

Other envoys went westwards, to the Almohad caliph Ya'qub al-Mansur. Relations with the North African dynasty had been poor, not least because of a major battle between Almohad and Ayyubid troops in Tunisia in October 1187, a struggle that ended the attempts to extend Saladin's dominions westwards. In spite of this, such was his need for naval help that he chose to strike a positive tone and effectively to acknowledge Almohad rule in North Africa. His letter revisited the fall of Jerusalem and then described the huge Christian response, centred upon the siege of Acre and created and sustained by their vast fleets. The sultan asked Ya'qub to send ships to assist him, or at least, to distract the Sicilian navy and to prevent it from troubling him further east. In the event, a combination of local priorities, principally conflicts with the Christian rulers of Spain and Portugal, as well as a residual mistrust, meant that on this occasion, Ya'qub chose not to respond.[25]

Saladin sought money and armaments from elsewhere, notably his brother Tughtekin, ruler of Yemen, specifically requesting the pure-blooded racehorses indigenous to the region. The Seljuk lord of Hamadan was asked for assistance too, but his recent conflicts with the Great Seljuk sultan Tughril III blocked any prospect of help from this direction.[26] It was all very well for such parties to show Saladin favour and respect after the capture of Jerusalem but it was actual, tangible support that he needed.

In late November Saphadin brought up the forces of Egypt, consisting of numerous men, both horse and foot, and much equipment. At the same time the Egyptian fleet prepared to set sail, now back under the leadership of the experienced emir Lu'lu. Numbering perhaps fifty vessels; it broke through a Christian blockade to reach Acre in late December 1189, a considerable boost to morale.[27]

At this time of gathering storm clouds, the advice of old friends was needed most, but on 19 December 1189 the sultan lost one of his closest associates, Isa the jurist. He was said to be afflicted 'with an illness that used to visit him when he was depressed'. Weakened in this way, a brutal bout of dysentery carried him off. He was a man famed for his wisdom and his consummate diplomatic skills; the ideal fixer. Isa was a person whose advice Saladin almost always followed, and it was said that he could speak to the sultan in terms 'so unceremonious that no other would dare to use them', a priceless asset to such a powerful leader who faced the danger of being told only what people thought he wanted to hear.[28] He was buried in Jerusalem, as were other members of his family who died in subsequent years. The spiritual value of this was, for Muslims and Christians alike, highly significant: 'Whoever is buried in Jerusalem is buried in heaven' asserted various (apparently apocryphal) hadith.[29]

As the winter weather set in, relentless cold and rain brought mud and misery to both sides and the fighting largely stopped. Saladin took the opportunity to send fresh troops, supplies and munitions into Acre. Noteworthy amongst the latter were catapults to project pots of Greek Fire, tubes of naphtha (the lord of Mosul had sent down white naphtha, a particularly rare and powerful form of this substance) and other incendiaries. Periodically the garrison of Acre would raid the crusader camp and one evening they struck at the tavern and brothel district, capturing a number of prostitutes. Imad al-Din took this as a cue to relate the arrival of a ship allegedly containing 300 Frankish prostitutes, generously responding 'to the call of sin' to offer their services to their co-religionists. The presence of prostitutes in any army is hardly a surprise, although the author took the opportunity to highlight what he saw as the moral inferiority of the Christians, indulging in one of his own literary flights and spending a couple of pages describing the attributes and athleticism of these fallen women in extraordinary detail.[30]

By the end of March 1190 the military situation was once more beginning to bubble. Saladin had received additional support from Syrian towns such as Hama, Homs and Damascus and moved his camp back towards Acre, settling again at Tell Keisan, around eight kilometres south-east of Acre.[31]

Over the winter the Franks had built three huge siege towers, each five storeys high and supposedly around twenty-seven metres tall. Timber was rare and expensive and the towers were protected by vinegar-soaked skins and clay. A platform on the top was large enough to accommodate a trebuchet, giving them a further lethal aspect. The crusaders' idea was to fill in the moat and then move their machines up to Acre's walls. Such was the height of the towers that they could overlook the battlements and drive away any defenders. The progress of these monstrous creations alarmed the garrison and they sent a swimmer to urge Saladin to act. For over a week the sultan dispatched wave after wave of men against the crusaders forcing them to fight the Muslims outside Acre as well as taking on the troops within the city, and thereby preventing them using the siege towers to the full.

Inside Acre, the fear engendered by these constructions grew and grew. Saladin's engineers had made repeated attempts to burn them but to little effect; Qaraqush, by now the commander of the city, was getting desperate. Fortunately for him, a Damascene inventor, the son of the master of the coppersmiths, had been experimenting with ways to enhance the strength of Greek Fire. He convinced Saladin to get himself smuggled into Acre, although some mocked his ideas and said that he was wasting his time and money. He approached Qaraqush, but given that the experts had failed to destroy the siege machines the emir expressed scepticism. Undeterred, the man formulated his brew in great copper vats until it steamed like burning coals. He launched a few pots at one of the towers, but to little effect, provoking derision on the part of the crusaders. But having established his range the Damascene now shot a full pot, this time with a lit fuse. The effect was astounding: the tower ripped into flames; a mountain of fire. A second and then a third pot slammed into the structure and it was quickly torched, incinerating most of the occupants inside. 'God gave them an early taste of fire in this world before the next', one author remarked with grim satisfaction. The other two towers, speedily abandoned by their crews, were also destroyed, a day of delight for the Muslim troops in both camps. The inventor was slipped out of the city and brought before Saladin. The sultan offered him land and money, although to the pleasure of all, the man declined saying that his work was for God alone.[32]

In late May 1190 Imad al-Din Zengi, the lord of Sinjar, arrived. We saw the lavish welcome that he received for the northern Syrian campaign of 1188 and once again he was enthusiastically feted. All of those who brought men to Acre were received with courtesy and gratitude but the presence of this important figure from Nur al-Din's line (he was a nephew), as well as his sizeable contingent of troops, caused much delight. Saladin was determined to accord him particular ceremony and the sultan's full entourage of judges, secretaries and his own sons came out to meet him. At a subsequent feast Zengi was 'honoured to the extent that [Saladin] placed a separate cushion for him next to his own', a sign of great favour. The customary fine gifts of satin cloth and Arab horses followed, accompanied by declamations of panegyrics and poetry.[33]

The need to smooth personal and political sensibilities was a central element in maintaining the siege of Acre. The fight against the Franks had been running, with some seasonal breaks aside, since the spring of 1187. It was a matter of extraordinary skill for Saladin to sustain support for the holy war and to provide his allies with sufficient material rewards, all against the prospect of ever-increasing pressure once the major crusading armies began to appear. The form and scale of the response to Saladin's multiple appeals for help through the winter and spring of 1190-1 were, in some respects, a measure of his personal standing and authority across the Muslim Near East, as well as the significance of the jihad. Of course, further political and diplomatic distractions nearer to an individual's home could just as easily lie behind a particular reaction, as we saw with some of the Seljuk lords. By the same token, failure to work with Saladin was not necessarily a reflection of a lack of piety or interest in the jihad but more of a wish not to benefit the Ayyubids.

The months between April and June 1190 saw the arrival of further contingents from lands ruled by members of Nur al-Din's Zengid clan, with the important and substantial forces of Jazirat, led by Sanjar Shah, as well as troops from Irbil and Mosul. In the case of the lord of Mosul (another of Nur al-Din's family, Izz al-Din Zengi), the dispatch of his son to Acre provoked tension because of the timing of his appearance, just as the winter started, and the fact that his father chose to remain at home which was taken as an insult. In the event, the young man's enthusiasm for the holy war and the large contingent that he brought rendered him a popular addition to the army. Keukburi, lord of Harran in the Jazira arrived with Turkmen and Arab troops all newly resolved to contribute to the holy war; likewise the Artuqid lord of Dara (near Mardin) reached the camp too.[34]

While these relationships were at least moving forwards, the ongoing coolness from the caliph of Baghdad remained a source of deep irritation. His reaction to Beha al-Din's embassy in the autumn of 1189 was pathetic: a stock of Greek Fire, some siege engineers and a contribution of 20,000 dinars. This was such a paltry sum that Saladin politely but pointedly declined it, although he made a great effort to show the ambassador the scale and effort being put into the siege.[35] The problem with the caliph's response was not really about the size of financial support, but more about putting his moral authority behind the sultan as he tried to get the Muslim Near East to join the jihad. The caliph's indifference was vastly frustrating. While he may have been dubious about Saladin's motives around the time of the takeover of Mosul in 1186, the capture of Jerusalem surely proved his credentials as a hero of the jihad, and Saladin's subsequent conquests had been made under the black banner of the Abbasid caliphate.

Had he offered a glowing endorsement of Saladin's successes then further support may have come forwards. But as we have seen, al-Nasir feared that Ayyubid expansion might threaten caliphal power in Iraq. Paradoxically, therefore, the greater Saladin's success, the less likely he was to get al-Nasir's backing. The caliph was also, at the time, very much preoccupied with the Seljuks and even asked Saladin to help, although the sultan was hardly inclined to act.[36] Beha al-Din, as a former envoy of the caliph, was reasonably restrained in his comments on this case, but other members of Saladin's household were not. A letter highlighted the role of the pope in encouraging people to go on crusade – an implicit contrast to the caliph's inactivity. They cited Islamic law that 'the imam of the community must watch over its defence and is not allowed to be exempt from warfare against its enemies'. The lacerating judgement of Qadi al-Fadil gives the sharpest insight into the Ayyubids' viewpoint: 'A letter from Baghdad is an insipid, dry, lifeless letter and whereas we are seeking gold in unity [fusion], it strikes the blade when it is cold.' Yet the caliph remained the spiritual head of Sunni Islam and while he was a passive hindrance to Saladin, the latter had no inclination to engage in any hostilities against Baghdad.[37]

17

The Siege of Acre, Part II:
The Threat from the North

*'The claws of [the crusaders'] ambition
were firmly fastened on the city'*

These exchanges at Acre were all played out against the backdrop of Frederick Barbarossa's apparently inexorable progress towards the Holy Land. As the German emperor marched through the Byzantine Empire his relations with the Greeks remained poor. Lack of promised supplies, mistreatment of German envoys and the presence in Constantinople of an embassy from Saladin did little to dampen down intense mutual suspicion. Frederick was even prepared to attack Constantinople, but in the end, after spending the winter months raiding Byzantine lands the two sides agreed to an uneasy peace and the Germans crossed the Bosporus in late March 1190.

Once into Asia Minor he faced the challenge of the Anatolian plateau, a harsh and bleak environment where Turkmen nomads harassed the crusaders and food supplies quickly ran low. Conditions became so grim that troops were reportedly reduced to drinking horse blood or chewing horse dung to extract moisture. Frederick himself had taken part in the calamitous march of the Second Crusade (1147) when the Germans tried to push their way through central Asia Minor and had been thrashed to near-extinction by the Seljuks. This time, over forty years later, German discipline held firm. In May 1190 Prince Qutb al-Din attempted to prevent Frederick's men from reaching the Seljuk capital at Konya but the Germans routed him in battle. They arrived at Konya in mid-May and laid siege to it; within a couple of days the city had surrendered – a stunning achievement by the emperor and the only time any crusaders ever held the place. But the expedition was not interested in conquering Seljuk lands and Frederick offered to return it in exchange for large supplies of food and guarantees of free passage. Next on his journey stood the Armenians, ruled by Leon II. Given that Frederick had brushed aside both the Byzantine emperor and the Seljuks, submission was clearly a prudent course of action. Leon duly acknowledged imperial overlordship and gave the Germans provisions and fodder.[1]

News of these apparently effortless successes filtered back to Aleppo and Acre, not least through a letter from the leader of the Armenian church who described the German army as 'serious in their enterprise and of prodigious discipline'.[2] Frederick looked set to pose an acute danger to the Ayyubid lands, and his eventual arrival at Acre could have added a fourth layer to the siege, pincering Saladin between the Germans and King Guy and the other crusaders. Just as he was poised to move into northern Syria, Frederick's forces camped by the River Saleph. It was a hot day and the emperor decided to cool himself in the water. Without warning he collapsed and died, presumably of a heart attack.[3] Once again, fate had dealt Saladin an astoundingly good card. The death of Frederick was arguably the most damaging blow suffered by the entire Third Crusade. His authority, his experience and his recent successes mean that he would have tipped the strategic balance strongly in favour of the Christians. The prospect of him retaking parts of northern Syria and then breaking into Acre could have squeezed Saladin's coalition close to collapse and also provided a tremendous platform for the English and French crusaders to follow.

Frederick was the sole casualty that day, but the political fallout from his death became a huge distraction to the senior German nobles. One of his sons, Duke Frederick of Swabia, took command of the army and headed for Antioch. Some of the other princes left for home, seeking to establish their allegiance to Barbarossa's eldest son, Henry (who was back in the West), and to safeguard their possessions. This still left a formidable German army in place, only for a severe outbreak of dysentery to tear through their camp killing thousands of men.

News of Frederick's death brought immense relief to Saladin's camp and those inside Acre too; the Muslims had been spared a hugely testing prospect.[4] Nonetheless, the sultan still deemed it prudent to send further contingents north, mainly from the Syrian towns and cities such as Baalbek and Shaizar, and these harassed the surviving German crusaders.[5]

By the same token, Frederick's demise and the disintegration of his army obviously hit Christian morale heavily, a situation compounded by a failed assault on the Muslim camp on 25 July 1190.[6] Given this damaging defeat, the arrival of Count Henry of Champagne, a man related to the ruling houses of both England and France, was very welcome indeed. The counts of Champagne had a lengthy crusading pedigree with multiple expeditions to the Holy Land. More importantly, Henry came with substantial financial resources and so he took responsibility for large numbers of extra troops while also reassuring the Franks that further waves of crusaders were en route to the Levant. His presence triggered an escalation in hostilities, although Saladin's armies were now reinforced by those freed from the need to guard against Frederick in northern Syria. A series of raids and counter-raids ensued, with the defenders of Acre sometimes making sorties as well. Intrepid swimmers, small boats and the use of carrier pigeons kept communications open between the city and the sultan's camp. Trebuchets sent rocks flying into the walls, pockmarking the surface; ballistas sent huge arrows, sometimes aflame, back into the crusader camp. Illness was an ever-present limitation on the capabilities of both sides, with several leading men falling sick such as Keukburi and one of Saladin's sons. These men recovered but many on both sides did not, and the drain, particularly on the crusaders, unused to the climate and bacteria of the Near East, was terrible.[7] Three notable casualties were amongst the non-combatants, namely Queen Sibylla and her two young daughters, Alice and Maria. Aside from the obvious personal tragedy this dealt a severe blow to King Guy's standing. He was king only by right of his marriage, meaning that Sibylla's sister, Isabella, could now claim the inheritance.[8]

In mid-September the defenders of Acre were desperately short of food. Qaraqush and Lu'lu wrote to Saladin telling him that their supplies were almost exhausted. The sultan spoke to no one of this, fearing the damage to morale and also because he knew that three Egyptian transport vessels were heading northwards. This was no time for subtlety; with a fair wind, these bulky, unwieldy vessels headed straight for the harbour. Knowing exactly how precarious the situation was inside Acre, the sultan was beside himself with anxiety, pacing the shore 'like a bereft mother, calling upon God for victory'. The Frankish fleet fought hard with the Egyptian escort vessels, but to the relief of all the Muslims, their precious convoy made it through to give the defenders another few weeks of food.[9] To show the level of concern in the Ayyubid camp, Saladin took the drastic step of ordering that the coastal towns of Sidon, Jaffa, Arsuf and Caesarea should be abandoned and their walls demolished. Qadi al-Fadil lamented 'the destruction of towns at a difficult time must undoubtedly strengthen the spirit of the enemy and weaken that of the Muslims ... we are saving the enemy the expense of destroying places that he would otherwise have to besiege'.[10] While this was designed to deny the Franks further ports, in the case of the last three locations, it would narrow the ability of the Egyptian fleet to reach Acre.[11]

While military matters dominated, Ayyubid court life did not entirely disintegrate. Saladin determinedly kept his circle of lawyers, Sufis, sheikhs and literary men around him to discuss and debate matters of interest.[12] He could also hunt when the opportunity arose, although several further periods of poor health are recorded, notably in the late summer of 1190 when he was in the grip of a particularly bad bout of colic.

This was the second year in succession that the sultan had fallen ill in the late autumn; he was to do so again in September 1191 as well.[13] Back in August 1189 he was observed not eating, his 'constitution suffering', and experiencing a 'recurring, painful colic' that caused 'intense pain'; military operations had to be delayed out of concern for his health.[14] This same problem appears to have flared up once more. Colic covers a broad spectrum of stomach troubles that affect the intestines, often starting with a fever, and then ranging from extreme constipation and stomach contractions through to the vomiting of bile. A stage of languor, and loss of appetite, feelings of nausea and a fluctuating pulse and temperature are documented too; a most advanced phase is described as loathing food, experiencing jaundice, vertigo and extreme bowel pain. Those prone to colic can be affected by cold and most especially by marshy conditions (the area near the River Belus being a plausible candidate); timing of colic was often said to be the autumn, as here. Contemporary Islamic medicine operated under the Hippocratic concept of the four humours of blood, phlegm, yellow bile and black bile, and the theory and practice of physicians was the subject of a huge and ever-increasing literature. Colic itself was the focus of various writings, and lengthy works by al-Razi (865–925) and Ibn Sina (c.980–1037) offered detailed analysis of the causes, symptoms and possible treatments; authors in Saladin's time added their own opinions as well.[15]

Colic can come and go, as in Saladin's case, and may be extremely debilitating. The tough conditions of a military campaign, moving from camp to camp, can hardly have helped. Ibn Jubayr commented that the sultan 'never retired to a place of rest, nor long abides at ease, nor ceases to make the saddle his council-chamber'.[16] The availability of a regular, healthy diet, even for a figure of high status who must have been given the best food and shelter possible, was potentially difficult. The presentation to the sultan of a regimen, or prescription for daily diet, shows the real relevance of this issue. We might suggest that the sultan had endured colic before. Saphadin's pointed comment to his brother outside Jerusalem in 1187 about the holy city remaining in Frankish hands if Saladin were to die of colic that night indicates that he had already suffered badly from the illness.[17]

The sultan's health was not just a matter of physical well-being. Beha al-Din wrote that in October 1189 Saladin was ailing because 'he had been affected with all that his mind had to bear and the tiredness that afflicted him from being in arms and full of cares at this time'. This is a very revealing comment, making the point that along with the physical issues in play, the huge mental strain of leading the holy war was exacting a massive cost. The loose pattern of illness striking towards the end of the campaigning season may be indicative of the cumulative pressure of each cycle of warfare taking its toll through the sapping summer months, peaking in the late autumn, with the 'off season' of the late winter and early spring giving the sultan time to regather his strength, both mental and physical, not least through being in easier living conditions. The 1190 illness progressed from 'a slight bilious fever' to 'being seized by a colic'. This was compounded by a terrible outbreak of boils that covered him from his waist to his knees, obviously causing him intense pain.[18] Again it is hard to make a more specific diagnosis other than to say that it probably indicates a depleted immune system. Such clear signs of distress obviously aroused great concern to those around him and Qadi al-Fadil urged the sultan to take care of his body, phrasing the fight for health as an inner jihad.[19] That said, suffering had a spiritual aspect (as it did in Christian theology), although in this instance, the illness seems real enough.[20]

Saladin and his companions were not without medical aid or advice. A circle of physicians was associated with the sultan throughout his career, some from his time in Egypt, some inherited when he took power in Damascus, while his fame as a patron attracted other men of skill and ambition. Our principal source of information here is the vast history of medicine and biographical dictionary *The Best Accounts of the Classes of Physicians*, written by Ibn Abi Usaybi'ah (which translates as 'the son of "Little Pinky"') in the middle decades of the thirteenth century.[21] His father was an Aleppan ophthalmologist who travelled to Egypt during Saladin's time in power there, perhaps seeking patronage. He later moved to Damascus where his son grew up to practise medicine and also began to assemble his 442-strong compendium of physicians ranging from the classical past to those active in his own lifetime. This lively text, peppered with poetry and anecdote gives, especially for his own time, a tremendous insight into the characters, skills and cultural environment of the medical profession. With regards to the men connected with Saladin, one is struck by the religious and geographical diversity of those who, at various times, were in his pay. We read of Christian doctors, Jews and a Samaritan, as well as a majority of Muslims either attending on, or being supported by, the sultan. They originated from places as far apart as Andalusia, Jerusalem, Cairo and Baghdad, and some had travelled to cities such as Mosul, Irbil and Constantinople to learn from others. Medicine was esteemed as a profession of the highest honour, and in the Eastern Mediterranean at least, it was also a career that moved across religious and cultural boundaries with some ease. Nur al-Din's great hospital in Damascus was a real focus for knowledge and the transmission of ideas, featuring frequently in the careers of many of these individuals. As well as visiting the great and the good, a number of them ministered free of charge to the poor, while the city's markets boasted numerous dispensaries selling medicines and treatments. They were not solely physicians, often combining other talents as ophthalmologists, teachers, writers, musicians, astronomers or poets; one was a skilled woodworker, another a clockmaker, another a philosopher.

Amongst the most important of Saladin's physicians was Radi al-Din, 'extolled by the elite and the common people and honoured by kings and others'. He had acquired a good reputation in Damascus and was allotted a monthly stipend by Saladin to work at the citadel and Nur al-Din's hospital. Radi was a man who believed firmly in the importance of diet, including red meat, a weekly bath, a day of rest and carefully evaluated eating patterns, although this calculated approach extended to a more prosaic element of self-help, namely a complete aversion to climbing ladders, which he regarded as being 'the saw which cuts off life'. Given that he lived to the age of ninety-seven, his point was well made, but his overt caution also meant that he utterly refused to accompany the sultan on campaign.[22]

The most prominent of the sultan's doctors was the Damascene Ibn al-Mutran, a convert from Christianity to Islam, a man who was present during his military endeavours and also came to be his chamberlain. He was described as a handsome individual of a haughty nature, given to luxury and display, although he was one of the physicians who cared for the poor as well. The sultan rewarded him for his work with marriage to a handmaiden of his first wife, Ismat al-Din Khatun, who blessed the union with a series of lavish gifts to the couple; they lived in a finely appointed house said to sport golden taps. The marriage may, in part, have been intended to quell rumours about the physician's personal relationship with a male servant, a matter that became the subject of widely circulated satirical verses written by al-Wahrani. Ibn al-Mutran's own interest in learning is shown by his employment of three scribes to copy medical texts, a decision that enabled him to amass a library of over 10,000 volumes.[23]

Al-Jilyani was an Andalusian by birth but a man who spent most of his career in Damascus. He was not only an esteemed physician and ophthalmologist, but also a prolific author who wrote widely on medicine, public speaking and philosophy, as well as producing the wonderfully ornamental descriptions of Saladin's wars and conquests we noted earlier.[24] Along with providing medical expertise, for which Saladin esteemed him highly, he wrote a lengthy poem, no less than eighty-two lines long, in praise of the sultan, delivered to him at his camp outside Acre in March 1191.[25] Entitled 'The Jewelled Precious

Gift', it was intended to encourage him as he prepared to face the next wave of crusaders, inevitably soon to arrive on the spring sailings.

> Do you think that the celestial spheres ever contained a king like Yusuf
> among the hosts that lived and passed in ancient times?
> ... For you are the one who awoke the party of Muhammad
> in a jihad when they were heedless as if asleep,
> And you fought for the Faith, not because of personal grudges,
> and you posted armies for the sake of God's pleasure, not for gain.

Al-Jilyani evokes the crusaders arriving with his phrase 'ships of tall warriors moving on the seas'. He writes of struggles with mounted knights and like many others, praises the sultan's perpetual labours:

> In winter and summer we never cease seeing you,
> evening and morning, as constant as the muezzin's call.

Such a gift still lay in the future, and the sultan's bilious fever of late October 1190 was hardly improved by the behaviour of Sanjar Shah, lord of Jazirat and a nephew of Imad al-Din Zengi, the lord of Sinjar. Sanjar Shah was an unenthusiastic participant in the siege of Acre, and from the early autumn of 1190 he relentlessly petitioned the sultan for permission to depart, having served there for only a short period. Sanjar was a troublemaker, making allegations that his uncle was intent upon attacking Saladin's lands and that he was inciting others to raid Ayyubid territory. The sultan declined Sanjar's request, pointing out that this departure would be a signal to others to follow. In the end the rebellious emir took matters into his own hands and told his men and baggage train to abandon the camp. He went to see the ailing Saladin in person, and insisted that he was leaving, in direct contravention to the sultan's wishes.

Saladin's nephew Taqi al-Din intercepted the renegade, who tried to bluff his way through and then changed tack to blame the sultan for not giving him a robe of honour. Finally, much to the Ayyubid emir's horror, he began to weep and beg for help. 'I was astonished first of all at his stupidity and secondly at his degradation', commented Taqi al-Din, who also described the emir as 'a child' who did not know the consequences of his actions. Sanjar realised he had no choice but to return to the camp where, with the intercession of Saphadin, a pardon was granted. Once again, given his need for military support, Saladin refused to burn bridges, although the sultan commented wryly: 'I never received a bad report about anyone without my finding him not as bad as was said, except for Sanjar Shah, for things were repeated about him that I thought terrible but when I saw him the reports were as nothing in my eyes [compared with the reality].'[26]

The endurance of these particular Turkish lords was problematic, and Sanjar's uncle was another to petition for leave to depart, probably in connection with the same issue. Imad al-Din Zengi was a senior figure and Saladin was both concerned and resolute. Saladin offered extra expenses and special winter tents but to no avail. Beha al-Din acted as an intermediary between the two men and described each of them as unmoving. In the end Imad al-Din Zengi produced a formal, written request. The sultan read it and then in his own hand wrote:

Whoever loses such as me,
Would that I knew what gain has he!

The underlying threat here was clear enough and Imad al-Din Zengi stayed put. This was another instance where wider political issues could impact heavily upon the siege of Acre and the struggle against the Franks.[27] It is also worth noting that numbers of Saladin's troops were paid men, serving to secure an income. In 1187 and 1188 the sultan's near-serial successes had offered rich pickings, but remaining tied down at Acre dramatically reduced such possibilities and at the same time generated massive costs. While the Ayyubids had obviously acquired significant resources of land (and hence could create income), much of this had already been given out to allies. Qadi al-Fadil ruefully summarised the response to appeals for support: 'tongues are generous with advice but hands are miserly with help'.[28]

In contrast, the arrival in Acre of a few thousand survivors of the German crusade, led by Duke Frederick of Swabia, gave the Franks some impetus.[29] Intense conflict often leads to innovation in military technology and Duke Frederick commissioned a device labelled by the Muslims as 'the Crawler'. This was a wheeled machine covered with sheets of iron that housed soldiers inside who hoped to manoeuvre it into a position where its large rounded 'head' could batter away at the Muslim defences. Another clever idea, probably made with the expertise of Genoese or Pisan woodworkers, was a prow attached to the forward turret of a transport ship that could be lowered to act as a bridge for soldiers to cross onto an enemy tower or wall. Doubtless this was conceived with the Tower of Flies in mind, the defensive structure on a rock at the entrance to Acre's harbour which, if captured, would enable the crusaders to control access to the port.

Duke Frederick ordered a major assault on Acre on 15 October 1190; yet again, Saladin was unwell, once more with a bilious fever, but he was at least able to ride out and view the assault. Qaraqush had prepared well and his men waited until 'the claws of [the crusaders'] ambition were firmly fastened on the city' when they surged out of the city gates to catch the crusaders gathered in the dry moat trying to get their machines up against the city walls. The Muslims managed to apply naphtha to the Crawler and then the 'cat' (a mobile covered hut that could protect the attackers inside), dragging the former back into the city where they extinguished the flames, later sending the 'head' as a trophy to the sultan. A couple of days later the transport ship was burned as well, bringing immense disappointment to the Germans.[30]

At this point in the season, as in the previous year, it was time to drop back to higher ground at Shafar'am to avoid the winter mud. The harsh conditions in both camps meant a continuous run of casualties, from all levels of society. The Muslims lost Zayn al-Din, the lord of Irbil, along with seven other emirs. Compounding the blow, his brother Keukburi, who played such a prominent role in recent campaigns, left to take over Irbil, thereby removing himself almost 600 kilometres east of Acre. With his new and distant preoccupations, he never returned.

Securing food for the garrisons of both Muslim Acre and the Christian camp continued to be a huge challenge. The strength of the Christian naval blockade called for imaginative means to break it. One captain ordered his crew to dress in the Frankish manner, to shave off their beards and to hoist flags bearing the cross atop their masts; for extra effect they even found a few pigs to snuffle around on deck. The ruse worked to perfection; none of the patrolling vessels challenged the ship too rigorously and it was able to slip into the harbour, bringing a great quantity of wheat, cheese, corn, onions and sheep, to the delighted defenders. By the early winter, with the sea lanes shutting down, it was the crusaders who struggled, paying enormously inflated prices for wheat and other basics. People killed and ate horses, some consumed grass and herbs or nibbled at discarded bones; fights broke out at the camp bakehouse. Curiously a trade in foodstuffs carried on between the two sides; the ability to starve the crusaders out seems like an obvious weapon but there are reports of several Muslim emirs selling provisions to the Christians.[31] With the siege well over a year old, people in the various camps had adjusted to the realities of daily life and created marketplaces, shops and institutional kitchens. One Muslim writer claimed that just one of these culinary outlets had twenty-eight cooking pots, each capable of holding nine sheep's heads. Those seeking to relax had to look no further than the Maghribi entrepreneurs whose clay-lined bathing tubs were filled with heated water, all on offer for a dirham per soak.[32]

The campaigning season drew to a close in November with a couple of major battles as the crusaders sought to exploit news of Saladin's continued ill health and to try to secure more supplies.[33] In one instance the Christians advanced well out of their camp and headed south towards Haifa. Each side tried to lure the other into a mistake. Saladin himself watched the proceedings from his tent on the hill of al-Kharruba but was unable to take part in person as skirmishers poured arrows into the crusader positions. He ordered his men forwards and they began to apply strong pressure; the Christians were seemingly moving eastwards along the river, maintaining very tight discipline. Their cavalrymen stayed hidden behind a wall of shields, and in spite of facing the hail of arrows, backed by the pounding of drums, the braying of trumpets and shouts of 'God is great!', their discipline held. At the heart of the crusader forces a cart carried a huge white flag bearing a red cross and this slowly moved back to the bridge of Da'uq over the River Belus. Casualties were heavy, with many members of Saladin's guard being killed or wounded; equally, the crusaders suffered serious losses with injuries to Count Henry and Marquis Conrad. This was a strange foray, apparently almost purposeless; most likely it was an attempt to gather supplies with some mention of targeting Haifa a few miles to the south.[34]

Several days later (23 November) a well-planned Muslim ambush succeeded in drawing out 200 knights, a blend of Templars, Hospitallers and other crusaders, and made many of these men prisoner. The delighted troops marched their captives to the sultan, and identified one of them as the commander of the French contingent, probably the royal butler, Guy of Senlis. The men were brought before Saladin who treated those of rank with due honour. Guy was given the sultan's own fur robe while the others were presented with a fur coat for the winter. The prisoners were then fed and sheltered in a tent close to his, with the commander invited to eat at the sultan's own table. Doubtless part of this was to gather intelligence about the crusaders' plans but this was also a familiar pattern of behaviour. A distinction here is that these were Frenchmen, rather than, for example, native nobles of the Latin East such as Reynald of Sidon. Recently arrived crusaders had been roused to take the Cross by stories of the hideous atrocities committed by the Muslims and their bloodthirsty leader. Quite how this reception matched up with their expectations is not recorded, but this – and as we will see, numerous other instances of what a European knight would recognise as chivalric conduct – did much to prepare the ground for Saladin's eventual transformation in the western eye from a 'son of Satan' to a figure of respect and admiration. The Frenchmen were permitted to contact their colleagues in the main crusader camp and to have clothes and belongings sent across before they were transferred to Damascus and imprisoned in heavy chains. Once again, to his great frustration, Saladin was forced to watch the battle from the sidelines, being unable to mount a horse and suffering further ill health for a couple of months.[35]

With the arrival of winter weather it was time to allow the troops from more distant territories to depart for their homelands. In spite of the troubles with both Imad al-Din Zengi of Sinjar and Sanjar Shah, they were both given splendid gifts and marks of honour, a recognition of the need to keep these men, and their vital military contribution, as sweet as possible for the next season's fighting. Likewise, the son of the lord of Mosul was given a letter that praised his personal qualities and he was sent off bearing racehorses, fine robes, vases from Egypt and precious metals.[36]

The absence of Frankish shipping over the winter afforded an opportunity to send in supplies and to change the garrison of Acre.

The men inside – 20,000 according to Imad al-Din – needed time off and replacement troops took over, although writers complained that only twenty emirs entered the city, compared to the sixty who left. Given the patently arduous nature of defending the place, even the most enthusiastic warrior may have hesitated about such an assignment. By the end of January 1191 the most important emirs to be in the city were the vastly experienced al-Mashtub, along with Izz al-Din Arsul, the commander of the Asadiyya regiment. Once again, we find criticism of Saladin's handling of this episode. Some advisors wanted him to keep the existing garrison in place, to give them ample money, stores and food and to rely on their experience and toughness to prevail. He disagreed, taking the view that these men were mentally exhausted and no longer able to endure. For that reason, he chose to replace them, although the determination of the new arrivals would – again, with the benefit of hindsight – be open to question. In the same episode, the loss of some of the supply ships, foundering in the rough seas, was a cause of great lamentation and, according to Beha al-Din, the first sign that the city would fall.[37]

18

The Arrival of Philip Augustus and Richard the Lionheart: The Fall of Acre

'The sultan was more affected than a bereft mother or a lovesick girl. I consoled him with such words of consolation as came to mind'

The harsh winter weather, mainly endless, depressing rains, turned the crusaders' earthworks into a horrible mud-bath. Mortality rates amongst the crusaders were high: Muslim writers suggest that over a hundred troops a day were dying; western sources describe what was happening: 'everyone coughed and sounded hoarse; their legs and faces swelled up ... they had such swelling that the teeth fell from their mouths'. This sounds like scurvy or trench mouth, excruciating and debilitating companions in such grim conditions. Corn and eggs were punishingly expensive, and a dead horse sold for more than a live one; wine, carob beans (usually fed to animals) and nuts were the only easily available sustenance. Most notable amongst the casualties were Duke Frederick of Swabia and Count Thibaut of Champagne. Yet in spite of these hardships the crusaders held firm, certain in the knowledge that reinforcements were on the way. Ships from both sides tried to get supplies to their men; Muslims and Christians lost vessels in these encounters and as the weather improved, the intensity of skirmishing increased as well.[1]

By early April 1191 the international sea lanes were open with the Christians eagerly anticipating the presence of King Philip Augustus of France who had wintered on Sicily and was now en route to the Holy Land. While the crusade finally seemed to be building to a peak, Saladin was becoming increasingly frustrated by the apparent indifference of the caliph. Anger and anxiety resonate in his letters: 'Islam asks aid from you as a drowning man cries for help.' In his irritation Saladin baited the caliph by pointing out that it was rumoured that 'the tyrant known as "The Aid of Christendom" [the pope] was on the move'. He complained that 'the slackness of Muslims in aiding their comrades in the cause of truth is matched by the eagerness with which these people aid their comrades in falsehood'. While a series of contingents arrived, including those from Aleppo, Damascus and Baalbek, larger numbers of Turkmen and Bedouin were required because 'the Franks were corn that could only be harvested by men as numerous as locusts'. These groups were, basically, hired hands and would have to be paid. Saladin argued that he was pouring all his personal revenues into the holy war and he suggested that the caliph should offer him support in all forms.[2]

The balancing of regional priorities, conflicting personalities and the needs of particular individuals was a perpetual juggling act for Saladin. He also had to think about the wider position of the Ayyubid clan, with its holdings in Yemen, Egypt and out east in the Jazira. Thus in early March 1191, the sultan's nephew Taqi al-Din went to assert his authority in his newly granted lands of Harran and Edessa and then, he promised, to gather more troops and return to Acre with an experienced and well-equipped force. Over the summer months, however, he began to take territory from the local Turkish lords. Just a few years earlier Taqi al-Din had aspired to establish his own domain in the Maghreb and it was plain that he could not be constrained forever. That said, his departure marked the loss of a skilled and successful commander.[3] Further absentees in the coming campaign were Izz al-Din Zengi of Mosul and Sanjar Shah. After the latter had returned home the previous autumn, regional rivalry between them had spilled into open conflict at Jazirat Ibn Umar up on the River Tigris – over 750 kilometres away from Acre.

Amidst all the strain of maintaining the siege, reports of Saladin's generosity and his sympathetic treatment of the weak and distressed still emerge. Beha al-Din is at pains to insist that he bore witness to such behaviour in person. In early April 1191 a group of Frankish prisoners was brought before the sultan, including a toothless old man. Through his interpreter, Saladin asked 'Why did you come here when you are so old? How far is it from here to your land?' A journey of ten months was the reply; 'as for why I came, it was just to go on pilgrimage to the [Holy] Sepulchre'. The sultan was impressed with the devotion of this venerable old fellow and gave him gifts and sent him back to the crusader camp on horseback.[4]

An attritional means of damaging crusader morale was for thieves to sneak into their tents and steal possessions, or sometimes to kidnap. One night they took an unweaned infant, just three months old, and sold it on the market. The mother was heartbroken and her grieving was noticed by the Frankish nobles. Beha al-Din relates that they told her of Saladin's mercy and urged her to go and talk to him. Thus she went to the Muslim advance guard and then through an interpreter was brought to the sultan; Beha al-Din himself was present. The woman's plight moved Saladin to tears and he gave instructions for the infant to be found. Alarmingly, it had already been sold, but a quick search revealed the purchaser. Saladin promptly paid this man his money back and had the baby returned to his tent. With tears from all those watching, the infant was reunited with its mother and then dispatched to the crusaders' camp.[5]

The spring sailing season finally brought the first of the western kings to the shore of the Levant. Philip of France appeared on 20 April, conveyed in a fleet of six large Genoese transport vessels with his household, troops, horses and equipment.[6] Some hoped for a larger force, and after the build-up he had been given, the Muslims were rather unimpressed, regarding him as weak-looking and lacking power. That said, Philip's presence, and that of his namesake the count of Flanders (who had already been a crusader in 1177–8) and Hugh, duke of Burgundy, gave renewed momentum to the campaign, not least because their financial resources enabled the crusaders to construct another series of elaborate siege machines.

Lurking in the background was the approaching menace of King Richard I of England. While technically subordinate to the French monarch, his substantial forces and rigorous levels of preparation, coupled with a confrontational and flamboyant leadership style, meant the Christians eagerly awaited his arrival. The news that he had swiftly captured Cyprus from its renegade Byzantine ruler, giving a further economic and strategic boost to his campaign, only served to heighten the sense of foreboding in the Muslim camp.[7]

By late May, Philip had sponsored the construction of seven large hand-pulled trebuchets and these began to take a heavy toll on the city walls; screens covered in iron protected his archers and cross-bowmen and they were able to deliver such concentrated fire that no one could show their face above the parapets. The garrison urgently requested diversionary tactics and by 4 June the situation had intensified with only a major assault on the crusaders' defensive ditches inducing them to turn aside from their efforts to breach the walls of Acre. The Muslims moved up to Tell al-Ayadiyya with Saladin at the centre of operations, passing amongst the troops urging them to wage jihad. This was a real game of cat and mouse, for as soon as the Muslims ceased pressing the crusaders the latter reapplied the pressure to Acre. The Christians wanted to get their rams right up to the city walls. To do so meant filling the moat and so rocks, wood, dead horses and, as both sides reported, human bodies, were used. To counter this, teams from the garrison had the grisly task of descending into the moat to cut up the corpses and throw them into the sea. The levels of exhaustion inside the city – physical and mental – must have been phenomenal. Food supplies were a desperate worry. Fears generated by weeks of almost ceaseless bombardment, and the knowledge that more and more crusaders were arriving, were compounded by the apparent inability of their leader to dislodge the attackers. This was not through lack of effort on Saladin's part, as he sent his officers and sons to head countless offencives against the besiegers' trenches. But over twenty months in, these earthworks had taken on a highly resilient form and were clearly capable of resisting pretty well any attempt to take them.[8]

The Ox Spring Tower and its adjacent walls near the north-east corner of Acre bore the particular brunt of crusader assault. A near-constant pounding had taken a serious toll on the stonework while a Pisan-made 'cat' was brought up to the wall to allow the miners inside to do their lethal work. Even though the shelter was set ablaze, the workmen had already managed to excavate sufficiently far underneath to construct a tunnel shored up with planks. When they set fire to it, the wall tumbled to the ground. A contingent of French crusaders scrambled through the dust into the city but al-Mashtub was well prepared and his men forced the enemy back out, killing a number of them. Ominously, this was the first proper breach of the walls and it reflected the increased intensity brought to the siege by the presence of King Philip.[9]

Events accelerated further on 8 June 1191 when 'the accursed king of England' reached Acre. Beha al-Din gives us a pithy commentary on Richard: 'His coming had great pomp. He arrived in twenty-five galleys full of men, weapons and stores. The Franks manifested great joy and delight at his coming ... Their princes had been threatening us with his arrival and deserters had been telling us that they were putting off the great push against the city until his arrival. He was wise and experienced in warfare and his coming had a dread and frightening effect on the hearts of the Muslims.' Beha al-Din's assessment of Richard was indeed well formed. Years of campaigning in the West, a forensic attention to planning and his own lethal ability as a warrior, coupled with a force of around 17,000, added a potentially decisive strength to the Christian armies.[10]

As Imad al-Din lamented, their infantry numbered like grains of sand. Saladin sent messages to settlements across the Near East, pleading for support: '[Acre] finds itself in grave danger ... if help does not arrive at this moment, when will it? To come at another time when not needed is pointless! Here is the moment to end prevarication ... it is the day of need and the moment of necessity ... this is not the time to make excuses ... the Muslims must think of nothing else.'[11] After nearly two years the siege was, finally, heading for its denouement with morale and momentum swung firmly towards the Christians. Another heavy blow to the Muslims inside Acre was the interception of a huge transport ship, crewed by 650 fighting men and carrying vast quantities of food and equipment.[12]

Attacks came in wave upon wave. The defenders beat a drum to signal the start of an assault, triggering Saladin to move on the Christian camp to try and draw the crusaders away. Now in the latter weeks of June the temperature was climbing into the 30s, debilitating for both sides and creating a natural break in fighting during the afternoon. Around 20 June, a crusader envoy appeared at Saphadin's camp and was conducted to Saladin's quarters. The man was a representative of King Richard and his presence marked the opening of what became one of the most important aspects of the Third Crusade, namely diplomacy. Running alongside the armed conflict there evolved a complex diplomatic game, in part about spying, in part about chivalric interplay, and in part an attempt to secure advantage and ultimate victory.[13] The envoy asked if Richard could meet Saladin, but the sultan responded crisply, 'Kings do not meet unless an agreement has been reached. It is not good for them to fight after meeting and eating together ... If we come to an agreement, the meeting can happen later', a principle that he held to throughout the crusade.[14]

Reports from inside Acre related ever-worsening conditions with utter exhaustion in the face of the constant crusader attacks. The arrival of six Genoese and twenty-five English ships (plus dozens of smaller vessels) pushed the war at sea far beyond the reach of Saladin's navy and further tightened the blockade.[15] Perhaps two slim chances still remained for the Muslims. Firstly there was the fact that both Philip and Richard were extremely sick. Philip was wrongly said to have been wounded, rather than suffering an illness, while Richard was afflicted with a severe fever, possibly an infectious disease that led to the loss of hair and nails, and red, peeling skin.[16] So, in spite of the progress of their respective armies, the leaders might die and, as we saw in the case of Frederick Barbarossa, the demise of such a figure could seriously fracture a crusading force. Already, on 1 June, one of the recent senior arrivals, Count Philip of Flanders, had died. Indeed, Richard's dire health caused a pause in the fighting in late June as the crusaders waited for him to recover.[17] Secondly, albeit very belatedly, some external help began to arrive. Armies from Sinjar, Mosul and Egypt reached the camp, although, as Beha al-Din commented, 'the noose around the defenders had become extremely tight'.[18]

By this time, parts of Acre's walls were crumbling very badly indeed. While trebuchets of this era did not usually fire the vast boulders that could simply shatter a wall, months of percussive attrition had taken their toll and it was reported that the top few metres had disintegrated. Even worse, the injection of money and materials had enabled the crusaders' engineers to construct machines that could fire heavier and more destructive projectiles. In fact, the ever-thoughtful Richard had transported stones, presumably of a particularly hard igneous type, from Messina, especially for use in the siege. The section of battlements near the top north-eastern corner of the city continued to receive special focus. The catapults had acquired names, with King Richard's 'Bad Neighbour' exchanging fire with the Muslims' 'Evil Cousin'. The Templars, the Hospitallers, the duke of Burgundy and Philip Augustus all now had catapults and cumulatively they gave the

Cursed Tower a terrible pounding and smashed the section above the Ox Gate too. A letter from Saladin to the lord of Mosul let slip that the Muslims were surprised at the level of damage caused by the Christian siege machinery. The French and English crusaders were so numerous that they could operate in shifts – just as Saladin's men had done when in a superior position during the 1188 campaign in northern Syria. For those inside Acre there was no respite at all, because they needed to man the walls, fire their own trebuchets, and also defend the harbour from attacks by the Christian ships. So numerous were the crusaders that they could even build up the barriers around their trenches, making it more difficult for the sultan's men to disturb their assault on the city.[19]

Saladin and especially Saphadin led desperate attacks on the Christian camp. The sultan was described as 'like a bereft mother, moving on horseback from division to division, urging people to perform their jihad duty'. He was said to have consumed no food at all and to be overcome by tiredness, dejection and grief. A message from inside the city reported that if nothing was done, so dire were their circumstances that they would seek terms themselves.[20]

For several days, two squadrons of French sappers had been burrowing towards the walls. On 3 July one group brought down a section near the Cursed Tower while the others were only stalled by a brave counter-mine. In the face of such grave threats the leaders inside Acre concluded their situation was beyond saving. Al-Mashtub sought a meeting with King Philip in which he argued that when the Muslims had besieged Frankish towns, if asked for terms, they would grant them and treat the defenders with honour and guarantee their lives. Philip was a newcomer to the East, and like all the other crusaders, he was saturated with the polemical preaching of the western clergy, as well as his own wish to demonstrate authority. He brusquely rejected such ideas: 'You are my servants and my slaves.' Al-Mashtub was furious and, much as the Franks in Jerusalem had resolved, swore that he and his men would sell their lives very dearly indeed: 'the lion that I know does not leave his den!'[21] The news of Philip's uncompromising stance aroused real fear in the city and a trio of important officers slipped out by boat, a clear indication that morale was at rock bottom. A letter sent almost immediately afterwards noted that some of the emirs inside Acre had lost their faith in God and that this encouraged the enemy and damaged the spirits of those remaining.[22] Matters were little better outside where an effort by Saladin himself to fill in the ditches on his side of the crusaders' earthworks was met with astonishing indifference: 'The troops gave him no help, but acted like malingerers,' an ominous sign of disintegrating morale.[23]

By now multiple diplomatic missions were taking place too. Richard presented Saphadin with some hunting birds; another negotiation saw him give Saladin a North African captive whom the sultan (naturally) freed. The king also sent envoys asking for fruit and ice. These men were shown the Muslim camp and the marketplace, presumably by way of advertising that the Muslims outside Acre, at least, were well provided for. Over the next few days other envoys, including Reynald of Sidon, fluent in Arabic as we saw earlier, came to talk with Saphadin and Saladin, although no substantive progress was reported.[24]

At this stage the wall of the outer defences (the barbican) had collapsed and the crusaders were making relentless progress towards filling in the moats. Fatigue, lack of food, ceaseless labour, fear as to what their fate might be, as well as continued personnel losses meant almost total despair within the city.

Saladin tried one last ploy to save at least the garrison, if not the city and its non-military inhabitants. A swimmer managed to enter Acre with orders for the troops to make a concerted push to get out on the north-western edge of the walls, while Saladin would simultaneously assault the crusader camp at exactly the same point. This seemed a sound idea but in another sign of weak morale someone inside the city alerted the Christians and they were ready to resist and stall the plan.[25]

On 7 July 1191 the defenders sent out a letter in which they pledged to die because 'our cause is lost'. Further Muslim troops reached Saladin from Shaizar and Homs and contingents of Turkmen appeared too, the latter led by the emir Dildirim. Improvised structures plugged the gaps in the walls but by this point, however valiantly the defenders fought, either defeat or surrender were inevitable. Well aware of their dominance the Christians negotiated hard. Thus a demand for all prisoners and the restoration of the coastal cities, a one-for-one prisoner exchange, and the return of the True Cross were proposed but refused. As Beha al-Din noted 'Our scope for finding ways of dealing with them became limited.'[26]

In spite of the flurry of diplomacy, there is a sense of the Muslim leadership failing to take the initiative here. The garrison had plainly fought with an extraordinary degree of courage and devotion. While it is true that the arrival of further reinforcements gave some hope of breaking the siege, Acre was patently a shattered shell and, as repeated messages made plain, the horrendous conditions inside the city meant that its days were very clearly numbered. Consciously or not, perhaps, Saladin did not want to be the man to make the surrender. But to not actively empower those within Acre to make such a deal, or to fail in formulating a joint negotiating position on behalf of himself and the garrison, seem errors of judgement.

Once more the crusaders were hard at work digging mines. The excavations crawled inexorably towards the Cursed Tower, and early in the morning of 11 July the timbers were fired, finally bringing down this tired and battered barrier. As the crusaders attempted to scramble over the mound of dusty stone, the garrison managed to stem the flow of attackers and, for one last day, Acre held out. With damage this severe, however, it was the end of the line as far as the defenders were concerned.

At first light on the morning of Friday 12 July a swimmer from the city reached the shore of the Muslim camps. He carried letters for the sultan containing disastrous news. The garrison had decided they faced certain death; whenever a city was taken by storm, a massacre almost inevitably followed. To avoid this fate they had struck a deal through an intermediary, Conrad of Montferrat, to surrender the city. In other words, they had lost faith in Saladin. The terms were to hand over all the ships, weapons and equipment therein, as well as a payment of 200,000 dinars, the release of 1,500 prisoners of common rank and a hundred prisoners to be specified by the crusaders, and to hand over the True Cross. In return the garrison, their women and children and their personal possessions could leave in safety. Conrad was to receive 10,000 dinars as the agent.[27]

Saladin was both angry and aghast. He, as the leader of the army, had not been party to this deal, yet apparently he was obliged to confirm it. His advisors could not agree on a response – presumably some expressed sympathy and support for the actions taken by Qaraqush and al-Mashtub, and felt that the garrison had to be saved; others condemned them. The sultan resolved to send a reply that expressed his strong disapproval, but by this stage he had been over-taken by events: 'Then, the next thing the Muslims knew the banners of Unbelief, its crosses, emblem and beacon were raised over the walls of the city. This was at midday. The Franks as one man gave a great shout while the Muslims were overcome by the disaster ... Great perplexity and confusion overwhelmed our people and the army resounded with cries, moans, weeping and wailing.'[28]

Christian banners appeared on the citadel, the minaret of the main mosque, the Templars' Tower and the Battle Tower. With no alterna-tive, the sultan had to confirm the agreement. Beha al-Din was along-side his master watching this calamity unfolding – after almost twenty-three months and incalculable levels of effort and sacrifice, the Muslims had lost Acre. The sultan 'was more affected than a bereft mother or a lovesick girl. I consoled him with such words of consola-tion as came to mind and reminded him to think [what he had achieved for Islam] and to put his mind to securing the release of the Muslims'.[29] Imad al-Din reports a more pungent reaction from the sultan who, after acknowledging the ways of God, launched into a devastating critique of Taqi al-Din's prolonged, and by implication, self-interested, campaign over towards the River Tigris, exacerbated by his failure to provide the large numbers of troops promised; this was claimed to be the cause of the shocking train of events that followed.[30] Many reasons explain the fall of Acre, but this was a rare occasion that Ayyubid clan unity had fractured. So many times over the decades they had worked together. Of course there had been periodic tensions but it seems that in this instance Taqi al-Din had put his own affairs ahead of Saladin's at a time when the needs of the sultan were, pretty obviously, paramount. This is not to say his presence would necessarily have stopped the crusader victory because so great was the impetus provided by Philip's and Richard's arrival. But, at the very least, Saladin had to try to explain to himself what had happened and why.

As the crusaders poured into Acre, Saladin's army dropped back and settled down to deal with the prisoner exchange. A group of crusaders soon arrived to go to Damascus to view the captives held there while Saladin sought clarification as to how long he had in which to fulfil the terms.

Imad al-Din wrote letters to the senior figures of the Near East, relating what had happened and making it clear that Saladin was not

beaten yet: 'This is not the moment to weaken; entirely the opposite!'
The Muslims were to pull together and stop the crusaders from
'obtaining the object of their desires'.[31] He described the huge crusader
armies, their perseverance, zeal and wealth and claimed that 50,000
had been killed. He also blamed the replacement garrison, the troops
sent into Acre at the start of 1191, for lacking the fortitude of their
predecessors, although it should be pointed out the earlier group did
not have to face such a vast array of crusaders. It was a time to look
forwards: 'But if the city is lost, Islam is not; if the city is killed, Islam
is not dead; if the city is conquered and occupied, the sovereignty of
Islam is not compromised.' His readers were to come and respond to
these calls.[32]

Aside from his despair at the fall of a city in which he had invested
so much emotional, political and financial capital, Saladin then had to
fulfil the terms of the surrender, terms that were not of his own
making.[33] The loss of much of the Egyptian fleet trapped inside Acre's
harbour added an unpalatable extra dimension to the situation and
marked the end of any serious attempt to understand and act upon
the need for Egypt to possess a proper navy.[34]

Another element of the deal was the return of the True Cross. The
relic was brought up to a camp near Acre in late July. Beha al-Din
reports that when various Christian envoys saw it, they hurled themselves to the dusty ground in veneration. Far more problematic was
the ransom money that Saladin was obliged to pay. The campaign had
cost a huge sum and we have seen Saladin repeatedly needed to appeal
for financial help. Generosity had been a key means to draw supporters
together, but now, without a recent success to generate cash and with
almost no money of his own, he was simply unable to come up with
the requisite 200,000 dinars.

Unsurprisingly the sources do not agree on this most contentious
of episodes but it appears that he managed to find half the money,
and an offer to hand over this and exchange half the agreed number
of prisoners seems to have been accepted. What remained a sticking
point was the status of these individuals amongst the Muslim captives.
Saladin repeatedly asked for assurances that they would include men
of status, rather than only common people. Without these guarantees
the timing of the exchanges started to slip, which in turn generated
mistrust and tension. As mid-August arrived, some in the Christian

camp suspected the sultan of playing them along in order to regather his armies and better prepare for the inevitable crusader march on Jerusalem. Eventually Saladin's refusal to budge on the identity of the Muslim prisoners was taken as a breach of the deal.

Richard's reaction to this ongoing prevarication was startling. With iron-willed practicality he escorted Muslim captives, bound by ropes, to a temporary camp near Tell al-Ayadiyya. There the prisoners held by the duke of Burgundy joined him. Saladin by this time had dropped back to Tell Keisan, eight kilometres to the south-east. The prisoners, numbering around 2,600 in total, were lined up and executed in cold blood, either by sword and spear thrusts, or beheading; an industrial-scale act of butchery. By the time the Muslim army realised what was happening it was too late; they could hurl themselves at the crusaders in anger and frustration, but to no avail. All that remained was for them to collect their dead and try to assimilate what had happened.

Saladin was utterly horrified; he had not remotely anticipated that Richard would act in such a brutal fashion and had badly underestimated the possible consequences of his quibbling over the peace terms. What prompted the king and, as Richard made clear in a letter home, his council, to decide to kill the prisoners? Surely he knew that some of his own men would perish in turn and that it would ratchet up Muslim resistance considerably. But it would also, as he must have anticipated, show Saladin in an even worse light after the fall of Acre, a man who had failed to save his men as well as losing his city.

Given the king's highly pragmatic approach to warfare one suspects that Beha al-Din's analysis is close to the mark: Richard desired to start marching southwards and did not wish to lose the initiative of his victory. He did not want to leave men to guard so many prisoners and was hardly going to release them. Thus, with Saladin apparently stalling he made a calculated decision to kill them. The sultan had, of course, executed hundreds of Frankish prisoners himself, most notably following Hattin and the capture of Jacob's Ford. In both cases these followed battles, rather than weeks of negotiation within the structure of a surrender agreement, however ill-formulated that deal may have been. This last point perhaps distinguishes these other grisly events from the massacre at Acre and explains why the latter has continued to cast such a long shadow over Christian–Muslim relations.[35]

19

Battles of Sword and Words: Arsuf and Diplomacy

'The Muslims and Franks are done for.
The land is ruined, ruined utterly at
the hands of both sides'

Within days of the massacre, Richard had gathered the crusader forces to start marching south. The curious settlements sprouting around Acre like a malign fungus had been home to thousands for months on end, but the time had come to leave these earthwork towns. What remained must have been a strange and ugly scene – in the case of Acre, comprising abandoned trenches, camping grounds, baths and latrine pits, scraggy allotments; a land stripped of vegetation and scarred by a lattice of temporary paths trodden hard into the earth, decorated with the discarded waste of people and animals living, cooking, trading and fighting. Somewhere in or around the camps lay improvised cemeteries, markers of the grim toll of twenty-three months of conflict; on Saladin's command post of Tell Keisan, a series of Muslim graves date from this period. But for many of these fallen souls there was not the tangible commemoration of a monumental grave but, like millions of soldiers before and after, a crude resting place, quickly hacked into the ground as the struggle continued.[1]

Saladin and his senior colleagues had to keep a sharp focus. The fall of Acre, coupled with the shocking execution of the Muslim prisoners, were devastating blows, but there was now a need to regroup and then to break the momentum of the crusaders. An army heading down the coast would get first to Caesarea (around sixty-five kilometres) and then to Jaffa (a further sixty kilometres). From there the Christians could either turn inland towards Jerusalem, or

continue south down the coast towards Ascalon (around fifty kilometres beyond Jaffa).

Almost as soon as the crusaders left Acre the mounted Muslim
archers started to harass them. Arrow-fire 'well-nigh veiled the sun'
and inflicted a steady casualty rate. Saladin's eldest son, al-Afdal, took
a leading role here and he is a figure who emerges with increasing
prominence over the next few months. The crusaders were aware of
Muslim anger after the massacre at Acre; Saladin himself had sworn
vengeance and all the westerners knew full well that captives could
expect no mercy. As Beha al-Din commented, for the next few weeks
those taken were 'most cruelly done to death', even including
nobles and knights, men whose higher status usually ensured they
were spared.[2]

By 31 August, Richard had reached Caesarea, a walled city and small
port where his men could rest and recuperate. He set up proper
co-ordination between his land forces and the fleet, creating a vital
supply line for the troops as they marched southwards. With the fall
of Acre, most of the Muslim navy had been lost or captured which
allowed the crusaders to operate such a system with relative impunity.
On 1 September the Christians set out once more and during this next
stage of the march the intensity of the fighting stepped up significantly.

Continuing their existing tactics, the crusaders moved in three
distinct contingents, although now the fleet tracked them just offshore,
a particularly skilful piece of seamanship given the prevailing wind in
the area runs from south to north, meaning the ships had to tack into
the breeze. (Historians delight in this textbook manoeuvre, although
it is worth noting that we saw something very similar executed by
King Guy in August 1189 in his progress from Tyre to Acre.[3]) Sometimes
the Templars took the vanguard, or on other occasions, the Hospitallers;
at times King Richard took the lead, or else it was King Guy and the
local nobles; periodically, the duke of Burgundy and the French held
the rear.[4] Visible from afar was King Richard's great standard, a banner
fluttering from a tall beam, sheathed in iron and mounted vertically
on a wheeled cart, a marker of his presence and a rallying point in
battle. An elite group of knights was responsible for the guardianship
of this striking talisman. As far as the main groups of soldiers were
concerned, foot soldiers formed a protective carapace for the cavalrymen and, importantly, safeguarded their precious horses. The

infantry themselves had taken precautions and wore full-length chain mail, better to endure the hail of arrow-fire they had to face. The crusaders' strategy was very well conceived, regularly rotating the men on the outer face of the formation with those in a safer position nearer the sea. An opportunity to recover was crucial, not least because in early September the temperature was still well over 30 degrees and writers on both sides lamented the toll taken by the heat. Most deadly of all, however, were the waves of Muslim horse archers, pouring in a bombardment of arrows, firing and then turning away at incredible speed; relentless, like rain. Beha al-Din, an eyewitness, reported that he saw men walking along with ten arrows sticking into them; his colleague Imad al-Din wrote that the closely packed crusaders resembled hedgehogs.[5] Both Richard and Saladin moved up and down the lines, encouraging their men while the customary cacophony of Muslim drums and bugles added a further dimension to the dust and chaos of battle. The crusaders were not simply slow-moving targets but could strike back too; their crossbowmen wrought destruction on the Muslim ranks, taking out horses and riders in large numbers, most notably a famous warrior, Ayas the Tall, whose death was lamented by the Muslim chroniclers and celebrated by their Christian counterparts. English longbowmen, firing at greater speed than the crossbowmen, inflicted serious damage as well.[6]

The coastal plain at the time was a mixture of sand dunes, swamps, scrublands and a large wooded area, the Forest of Arsuf. Richard was heading for the small town and castle of Arsuf, perched at the top of a twenty-five-metre sandstone sea cliff above a small artificial harbour. Saladin continued to scout out battle sites, a search that had become even more vital because around twenty-three kilometres to the south lay Jaffa, the first place the road turned east towards Jerusalem.[7]

One of the most distinctive aspects of the Third Crusade was the number of diplomatic encounters that took place during the campaign. A negotiated peace was always a possibility, even if the terms on offer fluctuated quite dramatically depending on the rise and fall in each side's fortunes. Some of these meetings were used simply as a means of keeping a dialogue open, others were undertaken in genuine hope of a resolution; but every encounter offered an opportunity to gauge an opponents' strengths and weaknesses. During the midst of this march south, one such encounter took place between Richard and

Humphrey of Toron, and Saphadin. Given the crusaders' recent victory at Acre, it is not surprising that the Christian demands were at the upper end of the spectrum, namely the return of all the land held at the time of King Baldwin the Leper. This was unlikely to be accepted, but Saphadin was content to spin out the discussions because it gave time for a Turkmen contingent to arrive in the area. The sultan and his brother conferred on their next move and it appears that this time they resolved to take decisive action.

The crusaders were camped by a small river close to the Forest of Arsuf and looking to head towards the town itself. On the morning of 7 September they marched off as usual. Muslim skirmishers were sent to draw out the Christian troops, the latter described by Imad al-Din as a nest of vipers wriggling under their brightly coloured shields. Both Saladin and Saphadin moved amongst their men, urging them on in the jihad. The crusaders held formation with, on this particular day, the Templars at the head of the march and the Hospitallers at the rear. This time, however, Turkmen archers began to extract such a heavy toll on the crusaders' horses that tensions flared within the ranks of the Military Orders. The Anglo-French writer Ambroise reports a conversation between the master of the Hospitallers, Garnier of Nablus, and King Richard, in which the familiar motifs of cowardice and honour were, as we saw at Cresson in May 1187, again laid out. 'St George, will you let us be defeated like this? Now, Christianity should collapse since no one offers battle to this pack of curs ... we are being harried shamefully and wrongfully and everyone is losing his mount', shouted Garnier. 'Put up with it, Master', was the king's crisp response.

Hugh of Champagne and Richard insisted that the men preserve their lines; this tight structure was, after all, what had enabled the armies to make such good progress in the first instance. In the end, though, the Hospitallers broke, and hurtled towards the Muslim forces, the bigger warhorses smashing into the Turkmen ponies. With his carefully nurtured strategy shattered, Richard reacted brilliantly to such an unwanted turn of events. Appreciating the need to prevent the Hospitallers from becoming isolated and then losing formation, he signalled for the entire crusader cavalry to charge. Three times the Christians thundered into the Muslim troops, driving back Saladin's men in the centre and on both flanks. The sultan's forces were in utter disarray but stationed further back, near the Forest of Arsuf, the yellow banners of his own regiment became a rallying point. Some Muslims fled into the forest and it seems that a combination of sterner resistance and the fear of an ambush caused the crusaders to call a halt. Given the Muslim propensity for a feigned retreat, this shows the prudence so characteristic of Richard's command. The crusaders had inflicted heavy casualties on their opponents, killing many foot soldiers, Kurdish horsemen and some senior emirs, including the esteemed warrior Buzghush, or 'Grey Falcon'. While the crusaders had carried the field, they too had suffered significant losses of men and material, with the death of the valiant James of Avesnes a notable setback.[8]

Night-time brought the battle to an end. Saladin was distraught and refused to accept food or consolation. Coming so soon after events at Acre this was another weighty blow to his prestige and the morale of his men. The following morning, though, he had to show resilience and he chose to lead out his troops in front of the crusaders as the latter entered Arsuf. In essence, however, the sultan's first plan had now failed. The crusaders quickly took Jaffa which was unoccupied and there they paused to regroup, delighted by the fertility of the surrounding area, rich in fruit, as well as the small port which allowed easy traffic to and from Acre.[9]

Saladin wrote to his lands in northern Syria and the Jazira urgently appealing for more men. What should he do next? In some ways he was trying to second-guess Richard. Both sides knew Jerusalem was the ultimate target of the crusade but it was Ascalon that complicated matters. This wealthy coastal city was a tempting target as it acted as the gatekeeper for one of the main routes to Egypt; holding it would allow the Christians to threaten the Nile Delta and Alexandria. Many on the Muslim side expressed a fear that if the crusaders laid siege to it, then there would be a repeat of the disaster at Acre. The fact that the Christians now had even more siege equipment, plus clear naval supremacy, compounded these concerns. Saladin lacked the resources to defend both Ascalon and Jerusalem – and the latter always had to be his priority. References to 'another Acre' keep surfacing, a mark of the deep wound to the Muslim psyche. The sultan himself was plainly in turmoil, barely sleeping. In the end, little alternative remained. Ascalon had to be demolished and abandoned. The inhabitants had feared a siege, but now they needed to cope with a different trauma.

People tried to sell their possessions, but prices crashed and the sight and sound of gangs of men tearing down the walls created an atmosphere of gloom and depression. Saladin hoped to accomplish this as fast as possible, fearful that the crusaders would rush down to interrupt the process; in this, at least, he succeeded, although the strength of the fortifications meant that some could only be set on fire and damaged rather than outright flattened. The destruction process took several days and the ploy of arranging more talks between Saphadin and the crusaders was used as a device to buy time. That said, once the latter learned of the fate of Ascalon they interpreted it – correctly in the context – as a sign of weakness from the sultan.[10]

Both sides seemed to pause a little at this point. With Ascalon broken, Saladin turned inland and ordered the demolition of the fortifications of Ramla and Lydda. His plan, therefore, was to deny Richard places of security en route to Jerusalem, lengthening his supply lines and increasing his vulnerability. Saladin also continued to struggle with his health and he was reported not to be riding in order to settle his condition, and later, to be leaving the camp only at night to avoid the effect of the heat. Some improvement must have happened by the end of September because the sultan made a quick visit to Jerusalem to check on the stores and the garrison there, information that he took back to his senior emirs to discuss and evaluate.

The crusaders took a while to rebuild Jaffa, doubtless a sensible move in their bid to safeguard the road to Jerusalem. Many westerners meanwhile were distracted by the more earthy pleasures on offer in Acre where a supply of 'excellent wine and beautiful girls' proved hard to resist. Richard himself had to sail up the coast to cajole the troops to return to the business of holy war, although his own ill health was said to have caused him to go back to Acre as well. Money was a further issue, prompting worried appeals to the West to send more resources with the spring sailings of 1192. Richard also reflected on the wider strategic aims of the crusade and the future of the Latin East. In mid-October 1191 he wrote to the leading men of Genoa to ask for their help in an invasion of Egypt. We have already seen that the wealth of Egypt was regarded as a key to the long-term viability of Frankish Jerusalem. Now the king offered the Genoese an enticing one-third of the conquest and to cover their expenses. He obviously needed their fleet and hoped that such a deal would appeal to their commercial sensibilities. More pertinently, it also showed the king had serious doubts as to the wisdom of a quick conquest of Jerusalem.[11]

While focusing on the immediate conflict between Saladin and the crusaders it is as well to remember that the sultan continued to rule vast areas of land to the north and north-east, as well as Egypt and Yemen. And, while his prestige had undoubtedly been dented by the fall of Acre and the battle of Arsuf, he remained the man who had recovered Jerusalem for Islam. In other words, people still looked to him for recognition and support, such as, for example, the Seljuk emir of Malatya (Mu'izz al-Din Qaysar Shah) who sought the sultan's backing in a high-level family dispute. Ever conscious of the need to forge advantageous and long-lasting relationships, Saladin sealed their meeting with a promise of marriage to a daughter of Saphadin's, and the emir's rival duly backed down. Ibn al-Athir gives us a nice vignette that describes how, when the visitor helped Saladin into the saddle, a young Zengid emir came forward to arrange the garments on Saladin's horse. Such courtesies were important parts of court etiquette and well understood to demonstrate authority and respect. An eyewitness admiringly commented 'O son of Ayyub, you should not worry how you might die, when a Seljuk prince and a descendant of Zengi help you to mount!'[12] By contrast, not long after this, relations with the caliphate reached a new low with Baghdad expressing outrage at Taqi al-Din's apparent empire-building, exemplified by his seizure of the city of Khilat (meaning 'to mix', a reference to its polyglot population of Armenian, Kurds and Turks), from one of Caliph al-Nasir's Turkmen allies up on the northern shore of Lake Van.[13]

Running alongside these events were further phases of diplomatic contact with the Christians. One part of this was an ongoing dialogue with Conrad of Montferrat who still regarded himself as the best candidate to become king of Jerusalem. The Muslim sources are consistently hostile about Conrad, a 'wicked, accursed man', but it was well worth Saladin trying to prise open this fundamental fault line of the Christians and to use Conrad's enmity with Richard as a lever in the diplomatic struggle.[14]

From the end of September and on through into mid-October 1191 the exchanges between Richard and Saphadin continued. The two men seem to have met frequently and engaged enthusiastically in the superficially gentle, but deadly serious, art of diplomatic one-upmanship. Court culture in the Near East was, as we have seen through Saladin's career, highly evolved.[15] The same applied in the West, shaped in part by the character and circumstances of individual rulers. Richard's mother, Eleanor of Aquitaine, came from the rich troubadour tradition of southern France and was a patroness of the writer of Arthurian romances, Chrétien of Troyes, while his father, Henry II, was a great supporter of poets such as Bertrand of Ventadour. Richard too was known for his interest in poetry and music. We can also see the currency of international diplomacy with gifts of fine cloth or here, of horses. Religious and linguistic differences aside, both men were from equestrian cultures and had a deep appreciation of horses – as did the absent Saladin. While the language of holy war, on both sides, emphasised 'otherness' and the alien and offensive nature of opponents, here such differences could sometimes be smothered by these shared values and reference points.[16]

Given the apparently regular meetings between Richard and Saphadin, the relationship evolved beyond initial courtesies. Yet underlying the pleasures of gift-giving and entertainment was the future of Jerusalem. With Saphadin busy commanding the outlying troops, Richard met the Ayyubid's secretary, al-San'ia, near Jaffa. Through this exchange the two sides set out their baseline negotiating stance. According to Beha al-Din, Richard wrote:

The Muslims and Franks are done for. The land is ruined, ruined utterly at the hands of both sides. Property and lives on both sides are destroyed … Now Jerusalem is the centre of our worship which we shall never renounce, even if there were only one of us left. As for these lands, let there be restored to us what is this side of the Jordan. The Holy Cross, that is a piece of wood that has no value for you, but is important for us. Let the sultan bestow it upon us. Then we can make peace and have rest from this constant hardship.[17]

After speaking to his council, Saladin responded:

Jerusalem is as much ours as it is yours. Indeed, for us it is greater than it is for you, for it is where our Prophet came on his Night Journey and the gathering place of the angels. Let not the king imagine that we shall give it up, for we are unable to breathe a word of that amongst the Muslims. As for the land, it is ours originally. Your conquest of it was an unexpected accident due to the weakness of the Muslims there at that time. While the war continues God has not enabled you to build up one stone there ... The destruction of the holy cross would, in our eyes, be a great offering to God, but the only reason we are not permitted to go that far is that some more useful benefit might accrue to Islam.[18]

What a fascinating exchange. At the very least, Beha al-Din's account gives us an insight into how the Muslim court perceived the relative positions of the two sides. Possession of Jerusalem was the rallying cry for Nur al-Din and Saladin's holy war; equally it had been the catalyst for the First Crusade and then, after the events of 1187, the trigger for the current Christian campaign. Given the powerful emotional register repeatedly used by preachers and leaders on both sides, it would require significant concessions to back down from these points, either willingly, or in a spirit of compromise brought on, for example, by sheer fatigue. In fact, over the next year the two sides' positions would prove much more flexible than they appear in this account.

After a couple of days' back and forth, Saphadin summoned a group of trusted emirs, most of whom held lands in Syria, and set out Richard's basic proposal: that Saphadin should marry Joan, Richard's sister (recently widowed after the death of the king of Sicily), and that Saladin should make his brother king of the coastal areas. Jerusalem would be the seat of their realm, the villages could be held by the Military Orders, the castles owned by the married couple, all prisoners released and the True Cross returned to the Christians; Richard would leave for home. When Saladin heard these ideas he expressed doubts as to their veracity and wondered whether Richard might actually deliver them, yet he indicated that he was prepared to agree in principle.[19]

At first this whole scheme might appear so outlandish as to seem a curious diplomatic joke and, in some respects, it was always rather a long shot. There were precedents in the Near East for marriages between Georgian and Armenian princesses and Seljuk rulers, but there were far fewer instances for diplomatic marriages that bridged the divide between Muslim lands and the Christian West. Even Iberia, with its long history of Christian–Muslim proximity, had seen a decline in this practice since the eleventh century, although there are occasional suggestions that it still took place into the thirteenth century. In the early 1170s during the positive diplomatic exchanges between the envoys of Frederick Barbarossa and Saladin, rumours of a possible marriage between Frederick's daughter Beatrice and one of Saladin's sons are recorded in a German source, but this does not seem to have been taken further.[20] Even if the marriage between Saphadin and Joan was unlikely ever to take place, more importantly, what would endure from Richard's proposal was the underlying principle of a division or sharing of lands.

This burst of diplomacy took place alongside a sense of imminent military activity. Skirmishing had continued throughout, with Saladin using Bedouin to creep into the crusader camp to kidnap or murder people. The castle of Latrun, perfectly located where the hills towards Jerusalem just start to rise from the coastal plain, had to be quickly destroyed to prevent the crusaders using it. More positively, troops were arriving from Anatolia and northern Syria and the escape of a Kurdish emir from captivity in Acre brought further cheer. This intrepid man had slipped out of the latrines and, even though in chains, had crossed the inner and outer walls of Acre, then hid on the Tell al-Ayadiyya, a few kilometres from the city, before managing to break his bonds and complete his getaway.[21]

News that the crusaders were on the verge of marching out towards Jerusalem brought the Muslims into battle order, with Saphadin in charge of the advanced guard. The holy city is often said to be in a weak position but in the strategic situation of the day, its location twenty-six kilometres from Richard's encampment along the steep and sinuous roads that twist through the stony terrain proved, for Saladin at least, one of its greatest defensive virtues.

Alongside the pressure of the conflict and diplomacy of the Third Crusade, personal and political events could exert their toll on the sultan as well. In the latter half of October, a cousin died in Damascus, an event that as Beha al-Din observed, Saladin took hard. Worse was to come. By the start of November, the two sides were near Ramla. Only 'a gallop' apart they were in a state of high anxiety with false alarms day and night ratcheting up the pressure. With what seems to be a sense that he knew bad news was coming, the sultan asked

Saphadin, Beha al-Din, Izz al-Din ibn al-Muqaddam and two other emirs to come to his tent and then he dismissed everyone else. He opened a letter, read it and began to weep and weep. Confused and worried, his companions were moved to tears themselves, showing empathy and support for the sultan. Finally he choked out the news that his nephew, Taqi al-Din, had died on campaign up in the north. We saw Saladin's anger with him after the fall of Acre but the reaction here likely shows how close a relationship these men had, not least because they were only two years apart in age; it is also interesting to see the 'support group' with whom Saladin chose to share the news first. The tensions of the time and nervous exhaustion compounded his distress and he insisted that no one should know of this, fearful they might see his emotional upset and view it as both a personal weakness and register the wider political loss as well. He called for rose water to clean his face. Duly composed, he emerged from the tent and managed to keep the news secret until the crusaders dropped back to Jaffa and the immediate crisis had passed.[22]

As if this was not enough trouble, the sultan's bumpy relationship with Baghdad had taken another turn for the worse. In mid-October a letter from Caliph al-Nasir had arrived. Written in pretty terse terms, it offered no formal greeting and chided Saladin for allowing Taqi al-Din to campaign against the powerful Turkmen emir Bektimur, although by now the death of the Ayyubid rendered this complaint redundant. He also grumbled about Keukburi's seizure of lands over to the east of the Tigris. In response, Saladin argued that these expeditions were largely dictated by the need to recruit more troops for the jihad. A summons to Qadi al-Fadil to come to Baghdad to explain matters more fully was parried by a statement regretting that he was unwell and in no condition to travel.[23] This relentlessly negative tone irked the sultan and his entourage and a letter to the caliph made the point that there had now been four relentless years of holy war. This, in case it had gone unnoticed, necessitated a huge outlay in men and materials. The letter pointedly thanked the lords of Mosul and Sinjar for their support, and made it clear that others had not been so forthcoming; the implication was plain: the caliph could and should provide greater encouragement for others to join the struggle for Jerusalem.[24]

Diplomatic channels with the crusaders continued to flourish. Saphadin and Richard held a particularly convivial gathering in November, both occupying large tents and involving the usual exchange of luxuries and special foods – plus, in the emir's case, sending seven valuable camels and a fine tent. The king asked to hear Muslim music and so Saphadin summoned a female harpist who performed to general approval. The two men continued to get on well, although writers on each side voiced suspicion as to their opponent's true motives. Richard persisted in the demand to return the lands held at the time of Baldwin IV and the tax formerly rendered by the Egyptians to the Franks; a stance that suggests he still felt confident in his ability to threaten Jerusalem. He also pushed Saphadin to try to facilitate a meeting between the two monarchs, but once more Saladin declined, arguing that he would only do so once a firm peace was made because he did not think it honourable to meet and then return to war. Beha al-Din noted that 'not one' of the sultan's advisors agreed with this course of action, perhaps indicative of their hope or belief that a face-to-face encounter between the two great men might yield a breakthrough. The apparently genial relationship between Richard and Saphadin drew criticism from some quarters of the crusaders, with a sense that the two men were, in the broader circumstances, overly friendly. Rather like the concern reported by William of Tyre around twenty years earlier when Saladin's good nature was said to be working too well on the Frankish nobility, Ayyubid charm was once more a cause of Christian trepidation. The sharper realities of conflict also bumped up against the diplomatic pleasantries when a particularly effective ambush on a group of Richard's troops by the Asadiyya and a force of Bedouin led to an angry exchange of messengers, with Richard complaining to Saphadin about the devious means employed.[25]

This was an intensive phase of diplomatic manoeuvring, with Conrad of Montferrat also in contact via the familiar figure of Count Reynald of Sidon. As we saw earlier, Reynald had met Saladin before, during the prolonged negotiations over the surrender of Beaufort, although their relationship soured once the sultan realised the count was stringing him along, and he had the nobleman imprisoned in Damascus. Now, though, Reynald was shown fine tents, cushions and all due honour as he outlined the ongoing split between Conrad and the crusaders over the succession to the throne of Jerusalem. Saladin encouraged Conrad to break openly with the crusaders, offering (unspecified) agreement on what he might concede in return, although nothing immediate ensued.[26]

Adding to the diplomatic merry-go-round, that very same evening Humphrey of Toron arrived with a new series of offers from Richard. This time, the king indicated that if Saphadin held the coastal regions, then he wanted Saladin to act as an arbiter to split those lands between his brother and Richard, thereby placing the sultan in a flattering position of power. He also wrote that 'it is essential that we have some hold on Jerusalem. My aim is that you [i.e. Saladin] divide the land in such a way that there should be no blame on him [i.e. Saphadin] from the Muslims and none on me from the Franks.'[27] This was, at last, a more realistic proposal, and one that recognised both leaders would face criticism if they did not achieve complete victory. The prospect of Conrad siding with the Muslims weakened the king's hand too.

Saladin's intentions here become murky. He remained worried about the danger posed by the Franks even if peace was concluded. Beha al-Din reported the sultan as preferring to keep fighting the jihad 'until we expel them from the coast or die ourselves'. It took much effort to persuade him to make peace. This may be the author determined to show Saladin's devotion to holy war, although the sultan's comment that 'If death should happen to strike me down these forces are hardly likely to assemble again and the Franks will grow strong' is a pithy assessment of his own extraordinary achievement in assembling an army from across the Near East and the centrality of his person to the Muslim cause. It also hints darkly at the sultan's understanding of his own all too apparent mortality.

Putting aside his reservations, Saladin summoned his senior emirs and advisors and placed before them various options. It was now mid-November 1191, and the chances of Richard laying siege to Jerusalem in the winter were perhaps fading, although the close of the sailing season meant that he would remain in the Holy Land and drag the crusade into 1192. Saladin indicated that Conrad wanted to have Sidon and in return would fight the crusaders. He then gave more details of Richard's idea of the Franks holding specified places on the coast while the Muslims occupied inland regions; the king also suggested that all settlements could be held according to the principle of *condominia*, that is shared between the two parties. Such arrangements had operated in borderlands over previous decades and saw revenues (from all sources) and jurisdiction split. Richard also proposed that priests would be present in certain religious sites in Jerusalem.[28]

So, Saladin asked his men, which of these options was preferable: to work with Richard, or with Conrad and the nobles of the Latin East? The response leaned very much towards King Richard on the basis that 'sincere friendship with the local Franks, such that they could mix together, was a remote possibility, and an association not safe from treachery'. This indicates that, presumably through Saphadin's representations, some of the Ayyubids felt the king trustworthy, although not Imad al-Din, who was openly scathing about the king's integrity. It also shows that the ill feeling after the massacre outside Acre had dissipated. On the other hand, the series of broken agreements with the Christians, such as Raymond of Tripoli's short-lived alliance, Reynald of Châtillon's attacks, Guy of Lusignan's actions after his release, Reynald of Sidon's gamesmanship at Beaufort, as well as a mistrust of Conrad of Montferrat, had created a cumulative and corrosive unwillingness to place faith in the locals' promises.[29]

More exchanges led to Richard explaining how his proposal that Saphadin marry Richard's sister Joan, who would then divide the coastal plain between them, had, in the face of some criticism from his people, necessitated sending an envoy to the pope (Joan's position as a widow meant that her remarriage required papal consent). If this was rejected, then he would put forward his young niece whom he was at liberty to marry off as he chose. While we have seen Saladin hinting at dissimulation, this three-month window seems convenient for Richard. He could make an attempt to take Jerusalem in the interim and, if it failed, then a satisfactory compromise was there ready to be taken up.

As always, alongside these talks, the two sides raided and harassed each other; on one occasion a reconnaissance mission led by Richard strayed too close to Muslim lines and it required one of his men to pretend to be the king to enable his monarch to escape. Constant calls to arms and false alarms drained the energy of both armies. A curious episode took place when Saphadin and Reynald of Sidon went out riding together to watch the Muslims and crusaders fight one another, an odd spectator sport for diplomats, although it was intended to pressure the crusaders into thinking that Conrad might definitively ally with the sultan.

By December, conditions were depressingly grim. Sources comment on bone-chilling rains, energy-sapping mud and perpetual gloom. In

Richard's army, Ambroise writes of the death of many horses, the decay of food and the rusting of chain mail; a belief that the Muslims were suffering too offered only mild compensation. There was a feeling that the crusaders were finally about to lay siege to Jerusalem, something that engendered anticipation and excitement in the Christian ranks. By this point, Saladin had gone in person to the holy city to take the lead in organising its defences. In anticipation of the siege fifty specialist stonemasons had been dispatched from Mosul to direct the strengthening of the city walls and ditches; an ample supply of Frankish prisoners provided the bulk of the workforce. The sultan himself was much in evidence, riding around and closely supervising the work, checking that each emir fulfilled his responsibilities in the section or tower designated to him. On one occasion, the masons ran out of stone and so the sultan sought out material from more distant places, helping bring it back and inspiring others to follow. This was tough physical labour that required financial outlay too, although money spent protecting the walls of the holy city could obviously be seen as well spent. The important Festival of Sacrifices was an opportunity to reinforce the spiritual strength of his men, and a great tent was erected on the Temple platform to allow the ceremony to take place. As always, Saladin strove to inform the wider Muslim world of his struggle and wrote to various senior figures in the Near East describing his intensive works on behalf of the faith 'to exalt his word and protect his people'.[30] The appearance of a large contingent of Egyptian troops led by Abu'l Hayja the Obese, as well as the arrival of the lord of Shaizar, added to Muslim resolve and helped them keep up the pressure on crusader supply lines through a series of raids in late December and early January.

We have seen the challenges faced by Saladin in gathering an army and then keeping it in the field for years on end. Probably (in psychological terms) the easiest phase in such a process is when moving towards a goal, a stage that creates expectancy and the wish to achieve an aim; in the sultan's case the capture of Jerusalem. While this took him many years, and was by no means a smooth process, the target was always there to look forwards to. Now, in an attritional defensive mode, things were harder. In Richard's case, he was still at the point of striving, seeking his aim. The loss of Jerusalem was a sharp shock to Christendom and the call for the crusade a relatively rapid reaction to this. Now, however, several years into the campaign, after a lengthy journey to the Levant, the triumph of the siege of Acre, the tough march down the coast and now this frustratingly incremental progress inland, he had to make a decision. A few miles further lay Jerusalem, the primary reason for calling the crusade and the object of the Christian army. If Richard was to lay siege to it and defeat Saladin, his renown would rival the heroes of the First Crusade. The king was painfully conscious that his men were eager and excited to achieve their goal. Yet as the commander of the army he had to take a wider, strategic perspective, informed not least by the views of the local military experts, the Templars and the Hospitallers. They emphasised something all too obvious to a man of Richard's extensive military experience: the supply lines from Jerusalem to the coast were simply too long and too vulnerable to sustain a serious siege.[31] The capture of Acre had been possible largely because ships had brought food and men to the Christian forces. Here, fifty kilometres inland, and with a particularly hilly route in its later stages, such a lifeline could not at present be guaranteed. Taking the various castles on the road was one option, but the prospect of the crusaders in front of Jerusalem then being attacked by Muslim relief armies from Aleppo and Mosul was a dangerous one. Or, if the crusaders did manage to capture the city quickly, what then? The majority of the crusaders would regard their work as done and, rightly, could complete their vow and return home.

Crucially, the Muslims had managed to decelerate the momentum of the losses at Acre and Arsuf in order to drag the crusader advance into midwinter. This was a considerable positive for Saladin; laying siege to anywhere in these unpleasant weather conditions would be a very tall order indeed. For the defenders inside Jerusalem, walls, houses and shelter would be far more comfortable than months under canvas.

This position reminds us of the extent to which Saladin had upended the strategic situation in 1187–8 with his destruction of the army of the kingdom of Jerusalem, the taking of so many towns, cities and castles and with the capture of the holy city itself. Reversing Saladin's achievement was never going to be simple and would require multiple phases, most probably including victory in a major field battle to break the sultan's forces and leave the land open for long enough to conquer it before a counter-response formed.

Richard could see that in the circumstances of December 1191, a siege was simply too risky. The strategist in him appreciated the balance of issues; a withdrawal to Ascalon, Acre and Jaffa would give time for his men to rest and regroup, and be reinforced by new arrivals in the spring sailings. Yet, as a man who had taken the Cross, and as the leader of thousands of men who, after considerable hardship, were almost within reach of their goal, he could see that this would be a searing blow to morale. The prospects of liberating Christ's city and, it must be observed, at least some spoils, were all too tangible. But as a leader with responsibility for his men, and as a man with a strong sense of his own reputation, he had to make the decision to turn around and return to the coast.[32] Meetings on 6 and 13 January 1192 set out the inexorable logic of the situation, and at the latter, Richard gave orders to drop back to Ramla, fifteen kilometres from the sea.

For Saladin this marked a moment of relief. The immediate prospect of a siege and the accompanying tension and stress was, for the moment, in abeyance. He could allow some of his men to return home to rest (although the newly arrived Egyptians were kept in place), and seek further support for the spring.[33] In any case, the well-formed diplomatic channels remained open, offering the prospect of a settlement away from the battlefield.

20

1192: Family Feuding, the Battle of Jaffa and the End of the Third Crusade

'Your Mamluks who beat people the day Jaffa fell and took their booty from them; tell them to charge'

Saladin and his entourage spent the whole winter in Jerusalem, a rare period of relative security in a more convivial environment. He stayed in the former patriarch's palace on the northern side of the Church of the Holy Sepulchre, a building that he had earlier given over to the Sufis and a place that still functions as a mosque under the name of al-Khanqah al-Salahiyya.[1]

While some troops had been sent home, others needed to remain *in situ*, or else Jerusalem would be vulnerable. To keep men on standby, away from their lands, was a costly business, as was the ongoing refortification of the holy city. Although the territories of the Ayyubids and their allies offered an extensive pool of resources, year upon year of intensive warfare had drawn deeply upon this, not least because of the absence of men. The ability to generate income had also been hampered by the closure or narrowing of various trade routes. As Ibn Jubayr saw in 1184, Acre was an outlet for goods from Muslim lands in Syria, but during the siege it had not functioned as such. Likewise, western shipping in Alexandria had been reduced. Commerce between Muslim lands carried on, but the loss of revenue from western merchants, especially when the Ayyubids were not in a phase of conquest, was damaging. As far as Egypt was concerned, Saladin was aware that Richard was considering an attack on the country and he ordered women and children to leave Damietta and Tanis and for the defences to be prepared. More seriously, in the autumn of 1191 the

Nile had risen too high and the land was inundated, causing big price rises in foodstuffs.[2]

The standing down of Saladin's men was not simply a matter of finance. Physical and mental exhaustion took a harsh toll on the leading nobles, their warriors and entourages. Ambroise reports this suffering, adding that the Turks still blamed Saladin for events at Acre. The crusaders too were tired, and also angry and dispirited. Richard's decision to retreat from Jerusalem had provoked considerable ill feeling within the army, a sense of frustration at being so close to their goal yet not actually grasping an opportunity that had already cost so many lives.

In March 1192 Richard sought renewed contact with Saphadin.[3] The sultan agreed to engage, albeit in rather inconsistent terms. On the one hand he instructed his brother to complain that previous talks had led nowhere and that this time the king should mean business or not bother talking at all; on the other hand he encouraged Saphadin to procrastinate to allow more Muslim troops to assemble in the spring. A memorandum provided the Ayyubid negotiator with the framework, and it included provision for *condominia*, the return of the True Cross, and permission for priests to reside in the Holy Sepulchre; the marriage of Saphadin and Joan had slipped quietly off the table by this point.

The small castle of Bethsan is about a hundred and fifty kilometres up the Jordan valley and it was here that Saphadin and his chamberlain Abu Bakr met with Humphrey of Toron. During this phase of diplomacy the projected peace settlements were at their most even-handed. A series of discussions, including Abu Bakr going on to see Richard himself, concluded with the principle that the Muslims would have the Dome of the Rock and the citadel, that the rest of the city and the villages around Jerusalem should be evenly divided, with the Christians having no 'distinguished commander' in the city.[4] This expression of shared ownership and joint possession has a curiously modern feel to it, perhaps because it seems so at odds with the hostile binaries of holy war. In theory, at least, the two sides had finally countenanced that both had a theoretical claim and a practical need to possess particular sacred sites within the walls of Jerusalem; sharing the city and surrounding lands seemed to be a way of safeguarding and sustaining this. In reality this never came to be tested, although it must mean that the concept of *condominia* had worked well enough before to be a recurrent negotiating tool acceptable to each party. Over the decades the polyglot population of the Near East had proven astoundingly adaptable to repeated changes of political leadership, and that in itself was another reason to place some hope in these ideas.

That such plans never came to pass was in part because, naturally enough, each side hoped for an outright victory; the schemes discussed above were born out of exhaustion, frustration and mutual failings, rather than the dominance of one party. During the course of early 1192, strengths and weaknesses started to emerge within both camps, and a wish to exploit or capitalise on these encouraged a search for more self-centred solutions.

As spring drew on the two sides prepared for an influx of returnees and new arrivals. Muslim troops began to reach Jerusalem while the crusaders anticipated fresh recruits from the West. In the case of the former, Shirkuh's son led his contingent down from Homs. Perhaps even more welcome was the release of al-Mashtub from captivity, almost eight months after the fall of Acre; his prestigious and valuable status as the commander of the city meant that he merited a large ransom. The very same day (16 April), Saladin issued orders to his son al-Afdal to take action in the Jazira. Now, however, a serious rebellion loomed on the horizon. The trouble centred upon al-Mansur, the son of Saladin's recently deceased nephew, Taqi al-Din, the man whose death had caused the sultan such upset. Al-Mansur wanted a formal grant to confirm his position in Mesopotamia, as well as the title to important holdings in Syria at Hama, Jabala and Latakia.[5] In no way was Saladin prepared to agree to this; one source indicates that he viewed al-Mansur as too young, although on the other hand the prospect of reassigning such wealthy districts to closer relatives was attractive. Such a tempting array of lands caught the eye of Saladin's eldest son, al-Afdal, who requested the territory by the Euphrates for himself. The stage was set for a collision.

With gifts of money, robes of honour and other precious objects from his father, al-Afdal had set out from Jerusalem in mid-February. Arriving at Aleppo his brother al-Zahir Ghazi gave him a sumptuous reception, presenting him with the keys of the city, fine Arab stallions and giving the visiting senior emirs robes of honour too.[6] Saladin's instructions to his eldest son were to take over al-Mansur's lands in the Jazira. The latter, of course, had heard about the expedition and tried to get Saphadin to intercede on his behalf, but this only enraged the sultan who was unused to such dissent from a junior figure. Equally pertinent, Richard's awareness of these problems meant that he now delayed making peace in the realisation that Saladin's ability to wage the jihad was potentially compromised. Likewise, al-Mansur could see the wider situation and this encouraged him to take his chances, and to play upon fears that he might join forces with the powerful Turkmen emir, Bektimur, lord of Khilat up near Lake Van. Saladin felt compelled to write to the lords of Mosul, Diyar Bakr and Sinjar, asking them to support al-Afdal, although doing so would drag valuable men away from fighting the crusaders and might damage outside perceptions of his ability to do so. Avoiding conflict was paramount and Saphadin managed to broker an agreement, although when Saladin was asked for a signed document confirming al-Mansur's holdings he refused, 'overcome with rage that he could be addressed in such a way on the part of a [relative]'.[7]

Beha al-Din was amongst those who tried to mediate, and it seems that Saphadin's emirs, led by Abu'l Hayja the Obese, laid out a no-nonsense evaluation that made plain to Saladin the need to compromise. This senior warrior expressed the view that al-Mansur's youth may have led him to make a poor choice but, more pointedly, he stated: 'We are unable to combine fighting Muslims with fighting infidels. If the sultan wants us to fight Muslims he will make peace with the infidels, march to those parts and we will fight under his leadership. If, however, he wishes to persevere in the Holy War he will make peace with the Muslims and be lenient.' Beha al-Din underlined the weight of this statement: 'This was the answer of them all.' In other words, Saladin was being told that he had got it wrong – not a situation that happened very often. Faced with the unwavering logic of this statement, the sultan backed down and duly provided the signed document.[8]

Having already had his hand somewhat forced, Saladin displayed an unusual clumsiness in the next stages of this episode, as if his generally expert political and personal skills were off balance. A complicated series of arrangements saw Saphadin take over the Ayyubid lands east of the Euphrates, as well as acquiring the important crossing point of Qalat Jabar. On top of this he was allowed to keep territories in southern Transjordan, including the great castles of Kerak and Shaubak, as well as half his personal holdings in Egypt; all his other lands and positions were to be relinquished. By contrast, Saladin's son al-Afdal lost out considerably in these new arrangements. From being in a prime position to become a major player in Mesopotamia, he was badly sidelined. Saphadin's role as mediator apparently prompted Saladin to decide that Saphadin was, in fact, the best man for the job of overseeing these crucial areas.[9] Given that the region in question was on the edge of Ayyubid lands and could face incursions from hostile Zengids, Artuqids and other local groups, there was some logic in allocating the territory to the experienced and reliable Saphadin. What is less easy to understand was the false start involving al-Afdal with the consequent political and personal fallout.

Saphadin needed to bring al-Mansur back into the Ayyubid fold and to make a show of authority in his own new lands. He made a journey begining in mid-May that took him far to the north for over two months. The imperative for such a senior figure to make this trip in spite of the crusaders' presence in Ascalon, Jaffa and Acre emphasises the importance of these regions and the value placed upon limiting the damage caused by this quarrel.[10] But the upshot of this family dispute was a significant undermining of the Muslims' military and diplomatic strength while Saphadin was away.

Divisive internal politics were rarely the exclusive preserve of the Muslims, but in mid-April the Christians started to put themselves in good order. The long-running struggle between the supporters of King Guy (including King Richard) and those who advocated that Conrad should take the throne of Jerusalem was finally resolved. It seems that the king of England had come to terms with the political reality that Conrad was the candidate with greater support. News from home that Prince John was causing serious disruption to the administration of England was another incentive for Richard to settle this affair.[11] Guy had, to some extent, redeemed himself through the siege of Acre, but because his wife and daughters had died in the summer of 1190 his claim to the throne was only by virtue of marriage, rather than blood. In the meantime, Conrad had pushed aside the husband of Isabella, the other royal claimant and, ignoring the fact that he was related to the princess, and the existence of his own two living wives, he managed to persuade a churchman to wed them in November 1190. In addition to his military skills he was now, therefore, well placed to assert his credentials to be king. A compromise was brokered in which Conrad would become king, and Richard compensated Guy with possession (via payment) of the island of Cyprus.[12]

Such a noxious dispute could not simply evaporate, though, and on 28 April, walking home after a meal through the streets of Tyre, the king-elect was set upon by two men who stabbed him to death. The assailants claimed that King Richard had commissioned them to act; plausible enough given his deep loathing of Conrad, but in reality probably far too crude an act of political score-settling. That said, it was a powerful enough rumour to achieve widespread credibility across Europe and badly blighted the king's reputation.[13] Ibn al-Athir and Ambroise suggested a different line, namely that Saladin had first asked the Assassins to kill Richard but because this was deemed too difficult, Conrad became the target, a choice apparently incentivised by a large reward. Two 'sleepers' ingratiated themselves into the entourage of the local Franks and became familiar figures to all. The story then slips into the narrative of the meal and the postprandial walk, in the course of which Conrad was killed.[14] Another version has Conrad seizing Assassin goods from a ship in the harbour of Tyre and refusing to return them. After due warning, he had to take the consequences. Further rumours blamed Guy, seeking revenge for his humiliation by Conrad outside Tyre in 1189.[15]

In any event, Isabella, pregnant by Conrad, found herself married again within a week, this time to Count Henry of Champagne, a man endorsed by his uncle, King Richard, and acceptable to all in the Frankish East. From this tumultuous series of events, by early May, therefore, the Christians found themselves reasonably unified.[16] As Imad al-Din noted, with Conrad alive, the Muslims had been able to exploit his rivalry with Richard, not least because the king became more malleable in his diplomatic dealings with Saladin when he knew Conrad was also talking to the sultan. Such a situation had helped to contain his demands, but this was no longer the case.[17]

Towards the end of May the crusaders readied themselves for another march towards Jerusalem, timing designed to avoid the deleterious effects of the winter weather and also take advantage of the absence of al-Afdal and Saphadin. Abu'l Hayja the Obese, along with recent arrivals from central Syria, Dildirim and Izz al-Din ibn al-Muqaddam, were sent out from Jerusalem to confront the enemy; worryingly, Saladin himself was unable to join them because of yet another bout of ill health.

In late May, after a four-day siege the crusaders seized the coastal fortress of Darum (south of Ascalon) and by 9 June Richard had moved inland to Latrun where he began to stockpile supplies and materials.[18] A day later they went to Beit Nuba, a day's march from Jerusalem itself. This swift advance was, rightly, a complete contrast to the laboured progress of the previous autumn. Ambroise reports feverish anticipation amongst the crusader rank and file as they moved confidently towards their goal, although Richard himself reportedly remained sceptical as to the prospects of lasting success.[19] Within Jerusalem, Saladin and his senior emirs each guarded specific sections of the walls. Meantime the advance guard under Dildirim acted as a roving hit squad, working with local Bedouin to try to disrupt the Christians. As ever, the loyalty of the nomads was fluid and one group of them favoured the crusaders, reporting that a large Muslim convoy was heading up from Egypt. Richard himself led the ambush, circling around the caravan under the cover of darkness. Just before dawn he pounced, splintering the Muslims, some of whom fled to Kerak, some into the desert, while others were taken captive. Important prisoners included a half-brother of Saphadin, as well as Husayn, an eminent surgeon. The spoils comprised horses, camels (perhaps 3,000 in number) and magnificent textiles, silks and linens, as well as spices, medicines and precious objects.[20] One traveller to suffer particular loss was the pilgrim and writer al-Harawi, a man who had occasionally acted as a diplomat for Saladin. The priceless notebooks for what later became his *Lonely Wayfarer's Guide to Pilgrimage* were part of the haul. The crusaders evidently took the trouble to go through their booty and identified the author. Richard was keen to meet such a figure, and sent several messages offering to return the books and compensate him if he came in person. Sadly this did not happen and al-Harawi apologised to his readers for any errors that may have resulted from the loss of his notes.[21]

News of the defeat hit Saladin badly and Beha al-Din struggled to console him. But this was a well-timed boost to the crusaders as they gathered themselves for the long-anticipated assault on Jerusalem.

With tension rising and in a sign that an imminent attack was expected, the Muslims poisoned the water sources near the city, such as the great Pools of Siloam and Mamilla and the Lake of St Lazarus.[22] The rocky ground around Jerusalem meant that it was almost impossible to dig a well, so this drastic measure would deny the besiegers a water supply. The last-minute arrival of al-Afdal also demonstrated that matters were reaching crisis point. Given his recent humiliation he had been understandably reluctant to attend, but the situation was so serious that he eventually moved southwards and reached Jerusalem on 2 July. Saladin realised the need to mend fences with his eldest son, and as a gesture of conciliation he dismounted from his horse to greet him. Such a public act, combined with the assignment of Hama and Latakia, started to patch matters up. Troops from the Jazira, including contingents from the Artuqid lord the 'Bald Lion' of Diyar Bakr, as well as men from Mosul, also bolstered the Muslim forces.[23]

A council of war gathered that same night with several veteran emirs present: al-Mashtub now restored to prominence; Abu'l Hayja the Obese, struggling with his great bulk and needing to perch on a stool, and Beha al-Din. The *qadi* urged all to emulate the Prophet and his companions, to gather at the Dome of the Rock and swear to support one another. Saladin himself stepped forwards and reminded them of their responsibility to protect the people of Islam. Rather pointedly, he noted that 'you are the ones who took on this task and have been supported by public treasury monies'. Al-Mashtub responded with a predictably robust affirmation of loyalty, crediting Saladin with making them powerful and rich: 'we have nothing but your lives and they are at your feet. By God, not one of us will give up fighting for you until he dies.' Thus it seemed that an agreement had been made to defend Jerusalem; all seemed well, and after a pleasant meal the group dispersed.

But after the late evening prayer, Saladin confided in Beha al-Din that, via Abu'l Hayja the Obese, a group of Mamluks and emirs had voiced serious criticism of the approach just advocated by the sultan and nominally supported by the senior commanders. They believed the decision to sit back and wait for the crusaders to besiege Jerusalem was far too passive. Once again, the trauma of Acre reared its head with fear that defeat at another siege might lead to the loss of the lands of Islam. These men preferred to risk a pitched battle, either gaining all with a victory, or else, even though failure could result in the fall of Jerusalem, the survival of the other lands and the chance to live to fight another day. There was also a demand that a member of Saladin's family should always remain in Jerusalem to bring a sense of unity to the place, 'for otherwise the Kurds will not submit to the Turks nor the Turks to the Kurds'.[24] The potential for tension between these groups was always just under the surface, and at times, with specific personalities or in particular contexts, it could break out into open conflict, as had happened in northern Syria in 1186. Beyond such obvious markers, an anecdote concerning the newly liberated al-Mashtub perhaps better illustrates the prejudices at play, from a Kurdish side at least. On meeting one of his sons he was angry to see that the child had a ponytail, a hairstyle he regarded as Turkish. Visibly displeased, he beckoned the boy over and said: 'The Kurds do not wear their hair in this way', then cut off the hair and warned the child not to repeat the offence.[25]

This series of pressures during the first few months of 1192, apparent even in the writings of the ultra-loyal Beha al-Din, illuminates the phenomenal stresses endured by Saladin at this time. By now, the strain of almost six years of near-continuous holy war had started to unsettle some of the political and personal balancing acts required to keep the Ayyubid Empire aligned in roughly the same direction. The recent family feud in the north, the questioning of the sultan's strategic planning, as well as the surfacing of long-running ethnic tensions between Turks and Kurds, demonstrated this all too clearly.[26] Looming over all these issues was the presence of the Third Crusade and the imminent threat to Jerusalem. Seamlessly, Beha al-Din tells his readers that, upon his own advice no less, Saladin made secret gifts of alms and petitioned God most earnestly for his favour. At Friday prayers in the al-Aqsa Mosque, Saladin prostrated himself and prayed with tears falling onto his prayer rug.

That same evening messengers arrived to report the crusaders had mounted up as if to set out, only to return to their tents. The following morning came news of disputes between the French and Richard. Just as the Muslims were divided over the best military approach, so too were the Christians. Ambroise reports that the king again raised fears over the length of supply lines to the coast, as well as the strength of the walls of Jerusalem. The lack of water supplies also worried Richard and he was unconvinced that an alternative source over ten kilometres away could be securely maintained. Fierce debate followed with many crusaders vigorously asserting the need to recover Jerusalem, the basic purpose of the campaign in the first place. In the end, however, on 4 July 1192, for the second time in seven months, the order was given to retreat. Saladin's prayers had been answered, proving to his admirers that he still merited God's favour. News of the crusaders' volte-face was a source of relief and celebration; Muslim Jerusalem had survived again.[27]

Such a development prompted another round of diplomacy with a series of embassies passing between Saladin, Count Henry and Richard. A request by the count to restore the coastal lands to him infuriated the sultan, but eventually a compromise emerged that recognised his hold over Acre and left the other territories open for discussion. Richard tried to insist that he remained a potential danger to the Muslims, but also observed, again, that both sides were 'ruined'. He suggested, a touch mischievously, that if he so instructed it, then Count Henry would accompany Saladin on a campaign in the East – a neat reminder that the king had not forgotten the nagging irritations from Muslim groups over towards the Euphrates.

While family disputes created real discomfort for the Ayyubids, so too did they trouble King Richard. The spring sailings of 1192 brought many more desperate pleas for the king to return home and fulfil his primary responsibility to his subjects – that of bringing order to his realm.[28] The near-exclusive focus required to conduct a crusade or jihad was a privileged position, and one that those not engaged in such an enterprise felt no obligation to grant. With the prospect of a siege of Jerusalem now passed, the strategic balance tilted strongly in Saladin's favour, something that became manifest in his conduct of both diplomatic and military activities. We can track this shift via the sharply declining scale of crusader demands for a presence in Jerusalem. No longer was there discussion about holding areas of the city, but a more basic request for pilgrims to be allowed to visit the holy sites. Ascalon remained the sticking point in talks, not least because of the vast sums of money Richard had spent rebuilding the place.[29] Still, however, notions of shared lands filtered into the discussions, largely in the context of the border regions between Frankish and Muslim territories. As ever, the conduct of diplomacy remained carefully orchestrated with the exchange of gifts being central. In mid-July Richard sent the sultan two beautiful hunting falcons, a gesture at the higher end of the spectrum and an act that piqued a competitive edge in Saladin. A fine (sadly, unspecified) present was dispatched in return because, as Beha al-Din asserted, 'in the matter of gifts he was not to be outdone'.[30]

Richard worked hard to keep hold of Ascalon and nearby Darum, arguing that such a stance was pushed upon him by the local Franks and only their intransigence on the matter prevented him from leaving. Beha al-Din marvelled at this guile: 'We pray to God to keep Muslims safe from his evil for they had never been tried by anyone more devious or more bold.' Further shuttling back and forth was of little effect; Ascalon remained the stumbling block.

Apparently stung by criticism of his passivity at Jerusalem (notwith-standing the fact that the crusaders had retreated), Saladin seized the initiative and launched a surprise attack. In mid-July, Saladin's favourite son al-Zahir Ghazi arrived, to be greeted with great honour and special affection, marked by an embrace and a kiss between the eyes.[31] The presence of his sons, the approach of Saphadin and many northern Syrian allies, all of whom would be keen to acquire rewards and to defeat the crusaders – combined with the strong feeling that Richard, while looking for an exit strategy, was playing games at this point – also prompted this more aggressive approach. News that the crusaders had gone northwards towards Beirut was the catalyst to act. Saladin gathered his forces and moved to Ramla, about twenty-five kilometres south-east of Jaffa, and after a quick recce, the full Muslim army, in its usual tripartite formation, set out for the coastal city on Tuesday 28 July 1192.

In this, their first major engagement for almost a year, the Muslim troops pressed hard, with a bombardment from trebuchets and mango-nels, coupled with a contingent of sappers. Christian resistance was, however, firm. A clever counter-mine caused the Muslim tunnel to start to collapse on itself and so the site of the digging was moved. After an initial burst of optimism, resolve in the Muslim ranks quickly ebbed and Saladin had to push hard to keep the pressure on. Nonetheless, by the end of the second day the town looked on the point of defeat.

Envoys came to the sultan and asked to discuss terms. Soldiers would be allowed to leave in exchange for the release of Muslim prisoners of the same rank. Non-combatants would be freed at the same prices as the inhabitants of Jerusalem in 1187, with the caveat that this would not come into operation until Saturday (1 August) unless help arrived. In other words, the defenders pinned their hopes on a rescue mission from the crusaders in Acre. Saladin rejected this, but the Muslim troops, thinking that a negotiated settlement was imminent, acted with little vigour. The crusaders, by contrast, were dynamic, heaving huge beams to block a section of wall brought down by a mine and then setting them on fire to prevent entry. We saw how such a ploy had literally backfired on the defenders of Jacob's Ford in 1179, but here it worked perfectly. So aggressive was the Christian defence they chose not to close the town gates and fought in front of them; the greater the resolve of those inside Jaffa, the more Saladin feared that his plan would fail.

Friday brought a renewed assault from the centre and the left wing of the Muslim troops; drums and trumpets spurred the men into action. Another section of curtain wall fell to the efforts of the sappers; fires that had been burning overnight finally achieved their purpose and with a noise 'like the clap of doom', the wall fell and 'a cloud of dust and smoke went up and darkened the sky'. Once more the defenders blocked the breach, a situation that prompted another round of surrender negotiations. The Christians who had rejected these terms retreated to the citadel, a move which left the town itself open to the sack. A buoyant Muslim army seized goods, crops, furnishings and even some of the booty taken from the captured Egyptian caravan back in late June. Their delight was abruptly brought up short when a group of Saladin's own Mamluks stationed at the city gates seized everything from them; those who objected were beaten until they handed the plunder over.[32] Quite why this happened is unclear; the men apparently expected to be able to keep what they could carry, suggesting that this was normal practice. The wish to centralise the haul might indicate that Saladin needed to gather all the resources he could muster; if this was the case then he, or certainly his personal troops, handled the situation poorly.

News came through that Richard had learned of the Christian resistance and was preparing to try to save Jaffa. Beha al-Din, who was present at the siege, voices a rare critical tone here, arguing there was no need for the delays caused by a negotiated surrender because the place had been about to fall anyway. Interestingly, he identified the fact that it had been a long time since the Muslims had taken somewhere 'ripe for plunder' and that doing so would have excited the troops' zeal.[33] These are fair points, although on most previous occasions we have seen that Saladin's default method of taking a city was by arrangement rather than by violence.

Exhaustion from the previous couple of days' fighting, exacerbated by the fierce July heat and the effects of smoke, meant that the attackers could not press home their advantage. A blast of trumpets from the citadel woke up the Muslim camp and conveyed most unwelcome news – a crusader fleet had arrived offshore. While Jaffa had a small natural harbour, landing either there or on the nearby beaches would be extremely hard. Saladin, meanwhile, sent a group of senior emirs to lead the remaining Christians out of the citadel, a slow and bureaucratic process as the man in charge insisted on writing down the details of those who left. Those who chose to depart at this point must have judged Richard's relief fleet too small to be of help and made the decision to save themselves. The leader of Saladin's Mamluk regiment feared disorder breaking out and, using considerable force, drove out any other Muslims roaming around inside the town. Those Christians who remained in the citadel held firm; the arrival of more vessels bolstered their spirits further. By this time, no less than fifty-five ships gathered offshore, although they hesitated to act, believing that they were too late because the town appeared full of Muslim troops and banners. Eventually, however, those at sea realised their co-religionists still held out in the citadel – now they had to move fast.

To the dread of the Muslims, there at the head of his troops was Richard the Lionheart. Here at Jaffa was the scene of one of his greatest acts of military virtuosity. The king swore 'by God's calves' that he would free the garrison; he urged his sailors to bring his galley close to land, jumped into the shallows and charged ashore, firing from a crossbow and armed with a Danish axe, inspiring his companions to plunge into the Turks 'like madmen'. The Muslims were quickly driven out of the port. Saladin had been talking with Christian envoys from the citadel when a flood of panicked people announced that the harbour was lost. The baggage train and markets were ordered to withdraw, although in their haste they abandoned much of the loot acquired only two days earlier. Richard meanwhile ploughed his way into Jaffa where 'the boldest king in the world' joyfully greeted the brave and resolute knights who had held on for his arrival. 'When the Turks saw his banner they trembled ... Richard the Great [was there].'[34]

What followed, as described by Beha al-Din, were a curious couple of scenes. First he reports that a number of Mamluks 'got to meet' Richard at the end of the siege 'and there was much conversation and merriment between them', a description that reads as if the Muslims were slightly in awe of Richard's celebrity and were pleased to have contact with him. The king soon took the initiative in asking to meet the chamberlain Abu Bakr, al-Mashtub, Dildirim and others. These were all men familiar to him from earlier discussions or their time as captives, and on this occasion, he was said to have knighted some of them. Once again we see the shared camaraderie of the equestrian classes comfortably crossing the religious divide and perhaps dulling the stark menace of holy war.[35]

In the negotiations that ensued, Richard dangled the prospect that if Ascalon was ceded to the Franks, then he would leave for home within a week. Otherwise – and this was meant as a threat – he would remain in the Holy Land for yet another winter, raising the prospect of the conflict dragging on yet further. Saladin was not, by this stage, particularly impressed by such an argument, knowing full well that domestic politics tugged extremely hard on the king. He sarcastically commented how easy it was for the young English king (he was thirty-five to Saladin's fifty-five) to spend time two months from his home, yet in contrast Saladin was in the middle of his own lands, surrounded by his sons and family and able to act as he pleased with armies available winter and summer. In other words, Richard would not win.

As ever, military manoeuvres continued alongside the talk, with Henry of Champagne bringing a large contingent of men down the coast as far as Caesarea. Looking to strike quickly Saladin learned that Richard had, rather casually, camped outside Jaffa with only a small group of men. Early in the morning of 5 August the Muslims made a surprise attack but the king's companions, knights of the highest quality, stood firm: 'like dogs of war they snarled, willing to fight to the death'. Richard, with the lion banner swirling above his men, was at his most lethal, hurling himself against the enemy, 'splitting them to the teeth' with the ferocity of his blows. Even within this savage confrontation, Ambroise was prepared to place an act of chivalric courtesy. The 'noble, kind and generous Saphadin' sent two fine Arab horses to the king in recognition of his valiant deeds.[36] That said, the knights numbered only a handful with perhaps 300 footmen. Capturing Richard should have been an easy task. Yet so stern was the crusaders' resolve that the Muslims, al-Zahir Ghazi aside, were not prepared to fight again, even when Saladin went around promising rewards to all. One emir remarked cynically, 'Your Mamluks who beat people the day Jaffa fell and took their booty from them; tell them to charge.'[37] In other words, the sultan's decision not to let Jaffa fall to the sack and then to allow the elite Mamluks to keep the spoils of war had dented the determination of the wider soldiery, and they no longer seemed willing to risk their lives for him. This was a grim moment for Saladin. Over the decades his ability to convince troops, certainly those in his presence, to fight the holy war for faith and for earthly rewards had been successful, even during the toughest of times at the siege of Acre. Now, however, the integrity and reliability of his good name had been compromised.

Richard was stung by the opportunist assault on Jaffa, and once Saladin had rejected his proposal for the exchange of Ascalon, the king announced that he was staying for the winter and that negotiations were at an end. His hand was beginning to weaken, however. Contingents from Mosul and Egypt arrived to support Saladin in early August, but of greater importance was the appearance of al-Mansur, with whom there had been such difficult relations earlier in the year.

Al-Mansur went first to the contingent of his Ayyubid patron, Saphadin. Given the gravity of the dispute with Saladin, the ground for their meeting needed to be well prepared and al-Zahir Ghazi prudently intervened to ask his father's permission to visit the newcomer. The two young men clicked and the Ayyubid took al-Mansur to meet his father. The sultan patently wished for the encounter to be a success and he showed due respect by rising and embracing the youth. Then, to the apparent surprise of all present, Saladin burst into tears. He managed to compose himself and then broke down again, crying 'in a way that had never been seen before'. Such a public display of emotion, with its apparent loss of control, were not Saladin's usual way. We have seen him master his emotions in public before, such as when he had to cope with the news of the death of his youngest brother, Taj al-Mulk, at the feast celebrating the takeover of Aleppo in 1183. More recently, news of the death of his nephew Taqi al-Din was choreographed to be absorbed amongst a group of trusted companions before the sultan pulled himself together to face the wider world. The situation here was not, of course, a matter of personal loss, and Beha al-Din's comment on the unprecedented nature of the sultan's reaction perhaps points to a release of tension triggered by the end of an enormously distracting series of disputes that had seriously threatened the Ayyubid confederation and potentially their hold on Jerusalem. The sultan's embrace of al-Mansur and the latter's obviously good relations with Saphadin and al-Zahir Ghazi brought some restoration of equilibrium.

Looking back on recent months this overt show of emotion was by no means an isolated occurrence. Beha al-Din's detailed character sketch of the sultan's virtues made much of his equanimity and even temperament, yet as the crusade dragged on it is noticeable that the author mentioned several instances of a major loss of temper.[38] There is a point in everyone where exasperation and frustration boil over, but reports of Saladin exceeding this mark are sporadic at best and thus the contrast becomes more evident. While the 'Mirrors for Princes' texts recognise anger as part of the human condition, they observe: 'Anger is a weapon that cannot be dispensed with but it should not be such that it takes over [one's] will without leave and dominate, contrary to reason and the Law ... curing anger is obligatory.'[39] In the context of Saladin's extraordinary labours – the years spent riding hundreds of miles around the Near East, fighting, motivating people, taking on the responsibility for leading the jihad against the crusaders and preserving the Muslim hold on Jerusalem, leading his family, not to mention his own serial health problems – it becomes understandable that from time to time, the longer these various hardships went on, so his bodily and mental well-being showed signs of creaking under such phenomenal strain. We saw that at the end of the 1189 campaigns his physical health was so bad that he was also described as being emotionally exhausted too: 'he had been affected by all that his mind had to bear and the tiredness that afflicted him from being in arms and full of cares at this time'.[40] A more extreme example of behaviour that was out of the ordinary took place earlier in 1192 when he ordered the crucifixion of al-Suhrawardi, a philosopher whose radical thinking deeply unsettled the religious establishment in Aleppo.[41] By the summer of that year, one can sense fatigue in his comments to crusader envoys about being an 'old man', as well as his teasing Richard about his relative youth.

For all Saladin's feelings of strain, he was not alone in such a condition. Saphadin had suffered poor health over the summer, as had Imad al-Din and many other emirs. Richard too endured bouts of serious sickness, as well as trying to fend off calls to return home; the French contingent had seemingly had enough and were looking to leave.[42] And in truth, it had become clear to Richard after the second retreat from Jerusalem that recapturing the holy city was simply not plausible. Now that the political situation of the Frankish kingdom was apparently settled and with plenty to take care of in England, it remained for Richard to finalise the security of the Latin East through the best possible deal on the coastal cities, before he sailed.

During the king's illness he had developed a craving for pears and plums. In delivering these delicacies the Muslims were able to ascertain that perhaps only 300 knights remained in Jaffa. Meanwhile the usual diplomats were busy as ever, and the chamberlain Abu Bakr was shuttling between Richard, Saladin and Saphadin, able to convey to the sultan the slow wilting of the English king's demands. By now Richard was reported as saying that he would give up Ascalon in return for financial compensation. The sultan instructed Saphadin to seize this opportunity to make peace, citing his own army's fatigue and lack of resources as a reason to bring matters to a close.[43]

A day later, even the requirement for money had gone and Dildirim was able to state that he believed the king's intentions to be sincere. A couple of detailed negotiating points concerned Ramla and Lydda (eventually ceded back to the Franks) and drafts of the deal were exchanged with Dildirim and Saphadin leading the work. Finally, on 1 September 1192 Imad al-Din himself, as befitted the sultan's senior secretary, drew up the treaty.[44] It was to last three years and eight months from that date. Jaffa, Caesarea, Arsuf, Haifa and Acre and their surrounding districts were to be held by the Franks, with some references to *condominia* around Ramla and Lydda. Ascalon was to be demolished by men from both sides; the lands of the Assassins were included in the division, indicating they were regarded as a sufficiently strong regional entity to require recognition; the Bedouin likewise. Bohemond III of Antioch and (since 1189) of Tripoli was also to be a signatory in order for the agreement to cover the whole of the Frankish East. Those observing the truce were free to visit the Holy Sepulchre too.[45]

Richard remained unwell but on 2 September he summoned the Christian leadership to receive the truce. He took the hand of the Muslim envoy and agreed to the arrangement, followed by Count Henry, the ruler of the kingdom of Jerusalem, and other important nobles, also supported by the Templars and the Hospitallers. Humphrey of Toron and Balian II of Ibelin rode back to Saladin's camp where they were welcomed with due honour. Just as the major figures of the Christian side had observed and approved the deal, so now gathered the Muslims.

Humphrey and Balian came forwards and took Saladin's hand as he swore to uphold the peace. The envoys insisted that others took the oath too, an observation on the need to guard against Saladin's possible death and the number of parties who held lands bordering on the Frankish territories. Thus Saphadin swore the oath, as did two of the sultan's sons, al-Afdal and al-Zahir Ghazi. The emirs al-Mashtub, Dildirim and al-Mansur also joined in.

At long last, the years of conflict would be over – for a while, at least. Heralds were sent out to proclaim the peace in the marketplaces and the camps. As Beha al-Din wrote, 'It was a memorable day. Both sides were overwhelmed with such joy and delight as God alone can measure.'[46] He claimed that in reality Saladin was unhappy with the outcome, fearing that it had formalised the Frankish presence on the coast and that they would only grow stronger. Imad al-Din wrote that the sultan made a case for continuing to fight, only for his emirs to hammer home the 'devastation and disarray' of the land, the utter lack of resources and energy of all his people; the crusaders, it was noted, wanted nothing more than to make peace. One suspects that Saladin was fully aware of this but had to make a show of wishing to continue the holy war, because he quickly accepted the advice of his friends and supporters.[47] In his letter to the caliph of Baghdad, Imad al-Din repeatedly placed collective responsibility for the unanimous decision to make peace on the leading emirs and men of religion.[48] It was blindingly obvious that a stalemate had been reached. Saladin's physical, mental and financial reserves were at the end of their tether; the troops were exhausted and, as he had observed in their behaviour at Jaffa, potentially questionable in their commitment; again, in part because of fatigue and a lack of resources. The Muslim Near East had been on a war footing for years; the land had to recover and troops needed to farm their properties. Imad al-Din's letter to the caliph made plain that he expected the crusaders to return, and this was a further reason to strengthen the defences of towns, castles, and above all, Jerusalem. He also made the point that the crusaders too had expended vast resources, thousands of men – and yet, most pertinently of all, they understood that 'the object of their desire is inaccessible'.

Within days, the troops of the two armies began to fraternise. Muslim traders went to Jaffa while the crusaders sought to fulfil their pilgrimage vows and visit Jerusalem. Many of the more distant contingents, such as those from Mosul, Hisn Kayfa, Irbil and Sinjar, started out for home. Saladin himself headed towards Jerusalem, meeting Saphadin en route to the shrine at Nebi Samuel, a few miles short of the holy city. Once again Saphadin had been unwell, but he managed to come and meet his brother, dismounting and kissing the ground as a sign of his respect. Together the two of them rode on to Jerusalem and entered the city with some feeling that, at last, they could relax a little.[49]

With the truce firmly in place, court life could begin to flourish again. Abd al-Latif Baghdadi was one of the foremost intellectuals of the age, a man with knowledge of grammar, law, philosophy, alchemy and especially medicine. This widely travelled man had earlier met the sultan and all his senior officials in his camp outside Acre and, through the patronage of Qadi al-Fadil, he secured a position in Cairo teaching at the mosque founded by the chamberlain (and sometime admiral of the Egyptian fleet) Lu'lu. There he had encountered numerous famous scholars, including Maimonides, the Jewish doctor who had, at times, ministered to Saladin. When Abd al-Latif heard of the peace agreement he hurried over to Jerusalem to see the sultan. In his account of this meeting he was suitably admiring, writing of 'a great sovereign, generous, affectionate and awesome to behold. He filled the hearts of those near and far with love.' He described there an assembly of men of learning, discussing numerous fields of knowledge, including, at one point, a highly practical turn with a review of the fortification of the walls of Jerusalem that featured the sultan's personal expertise. Just as other writers had claimed, Abd al-Latif related how Saladin was reported to have taken a lead in the carrying of stones, labouring from before sunrise until the evening, his work in the holy war barely ceasing. Of course, as with so many of those who thronged around the courts of the leading men of the day, Abd al-Latif was seeking patronage, hoping to earn with his praise of the sultan the financial support that would allow him to lecture in a mosque and, in his case, study the scientific works of the ancients and continue his prolific literary output. Abd al-Latif was successful, and through Saladin and his sons, he arranged a healthy monthly stipend in the Great Mosque and he quickly moved over to Damascus.[50]

Saladin received a number of visiting crusaders as well, treating them with courtesy and respect and ensuring that they were able to travel in safety to and from the coast. Given that the sultan had deliberately kept his distance during the diplomatic dance of the last three years, it was rare for western crusaders to encounter him face to face. One man who we know came to Jerusalem and met him there was Hubert Walter, bishop of Salisbury (later archbishop of Canterbury). His experiences and those of other pilgrims were portrayed by Ambroise. In one episode it is reported that a group of crusaders were careless in organising their escorts to Jerusalem, and some of the Muslims pleaded with Saladin to be allowed to massacre the Christians in revenge for those slaughtered at Acre. But the senior Muslim lords, Dildirim, al-Mashtub and Saphadin, spoke of the need not to break the truce and the sultan insisted on the proper security in order to be seen to be good to his word. Saladin is also reported to have shown the knights the True Cross. In another vignette, the bishop himself is treated with immense respect and presented (inevitably!) with fine gifts before having a meeting with the sultan. Saladin shows him the True Cross too and they talk through interpreters for a long time. At one point the sultan asks for more information about King Richard. In the bishop's reply (or the comments imagined by Ambroise), Richard is described as the best warrior, generous and talented, but 'if one were to take your [Saladin's] qualities and his together, then we will say that nowhere in the world would ever two such princes be found, so valiant and so experienced'. The author's praise of Richard is to be expected; its praise of Saladin we might understand to reflect well on the Lionheart too, showing how the king faced a worthy opponent in the sultan. Saladin then gives his assessment of Richard and, while acknowledging his valour, says that 'he rushes into things so foolishly ... I would prefer to exercise generosity and judgement with moderation, rather than boldness without moderation.'[51] Whether these comments are accurately recorded or not, it was true that Saladin was much less in the habit of leading his troops from the front, a contrast evident to all, especially after Richard's actions at Jaffa. In the course of their conversation, Ambroise relates how the sultan offers the bishop the chance to ask for a gift and in reply Hubert requests that two Latin priests and two deacons should be allowed to worship in the Holy Sepulchre, Bethlehem and Nazareth, giving the Christians at least a token presence at these exalted sites. Saladin duly agrees.

At last, on 10 October 1192, Richard left for home. He vowed to return to the Near East and complete his efforts to recover Jerusalem with, seemingly, a clear plan to attack Egypt as a precursor to making any capture of the holy city sustainable in the long term. Richard, in conjunction with the efforts of the French crusaders, had, nonetheless, given the Franks a viable coastal entity, and with his conquest of Cyprus, an ideal stepping stone to the mainland. Compared to the situation in August 1187 with Tyre on the verge of surrender (before Conrad of Montferrat arrived), this was a transformative step. Richard's reputation as a great warrior had echoed across the Mediterranean, burnished by chroniclers East and West, not least because in Saladin he was up against a man of such standing and achievement.[52]

On the news that Richard had departed, Saladin set out for a quick tour of various fortresses and towns including Nablus, Jenin, Bethsan, Belvoir, then up to Safad and finally over to Beirut. The governor there, Izz al-Din Usama, hosted a great reception where Saladin dispensed many gifts, his habitual generosity remaining undimmed. He distributed a variety of rich cloth, including on this occasion woollen cloth from Europe, presumably acquired from the departing crusaders. He also met Prince Bohemond III of Antioch. This was the moment to affirm the peace arrangement with him, and the grant of a couple of towns near his capital city was a welcome gesture of goodwill. Saladin treated the prince with great courtesy, according him a place of honour at his side, as well as bestowing robes of honour on his fourteen nobles. Bohemond had been rather nervous about the meeting but was suitably charmed and departed with feelings of admiration and gratitude.[53]

Of great delight was, at last, the release of Saladin's most loyal associate, Qaraqush. The master builder of Cairo and then the man charged with leading the final defence of Acre had remained a prisoner throughout the remainder of the crusade. On 20 October he was liberated and, as Beha al-Din rightly noted, 'the sultan and Islam owed him much'.[54] Qaraqush, too, owed much, although in his case it was the cost of his ransom – a hefty 80,000 dinars.[55]

His brief tour complete, Saladin headed towards Damascus. As he approached what had become his 'home', people came out to greet him and to present gifts and tokens to their returning hero. On 4 December he entered the city – a truly memorable day and celebrated with great festivity by all. It was at this point Saladin and his people could feel their labours were at an end, in the medium term at least. Here were his sons al-Afdal and al-Zahir Ghazi (his favourite), al-Zafir and all the others. He could resume giving justice and restore economic order; meanwhile the poets and the holy men of the city visited him, declaimed of his great deeds and waited for his generosity to reward them. As Imad al-Din commented, at the end of this year 'the sultan reached the apogee of his greatness', with his fame at its peak, with lands to the east and the west asking for his support, and a stream of ambassadors arriving at his palace over the next few weeks.[56]

Saladin's relationship with his eldest son al-Afdal continued to be slightly awkward after the rather clumsy allocation to him, and then reallocation to Saphadin, of the lands near the Euphrates. Despite their reunion outside Jerusalem in the summer, a later meeting in the holy city had been difficult. Saladin seems to have recognised the need to make a more public gesture to show that all was well, and when his son al-Zahir Ghazi organised a splendid banquet for his older brother, their father attended by way of an act of goodwill towards his designated successor.[57]

Another sign of this more relaxed ambiance was the opportunity for the family to hunt gazelles, partridges and ducks down in the Hauran and closer to Damascus itself.[58] In Jerusalem Saladin had spoken enthusiastically about making the haj, the pilgrimage that he, for obvious reasons perhaps, had failed to make. Back in the late 1170s, in line with contemporary convention, Saladin had sent a proxy (a prominent Sufi) to make the pilgrimage on his behalf, but now he wanted to go in person.[59] With the military situation calm, he had discussed setting in train the arrangements for a large party of pilgrims to head towards Arabia, possibly via Egypt. In the event little was done to put this into practice, in part because Qadi al-Fadil advised him of the need to secure a better relationship with the caliph in case the latter interpreted the movement eastwards of the sultan, accompanied by a large body of men, as a threat to his own position.

On 19 February 1193 a group of emirs from northern Syria arrived in Damascus, passing through on their way home from Mecca. This was a formal occasion, always witnessed by a large crowd. In the company of al-Afdal the sultan rode out to meet them. This was to be his final public appearance.

21

Peace at Last

*'This was a day such as had not befallen
the Muslims and Islam since the loss of the
rightly guided caliphs'*

By this point Saladin's well-being had started to trouble those close
to him. He had shown signs of severe fatigue and a lack of energy.
His usual sharpness was absent too: forgetting to wear his leather
undergarment in public at the meeting with the pilgrims was out of
character. It also showed the precautions necessary, then as now, for
a major public figure. The day after (20 February) he complained of
a bilious fever coupled with excessive catarrh in the stomach. This can
be brought on by an inability to digest fatty foods, notably meat,
reminding us that Saladin's uncle Shirkuh had died (fairly rapidly) after
eating an excess of rich meats. Catarrh can block the liver duct and
the bile duct, exacerbating the pain. Vomiting of acid and bile can
also occur. Beha al-Din and Qadi al-Fadil faithfully visited the citadel,
sometimes conversing with their bedridden leader, although he was
now troubled by persistent, acute headaches akin to what we might
call a severe migraine. Al-Afdal, at Saladin's request, sat in the sultan's
place during regular court meals, a move seen as an ominous portent.
Doctors were in constant attendance on Saladin, although his primary
doctor was away elsewhere. One doctor bled the patient, but Abd
al-Latif Baghdadi was especially scathing about this man and blamed
his incompetence for Saladin's death. Another medic prescribed a
laxative to try to remove the bile. By the time the illness moved into
its second week, the sultan's mind was starting to wander and he was
suffering from fainting fits.[1]

With no sight of Saladin in public, rumours started to spread; the prospective loss of such a revered man inevitably provoked a mixture of deep sorrow and anxiety over possible political turmoil. By the tenth day, enemas brought the sultan brief relief, but a couple of days of intense fever and perspiration broke his strength completely. His womenfolk started to deny access even to his old companions, a sign that the end was near. Al-Afdal began to take practical measures and summoned a number of emirs to one of the Damascus palaces to swear what was described as a 'precautionary' oath of allegiance to both Saladin and himself. Local emirs, as well as some from northern Syria, complied, although a couple used the opportunity to extract better lands for themselves. Al-Afdal suggested that Beha al-Din and Qadi al-Fadil spend the night in his company, looking to align himself with these pillars of his father's regime. In the event, a Damascene imam was summoned to the palace and sat next to the dying man, reciting the Quran and calling him to remember God.

The end came just after dawn on 4 March 1193 with Qadi al-Fadil and the imam at his side.[2] Imad al-Din wrote: 'With him died the hope of humanity, when the sun went down, the huge area of his rule was covered with darkness; enemies multiplied; the survivors exhausted; the horizons obscured; those who had hoped were disappointed; those who had asked for refuge vanished.'[3] Beha al-Din gives us his sense of the loss: 'This was a day such as had not befallen the Muslims and Islam since the loss of the rightly guided caliphs.'[4] Ibn al-Athir, generally described as a partisan of the Zengids, gave a positive summary of the man who had uprooted his favoured dynasty from its principal seats of power, when he praised the sultan for his generosity, humility, religious learning and forbearance, 'in short, he was a rare individual in his age, with many good qualities and good deeds, mighty in jihad against the infidels, for which his conquests are the proof'.[5]

Al-Afdal received the condolences of the leading emirs, while poetry and sermons were banned in the chamber as a mark of respect. The appearance of Saladin's numerous distraught children added to the atmosphere of grief. As is customary in Islam, the funeral was extremely rapid with the body washed and shrouded before burial. Famously it is reported that the sultan's generosity had almost entirely emptied his personal treasury, leaving only one dinar of Tyre and thirty-six Nasiri dirhams; money had even to be borrowed to complete the burial arrangements because he possessed no houses, gardens or estates himself.[6] Countless benedictions were said over the body, led by the *qadi* of Damascus, Muhyi al-Din, appropriately the man who had delivered the first Friday sermon in the al-Aqsa Mosque that marked Saladin's greatest achievement.

Once the immediate outpouring of grief at the sultan's death had passed, the Ayyubid clan and their client emirs, as well as rivals and neighbours in the Muslim Near East – not to mention the splintered remnants of the Frankish states – started to adjust to life without the most prominent figure on the political landscape. Succession in the Near East was a tricky business and back in the 1170s Saladin himself had ruthlessly exploited the demise of Nur al-Din. The brief machinations that followed the sultan's own serious illness in 1185–6 revealed the potential for trouble around his own dynasty. Then his eldest sons had been too young to take power, but seven years later they were of age. What Saladin never really experienced, largely as a testament to his own personal charisma and authority, was open conflict within his family. There were moments of tension, of course, as well as occasions when he had to cut individuals some slack, such as allowing Taqi al-Din to go to northern Iraq in 1191, along with times where he needed to appease people, including his own son al-Afdal. Yet within months of Saladin's death, the Ayyubids were in chaos.[7]

Initially, all looked well as the twenty-two-year-old Al-Afdal took control of Damascus, but matters soon deteriorated. First the Zengids of northern Syria sought to recover some of their former lands, while in Damascus, al-Afdal struggled to assert his authority over a well-established ruling elite. His father had permitted him little experience of government and he proved unable to keep Saladin's crucial inner circle of advisors around him. Beha al-Din left to take up a position with Saladin's favourite son al-Zahir Ghazi in Aleppo, while Qadi al-Fadil headed back to his original stamping ground in Cairo, taking his skills to the court of al-Aziz Uthman, Saladin's second son, in Egypt.[8]

As early as the spring of 1194 relations between Cairo and Damascus frayed and an armed stand-off between their troops took place outside the Syrian capital in May. The Ayyubids' internal discipline had slipped away with remarkable ease, contaminating the family itself and their client emirs, as well as powerful entities such as the Salahiyya and Asadiyya regiments. The dispatch of Saladin's arms and armour to the caliph of Baghdad were designed to symbolise the sultan's labours on behalf of Islam, as well as to gain approval and endorsement for al-Afdal. One further part of this diplomatic presentation is uncomfortable to modern eyes and jars with Saladin's chivalrous reputation towards women: amongst the gifts were four young Frankish slave girls, including daughters of Balian of Ibelin and Hugh of Jubail, taken after the fall of Jerusalem. Their parents and other siblings had been released long ago, but in spite of their status they were kept, perhaps as a way of humiliating the Franks. The girls' fate in Baghdad is unknown.[9]

Over the next four years, a complex series of campaigns ebbed and flowed between the various groups; while in the background the familiar figure of Saphadin managed to steer a path between his two nephews. When al-Aziz Uthman died unexpectedly in 1198 the emirs of Egypt invited Saphadin to act as regent, in part acknowledging his previous experience in ruling the country on Saladin's behalf. A year later Saphadin became sultan in his own right. Displaying his well-honed political skills he brought the Syrian Ayyubid lands under his authority, earning a diploma of investiture from the caliph as well. The Franks applied occasional pressure, with the German Crusade of 1197–8 recovering Beirut and Sidon, although the Fourth Crusade (1202–4) infamously sacked Christian Constantinople rather than achieving much of note in the Levant.

The ruler of Egypt had the economic wealth of Alexandria and the Nile at his disposal (although a devastating drought in 1203 inflicted terrible suffering on the population), while Damascus was the main cultural and intellectual centre of the Islamic Near East. Saphadin managed to extend his authority into Syria but in reality what had been Saladin's empire existed under the control of the ruling family, rather than one man. Aside from Egypt and Damascus, the cities of Aleppo and Mayyafariqin (in north-eastern Syria) were the main centres of power with a raft of smaller cities underneath, all vying for position. Just as the First Crusade had benefited from the divisions amongst the Muslims of the Levant to establish the Frankish East, a similar pattern re-emerged with different Christian and Muslim groups sometimes working alongside one another against their co-religionists in order to advance their own standing; a sense that the Syrians did not wish to be subject to the authority of Egypt also emerges strongly.

Periodically the Muslims drew together at a time of crisis, such as the Fifth Crusade (1217–21) which captured Damietta and threatened Cairo. In this instance, the arrival of Syrian Ayyubid forces certainly helped to save the day. Yet within a decade, the prospect of Emperor Frederick II of Germany leading a major expedition caused al-Mu'azzam of Damascus to hand over Jerusalem to the Christians, rather than face a possible alliance between the crusaders and his brother, al-Kamil of Egypt. Disregarding al-Mu'azzam's pragmatic assessment that this was only an interim measure, this apparent betrayal of the holy places caused outrage. We may be certain that Saladin himself would not have endorsed such an approach, not least because of the effort required to recover the city in the first instance.

There is a sense that the jihad spirit so carefully fostered by Nur al-Din and Saladin was in decline. This may hold true in the sense that the lesser jihad, that is fighting the enemies of the faith in the world, was less prominent because in the years after Saladin's death the Franks posed only a minimal threat to the Ayyubids. The greater or internal jihad, however, came strongly to the fore with a huge growth in places of learning in Damascus especially, often sponsored by Ayyubid family members and particularly by women.[10] Jihad poetry and treatises were composed and circulated as well. The thirteenth century, across both the Ayyubid and the subsequent Mamluk dynasties, was also the era in which historians and biographers such as Abu Shama, Ibn al-Athir, Sibt Ibn al-Jawzi, Ibn al-Adim, Ibn Khallikan and Ibn Wasil wrote their accounts of the period, often looking back to the previous century with admiring eyes and delivering a significant corpus of material concerning Saladin and Nur al-Din.[11]

The 1230s was a low point for family unity and it was not until the sultan al-Salih Ayyub established his power in Egypt that, with the assistance of various allies, Jerusalem was recovered in 1244. But the conjunction of a series of powerful external threats, coupled with destructive internal squabbling, soon brought the Ayyubid dynasty to breaking point. The fall of Jerusalem to the latest invaders from the east, the Khwarazmians, prompted the Seventh Crusade (1248–54), a major expedition led by Louis IX of France, a man of immense personal piety determined to advance the Christian cause. Disastrously for the

Ayyubids, Sultan al-Salih Ayyub's successor, Turanshah, then alienated one of the powerful army factions, the Bahriyya Mamluks. These highly trained soldiers had become central to the regime in Egypt, and when the young sultan tried to place his own northern Syrian associates in positions of power there, the Mamluks rose in revolt. In spite of desperate efforts to escape, the Ayyubid sultan was left lying dead on the banks of the Nile, an ignominious fate. His father's slave concubine, Shajar al-Durr, was proclaimed sultana, an extraordinarily rare instance of female rule, but when she was pushed aside a few months later, this marked the effective end of Ayyubid authority in Egypt.[12] Turanshah had, in fact, helped to defeat Louis' crusade yet it was the Mamluks who derived the benefit of seeing this dangerous expedition shattered.

But around the same time, the most serious threat to Ayyubid power – and indeed to Sunni Islam – was gathering momentum elsewhere.[13] Further to the east, the Mongols, central Asian nomads, had appeared periodically in Persia since the 1220s, and were now looking to extend their conquests into the Near East. In 1258 they tore into Baghdad, obliterated the city and slaughtered the caliph. Swiftly moving eastwards they ejected the Ayyubid rulers of Damascus and Aleppo – taking cities the crusaders had never captured – to terminate the last major centres of Ayyubid power.

The Mamluks, however, managed to resist and at the Battle of Ayn Jalut, fighting against a small Mongol army, they won a famous victory. Soon afterwards the Mongol force retreated, probably on account of a lack of pasture and the need to elect a new great khan. In a fashion that Saladin's publicity machine would have been proud of, the Mamluks claimed that the Battle of Ayn Jalut had saved Sunni Islam. This sign of divine approval for the new regime became one of the defining moments in Egyptian history, recalled on many occasions down to the modern age. With the ruthless leadership of the Sultan Baibars (1260–77), the Mamluks extended their power in Syria where they continued to resist the Mongols, and over the next few decades picked off the Franks' remaining fortresses and cities, until in May 1291 the fall of Acre marked the end of Christian rule in the Holy Land.

The fact that Saladin's dynasty held on to Egypt only until 1250 and lost Damascus in 1260 has led some to dismiss it as lightweight and to intimate that Saladin was in some ways responsible for failing to put down proper foundations.[14] Yet such charges do not take into account the basic parameters within which his empire operated. As the sultan himself fully appreciated, Egypt, Syria and the Jazira were areas of vastly contrasting history and character. While his own fecundity in producing perhaps seventeen sons added to the problem, the fact that they lacked the ability or determination to preserve a sense of unity, in the face of such diversity, was out of his control.

In spite of several huge expeditions, and a brief period of rule over Jerusalem from 1229 to 1244, the crusaders never managed to restore a presence anything like the one which Saladin had so shattered at Hattin in the summer of 1187. Ultimately, while it was the Mamluks who succeeded in terminating the crusader states, it was the Ayyubid sultan who had broken their power. Without the unifying call provided by the recovery of Jerusalem, and lacking perhaps the political dexterity of Saladin, his successors lost two of their dynasty's greatest attributes: cohesion and clan loyalty.

PART II

Afterlife

On 8 November 1898 the shadowy calm of Saladin's mausoleum was disturbed by the arrival of some unusual visitors. Pilgrims and travellers had paid their respects to the sultan down the centuries but none had the global standing of Kaiser Wilhelm II of Germany. As the nineteenth century drew to a close, Wilhelm sought to advance German power through forming closer ties with Sultan Abdul Hamid II and the Ottoman Empire. In the late autumn of 1898, he followed a major state visit to Istanbul with a journey to Palestine and Syria.[1]

An enthusiastic reception from the Damascenes delighted Wilhelm and his wife Auguste Viktoria, and the imperial couple began their tour with an inspection of the city's centrepiece, the magnificent Umayyad Mosque. Just adjacent to the spiritual heart of Damascus stands Saladin's mausoleum. As the imperial party entered they were confronted by not one but two tombs (see picture section). By the 1870s the wooden original had been showing understandable signs of wear and tear, a situation that prompted the local governor to give orders to smarten it up. More dramatically, Sultan Abdul Hamid II had commissioned a marble cenotaph to stand next to the thirteenth-century wooden sarcophagus, a timing that likely reflected Abdul Hamid's wish to bolster his image in Syria after the sweeping territorial losses his lands suffered at the Congress of Berlin in 1878. An inscription linked him to the Ayyubid ruler as a warrior who defended both his people and his faith against invaders. The cenotaph itself is of an Ottoman baroque style, a mark of modernity at the time, and it remains in place today, looking uncomfortably bulky next to its venerable stablemate.[2]

Inside the mausoleum the empress laid a fine bronze wreath on the Ottoman tomb.[3] Wilhelm himself was reported to have remained silent at this point; he then spread his hands, a gesture the local press understood as a request for mercy for the dead. Later that evening the Ottoman governor hosted a splendid dinner party at which the kaiser emphasised the bonds of friendship between the two regimes and his own peaceful intentions.[4] In attendance was the British diplomat William Shortland Richards, who reported the kaiser's words:

> I remember that I am now in a city in which once lived the greatest prince whose name is recorded in history, the valorious hero, who by his courage, his elevation and nobility of character and his devotion to his religion was an example in heroism even to his enemies. I refer to the great sultan Saladin of the dynasty of Ayyub when I think of this.[5]

For a man of this profile to lavish such praise on Saladin undoubtedly cast a sharp spotlight on the sultan, especially in the Near East where the kaiser's words were widely reported by the emerging Arab press across Syria, Lebanon and Egypt. The way in which this was done indicates that Saladin's deeds and personality were familiar to the readership; the newspapers had no need to introduce him. The new Egyptian weekly, Al-Manar, outlined why Wilhelm praised Saladin: 'William II is a warrior because he is the leader of the best army of the world. Salah al-Din was the best warrior of his time. It is typical of man that somebody distinguished by something will pay respect to his equal.'

The newspaper al-Mu'ayyad argued that the kaiser was drawn towards Saladin's honourable characteristics, and so, setting aside the fact that Wilhelm was 'propagating Christianity in the nineteenth century while Salah al-Din was protecting and propagating Islam' in the medieval age, he became like him. Writers warned of the 'greedy vultures flying eagerly over the lands of the Ottoman Empire', a reference to British, French and Russian interests in the Near East, yet in the person of Saladin was a man who had successfully defended Islam against the invading crusaders.[6]

Ahmad Shawqi, at the time a court poet for the Egyptian viceroy and an Ottoman patriot (he was later an Arab nationalist), wrote a poem for the occasion and the following year produced a piece in *al-Mu'ayyad* in which he said that after the first four rightly guided caliphs, no Muslims were more meritorious than Saladin and the Ottoman Sultan Mehmet II (conqueror of Constantinople in 1453). He wondered how Muslim writers had been so tardy to awaken to their memory; as we will see, a largely rhetorical question rather than a wholly realistic assessment of the contemporary standing of these two heroes, especially Saladin.[7]

For Saladin to be so attractive and so relevant to these two diametrically different constituencies – the inhabitants of the Levant, and one of the most powerful figures in Europe – is an intriguing and, in some respects, an extraordinary situation, not least because he had been dead for over 700 years by this point. How and why could he hold such appeal for both a western European emperor and the people of the Near East?

The remainder of the book follows this detective trail down the centuries, looking firstly at his reputation in the West where it ranges from his demonisation as the man who captured Jerusalem to the figure so lionised by Kaiser Wilhelm. In parallel to this we can explore how Saladin's memory also endured in the Near East – despite the consensus across decades of historians that Saladin and the crusades were more or less forgotten there until Kaiser Wilhelm's visit – and see why it became so enfolded in the popular psyche that by the end of the nineteenth century the local press could take it for granted. Down into the twentieth century, hugely stimulated by contemporary events, the image of Saladin came to be utilised again and again. Inevitably intertwined with this is the legacy of the crusades in the Near East, an issue that has evoked (and continues to evoke) powerful emotions and often forms a basic context for engaging with the sultan's memory.

People connect with the past in a multiplicity of different ways, and many of the ideas and sentiments expressed about Saladin have coalesced to form a series of collective memories.[8] Saladin's life story was such as to be attractive (or indeed repellent to some, of course) and accessible to an incredible array of players. His durability lies in a combination of the intrinsic importance of some of these events and the kaleidoscopic variety of circumstances that his career and character can be adapted to fit. Strict accuracy, as best as we can discern it anyway, is not always the priority of those invoking Saladin – and why should it be? Headline images and propaganda care little for nuance, and in any case, what is deemed 'true' by historians in one era can be disregarded by later generations.[9] At its heart, cultural memory depends largely on contemporary interests and these naturally change and evolve over time and space. In other words, memories and images are related to contemporary situations and put the strictly objectivised meaning into their own perspective. It is that which gives them relevance.[10] With this in mind, many of the reasons why Saladin's image has demonstrated such extraordinary resonance become apparent.

22

Saladin's Reputation in the West

'Think of generous Saladin; he said that
a king's hands should have holes in them'

Saladin is a man of myriad guises in the memory and the imagination of the West. The sheer diversity on display is astonishing: time traveller, master of disguise, a just ruler and a pillar of nobility, or an unscrupulous chancer, a rapist and tormenter of the Christian faith are just a few of the vices or virtues attributed to the sultan. The starting point for what ultimately became a positive characterisation was an unlikely one. The capture of Christendom's most holy sanctuary by 'the son of Satan' inflicted immeasurable spiritual harm on the West, yet over time, a blend of fact and fiction came to dilute and then to transform Saladin's image.

In every instance, it is the particular context and audience that steer such perceptions, but because the Muslim conquest of Jerusalem was such a profound blow to the people of western Europe – to some, a sign of the impending apocalypse – any change in attitude towards the author of this calamity warrants our attention. For the transformation to be, at times, so complete and certainly so durable, running down even to the present day, is curious. Given this longevity, the framework is vast, drawing in the centuries-long history of crusading and encompassing the evolving relationship between Christians and Muslims. From beneath these great themes Saladin has emerged to hold an overwhelmingly positive image in the West. It is, I would venture, impossible to think of another figure from history who dealt such a deep wound to a people and a faith, and yet became so admired.

The Saladin whom we encounter is, in many senses, a literary construct, yet one with tangible historical foundations, upon which have accumulated layer upon layer of authorial agenda and aspiration.

The Latin West first learned of Saladin through reports of his involvement in Shirkuh's campaigns to Egypt. As Saladin's power in Egypt and then Syria increased, so grew a recognition of the threat that he posed.[1] Any image of the sultan would feed into existing western views of the Muslims – or pagan Saracens, as they were usually known – and these were in large part hostile, especially where actual ownership of the holy places was at issue.[2] But in the context of warfare there emerged something more positive – a tradition of the valiant Muslim opponent. This was, in part, the matter of needing to have a worthwhile adversary against whom to show oneself, but also a sense that the warrior classes could share a measure of mutual respect. An anonymous writer on the First Crusade wrote: 'They [the Turks] have a saying that they are of common stock with the Franks, and that no men, except the Franks and themselves, are naturally born to be knights. This is true ... you could not find stronger, or braver or more skilful soldiers; and yet by God's grace they were beaten by our men.'[3]

The crushing defeat at the Battle of Hattin and the fall of Jerusalem entirely obscured such views and transformed Saladin's profile. This unprecedented tragedy triggered appeals to the people of Europe to liberate Christ's sanctuary from the man who had delivered such a terrible blow, a man of 'evil ... sated with Christian blood'; 'the whore of Babylon', drunk on the blood of saints; the individual responsible for having the Cross removed 'from the Temple of the Lord and publicly beaten for two days as it was being carried around the city'.[4] This was not the time to seek shared values but a moment to accentuate and to emphasise differences between the Christian West and 'the filthy Saladin and his sect'.[5]

An angry and vicious Latin poem presented the sultan as a man of lowly origins also responsible for the murders of the Fatimid caliph, plus Nur al-Din and his son, as well as the rape of Nur al-Din's wife. For Joachim of Fiore, the influential Calabrian mystic, the stakes were even higher. In Joachim's understanding of the Apocalypse, the Prophet Muhammad and Saladin took key roles in the approach of the Last Days. The sultan featured as one of the seven heads of the Beast of the Apocalypse, as a stunning manuscript illustration by Joachim's pupils revealed to Richard the Lionheart in late 1190 (see picture section). The opening chapters of one of the earliest accounts of the Third Crusade, the *Itinerarium peregrinorum*, accused the sultan of living off the workings of prostitutes in Damascus and killing the caliph; he was characterised as a fortuitous, opportunistic chancer. Saladin was often described as a stick, a scourge sent by God to beat the Christians for their sins or, as one writer put it, if Nur al-Din was a stick, then Saladin was a hammer.[6] To compound these spiritual matters, the sultan's victories in the Holy Land prompted the kings of England and France to launch the 'Saladin tithe', a punishing 10% levy on revenues and movables; to have one's name attached to a major tax rarely constitutes an attractive legacy.[7]

But amidst this hail of invective, one crucial plank in the construction of a more positive image had already been put in place, namely the incontrovertible fact that Saladin had not massacred the Christian defenders of Jerusalem, a stark antithesis to the savagery meted out to its Muslim inhabitants by the armies of the First Crusade. Setting aside that he may initially have been inclined to act harshly, and that in 1187 the garrison of Jerusalem negotiated a surrender in a way that those in 1099 had not done so, this distinctive and contrasting aspect in the fall of the holy city was, once the trauma of its loss had been absorbed, something very much in his favour.[8]

The duration of the Third Crusade brought westerners into contact with the Muslims and the Levantine Franks for a considerable period of time. This was, of course, a holy war, an armed struggle to secure authority over, or to share control of, the holy places in Jerusalem. Yet the campaign also generated substantial diplomatic interaction between the crusaders and the Muslims. A few of the crusaders actually encountered Saladin himself, such as Guy of Senlis, the French royal butler, who was treated with great courtesy before he was packed off to prison in Damascus. Many more dealt with the sultan's brother, Saphadin, whose admirable charm did much to keep diplomatic channels open; Richard himself faced criticism for becoming too amicable with him. The apparent camaraderie between the crusader nobles and Saladin's emirs at Jaffa in 1192, with reports of Muslims being knighted, speaks to a similar theme.[9] By the end of the crusade, it seems that the Muslims, and Saladin and Saphadin in particular, did not entirely match the caricatures that had been ascribed to them. The crusaders, especially Richard, also needed to accept that while they had achieved some notable military successes, Jerusalem remained elusive. This required explanation, and the quality – and indeed, the qualities – of their opponents helped them to do this. Ralph the Black, writing in 1193, was a critic of crusading, and the Muslims and the Franks of the Levant, yet standing alone above this wicked scene was Saladin, 'a man of indescribable glory, raised high by victories unheard of'.[10] Saladin came to emerge from the crusade as a man of generosity, integrity, faith and culture. These were, of course, in his own terms, signs of *adab* and entirely appropriate, or indeed necessary, for a man of his status.[11] In the West they found a loose parallel in the gradually evolving set of practices wrapped up under the broad and elastic label of chivalry.

It is remarkable how quickly aspects of Saladin's positive personal reputation gained wider cultural acceptance in Europe.[12] Writing before 1208, the German court poet Walther von der Vogelweide criticised his master, Philip of Swabia, the king of Germany, for not dishing out small sums of money when times were good, as against the need to hand over much larger amounts to secure allegiance when it was required urgently. Walther saw that the act of giving gained admiration and honour and he regarded generosity as a marker of lordship:

> King Philip, those who observe you closely accuse you of not being
>   generous voluntarily
> It seems to me that you lose much more than that.
> You might more gladly give a thousand pounds voluntarily than thirty
>   thousand involuntarily
> You do not know how one acquires esteem and honour through giving.
> Think of generous Saladin; he said that a king's hands should have
>   holes in them;
> In that way they would be feared and also loved ...
> One loss is good if it brings two gains.

Walter was, therefore, endorsing Saladin's own model of behaviour and one of the most prominent characteristics of his rule. More significantly, he demonstrated that around a decade after the sultan's death his reputation for generosity in Europe was such that he could

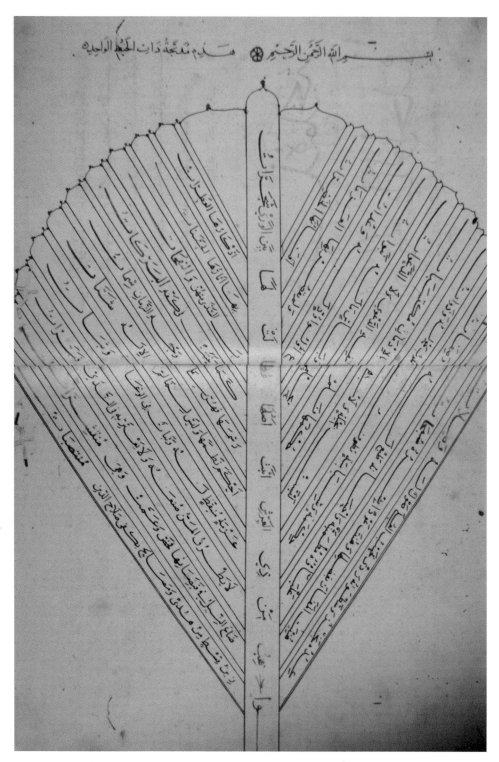

One of the many complex and highly decorative poems composed for the sultan by al-Jilyani, a physician and writer. This example of his work is in the shape of a tree and praises Saladin's generosity.

Saladin initiated a major building programme in Cairo in the 1170s including this new section of the city walls, recently excavated by the Aga Khan Foundation.

Mosque and water wheels in Hama, Syria, a complex originally constructed by Nur al-Din in 1164.

Gold dirham of Saladin from AH 586/1190 CE.

Silver half-dirham of Saladin from Aleppo, AH 580/1184–5, featuring a six-pointed star, linking the sultan to the Quranic prophet and king, Solomon.

This depiction of Saladin from Thomas Fuller's *History of the Holy Warre*, published in England in 1639, highlights the sultan's enduring reputation in the West for personal austerity.

A postage stamp of
Saladin issued in Syria
during the 1930s under
the French mandate;
it uses a representation
of the sultan that
has been displayed
alongside his tomb
since the 1870s.

Palestinian artists often painted pictures of Saladin as they recalled his victories over the West.
Here Mubarak Saad's 1945 work shows the sultan's triumphal entry into Jerusalem in 1187.

President Nasser of Egypt (with the future President Sadat, behind to his right) visiting Saladin's tomb in Damascus with the president of Syria, al-Quwatli, as the two countries forged the short-lived United Arab Republic, February 1958.

President Hafiz al-Asad often linked himself to Saladin's legacy; here his image is imposed in front of a painting of the Battle of Hattin.

Stamps and coins are a highly visible means for modern regimes to connect Saladin's life and achievements to the present day. Above, a First Day Cover from Egypt celebrates the 800th anniversary of the sultan's birth. To the left, Saladin represents a powerful symbol of Kurdish identity and is shown on a coin from Iraqi Kurdistan of 2003. Below, a stamp issued in the aftermath of the Suez Crisis (1956) indicates the fate of those who attack Egypt or her rulers, hence 'Tomb of the Aggressors', recalling Saladin's great victory over the Franks at Hattin in 1187.

Jordan is another modern country to draw upon Saladin's legacy, marked by this equestrian statue of the sultan in the town of Kerak, the scene of three long sieges by the sultan's forces.

Saladin featured in a lively 2010 Malaysian television cartoon, aiming to showcase many admirable facets of his character within a series of historically-based adventures.

Saladin's image is used by demonstrators in Nablus on the West Bank, marking the anniversary of the Second Intifada, 29 September 2001, and making the point to President George W. Bush that the legacy of their great hero is one of victory over the West.

Damascus, 2009: Saladin leads his troops in a scene from the Enana Dance Group's energetic portrayal of the sultan's success at Hattin and conquest of Jerusalem.

be unblinkingly imagined as a benchmark for one of the basic identi-
fiers of a good monarch. Saladin's faith was not mentioned, although
this may be understood to shame Philip further. The essential point
remains: the sultan's standing was comfortably sufficient for him to
hold a place of esteem within high-level political and cultural debate
in the medieval West.[13]

Not every reference to Saladin was framed in positive terms. A
seemingly unique turn of phrase was coined by Bishop Vincentius of
Cracow in the *Chronica Polonorum*, written prior to 1208 at the request
of Kazimierz II, *princeps* of Poland. The latter led an expedition against
a pagan Prussian tribe in 1192, in part inspired by the recent crusade
preaching. Vincentius wrote that the prince 'has the whole army
receive the salving Host and the Holy Sacrifice ... Rightly so because
those who were to fight against the *Saladinistas*, against the enemies
of the Holy Faith, against the shameful idolators, should trust in the
shield of their Faith rather than their weapons.' The meaning of this
seemingly newly minted word was obvious to all. With his use of
Saladinistas, that is, kinsmen of Saladin, the author was showing his
Polish audience the merit of the fight against the Prussians, and in
giving them parity with the conqueror of Jerusalem he tried to link
the threat posed by the pagans to that of the Christian world's great
contemporary bogeyman.[14]

By the second decade of the thirteenth century, as some writers
looked to praise Richard and thereby came to accommodate
Saladin's positive characteristics into their narrative, his image grew
further. Translations and continuations of William of Tyre's history
circulated widely in the West and they added to a softening image
of the conqueror of Jerusalem. Witness, for example, the story of
the sultan allowing Balian of Ibelin's two young sons to leave the
siege of Jerusalem unharmed and treated with kindness and respect.
Likewise, his decision not to bombard the chamber of the newly-
weds Humphrey of Toron and Isabella of Jerusalem during the
siege of 1184.[15]

The loss of Jerusalem became assimilated into the western psyche
and Saladin came to evolve a separate life, a literary career, alongside
the narratives of the crusades and the ongoing efforts to recover the
holy city. One way in which he came to experience such longevity,
based initially on the accounts of the Third Crusade and the reports

that came back from the Holy Land, was through a process of drawing him into the life of the West. He was far less 'the other' but became adopted and absorbed into European culture and values; while the Holy Land may have been lost to Saladin, with time and distance, the West managed to 'capture' him.[16]

Historical legends, such as Richard and Saladin fighting in single combat, circulated freely by the 1250s. To preserve the inconvenient truth that these two central figures never met denied an author the chance to formulate a climactic encounter between the two great men. Various verse accounts of the struggle emerged in Middle English and Old French by the mid-thirteenth century and the duel became the subject of artistic works too, with King Henry III of England commissioning such an image for his palace at Clarendon in 1251.[17]

Romantic stories, some of which were intended to help recruit crusaders, as well as to entertain, embedded the sultan much more deeply into the consciousness of the West. From the middle of the thirteenth century emerged *La fille du comte de Ponthieu*, a story that circulated in its own right and was also taken up and incorporated into other popular texts such as the Old French *History of Outremer and the Birth of Saladin*. In this complicated tale of abduction and adventure it emerges that Saladin was descended on his mother's side from the counts of Ponthieu, a powerful northern French family, thought to be the original patrons of the piece. With Saladin's great-grandmother providing the bloodline, this was a sufficient distance from anyone alive yet offered the reflected prestige of a tie to the great sultan. The story proved highly popular and a later epic poem simplified it by cutting out the intervening generations to make Saladin's mother the lady of Ponthieu.[18]

The sultan's increasing reputation as a towering exemplar of honour, generosity and courtesy was fertile ground for what had become a central aspect of cultural life in medieval Europe, namely, chivalry.[19] The chivalric ethos emerged from the shared identity of elite mounted warriors and was a sign of status and fighting prowess. But by the end of the twelfth century it had come to include a moral code in which the very values that Saladin's behaviour, and the stories accruing around him, seemed to match. The text known as *The Order of Chivalry* proved immensely popular and was widely diffused (in variant forms) across the West. The story had the Frankish noble Hugh of Tiberias as a prisoner of the Muslims. Saladin asked to be instructed in the practices of chivalry but at first Hugh refused, exclaiming that the stench of unbelief could not be hidden under the silken cloth of chivalry.[20] Yet by the end of the prose version of the tale Saladin had been dubbed a knight. Placing him at the centre of the story demonstrated his standing as a man who represented the values so esteemed, and in reverse, reflected prestige on the ritual itself. Here the ceremony was a secular event; there was here no promise to defend the Church, which was one reason why Saladin could be involved. In this instance chivalry was a secular 'club' that could embrace the heroes of antiquity and the sultan with equal ease.[21]

Saladin's repertoire of talents soon extended further. He frequently became a master of disguise, and texts in Middle Dutch, Old French and Occitan, as well as works produced in Italy and Spain, bear testimony to his character's wide literary appeal. Such skills enabled him to come to the West to learn more about, variously, the Christian faith, the strength of western Europe (a sort of pre-crusade recce), and to meet western ladies. The Saladin of literature had a prolific romantic career in Europe. Occasionally he was rebuffed, but there was a long list of other conquests, including the chronological challenge of Eleanor of Aquitaine. Setting aside the fact that Saladin was aged only eleven when she was in the Near East, the Minstrel of Rheims, author of a collection of entertaining anecdotes and stories from the crusades, tells us that Eleanor, fed up with the rather dull Louis VII, learned of the prowess, wisdom and generosity of Saladin. She offered to renounce her faith and to be his lady. The sultan sent a ship to collect her but a servant warned Louis and the escape bid was foiled. When asked by the king to explain herself she answered that Louis was not worth 'a rotten apple. And I have heard so much good said about Saladin that I love him more than you.' The couple returned home and the king repudiated her. Multiple variations on this tale emerged in the popular imagination, all glossing the image of Eleanor as a flighty adventuress and of Saladin as a glamorous and charming infidel.[22]

With his knightly worth, his romantic allure and an ability to visit the Latin West incognito, it was only one small step further to bring Saladin into the Christian fold. Crusade epics frequently included tales of an admirable opponent who converted to Christianity which implies this was a reasonably familiar path, although not for a man of such high profile. Another literary tradition that first dates from the eleventh century is that of a parable that weighs up the claims of Christianity, Islam and Judaism, and by the late thirteenth century Saladin began to feature in these stories, most fully realised by Boccaccio (see below). A further variant was the sultan, on his deathbed, ordering a debate between the caliph of Baghdad, the wisest of the Jews and the patri- arch of Jerusalem.

It was the populist Minstrel of Rheims who finally ushered Saladin over the religious boundary line, albeit not entirely without a whiff of ambiguity. Given the understandable presence of the sultan's family at his deathbed he had to perform a covert auto-baptism, asking for a bowl of water, making a secret sign of the cross and then pouring the water over his head and muttering three words in French that no one managed to catch. Needless to say, other authors repeated the story, or something akin, with one widely circulated version conflating the religious debate with the auto-baptism. Regardless of the utter implausibility of these various scenarios, the basic point remains that Saladin possessed many of the virtues that the West admired. These 'compensating fictions' enabled writers to embrace him in their literary and historical worlds, deflecting from the harsh reality of his achieve- ments and forming a more attractive and palatable alternative.[23]

Within the *Divine Comedy*, Dante's landmark narrative poem completed in 1320, are the three divisions of Hell, Purgatory and Paradise. In the first circle of Hell stands a fine castle reserved for noble pagans and in the main inhabited by classical poets, philosophers and heroes, unable to enter heaven, but nonetheless entirely worthy of comfort and recognition. Only three Muslims are allowed to join them. Two of them, Ibn Sina (Avicenna) and Ibn Rushd (Averroes), were philosophers; the third, 'by himself, apart', was Saladin, the only man to have tangibly inflicted damage upon Christendom, yet by virtue of his character, present in this privileged company. Dante's poetry also recalled Saladin's munificence.[24]

A few decades later Giovanni Boccaccio wrote his influential *Decameron*, a collection of stories within which Saladin appeared prom- inently on two occasions, displaying his famous generosity, acuity and good graces. Boccaccio later produced his *On the Fates of Famous Men* in which Saladin featured as one of the fifty-six individuals selected.[25] In

Castile, the nobleman Don Juan Manuel wrote his *Luanor* in the 1340s and deployed Saladin as an interlocutor on contemporary politics and moral life. In his search of the most important human virtue, chivalry, he travelled into France and to the papacy, his Muslim origins far removed from the southern Iberian and North African Moors encountered by the author at the time.[26] Soon after this, the Italian poet and scholar Petrarch composed *The Triumph of Fame* in which he wrote that the foremost figure amongst the furthest tribes was 'mighty Saladin, his country's boast, the scourge and terror of the baptised host'.[27]

As was evident to all, Saladin was a man of huge generosity. At his death, contemporary Muslim sources reported that he was practically penniless, and from this vein probably emerged another enormously pervasive anecdote.[28] As he lay dying the sultan supposedly commanded one of his retainers to walk through his lands bearing a shroud or shirt suspended on a spear and to proclaim that this was the only possession that he would take with him when he died. It was a story that quickly made its way across to the Franks. Jacques of Vitry, a leading churchman of the early thirteenth century and a man usually highly critical of the sultan, employed it in his sermon *c.*1213–21 on a good death; worldly possessions should be shunned and Saladin's humility was cited as a particularly fine exemplar. The Dominican Stephen of Bourbon took up the tale as did many more preachers and historians; likewise chroniclers repeated it across France, in Italy, Spain and the Netherlands.[29]

While it is easy enough to cite what can be familiar instances of Saladin's presence in famous works it is worth tracing the wider diffusion of some of these images. From the latter decades of the fifteenth century the emergence of printing presses slowly began to bridge the gap between elite and popular cultures in western Europe. Rising literacy was both a trigger and a response to this, meaning there was a growing market for the printed word, from its most elevated form to the most trivial. Between 1660 and 1800 it is argued that over 300,000 book and pamphlet titles appeared in England alone, producing sales of perhaps 200 million copies. The issue of the reception of texts involving Saladin is difficult to ascertain; were they regarded as fact, or fiction, or both? In the broadest sense, their very existence, coupled with their range of literary use, is arguably of sufficient relevance to our present purpose.[30] Three, of many extant examples that are entirely unrelated (in terms of authorship), serve to show how the theme of the vanity of earthly power could reference Saladin.

Matthieu Coignet was a French lawyer and royal advisor whose advice book *Instruction aux princes pour garder la foi promise* of 1583 was swiftly translated into English; here the tale of the shroud was related in the context of the humility of kings.[31] In 1653, William Ramsey, a physician and astrologer, wrote *An Introduction to the Knowledge of the Stars*, and in a lengthy opening section he reflected on God's power and that when humans died, they took nothing of material value with them, thus: 'you have heard what the great conqueror of the East, Saladin, carried to his grave of all he had gained: but a black shirt'.[32] Here the hero of Islam is slotted comfortably alongside, and into, Christian theology. Finally, in 1781, the Scottish Enlightenment figure Henry Home, Lord Kames, wrote his *Loose hints upon education, chiefly concerning the culture of the heart* and was pleased to praise the actions of a man for whom 'there was no vanity here, but an angelic moderation preserved amid illustrious victories'.[33] The didactic potential of this tale was plainly too strong to resist.

Not all of these stories were in as weighty a context, and accounts of Saladin's amorous adventures were likewise circulated and repeated in multiple forms, just one example being the translation of *The Royal Mistresses of France, Secret History of the Amours of all the French Kings*, in 1695. The sultan's romantic liaison with Eleanor of Aquitaine is enthusiastically reported with her attraction to the young warrior easily explained: ''Twas said of him he was a person well shaped, nimble in all manner of exercises, valiant, generous, liberal, courtly, and in a word, that he was endowed with French manners.'[34]

More serious historical enquiry concerning the crusades in this period tended to divide on confessional lines, although by the seventeenth century more nationalisitic readings of (often) French scholars were set against a background of ongoing tensions with the Ottomans; within this Saladin could emerge creditably as the dignified conqueror of Jerusalem. In 1639, Thomas Fuller produced his successful *Historie of the Holy Warre*. The frontispiece features an image of the sultan framed by the phrase 'This black shirt is all Saladin, conqueror of the East, hath to his grave', perpetuating this popular belief. In the text itself, Fuller suggested that historians often described princes as how they should be rather than how they were, 'but finding this Saladin so generally commended of all writers, we have no cause to distrust his character'.[35]

Another curious signal of cultural admiration is the use of Saladin as a given, or first, name. By 1241 we find a man called Saladin of Garsington, located just south-east of Oxford, standing as surety in a land case involving, of all people, the Knights Hospitaller.[36] Documents from the northern Italian city of Genoa contain several charters witnessed by individuals named 'Saladinus', including one from the illustrious Doria family.[37] So, just a few decades after the Battle of Hattin and the fall of Jerusalem it was, apparently, acceptable to carry the name of the hammer of the Christians. The most enduring example of this concerns the lords of Anglure in Champagne. From the fourteenth century onwards tales appear in which Saladin chose to release a French knight from prison in order that the man could travel home to gather his ransom. When he was unable to raise the money he returned to Saladin only for the sultan to be so impressed by this honourable behaviour that he set him free on three conditions: the man should add Muslim crescents to his coat of arms, adopt 'Damascus!' as his battle cry, and that his firstborn son, and that of future generations, should be called Saladin. Whatever the origins of this, the name Saladin d'Anglure was found in the late thirteenth century and is still in existence today.[38]

By nice connection, Rifa'a Rafi al-Tahtawi, a man sent to Paris as part of an Egyptian educational mission in the 1820s and later the author of an influential account of his encounter with Enlightenment Europe, made friends with a Treasury official named Jules Saladin. This man was, he reported, the 'offspring of a great family called "the Saladins" whose name goes back to Salah al-Din al-Ayyubi'.[39]

It is as well to restate, however, that on occasion Saladin's actions in capturing Jerusalem meant that he was restored to his twelfth-century status as an agent of the Devil, although here within the framework of Christian sectarian tension. Daniel Defoe was a Protestant Dissenter and in his *Political History of the Devil* of 1726 the crusades were a 'religious madness called in those days Holy Zeal to recover the Terra Sancta ... though true religion says it was the accursed city and not worth spending one drop of blood for ... This religious bubble was certainly of Satan who ... animated the immortal Saladin against them.'[40] Just to make a further point about diffusion,

Defoe's book was itself owned by the author George Eliot who has a character read it in her novel *Mill on the Floss*.[41]

A landmark moment in the reception of Saladin in the West was the first translation from Arabic to Latin of Beha al-Din's account of the sultan's life by Schultens (1732), which enabled the voice of one of his closest admirers to be heard for the first time with relative ease. The author also included a selection from Imad al-Din's *Fath al-Qussi*. As we have seen, Beha al-Din was largely very positive about his master, and in effect the appearance of this text added another highly favourable witness to the sultan's corner. The translation of further Arabic narratives was a slow and complicated affair with many of the projects struggling to see the light of day, hampered further by contemporary editorial practices which meant they omitted material adjudged irrelevant, such as much of the poetry from Abu Shama, and provided poor-quality translations into the bargain.[42]

By the time of the Enlightenment the crusades were subject to withering disdain. Voltaire viewed the campaigns as an irrational and pointless exercise. Saladin, however, emerged in a more positive light as a tolerant, civilised character. In the 1750s Voltaire chose to blend some of the history with a couple of the more legendary aspects of the sultan's reputation, including his single combat with Richard and deathbed auto-baptism.[43]

Soon after this, François-Louis-Claude Marin published the first western language *Histoire du Saladin* (1758), a serious scholarly attempt to evaluate the sultan. In the context of Enlightenment criticism of 'fanatical' religions, and a view of Muslim rulers as cruel and ruthless despots, Saladin emerges remarkably well, governing through moderation, generosity and clemency. The author was unconvinced by the stories of Saladin's various romantic adventures in the West, although he indicated his belief that the sultan had been dubbed a knight. 'Finally,' Marin concluded, 'an astonished Europe admired in a Muslim, virtues unknown to the Christians of that century.'[44] In terms of profile, mention must also be made of Edward Gibbon's monumental *History of the Decline and Fall of the Roman Empire* (1776–8). Saladin's clear sense of ambition was made plain, although his merciful treatment of the defenders of Jerusalem won lavish praise.[45]

It is intriguing to follow the intertwining of history and fiction as authors of novels and plays sought material from historians and their literary colleagues. Thus Gotthold Ephraim Lessing's drama *Nathan the Wise* (1779) was adapted in part from Boccaccio's *Decameron* and also reflected the author's use of Marin's biography. Lessing made the point that Christians do not have a monopoly on religious truth, a sentiment that provoked a harsh reception from many censors and earned the play a place on the Catholic Church's list of banned works. Saladin took a leading role and his moral excellence was used as a means to deliver Lessing's message of tolerance across Judaism, Christianity and Islam. A short extract demonstrates this for the latter two:

> Saladin (addressing a Templar prisoner): So you'll stay with me, and as part of my court? As Christian, as Muslim, it's all the same! ... It doesn't matter! I've never demanded that every tree grow one bark.
> Templar: Otherwise you'd hardly be who you are: the hero who would rather be God's gardener.
> Saladin: Well then, if you don't think worse of me, then we're already halfway there?
> Templar: All the way!

While this is obviously a fictional exchange, Lessing was able to employ Saladin as his vehicle because of the sultan's historical reputation for mercy to Christians.[46]

The most influential picture of Saladin emerged from the pen of Sir Walter Scott in *The Talisman* (1825). Scott 'turned history into a pageant' and his practice of 'inserting sympathetic, enterprising characters into the company of real kings and queens' was extremely popular. *The Talisman* itself was immensely successful and soon translated into numerous European languages, including German, Norwegian, Italian, Russian and French, and it sold well in the United States too. This was also a time in which the technology of printing and paper production stepped forwards again, as did the ease of distribution of the printed word. Governments began to introduce legislation that encouraged formal education, further increasing literacy levels while lending and circulating libraries had already emerged to create greater accessibility to the printed word.[47] *The Talisman* went into multiple editions, inspiring dozens of works of art and theatre, again across Europe and also prompting further fictional accounts. Saladin stands as an obvious exception to the largely negative contemporary image of the Orient and he reverses stereotypes. As Scott wrote: Richard 'showed all the cruelty and violence of an Eastern sultan. Saladin, on the other hand, displayed the deep policy and prudence of a European sovereign.' The famous scene in which he visited Richard in his tent to heal him of illness is likely the product of the long tradition of his acts of disguise. Given the range of diffusion achieved by Scott's works, with *Ivanhoe* being considerably more popular again, it is hard to understate 'his influence in the creation of the nineteenth-century image and public perception of the crusades'. The fact that Kaiser Wilhelm read Scott's works is interesting to note too.[48]

Moving through the nineteenth century, the western view of the crusades became more positive. In part this was propelled by an increased European presence in the Levant, but also through a vogue for the medieval age, seen in architecture, theatre and fiction. The crusades, often in a secularised, chivalric form, constituted part of this, and Saladin, in the various guises he had now taken, naturally fitted in.[49] It is also pertinent to register the emergence of the use of crusade as a metaphor, usually taken to mean a cause with moral right. Voltaire called for a crusade against smallpox (1767), while Thomas Jefferson wrote of a 'crusade against ignorance' (1786).[50] This would prove a hugely popular practice and remains in perpetual use to the present day, certainly in English-speaking countries. As we will see, however, this positive aspect of the legacy of the crusades in the West does not sit at all well in the Near East.

Taken cumulatively, this means that by the time of Kaiser Wilhelm's visit to Damascus in 1898 the image of Saladin as a religiously tolerant and chivalric persona was firmly fixed in western culture; the sultan was indeed a noble figure whom Wilhelm could understand in the most positive terms and express his admiration for; the ferocity of holy war had receded considerably.

23

The View from the East: From the Medieval Age to the late Nineteenth Century

'Books of history are overflowing with honour and praise for that noble individual'

Amongst the most eminent writers of the Ottoman era was the palace administrator and historian Naima (d.1716). He cited an advice book that counselled Saladin to be upright in his life and argued that in doing so he would 'become such a world conqueror as was Alexander'. 'It is the truth', continued Naima, 'that he served religion and the state in a way which has been granted to few other kings. Books of history are overflowing with honour and praise for that noble individual.'[1] This last, almost throwaway, comment is especially revealing; the surfeit of writing about the sultan had made his achievements and his qualities so ubiquitous as to almost remove the need to mention them. The centrality of his character testifies to the durability and attractiveness of these aspects of his legacy as well. In other words, for Naima, the sultan's importance lay not just in the recovery of Jerusalem.[2] As we look to follow the trail of Saladin down the centuries it is as well to bear this in mind and to see that alongside his liberation of the holy city, the personality traits ascribed to him often explain why his memory endures.

Historians have persistently suggested that Saladin and the crusades were largely forgotten in the Near East between the end of Christian rule in the Levant (1291) and the late nineteenth century. The Frankish presence in the area is said to have been a brief and meaningless episode that was of little importance or relevance until Kaiser Wilhelm's ostentatious visit to Damascus in 1898. After this generous prompt the sultan was duly wheeled out as a symbol of resistance to the invading imperial powers.[3]

It is certainly true, as we will see in a later chapter, that from around this time a conjunction of political and cultural factors generated a formidable surge in the profile of Saladin and the crusades. But such prominence did not spring from a vacuum, nor was it driven only by external forces. With a careful sense of perspective, it is possible to assemble a substantial body of evidence that reveals a very different picture. From this more refined viewpoint emerges the sense that Saladin and the crusades had not wholly disappeared from the mental landscape of the Near East, but had, in fact, remained a manifest part of cultural memory and tradition across the region. With that duly acknowledged it then becomes easier to explain how Saladin's memory and legacy were so strongly embraced come the start of the twentieth century. By this point, various external stimuli such as the kaiser's visit were, in metaphorical terms, encountering a lot of dry tinder.

First of all, some context. Simply because the Franks were driven out of the Holy Land by the Mamluks in 1291 did not mean the end of the crusades. For decades after, kings and nobles formulated plans to try to return to the Levant. While these ideas failed to inspire an actual expedition, their existence shows the possibility of a new crusade was plain to all, both in Europe and the Near East. More importantly, there remained a strong Christian presence in the Eastern Mediterranean; on Cyprus, on the many islands of the Aegean Sea controlled by the Italian trading city of Genoa and, especially through the Knights of St John (the Hospitallers) on Rhodes and later Malta. Furthermore, the Byzantine Empire had survived in Greece, Asia Minor and, of course, in Constantinople. Down the centuries, the Mamluks and then the Ottomans became involved in conflicts against Christian powers in the region.[4] In essence, ongoing crusades, or the prospect of them, underpinned by the presence of overtly crusading organisations such as the Hospitallers, had the effect of reminding people of the Frankish conquests of the past and when a new campaign took place, it prompted the locals to see continuity with, and repetition of, the earlier crusading period.

Our principal reservoir of material is a range of historical, travel and religious texts. Some of these were built on the writings of earlier historians whom we have already encountered and in doing so gave further and continued prominence to Saladin. Others, such as Naima, wrote of their own times and looked to the past to inform them about their present, or to offer the exemplar of an individual who might inspire contemporaries. An exhaustive trawl through the literary output of the period is a major project in itself and one well beyond the capability of this author.[5] Yet taking the work of a few writers, some well known, others more obscure, can give a measure of the presence of Saladin and the crusades within the consciousness of the literary circles of the Near East and the people with whom these authors engaged, often the ruling classes and the religious hierarchy. From travel writers and local historians we have glimpses of greater and deeper diffusion, not least because particular locations have the potential to trigger associations and resonances.[6] Travel writers looked to give a sense of the importance of places they visited, to make reference to events there, and for our purposes, to relate to battles, buildings, or a specific incident or decision, that had involved Saladin. In doing so they might evince their own historical knowledge but they often reported what locals said or did, thereby reflecting and refracting traditions and cultural memories. Court records and official letters can also provide important and immediate insights. But, to restate the need for a large measure of perspective, these writers had a myriad of other interests, often concerning their own day, that moved far beyond coverage of the Ayyubid sultan. Saladin's ongoing presence in the historical record of the Levant is not some huge metaphorical mountain range that historians have missed, but it is, I would contend, a small, but important hill. As the man who recovered Jerusalem for Islam and as the first ruler of a dynastic house of the Near East, Saladin does have a natural role in historical texts. Beyond the statement of these important and incontrovertible achievements, it is interesting to see him – as Naima did – as being advanced as (variously) an ideal ruler, as a man of generosity and justice, as an upholder of faith. Sometimes events are referenced as coming from the time of his rule, because being able to boast a heritage from the age of Saladin could give a decision or a text a weight and a significance through an association with him. On the other hand, there are also occasions where he is mentioned only briefly, or in a more negative fashion, a spectrum that could range from satire to outright hostility.

One further caveat, though: within the broad spectrum of the ongoing memory of the medieval period, the Mamluk sultan Baibars has a strong profile too. Baibars was involved in defeating the crusade of King Louis IX of France (1250), he gave the Mamluk dynasty a firm foundation, and fought off the grievous threat to Islam posed by the Mongols. A number of the writers discussed below worked during the Mamluk era and it is not surprising that Baibars featured prominently therein. He was also the subject of an epic narrative, an immensely popular genre, with the *Sirat al-Baibars* widely presented down the centuries. A western visitor to Cairo in the 1830s observed around thirty street performers recounting Baibars' life in this way. Such stories were primarily works of entertainment, but they can be seen as transmitting preoccupations and stereotypes. Crusaders are far from the most dominant figures here, but when they do appear it is as dangerous, threatening men with wicked and cunning leaders – again, constituting a seedbed of memory to be tapped into later.[7]

From the extensive range of possible writers, a quintet of prominent historians give us a basis upon which to take soundings on Saladin's profile. Ibn Khaldun (d.1406) was a historian, intellectual and diplomat who led a complicated existence in the febrile and dangerous courts of the Maghreb, Egypt and Muslim Spain. His masterpiece the *Muqaddima* (the *Prolegomena*, or 'Introduction') on the principles of history was completed by 1377. He came to formulate 'laws that governed the formation and dissolution of communities', in other words, the cyclical process of rise and fall. He also produced a vast history: *Book of Warnings and the Collection of Beginnings and Historical Information* as well as a much shorter account of some of his travels.[8]

Saladin was worthy of particular praise as an exceptional figure who had 'cleansed the holy places of infidelity, who fought the Franks and abolished the trinity of God'. The sultan was described as being of the Turkish dynasty, although his name was given as 'Salah al-Din al-Kurdi'. His behaviour stood as greatly admirable, abolishing unjust taxes and ending Shi'ite rule in Egypt; the author was also a great admirer of the virtue of poverty.[9] A closer and more personal connection with the sultan was Ibn Khaldun's appointment as the head of the al-Qamhiyya madrasa in Cairo, an institution founded by Saladin in 1170.[10] Ibn Khaldun has often been regarded in the West (from the nineteenth century onwards when his works were translated) as one of the finest, if not the finest, mind of the Arab world. Within the Near East, while a few copies of his work were in the libraries of the Maghreb, it was the Ottoman Turks who brought him to real prominence. He attracted some attention from the mid-seventeenth century, but in the early eighteenth century, Naima proclaimed him 'the greatest of all historians'; translations into Turkish followed, transmitting his thoughts more widely.[11]

A real advocate of the Ayyubid sultan was an Egyptian writer from the end of the Mamluk era. Al-Suyuti (d.1505) was a vastly prolific author and compilator who saw the earlier period as a golden age with Saladin standing as 'an ideal Muslim prince'. A long section on his good, just rule, his allegiance to the caliph of Baghdad and support for Sunni religious groups underpinned al-Suyuti's admiration for the sultan. Al-Suyuti's writings are often quite derivative and preserve and transmit earlier texts such as those by Ibn al-Athir and Ibn al-Jawzi, as well as numerous poets. His role lies not in his limited originality, but as a channel to be used by subsequent authors such as Çelebi and al-Khiyari. Al-Suyuti's works were widely copied and diffused across Egypt, Syria, the Maghreb, Asia Minor, the Hijaz and India.[12]

A contemporary of al-Suyuti was the highly learned *qadi* of Jerusalem, Mujir al-Din (d.1522).[13] He produced a history spanning from the Creation until 1491, and wrote at length on Egypt and Ayyubid Syria with the sultan taking centre stage in the latter section. He also composed a detailed and popular history of Jerusalem and Hebron, dated to 1490. Multiple references to Saladin's conquests and the crusades are contained in this book, with focus on the restoration of Jerusalem and the sultan's many other foundations and endowments. The author described Saladin's conquest in 1187 as 'the like of the night of the Ascension of the Prophet' giving it a particularly weighty setting. Bringing the story down to his own lifetime, Mujir al-Din mentioned the tomb of a sheikh found near the village of Arsuf, the location of Saladin's and Richard's great battle in 1191. He reported that in 1484 a sheikh had restored the tomb, including the tower where he hoarded weapons in case they needed to be used in a holy war against the Europeans. This torrent of information, a blend of written history and anecdote, bears vivid testimony to the fact that Saladin was a prominent figure in the cultural memory of the Holy Land at this time.[14]

Other writers of note included the Egyptian scholar al-Maqrizi (d.1442), who produced popular histories of Cairo and of Egypt.[15] The historian Ibn Kathir (d.1373) wrote an important account of Ayyubid and Mamluk Syria, and was also commissioned to compose a jihad treatise by the governor of Damascus in the aftermath of the crusading attack on Alexandria in 1365 and Cypriot raids on Tripoli.[16]

The authors discussed so far were all well-known individuals and in the last four cases, their writings were soon widely copied and circulated. By way of demonstrating the diffusion of the memory of the crusader era beyond such heavy hitters, it is worth citing a largely unknown tract, *The Exposition and Explanation of the Cursed Franks' Departure to the Muslim Lands*, written in September 1520 by Ahmad al-Harari, a Syrian author. The text describes the conquests of the crusaders in a chronological fashion and then, as the tide turned, covers Saladin's recovery of Jerusalem; a pietistic eulogy rounds out the section on the sultan.[17] Further pilgrimage texts and local histories of Jerusalem and Damascus make reference to Saladin, not least because it was impossible to separate him from the history of religious sites in the Near East.[18]

The points made by most of the writers cited above very much show Saladin in a positive, often exemplary, light. But not every regime felt so generously towards their predecessors and could criticise or, in the case of the Ottoman Mustafa Ali (1541–1600), satirise him.[19] Mustafa visited Cairo in 1599 and wrote a detailed description of the city. From what we have just seen we might expect comments on Saladin's achievements as a great builder or as the man who ended the Fatimid dynasty. Instead, after Mustafa relates Saladin's acquisition of the throne as 'an unexpected stroke of good luck' (not entirely wrong) he describes the 'Kurdish Ayyubid's' assessment of the wonders of the royal treasury. What follows was based upon a story we encountered earlier, that of the drum that cured colic. Here, Saladin becomes the butt of the joke through the assertion that he always carried a drumstick. As was his supposed habit, he struck the drum. 'No sooner had the drum sounded from over there when the [other] drum, namely his belly, over here, also gave a sound. In other words, he unintentionally broke wind a few times. However, among the Kurds there is nothing more disgraceful to do, and among them the ignominy of passing wind is the greatest of all. Consequently, he struck the drum he was holding to the ground and full of shame and anger, he broke it. It was, it turned out, a magic cure for gas troubles; its property had gone to waste.' Mustafa followed this with a couple of impromptu verses, not perhaps a creative high point for the genre, but a good way to round out the tale:

> When the sultan saw the situation that is so embarrassing to the Kurds
> He struck the drum to the ground in anger; immediately
> That unaware one started suddenly to break wind
> As if sighs were escaping from his lower mouth.[20]

Beyond the Arabic sources that have provided our information thus far is a narrative produced in Persian in 1597. This was Prince Sharaf al-Din Bitlisi's *Sharafnama* ('The Book of Honour'), the first specific history of the Kurds that ran from the tenth century to his lifetime. The author, the lord of Bitlis (around twenty kilometres west of Lake Van in eastern Anatolia), wrote with the intention that 'the noble and grand ruling houses of Kurdistan should not remain obscured'. In light of Saladin's Kurdish ethnicity it is no surprise that the Ayyubids were given a lengthy and positive coverage. The practice of heavy reliance on earlier authors is again highly visible with Ibn al-Athir and Ibn Khallikan prominent. The *Sharafnama* was soon copied and translated into Arabic and Turkish to take its own place in the works consulted, absorbed and repeated by others.[21]

This last text aside, our focus thus far has been on historians of the Near East writing in Arabic, but of course the Islamic world extends far beyond that. Lands to the east produced a wealth of literature, mostly in Persian, in an area where Saladin's life and career exerted little direct influence.[22] Yet the sultan does form part of the historical record here – not as the victor over the crusaders, but instead as the man who removed the Fatimid Shi'ites. As ever, writers reflect their own concerns and priorities and in this case it was understanding and assimilating the devastating conquests of the Mongols (with the death of huge numbers of Sunni Muslims), that began in the early decades of the thirteenth century and culminated in the Sack of Baghdad in 1258.[23] One way to explain this was to position the Mongols as a scourge from God, provoked by the presence of a large group of the Ismaili Shi'ite Assassins whom the invaders subsequently removed. Because

Saladin had earlier ended Shi'ite rule in Egypt he was an important exemplar. Authors such as al-Juvaini (d.1283) described Saladin's achievements as 'praiseworthy' and noted that 'the circumstances of his life are well known'.[24] The influential text of Rashid al-Din also laid emphasis on the destruction of the Fatimids and the preservation of sacred law. These two sources were in turn used as templates and copied and synthesised through the fourteenth and fifteenth centuries, running into the Timurid era where writers continued to fit Saladin into their work for his overthrow of the Fatimids.

An example of just how strongly the memory of Saladin and his achievements adhered to the people and the city of Jerusalem is evident in the early seventeenth-century poem written by a Sufi mystic and sheikh Muhammad al-Alami.[25] The context was a dispute over the custody and associated privileges of the Salahiyya lodge founded by Saladin in the palace of the patriarch of Jerusalem in 1189. After a lengthy court case the poet's son took control of the institution and the family chose to justify their actions by reason that the existing owners had utterly neglected both the upkeep and Saladin's original ethos for the place. The poem was a way to cele-brate the family's legal success and was designed for broad public consumption. Once more we see the role of poetry in Near Eastern culture. The verse presumes complete awareness of the sultan in its audience and is a really vivid example of looking back to the Ayyubid as the man who had purified Jerusalem and restored it to its full glory.

> Look to the *khanqah*, erected in the cause of our faith, by the hand of
>   the righteous
> Salah al-Din, the high-minded one;
> By him I mean the deceased king, may God's pleasure with him increase,
>   he who saved Jerusalem from godlessness and injustice.

An enormously rich source for the history and culture of the Near East was composed by the Turkish writer Evliya Çelebi (1611–c.1685) in an epic ten-volume account of his travels. He also made occasional use of the works of many other writers, including as-Suyuti and Sharaf al-Din Bitlisi. For our purposes he can show that people sustained a memory of Saladin and an awareness of the crusades in a number of different contexts, in the case of the latter often in a much more immediate vein such as the Ottoman conquest of Crete in 1669.[26]

In the mid-seventeenth century Çelebi travelled through the Holy Land, making brief references to Saladin's role in recovering particular sites. Çelebi also reminds us of contemporary concerns with a discussion of the dangers posed by the Knights Hospitaller on Malta.[27] Saladin's imprint as the ruler of Egypt emerges from time to time too. In Cairo, Çelebi marvelled at 'Yusuf's Well'. He described Saladin's insistence that the citadel had a reliable water supply and he related the need for ramps 3,000 paces long for cattle and men to make the hour-long descent to the water. He was keen to correct the attribution to Saladin, rather than the prophet Joseph, as some claimed, and he wrote of the pale cattle stabled far below ground labouring to turn the wheels that raised the water: 'the world traveller who has not seen this Joseph's Well has no idea of what craftsmanship there is in the world'. He did, however, comment that the water was rather bitter.[28]

From time to time, the inhabitants of Jerusalem became jittery about the prospect of a repeat of the traumas of the crusading era.[29] A similar groundswell of popular discontent bubbled to the surface in 1701 after a decision by the Ottoman authorities in Istanbul to allow the French consul of Sidon to stay in Jerusalem. Leading families and lesser folk mounted a furious protest at the Dome of the Rock and the al-Aqsa Mosque, and signed a petition to Sultan Mustafa II demanding that he revoke this permission. The presence of a foreign diplomat was said to have been forbidden since the first conquest of Jerusalem by Umar in the seventh century, and from the time of Saladin's recovery of the city in 1187. Jerusalem's sanctity within Islam was also heavily emphasised. The idea that the consul's stay represented an instance of current infidel interest in the region was made explicit in the fear that 'we will be occupied as a result of this, as happened repeatedly in past times'.[30] Likewise, a local sheikh, Muhammad al-Khalili (d.1734), wrote about contemporary Jerusalem and Hebron, and in doing so produced a lengthy and generous account of Saladin's successes. The same author was responsible for a legal document which warned against the ambition and covetousness of external forces.[31]

One final example from the eighteenth-century Ottomans is a treatise, surviving in manuscript only, from the statesman Durri Mehmed, who wrote his 'Selected Wishes for the Emendation of Mischief' as a reflection on recent disorder and war with Russia and Austria. Probably influenced by Naima, he explained how Saladin, through following Sharia law, corrected mischief and disorder by reducing luxury, gave money to those in need, and made good appointments to key offices. As a result, he was able to fight off his enemies and recover what had been lost in the past. Saladin's upright behaviour was seen as a key to success in this didactic invocation of the Ayyubid sultan.[32]

Cumulatively, therefore, this swift survey of histories, of travel writings and legal documents gives a clear signal that Saladin and the crusades were by no means forgotten in the Near East. At the end of the eighteenth century, however, relations between the Near East and the West experienced a momentous jolt as Napoleon's bold invasion of Egypt signalled an era of increasing European dominance over the Muslim world.

In June 1798 the French army camped outside Cairo on the western bank of the Nile. Behind them in the distance lay the great pyramids of Giza; ahead the French invaders surveyed the absorbing skyline of Cairo, a vista peppered by hundreds of minarets set against the backdrop of Saladin's great citadel. The following day, a couple of miles north, the closely drilled troops of the French army formed up in their customary huge squares and prepared to face wave after wave of Mamluk cavalry charges. For just over two hours, French artillery fire ripped into them. Local troops had no idea how to break down their opponents; the Mamluks were either slaughtered on the spot or forced to flee.[33]

The arrival of a large European army headed by the military genius of his age and accompanied by a panoply of scholars, artists and archaeologists can be seen as the point that launched Europe into a series of aggressive, imperialist conquests in the Mediterranean and led to the imposition of western power, technology and values on the Muslim Near East.[34] As we saw earlier, there was in at least one sense, some continuity. The prospect of a European presence in the Levant had evoked local memories of the crusading age prior to 1798 and did so again in the future. What did change, for a whole range of reasons encompassing global politics, technology and trade, was the scale and frequency of these threats. More to the point, there was a shift from a largely theoretical fear to a far more tangible phenomenon. By the late nineteenth century, Europeans had either conquered lands outright, or established political, economic and religious influence across the Muslim Mediterranean.

A successful landing close to Alexandria was followed by his victory at the Battle of the Pyramids (July 1798). Once in control of Cairo, Napoleon wished to portray himself as an admirer of Islam, although a decree intended to underpin this convinced no one, largely because it was issued in what turned out to be the most laughably illiterate Arabic. The French also argued that they were agents of reform, and they wanted the Egyptians to participate in their own government. Napoleon proposed to free the people from the immediate oppression of their harsh Mamluk rulers, and he claimed to be working alongside the theoretical overlords of the country, the Ottoman sultanate.

Within weeks, what emerged was a French military dictatorship that tolerated no resistance. Stark cultural differences soon became apparent. The French were unprepared and uncomprehending of the East. The troops' heavy drinking and their often appalling treatment of women caused outrage. In late October a revolt broke out, intent upon ejecting the invaders. The Ottoman sultan Selim III pronounced a jihad against the French in September 1798 and the language of those involved in Cairo also spoke of a fight against the enemies of religion, the dangers facing Islam and the duty of all good Muslims to resist.[35] The response of the French was, inevitably, more brutality. In January 1799 an invasion of Syria and Palestine tried to draw in Christian locals against the Ottomans and the sultan's governor of Damascus warned the hierarchy of Jerusalem that their city remained, as always, the infidels' top target. Similarly, the governor of Gaza alerted Jerusalem to the 'cursed French infidels, may God destroy them all'.[36] A terrible massacre at Jaffa was followed by a failed attempt to capture Acre in May 1799. With British help this was repulsed by the Ottomans and in August that same year Napoleon slipped quietly back to France, his grandiose and increasingly deluded strategy stopped short by the culture and the climate of the Near East; two years later the rest of his compatriots followed.[37]

Two writers of very contrasting backgrounds give us a stark insight into how the French presence was viewed.[38] Al-Jabarti was part of

Egypt's educated elite; he also wrote a series of narratives, including a history of Egypt and an account of the French invasion. He distrusted the Europeans' assurances that they would respect the Islamic religious community. In one text, completed at the end of 1801 after the re-establishment of Ottoman rule, he explained that God's will, demonstrated by the arrival of troops led by the Ottoman grand vizier Yusuf Zia Pasha, had saved the country from Napoleon. Whenever Egypt had been in danger it was a man named Yusuf who came to the rescue. Al-Jabarti cited Yusuf the Righteous (that is, Joseph, the son of Jacob), and Yusuf Pasha, the vizier of Selim I and, of course, it was Saladin (Salah al-Din Yusuf) who, in his view, had saved Egypt from the heresy of the Shi'ite Fatimids and had set forth the party of the *sunna*.[39] He also wrote that the French troops saw themselves 'as fighters in a holy war', something that made them even more of a threat, above and beyond their violent behaviour.[40]

Another commentator on Napoleon's campaign hailed from an entirely different perspective. Al-Niqula, or 'Nicholas the Turk', was a Greek Orthodox Christian from the Lebanon sent to Egypt to report on the events taking place there by his patron. Nicholas was overtly hostile to the French and he wrote that the locals saw their presence as being in a clear continuum with the medieval crusaders. The fact that Nicholas was based in the town of Mansourah, the site of the captivity of King Louis IX of France during his disastrous crusade of 1250, meant that he picked up on local references to the humiliating fate of this earlier Gallic invader: 'The Egyptians could not remotely stand the French because of differences of religion, language and clothes; not to mention the old enmity that had existed between them since the time of the sultan Baibars. The troops of King Louis of France came to their defeat here at the hands of the Muslim army, and the memory of this is perpetuated by the name given to the town – Mansourah (meaning "the victorious").' Nicholas commented that the French had never managed to take Mansourah in the past and that Louis' dismal failure was reported by the histories, a nice indication of the written record being recalled alongside popular memory.[41]

While the people of the Near East could take pleasure in defeating Napoleon, the ferocity of the fighting and the harsh and callous French regime would not be forgotten. For the French, aside from their scientific and archaeological discoveries, the campaign had only engendered in them a greater fear and mistrust of the people of the Orient. It also left them with an 'unshaken, even strengthened, belief in their own culture's superiority to the Orient's which had not been there before', an unhealthy and corrosive sentiment that proved hugely persistent, something that could only encourage historical enmities to revive as well.[42] As the nineteenth century progressed, western powers began to exert control over, or to occupy and annex, ever more Muslim lands in the Mediterranean and the Near East. The French conquered Algeria in 1830; thirty years later Spain declared war on Morocco in a dispute over its enclave at Ceuta. Economic and religious rivalries caused the main powers to establish a permanent presence in the Levant. France wished to preserve its role as protector of Maronites and Catholics in the Holy Land; the Russians were the champions of the Orthodox Church and wanted to weaken the Ottomans; the Germans, on the other hand, looked to support the Turks.[43] The issue of a western presence in Jerusalem was a highly sensitive subject but against a background of Ottoman weakness, resistance to such a prospect was no longer tenable. Thus the British established a consulate in 1839, followed soon by the Germans (1842) and the French (1843), then the Russians in 1858.[44] The restoration of senior religious representatives was now almost inevitable and in 1844 a Greek Orthodox patriarch returned to Jerusalem, joined four years later by his Latin counterpart.[45]

Tensions within the Ottoman Empire manifested themselves in revolt and rebellion. Attempts to stabilise the situation resulted in the European-influenced reforms known as the Tanzimat (issued 1839–76), measures that included the principle of equality between the Muslims and non-Muslims of the empire, a major shift from the previous situation whereby the latter (often meaning Christians) had been an inferior but protected class (dhimmi), who paid special taxes.[46] Set against the wider background of international political and economic competition, attempts to assert particular rights and privileges came to focus on French and Russian claims to the Holy Places, a dispute that led eventually to the Crimean War (1853–6).[47]

An especially useful commentator to us is James Finn, the British consul in Jerusalem from 1845 to 1863. In May 1855 he noted that the idea of a French army of occupation was present 'in the minds of the city's inhabitants'. Finn's extensive memoirs were heavily coloured by the outbreak of the Crimean War and he worried that it evoked memories of the crusading age for the local Muslims, a parallel that could have dire consequences for the Christian community in the East. In 1853 Arab troops asked the Turkish commandant of Jerusalem: 'Who are these upstart Russians? We have heard of the French, the English and the Germans as being honourable foes of Saladin, but who are these dead dogs with burnt fathers, the Russians?'[48] Finn wrote of the curiosity whereby the French were fighting in defence of the Muslim holders of Jerusalem against a new crusading power, the Russians.[49] Perhaps the most pertinent observation for us is his observation on the duration of historical memories amongst the locals: 'The lapse of the centuries does not tell us much in the East ... the people judge history rather by their own lasting impressions than by dates of chronology.' The great battles of the past, such as Yarmuk (636), Hattin (1187), Mount Tabor and the French siege of Acre (both 1799) were, he asserted, of far greater familiarity than more recent events that concerned 'only the Turks and the yellow-haired Russians'.[50] That said, the contemporary struggle had plainly evoked a popular memory of the medieval period with Saladin at the head of the Muslim armies. While the Russians were, from his perspective, the aggressors, he was also concerned that the French claim 'to be regarded as the hereditary successors of the crusaders' could only aggravate the situation.[51]

Sectarian tensions grew and grew, exacerbated by increased foreign trade which seemed to benefit the Christian communities at the expense of the Muslims; in Aleppo, placards encouraged a pre-emptive assault on Christians, and in the port of Latakia, Muslims were reported as saying 'We know that our country will be taken by the Europeans but before that we will destroy as many Christians as we can.'[52] In early 1860, civil war broke out in the Lebanon between the Christian Maronites and the Shi'ite Druze. By the summer the violence spread to Damascus where thousands of Christians died and their property was destroyed. An English missionary in Damascus wrote of his fear that he would be identified as 'A Frank or a Christian', as the mob tore through the streets.[53] In response the French dispatched a fleet to the region to work with the Ottoman authorities to restore order and to defend the Christians. Napoleon III sent his men off with the reminder that they were 'the dignified children of those heroes who gloriously brought the banner of Christ to that land'. His commander was the inflexible and pompous General Beaufort who stated he was there 'in the name of civilised Europe ... to help the sultan's troops avenge humanity disgracefully vilified ... In these famous lands Christianity was born, and Godfrey of Bouillon and the crusaders, General Bonaparte and the heroic soldiers of the Republic honoured themselves.' In the event the French made little progress and returned home the following summer.[54]

Westerners did not always arrive in such a bellicose context. Thousands of traders, pilgrims and tourists, of imperial rank and down, came to the Near East.[55] Sometimes these westerners offer us snippets of information. Josias Leslie Porter was a Presbyterian missionary and traveller who spent time in Damascus and wrote a description of the city. He included an account of Saladin's life thus: 'In Damascus, where his subjects had the best opportunities of witnessing his justice and clemency, the people mourned as for a father and benefactor; and to this day his name is venerated by every Muslim.'[56] Once again, we see Saladin as a figure in the contemporary cultural memory remembered in this instance as a figure of virtue and mercy, rather than simply a fighter.

It was not only visiting Christians who evoked the crusading era – the local Muslim population could do the same. Finn observed an important link with the medieval age in the form of the Nebi Musa festival.[57] This was a major pilgrimage that took place about five miles south-west of Jericho at the traditional site of the tomb of Moses. It was an event popularly believed to have been founded by Saladin, although in fact the shrine itself had been commissioned in 1269 by Baibars.[58] Coupled with its central function as a place of pilgrimage, the visitors, often accompanied by a substantial entourage, enjoyed a celebration with associated culinary and musical entertainments as well as mock battles and horseback manoeuvres. Mujir al-Din had mentioned this event in his account back in the late fifteenth century but in the highly charged atmosphere of the 1850s and 1860s it was particularly energised.[59] The exact content of the military displays that Consul Finn witnessed is not clear, but for him the festival's proximity to Easter, coupled with the fact that the pilgrims gathered in Jerusalem to make the short journey to the shrine, marked out potential flashpoints for 'fanatics' from either side.[60] Down into the twentieth century, Nebi Musa has often remained a trigger for trouble.

In the course of the nineteenth century, therefore, western powers establishing and advancing their political, religious and economic position in the Near East did much to reaffirm and remind the local population of the history of the crusades. The memory of Saladin as a fine, successful ruler who had recovered and then defended Jerusalem from external invaders had already endured down the years. In the course of the nineteenth century he became increasingly appropriate to invoke, and in turn came to attract even greater interest and attention.

24

Early Arab Nationalism Expressed Through Theatre, Books and Newspapers

'Unity! Unity between all the inhabitants
of our lands!'

From the 1850s newspapers began to appear across the Muslim world in Arabic, Turkish and, further east, Farsi and Urdu. In 1858 came the Lebanese *Garden of News* and soon it included a serialisation of 'The Two Gardens', Abu Shama's admiring history of Nur al-Din's and Saladin's struggles to defeat the Franks, originally written in the thirteenth century. Manuscript versions had been painstakingly copied and circulated down the years, but to be featured in a newspaper in the 1860s indicates that the editor judged the content of interest to contemporary readers. It is intriguing that an original medieval text was chosen, not least because this was before more modern accounts of Saladin's life began to appear.[1] Other narratives from the medieval age started to materialise in print as well, all giving a higher profile to the life and achievements of the sultan.[2]

The broader relationship between the western European powers and the peoples of the Near East is, of course, a complex and multifaceted subject. Throughout this time the environment became ever more ripe to build upon and to exploit the existing legacy of Saladin and the crusades. Cultural factors exerted a particular impact, not least in helping to create and transmit ideas of shared identity, such as nationalism, that would become so powerful. As we have just seen, one such driver was through the flourishing of print publishing houses. Likewise, Arab theatre blossomed, the Arabic language evolved further, and there was also a rise in education that encompassed both schooling and academic advance. All of these factors contributed to the faster spread of ideas and to the de-localisation of society; they also offer a rich seam of material for us to follow the growing profile of Saladin and the crusades.[3]

Political events provided much of the impetus for many such developments. Egypt's attempts to modernise itself with, for example, the construction of the Suez Canal, caused devastating financial problems, exacerbated by rapacious foreign creditors. Overseas commissioners stepped in to approve government spending which stirred huge resentment. 'Egypt for the Egyptians' rallied the people, and in 1882 an uprising resulted in the British navy landing troops to occupy Egypt. The country became a colony 'in fact but not in name', a distinction to keep it nominally within the Ottoman orbit and to forestall other countries dismembering the ailing Turkish Empire further. This early stirring of nationalism was symptomatic of a wider desire to cast off outside control from Istanbul as well, but even more so, represented hostility to the western powers.[4]

By this time a number of books on the history of the crusades had begun to emerge, perhaps inspired in part by the publication of medieval Arabic texts, while European authors came to influence historical writing in the region as well.[5] In the mid-1850s Ahmed Jevdet's history of the Ottoman Empire included a section on the crusades, while the first biography of Saladin was written by the Turk Namik Kemal in 1872. He was a prominent historian of the time who lived briefly in France before returning to Istanbul. His biography was in some measure a response to the Turkish translation of Frenchman Joseph-François Michaud's imperialistic *Histoire des Croisades* (1811–22). Kemal wanted to use Muslim sources to give a more representative picture of the sultan.[6] The first Arabic language history of the crusades from this era was published in Jerusalem in 1865, itself based on a French work of 1840 by Maxime de Montrond, in turn heavily reliant on Michaud. It was translated into Arabic by Maximos Mazloum III, the Melkite patriarch of Jerusalem, Antioch and Aleppo, with a suitable toning down of some of de Montrond's more offensive phrases, such as 'barbaric', 'infidel' and 'false prophet'.[7]

The first modern Muslim-authored crusading history, *Splendid Accounts in the Crusading Wars* (1899) by the Egyptian Sayyid Ali al-Harari, is significant for tackling the subject as a distinctive topic in itself, rather than placing it in a grand narrative of Islamic history. Al-Harari made considerable use of medieval Islamic sources, texts that as we have seen were becoming much more accessible in printed form. Taking a cue from the very top, the author quoted Sultan Abdul Hamid II himself to emphasise the parallels between the medieval era and the present day: 'Our most glorious sultan has rightly remarked that Europe is now carrying out a Crusade against us in the form of a political campaign.'[8]

What we see here is a merger of long-standing local memories of crusades, running into the self-image of new European settlers and visitors who felt they were following in the footsteps of their medieval ancestors. We noted earlier how the French armies of the 1860s viewed themselves, and registered the concerns of Consul James Finn as to how this might be received. By the end of the century, Jerusalem contained a number of buildings with recently created representations of crusaders, most strikingly the hospital of St Louis with its fine images of knights and copies of dozens of the shields of early crusaders. Pilgrims caused particular problems, with the French ambassador to Istanbul being warned that the behaviour of visitors to Jerusalem dressed up as crusaders caused grave offence to the local population.[9]

The relentless military and commercial power of the West, as well as a rapid cultural penetration through, for example, the translation of books and plays, created what seemed to be an unstoppable imperative to change; cumulatively these factors were overwhelming the Muslim world. There was a need for self-examination, to have an understanding of what had happened, and then react to it. As the European powers began to bear down ever more heavily on the lands of the Near East, people sought to formulate ideologies of resistance and renewal. Looking to Islam was one option.

An individual who came to exert a powerful influence in Islamist thought (and hence on those who came to invoke Saladin and the crusades into the twentieth century) was the restless and controversial character, Jamal al-Din al-Afghani (d.1897). He sought political independence from the West and a return to the fundamentals of Islam. He regarded the Christian world, in spite of its divergences of races and nationalities, as united in a desire for the destruction of Muslim countries and argued that the crusades had survived to the modern age. Al-Afghani tried to persuade Abdul Hamid II that he could draw the Muslim people to the sultan's leadership and called for 'the banner of unity of Islam' to engage in holy war, but this pan-Islamic appeal fell flat.[10] His sometime companion, a more moderate and gradualist reformer, Muhammad Abduh, is also of note because his *Theology of Unity* (1897) referenced the crusades in an interesting way. Given the almost ubiquitous link between the crusades and imperialist greed drawn by the next few generations, admittedly mainly nationalists, Abduh was clear that it was 'unprecedented zeal and fervour for religion that drove them to overrun Muslim lands', an idea that would return to the fore over half a century later.[11]

In the short term at least, these Islamic movements achieved little, and it was a more secular concept, that of nationalism, that proved to have greater traction. One of the engines that powered European expansion had been an 'emotional identification with a hitherto abstract idea, the nation'. This had energised the French under Napoleon, while later on it came to shape Germany and then helped to drive the Italian Risorgimento. While these views took a while to drop anchor in the Near East, some of the principles therein came to have a significant impact on the area: the ideas of unifying of states, the removal of corrupt and ossified regimes and lifting the hand of clerical authority all came to find receptive minds. In the circumstances of the day, Islamic society had spread too far for the unity promoted by the Quran to still adhere. There also emerged a growing sense of identification with place, a secular concept, rather than having a community defined simply by belief. Of course, nationalism and Islam are not mutually exclusive and the basic environment in which the broader movement of Arab nationalism emerged was undoubtedly an Islamic one with the Prophet as a foundational, spiritual hero of the people.[12]

A fundamental principle of nationalism is that of shared origins; in part, therefore, it encourages a looking back to learn about great deeds of the past, to formulate a particular heritage and to create an identity manifest to all. In the context of such a framework, Saladin's role in drawing people together, his success in defeating the Franks and recovering Jerusalem, and then his resistance to the western crusaders was prime material. To make this even more appealing, his personal qualities as a man of justice, mercy, religion and generosity provided a splendid spectrum of behaviour for writers, politicians and religious figures to admire and emulate, and for their audiences in the wider public to recognise and identify with as they sought to throw off the modern invaders.

Within this dynamic environment, a number of individuals enjoyed careers that criss-crossed the emerging cultural forms of the day. These entrepreneurial characters were passionate about the achievements of the Arab people and wanted to reflect contemporary interests. Their works hit a real chord with a public eager to understand their heritage and identity. The growing popularity of clubs, cafés and theatres facilitated the discussion and dissemination of new ideas about nation and empire.

Jurji Zaydan was a Beirut-born Greek Orthodox Christian; as a non-Muslim who wrote largely about Islamic history such a background sometimes met with hostility and suspicion. His main purpose in writing was 'to arouse the desire of the public to read history and to read it abundantly'.[13] In 1892 he launched the monthly *al-Hilal* ('the Crescent'), a publication still in existence today. With a remit to popularise Arab and Islamic heritage, by June 1894 Saladin was featured in an illustrated biographical piece.[14] Zaydan also acted as a war correspondent and in 1884 had taken part in the effort to rescue General Gordon from Khartoum. Soon afterwards he visited London where he used the British Library to research Arabic history, adopting a western-style critical reading of the original sources, something of a departure for contemporary Arab historiography. His *History of Modern Egypt* encompassed the period 643–1879 and included a lengthy section on the crusades, a subject he framed in terms of a coalition of Europeans defeating and enslaving a divided Near East, an obvious reflection of his interpretation of contemporary times. He excoriated those responsible for allowing and encouraging the Franks to invade Egypt in the 1160s and he disliked phases of co-operation between the people of the Near East and the westerners. The troubled dealings between Saladin and Nur al-Din had to be covered in rather opaque terms and the two great men were depicted in a positive relationship, not least to show the power of the combined strength of Syria and Egypt and the fear this might engender amongst the Franks. Saladin himself represented the grandeur of Arab culture.[15]

Zaydan also wrote twenty-two historical novels that were widely read and often republished. The immediate popularity of his work suggests that his secular approach to Islamic history, blending fiction with a strong dose of instructional rigour, found a receptive audience. One of these books nominally concerned Shajar al-Durr, the wife of the last Ayyubid ruler of Egypt, but in fact was far more interested in Baibars and the Mongol attack on Baghdad in 1258. A further volume, *Salah al-Din Ayyubi* (1913), also translated into Persian and Kurdish, is of note to us here not least because of its message of Muslim–Christian (Arab) unity and its explicit use of the historian Abu Shama at certain points in the text.[16]

One of Zaydan's rivals in the newspaper business was another Lebanese-born Christian, Farah Antun, who moved to Egypt in 1897 and two years later established his own journal. Initially he was a strong supporter of a secularised Ottoman state (Ottomanism), political adherence to the empire underpinned by civic rather than faith-based affiliation. But this was an immensely fluid political climate, moving between Ottomanism, through more nationalist groups, including Turks and Egyptians, over to the pan-Islamic ideals of Sultan Abdul Hamid II, whose empire was 'a political entity within whose framework Islamic reform could be carried out'.[17] A decade later, Antun himself had steered towards Egyptian nationalism, perceiving that his previously strong allegiance to Ottomanism was a mistake. Overt criticism of the British became a clear element of his work. With regards to the crusades, he saw them as 'the origins of western aggression' against the Near East. The vehicle through which he came to make one of his most significant contributions to the wider debates of the day was the theatre.[18]

Antun had already discovered that writing what is best described as 'light entertainment' was a lucrative business. He was also responsible for the translation and adaptation of a number of western plays, a commonplace practice at the time. Theatre had blossomed in the Near East over the recent decades, building on a centuries-long tradition of popular entertainments, including the shadow plays enjoyed by Saladin. Performances were comedic or satirical in character and presented in colloquial Arabic in a blend of verse and prose but by the 1870s, as the influence of Cairo-based French and Italian operatic and drama companies took effect, there was a move to establish an indigenous theatre in Egypt.[19]

In 1914 Antun's growing sense of political activism and nationalist feeling prompted him to write *The Sultan Saladin and the Kingdom of Jerusalem*, a piece that tackled contemporary social and political issues through the storyline of the medieval hero. The play had a more Islamic accent than Antun's previously very secular work. Saladin explains that 'This victory comes from God, I am only his servant.' But the main theme was anti-imperialist, with Saladin's statement that 'Jerusalem will remain ours forever, and our land will remain our land' echoing this. Alongside the sultan's obvious virtues of wisdom, loyalty and faith, Saladin is held up as a man who unified and liberated his people in defiance of deceitful and rapacious invaders. The first two acts take place in Cairo where Saladin wisely declines various western efforts to snare him into political alliances. It is Reynald of Châtillon's unilateral attack on the peaceful Muslim caravan that triggers him to war. Act Three takes place in a tent on the battlefield at Hattin where Reynald pays the inevitable price for his wickedness and is executed. The final act (set in 1189–90) is situated in front of the walls of the liberated holy city of Jerusalem. There Saladin receives various envoys, including, in disguise, Maria, a (in reality, mythical) sister of Reynald of Châtillon. Maria is seeking revenge and tries to assassinate the sultan, but once she is restrained, Saladin demonstrates his habitual mercy and sets her free.

The play ends with a call: 'Unity! Unity between all the inhabitants of our lands!' A crowd pours onto the stage in response, rallying around a theme that would grow ever stronger down the decades. As an aside, Maria shows that Antun also understood Saladin's high reputation in the West by her words that 'in the future, in times of peace as in times of war, he will have the same standing as Charlemagne, Caesar and Alexander carry for us'.

The play emerged just after the Ottoman Empire had entered the First World War and Sultan Abdul Hamid called for a jihad against his enemies. The British in Egypt severed ties with Istanbul and established a protectorate under martial law. In such circumstances the authorities frowned heavily on the content of Antun's work and imposed strict censorship, requiring a number of amendments to get it back on stage – the play was then performed in Egypt, Syria and Palestine.[20]

Antun was not the first playwright to use Saladin as a vehicle for his beliefs. In 1895 the Egyptian Najib Haddad produced a popular and highly durable work called *The History of Saladin Ayyubi*. This was put into print three years later and over the next four decades was widely repeated across the Near East. Saladin represents pan-Islamic pride in a work that was partially influenced by Sir Walter Scott's *The Talisman*. In contrast to the novel, Saladin takes the leading role and through monologues and exchanges with Imad al-Din (who was not in Scott's book), he is able to convey his messages and also to evade the crusaders. The famous scene in which Saladin slips into the crusader camp in disguise to heal King Richard is faithfully preserved, not least to reinforce the sultan's personal kindness and intelligence, but also to restate the cultural superiority of his people, that is, the Arabs. Haddad's play was performed in Egypt and then in Algeria in 1913 and 1921, in Tunisia in 1913 and Morocco in 1927. A British academic visitor surveying Egyptian theatre in 1932–3 tersely described the *Talisman*-influenced play as a 'stock piece' still regularly staged.[21]

It was not just western plays and operas that were translated into Arabic, with novelists such as Dumas and Tolstoy proving highly popular too. Scott was prominent as well, and *The Talisman* was published in Arabic in the scientific and literary journal *al-Muqtataf* as early as 1887. Again, a high-profile outlet for the story suggests an anticipation of public interest although the translator changed the title to *The Lionheart and Saladin* and, as he admitted, took the opportunity to omit, add and alter parts of the story to suit his audience's taste.

One further novel might be adduced at this point, largely to show how quickly and how far the image of Saladin was being taken up by novelists in the Arabic-language world. This unique marker of the diffusion of Saladin's image straddles the Near East and the West, or more specifically, the United States. Ameen Rihani, a Lebanese-born Maronite (later excommunicated), wrote what has been described as 'the first Arab–American novel'. Rihani had emigrated aged eleven, and then moved back and forth between the US and Lebanon. He wrote about Arab nationalism and religious reform, but also the immigrant experience; he was influenced by contemporary American authors, but also translated medieval works of philosophy. He composed *The Book of Khalid* in Lebanon in 1910, that is just after the great changes effected in the Ottoman Empire by the 'Young Turk' movement and the Committee of Union and Progress. These had forced Abdul Hamid II to return to a more constitutional authority and to relax the repression and censorship so prevalent by this time.

Rihani reflected the Arab–Turkish tension often on display in contemporary Egyptian and Lebanese poetry as well.

One scene is a conversation in the context of 'the renaissance of Arabia, the reclaiming of her land, the resuscitation of her glory'. Khalid has before him antique colour prints from the bazaar in Damascus representing heroes of Arabia, including Saladin, each with a verse of poetry underneath.

> Khalid ... lays the picture of Saladin on the table, lights another cigarette, looks intently upon his friend, his face beaming with his dream ... 'We need another Saladin today – a Saladin of the idea, who will wage a crusade not against Christianity or Mohammedanism, but against those Tartaric usurpers who are now toadying to both.'
> 'Whom do you mean?'
> 'I mean the Turks. They were given a last chance to rise; they tried and failed ... But out in the deserts is a race which is always young, a race that never withers, a strong, healthy, keen-eyed, quick-witted race ... that gave Europe a civilisation, that gave the world a religion ... and with a future too, if we had an Ali or a Saladin. But He who made those heroes will make others like them, better.'[22]

So here Saladin is an Arab crusader against Turks, an ethnically defined warrior, working outside of his usual prism of the vanquisher of the imperialist West and standing as a metaphor for a fighter for a just cause, albeit with a particularly distinctive twist.

With ideas of national identity very much in the ascendancy, it is not surprising to see another group, in this case the Kurds, choosing to seize the moment as well. Reformers in the Ottoman Empire were concerned with issues of Turkishness: Turkish history, literature and language. Many Kurds felt excluded by this and in response emerged associations that were determined to signal their identity in the face of what they viewed as a history of Ottoman domination. In 1898 exiles from Cairo founded the first Kurdish newspaper, *Kurdistan*. There was a move to mark out the Kurds as a distinct group with a particular past, a powerful language (although much in need of revival at the time) and great leaders – most especially, Saladin. Those behind this concept looked to establish a Kurdish character from within, intending to develop and clarify their culture, history and language.

Another newspaper appeared: *Rojë Kurd* ('the Daily Kurd'), designed to awaken these issues amongst the people.[23]

The cover of the first issue (1913) featured an image of Saladin himself, using the Ottoman-era portrait over his tomb in Damascus. The sultan symbolised military strength, but he was also put forward as a model character to inspire. A few years earlier a celebrated Kurdish poet, Sheikh Riza Talabani (d.1910), wrote of being free from the House of Osman and drew a link between the medieval hero and his own favoured family as well as pointing out that it was a Baban Kurd, Saladin, who had achieved the greatest success, more so even than the Arabs:

> Arabs! I do not deny your excellence; you are the most excellent, but Saladin who took the world was of Baban–Kurdish stock.[24]

The sultan also featured in one of the most powerful and controversial themes to emerge in the course of the twentieth century, that of Zionism, the effort to re-establish a Jewish homeland in Palestine. The First Zionist Congress took place in Basel in 1897 and as the number of Zionist settlements in Palestine grew, hostility mounted. In one case a central theme of resistance drew heavily upon the figure of Saladin. Shukri al-Asali, the district commissioner of Nazareth, wrote widely in the newspapers in Istanbul and Syria under the pseudonym 'Salah al-Din al-Ayyubi'.[25] In late 1910 he objected to the sale of an area of land to Zionists, and in his emotional opposition to the deal and to the removal of the peasants who lived there he made play of the fact that the area included the castle of al-Fula, captured from the Franks by Saladin in late 1187. To give his case historical underpinnings he cited the thirteenth-century writer Ibn al-Athir, while a cartoon from the Beirut weekly magazine *al-Himara* ('the She-Ass') shows Saladin threatening a crudely caricatured Jew who pours gold into the hands of an Ottoman official while behind them looms the fortress. Saladin is captioned as saying 'Keep away from this fortress you swindler, or else I shall set on you the armies of my descendants and you will not come near a fortress which I conquered with Muslim blood.' In response, the Jew states that money and bribery will prevail. Saladin's status as a hero for Muslims and Arabs meant this was an early example of something repeatedly used in later conflicts between these groups and the Israelis.[26]

Across this generous spread of religious, geographical and ethnic scenarios, the idea of a nationally based community had become especially potent, not least in conjunction with wide-ranging political and cultural developments. Within this, Saladin had been eagerly adopted as a figure who could stand tall as a representative of the aims and aspirations of the peoples of the Near East, wishes that would soon gather even greater momentum.

25

Struggles for Independence in Syria, Egypt and Palestine

'Awake, people, before you are expelled from a country
where the bones of your ancestors are buried!
What would you say to Saladin ... ?'

In August 1920, General Henri Gouraud of France snuffed out an attempt to set up an independent Syrian state. Upon entering Damascus he marched into Saladin's mausoleum. Infamously, he is said to have kicked the sultan's tomb and then barked: 'Saladin, we have returned.' It is a matter of some controversy as to the exact words used, whether Gouraud said them or not, or if the phrase was uttered by one of his associates.[1] The general had already described himself and the French as 'descendants of crusaders' and in doing so he merely reflected an attitude we have seen in play from the age of Napoleon onwards, a view bolstered by contemporary French academics.[2] In any event, the phrase has stuck badly in the craw of the people of the Near East and has been repeated as a near-canonical point of evidence that westerners want the crusades to continue. Implicit in the statement is a blend of condescension, contempt and niggling antagonism, a deliberate show of disrespect to their historical hero at the monument that contains his mortal remains. For the inhabitants of the area, it is a challenge both to their medieval role model, and to their contemporary rulers, to take up the fight against the returning crusaders and, of course, to defeat them again. The words have been cited by people ranging from members of the Islamist organisation the Muslim Brotherhood, including its leader Sayyid Qutb, and were also included in the charter of the Hamas movement (1984).[3] The Arab nationalist President Nasser of Egypt repeated them in the 1960s, and they endure in Syrian school textbooks. Most powerful of all, perhaps, are the words of the poet Haroun Hashim Rashid:

We have returned
Saladin
We returned ...
We came to Egypt
We came to al-Sham ...
You are here
Saladin
Confined to the grave and hollowed walls
Saladin O man
And O the one who honoured men
We have now returned
As we once did
Tearing the flag of *Iman* [faith]
And raising the flag of tyranny
Saladin, we have returned
Keeping the dead awake.[4]

Gouraud's comment emerged in the context of the disintegration of the Ottoman Empire, a process that was vastly accelerated by the First World War. Western powers' involvement in the Near East inevitably came to form part of the wider conflict and in doing so provided multiple further scenarios in which the struggles of the medieval age would resonate. In the summer of 1914 Kaiser Wilhelm tried to exploit his links with Sultan Abdul Hamid II to prompt a holy war against the Allies, notably the British in India and Egypt. By early November the Ottomans had entered the war and soon afterwards the grand mufti declared a jihad against Russia, Britain and France. The faithful were assured of a place in paradise if they fell as martyrs; in early 1915 an attack on the Suez Canal was the first, unsuccessful, manifestation of this alliance.[5]

Britain and France settled upon strategic objectives particular to the Near East, aims that would have enormous long-term consequences and, pertinent to our tightly focused purposes here, lead to a variety of new ways in which Saladin's legacy was reimagined. The British wanted a barrier in the Near East (running from Suez to Iran) to preserve access to the oilfields of Iran and to protect the vast wealth of India. The French desired to control lands they regarded as historically theirs in Syria, the Lebanon and southern Turkey; other theoretical provisions rewarded Russia and Italy. The result was the infamous Sykes–Picot Agreement of January 1916, dividing up the Near East and representing 'the high-water mark in the flood tide of imperialism' in the area, although the plan was not, as yet, revealed to the wider world.[6]

The war spread to the Middle East and, in the autumn of 1917, the approach of an English military leader, General Allenby, towards Jerusalem was simply too tempting a parallel with Richard the Lionheart and the Third Crusade for the British media to resist. Allenby himself was horrified at the prospect of a comparison with the crusades, not least because he was fully aware of the insensitivity of such a move. He understood the depth of feeling the crusades could arouse amongst Muslim peoples, something the contemporary British public had practically no conception of. The fact that his army had significant Muslim contingents, not to mention the provocation to the Islamic inhabitants of India and Egypt, underlay his fears. At first the government went along with this by issuing a D-notice that banned such references, but once Allenby entered the holy city on 11 December 1917, popular sentiment and the national press overwhelmed this. Headlines broadcast a sense of pride and excitement in recalling the medieval age.[7] Allenby's personal scruples aside, this overt symbolism obviously raised the profile and the perceived relevance of the crusades further.

One small side effect of the Ottoman loss of Jerusalem was the closure of the city's Saladin University, founded by the Turkish authorities in 1915. This institution occupied premises in and around the madrasa complex created by Saladin in 1192, pointedly linking itself to the person, place and original educational purpose of the Ayyubid sultan. It was intended to promote Ottoman values, but quickly became a centre for the dissemination of Arab nationalist thought.[8]

A few weeks before Allenby entered Jerusalem the situation had become even more complex. The Balfour Declaration (issued 2 November 1917) set out British support for a Palestinian home for the Jewish people, albeit one that would not 'prejudice the civil and religious rights of existing non-Jewish communities in Palestine'. Three weeks later (26 November), the disclosure of the Sykes–Picot document compounded the sensitivities and complexity of the situation for the foreseeable future.

This was especially so in Syria. In late November 1917, Jamal Pasha, the Ottoman military governor of Syria, wrote to Emir Faisal (the son of Sharif Husayn of Mecca who had led the Arab Revolt against the Ottomans in 1916) and to Ja'far al-Askari (the commander of Husayn's army) in an attempt to exploit the revelation of the Sykes–Picot Agreement to set up a separate Turko-Arabic peace deal. In quite pointed terms he expressed distress that al-Askari, having fought on behalf of the Turks early in the war, was now in revolt against the Ottomans and thereby aiding the British cause. He cast his appeal in terms of betraying the specific legacy of Saladin: 'I like to believe that you have chosen this course of action out of a pure desire to defend the rights of the nation to which you belong. But whatever may have been the customs and circumstances which have caused this evil to enter your heart, you should not forget that the British Army, commanded by General Allenby, is today conquering Palestine which Salaheddin defended.'[9]

Faisal aimed to form an independent Syrian state and in October 1918 he made a well-orchestrated entrance on horseback into Damascus. Shortly before this, his representatives had removed the kaiser's bronze wreath from Saladin's tomb, an emblematic liberation from the Ottomans and their German ally. Faisal established an embryonic Sunni Arab government in Damascus.[10] Tensions continued to rise with the prospect of open conflict with the French. Europeans in Damascus were subject to hostility, and in late October a meeting of the Syrian National Congress heard calls for the conquest of the country's western region. Within days a document based on this speech was distributed on the streets of Damascus and reproduced in newspapers across the Middle East. 'The First Call' was a powerful attempt to rally the Arab people against the despotic colonising powers who, they claimed, wanted to:

> enslave the Arabs, to violate their women, to rob their money, to destroy their religion and to annihilate the Arab nation. See how the Jews who are enslaved and simple have risen now to demand Palestine, pretending it to be the land of their ancestors. Do you not wish to

follow their example? Do you not want to safeguard the land of your forefathers who defended her from the offence of the crusaders in the days of Salah al-Din? Why do you not stand in their faces now?'[11]

The danger posed by such an appeal was recognised in London. The head of intelligence sent a copy directly to the Undersecretary of State at the Foreign Office who assessed it as 'a most dangerous pamphlet ... the writer is as able as he is dangerous'.[12]

An article in a nationalist Damascene newspaper from 5 December 1919 commemorating the Prophet's birthday made clear the feelings in play. It is especially striking to see the French so overtly identified as crusaders and with all the negative connotations therein:

> Muslims do not regard the Prophet – much as they venerate him – as being more than a man and a prophet; and when they pray, they pray to God alone. The colonisers who have descended on Muslims, particularly the French, who boast of their descent from the crusaders, continue to suppose, as their fathers did, that the Muslims of Syria worship Mohamad and believe that their souls return to him after death. We have been told that when a certain young Muslim was saved from drowning, some Frenchmen who were on their way to occupy Syria, said: 'Why do you fear death, when if you died, your soul would go to Mohamad?' The youth smiled scornfully and explained the matter, after which he expressed his regret that the French, who claimed to have mastered every science, should continue to persist in such ignorance, and wondered how they could be so ambitious as to colonise a Muslim country and associate with Muslims, while they still have the same notion about them as their crusading ancestors in the Middle Ages.[13]

In spite of the proclamation of Faisal as king of the United Syrian Kingdom (Syria, Lebanon and Palestine) in March 1920, the attempt to break free of France failed. But in these circumstances, in this location, it was not solely from the Arab side that the actions of medieval forefathers seemed relevant.[14] Within months the French under Gouraud took control over Syria and the notorious statement discussed above emerged. Faisal, meanwhile, was being put forward as a candidate to govern the British Mandate in Iraq. T. E. Lawrence, who had been prominent in the Arab Revolt and taken a major role at the Paris

Peace Talks, encouraged this through describing him as 'the greatest Arab leader since Saladin'.[15]

It was not simply in a Syrian context that the crusades resurfaced. The Turkish War of Independence of 1919 to 1922 brought an end to the Ottoman Empire. Given that Saladin and the crusaders had been periodically invoked by the imperial regime, it is interesting to see them occasionally pressed into service by the Turkish nationalist movement of Mustafa Kemal. Pan-Islamic solidarity was important at this stage of affairs, and in March 1921 a Kemalist newspaper set out a rallying call against western crusader aggression in preparation for the forthcoming Congress of Muslim Nations to be held in Ankara.[16] It wrote that: 'The corporeal and spiritual European nations are apparently still not far from showing the extremely fanatical and implacable enmity towards Muslims as did the crusaders of old ... The call of the *ezan* [i.e. the summons to worship] from the heights will be reduced to silence before the centuries-old fanatical attack of the West and the crusaders' army ... a labour which has lasted from the Middle Ages.'[17]

The Young Turks could not reconcile western Christian imperialism with Turkish and Muslim identity. The Turks were the people to fight off these invaders. Thus, in the context of the day it was once more Christianity against Islam with, as the official history of the Turkish Independence War (1925) suggested, 'the Turkish nation as the first and last bastion against this occupationist drive'.[18] Kemal's victories in Anatolia attracted considerable praise across the Near East, particularly in Egypt, where the Islamic dimension of his struggle as a Muslim resisting western domination played well as a contrast to the passive Ottomans. In September 1922, rumours began to circulate in Egypt that Kemal might start a jihad to liberate Egypt from the British.[19] Poets and illustrators compared him to the Prophet's companion and great general, Khalid ibn al-Walid, and to Saladin.[20]

In the aftermath of these tumultuous changes, as elsewhere in the Near East, different groups worked to formulate understandings of their past and ideologies for the future, assessing where their values, morals and identity lay. Establishing a contrast between western materialism as against Islamic reformers or traditionalists was one way to address this. The twin pillars of nationalism and Islam formed the basic underpinning of many of these concepts, although the relative balance between the two varied considerably. In each case, the time of Saladin and the crusades constituted part of their historical discourse, employed to carry a different ideological emphasis appropriate to the interests and beliefs of particular groups.[21]

In the course of the 1930s other narratives came into play, some of which placed the role of Islam much more to the fore. Islamic nationalism adjudged Egypt to be the leader of the Muslim and Arab worlds; Islamic Egypt had repelled the crusaders in an Islamic, not an Egyptian war; the country was the shield of Islam against the crusaders and had a destiny to lead the Islamic people.[22] 1928 saw the foundation of the Muslim Brotherhood, an organisation that aims for a pan-Islamic reach and whose teachings have sometimes been used to stir extreme violence. The founder, Hasan al-Banna, saw Islam through Sharia law as the solution to the wider troubles that faced the people and lands of the Muslim world. In the first instance this could only happen with independence, thus the need to drive out the British; beyond this was the hope to extend Sharia law across all Muslim lands and to recreate the caliphate. Al-Banna was key in moving Islamic rhetoric of this era from the more rarefied circles of the religious and academic classes to a more populist political philosophy.

With the emphasis on the decline of Islam after the age of the first four caliphs, much of what followed is seen by the Brotherhood as marred by the failings of its leadership with episodes such as the crusades one part of the series of catastrophes that struck Islam. Within that narrative, al-Banna reflected upon the remarkable emergence of the first heroes of Islam, cited here as the second caliph, Abu Bakr, Ali and al-Abbas (an uncle and companion of the Prophet). The only other historical figure accorded such admiration was Saladin: 'Who would have imagined that Salah al-Din the Ayyubid would hold his ground for long years and hurl back the kings of Europe on their heels, defeated, despite their enormous numbers and the brave show of their armies, until twenty-five of their greatest kings banded against him?'[23]

Al-Banna generally advocated a gradual, practical approach to change, but the Palestinian question caused him to call for a jihad in 1947. Rising violence meant the Muslim Brotherhood was ordered by the British to disband, a move that provoked the assassination of Egyptian prime minister Mahmoud El-Nokrashy Pasha in 1948; the following year, al-Banna himself was killed, probably by government operatives.

The crushing of the Egyptian army in the Arab–Israeli War of 1948 added more fuel to the fire in a period of intense political turmoil. Emerging from this context Sayyid Qutb formulated his *Social Justice in Islam*, an influential attempt to try to present a case to improve the lot of the wider population, ignored by, as he saw it, the elites and ruling classes, through the renewal of Islamic life; he was vehemently against nationalism, which he believed to be a materialist and flawed creed.[24]

This ethos was in many respects a reaction against the western presence and values that had arrived in the Near East since the nineteenth century. A distinctive element of this ideology was an attack on cultural imperialism, and with the caveat that this was only a part of his much wider concerns, the language of 'crusading' was used, often identifying Zionism with western crusading imperialism. Furthermore, as religion was synonymous with society and culture in Qutb's view, western crusading imperialism related not just to the conquest of land, but was an effort to subvert Muslim society as well. The use of crusading widened: 'The evil stirred up by the crusaders was not limited to the clash of arms but was first and foremost a cultural evil.'[25] Qutb had, in fact, heavily borrowed this idea from an Islamic convert, originally a Jewish journalist from Austria who became a Muslim and took the name Muhammad Asad. He had suggested that the West and Islam should be able to exist alongside one another but blamed the crusades as, primarily, 'an intellectual evil, poisoning the European mind against the Muslim world ... the spirit of the crusades – in a very diluted form to be sure – still lingers over Europe and the attitude of its civilisation towards the Muslim world bears traces of that diehard ghost'.[26] This explicit broadening out of the understanding of the historical crusades into a cultural war seems to me to mark a significant change, not least because once adopted by Qutb it came from such a prominent platform. Saladin was singled out by name as 'one whose lofty Islamic spirit is preserved in the history of these wars', and when the tide of war turned against the crusaders, 'the Muslims' treatment of them was marked by the spirit of Islam which was able to curb the desire for revenge in the souls of Muslims and keep them within the bounds of humanity and religion'.

Qutb suggested that 'the crusader spirit runs in the blood of all westerners'. We saw back in 1798 Nicholas the Turk's rejection of Napoleon's forces' language, clothes and religion, a loosely parallel dislike of western culture. In contrast, the Syrian–French conflict of 1919–20 was cast largely in terms of reversing Saladin's physical conquest. Qutb here wraps his broad-ranging hostility into the crusade label to deploy this catalysing word in a more penetrative and transferable way.

He wrote of 'inherited crusader hostility' that was trying to kill the Islamic spirit. He argued that the slow destruction of Muslim Spain (from the eleventh century to 1492) had done much to build upon the distorted image of Islam propagated by western leaders and meant that anti-Islamic feeling in the West became permanent. He cited a form of the controversial words sometimes put into the mouth of General Gouraud at Saladin's tomb in Damascus in 1920, but according to Qutb from the lips of Colonel Catroux: 'We are the descendants of the Crusaders and anyone who does not like our rule can leave.' His *Social Justice in Islam* also included a description of the massacre of the Muslims of Jerusalem in 1099, slaughtered after the crusaders broke their own pledge of security. Qutb later joined the Muslim Brotherhood and continued to grow in profile. He is known as the 'prophet' of militant Islam, not least for his *Milestones* (1966) which set Saladin forward as a man who cast aside differences of nationality and triumphed through his unwavering faith.[27]

Antipathy towards (especially) the British following the revelation of the Balfour agreement grew during the 1920s and 1930s and culminated with the Arab Revolt of 1936–9. Fury at this betrayal was apparent in a vast array of political and cultural forms, ranging from violent uprisings to polemical speeches, through drama, art and poetry. Needless to say, historical reference points from the medieval period (amongst others) emerged, especially in poetry.[28] In the context of the 1920s and 1930s, poets frequently looked to earlier Arab heroes for the inspiration, encouragement and confidence to defend their cause. As the most obvious candidate to protect Palestine from the 'new crusaders', Saladin was referred to far more than anyone else. Poets appealed for the sultan to rise from his grave and defeat the crusaders again:

> Saladin! Your people are calling upon you to rise from the dead; your
> chivalry would not allow you to sleep while they are on the alert.
> The Crusaders have forgotten the lesson they received at your hands,
> so come back and remind them.[29]

The poet Burhan al-Din al-Abbushi urged his people to come to their senses before this happened, and reminded them of times past:

Awake, people, before you are expelled from a country where the bones of your ancestors are buried!
What would you say to Saladin and Khalid ibn al-Walid if you were meekly expelled?[30]

Particular events such as the Bludan Conference of 1937 in Syria, an attempt by the wider Arab world to organise itself against Zionism, prompted a flurry of verse. The poet Sulayman Zahir connected the earlier failure of the crusaders with what would happen to them once more: 'Those who, in the past, scoffed at the lightning coming from your marching troops, those who saved the country when your armies covered all its highlands and lowlands; and those whose Saladin drove you back like a camel-herdsman driving back a runaway she-camel, will not be scared of the thunder coming from you.'[31]

Theatre continued to engage with the memory of Saladin. A play from this period by Nasri al-Juzi called *The Ghosts of the Freedom Knights* addressed the issue of selling land to the Zionists. The drama depicts a hard-pressed landowner planning to make just such a sale but his son, aided by a trio of ghostly heroes – Caliph Umar, Khalid ibn al-Walid and Saladin – reminds him of the sacrifices of early generations of Arabs, and he eventually changes his mind.[32]

Secular art also began to emerge in Palestine during the 1930s. One such painter was Zulfa al-Sa'di, whose pictures were exhibited at the First National Arab Fair in Jerusalem in the summer of 1933. Her work included portraits of Arab heroes such as Saladin alongside those of contemporary cultural or political figures, constituting a clear anti-colonial message.[33]

A much more direct engagement in the Palestinian issue can be seen in the political–religious aspect of an event masterminded by the Istiqlal ('Independence') party, one of the numerous groups who looked to take a lead in Arab political activity in Palestine at the time of the Mandate. One way to signal their antipathy towards the British was to invoke Saladin's crushing defeat of the Christians at the Battle of Hattin. This organisation was drawn mainly from the professional classes and it sought to mobilise support through educational and youth movements. With that in mind, in August 1932 it drew many thousands from across the Near East to events in Safad, and especially, Haifa to celebrate Saladin's victory. This was, in part, a process of forming a national past with Palestine as a part of a larger Arab community. Thus speeches were made calling for the revival and independence of the Arab nation, and the unity of Christian and Muslim Arabs. Some Christian newspapers objected to the event, regarding the Hattin theme as an attack on them, but elsewhere, elements of the Arab press suggested it should be treated as a secular gathering that symbolised the victory of the East over the West. The following year, numbers were down, although more provocatively, one newspaper insisted that 'we want another Battle of Hattin'.[34]

In the mid-1930s, the continued failure of the Palestinians to persuade the British to allow them to form their own national government, exacerbated by dire economic conditions and a growing influx of Jews fleeing from the Nazis, generated tensions that produced armed conflict. The death of the Palestinian leader Sheikh Izz al-Din al-Qassam prompted a general strike which in turn led to a three-year uprising that was only brought to a close after the British deployed serious military force and inflicted heavy casualties on the Palestinians, and killed or sent into exile their senior commanders. In the context it seemed entirely appropriate to reference Saladin and the crusaders, as the insurgents in Nablus in 1938 were urged to represent the Muslim world with pride. They were described as 'keepers of the Aqsa Mosque and successors of Salah al-Din', drawing parallels with their fight and the Yarmuk campaign (638), and between Saladin's triumph at the Battle of Hattin and the jihad of the present.[35]

Syria also saw a major public event that underpinned the relevance of Saladin in the context of contemporary Arab nationalism. Yasim al-Hashimi was the recently exiled former prime minister of Iraq, a strong supporter of the Arab Revolt of 1936 and when he died in Beirut in January 1937 he was widely mourned across the Near East. A new government had just taken office in Syria and was looking to enhance its nationalist credentials. A funeral service took place in Damascus, a public ritual for a secular hero. The carefully choreographed procession and service attracted enormous crowds. Speeches outlined the Arab cause and naturally included Saladin's victories as well as references to the Battle of Maysalun, the Syrians' last stand against the French in 1920. Prime Minister Jamil Mardam Bey spoke, first of all taking a swipe at the Iraqis for exiling al-Hashimi and describing them as deserters from the cause of Arabism; Syria in contrast, still held up its beacon. He continued: 'Damascus ... wanted that her earth, which is moist with the blood of martyrs, enclose his body, too, and she wanted to build him a grandiose mausoleum at the side of ... Salah al-Din.' In other words, al-Hashimi would lie close to the secular saint of the Arab nationalist cause.[36]

By the eve of the Second World War, therefore, the demise of the Ottoman Empire and the post-First World War settlements in the Near East had generated movements, of varying degrees of strength and effectiveness, seeking independence. Nationalism and Islamism offered two essential themes for the many different groups looking to achieve these goals, and the relative importance of one to the other was constantly shifting. Through ideology and culture, manifest in history, drama and commemoration, the invocation of Saladin, the most successful of all the West's opponents, constituted an evocative part of the call to arms for leaders and listeners of all persuasions. Or, to put it another way, Saladin and the crusaders offered a shared reference point, providing a powerful commonality that ranged across what can otherwise seem the purely national histories of Turkey, Syria, Lebanon, Palestine and Egypt.

26

Looking for a New Saladin,

c.1950–2001

*'It seems to me that within the Arab circle there
is a role wandering aimlessly in search of a hero'*

In the autumn of 1963 cinemagoers packed the movie houses of the
Near East. The opening scene of Youssef Chahine's epic *El-Naser Salah
Ad-Din*, a play on President Nasser's name and translated as 'Saladin the
Victorious', showed the terrible state of the Arabs in the kingdom of
Jerusalem at the time of the crusades. Driven from their lands and living
in terror, they are bullied by the brutal crusaders; starving refugees trail
across a barren desert. In these grim conditions the people dream of
redemption and that God will send them a liberator. As the camera
pans across the silent, anxious faces of this poor band, a wind picks up.
Slowly the crowd start to hear distant drums, the people gather and
begin to stir. As the noise becomes louder, a banner appears on the
horizon: 'He has come!' exclaims a man, giving voice to an almost
divine deliverance. A mighty blast of trumpets overwhelms the viewer
and the title of the film bursts onto the screen. Saladin has arrived! The
plea to lead his people into battle is impossible to resist: 'I cannot ignore
their call. My dream is to see the Arab nation united under one flag.'

The film was a roaring success and in Cairo and Alexandria the
audience chanted the name of their president, linking the battles of
the twelfth century to those of the present. It was 'a film that made
us all proud', as one newspaper wrote. Even more pointedly another
critic proclaimed 'this is a historical moment we need to once again
look at and absorb. Saladin did an excellent job of reminding us of
that moment.'[1]

From the late 1950s onwards a series of powerful, authoritarian figures emerged across various of the lands of the Near East. For many of these men, and their peoples, Saladin exerted an immense attraction as a role model and an exemplar to be evoked and employed to encourage ideas of unity and successful resistance to the West, a chance to be 'the new Saladin', the man to take them to victory. That said, having set oneself up for comparison with Saladin the bar is high, meaning lapses and failure can be measured against the sultan too.

The use of the memory of Saladin in the context of Arab nationalism had its highest profile during the years of President Gamal Abdel Nasser, the man who governed Egypt from 1954 to 1970.[2] In 1954 he wrote his *Philosophy of the Revolution* outlining his views and his sense of history: 'I believe that we must also dwell at length on our history through the Middle Ages since it was the vicissitudes of that period which contributed so much to what we think and how we act today. If the crusades were the beginning of the Renaissance in Europe, they were the beginning of the Dark Ages for our country. Our people alone bore most of the sufferings of the crusades, out of which they emerged poor, destitute and exhausted.' He argued that the Egyptians had been slow to adapt to the modern world after centuries of darkness. Nasser suggested that Egypt needed a new hero: 'It seems to me that within the Arab circle there is a role wandering aimlessly in search of a hero.' This man should look to the past for reference points with the aim of harnessing the 'tremendous power latent in the area around' to build a positive future.[3]

His decision to nationalise the Suez Canal in 1956 brought him into conflict with the British and the French, a struggle rich with opportunities to summon up crusading precedents for the defeat of invading westerners. Propaganda encouraged civilian resistance in the cause of national defence, and an article in the long-standing political magazine *Ruz al-Yusuf* titled 'How Can You Become a Resistance Fighter?' stated that the first real anti-imperialist Egyptian patriot was a warrior in Saladin's army against the crusaders.[4]

While the forces of Israel, France and Britain achieved military successes against the Egyptians, American diplomatic intervention led to these powers being condemned by the United Nations and the insertion of a peacekeeping force into Suez. Such an outcome was regarded as a great achievement by the Arab world and Nasser's popularity soared. He had stood up to the imperialists and transformed an aspiration to take on the West into a reality. The notion of the Arab people working together was central to the president's ideology, and Saladin's role as the ruler of Egypt and Syria neatly matched his aims. Syria had, in its constitution of 1950, stated that the Syrian people were part of an Arab Nation and, in the post-Suez era, enthusiasm for the joining of these 'northern and southern poles' of the Arab peoples ran high in both countries.[5] Thus, 1 February 1958 saw the foundation of the United Arab Republic. To mark the occasion Nasser travelled to Damascus where he visited Saladin's tomb; accompanying him was Anwar Sadat, at the time, speaker of the UAR parliament and later president of Egypt himself.[6]

Nasser was keen to emphasise the historic roots of Arab nationalism. He argued that unity amongst Arabs meant victory and that division brought defeat. He described the crusader invasion of Egypt and noted that 'they got as far as the gates of Cairo'. He rightly credited Nur al-Din with sending the armies of Syria to join with the Egyptians to drive the crusaders away. After this, Saladin defeated the imperialists at the Battle of Hattin and recovered Jerusalem; 'this was the basis of Arab unity'. The present was a time of 'a rebirth of Arab nationalism and a means of defeating imperialists ... Naturally, they recall events that took place as far as 800 years back and note that whenever any Arab country was attacked it could never withstand invasion on its own ... but when united they invariably succeeded.'[7] His speeches included references to many other events such as the betrayal of the Arabs by the Ottomans and the defeat of Napoleon. This earlier triumph over the French, coupled with events at Suez, were an obvious cue for comparisons to the demise of the crusade of Louis IX at Mansourah in northern Egypt in 1250. Just as we saw the Egyptians remembered Louis' defeat during Napoleon's invasion, so too did Nasser.[8]

On numerous other occasions Nasser chose to evoke victories over the crusaders.[9] Saladin 'as you know from history' was one of those who had achieved this.[10] Saladin, as the man who recovered Jerusalem was, therefore, representative of a central aspiration of the Arab peoples, although the claim that 'he was able to take Richard prisoner of war' was wishful thinking.[11]

Nasser repeatedly quoted General Allenby's supposed comment when he entered Jerusalem in December 1917: 'Today, the war of the crusades has ended.' Likewise he mocked General Gouraud's 'Saladin, we have returned', saying that if Gouraud imagined he had succeeded where his forefathers, the crusaders, had failed and if he believed that he could destroy Arab nationalism 'which the crusaders failed to destroy during a period of 200 years', then he was severely wrong.[12] These phrases had obviously taken a firm hold in the Near East and persisted as a means to challenge the West's purported narrative. But, as with so much to do with myth and image, they were seen as plausible in the circumstances and fitted perfectly the agenda of those who invoked them.

Contemporary stamps featured, amongst many designs, the so-called Eagle of Saladin, said (wrongly) to have been his battle standard. Egyptian stamps of the day celebrated the events at Suez with a series that included the Battle of Hattin and the defeat of Louis IX at Mansourah. Stamps may seem deeply mundane objects but as the product of a government they represent a message that it wishes to transmit; likewise public displays and parades featured the Ayyubid hero as well. Further biographies of Saladin appeared, as did histories of the crusades and beyond, including one survey titled *East and West from the Crusades to the Suez War*.[13]

One of the most enduring relics of the Nasser-era fascination with Saladin is Youssef Chahine's film noted at the start of the chapter. While the United Arab Republic fractured in the course of the movie's production, the issue of Arab unity was still high on the political agenda. In fact, this was not the first Arab film about Saladin; an earlier (1941) effort had tried to cover his story but for a number of reasons fell alarmingly short. The director, Ibrahim Lama, cast his brother, who apparently had aspirations to be the Arab Rudolph Valentino, in the lead role. Hampered by a script written by an unknown poet and wildly at variance with historical events, the decision to bootleg parts of Cecil B. DeMille's 1935 Hollywood epic *The Crusades* proved unwise, not least because people pointed out that the Arab soldiers possessed foreign features. On learning of this criticism, Lama removed the offending scenes but this only compounded the fiasco. Panoramic battlefields had a grand total of twelve brave knights heading into the fray. 'Are they on their way to liberate a city or open a shop?' ruminated one reviewer.[14]

Limitations on cast numbers would not be an issue for Chahine, whose film proved far more successful and durable.[15] In essence, the

Saladin in the film is a man of simple tastes, admirably modest in dress, who pursues the interests of Arabs in his uniting of Egypt and Syria. Through his personal boldness, moral integrity and high political skills he was able to defeat the crusaders who were motivated by base imperialist desires. These characteristics were all, of course, meant to telegraph Nasser.

After the opening scenes, the story runs through Reynald of Châtillon's sanguinary attack on the caravan (here containing pilgrims rather than merchants), the Battle of Hattin which elides into the fall of Jerusalem, the siege of Acre and then the Third Crusade itself. Chahine wanted to show that the Egyptians could produce a Hollywood-style epic themselves and he certainly achieved this aim, with a cast of thousands, no less than seven battle scenes and a duration of over three hours for the cinematic original. By the end of the movie, Saladin defeated the crusaders, people who, under the guise of religion, came and took over a sacred Arab city and dispossessed its rightful owners. Israel was the obvious parallel here, which gave the film another powerful resonance across the Arab world. The position of Israel as the supposed successor to the crusader states is a theme that would emerge with great frequency in the coming decades.

Saladin himself is a noble, courteous, culturally superior leader; the crusaders are, with the exception of Richard the Lionheart, greedy and corrupt. Curiously, given that the massacre of the Muslim prisoners at Acre in 1191 is (rightly) held out as an atrocity, the English king is largely absolved from blame. Instead, the fault falls upon other crusade leaders who murdered his messengers to the sultan and yet pinned the blame on Saladin, thus causing Richard to order the execution. Once the matter is explained, Saladin can accept his apology.

Saladin and Richard come face to face and make peace: 'Tell all those in Europe that war is not always the solution ...'. The point related is: 'Since when do aggressors impose conditions on legitimate owners? You started this war, if you want peace truly, leave my country.' By the end of the movie the message was clear; Saladin was a humane and cosmopolitan ruler and a worthy guardian of Jerusalem. He concluded: 'Christianity is respected here; you know that. Jerusalem belongs to the Arabs. Stop this bloodshed. That would satisfy God and Christ.' Yet there was stern underpinning to this message: 'I hate war. Islam and Christianity condemn bloodshed. Yet we shall fight if necessary to save our land.'

Strict historical accuracy was questionable and this did attract some criticism when the film appeared. A rather forced scene towards the end of the movie blends a muezzin's call to prayer at midnight (this does not happen) with a heavenly choir singing a Christmas carol while snow falls on a harmonious holy city. Richard meeting Saladin, or the English king entering Jerusalem once, let alone twice, are just two examples; an anachronistic use of binoculars is another. Some anecdotes from the medieval age, such as Saladin reuniting the Frankish mother with her infant daughter, did find their way into the film, although the sultan's medical skills and his presence at the bedside of a sick King Richard are drawn from the enduring imagination of Sir Walter Scott (presumably via the 1898 Haddid play and/or the 1935 Cecil B. DeMille *Crusades* epic), rather than the pen of a medieval writer. On the other hand this was, after all, a movie, not a documentary. It was also a film of its time, rewriting and reinterpreting history with an eye to the present. For this reason, Saladin is portrayed as practically flawless, obviously far from reality, although this was hardly the moment to highlight his failings.

In the later years of Nasser's rule his engagement with the memory of Saladin had a lower profile, not least because of the disastrous 1967 Six Day War. This saw the loss to the Israelis of Gaza, Sinai, the Golan Heights and, most significantly of all, the West Bank, including East Jerusalem (the old medieval city), a defeat that many compared to the capture of the city by the First Crusaders in 1099.[16]

Given how obvious a model Saladin seemed to offer and with the influence of years of his use by Nasser it is unsurprising that his successor, Anwar Sadat, periodically drew upon the memory and the legacy of the crusades. In some contexts it was too tempting to ignore, for example when trying to forge a union between Egypt, Libya and the Sudan and to work with Syria. In a broadcast to the nation Sadat argued: 'The Crusader invasion lasted for 80 years ... they used the Cross only as a pretext, for in reality that was an Imperialistic invasion to conquer this area. Now, History has mentioned, and History books still mention, that if it were not for the union between Egypt and Syria under Saladin's leadership there would have been no way to rescue the area from the Crusader invasion.'[17]

On numerous occasions between 1971 and 1975 Sadat referenced Saladin as a creator and symbol of Arab unity.[18] But as relations with Israel improved he made a historic visit to the Knesset (the Israeli parliament) and in his address of 20 November 1977 he completely inverted decades of Arab rhetoric to reject awakening 'the hatreds of the crusades'. Seeking to establish a more constructive atmosphere he drew upon the many positive aspects of Saladin's reputation as a man whose 'spirit of tolerance and respect for rights' was an example of the approach needed to make a lasting peace.[19]

Yet the sultan was not invoked solely by politicians looking to wrap themselves in his glorious history, although the use of it by such figures certainly embedded the image ever more deeply within the public consciousness. Dramatists employed Saladin in complex socio-political situations, most notably in the aftermath of Nasser's humiliating defeat in the 1967 war. Produced four years after this event, and with Nasser now dead, Mahmud Diyab's epic *The Gateway to Conquest* was written in literary Arabic. It was a pointed encouragement to elites to give people political freedom.[20] In the play a group of young men discuss the desolation they feel after 1967. They fashion a game in which historical events become closer to their own hopes and the action moves between the medieval and the modern ages. Saladin is held up as a man of courage and inspiration, but the main protagonists argue that historians have ignored the role of the people in his achievements. Usama, a fictional hero from Muslim Spain, leaves his divided, squabbling homeland to show Saladin a book that he has written about the shared interests of the Arab nation. The sultan's secretary is horrified by what appear as revolutionary ideas and the book is burned and Usama killed, although not before many are attracted to his views. The hero had hoped to show Saladin that his counsellors formed a wall between the sultan and his people, the group for whom he was fighting. Yet as things stand only the rich would benefit, making even the sultan's victories at Hattin and Jerusalem short-lived and superficial; 'a war by the people, not for the people'. Thus the medieval sultan is lifted clear of any blame and it seems that those around the leader were the contemporary targets of the playwright's pen.[21]

Another dramatist, Abd al-Rahman al-Sharqawi, produced an epic pair of plays about Saladin called *Saladin, the Red Eagle* (1976). The sultan's virtues as a pious and chivalric holy warrior, who resisted oppression in all its forms, were the characteristics emphasised here. In a sharper tone Saladin is advised to prioritise justice at home over the pursuit of war and foreign affairs, presumably a reflection of al-Sharqawi's own concerns over Sadat's policies.[22]

A less convincing nod to the memory of Saladin in the context of Egyptian history emerged at a state dinner for President Mubarak in London in March 1985. Prime Minister Margaret Thatcher welcomed the Egyptian premier with the slightly alarming remark: 'Relations between Britain and Egypt are excellent. Of course, they go back quite a long time. We were already on good terms in the days of Saladin and Richard the Lionheart.'[23]

One of the most familiar figures to draw upon the image of Saladin was Saddam Hussein, president of Iraq from 1979 until his overthrow in 2003. He was attracted to an Arab nationalist ideology and having observed Nasser use Saladin within this broad framework, it was logical for Saddam to do so as well. Reasons for this went far beyond external influences, though. In the 1930s and 1940s Iraqi education ministers had emphasised nationalism through encouraging the study of history because it was 'filled with sentiments to awaken national pride' as demonstrated by the virtuous, brave and glorious heroes of the past, featuring Saladin, of course.[24] For Saddam himself, the fact that they were both born in the town of Takrit provided an obvious cue for him, and such was the president's enthusiasm for the link that he changed his official year of birth from 1939 to 1937 in order to connect his own birth with that of the medieval sultan (b.1137).

The Iraqi regime focused intensively on honing a cult of personality around their leader.[25] A number of individuals were given prominence with, amongst others, Saladin coming periodically to the fore. The First Gulf War, triggered by the Iraqi invasion of Kuwait, provided the opportunity to employ such imagery. With his seeming penchant for anniversaries, just as Saladin had (apparently) foiled the crusaders in 1191, so in 1991 the president predicted that he would defeat the new crusaders. Phrases such as 'we can smell the smell of Hattin' also showed a connection to the sultan's success.[26] That Saddam's affinity with the sultan had registered on a wider scale was shown when Margaret Thatcher queried his use of women and children as human shields in Kuwait as being 'strange for someone who claims to be the leader of the Arab world and a latter-day Saladin'.[27]

More commonplace was the use of Saladin on stamps and currency, on posters, monumental wall paintings and statues. Saddam himself was presented with a golden statue of the sultan in 2002. All of this embedded, fortified and conveyed the appropriate resonance and identity; schoolbooks and education played their part too. The 800th anniversary of the Battle of Hattin prompted a children's book, *The hero Saladin*, that included a brief history of the medieval sultan, followed by a much lengthier account of the life of 'Saladin II Saddam Hussein'; an illustration showing Saladin blessing the Iraqi president also appeared. Much more contentious was Saddam's attitude towards the Kurds. They were fellow Sunnis, but they were deemed un-Iraqi, and were the subject of savage persecution. The grim irony of Saladin's Kurdish ancestry was ignored, with Saddam describing the medieval sultan as an Arab.[28]

A particularly personal insight into Saddam's view of history was gained in the course of the extensive debriefing of the president conducted in December 2003 and January 2004 by the senior CIA leadership analyst John Nixon. Saddam 'felt a strong kinship with the great warrior', not least as a fellow native of Takrit and, as Nixon recalls, he recounted the sultan's capture of Jerusalem from the crusaders in detail. Sometimes he answered questions on his presidency via long, rambling lectures, at times going back to the rule of Saladin, in order, as he saw it, to explain why he had acted in a certain way.[29]

Saddam discussed Saladin's personality as well, describing here his most esteemed attribute, although given the particular circumstances, Nixon himself commented: 'I couldn't help but think if Saddam was trying to get across to us the need for clemency in any future judgement on him or his regime.' Saddam said:

> Reading history now, we are more enlightened. The one that always attracted me was Saladin, not because of his successful battles but because of his humane treatment of his enemies. There was an alliance against him [a crusade], and one of the European kings got sick and he [Saladin] put on a disguise, entered his tent, treated him and left for a while. They discussed who had treated the king until they realised it was him. When Richard the Lionheart was captured, they respected him and gave him all of his weapons and supplies back for him to go home with after his troops were scattered.[30]

In reality, as we saw, Richard and Saladin never met, yet what Saddam seems to have referenced is a scene from Youssef Chahine's 1963 movie. In this, as Saddam stated, the sultan disguised himself and crept into the king's tent to cure him of an illness. The origins of this story lie within, of all places, the pages of The Talisman, Sir Walter Scott's novel from 1825. The situation whereby an imprisoned ex-president of Iraq faithfully relays a scene that emanated from the mind of a Scottish Anglican nobleman almost 200 years previously is quite surreal, although more likely a testament to the enormous popularity of Chahine's film (itself running through the Scott-influenced Egyptian plays of the late nineteenth century) than anything else. Saddam, it seems, tapped into a collective public memory that had plainly become part of a popular cultural tradition.[31]

Elsewhere in the Near East, soon after President Nasser died (September 1970) another leader in the region stepped forwards to try to claim the mantle of Saladin. Hafiz al-Asad (b.1930) grew up in north-western Syria in an area where the medieval sultan had captured several crusader castles. Educated in Arab nationalist beliefs and living in a country that had long made reference to its illustrious hero, it is unsurprising that Asad was a great admirer of Saladin, as he was of President Nasser too.[32] Once he solidified his grip on power, the Syrian president formed a huge cult of personality with the media driving forwards his position as 'the father of the nation', 'the first teacher', the 'gallant knight', or indeed, 'the premier pharmacist'.[33]

The Ba'ath Party was keen on the markers of shared language and history as the foundations of Arab nationalism. Syrian academics met on a number of occasions to discuss and define history and to examine the history of Arab unity, in a cultural, rather than strictly political, sense.[34] An event focused on the 800th anniversary of the Battle of Hattin inevitably formulated a strong degree of historical continuity between Saladin and Asad, and the crusades and Zionism. It also drew close attention to the city of Damascus, Saladin's favoured base during the medieval period and declared that 'Asad's Damascus is the source of unity and liberation as it was in the days of Saladin'. The medieval sultan's endless toil in the effort to defeat his enemies was said to be matched by Asad:

Mr President, we are mindful of the similarity and the link between the Frankish invasion of the Arab Middle East and Israeli aggression against Arab countries. From the historical documents in our possession and according to the research presented at the conference, we know that the crusaders and the Zionists had but a single purpose, namely occupation, settlement, pillage, slaughter and deportation ... We are certain that your wise and courageous leadership will take the Arab nation to victory as Salah al-Din led the Arab East to triumph. There is no doubt that the Arab soil that presented our nation with Salah al-Din al-Ayyubi is the very same soil that has given the nation Hafiz al-Asad, that tomorrow's heroism will be as great as yesteryear's.[35]

This scholarly endeavour emphasised Asad's legitimacy and his claim to Saladin's heritage, not least in the face of the neighbouring Saddam Hussein's growing proclivity to hitch himself to the victor over the crusaders. Holy war tended to be low in the rhetoric for Asad, not least because Saladin had removed the Shi'ite caliph (the Alawites are an offshoot of Shi'ism) and he had fought the Christians, who constituted 14% of the Syrian population under Asad.[36]

Various other aspects of visual culture featured Saladin, all in the context of a tightly controlled media. He appeared on issues of bank-notes in 1977 and 1997; the October War Memorial, a gift of the North Koreans, features diorama images of the 1973 conflict and includes one of Saladin taking Jerusalem. In 1992 a large equestrian statue was erected outside the citadel of Damascus. This striking memorial stands alongside a major road and is just next to the main entrance of the medieval walled city, about as visible a position as could be imagined. A proud and confident Saladin rides his horse to victory, while behind him two defeated crusaders slump dejectedly below his horse; the imperialists in defeat. Annual commemorations of the sultan's death were prominent under Hafiz al-Asad. Roadside paintings and privately created images above shops link his successor, Bashar, to the medieval sultan, and also indicate the continued attraction of this message.[37]

Saladin's victory at Hattin was used to provide a rather stretched historical comparison to the 1973 October War when an attempt to take the Golan Heights from Israel was, after early successes, driven back. At the time this was described as a glorious victory and 'a fatal blow to imperialism and Zionism' and later posters showed Asad next to Saladin.[38] The triumph at Hattin was also the subject of a painting hung behind the president's desk. Former US president Jimmy Carter visited Damascus in 1984. Carter wrote: 'As Asad stood in front of the brilliant scene and discussed the history of the crusades and the other ancient struggles for the Holy Land, he took particular pride in retelling the tales of Arab successes, past and present. He seemed to speak like a modern Saladin, feeling that it was his dual obligation to rid the region of all foreign presence, while preserving Damascus as the only focal point of Arab unity today.'[39]

Further afield, yet another leader to link his name to Saladin was the Libyan leader Muammar Gaddafi, who took care to plant the connection in the minds of his people from their schooldays onwards. On the other hand he was described by one British ambassador as an 'unbalanced' and 'paranoic latter-day Saladin'.[40]

Along with their own national and domestic political concerns, all of the leaders above sought to advance the cause of the Palestinians. In the aftermath of the 1948–9 war the emergent state of Israel kept hold of large areas of territory designated to the Palestinians; Transjordan took control of the West Bank, the Gaza strip came under the rule of the Egyptian army, and a massive exodus of refugees flooded the neighbouring Arab countries. The governments of Egypt and Syria, both facing criticism for their failure to defend the Arab lands, started to support various partisan groups with the first to come to prominence being *Fatah* (meaning 'conquering') founded by the Cairo-born Yasser Arafat in Gaza in 1954. Early in life he was influenced by the Muslim Brotherhood, although his later admiration of President Nasser signals his Arab nationalist ideology; by 1968 he had become chairman of the Palestine Liberation Organization.[41]

At the heart of Palestinian identity is a focus on the guardianship of the holy places of Jerusalem, a situation that gave the paradigm of Saladin and the crusades a particularly natural resonance. As Arafat was sworn in as president of the Palestinian Authority c.1996 he was introduced with the phrase 'We are living this day for our Arab and Islamic nation, the triumph of Saladin.'[42] A few years later a Palestinian minister observed that 'Jerusalem was the unifying factor for Muslims in the Crusader period, and it is what will unify Muslims and Arabs today, with Allah's help.' He also wrote that 'we are aspiring for a new Umar or Saladin who would return to us our al-Quds [i.e. Jerusalem] and our dignity'.[43]

The Palestinian authorities devote much attention to the presentation of history; as we have seen, collective memory helps to form a contemporary self-image. The nationalism of the PLO employs a great deal of religious imagery as well, a logical step given that most Palestinians are Muslims. Arafat could formulate the Palestinian cause as one of religious struggle and mission.[44] A very open affirmation of the link with Saladin and the crusades took place in the late 1990s with the revival of the Nebi Musa festival, an event that had been a serious flashpoint in the past. The mufti of Jerusalem stated that 'Nebi Musa symbolises the liberation from the occupation of the *franj* ... [Now] there are no crusaders, but there is still the West. The West has replaced the crusaders and the West supports Israel in its occupation of our country. We consider this another form of crusader war.' This potent blend of pilgrimage, politics and folklore offered a platform for speakers to extol the 'new Saladin', Yasser Arafat, the man to lead the Palestinians to victory.[45]

Saladin was held out as the unifier of Palestinians and of a nation that had not changed since the twelfth century; pictures of the sultan next to Arafat appeared on the walls of the Nebi Musa sanctuary; an implicit equivalence between the two men. A popular slogan from the organisers was 'Lead us [Arafat], to Jerusalem like Saladin, we are your knights!' Through the Nebi Musa event, Saladin acts as a binding force, a saint to be celebrated in public, at a nationalist festival with, of course, his most heroic characteristics to the fore and carrying the hope of victory to come.[46]

Arafat, as with all the other individuals discussed earlier, had a far wider range of concerns above and beyond that of Saladin, although the presence of the medieval ruler was reinforced on television and in other media. The link between Arafat's aspirations, contemporary politics and the Ayyubid emerged with the reconstruction of the pulpit, originally commissioned by Nur al-Din, in the al-Aqsa Mosque. A lunatic had burned the original to the ground in 1969 but the Jordanians undertook a painstakingly precise restoration. Naturally, King Hussein wanted a public ceremony to reinstall it, but doing so would acknowledge Jordanian claims to Jerusalem's Islamic sites and would also block Arafat's own wish to bring with him 'Saladin's pulpit' in a triumphal entry to the holy city. In the event, this beautiful object was returned to the al-Aqsa in 2007, three years after Arafat's death.[47] Jordan, incidentally, also nurtures Saladin's legacy through commemorations of the victory at Hattin, in taking great pride in the existence of the castle of Ajlun, constructed by the sultan in the 1180s, through his presence in schoolbooks and, in the 1990s, the creation of their own equestrian statue of him in the town of Kerak.[48]

Alongside high-profile political leaders it is as well to acknowledge briefly other markers; the genre of poetry, as we have seen throughout this book, remains a powerful and emotive channel. Amongst the most prominent of all Palestinian poets was Mahmoud Darwish (d.2008), a man with close involvement in political life, especially with Yasser Arafat. Darwish made a number of references to Saladin and the crusades in his extensive *oeuvre*, especially in 'Memory for Forgetfulness', written about his experiences in Beirut in 1982. A lengthy section invokes the medieval age and contrasts the harshness of the Israelis ('leftover crusaders') with the magnanimity of Saladin, who sent fruit and ice to his opponents. Darwish's 'Tragedy of Narcissus: The Comedy of Silver' includes the well-worn General Gouraud quote, while his 'Passers in Passing Words' was put to music for the opening credits for the 2002 Syrian television series on the sultan.[49]

Film continues to act as a powerful conduit of political expression with Michel Khleifi's *Tale of the Three Jewels* (1994) set in a Gaza refugee camp where people yearn to return to their homes. The young protagonist, Yusuf, wants to escape the trauma of the present into an idyllic Palestine of the past, a place without borders. The film begins with a dream sequence in which he meets Saladin (who gives him a gun), with whom he shares, of course, his given name. In 2001 Tawfik Abu Wael made *Waiting for Saladin*, a film about the lives of the Palestinian residents of East Jerusalem. It starts with brief statements about the 'immortalised' medieval sultan 'who unified the Islamic–Arab state' and 'released' Jerusalem from the crusaders. As the film follows everyday people caught in barren, static lives, a voiceover anticipates that eventually 'destiny will come from the cape of time, from the battles of Badr, Yarmuk and Hattin' and from Saladin's sword. At a wider cultural level, it is unsurprising that Saladin featured in popular chants – 'tell Shamir, tell Rabin, we are the sons of Saladin' – and on banners carried during the first and second intifadas, or in the writings of many other poets such as Atallah Jabr.[50]

One final example from a Palestinian context gives the flavour of yet another setting in which Saladin's name and legacy have been invoked. What started as a seemingly minor affair in the northern

Israeli town of Nazareth expanded to become an international dispute that brought in an explicitly Christian dimension to the story. Plans to construct a plaza adjacent to the Church of the Annunciation prior to the flood of tourists expected for the millennial visit of Pope John Paul II ran into serious trouble. The ostensible reason was that within the area designated for the plaza lay the tomb of Shihab al-Din, a Muslim saint. This stood on land said to belong to an Islamic endowment (*waqf*) whose custodians wanted to build a mosque on top of the tomb. The construction of a basement in late 1997 sparked a three-week riot and the affair began to draw in the Israeli government and international Christian groups. Rising Islamist power in the locality put pressure on the Israeli–Arab community, as well as the Christians, with the issue revolving around the status of the *waqf*. It was in these circumstances that the memory of Saladin became relevant. Shihab al-Din was a largely unknown saint whose tomb seems to have been neglected for decades. To justify this level of controversy, exacerbated by the proximity of the Church of the Annunciation, the saint needed to have, or to acquire, a suitable pedigree. One version had him as a Damascene judge and preacher from the Mamluk era. By 1999, and perhaps as a reflection of some of the Saladin-related gestures we have seen from the PLO and Hamas, a more elaborate alternative emerged. Shihab was, apparently, the son of Saladin's sister, said to have been killed by Reynald of Châtillon in his infamous attack on the Muslim caravan in the spring of 1187. It was this act that triggered the Hattin campaign in which Shihab and his brother fought, only to be wounded and brought back to Nazareth where they died and were buried. This was, therefore, a narrative designed to link Shihab to Saladin and to give him an elevated significance on the symbolic landscape at a local, national and Islamic level. The wish to construct a mosque on the site 'was a continuation of the Muslim struggle against the Christian crusaders'. Further outbreaks of violence and various investigations ensued. The Israeli government became involved and ruled first, in 1999, that the mosque could be built on an area of the planned plaza, but then after pressure from the papacy and President George W. Bush reversed its decision and in 2003 the basement was demolished and by 2006 the plaza completed.[51]

Saladin's drawing together of the Near East to fight westerners and to expel them from Jerusalem, burnished by his courteous and merciful behaviour, made him a powerful and emotive figure during the decades that Arab nationalism rode high. Each of the leaders here tried to channel his legacy. Nasser and Saddam Hussein, in different ways, felt or formed a particularly personal affinity with the sultan. All of them brought into play the full weight of contemporary government to harness what was by now a very deeply rooted set of images to convey wider political aspirations to their own people and to the outside world. Towards the close of the twentieth century, however, Arab nationalism had achieved little in the way of tangible success; once more religion re-emerged as a prominent framework with which to engage with the West.

A bitter rival of the PLO is the Islamist group Hamas, founded in Gaza in 1987 by Ahmad Yasin and with close ties to the Muslim Brotherhood in Egypt. The Hamas charter of 1988 sets out the ideology of the Islamic Resistance Movement and its aim to draw in the 'divided Arab and Islamic world' until the land of Palestine is free. The document argues hard for the permissible and obligatory nature of jihad in achieving its goals. The language of 'the crusading West' and the characterisation of the struggle as one beyond a military conflict, having 'an ideological invasion of the Arab world', shows a close ancestry to the writings of Sayyid Qutb and Mohammad Asad. General Gouraud's 'Saladin, we have returned' phrase is again pressed into service while a lengthy historical context makes reference to the sultan's unifying leadership as vital in the defeat of the crusaders.[52] Saladin's victory also featured on Hamas banners flown at festivals and marches.[53]

Towards the end of the twentieth century another Islamist group began to gather ideas and to confront those whom it saw as inimical to their faith. Once more we see the influence of Sayyid Qutb, in this case perpetuated through his younger brother Muhammad, who lectured in Saudi Arabia for many years. There he taught a young Osama bin Laden who turned away from his wealthy family to go and fight the Soviet atheists in Afghanistan. Subsequently he set up training camps and, combining forces with the veteran jihadist the Egyptian Ayman al-Zawahiri, they created the 'World Islamic Front for Jihad against Jews and Crusaders' in 1998, with Zawahiri emerging as the principal ideologue. Numerous attacks followed.[54] Bin Laden issued a series of publications and broadcasts, embracing the emerging potential of the Internet to reach a global audience. His speeches were underpinned with texts from the Quran, from hadith, and by medieval scholars such as Ibn Taymiyya. Bin Laden wrote of the Judaeo-Crusader alliance against Islam and the struggle between Muslims and the global crusaders, casting the conflict very much as a war of religion, and emphasised the religious duty of all Muslims to expel enemies from their lands and the obligation on all believers to defend the Islamic community.[55]

On 9/11 came the ghastly attacks that hit the World Trade Center, the Pentagon and took down a further plane in Pennsylvania, costing almost 3,000 lives, an unprecedented strike at the United States. A few days later, President George W. Bush, in an unscripted response said: 'This crusade, this war on terrorism, is going to take a while.'[56] Unknown to Bush, he had reached for a word with toxic resonance in the Muslim world. A generous interpretation would lean towards the president invoking a morally right cause, as the word 'crusade' has so often come to mean in the West; indeed, as his press spokesman said a couple of days later: 'I think to the degree that that word has any connotations that would upset any of our partners, or anybody else in the world, the president would regret if anything like that was conveyed. But the purpose of his conveying it is in the traditional English sense of the word. It's a broad cause.'[57]

But this was the commander-in-chief of the US armed forces, a man known for his deeply held religious beliefs, seemingly demanding a holy war. To bin Laden, this was a gift: 'Bush left no room for the doubts or media opinion. He stated clearly that this war is a crusader war. He said this in front of the whole world to emphasise the fact ... the truth is that Bush has fought a crusade and raised his banner high and stood at the front of the procession.' Bin Laden spoke of 'the fiercest, and most violent crusader war against Islam since Muhammad was sent'.[58]

This exchange was broadcast across the world: what exactly Bush meant, and that crusading in a strict sense had been dead for centuries, were both irrelevant. The president himself, then expertly amplified by bin Laden, had tapped directly into an image of western aggression and an apparent disregard for Islamic faith and culture.

These ideas had been bubbling away for well over a century, and for people in the Near East especially, in terms of seeing connections between the medieval crusades and contemporary times, they had not really disappeared at all.

Bin Laden himself was keen to place the efforts to resist the American and British invasion of Iraq into a historical continuum that stretched from Muhammad's first victories, through the early centuries of Islam to a time when the al-Aqsa Mosque was lost and then regained 'at the hands of a wise leader who pursued a sound approach. The leader was Salah al-Din, may God bestow mercy on him, and the approach was Islam.'[59] Bin Laden also used poetry to invoke Saladin's spirit:

> I envision you all as Salahuddin Ayubi himself, wielding his all-conquering sword dripping with the blood of the infidels.
> I envision Salahuddin Ayubi coming out of the clouds, and in our hearts and minds is recreated the remembrance of the battles [of the Prophet Muhammad].[60]

Bin Laden's colleague, al-Zawahiri, was the unofficial spokesman for al-Qaeda (meaning 'the base') and made numerous broadcasts, as well as writing *Knights under the Prophet's Banner* explaining the development of jihadist ideas that led to 9/11 and setting out how to kill his enemies. He also included historical references, adding Nur al-Din alongside Saladin as a man of achievement, praising the former for seizing Damascus from 'the hypocrites' who had been in alliance with the crusaders of Jerusalem, an interestingly specific historical exemplar that showed al-Zawahiri's view on those who worked with outside powers.[61]

A noteworthy understanding that Saladin can be used to represent a figurehead for opposition came from Michael Scheuer, head of the CIA unit charged with hunting down bin Laden. Scheuer recognised that bin Laden's personal piety, eloquence, generosity and courage were qualities that made him 'an Islamic hero, as that faith's ideal type, and almost a modern-day Saladin'.[62]

As a symbol of resistance and victory over the invading West, as the man to unify the Near East under, variously, the sometimes overlapping banners of Islam, Palestine and the Arabs, Saladin's image endured and flourished across the Near East in the latter half of the twentieth century. Through relentless political exposure in speeches and broadcasts, on banners, coins, stamps, statues and posters, on film, the stage, in literature and educational material, his profile and his allure have grown ever stronger and wider.

Conclusion

This book has tried to understand how and why Saladin remains a figure of such profile and esteem over 800 years after his death. In one sense, the answer is simple – he conquered Jerusalem from the Christians and returned Islam's third most holy site to Muslim hands. But while this spectacular victory will always remain central, there was rather more to the sultan than this one great triumph, regardless of its unparalleled symbolic importance. I have attempted to discern what underlay his success, both in military, religious and political terms, and also look at the challenges he faced in a more personal way, in terms of the physical and mental demands upon him. What was it about Saladin that took the sultan beyond a landmark historical accomplishment and enabled him to evolve into a figure admired and at times mythologised in both East and West?

What emerges is an interpretation of his character, or the various representations of his character, left by the sources for us to assimilate and evaluate. This both slides and elides into a memory and a legacy, undoubtedly given massive momentum by the events of 1187, but also energised by what we can discern of his personality. Faith, generosity, mercy and justice are fundamental to many aspiring rulers and regimes, and they are features that followers and indeed enemies can admire. They are cross-cultural qualities, transferable outside the strictures of contemporary dynastic or ethnic rivalries in the Near East, beyond disputes between political and religious classes, or tension and war between Muslims and the various Christian groups with whom they interacted.

Set against a combination of wider cultural, religious and historical events, a blend or a selection of Saladin's personal attributes and achievements can be fitted to the needs and interests of a multitude of individuals, ideologies and situations. In many cases, the resultant image is defined primarily by these needs and may bear little or no resemblance to the historical record. But that, in some ways, is beside the point; part of my curiosity has been to see just how far and how flexibly his legacy and memory have been taken as people from a vast spectrum of standpoints look to appropriate or identify with him. To many he is a hero, a person who unifies individuals and a collective; a person about whom it is possible to invent traditions.[1] Yet it goes without saying that one person's hero is another's villain, and in a life as complex and frequently confrontational as Saladin's, he inevitably attracted considerable criticism and hostility. Watching some of this melt away over time is interesting in itself, but it does not evaporate entirely, of course. His removal of the Shi'ite caliph condemns him in the eyes of many modern adherents to this branch of Islam. Historians too have occasionally taken a harsh line, notably the American academic Andrew S. Ehrenkreutz who calls him 'a pragmatist pursuing power-oriented self-serving ambitions'.[2]

While Saladin was in no way without flaws or inconsistencies it is hard not to admire him, not least for his restless energy. That said, his shortcomings as a military leader at Montgisard, Tyre, Acre, Arsuf and Jaffa constitute a problematic tally. Set against that was the crushing triumph at Hattin and the huge number of towns and fortresses taken in decades of fighting Franks and Muslims. At the summit, of course, stands Jerusalem. As Imad al-Din wrote, 'blessed is the man who has lived long enough to see this day on which Islam has arisen and taken wing'.[3] Hattin and Jerusalem gave Saladin the authority and the divinely endorsed credibility to weather these other setbacks and ultimately, in conjunction with other factors, to see the leaders of Christian Europe return home having failed to secure their dearest wish.

But warfare is not simply about battles and sieges. To gather the troops needed to fight year upon year of holy war required immense financial resources, both in terms of running costs and to incentivise and reward the troops. Exacerbated by his relentless generosity there were times these costs ran beyond his means. Yet as Qadi al-Fadil wrote concerning an expensive expedition: 'no money is wasted that leaves a legacy of praise'. It also required brilliant motivational skills and Saladin's personal piety, his leading by example and his endurance all played a part. He joined the interests of his own family in forming

an Ayyubid empire alongside the call to jihad so desired by the religious classes and embraced and stimulated by Nur al-Din. Achieving
these dynastic ambitions required the submission of the Zengid family
but in preserving and realising his spiritual aims, Saladin was able to
secure enough support to take on and defeat the Franks. The wider
diplomatic skills needed to neutralise peripheral forces such as the
Seljuks, the Assassins, the Byzantine Empire, the Maghrebis, not to
mention struggling with a deeply recalcitrant Sunni caliph, cumulatively constitutes one of his most impressive, and unremarked upon,
achievements. Likewise, it is easy to be drawn into the fast-paced
narrative of the years 1186 to 1192 without appreciating the hundreds
of days that Saladin spent in the saddle and the months camped outside
fortresses and cities come winter rains, or the hottest of summers.
Coupled with the responsibility of first taking, and then holding on
to, the holy city of Jerusalem, not to mention the diplomatic, financial
and familial pressures that accreted over the years, it is unsurprising
that his physical health was often dire and, as his contemporaries
acknowledged, the mental strain on him was sometimes hard to bear.

The Ayyubid clan was central to Saladin's success, and rarely
wavered in their loyalty to him. It was not until the later stages of
the siege of Acre, not a good time to pick, admittedly, that real cracks
began to appear. By any standards this was a remarkable record and
it showed the Ayyubids' appreciation of Saladin's leadership abilities
and reflects upon his strength of personality and charisma. It is also
clear that he came to rely heavily upon his younger brother Saphadin,
often his first source of advice and support in difficult times and his
de facto deputy. In terms of personality they were, in some respects,
quite different. On the one hand, Saphadin's diplomatic skills during
the Third Crusade suggest they shared an ability to engage and negotiate; the younger brother was also an active military commander. On
the other hand, he is described as a glutton for rich meats and sex.[4]
While Saladin had at least seventeen children, he was certainly not a
heavy eater and in terms of comportment he seems comparatively
austere, as befitted the leader of the holy war. Not that he failed to
enjoy himself entirely – his passion for polo, horses and hunting was
famous. He was clearly comfortable in hosting splendid celebrations,
such as the lavish welcome accorded to his ally for the northern Syrian
campaign of 1188, although he was well aware that this was all very

much part of the language of power and reciprocity too. His love of poetry and learning was such that a panoply of scholars, poets, doctors and theologians (sometimes one and the same person) were in his entourage; attracted too, it should be said, by his legendary patronage. Saladin could be affectionate towards his younger children although relations with his eldest boys veered between obvious affinity (al-Zahir Ghazi) to, at times, the utterly glacial (al-Afdal). Of his womenfolk, it was his wife Ismat al-Din Khatun who seemingly meant the most to him, as we saw from his constant correspondence with her from his sickbed in Mosul. A nice human touch is his apparent, if understandable, dislike of the first appearance of grey hairs although he declined to resort to dye.[5]

The most underestimated element of Saladin's career is to be found during his early years in Egypt. At the time of his uncle Shirkuh's unexpected death, he formed part of a compact force of invaders from Syria, he was a Sunni Kurd in a country ruled by the Shi'ite Fatimids, and he had seemingly limited top-level experience. Yet he was chosen to be vizier. This was an extraordinarily vulnerable position but it is striking how rapidly Saladin understood and assimilated the challenges that he faced. He dispensed land and money to secure immediate support and, given the immense wealth of the Fatimids, he was fortunate in having considerable resources at his disposal. To make all this work he swiftly meshed with the Fatimid bureaucrats, some of whom became lifelong members of his inner circle. A hallmark of his career was an ability to identify and to bring on board the very best administrators; it meant that the sultan had a reliable and talented group around him at all times. It is no coincidence that almost immediately he oversaw the first recalibration in decades of a basic tax indicator, likewise the commission by him or his office of a major land survey (the Domesday Book would be a loose parallel), showing an interest in government and resources and in understanding what was available to him and how the country functioned. Such riches also allowed him to display what would become one of his most feared and famous attributes, that of generosity. Money spent on the patronage of court poets was wise because they would broadcast his merits to the outside world. Likewise, vigorous support of religious institutions – for reasons of personal piety and the approval this would merit, both from the secular and the divine – was highly effective. Finally, Saladin's engagement with the centuries-old rituals of the measuring of the Nile and the Cutting of the Canal show him to be sensitive to local customs and astute enough to exploit the vast ceremonial potential of these events to his own advantage.

While Saladin is famous for his mercy, most notably at Jerusalem, he was savage in his treatment of Reynald of Châtillon and the Military Orders at Hattin, as well as ordering executions after several of his earlier battles against the Franks and in the aftermath of the Acre massacre. He also put down revolts in Egypt with considerable harshness. Hattin aside, the need to be seen to act firmly after a recent setback often seems the trigger for these killings.

Overall, however, he was widely regarded in his lifetime. As Abd al-Latif, a visitor to the sultan in the last months of his life, wrote: 'I found a great king who inspired both respect and affection, far and near, easy-going and willing to grant requests. His companions took him as a model ... men grieved for him as they grieve for prophets. I have seen no other ruler for whose death the people mourned, for he was loved by good and bad, Muslim and unbeliever alike.'[6]

The memory of Saladin is open to manipulation and appropriation and as we have seen offers a vast range of elements to be borrowed or admired. In the West, early in the thirteenth century, Gervase of Canterbury summed up the problem perfectly: the sultan was 'a pagan man but a distinguished knight'. The Third Crusaders had, contrary to expectation, discovered an individual worthy of their estimation and, his faith aside, bearing so many of the characteristics they esteemed themselves. The failure of the crusade also meant a need to accord their opponent respect, not least for the reputation of the great warrior-king, Richard the Lionheart. In conjunction with the dominant cultural movement of the day, chivalry, came the audacious literary kidnapping of someone from a culture and a faith usually regarded with hostility. Saladin acquired not only the ability to move across continents, but to seduce western women, to have a western family heritage, to become a knight and also, on occasion, to even become a Christian. His reputation for generosity and mercy have fused him into the consciousness of Europe down to this day.

In the Near East his memory endured by reason of his success in recovering Jerusalem for Islam and resisting the might of western Europe. His personal qualities were acknowledged and burnished his memory brighter, although some critical voices can be heard, most notably from the Shi'ites on account of his termination of the Fatimid caliphate. The ongoing fear of crusades in the centuries after the end of Frankish rule in the Levant helped to preserve Saladin's memory as well, and once the western imperialist powers started to engage directly with the Near East on a large scale, Saladin was already there, enfolded into the region's consciousness and collective heritage to be utilised as part of the response to this. His accomplishments and personal qualities have been taken on by a remarkable, and ever-growing range of actors, ideologies and institutions; to this day the name Saladin conjures hope and admiration. In 2001, the film director Youssef Chahine commented, 'The legend will not go away easily. It triggers a feeling of pride, a feeling of strength ... When [people] go back and say, Saladin, they are trying to find somebody that is as honourable, who is as charitable, as tolerant, and as great as Saladin.'[7]

To support the depth to which this feeling permeates I can only proffer an anecdote. A couple of years ago I gave a public lecture on Saladin in Oakland University, Michigan, not far from Detroit, a city with a significant Syrian refugee community. Afterwards a student came up to chat. We talked about the lecture and then she told me how she and her friends in their home town of Hama remembered and connected with Saladin: he was the screensaver on their mobile phone. Beautifully mundane and beautifully modern. This, to me, was in some respects a thousand times more revealing than seeing the grand gestures of politicians. A screensaver is a pretty basic tech-nological object of the early twenty-first century. Yet there was Salah al-Din ibn Ayyub, the Righteousness of the Faith, and the fact that it was something so very personal demonstrates perfectly just what symbolic power Saladin still bears. He has evolved to the point where there is no need for him always to be affixed to an individual or an ideology; in this instance he is acting for people looking to a leader whom they could admire without fear.

Writing the History of Saladin

Given the predominantly glowing portrayal of Saladin, 'Is it all too good to be true?' represents a fair question and one posed with varying degrees of restraint by historians in recent decades.[1] Many of our principal sources of information were individuals closely affiliated to the sultan, loyal members of his household who spent years engaging in the labours and the ideology of holy war and sharing the highs and lows of his career; the writings of Imad al-Din and Beha al-Din are particularly fulsome. They are also open to accusations of straying too near the literary genre known as 'Mirrors for Princes'.[2] The symmetry between those qualities attributed to Saladin and the content of books of advice for an ideal ruler can seem uncannily close, potentially compressing history into a literary convention. In both cases – as with any writer – there is a need to recognise the influence of contemporary cultural milieu on the style and content of their output. It is true that the opening section of Beha al-Din's biography setting out Saladin's virtues treads on the edge of hagiography. That said, books of advice were a familiar part of a court environment and outlined practices compatible with success. The sultan was undeniably an accomplished ruler and it is not surprising, therefore, to find Saladin acting in ways (with regards to generosity, piety, mercy and justice, for example) that fitted his own needs and wishes, but happen to match, in broad terms, the literary exemplars. Not every anecdote can stand close scrutiny, nor perhaps was it meant to; as we have suggested at times above, some were constructed by authors to praise a patron, to illustrate a style of ruling and/or to entertain. But the core characteristics noted here are recorded by a wide range of sources well beyond the immediate household; they form plausible behaviours that also help explain Saladin's achievements.

It is also relevant to note that Beha al-Din's main account of Saladin's career is not wholly uncritical, an issue rarely drawn out by historians. Thus, the author registers discontent over the sultan's failure to meet Richard, his nobles' dissatisfaction at his handling of the issue of al-Mansur's inheritance, opposition to his strategy for resisting the crusader advance on Jerusalem, and the breakdown in morale at the siege of Jaffa – cumulatively quite a robust list, although one that allows us to distinguish particular errors within the historical narrative, as distinct from Saladin's more universal personal qualities and his skills as a ruler. Likewise, Imad al-Din cites letters from hostile sources such as the caliph of Baghdad, from which one can discern clear contemporary disapproval for the sultan's behaviour and his dynastic ambitions.

In respect of the almost relentlessly positive tone of these narratives, as well as the many letters and poems produced at his court, it is clear that Saladin and his household were highly attuned to the need to generate positive publicity. In modern terms, we would say they liked to control the news story, not least to demonstrate the virtue of their actions, to celebrate successes and to attract support. There was nothing odd or sinister about this; we should simply acknowledge that the Ayyubid sultan was particularly good at it. Likewise, the array of poets, doctors, theologians and lawyers drawn to his court were there to seek patronage; to advance the praises of their sponsor was a logical and conventional response.

The many other sources in play offer further checks and balances.[3] Ibn al-Athir's loyalty to the Zengid clan meant that he expressed strong praise for Nur al-Din's achievements in the holy war, but at times made sharp criticism of Saladin. A particularly valuable author is the Spanish pilgrim Ibn Jubayr, who returned to his homeland after visiting the Near East in 1184 and whose writing was uncoloured by the need to satisfy an Ayyubid patron; his veneration of Saladin is plain. Even the contemporary Frankish author William of Tyre recognised many virtues within a man who posed such a threat to the Christians – while naturally reserving some barbs for him too.[4]

To answer the question posed at the start of this chapter: there is certainly a need to be cautious about the material available and much of it is concerned to paint the sultan in an advantageous light, in itself revealing something about the both the creators and their context.

But that does not devalue it entirely, not least because we are still left with the task of understanding how Saladin was able to achieve what he did.

We have seen how this basic corpus of contemporary and near-contemporary material has been used and shaped by writers down the centuries and it is worth closing with a few brief comments on more recent assessments of the sultan. Stanley Lane-Poole's 1898 *Saladin and the Fall of the Kingdom of Jerusalem* was a popular but romanticised view of the sultan, heavily refracted through the (almost inevitable) lens of Walter Scott's *Talisman* (1825). Hamilton Gibb's many far more scholarly works (including a 1973 biography) identified a modest and highly admirable man, who 'by sheer goodness and firmness of character, raised Islam out of the rut of political demoralisation ... by standing out for a moral ideal and expressing that ideal in his own life and action, he created around him an impulse for unity'.[5] A harsh counterblast to this positive perspective came from the American scholar Andrew Ehrenkreutz's *Saladin* (1977). The sultan's rule in Egypt was 'a depressing record of callous exploitation for the furthering of his own selfish political ambitions'. Ehrenkreutz depicted his subject as a ruthless, vindictive, calculated opportunist, ready to compromise religious ideals to political expediency.[6] Such a savage view certainly prompted a reassessment. In conjunction with a number of careful evaluations of the source material in articles by Richards and Holt, perhaps the more romantic interpretations fell by the wayside.[7] Lyons' and Jackson's 1982 *Saladin and the Politics of the Holy War* stands as a particular landmark, characterised by its close engagement with the letters of Qadi al-Fadil (still to this day not fully edited). From this formidable work, which is not an easy read, Saladin emerges as a pious, conventional and highly skilled politician. More recently, Möhring's balanced and incisive *Saladin: The Sultan and His Times, 1138–1193* (2009 in English, German 2005) offers sharp insights into Saladin's wider diplomacy across the Near East. Humphreys' *From Saladin to the Mongols* (1977) gives a strong sense of the Ayyubid lands as a whole; Lev's *Saladin in Egypt* (1999) has rightly shone a spotlight on many aspects of Saladin's rule in Egypt, and Azzam's *Saladin* (2009) helpfully corrects the often western-centric assessment of Saladin's impact on the medieval Muslim world. The broader relationship between the Muslim Near East and the Crusaders was drawn into a rich foundational framework by Hillenbrand in her *Crusades: Islamic Perspectives* (1999) while Cobb's *Race for Paradise* (2014) adds a supple examination of the wider interaction between Muslims and Christians from Baghdad to Islamic Spain. Of particular significance here is Eddé's *Saladin* (2011 in English, French 2008), an erudite and substantial book that is a blend of narrative, heavily overlain by thematic discussions, making a particular priority of evaluating the literary agendas of the sources. Her use of a vast range of materials renders this a vital resource.[8]

The detailed study of recent historical writings in the Near East constitutes a further dimension to Saladin's broader cultural and political importance in itself. Modern Arabic historiography can run down sectarian lines with some Shi'a authors extremely hostile to Saladin because of his overthrow of the Fatimid caliphate. Naturally enough, Sunni writers paint a highly positive picture of the sultan, emphasising his achievements on behalf of his people and his faith. Detailed studies by Sivan, Chamberlain, and especially that of Bhatia – who draws in an impressive range of material from literature and theatre – are the most valuable works here.[9]

An interesting crossover to the West is the Lebanese author Amin Maalouf's widely translated and polemical history of the crusades, first published in 1983. Appearing in English as *The Crusades Through Arab Eyes*, the French subtitle, which translates as 'Christian Barbarism in the Holy Land', signals its strong leanings towards a 'clash of civilisations' narrative that gives limited space to the complexities of the medieval age.[10]

One way to illuminate these matters better is through the increasing availability of high-quality translations of Arabic texts. Historians (not least myself), teachers and students owe much to the work of, especially, Donald Richards, but also to the many others who bring narratives, sermons, poems, travel writings and medical dictionaries into English. In doing so they create the opportunity for more of us to see a much broader perspective; long may that last.

Acknowledgements

Writing this book has been an enormously enjoyable process, both for the experience of immersing myself in the medieval Near East and then following the absorbing and addictive detective trail tracking Saladin down the centuries. In the course of this work, many friends and colleagues have provided generous advice and/or given me the chance to test and evolve my ideas in public – a particular kindness as a historian of the crusades trespasses onto less familiar ground. I would like to thank Carole Hillenbrand, Thomas Madden, Cecilia Gaposchkin, Jay Rubenstein, James Naus, Nicholas Paul, Kurt Villads Jensen, Torben Kjersgaard Nielsen, Simon Møberg Torp, Beni Kedar, Ronnie Ellenblum, Adrian Boas, Iris Shagrir, Judith Bronstein, Jonathan Rubin, Vardit Shotten-Hallel, Gil Fishof, Felix Hinz, Johannes Mayer-Hamme and Tom Sutton for these opportunities.

Many people have offered valuable insight and information; my appreciation to: Mike Horswell, Konrad Hirschler, Jessalynn Bird, Rafi Lewis, Michael Ehrlich, Jan Vandeburie, Don Matthews, Jonathan Harris, Jamie Doherty, Molly Tarhuni, Stephane Pradines, Stefano Jossa, Adam Knobler, Taef el-Azhari, John Nixon, Ethan Menchinger. A special thanks to Emilie Savage-Smith, Geert van Gelder and Peter Joosse from the Ibn Abi Usaybi'ah project for so willingly sharing their exciting unpublished material with me, and to Julia Bray for her insights into the spectacular poetry of al-Jilyani.

As the endnotes make plain, I owe a particular debt of gratitude to Dr Osman Latiff for his patient responses to my repeated calls upon his linguistic skills, as well as his thoughtful comments and excellent company. I must also thank William Purkis, Andrew Jotischky, Myra Bom and Steve Tibble for their camaraderie as we tracked down (and trekked up) various sites of interest, as well as their candid assessments of the text and the presentation of the ideas therein.

The MA in Crusader Studies at Royal Holloway, University of London includes a unit on the 'Memory and the Legacy of the Crusades', to my knowledge the only such course in existence and one that evolves and diversifies in content every year; my appreciation to the imaginative students who have cheerfully joined me on this journey into the unknown.

My thanks also to the many audiences in colleges, schools and Historical Association events where some of these ideas have been broadcast – it is always a genuine delight to meet the staff who do so much to enthuse new generations of historians, and to talk to their interesting and engaged students.

Others have provided invaluable support and encouragement over recent years: Andrew Taylor, Robert and Pilar McIntosh, Bruno Heisey, Lisa Drage, Sir Idris Pearce, Liz Medaglia and Joe Sinnott, Andrew and Kate Golding, Michael-Ann Haders, Rosie Meek, Alister Miskimmon, Peregrine Horden, Penelope Mullens and Alex Windscheffel. Ann Carr and all at 'Voyages to Antiquity' have helped me visit numerous locations in very good company.

A special acknowledgement to David Eldridge for inviting me to become involved in his play *Holy Warriors* at the Globe Theatre in 2015. It was an extraordinary privilege to see first-hand the pressures and rewards in delivering live drama.

As ever, I am grateful to my splendid agent, Catherine Clarke and her colleagues at Felicity Bryan Associates, to Andrew Nurnberg Associates for their efforts in the markets overseas, and to Sarah Fuentes of Fletcher and Company in New York for her energetic work in North America.

It has been my particular good fortune to work with Will Hammond at Bodley Head; his calm and perceptive views have been essential in bringing this project to fruition. I would also like to thank Will Sulkin for commissioning the book and Stuart Williams for keeping the faith over its long gestation. Once again, it has been an easy experience to copy-edit with the ever-sharp David Milner; my gratitude also to Alison Worthington, Bill Donohoe and Alison Davies.

My family have tolerated the presence of Saladin with extraordinary good grace. Sadly my parents did not live to see the finished work but their love and enthusiasm will always remain with me. Heartfelt thanks to my pride and joy, Tom and Marcus, both great company on the road too; and equally to my wonderful wife, Niki, for her unwavering love and support. Finally, I must thank my brother-in-law, John Wallace, and especially my sister, Sophie, for their cheerful and unreserved companionship down the decades; it is with great pleasure that I dedicate this book to them.

Illustration Credits

All images are from the author's collection except the following:

Colour section: page 2, top: Khaled El-Adawy / Shutterstock.com; page 2, bottom: Courtesy of Trustees of the British Museum; page 3, top: Jane Taylor Photography; page 4, top: Alistair Duncan and the Altajir Trust; page 6, top: by permission of the President and Fellows of Corpus Christi College, Oxford CCC MS 255a, 7; page 6, bottom: ClimaxAP / Shutterstock.com; page 7, bottom: Shakespeare's Globe Theatre, London.

Black and white section: page 1: Uppsala University Library, O Sp. 28, fol. 53v, 54r; page 2, top: Courtesy of Stephane Pradines; page 3, bottom: Royal Holloway, University of London Library; page 4, bottom: The Palestinian Museum, Birzeit; page 5, top: SyrianHistory.com; page 5, bottom: Courtesy of Carole Hillenbrand; page 7, top: Courtesy of Tom Sutton; page 7, bottom: Malaysian Digital Economy Corporation; page 8, top: Ricki Rosen / Corbis; page 8, bottom: Enana Dance Theatre, Dubai. Every best effort has been made to secure the permission of the rights holders in the images on page 4, bottom, and page 7, bottom.

Bibliography

Archives

FCO 93/351

FO 141/514/2

FO 195/2024

FO 371/4185

FO 371/4186

FO 371/16926

FO 684/10

FO 686/38

SP 97, 16 May 1614

Thatcher Archive, Churchill College, Cambridge, THCR 1/17/123

Primary sources, pre-1750

Abd al-Latif al-Baghdadi, *The Eastern Key: Kitab al-ifadah wa'l-l'tibar of Abd al-Latif al-Bagh-dadi*, trs. K. Hafuth Zand, J. A. and I. E. Videan (London, 1965).

Abu Shama, 'Le Livre des deux Jardins', *Recueil des historiens des croisades: Historiens orien-taux*, 5 vols. (Paris, 1872–1906), 4.3–522; 5.3–206; all references to volume 4 unless stated. Unpublished English translations by O. Latiff, 2017, from I. Shams al-Din (ed.), *Kitab al-Rawdatayn fi akhbar al-dawlatayn al-nuriyya wa-l-salahiyya*, 4 vols. (Beirut, 2002).

Ambroise, *The History of the Holy War: Ambroise's Estoire de la Guerre Sainte*, eds. and trs. M. Ailes and M. C. Barber, 2 vols. (Woodbridge, 2003). All references to volume 2.

Beha al-Din Ibn Shaddad, *The Rare and Excellent History of Saladin or al-Nawadir al-Sultaniyya wa'l-Mahasin al-Yusufiyya by Baha' al-Din Ibn Shaddad*, tr. D. S. Richards, *Crusade Texts in Translation 7* (Aldershot, 2001).

Bar Hebraeus, *The Chronography of Bar Hebraeus, Volume 1*, tr. E. A. Wallis Budge (Oxford, 1932).

Book of Gifts and Rarities, tr. G. H. al-Qaddumi (Harvard, 1996).

Caffaro of Genoa and the Twelfth-Century Crusades, trs. M. A. Hall and J. P. Phillips, *Crusade Texts in Translation 26* (Farnham, 2013).

Calendar of the Fine Rolls of the Reign of Henry III. Volume III: 1234–42, eds. P. Dryburgh and B. Hartland, technical eds. A. Ciula and J. M. Vieira, 2 vols. (Woodbridge, 2009).

'Chronica regia Coloniensis' in G. H. Pertz (ed.), *Monumenta Germaniae Historica, Scriptores*, 32 vols. (Hanover, 1826–1934), 18.121–5.

'Chronicle of Magnus of Reichersberg' in *The Crusade of Frederick Barbarossa: The History of the Expedition of the Emperor Frederick and Related Texts*, tr. G. A. Loud, *Crusade Texts in Translation* 19 (Aldershot, 2010), pp. 149–67.

Chronicle of the Third Crusade: The Itinerarium Peregrinorum et Gesta Regis Ricardi, tr. H. J. Nicholson, *Crusade Texts in Translation* 3 (Aldershot, 1997).

The Conquest of Jerusalem and the Third Crusade, tr. P. W. Edbury, *Crusade Texts in Translation* 1 (Aldershot, 1996).

Crusade and Christendom: Annotated Documents in Translation from Innocent III to the Fall of Acre, 1187–1291, eds. and trs. J. Bird, E. Peters and J. M. Powell (Philadelphia, PA, 2013).

The Crusade of Frederick Barbarossa: The History of the Expedition of the Emperor Frederick and Related Texts, tr. G. A. Loud, *Crusade Texts in Translation* 19 (Aldershot, 2010).

Dante Alighieri, *Il Convivio*, tr. R. H. Lansing (New York, 1990).

Evliya Çelebi, *Evliya Tshelebi's Travels in Palestine (1648–1650)*, tr. St H. Stephan (Jerusalem, 1980).

Evliya Çelebi, *An Ottoman Traveller: Selections from the Book of Travels of Evliya Çelebi*, eds. and trs. R. Dankoff and S. Kim (London, 2010).

Evliya Çelebi, *Ottoman Explorations of the Nile: Evliya Çelebi's 'Matchless Pearl These Reports of the Nile' map and his accounts of the Nile and the Horn of Africa in 'The Book of Travels'*, eds. and trs. R. Dankoff, N. Tezcan and M. D. Sheridan (London, 2018).

Fuller, T., *Historie of the Holy Warre* (Cambridge, 1639).

Gesta Francorum, The Deeds of the Franks and the Other Pilgrims to Jerusalem, ed. R. Mynors, tr. R. M. T. Hill (London, 1962).

Giovanni Boccaccio, *Tutte le opere 4: Decameron*, ed. V. Branca, 2 vols. (Florence, 1951–2).

Giovanni Boccaccio, *Tutte le opere 9: De casibus virorum illustrium*, eds. P. G. Ricci and V. Zaccaria (Milan, 1983).

Gouvernance et libéralités de Saladin d'après les données inédites de six documents arabes, eds. and trs. J-M. Mouton, D. Sourdel and J. Sourdel-Thomine (Paris, 2015).

Gregory the Priest, *Armenia and the Crusades, 10th to 12th Centuries*, ed. and tr. A. E. Dostaurian (Lanham, MI, 1993).

Harawi, al-, in 'Les Conseils du Sayh al-Harawi à un prince Ayyubide', ed. and tr. J. Sourdel-Thomine, *Bulletin des études orientales* 16 (1961–2), pp. 205–66.

Harawi, al-, *A Lonely Wayfarer's Guide to Pilgrimage*, tr. J. W. Meri (Princeton, NJ, 2004).

Hariri, al-, A., *al-I'lām wa-al-tabyīn fī khurūj al-Firanj al-malā'īn 'alā diyār al-muslimīn* ('The Exposition and Explanation of the Cursed Franks' Departure to the Muslim Lands'), ed. S. Zakkar (Damascus, 1981), unpublished translations by O. Latiff, 2017.

History of the Patriarchs of the Egyptian Church, Volume 3, trs. A. Khater and O. H. E. Burmester (Cairo, 1968).

Ibn Abi Usaybi'ah, *A Literary History of Medicine: 'Uyūn al-anbā' fī ṭabaqāt al-aṭibbā' of Ibn Abī Uṣaybi'ah (d.1270)*, eds., trs. and analysed by E. Savage-Smith, S. Swain and G. J. van Gelder, with I. Sánchez, N. P. Joosse, A. Watson, B. Inksetter and F. Hilloowalla, 4 vols. (Brill, 2019).

Ibn al-Athir, 'Histoire des Atabegs de Mosul', *Recueil des historiens des croisades, historiens orientaux*, 5 vols. (Paris, 1872–1906), 2.ii.5–375.

Ibn al-Athir, *The Chronicle of Ibn al-Athir for the Crusading Period from al-Kamil fi 'l-Ta'rikh. Part 2, The Years 541–589/1146–1193: The Age of Nur al-Din and Saladin*, tr. D. S. Richards, *Crusade Texts in Translation* 15 (Aldershot, 2007).

Ibn Asakir, 'Un document contemporain de Nur ad-Din: Sa notice biographique par Ibn Asakir', tr. N. Elisséeff, *Bulletin d'études orientales* 25 (1972), pp. 125–40.

Ibn Asakir, in *The Intensification and Reorientation of Sunni Jihad Ideology in the Crusader Period: Ibn Asakir of Damascus (1105–1176) and His Age, with an Edition and Translation of Ibn Asakir's The Forty Hadith for Inciting Jihad*, eds. and trs. S. A. Mourad and J. E. Lindsay (Leiden, 2013).

Ibn al-Qalanisi, *The Damascus Chronicles of the Crusades*, tr. H. A. R. Gibb (London, 1932), fuller text translated into French as: Ibn al-Qalanisi, *Damas de 1075 à 1154*, tr. R. Le Tourneau (Damascus, 1952).

Ibn Jubayr, *The Travels of Ibn Jubayr*, tr. R. J. C. Broadhurst (London, 1952).

Ibn Khaldun, *The Muqaddimah: An Introduction to History*, tr. F. Rosenthal, second edition, 3 vols. (London, 1967).

Ibn Khallikan, *Ibn Khallikan's Biographical Dictionary*, tr. W. M. de Slane, 4 vols. (Paris, 1843–71).

Ibn Mammati, 'Ibn Mammati's Rules for the Ministries: Translation with a Commentary of the Qawanin al-Dawawin', R. S. Cooper, unpublished doctoral thesis, University of California, Berkeley, 1973.

Ibn Tubayr al-Qaysarani, *Nuzhat al-muqlatayn fī akhbār al-dawlatayn Ibn aṭ-Ṭuwayr*, ed. A. F. Sayyid (Beirut, 1992), unpublished translations by O. Latiff, 2018.

I Libri Iurium della Repubblica di Genova, ed. A. Rovere et al., 9 vols. (Rome, 1992–2002).

Imad ad-Din al-Isfahani, *Al-barq al-shami*, ed. R. Sesen (Istanbul, 1971), partial translation into English in H. A. R. Gibb, 'Al-Barq al-Shami, the History of Saladin by the Katib Imad al-Din al-Isfahani', *Wiener Zeitschrift für die Kunde des Morgenlands* 52 (1953), pp. 93–115, also unpublished translations by O. Latiff, 2017.

Imad ad-Din al-Isfahani, *Conquête de la Syrie et de la Palestine par Saladin*, tr. H. Massé (Paris, 1972); partial translation into English in F. Gabrieli, *Arab Historians of the Crusades* (Berkeley, CA, 1969).

Itinerarium peregrinorum et Gesta Regis Ricardi, translated in *Chronicle of the Third Crusade: A Translation of the Itinerarium peregrinorum et Gesta Regis Ricardi*, tr. H. J. Nicholson, *Crusade Texts in Translation* 3 (Aldershot, 1997).

Jacques de Vitry, *Exempla, or Illustrative Stories from the Sermones Vulgares of Jacques de Vitry*, ed. T. F. Crane (London, 1890).

Jilyani, al-, Abd al-Mun'im ibn Umar ibn Ḥassān al-Jilyānī al-Andalusī, *Dīwān al-tadbīj: Fitnat al-ibdā 'wa-dhurwat al-imtā*, eds. K. Abū Deeb and D. Bakhsh (London and Oxford, 2010).

Juvaini, Ata-Malik, *Genghis Khan: The History of the World Conqueror*, tr. and ed. J. A. Boyle (Manchester, 1997).

Kemal al-Din, in 'Kamal al-Din's biography of Rasid al-Din Sinan', tr. B. Lewis, *Arabica* 13 (1966), pp. 225–67.

Kemal al-Din, 'L'histoire d'Alep', *Revue d'Orient Latin* 3 (1895), pp. 509–65.

La fille du comte de Ponthieu. Nouvelle du xiii s.: 'Roman' du xv s., ed. and tr. R. Dubois (Paris, 2010).

Letters from the East: Crusaders, Pilgrims and Settlers in the 12th–13th Centuries, *Crusade Texts in Translation* 18, trs. M. Barber and K. Bate (Farnham, 2010).

Libellus, 'De Expugnatione Terra Sanctae per Saladinum' in Ralph of Coggeshall, *Chronicon Anglicanum*, ed. J. Stevenson, Rolls Series, no. 66 (London, 1875), pp. 209–62.

Maqrizi, al-, *The History of the Ayyubid Sultans of Egypt*, tr. R. J. C. Broadhurst (Boston, MA, 1980).

Medieval Latin Lives of Muhammad, ed. and tr. J. Yolles and J. Weiss (Cambridge, MA, 2018).

Mujir al-Din al-Ulaymi, *Histoire de Jérusalem et d'Hébron depuis Abraham jusqu'à la fin du xv s.*, tr. H. Sauvaire (Paris, 1876).

Mustafa Ali, *Mustafa Ali's Description of Cairo of 1599*, ed. and tr. A. Tietze (Vienna, 1975).

Niketas Choniates, *O City of Byzantium*, tr. H. J. Magoulias (Detroit, 1984).

Nizam al-Mulk, *The Book of Government or Rules for Kings*, tr. H. Darke (London, 1960).

Old French Continuation of William of Tyre in *The Conquest of Jerusalem and the Third Crusade*, tr. P. W. Edbury, *Crusade Texts in Translation* 1 (Aldershot, 1996), pp. 11–145.

Paris, G. (ed.), 'Un poème latin contemporain sur Saladin', *Revue d'Orient latin* 1 (1893), pp. 433–44.

Peter of Blois, 'Passio Raginaldi principis Antiochie' in *Tractatus duo*, ed. R. B. C. Huygens, *Corpus Christianorum continuatio mediaevalis* 194 (Turnhout, 2002).

Petrarch, F., *Francesco Petrarca: Trionfi, Rime estravaganti, Codice degli abbozzi*, eds. V. Pacca, L. Paolino and M. Santagata (Milan, 2013).

Pilgrimage to Jerusalem and the Holy Land, 1187–1291, tr. D. Pringle, *Crusade Texts in Translation* 23 (Aldershot, 2012).

Qalqashandi, al-, *Selections from Subh al-A'sha by al-Qalqashandi, Clerk of the Mamluk Court*, eds. and trs. H. El-Toudy and T. G. Abdelhamid (London, 2017).

Razi, al-, *Kitab al-Qulang (Le livre de colique)*, ed. and tr. S. M. Hammami (Aleppo, 1983).

Rules and Regulations of the Abbasid Courts, tr. E. Salem (Beirut, 1977).

Sea of Precious Virtues, tr. J. S. Meisami (Salt Lake City, UT, 1991).

Sharaf al-Dîn Bitlîsî, *The Sharafnâma: Or the History of the Kurdish Nation – 1597, Book One*, tr. M. R. Izady (Costa Mesa, CA, 2005).

Sulami, al-, *The Book of the Jihad of Ali ibn Tahir al-Sulami (d.1106): Text, Translation and Commentary*, N. Christie (Farnham, 2015).

'Two *excitationes* for the Third Crusade: The Letters of Brother Thierry of the Temple', ed. J. H. Pryor, *Mediterranean Historical Review* 25 (2010), pp. 147–68.

Urkunden der lateinischen könige von Jerusalem, ed. H. E. Mayer, 4 vols. (Hanover, 2010).

Uthman ibn Ibrahim al-Nablusi, *The Sword of Ambition: Bureaucratic Rivalry in Medieval Egypt*, ed. and tr. L. Yarborough (New York, 2016).

Wahrani, al-, in G. J. Van Gelder, 'A Conversation on Contemporary Politics in the Twelfth Century: "al-Maqama al-Baghdadiyya" by al-Wahrani (d.575/1179)' in *Texts, Documents and Artefacts: Islamic Studies in Honour of D. S. Richards*, ed. C. F. Robinson (Leiden, 2003), pp. 103–119.

William of Tyre, *Chronicon*, ed. R. B. C. Huygens, 2 vols., *Corpus Christianorum continuatio mediaevalis 63* (Turnhout, 1986), translated as: William of Tyre, *A History of Deeds done Beyond the Sea*, trs. E. A. Babcock and A. C. Krey, 2 vols. (New York, 1943).

Primary sources, post-1750

Abduh, M., *The Theology of Unity*, trs. I. Musa and K. Cragg (New York, 1980).

Asad, M., *Islam at the Crossroads* (Delhi, 1934).

Banna, H. al-, *Five Tracts of Hasan al-Banna (1906–1949)*, tr. C. Wendell (Berkeley, CA, 1978).

Burdett, A. P. (ed.), *Islamic Movements in the Arab World, 1913–66*, 4 vols. (Slough, 1998).

Darwish, M., *If I Were Another*, tr. F. Joudah (New York, 2011).

Darwish, M., *Memory for Forgetfulness: August, Beirut, 1982*, tr. I. Muhawi (Berkeley, CA, 2013).

Dumas, A., *The Black Tulip*, tr. D. Coward (Oxford, 1993).

Eldridge, D., *Holy Warriors: A Fantasia on the Third Crusade and the History of Violent Struggle in the Holy Lands* (London, 2014).

Finn, J., *Stirring Times: Or, Records from Jerusalem Consular Chronicles of 1853 to 1856*, 2 vols. (London, 1878).

Jabarti, al-, *Napoleon in Egypt: Al-Jabarti's Chronicle of the French Occupation*, tr. S. Moreh, introduction, R. Tignor, expanded edition (Princeton, NJ, 2004).

Lane. E. W., *An Account of the Manners and Customs of the Modern Egyptians* (London, 1860).

Lessing, G. E., *Nathan the Wise with Related Documents*, ed. and tr. R. Schechter (Boston, 2004).

Marin, F-L. C., *Histoire du Saladin*, 2 vols. (Paris, 1758).

Nasser, G. A., *Egypt's Liberation: The Philosophy of the Revolution* (New York, 1956).

Nasser, G. A., *President Gamal Abdel Nasser's Speeches and Press Interviews 1958* (Cairo, 1959).

Nasser, G. A., *President Gamal Abdel Nasser's Speeches and Press Interviews 1959* (Cairo, 1960).

Nasser, G. A., *President Gamal Abdel Nasser's Speeches and Press Interviews October to December 1960* (Cairo, 1961).

Nicolas le Turc, *Chronique d'Égypte 1798–1804*, ed. and tr. G. Wiet (Cairo, 1950).

Osama bin Laden, *Messages to the World: The Statements of Osama bin Laden*, ed. B. Lawrence, tr. J. Howarth (London, 2005).

Palestine and Transjordan Administration Reports 1918–1948, Volume 4, 1932–33 (Gerrards Cross, 1995).

Porter, J., *Five Years in Damascus: With Travels and Researches in Palmyra, Lebanon, The Giant Cities of Bashan and the Hauran*, second edition (London, 1870).

Al-Qaeda in its own Words, ed. G. Keppel and J-P. Milelli, tr. P. Ghazaleh (Cambridge, MA, 2008).

Qutb, S., in W. E. Shepard, *Sayyid Qutb and Islamic Activism: A Translation and Critical Analysis of 'Social Justice in Islam'* (Leiden, 1996).

Qutb, S., *Milestones* (repr. New Delhi, 2002).

Rashid, Harun Hashim, poem on Saladin, in 'Salah al-Din al-Ayyubi fil-Shi'r al'Arabi al-Mu'asir', S. J. al-Tu'ma, *al-Adab* 11 (November, 1970), unpublished translation here by O. Latiff, 2018.

Revue du monde musulman 22 (March 1913).

Rihani A., *The Book of Khalid*, afterword by T. Fine (Brooklyn, NY, 2012).

Rojë Kurd 1 (1913).

Russell, A., *The Natural History of Aleppo*, 2 vols. (London, 1794).

Sadat, el-, A., *Speech by President Anwar el-Sadat to the Knesset, 20th November 1977* (Cairo, 1978).

Sadat, el-, A., *The Public Diary of President Sadat, Part One: The Road to War (October 1970– October 1973)*, ed. R. Israeli (Leiden, 1978).

Sadat, el-, A., *The Public Diary of President Sadat, Part Two: The Road of Diplomacy (November 1973–May 1975)*, ed. R. Israeli (Leiden, 1979).

Scott, W., *The Talisman* (London, 1832).

Tahtawi, al-, R. R., *An Imam in Paris: Account of a Stay in Paris by an Egyptian Cleric (1826–31)*, tr. D. L. Newman, second edition (London, 2011).

Zaidan, J., *Tree of Pearls, Queen of Egypt*, tr. S. Selim (Syracuse, NY, 2012).

Zaidan, J., *Saladin and the Assassins*, tr. P. Starkey (Bethesda, MA, 2011).

Secondary materials

Abdel-Malik, K., *The Rhetoric of Violence: Arab-Jewish Encounters in Contemporary Palestinian Literature and Film* (Basingstoke, 2016).

Aberth, J., *A Knight at the Movies: Medieval History on Film* (New York, 2003).

Abouali, D., 'Saladin's Legacy in the Middle East before the Nineteenth Century', *Crusades* 10 (2011), pp. 175–89.

Abu Eid, M., *Mahmoud Darwish: Literature and the Politics of Palestinian Identity* (London, 2016).

Abulafia., D., *The Great Sea: A Human History of the Mediterranean* (London, 2011).

Ailes, M. J., 'The Admirable Enemy? Saladin and Saphadin in Ambroise's *Estoire de la guerre sainte*' in *Knighthoods of Christ: Essays on the History of the Crusades and the Knights Templar presented to Malcolm Barber*, ed. N. Housley (Aldershot, 2007), pp. 51–64.

Amine, K. and Carlson, M., 'Islam and the Colonial Stage in North Africa', *Performance and Spirituality* 3 (2012), pp. 1–12.

Amitai, R., 'Some Remarks on the Inscription of Baybars at Maqam Nabi Musa' in *Mamluks and Ottomans: Studies in Honour of Michael Winter*, eds. D. Wasserstein and A. Ayalon (Abingdon, 2006), pp. 45–53.

Anderson, B., *Imagined Communities: Reflections on the Origins and Spread of Nationalism*, revised edition (London, 2016).

Ankori, G., *Palestinian Art* (London, 2006).

Antrim, Z., 'Ibn Asakir's Representations of Syria and Damascus in the Introduction to the *Ta'rikh Madinat Dimashq*', *International Journal of Middle Eastern Studies* 38 (2006), pp. 109–29.

'Apologetic Commentary on the Creed' in *Christian–Muslim Relations: A Bibliographical History, Volume 3 (1050–1200)*, eds. D. Thomas and A. Mallett (Leiden, 2011), pp. 671–5.

Arberry, A. J., 'Hafiz Ibrahim and Shauqi', *Journal of the Royal Asiatic Society* 35 (1937), pp. 50–8.

Asali, K., 'Jerusalem under the Ottomans, 1516–1917' in *Jerusalem in History* (London, 1989).

Asbridge, T. S., *The Crusades: The War for the Holy Land* (London, 2012).

Asbridge, T. S., 'Talking to the enemy: the role and purpose of negotiations between Saladin and Richard the Lionheart during the Third Crusade', *Journal of Medieval History* 39 (2013), pp. 275–96.

Assmann, J., 'Collective Memory and Cultural Identity', *New German Critique* 65 (1995), pp. 125–33.

Aubin-Boltanski, E., 'Salah al-Din, un héros à l'épreuve: Mythe et pèlerinage en Palestine', *Annales. Histoire, Sciences Sociales* 60 (2005), pp. 91–107.

Ayalon, A., *The Press in the Arab Middle East: A History* (Oxford, 1995).

Ayalon, D., *Eunuchs, Caliphs and Sultans: A Study in Power Relationships* (Jerusalem, 1999).

Azhari, el- T.K., *The Saljuqs of Syria during the Crusades, 463–549 AH / 1070–1154 AD* (Berlin, 1997).

Azhari, el-, T. K., *Zengi and the Muslim Response to the Crusades: The Politics of Jihad* (Abingdon, 2016).

Azzam., A. R., *Saladin* (Harlow, 2009).

Baadj, A. S., *Saladin, the Almohads and the Banū Ghāniya: The Contest for North Africa (12th and 13th Centuries)* (Leiden, 2015).

Bach, E., *La cite de Gênes au xii siècle* (Copenhagen, 1955).

Badawi, M. M., *Early Arabic Drama* (Cambridge, 1988).

Badawi, M. M., *Modern Arabic Drama in Egypt* (Cambridge, 1988).

Badawi, M. M. (ed.), *Modern Arabic Literature* (Cambridge, 1992).

Barber, M. C., 'Frontier Warfare in the Latin Kingdom of Jerusalem: The Campaign of Jacob's Ford, 1178–9' in *The Crusades and their Sources: Essays presented to Bernard Hamilton*, eds. J. France and W. G. Zajac (Aldershot, 1998), pp. 9–22.

Barber, M. C., 'The Reputation of Gerard de Ridefort' in *Military Orders Volume 4: On Land and by Sea*, ed. J. Upton-Ward (Aldershot, 2008), pp. 111–20.

Barber, M. C., *The Crusader States* (London, 2013).

Barbour, N., 'The Arabic Theatre in Egypt', *Bulletin of the School of Oriental Studies* 8 (1935), pp. 173–87.

Barr, J., *A Line in the Sand: The Anglo-French Struggle for the Middle East, 1914–1918* (New York, 2012).

Barton, S., 'Marriage across frontiers: sexual mixing, power and identity in medieval Iberia', *Journal of Medieval Iberian Studies* 3 (2011), pp. 1–25.

Bar-Yosef, E., *The Holy Land in English Culture, 1797–1917: Palestine and the Question of Orientalism* (Oxford, 2005).

Bashkin, O., 'My Sister Esther: Reflections on Judaism, Ottomanism and Empire in the Works of Farun Antun' in *The Long 1890s in Egypt: Colonial Quiescence, Subterranean Resistance*, eds. M. Booth and A. Gorman (Edinburgh, 2014), pp. 315–41.

Bauden, F., 'Taqi al-Din Ahmad ibn Ali al-Maqrizi' in *Medieval Muslim Historians and the Franks in the Levant*, ed. A. Mallett (Leiden, 2014), pp. 161–200.

Beben, D., 'Remembering Saladin: The Crusades and the Politics of Heresy in Persian Historiography', *Journal of the Royal Asiatic Society*, Series 3, 28 (2018), pp. 231–53.

Belli, M. N., *An Incurable Past: Nasser's Egypt Then and Now* (Gainesville, FL, 2013).

Bengio, O., *Saddam's Word: Political Discourse in Iraq* (Oxford, 1998).

Bennison, A. K., *The Almoravid and Almohad Empires* (Edinburgh, 2016).

Benvenisti, M., *The Crusaders in the Holy Land* (New York, 1970).

Berkey, J., *Popular Preaching and Authority in the Medieval Islamic Near East* (Seattle, 2001).

Bhatia, U., *Forgetting Osama bin Munqidh Remembering Osama bin Laden: The Crusades in Modern Muslim Memory* (Nanyang, 2008).

Bird, J., 'Memory and the Crusades: Sermons as Vectors for Commemoration and Contextualization' (forthcoming).

Birnbaum, L., 'Historical Discourse in the Media of the Palestinian National Authority' in *Palestinian Collective Memory and National Identity*, ed. M. Litvak (Basingstoke, 2009), pp. 135–41.

Bjørneboe, L., *In Search of the True Political Position of the Ulama: An analysis of the aims and perspectives of the chronicles of Abd al-Rahman al-Jabarti (1753–1825)* (Aarhus, 2007).

Black, E., *Parallel Realities: A Jewish/Arab History of Israel/Palestine* (Minneapolis, MN, 1992).

Boas, A., *Crusader Archaeology: The Material Culture of the Latin East*, second edition (Abingdon, 2017).

Bonney, R., *Jihad: From Qur'an to bin Laden* (Basingstoke, 2004).

Bora, F., 'Did Salah al-Din Destroy the Fatimids' Books? An Historiographical Enquiry', *Journal of the Royal Asiatic Society* 25 (2015), pp. 21–39.

Bossémo, C., *Youssef Chahine l'Alexandrin: CinémAction* 33 (1985).

Boudot-Lamotte, A., *Ahmad Sawqi, l'homme et l'oeuvre* (Damascus, 1977).

Bray, J., 'Picture Poems for Saladin: Abd al-Mun'im al-Jilyani's *mudabbajat*', in *Syria in Crusader Times: Conflict and Co-existence*, ed. C. Hillenbrand (Edinburgh, 2019).

Bray, J., 'From Spain to Syria: What did al-Jilyani bring with him?', in *Re-Defining a Space of Encounter. Islam and Mediterranean: Identity, Alterity and Interactions: Proceedings of the 28th Congress of the Union Européenne des Arabisants et Islamisants, Palermo 2016*, eds., A. Pellitteri, N. Elsakaan, M. G. Sciortino, D. Sicari (Leuven, forthcoming).

Brett, M., *The Fatimid Empire* (Edinburgh, 2017).

Broers, M., *Napoleon, Soldier of Destiny* (London, 2014).

Buck, A., *The Principality of Antioch and its Frontiers in the Twelfth Century* (Woodbridge, 2017).

Bull, M. G., *Eyewitness and Crusade Narrative: Perception and Narration in Accounts of the Second, Third and Fourth Crusades* (Woodbridge, 2018).

Cahen, C., 'Un traité financier inédit d'époque fatimide-ayyubide' in *Makhzumiyyat: Études sur l'histoire économique et financière de l'Égypte médiévale* (Leiden, 1977), pp. 1–21.

Cahen, C., 'Douanes et commerce dans les ports Méditerranéens de l'Égypte médiévale d'après le *minhadj* d'al-Makhzumi' in *Makhzumiyyat: Études sur l'histoire économique et financière de l'Égypte médiévale* (Leiden, 1977), pp. 57–152.

Cahen, C., 'L'administration financière de l'armée fatimide d'après al-Makhzumi' in *Makhzumiyyat: Études sur l'histoire économique et financière de l'Égypte médiévale* (Leiden, 1977), pp. 155–63.

Centlivres, P., Fabre, D. and Zonabend, F., *La Fabrique des héros* (Paris, 1999).

Chamberlain, M., *Knowledge and Social Practice in Medieval Damascus, 1190–1350* (Cambridge, 1994).

Chamberlain, M., 'The Crusader Era and the Ayyubid Dynasty' in *The Cambridge History of Egypt, Volume 1, Islamic Egypt, 640–1517*, ed. C. F. Petry (Cambridge, 1998), pp. 211–41.

Christie, N., *Muslims and Crusaders: Christianity's Wars in the Middle East, 1095–1382, From the Islamic Sources* (Abingdon, 2014).

Christie, N., 'Ibn al-Qalanisi', *Medieval Muslim Historians and the Franks in the Levant* (Leiden, 2014), pp. 7–28.

Cobb, P. M., *Usama ibn Munqidh: Warrior Poet of the Age of the Crusades* (Oxford, 2005).

Cobb, P. M., *The Race for Paradise: An Islamic History of the Crusades* (New York, 2014).

Cohen, A., 'Al-Nabi Musa – an Ottoman festival (*mawsim*) resurrected?' in *Mamluks and Ottomans: Studies in Honour of Michael Winter*, eds. D. Wasserstein and A. Ayalon (Abingdon, 2006), pp. 34–44.

Cole, J., *Napoleon's Egypt: Invading the Middle East* (New York, 2007).

Cole, P. J., *The Preaching of the Crusades to the Holy Land, 1095–1270* (Cambridge, MA, 1991).

Cooper, J. P., *The Medieval Nile: Route, Navigation and Landscape in Islamic Egypt* (Cairo, 2014).

Connerton, P., *How Societies Remember* (Cambridge, 1989).

Daftary, F., *The Assassin Legends: Myths of the Isma'ilis* (London, 1995).

Dajani-Shakeel, H., 'Al-Quds: Jerusalem in the Consciousness of the Counter Crusader' in *The Meeting of Two Worlds: Cultural Exchange between East and West during the Period of the Crusades*, ed. V. P. Goss (Kalamazoo, MI, 1986), pp. 201–21.

Dankoff, R., *An Ottoman Mentality: The World of Evliya Çelebi*, revised second edition (Leiden, 2006).

Debeuf, K., *Inside the Arab Revolution: Three Years on the Frontline of the Arab Spring* (Tielt, 2014).

Degeorge, G., *Damascus* (Paris, 2004).

Deheuvels, L. W., 'Le Saladin de Farah Antun du mythe littéraire arabe au mythe politique', *Revue des mondes musulmans et de la Méditerranée* 89–90 (2000), pp. 189–203.

Determann, J. M., 'The Crusades in Arab School Textbooks', *Islam and Christian–Muslim Relations* 19 (2008), pp. 199–214.

De Vasselot, C., 'A Crusader Lineage from Spain to the Throne of Jerusalem: The Lusignan', *Crusades* 16 (2017), pp. 95–114.

Dupont, A-L., 'Le grand homme, figure de la "Renaissance arabe"' in *Saints et héros du Moyen-Orient contemporain*, ed. C. Mayeur-Jaouen (Paris, 2002), pp. 47–73.

Ecochard, M., 'Trois Bains Ayyoubides de Damas' in *Les Monuments Ayyoubides de Damas, Volume II* (Paris, 1940), pp. 51–112.

Edbury, P. W. and Rowe, J. G., *William of Tyre: Historian of the Latin East* (Cambridge, 1988).

Eddé, A-M., 'Religious Circles in Jerusalem in the Ayyubid Period' in *Ayyubid Jerusalem: The Holy City in Context, 1187–1250*, eds. R. Hillenbrand and S. Auld (London, 2009), pp. 195–201.

Eddé, A-M., *Saladin*, tr. J. M. Todd (Cambridge, MA, 2011).

Edmonds, C. J., *Kurds, Turks and Arabs: Politics, Travel and Research in North-Eastern Iraq, 1919–1925* (London, 1957).

Ehrenkreutz, A., 'The Place of Saladin in the Naval History of the Mediterranean Sea in the Middle Ages', *Journal of the American Oriental Society* 75 (1955), pp. 100–16.

Ehrenkreutz, A., 'The Crisis of the Dinar in the Egypt of Saladin', *Journal of the American Oriental Society* 76 (1956), pp. 178–84.

Ehrenkreutz, A., *Saladin* (Albany, NY, 1972).

Ehrlich, M., 'The Battle of Hattin: A Chronicle of a Defeat Foretold?', *Journal of Medieval Military History* 5 (2007), pp. 17–27.

Ehrlich, M., 'St Catherine's Day Miracle: The Battle of Montgisard', *Journal of Medieval Military History* 11 (2013), pp. 95–106.

Ehrlich, M., 'The Battle of Arsur: A Short-Lived Victory', *Journal of Medieval Military History* 12 (2014), pp. 109–18.

Elad-Bouskila, A., *Modern Palestinian Literature and Culture* (London, 1999).

Eliassi, B., *Contesting Kurdish Identities in Sweden: Quest for Belonging amongst Middle Eastern Youth* (New York, 2013).

Elisséeff, N., 'Corporations de Damas sous Nur al-Din: Matériaux pour une topographie économique de Damas au xiie siècle', *Arabica* 3 (1956), pp. 61–79.

Elisséeff, N., *Nur ad-Din: un grand prince musulman de Syrie au temps des croisades (511–569 H. /1118–74)*, 3 vols. (Damascus, 1967).

Elisséeff, N., 'The Reaction of the Syrian Muslims after the Foundation of the First Latin Kingdom of Jerusalem', *Crusaders and Muslims in Twelfth Century Syria*, ed. M. Shatzmiller (Leiden, 1993), pp. 162–72.

Ellenblum, R. E., 'Frontier Activities: The Transformation of a Muslim Sacred Site into the Frankish Castle of Vadum Iacob', *Crusades* 2 (2003), pp. 83–98.

Ellenblum, R. E., *Crusader Castles and Modern Histories* (Cambridge, 2007).

Ellenblum, R. E., *The Collapse of the Eastern Mediterranean: Climate Change and the Decline of the East, 950–1072* (Cambridge, 2012).

Encyclopaedia of Archaeological Excavations in the Holy Land, ed. E. Stern, 4 vols. (New York, 1993).

Ende, W., 'Wer ist ein Glaubensheld, wer ist ein Ketzer? Konkurrierende Geschichtsbilder in der modernen Literatur islamischer Länder', *Die Welt des Islams* 23–4 (1984), pp. 70–94.

England, S., *Medieval Empires and the Culture of Competition. Literary Duels at Islamic and Christian Courts* (Edinburgh, 2017).

Epstein, S. A., *Genoa and the Genoese, 958–1528* (Chapel Hill, NC, 1996).

Faulkner, N., *Lawrence of Arabia's War* (London, 2016).

Fawal, I., *Youssef Chahine* (London, 2001).

Fawaz, L., *An Occasion for War: Civil Conflict in Lebanon and Damascus in 1860* (London, 1994).

Fischel, W. J., *Ibn Khaldun in Egypt: His Public Functions and His Historical Research (1382–1406). A Study in Islamic Historiography* (Berkeley, CA, 1967).

Fleischer, C. H., *Bureaucrat and Intellectual in the Ottoman Empire: The Historian Mustafa Ali (1541–1600)* (Princeton, NJ, 1986).

France, J., 'Saladin, from Memory towards Myth in the Continuations' in *Deeds Done Beyond the Sea: Essays on William of Tyre, Cyprus and the Military Orders Presented to Peter Edbury*, eds. S. B. Edgington and H. J. Nicholson, *Crusades Subsidia* 6 (2014), pp. 69–82.

France, J., *Hattin* (Oxford, 2015).

Freed, J. B., *Frederick Barbarossa: The Prince and the Myth* (London, 2016).

Freitag, U., 'In Search of "Historical Correctness": The Ba'ath Party in Syria', *Middle Eastern Politics* 3 (1999), pp. 3–10.

Flori, J., *Richard the Lionheart: King and Knight*, tr. J. Birell (Edinburgh, 2006).

French, R., 'The Religion of Sir Walter Scott', *Studies in Scottish Literature* 2 (1964), pp. 32–44.

Frenkel, Y., 'Political and Social Aspects of Islamic Religious Endowments (*awqaf*): Saladin in Cairo (1169–73) and Jerusalem (1187–93)', *Bulletin of the School of Oriental and African Studies* 62 (1999), pp. 1–20.

Fromherz, A. J., *Ibn Khaldun, Life and Times* (Edinburgh, 2010).

Gal, Z., 'Saladin's Dome of Victory at the Horns of Hattin' in *The Horns of Hattin*, ed. B. Z. Kedar (Jerusalem, 1992), pp. 213–15.

Ganim, J. M., 'Reversing the Crusades: Hegemony, Orientalism and Film Language in Youssef Chahine's *Saladin*' in *Race, Class and Gender in 'Medieval' Cinema*, eds. L. T. Ramey and T. Pugh (Basingstoke, 2007), pp. 45–58.

Gaposchkin, M. C., *Invisible Weapons: Liturgy and the Making of Crusade Ideology* (Ithaca, NY, 2017).

Garcin, J., 'Histoire, opposition politique at piétisme traditionaliste dans le Husn al-Muhadarat de Suyûti', *Annales Islamologiques* 7 (1967), pp. 33–89.

Gelvin, J. L., *Divided Loyalties: Nationalism and Mass Politics in Syria at the Close of Empire* (Berkeley, CA, 1998).

Gemignani, M. (ed.), *Le bandiere della Chiesa di Santo Stefano dei Cavalieri di Pisa: Loro storia, significato e restauro/The Flags of the Church of Saint Stephen of the Knights in Pisa: Their History, Meaning and Restoration* (Pisa, 2015).

Gerber, H., *Remembering and Imagining Palestine: Identity and Nationalism from the Crusades to the Present* (Basingstoke, 2008).

Gershoni I. and Jankowski, J. P., *Egypt, Islam and the Arabs: The Search for Egyptian Nationhood, 1900–1930* (Oxford, 1986).

Gershoni, I. and Jankowski, J. P., *Redefining the Egyptian Nation, 1930–1945* (Cambridge, 1995).

Gertwagen, R., 'The Crusader Port of Acre: Layout and problems of maintenance' in *Autour de la première croisade*, ed. M. Balard (Paris, 1996), pp. 553–82.

Gertz, N. and Khleifi, G., *Palestinian Cinema: Landscape, Trauma and Memory* (Edinburgh, 2008).

Gertz, N. and Khleifi, G., 'A Chronicle of Palestinian Cinema' in *Film in the Middle East and North Africa: Creative Dissidence* (Austin, TX, 2011), pp. 187–97.

Gertz, N. and Khleifi, G., 'Tale of Three Jewels: Children Living and Dreaming amid Violence in Gaza' in *Film in the Middle East and North Africa: Creative Dissidence* (Austin, TX, 2011), pp. 208–17.

Gibb, H. A. R., 'The Arabic Sources for the Life of Saladin', *Speculum* 25 (1950), pp. 58–72.

Gibb, H. A. R., 'Al-Barq al-Shami: The History of Saladin by the Katib Imad ad-Din al-Isfahani', *Wiener Zeitschrift für die Kunde des Morgenlandes* 52 (1953), pp. 93–115.

Gibb, H. A. R., 'The Armies of Saladin' in *Saladin: Studies in Islamic History*, ed. Y. Ibish (Beirut, 1972), pp. 138–57.

Gillingham, J. B., *Richard I* (London, 1999).

Girouard, M., *The Age of Camelot* (London, 1981).

Goitein, S. D., *A Mediterranean Society: The Jewish Communities of the World as Portrayed in the Documents of the Cairo Geniza*, 6 vols. (Berkeley, CA, 2000).

Gonnella, J., 'Die Ayyubidische und Mamlukische zitadelle von Aleppo' in *Burgen und Städte der Kreuzzugszeit*, ed. M. Piana (Petersberg, 2008), pp. 139–47.

Haddad, G. M., 'The Historical Works of Niqula El-Turk 1763–1828', *Journal of the American Oriental Society* 81 (1961), pp. 247–51.

Halim, H., 'The Signs of *Saladin*: A Modern Cinematic Rendition of Medieval Heroism', *Alif* 12 (1992), pp. 78–94.

Hamblin, W. J., 'Saladin and Muslim Military Theory' in *The Horns of Hattin*, ed. B. Z. Kedar (Jerusalem, 1992), pp. 228–38.

Hamilton, B., 'The Elephant of Christ: Reynald of Châtillon' in *Religious Motivation: Biographical and Sociological Problems for the Church Historian*, ed. D. Baker, *Studies in Church History* 15 (1978), 97–108.

Hamilton, B., *The Leper King and His Heirs: Baldwin IV and the Crusader Kingdom of Jerusalem* (Cambridge, 2000).

Hamarneh, W., 'Jurji Zaydan' in *Essays in Arabic Literary Biography, 1850–1950*, ed. R. Allen (Wiesbaden, 2010), pp. 389–92.

Harawi, M., 'Ayyubid Monuments in Jerusalem' in *Ayyubid Jerusalem: The Holy City in Context, 1187–1250*, eds. R. Hillenbrand and S. Auld (London, 2009), pp. 216–75.

Harris, J., 'Collusion with the infidel as a pretext for western military action against Byzantium (1180–1204)' in *Languages of Love and Hate: Conflict, Communication and Identity in the Medieval Mediterranean*, eds. S. Lambert and H. Nicholson (Turnhout, 2012), p. 99–117.

Harris, J., *Byzantium and the Crusades*, second edition (London, 2014).

Harvey, E., 'Saladin Consoles Baldwin IV over the Death of his Father', *Crusades* 15 (2016), pp. 27–34.

Heidemann, S., *Die Renaissance der Städte in Nordsyrien und Nordmesopotamien: städtische Entwicklung und wirtschaftliche Bedingungen in ar-Raqqa und Ḥarrān von der Zeit der beduinischen Vorherrschaft bis zu den Seldschuken* (Leiden, 2002).

Heidemann, S., 'Memory and Ideology: Images of Saladin in Syria and Iraq' in *Visual Culture in the Modern Middle East*, eds. C. Gruber and S. Haugbolle (Bloomington, IN, 2013), pp. 57–81.

Heng, G., *The Invention of Race in the European Middle Ages* (Cambridge, 2018).

Hillenbrand, C., 'The First Crusade: The Muslim Perspective' in *The First Crusade: Origins and Impact* (Manchester, 1997), pp. 130–41.

Hillenbrand, C., *The Crusades: Islamic Perspectives* (Edinburgh, 1999).

Hillenbrand, C., '"Abominable Acts": The Career of Zengi' in *The Second Crusade: Scope and Consequences*, eds. J. P. Phillips and M. Hoch (Manchester, 2001), pp. 111–32.

Hillenbrand, C., 'The Imprisonment of Reynald of Châtillon' in *Texts, Documents and Artefacts. Islamic Studies in Honour of D. S. Richards*, ed. C. F. Robinson (Leiden, 2003), 79–99.

Hillenbrand, C., *Islam: A New Historical Introduction* (London, 2015).

Hillenbrand, C., 'The Sultan, the Kaiser, the Colonel, and the Purloined Wreath', in *The Making of Crusading Heroes and Villains: Engaging the Crusades*, eds. M. Horswell and K. Skottki (Abingdon, forthcoming).

Hillenbrand, R., 'The Ayyubid Aqsa: Decorative Aspects' in *Ayyubid Jerusalem: The Holy City in Context, 1187–1250*, eds. R. Hillenbrand and S. Auld (London, 2009), pp. 301–26.

Hilsum, L., *Sandstorm: Libya from Gaddafi to Revolution* (London, 2012).

Hinz, F. and Mayer-Hamme, J., *Controversial Histories – Contemporary International Views on the Crusades: Engaging the Crusades* (Abingdon, forthcoming).

Hirschler, K., *Medieval Arabic Historiography: Authors as Actors* (Abingdon, 2006).

Hirschler, K., *The Written Word in the Medieval Arabic Lands: A Social and Cultural History of Reading Practices* (Edinburgh, 2012).

Hirschler, K., 'The Jerusalem Conquest of 492/1099 in the Medieval Arabic Historiography of the Crusades: From Regional Plurality to Islamic Narrative', *Crusades* 13 (2014), pp. 37–76.

Hirschler, K., *Medieval Damascus: Plurality and Diversity in an Arabic Library. The Ashrafiya Library Catalogue* (Edinburgh, 2016).

Hirschler, K., 'Frankish–Muslim Relations in the Ayyubid Period, c.1193–c.1250' in *The Cambridge History of the Crusades*, Volume 2, eds. A. Jotischky and J. P. Phillips, 2 vols. (Cambridge, 2020).

Hodgson, M. G. S., *The Secret Order of Assassins: The Struggle of the Early Nizârîl Ismâ'îlîs against the Islamic World* (Philadelphia, PA, 1955).

Horswell, M. J., *The Rise and Fall of British Crusader Medievalism, c.1825–1945* (Abingdon, 2018).

Hosler, J. D., *The Siege of Acre, 1189–91: Saladin, Richard the Lionheart and the Battle that decided the Third Crusade* (London, 2018).

Hosler, J. D., 'Clausewitz's Wounded Lion: A Fighting Retreat at the Siege of Acre, November, 1190' in *Acre and its Falls*, ed. J. France (Leiden, 2018), pp. 30–48.

Housley, N., *The Later Crusades: From Lyons to Alcazar, 1274–1580* (Oxford, 1992).

Humphreys, R. S., *From Saladin to the Mongols: The Ayyubids of Damascus, 1193–1260* (Albany, NY, 1977).

Humphreys, R. S., 'Women as Patrons of Religious Architecture in Ayyubid Damascus', *Muqarnas* 11 (1994), pp. 35–54.

Irwin, R., *The Arabian Nights: A Companion* (London, 1994).

Irwin, R., 'Orientalism and the Development of Crusader Studies' in *The Experience of Crusading 2. Defining the Crusader Kingdom*, eds. P. W. Edbury and J. P. Phillips, 2 vols. (Cambridge, 2003), 2.219–29.

Irwin, R., *Ibn Khaldun: An Intellectual Biography* (Princeton, NJ, 2018).

Isphording, B., *Germans in Jerusalem, 1830–1914* (Jerusalem, 2009).

Jackson, D. E. P., 'Some Preliminary Reflections on the Chancery Correspondence of the Qadi al-Fadil' in *Egypt and Syria in the Fatimid, Ayyubid and Mamluk Eras I*, eds. U. Vermeulen and D. de Smet (Leuven, 1995), pp. 207–17.

Jacoby, D., 'Aspects of Everyday Life in Frankish Acre', *Crusades* 4 (2005), pp. 73–105.

Jackson, P., *The Mongols and The Islamic World: From Conquest to Conversion* (London, 2017).

James, L., *Nasser at War: Arab Images of the Enemy* (Basingstoke, 2008).

Jensen, M. I., *The Political Ideology of Hamas: A Grassroots Perspective* (London, 2008).

Jerusalem 1000–1400: Every People under Heaven, eds. B. Boehm and N. Holcomb (New York, 2016).

Johns, C. N., 'Medieval Ajlun', *Quarterly of the Department of Antiquaries in Palestine* 1 (1931), pp. 21–33.

Jones, M. H., 'Richard the Lionheart in German Literature of the Middle Ages' in *Richard Coeur de Lion in History and Myth*, ed. J. L. Nelson (London, 1992), pp. 70–116.

Jubb, M., 'Enemies in Holy War, but Brothers in Chivalry: The Crusaders' View of their Saracen Opponents' in *Aspects de l'épopée romane, mentalités, idéologies, intertextualités*, eds. H. van Dijk and W. Noomen (Groningen, 1995), pp. 251–9.

Jubb, M., *The Legend of Saladin in Western Literature and Historiography* (Lewiston, NY, 2000).

Kansteiner, W., 'Finding Meaning in Memory: A Methodological Critique of Collective Memory Studies', *History and Theory* 41 (2002), pp. 179–97.

Karsh, E., *Arafat's War: The Man and his Battle for Israeli Conquest* (New York, 2004).

Kedar, B. Z., 'Noms de saints et mentalité populaire à Gênes au XIVe siècle', *Moyen Age* 73 (1967), pp. 31–46.

Kedar, B. Z., 'The Battle of Hattin Revisted' in *The Horns of Hattin*, ed. B. Z. Kedar (Jerusalem, 1992), pp. 187–212.

Kedar, B. Z., 'Croisade et jihad vus par l'ennemi: une étude des perceptions mutu-elles des motivations' in *Autour de la première croisade*, ed. M. Balard (Paris, 1996), pp. 345–55.

Kedar, B. Z., 'A Western Survey of Saladin's Forces at the Siege of Acre' in *Montjoie. Studies in Crusade History in Honour of Hans Eberhard Mayer*, eds. B. Z. Kedar, J. S. C. Riley-Smith and R. Hiestand (Aldershot, 1997), pp. 113–22.

Kedar, B. Z., 'Convergence of Oriental Christian, Muslim and Frankish Worshippers: the Case of Saidnaya and the Knights Templar' in *The Crusades and the Military Orders: Expanding the Frontiers of Medieval Latin Christianity*, eds. Z. Hunyadi and J. Laslovszky (Budapest, 2001), pp. 89–92.

Kedar, B. Z., 'The Jerusalem Massacre of 1099 in the Western Historiography of the Crusades', *Crusades* 3 (2004), pp. 15–76.

Kedar, B. Z., 'King Richard's Plan for the Battle of Arsuf/Arsur, 1191', in *The Medieval Way of War: Studies in Medieval Military History in Honor of Bernard S. Bachrach* ed. G. I. Halfond (Farnham, 2015), pp. 117–32.

Kedar, B. Z. and Pringle, D., 'La Fève: A Crusader Castle in the Jezreel Valley', *Israel Exploration Journal* 35 (1985), pp. 164–79.

Kedar, M., *Asad in Search of Legitimacy: Message and Rhetoric in the Syrian Press under Hafiz and Bashar* (Brighton, 2005).

Keddie, N. R., 'The Pan-Islamic Appeal: Afghani and Abdülhamid II', *Middle Eastern Studies* 3 (1966), pp. 46–67.

Keddie, N. R., *An Islamic Response to Imperialism: Political and Religious Writings of Sayyid Jamal al-Din 'al-Afghani'* (Berkeley, CA, 1983).

Keen, M., *Chivalry* (London, 1984)

Kennedy, H., *Crusader Castles* (Cambridge, 1994).

Khalidi, R., 'The Role of the Press in the Early Arab Reaction to Zionism', *Peuples Méditerranéens* 20 (1982), pp. 105–23.

Khalidi, R., 'Contrasting Narratives of Palestinian Identity' in *The Geography of Identity*, ed. P. Yaeger (Ann Arbor, MI, 1996), pp. 187–222.

Khalidi, R., *Palestinian Identity: The Construction of Modern National Consciousness* (New York, 2009).

Khouri, M., *The Arab National Project in Yousef Chahine's Cinema* (Cairo, 2010).

Khoury, P. S., *Syria and the French Mandate: The Politics of Arab Nationalism, 1920–1945* (London, 1987).

Köhler, M-A., *Alliances and Treaties between Frankish and Muslim Rulers in the Middle East*, trs. P. M. Holt and K. Hirschler (Leiden, 2013).

Kool, R., 'Coins at Vadum Jacob: New Evidence on the Circulation of Money in the Latin Kingdom of Jerusalem during the Second Half of the Twelfth Century', *Crusades* 1 (2002), pp. 73–88.

Korn, L., '"Die Bauten Saladins": Kairo, Damaskus, und Jerusalem in der Baupolitik des an-Nasir Salah ad-Din Yusuf Ibn Ayyub' in *Egypt and Syria in the Fatimid, Ayyubid and Mamluk Eras II*, eds. U. Vermeulen and D. de Smet (Leuven, 1998), pp. 209–35.

Korn, L., *Ayyubidische Arkitektur in Ägypten und Syrien. Bautätigkeit im Kontext von Politik und Gesellschaft 564–658/1169–1260*, 2 vols. (Heidelberg, 2004).

Korn, L., 'Ayyubid Mosaics in Jerusalem' in *Ayyubid Jerusalem: The Holy City in Context, 1187–1250*, eds. R. Hillenbrand and S. Auld (London, 2009), pp. 377–87.

Krämer, G., *Hasan al-Banna* (Oxford, 2010).

Krüger, J., 'William II's Perception of Sacrality' in *Baalbek: Image and Monument, 1898–1998*, eds. H. Sadler, T. Scheffler and A. Neuwirth (Beirut, 1998), pp. 89–95.

Kubiak, W., 'The Burning of Misr al-Fustat in 1168: A Reconsideration of Historical Evidence', *Africana Bulletin* 25 (1976), pp. 51–64.

Kupferschmidt, U. M., *The Supreme Muslim Council: Islam under the British Mandate for Palestine* (Leiden, 1987).

La Guardia, A., *Holy Land, Unholy War: Israelis and Palestinians* (London, 2001).

La Mazière, P., *Partant pour la Syrie* (Paris, 1926).

Lambton, A. K. S., 'Islamic Mirrors for Princes' in *Theory and Practice in Medieval Persian Government* (London, 1980), 6:419–42.

Landau, J., *Studies in the Arab Theatre and Cinema* (Philadelphia, PA, 1958).

Laoust, A., 'Ibn Katir, historien', *Arabica* 2 (1955), pp. 42–88.

Latiff, O., *The Cutting Edge of the Poet's Sword: Muslim Poetic Responses to the Crusades* (Leiden, 2018).

Layish, A., 'The *Sijill* of Jaffa and Nazareth *Shari'a* courts as a source for the Political and Social History of Ottoman Palestine' in *Studies on Palestine during the Ottoman Period*, ed. M. Ma'oz (Jerusalem, 1975), pp. 525–32.

Leiser, G., 'The Crusader Raid on the Red Sea in 578/1182–3', *Journal of the American Research Center in Egypt* 14 (1977), pp. 87–100.

Leiser, G., 'The *Madrasa* and the Islamization of the Middle East: The Case of Egypt', *Journal of the American Research Center in Egypt* 22 (1985), pp. 29–47.

Leopold, A., *How to Recover the Holy Land: The Crusade Proposals of the Late Thirteenth and Fourteenth Centuries* (Aldershot, 2000).

Lev, Y., *Saladin in Egypt* (Leiden, 1999).

Lev, Y., 'The Dismemberment of the Fatimid State and the Emergence of a New Ayyubid Elite in Egypt', *Egypt and Syria in the Fatimid, Ayyubid and Mamluk Eras V*, eds. U. Vermeulen and K. D'Hulster (Leuven, 2007), pp. 130–52.

Lev, Y., 'Saladin's Economic Policies and the Economy of Ayyubid Egypt' in *Egypt and Syria in the Fatimid, Ayyubid and Mamluk Eras V*, eds. U. Vermeulen and K. D'Hulster (Leuven, 2007), pp. 307–48.

Lev, Y., 'The "jihad" of Sultan Nur al-Din of Syria (1146–1174): History and Discourse', *Jerusalem Studies in Arabic and Islam* 35 (2008), pp. 228–84.

Lewis, B., *The Assassins* (London, 1967).

Lewis, B., *Islam from the Prophet Muhammad to the Capture of Constantinople* (New York, 1974).

Lewis, B., *History Remembered, Recovered, Invented* (Princeton, NJ, 1975).

Lewis, B., *The Muslim Discovery of Europe* (New York, 1982).

Lewis, K. J., *The Counts of Tripoli and Lebanon in the Twelfth Century: Sons of Saint-Gilles* (Abingdon, 2017).

Lewis, R. Y., 'Crusader Battlefields: Environmental and Archaeological Perspectives' in *The Crusader World*, ed. A. Boas (Abingdon, 2016), pp. 460–89.

Little, D. P., *An Introduction to Mamluk Historiography* (Wiesbaden, 1970).

Little, D. P., 'Mujir al-Din al-Ulaymi's vision of Jerusalem in the ninth/fifteenth century', *Journal of the American Oriental Society* 115 (1995), pp. 237–47.

Little, D. P., 'Historiography of the Ayyubid and Mamluk epochs', *Cambridge History of Egypt. Volume 1, Islamic Egypt, 640–1517*, ed. C. F. Petry (Cambridge, 1998), pp. 412–44.

Litvak, M., 'Constructing a National Past: The Palestinian Case', *Palestinian Collective Memory and National Identity*, ed. M. Litvak (Basingstoke, 2009), pp. 97–113.

Loomis, R. S., 'The "Pas Saladin" in Art and Heraldry' in *Studies in Art and Literature for Belle da Costa Greene*, ed. D. Milner (Princeton, NJ, 1954), pp. 83–91.

Lyons, M. C., 'The Crusading Stratum in the Arabic Hero Cycles' in *Crusaders and Muslims in Twelfth Century Syria*, ed. M. Shatzmiller (Leiden, 1993), pp. 147–61.

Lyons, M. C, *The Arabic Epic: Heroic and Oral Story-Telling*, 3 vols. (Cambridge, 1995).

Lyons, M. C. and Jackson, D. E. P., *Saladin: The Politics of the Holy War* (Cambridge, 1982).

MacEvitt, C., *The Crusades and the Christian Worlds of the East: Rough Tolerance* (Philadelphia, PA, 2008).

MacKenzie, N. D., *Ayyubid Cairo: A Topographical Study* (Cairo, 1992).

Mallett, A., 'A Trip Down the Red Sea with Reynald of Châtillon', *Journal of the Royal Asiatic Society* 18 (2008), pp. 141–53.

Mallett, A., 'Ibn al-Jawzi' in *Christian–Muslim Relations: A Bibliographical History, Volume 3 (1050–1200)*, eds. D. Thomas and A. Mallett (Leiden, 2011), pp. 731–5.

Mallett, A. (ed.), *Medieval Muslim Historians and the Franks in the Levant* (Leiden, 2014).

Mallett, A., *Popular Muslim Reactions to the Franks in the Levant, 1097–1291* (Farnham, 2014).

Mandel, N., *The Arabs and Zionism before World War I* (Berkeley, CA, 1978).

Manna, A., 'The *Sijill* as a Source for the Study of Palestine' in *Palestine in the Late Ottoman Period: Political, Social and Economic Transformation*, ed. D. Kushner (Jerusalem and Leiden, 1986), pp. 351–62.

Maqdsi, M., 'Charter of the Islamic Resistance Movement (Hamas) of Palestine', *Journal of Palestine Studies* 22 (1993), pp. 122–34.

Mason, H., *Two Statesmen of Medieval Islam* (The Hague, 1953).

Masri, P. and Swanson, M. N., 'Apologetic Commentary on the Creed' in *Christian–Muslim Relations: A Bibliographical History, Volume 3 (1050–1200)*, eds. D. Thomas and A. Mallett (Leiden, 2011), pp. 671–5.

Masters, B., *Arabs of the Ottoman Empire, 1516–1918* (Cambridge, 2013).

Matthews, D., *Confronting an Empire, Constructing a Nation: Arab Nationalists and Popular Politics in Mandate Palestine* (London, 2006).

Mazza, R., *Jerusalem from the Ottomans to the British* (London, 2009).

McCracken, P., 'Scandalizing Desire: Eleanor of Aquitaine and the Chroniclers' in *Eleanor of Aquitaine: Lord and Lady*, eds. B. Wheeler and J. C. Parsons (Basingstoke, 2002), pp. 247–63.

Menchinger, E. L., *First of the Modern Ottomans: The Intellectual History of Ahmed Vasif* (Cambridge, 2017).

Meri, J. W., *The Cult of Saints amongst Muslims and Jews in Medieval Syria* (Oxford, 2002).

Mesqui, J., 'Bourzey, une forteresse anonyme de l'Oronte' in *La Fortification au temps des croisades*, eds. N. Faucherre, J. Mesqui and N. Proteau (Rennes, 2004), pp. 95–133.

Mesqui, J., 'Die Burg Saône' in *Burgen und Städte der Kreuzzugszeit*, ed. M. Piana (Petersberg, 2008), pp. 356–66.

Metcalfe, A., *The Muslims of Medieval Italy* (Edinburgh, 2009).

Meynier, G., *L'Algérie révélée: la guerre de 1914–1918 et le premier quart du XXe* (Geneva, 1981).

Milwright, M., 'Reynald of Châtillon and the Red Sea Expedition' in *Noble Ideas and Bloody Realities: Warfare in the Middle Ages*, eds. N. Christie and M. Yazigi (Leiden, 2006), pp. 235–57.

Milwright, M., *The Fortress of the Raven: Karak in the Middle Islamic Period (1100–1650)* (Leiden, 2008).

Minorsky, V., *Studies in Caucasian History* (London, 1953).

Mitchell, P. D., 'An Evaluation of the Leprosy of King Baldwin IV of Jerusalem in the Context of the Medieval World' in B. Hamilton, *The Leper King and His Heirs: Baldwin IV and the Crusader Kingdom of Jerusalem* (Cambridge, 2000), pp. 245–58.

Mitchell, P. D., *Medicine in the Crusades: Warfare, Wounds and the Medieval Surgeon* (Cambridge, 2004).

Mitchell, P. D., Nagar, Y. and Ellenblum, R., 'Weapon Injuries in the 12th Century Crusader Garrison of Vadum Iacob Castle, Galilee', *International Journal of Osteoarchaeology* 16 (2006), pp. 145–55.

Mitchell, R. P., *The Society of the Muslim Brothers* (Oxford, 1993).

Mo'az, M., *Ottoman Reform in Syria and Palestine, 1840–1861: The Influence of the Tanzimat on Politics and Society* (Oxford, 1968).

Mo'az, M., *Asad: The Sphinx of Damascus: A Political Biography* (New York, 1988).

Moctar, el-, M., 'Saladin in Sunni and Shi'a Memories' in *Remembering the Crusades: Myth, Image and Reality*, eds. N. Paul and S. Yeager (Baltimore, 2012), pp. 198–201.

Möhring, H., 'Zwischen Joseph-Legende und Mahdi-Erwartung: Erfolge und Ziele Sultan Saladins im Spiegel zeitgenössicher Dichtung und Weissagung' in *War and Society in the Eastern Mediterranean, 7th–15th Centuries*, ed. Y. Lev (Leiden, 1997), pp. 177–223.

Möhring, H., *Saladin: The Sultan and his Times, 1137–1193*, tr. B. S. Bachrach, introduction P. M. Cobb (Baltimore, MD, 2008).

Montada, J. P., 'Al-Afghânî, a Case of Religious Unbelief?' *Studia Islamica* 100/101 (2005), pp. 203–20.

Moosa, M., *The Origins of Modern Arabic Fiction* (Washington DC, 1983).

Morton, N. E., *Encountering Islam on the First Crusade* (Cambridge, 2017).

Morton, N. E., *The Field of Blood: The Battle for Aleppo and the Remaking of the Medieval Middle East* (New York, 2018).

Mottahedeh, R. P., *Loyalty and Leadership in an Early Islamic Society*, revised edition (London, 2001).

Mouton, J-M., *Damas et sa principauté sous les Saljoukides et les Bourides, 468–549/1076–1154* (Cairo, 1994).

Mouton, J-M., *Sadr: Une forteresse de Saladin au Sinai. Histoire et archéologie*, 2 vols. (Paris, 2010).

Mouton, J-M. and Abd al-Malik, S., 'La forteresse de l'Ile de Graye (Qal'at Ayla) à l'époque de Saladin: Étude épigraphique et historique', *Annales Islamologiques* 29 (1995), pp. 75–90.

Murray, A. V., 'Mighty against the enemies of Christ' in *The Crusades and their Sources: Essays presented to Bernard Hamilton*, eds. J. France and W. Zajac (Aldershot, 1998), pp. 217–38.

Murray, A. V., 'Finance and Logistics of the Crusade of Frederick Barbarossa' in *In laudem Hierosolymitani: Studies in Crusades and Medieval Culture in Honour of Benjamin Z. Kedar*, eds. I. Shagrir, R. Ellenblum and J. S. C. Riley-Smith, Crusades Subsidia 1 (Aldershot, 2007), pp. 357–68.

Musallam, A. A., 'Sayyid Qutb and Social Justice, 1945–1948', *Journal of Islamic Studies* 4 (1993), pp. 52–70.

Myers, D., 'An Overview of the Islamic Architecture of Ottoman Jerusalem' in *Ottoman Jerusalem: The Living City 1517–1917*, eds. S. Auld and R. Hillenbrand 2 vols (London, 2000), 1.326–38.

Nammour, M., 'La perception des croisades chez Jurjy Zaidan (1861–1914)' in *Chrétiens et Musulmans au temps des croisades: Entre l'affrontement et la rencontre*, eds. L. Pouzet and L. Boisset (Beirut, 2007), pp. 141–61.

Natsheh, Y., 'The Architecture of Ottoman Jerusalem' in *Ottoman Jerusalem: The Living City, 1517–1917*, eds. S. Auld and R. Hillenbrand (London, 2000), 1.583–655.

Nicault, C., 'Foi et politique: les pèlerinages français en Terre Sainte' in *De Bonaparte à Balfour: La France, L'Europe occidentale et la Palestine, 1799–1917*, eds. D. Trimbur and A. Aaronsohn (Paris, 2001), pp. 295–325.

Nicholson, H. J., '"Martyrum collegio sociandus haberet": Depictions of the Military Orders' Martyrs in the Holy Land, 1187–1291' in *Crusading and Warfare in the Middle Ages: Realities and Representations. Essays in Honour of John France*, eds. S. John and N. E. Morton (Farnham, 2014), pp. 101–18.

Nicolle, D., *Saladin and the Saracens* (Botley, 1986).

Nixon, J., *Debriefing the President: The Interrogation of Saddam Hussein* (London, 2016).

Nora. P., 'Between Memory and History: Les Lieux de Mémoire', *Representations* 26 (1989), pp. 7–24.

Northrup, L. S., 'The Bahri Mamluk sultanate, 1250–1390' in *The Cambridge History of Egypt. Volume 1, Islamic Egypt, 640–1517*, ed. C. F. Petry (Cambridge, 1998), pp. 242–89.

Ohana, D., *The Origins of Israeli Mythology: Neither Canaanites nor Crusaders* (Cambridge, 2012).

Olsaretti, A., 'Political Dynamics in the Rise of Fahkr al-Din, 1590–1633: Crusade, Trade, and State Formation along the Levantine Coast', *International History Review* 30 (2008), pp. 709–22.

Pahlitzsch, J., 'The Transformation of Latin Religious Institutions into Islamic Endowments by Saladin in Jerusalem' in *Governing the Holy City: The Interaction of Social Groups in Medieval Jerusalem*, eds. L. Korn and J. Pahlitzsch (Wiesbaden, 2004), pp. 47–69.

Pahlitzsch, J., 'The People of the Book' in *Ayyubid Jerusalem: The Holy City in Context, 1187–1250*, eds. R. Hillenbrand and S. Auld (London, 2009), pp. 435–40.

Peacock, A. C. S., *The Great Seljuk Empire* (Edinburgh, 2015).

Philipp, T. D., 'Approaches to History in the Work of Jurji Zaydan', *Asian and African Studies* 9 (1973), pp. 63–85.

Philipp, T. D., 'The French and the French Revolution in the Works of al-Jabarti' in *Eighteenth-Century Egypt: The Arabic Manuscript Sources*, ed. D. Crecelius (Claremont, CA, 1990), pp. 127–40.

Phillips, J. P., *Defenders of the Holy Land: Relations between the Latin East and the West, 1119–1187* (Oxford, 1996).

Phillips, J. P., *The Second Crusade: Extending the Frontiers of Christendom* (London, 2007).

Phillips, J. P., 'The Travels of Ibn Jubayr and his View of Saladin' in *Cultural Encounters during the Crusades*, eds. K. Villads Jensen, K. Salonen and H. Vogt (Odense, 2013), pp. 75–90.

Phillips, J. P., 'The Third Crusade in Context: Contradiction, Curiosity and Survival' in *Christianity and Religious Plurality*, eds. C. Methuen, A. Spicer and J. Wolffe, *Studies in Church History* 51 (Woodbridge, 2015), pp. 92–114.

Phillips, J. P., 'Unity! Unity between all the Inhabitants of our Lands!' in *Perceptions of the Crusades from the Nineteenth to the Twenty-First Century*, eds. M. J. Horswell and J. P. Phillips, *Engaging the Crusades* 1 (Abingdon, 2018), pp. 79–106.

Phillips, J. P., 'Saladin and Gift-Giving' in *Syria in Crusader Times: Conflict and Co-existence*, ed. C. Hillenbrand (Edinburgh, 2019).

Piana, M. (ed.), *Burgen und Städte der Kreuzzugszeit* (Petersberg, 2008).

Pipes, D., *Greater Syria: The History of an Ambition* (Oxford, 1990).

Podeh, E., *The Decline of Arab Unity: The Rise and Fall of the United Arab Republic* (Eastbourne, 1999).

Polk, R., *Crusade and Jihad: The Thousand Year War between the Muslim World and the Global North* (London, 2018).

Pormann, P. E. and Savage-Smith, E., *Medieval Islamic Medicine* (Edinburgh, 2010).

Porter, R., *Enlightenment: Britain and the Creation of the Modern World* (London, 2000).

Pradines, S., 'Burj al-Zafar: Architecture de passage des fatimides aux ayyoubides' in *Egypt and Syria in the Fatimid, Ayyubid and Mamluk Eras VIII*, eds. U. Vermenlen, K. D'Hulster and J. Van Steenbergen (Leuven, 2016), pp. 51–119.

Pringle, D., 'Richard I and the Walls of Ascalon', *Palestine Exploration Quarterly* 116 (1984), pp. 133–47.

Pringle, D., *The Churches of the Crusader Kingdom of Jerusalem: A Corpus*, 4 vols. (Cambridge, 1993–2009).

Pringle, D., 'Town Defences in the Crusader Kingdom of Jerusalem' in *The Medieval City Under Siege*, eds. I. A. Corfis and M. Wolfe (Woodbridge, 1995), pp. 69–122.

Pringle, D., 'The Castles of Ayla (al-Aqaba) in the Crusader, Ayyubid and Mamluk Periods' in *Egypt and Syria in the Fatimid, Ayyubid and Mamluk Eras IV*, eds. U. Vermeulen and J. Van Steenbergen (Leuven, 2005), pp. 333–53.

Provence, M., *The Last Ottoman Generation and the Making of the Modern Middle East* (Cambridge, 2017).

Prusskaya, E., 'Arab Chronicles as a Source for Studying Bonaparte's Expedition to Egypt', *Napoleonica. La Revue* 24 (2015), pp. 48–60.

Pryor, J. H., *Geography, Technology and War: Studies in the Maritime History of the Mediterranean, 649–1571* (Cambridge, 1988).

Pryor, J. H., 'A Medieval Siege of Troy: The Fight to the Death at Acre, 1189–91, or the Tears of Salah al-Din' in *The Medieval Way of War: Studies in Medieval Military History in Honor of Bernard S. Bachrach*, ed. G. I. Halfond (Aldershot, 2015), pp. 97–115.

Rabbat, N. O., *The Citadel of Cairo: A New Interpretation of Royal Mamluk Architecture* (Leiden, 1995).

Rabbat, N. O., 'My Life with Salah al-Din: The Memoirs of Imad al-Din al-Katib al-Isfahani', *Edebiyat* 7 (1997), pp. 267–87.

Rabie, H., *The Financial System of Egypt, A. H. 564–741/A. D. 1169–1341* (Cambridge, 1972).

Rafeq, A., 'Ottoman Jerusalem in the Writings of Arab Travellers' in *Ottoman Jerusalem: The Living City, 1517–1917*, 2 vols., eds. S. Auld and R. Hillenbrand (London, 2000), 1.63–72.

Ragab, A., *The Medieval Islamic Hospital: Medicine, Religion and Charity* (Cambridge, 2015).

Raphael, K., *Muslim Fortresses in the Levant: Between Crusaders and Mongols* (Abingdon, 2011).

Reid, D. M., *The Odyssey of Farah Antun: A Syrian Christian's Quest for Secularism* (Minneapolis, MN, 1975).

Reiter, Y., *Jerusalem and its Role in Islamic Solidarity* (Basingstoke, 2008).

Reiter, Y., *Contested Holy Places in Israel-Palestine: Sharing and Conflict Resolution* (Abingdon, 2017).

Reynolds, D. F., *Interpreting the Self: Autobiography in the Arabic Literary Tradition* (Berkeley, CA, 2001).

Richard, J., 'National Feeling and the Legacy of the Crusades' in *The Crusades*, ed. H. Nicholson (Basingstoke, 2005), pp. 209–18.

Richard, J., 'Les esclaves franques de Saladin' in *Gouvernance et libéralités de Saladin d'après les données inédites de six documents arabes*, eds. and trs. J-M. Mouton, D. Sourdel and J. Sourdel-Thomine (Paris, 2015), pp. 123–5.

Richards, D. S., 'The Early History of Saladin', *Islamic Quarterly* 17 (1973), pp. 140–59.

Richards, D. S., 'A Consideration of Two Sources for the Life of Saladin', *Journal of Semitic Studies* 25 (1980), pp. 46–65.

Richards, D. S., 'Imad al-Din al-Isfahani: Administrator, Littérateur and Historian' in *Crusaders and Muslims in Twelfth Century Syria*, ed. M. Shatzmiller (Leiden, 1993), pp. 133–46.

Richards, D. S., 'Biographies of the Ayyubid Sultans' in *Ayyubid Jerusalem: The Holy City in Context, 1187–1250*, eds. R. Hillenbrand and S. Auld (London, 2009), pp. 441–55.

Richter-Bernberg, L., 'Between Marvel and Trial: al-Harawi and Ibn Jubayr on Architecture' in *Egypt and Syria in the Fatimid, Ayyubid and Mamluk Eras VI*, eds. U. Vermeulen and K. D'Hulster (Leuven, 2010), pp. 115–46.

Richter-Bernburg, L., 'Imad al-Din al-Isfahani' in *Medieval Muslim Historians and the Franks in the Levant*, ed. A. Mallett (Leiden, 2014), pp. 29–51.

Rikabi, J., *La poésie profane sous les Ayyubides et ses principaux représentants* (Paris, 1949).

Riley-Smith, J. S. C., 'Islam and the Crusades in History and Imagination, 8 November 1898–11 September 2001', *Crusades* 2 (2003), pp. 151–67.

Rogers, R., *Latin Siege Warfare in the Twelfth Century* (Oxford, 1992).

Röhl, J. C. G., *Young Wilhelm: The Kaiser's Early Life, 1859–1888*, tr. J. Gaines and R. Wallach (Cambridge, 1988).

Röhl, J. C. G., *Wilhelm II: The Kaiser's Personal Monarchy, 1888–1900*, tr. S. de Bellaigue (Cambridge, 2003).

Rubenstein, J., *Nebuchadnezzar's Dream: The Crusades, Apocalyptic Prophecy and the End of History* (New York, 2019).

Saleh, M. J., 'Al-Suyuti and His Works: Their Place in Islamic Scholarship from Mamluk Times to the Present', *Mamluk Studies Review* 5 (2001), pp. 73–89.

Sanders, P., 'From Court Ceremony to Urban Language: Ceremonial in Fatimid Cairo and Fustat', *The Islamic World from Classical to Modern Times: Essays in Honour of Bernard Lewis*, eds. C. E. Bosworth et al. (Princeton, NJ, 1989), pp. 311–21.

Sanders, P., *Ritual, Politics and the City in Fatimid Cairo* (Albany, NY, 1994).

Sanders, P., 'Robes of Honor in Fatimid Egypt' in *Robes and Honor: The Medieval World of Investiture*, ed. S. Gordon (Basingstoke, 2001), pp. 225–39.

Sartain, E. M., *Jalal al-din Suyuti*, 2 vols. (Cambridge, 1975).

Sayyid Marsot, A., 'A Comparative Study of Abd al-Rahman al-Jabarti and Niqula al-Turk' in *Eighteenth-Century Egypt: The Arabic Manuscript Sources*, ed. D. Crecelius (Claremont, CA, 1990), pp. 115–26.

Scheuer, M., *Imperial Hubris: Why the West is Losing the War on Terror* (Lincoln, NE, 2007).

Scheuer, M., *Osama bin Laden* (New York, 2011).

Schiller, E., *Wall Paintings at the St Louis Hospital in Jerusalem* (Jerusalem, 2016), in Hebrew.

Schmid, A., *The Final Crusade: A Study of the Crusades in ISIS Propaganda* (Bloomington, IN, 2018).

Sedgewick, M., *Muhammad Abduh* (Oxford, 2010).

Seligman, J., 'A Wall Painting, a Crusader Flood Diversion Facility and other Archaeological Gleanings from the Abbey of the Virgin Mary in the Valley of Jehoshaphat, Jerusalem' in *Christ is Here! Studies in Biblical and Christian Archaeology in Memory of Michele Piccirillo ofm*, ed. L. D. Chrupcala (Jerusalem, 2012), pp. 185–220.

Shafik, V., *Popular Egyptian Cinema: Gender, Class and Nation* (Cairo, 2007).

Shagrir, I. and Amitai-Preiss, N., 'Michaud, Montrond, Mazloum and the First History of the Crusades in Arabic', *al-Masaq* 24 (2012), pp. 309–12.

Shalit, Y., *The European Powers' Plans regarding Jerusalem towards the Middle of the 19th Century* (Berlin, 2004).

Siberry, E., *The New Crusaders: Images of the Crusades in the Nineteenth and Early Twentieth Centuries* (Aldershot, 2000).

Siberry, E., 'The Crusades: Nineteenth-Century Readers' Perspectives' in *Perceptions of the Crusades from the Nineteenth to the Twenty-First Century*, eds. M. Horswell and J. P. Phillips, *Engaging the Crusades* 1 (Abingdon, 2018), pp. 7–26.

Simon, R. S., 'The Teaching of History in Iraq before the Rashid Ali coup of 1941', *Middle Eastern Studies* 22 (1986), pp. 37–51.

Singer, L. (ed.), *The Minbar of Saladin: Reconstructing the Jewel of Islamic Art* (London, 2008).

Sinno, A-R., 'The Emperor's Visit to the East as Reflected in Contemporary Arabic Journalism' in *Baalbek Image and Monument, 1898–1998*, eds. H. Sader, T. Scheffler and A. Neuwirth (Beirut, 1998), pp. 115–33.

Sivan, E., 'Modern Arab Historiography of the Crusades', *Asian and African Studies* 8 (1972), pp. 109–49.

Sivan, E., 'Saladin et le calife al-Nasir', *Scripta Hierosolymitana* 23, *Studies in History* (Jerusalem, 1972), pp. 126–45.

Sivan, E., *Mythes politiques arabes* (Paris, 1995).

Skottki, K., 'The Dead, the Revived and the Re-created Pasts: "Structural Amnesia" in Representations of Crusade History' in *Perceptions of the Crusades from the Nineteenth to the Twenty-First Century*, eds. M. Horswell and J. P. Phillips, *Engaging the Crusades* 1 (Abingdon, 2018), pp. 107–32.

Skovgaard-Petersen, J., 'The Crusades in Arab Film and TV: The Case of Baybars' in *Cultural Encounters during the Crusades*, eds. K. Villads Jensen, K. Salonen and H. Vogt (Odense, 2013) pp. 299–312.

Smail, R. C., 'The Predicaments of Guy of Lusignan, 1183–87' in *Outremer. Studies in the History of the Crusading Kingdom of Jerusalem presented to Joshua Prawer*, eds. B. Z. Kedar, H. E. Mayer and R. C. Smail (Jerusalem, 1982), pp, 159–76.

Smith, G. R., *Ayyubids and Early Rasulids in the Yemen (567–694/1173–1295)*, 2 vols. (London, 1978).

Smoor, P., 'Fatimid Poets and the "Takhallus" that Bridges the Nights of Time to the Imams of Time', *Der Islam* 68 (1991), pp. 232–62.

Smoor, P., 'Umara's Political Views of Shawar, Dirgham and Salah al-Din as Viziers of the Fatimid Caliphs' in *Culture and Memory in Medieval Islam: Essays in Honour of Wilferd Madelung*, eds. F. Daftary and J. W. Meri (London, 2003), pp. 410–32.

Sourdel, D. and Sourdel-Thomine, J., *A Glossary of Islam* (Edinburgh, 2007).

Spagnolo, J., *France and Ottoman Lebanon 1861–1914* (London, 1977).

Spengler, W. F. and Sayles, W. G., *Turkoman Figural Bronze Coins and their Iconography*, 2 vols. (Lodi, WI, 1992–96).

Stanton, C. D., *Norman Naval Operations in the Mediterranean* (Woodbridge, 2011).

Starkey, P., 'Romances of History: Jurji Zaydan and the Rise of the Historical Novel' in *The Long 1890s in Egypt: Colonial Quiescence, Subterranean Resistance*, eds. M. Booth and A. Gorman (Edinburgh, 2014), pp. 343–53.

Staunton, M., *The Historians of Angevin England* (Oxford, 2017).

Strathern, P., *Napoleon in Egypt: 'The Greatest Glory'* (London, 2008).

Strickland, M., *Henry the Young King, 1155–1183* (London, 2016).

Strohmeier, M., 'Al-Kulliyya al-Salahiyya: A Late Ottoman University in Jerusalem' in *Ottoman Jerusalem: The Living City, 1517–1917*, eds. S. Auld and R. Hillenbrand, 2 vols., (London, 2000), 1.157–62.

Strohmeier, M., *Crucial Images in the Presentation of a Kurdish National Identity: Heroes, Patriots, Traitors and Foes* (Leiden, 2003).

Sturtevant, P. B., 'SaladiNasser: Nasser's Political Crusade in *El Naser Salah Ad-Din*' in *Hollywood in the Holy Land: Essays on Film Depictions of the Crusades and Muslim-Christian Clashes*, eds. N. Haydock and E. L. Risden (Jefferson, NC, 2009), pp. 123–46.

Sturtevant, P. B., *The Middle Ages in Popular Imagination: Memory, Film and Medievalism* (London, 2018), pp. 117–43.

Sulaiman, K. A., *Palestine and Modern Arab Poetry* (London, 1984).

Tabbaa, Y., 'Monuments with a Message: Propagation of *jihad* under Nur ad-Din (1146–74)' in *The Meeting of Two Worlds: Cultural Exchange between East and West during the Period of the Crusades*, ed. V. P. Goss (Kalamazoo, MI, 1986), pp. 223–40.

Tabbaa, Y., *The Transformation of Islamic Art during the Sunni Revival* (Washington DC, 2001).

Tabbaa, Y., *The Ayyubid Era: Art and Architecture in Medieval Syria* (Vienna, 2015).

Talmon-Heller, D., *Islamic Piety in Medieval Syria: Mosques, Cemeteries and Sermons under the Zangids and Ayyubids (1146–1250)* (Leiden, 2007).

Talmon-Heller, D., Kedar, B. Z. and Reitel, Y., 'Vicissitudes of a Holy Place: Construction, Destruction and Commemoration of Mashad Husayn in Ascalon', *Der Islam* 93 (2016), pp. 182–215.

Tauber, E., *Arab Movements in World War I* (London, 1993).

Tauber, E., *The Formation of Modern Syria and Iraq* (London, 1995).

Tell Keisan (1971–1976) une cité phénicienne en Galilée, eds. J. Briend and J-B. Humbert (Fribourg, 1980).

Temperley, H., *England and the Near East: The Crimea* (London, 1936).

Thomas, L. V., *A Study of Naima*, ed. N. Itzkowitz (New York, 1972).

Tibawi, A. L., *Anglo-Arab Relations and the Question of Palestine, 1914–1921* (London, 1978).

Tibble, S., *The Crusader Armies, 1099–1187* (London, 2018).

Tolan, J. V., *Saracens: Islam in the Medieval European Imagination* (New York, 2002).

Tolan, J. V., 'Saladin in the Medieval European Imagination', *Sons of Ishmael. Muslims through European Eyes in the Middle Ages* (Gainesville, FL, 2008), pp. 79–100.

Trotter, D. A., *Medieval French Literature and the Crusades (1100–1300)* (Geneva, 1988).

Tyerman, C. J., *England and the Crusades, 1095–1588* (Chicago, 1988).

Tyerman, C. J., *God's War: A New History of the Crusades* (London, 2006).

Tyerman, C. J., *The Debate on the Crusades* (Manchester, 2011).

Van Gelder, G. J., 'Mirror for princes or vizor for viziers: the twelfth century Arabic popular encyclopedia *Mufid al-ulum* and its relationship with the anonymous Persian *Bahr al-fawa'id*', Bulletin of the School of Oriental and African Studies 64 (2001), pp. 313–38.

Vannini, G. and Nucciotti, M. (eds), *Da Petra a Shawbak: Archeologia di una frontiera* (Florence, 2009).

Verbruggen, J. F., *The Art of Warfare in Western Europe during the Middle Ages* (Woodbridge, 1997), pp. 232–9.

Vienne-Guerrin, N., *The Unruly Tongue in Early Modern England: Three Treatises* (New York, 2012).

Von Güttner-Sporzynski, D., *Poland, Holy War and the Piast Monarchy, 1100–1230* (Turnhout, 2014).

Von Güttner-Sporzynski, D., 'Bishop Vincentius of Cracow and his *Chronica Polonorum*' in *Writing History in Medieval Poland: Bishop Vincentius of Cracow and the Chronica Polonorum*, ed. D. von Güttner-Sporzynski (Leiden, 2017), pp. 1–17.

Wagner, T. G. and Mitchell, P. D., 'The Illnesses of King Richard and King Philippe on the Third Crusade: An Understanding of "*arnaldia*" and "*leonardie*"', *Crusades* 10 (2011), pp. 23–44.

Walker, P. E., 'Succession to Rule in the Shiite caliphate', *Journal of the American Research Center in Egypt* 32 (1995), pp. 239–64.

Walker, P. E., 'Al-Maqrizi and the Fatimids', *Mamluk Studies Review* 7 (2003), pp. 83–97.

Webb, W., *An Inaugural Dissertation on Colic* (Philadelphia, PA, 1798).

Weber, S., *Damascus: Ottoman Modernity and Urban Transformation (1808–1918)*, 2 vols. (Aarhus, 2009).

Weedon, L., *Ambiguities of Domination: Politics, Rhetoric and Symbols in Contemporary Syria* (Chicago, 1999).

Weigert, G., 'A Note on *Hudna*: Peacemaking in Islam' in *War and Society in the Eastern Mediterranean, 7th–15th Centuries*, ed. Y. Lev (Leiden, 1997), pp. 399–405.

Where Heaven and Earth Meet: Jerusalem's Holy Esplanade, eds. O. Grabar and B. Z. Kedar (Jerusalem, 2009).

Wien, P., 'The Long and Intricate Funeral of Yasim al-Hashimi: Pan-Arabism, Civil Religion, and Popular Nationalism in Damascus, 1937', *International Journal of Middle East Studies* 43 (2011), pp. 271–92.

Wien, P., *Arab Nationalism: The Politics of History and Culture in the Modern Middle East* (Abingdon, 2017).

Woltering, R., *Occidentalisms in the Arab World: Ideology and Images of the West in the Egyptian Media* (London, 2011).

Woodward, D. P., *Hell in the Holy Land: World War I in the Middle East* (Lexington, KY, 2006).

Yovitchitch, C., 'Die Aiyubidische burg Aglun [Ajlun]' in *Burgen und Städte der Kreuzzugszeit*, ed. M. Piana (Petersberg, 2008), pp. 118–25.

Yovitchitch, C., 'Bosra: Eine Zitadelle des Fürstentums Damaskus' in *Burgen und Städte der Kreuzzugszeit*, ed. M. Piana (Petersberg, 2008), pp. 169–77.

Ze'evi, D., *An Ottoman Century: The District of Jerusalem in the 1600s* (New York, 1996).

Ze'evi, D., 'Back to Napoleon: Thoughts on the beginning of the Modern Era in the Middle East', *Mediterranean Historical Review* 19 (2007), pp. 73–94.

Zilberman, I., 'The Renewal of the Pilgrimage to Nabi Musa' in *Sacred Space in Israel and Palestine: Religion and Politics*, eds. M. Breger, Y. Reiter and L. Hammer (Abingdon, 2012), pp. 103–15.

Unpublished theses

Chamberlain, J. M., 'Imagining Defeat: An Arabic Historiography of the Crusades' (Naval Postgraduate School, Monterey, CA, 2007).

Cooper, R. S., 'Ibn Mammati's Rules for the Ministries: Translation with Commentary of the Qawanin al-Dawawin' (University of California, Berkeley, CA, 1973).

Determann, J. M., 'The Crusades in Arabic Schoolbooks' (University of Vienna, 2007).

Murrell, W. S., 'Dragomans and Crusaders: The Role of Translators and Translation in the Medieval Eastern Mediterranean, 1098–1291' (Vanderbilt University, Nashville, TN, 2018).

Rajohnson, M., 'L'Occident au regret de Jérusalem. L'image de la Ville sainte en chrétienté latine (1187–fin du xiv s.)' (University of Paris, Nanterre, 2017).

Internet resources/references

(EEBO = Early English Books Online; ECCO = Eighteenth Century Collections Online)

http://www.fineart.gov.eg/Eng/musem/Musem.asp?IDs=9

https://www.thefreelibrary.com/%27From+The+Days+of+Saladin%27%3A+thinking+outside+the+box. -a0260918007

http://www.saladindays.com/

https://www.independent.co.uk/voices/commentators/fisk/why-ridley-scotts-story-of-the-crusades-struck-such-a-chord-in-a-lebanese-cinema-492957.html

www.beliefnet.com/entertainment/movies/2005/05/a-modern-saladin-speaks-his-mind.aspx

https://baheyeldin.com/writings/culture/shaaban-abdel-rahim-popular-egyptian-singer-cautious-about-obamas-win.html

https://www.youtube.com/watch?v=CYVoTTiNxpI

https://www.tccb.gov.tr/en/news/542/87719/tum-ulkeleri-kudusu-filistin-devletinin-baskenti-olarak-tanimaya-davet-ediyorum.html

https://www.voanews.com/a/egypt-reforms-school-textbooks-to-counter-extremism/2730247.html

https://georgewbush-whitehouse.archives.gov/news/releases/2001/09/20010916–2.html

https://georgewbush-whitehouse.archives.gov/news/releases/2001/09/20010918–5.html

http://americanradioworks.publicradio.org/features/resentment/angryprint.html

EEBO 1586. https://data-historicaltexts-jisc-ac-uk.ezproxy01.rhul.ac.uk/view?pubId=eebo-99844109e&terms=saladin%20shirt&pageTerms=saladin%20shirt

EEBO 1653. https://data-historicaltexts-jisc-ac-uk.ezproxy01.rhul.ac.uk/view?pubId=eebo-ocm12404310e&terms=saladin%20shirt&pageTerms=saladin%20shirt&pageId=eebo-ocm12404310e-61337–1

ECCO 1781. https://data-historicaltexts-jisc-ac-uk.ezproxy01.rhul.ac.uk/view?pubId=ecco-0386401200&terms=saladin%20shirt&pageTerms=saladin%20shirt&pageId=ecco-0386401200–10

EEBO 1695. https://data-historicaltexts-jisc-ac-uk.ezproxy01.rhul.ac.uk/view?pubId=eebo-ocm12075953e&terms=saladin&date=1695&undated=exclude&pageTerms=saladin&pageId=eebo-ocm12075953e-53606–75

ECCO 1777. https://data-historicaltexts-jisc-ac-uk.ezproxy01.rhul.ac.uk/view?pubId=eccoii-1383800600&terms=saladin&date=1777&undated=exclude&pageTerms=saladin&pageId=eccoii-1383800600–130

https://www.bl.uk/collection-items/the-political-history-of-the-devil-by-daniel-defoe

Abbreviations

AM	Maqrizi, al-, *The History of the Ayyubid Sultans of Egypt*, tr. R. J. C. Broadhurst (Boston, MA, 1980).
Ambroise	Ambroise, *The History of the Holy War: Ambroise's Estoire de la Guerre Sainte*, eds. and trs. M. Ailes and M. C. Barber, 2 vols. (Woodbridge, 2003). All references to volume 2.
AS	Abu Shama, 'Le Livre des deux Jardins', *Recueil des historiens des croisades, Historiens orientaux*, 5 vols. (Paris, 1872–1906), 4.3–522; 5.3– 206. All references to volume 4 unless stated.
BaD	Beha al-Din Ibn Shaddad, *The Rare and Excellent History of Saladin or al-Nawadir al-Sultaniyya wa'l-Mahasin al-Yusufiyya by Baha' al-Din Ibn Shaddad*, tr. D. S. Richards, *Crusade Texts in Translation* 7 (Aldershot, 2001).
CCKJ	Pringle, D., *The Churches of the Crusader Kingdom of Jerusalem: A Corpus*, 4 vols. (Cambridge, 1993–2009).
FO	Foreign Office.
IA	Ibn al-Athir, *The Chronicle of Ibn al-Athir for the Crusading Period from al- Kamil fi'l-ta'rikh. Part 2, The Years 541–589/1146–1193: The Age of Nur al-Din and Saladin*, tr. D. S. Richards, *Crusade Texts in Translation* 15 (Aldershot, 2007).
IaDG	Imad al-Din al-Isfahani, 'Al-Fath al-qussi fi l-fath al-qudsi' ('Ciceronian Eloquence on the Conquest of the Holy City'), partial translation in F. Gabrieli, *Arab Historians of the Crusades* (Berkeley, CA, 1969).
IaDM	Imad al-Din al-Isfahani, *Conquête de la Syrie et de la Palestine par Saladin*, tr. H. Massé (Paris, 1972).
IJ	Ibn Jubayr, *The Travels of Ibn Jubayr*, tr. R. J. C. Broadhurst (London, 1952).
IK	Ibn Khallikan, *Ibn Khallikan's Biographical Dictionary*, tr. W. M. de Slane, 4 vols. (Paris, 1843–71).
IQ	Ibn al-Qalanisi, *The Damascus Chronicles of the Crusades*, tr. H. A. R. Gibb (London, 1932).
Itinerarium	*Chronicle of the Third Crusade: A Translation of the Itinerarium peregrinorum et Gesta Regis Ricardi*, tr. H. J. Nicholson, *Crusade Texts in Translation* 3 (Aldershot, 1997).
OFCWT	Old French Continuation of William of Tyre in *Conquest of Jerusalem and the Third Crusade*, tr. P. W. Edbury, *Crusade Texts in Translation* 1 (Aldershot, 1996), pp. 11–145.
TNA	The National Archives
WT	William of Tyre, *A History of Deeds done Beyond the Sea*, trs. E. A. Babcock and A. C. Krey, 2 vols. (New York, 1943). Latin edition: *Chronicon*, ed. R. B. C. Huygens, 2 vols., *Corpus Christianorum continuatio mediaevalis* 63 (Turnhout, 1986) used as specified.

Notes

Dramatis Personae and a Note on Names

1 As N. Christie outlines neatly in his *Muslims and Crusaders: Christianity's Wars in the Middle East, 1095–1382, From the Islamic Sources* (Abingdon, 2014), pp. xxxix–xl.

Introduction

1 The outbreak of civil war in Syria saw the Enana Dance Group, the company that staged the event in Damascus, relocate to Qatar and continue their performances of the play there, and in Algeria and Dubai.

2 https://www.thefreelibrary.com/%27From+The+Days+of+Saladin%27%3A+thinking+outside+the+box.-a0260918007. Another play to note was produced in 2004 by the ruler of the emirate of Sharjah, Sheikh Sultan bin Muhammad al-Qassimi; see U. Bhatia, *Forgetting Osama bin Munqidh, Remembering Osama bin Laden: The Crusades in Modern Muslim Memory* (Nanyang, 2008), pp. 8–9.

3 http://www.saladindays.com/.

4 D. Eldridge, *Holy Warriors: A Fantasia on the Third Crusade and the History of Violent Struggle in the Holy Lands* (London, 2014), p. 93.

5 https://www.independent.co.uk/voices/commentators/fisk/why-ridley-scotts-story-of-the-crusades-struck-such-a-chord-in-a-lebanese-cinema-492957.html.

6 P. B. Sturtevant, *The Middle Ages in Popular Imagination. Memory, Film and Medievalism* (London, 2018), pp. 117–43; www.beliefnet.com/entertainment/movies/2005/05/a-modern-saladin-speaks-his-mind.aspx.

7 J. Skovgaard-Petersen, 'The Crusades in Arab Film and TV: The Case of Baybars' in K. Villads Jensen, K. Salonen and H. Vogt (eds.), *Cultural Encounters During the Crusades* (Odense, 2013), pp. 299–312.

8 https://baheyeldin.com/writings/culture/shaaban-abdel-rahim-popular-egyptian-singer-cautious-about-obamas-win.html.

9 https://www.youtube.com/watch?v=CYVoTTiNxpI.

10 K. Debeuf, *Inside the Arab Revolution: Three Years on the Frontline of the Arab Spring* (Tielt, 2014), pp. 193, 196.

11 Saladin's name (Selahattin in Turkish) appeared alongside Erdoğan's on posters during the 2017 referendum; around the same time he denounced a meeting between Pope Francis I and EU leaders as 'an alliance of crusaders.' https://www.tccb.gov.tr/en/news/542/87719/tum-ulkeleri-kudusu-filistin-devletinin-baskenti-olarak-tanimaya-davet-ediyorum.html. More recently, the US recognition of Jerusalem as Israel's capital led to a meeting between the two men, both deeply unhappy at this development.

12 B. Eliassi, *Contesting Kurdish Identities in Sweden: Quest for Belonging amongst Middle Eastern Youth* (New York, 2013), pp. 84–6.

13   A. Schmid, *The Final Crusade: A Study of the Crusades in ISIS Propaganda* (Bloomington, IN, 2018).

14   https://www.voanews.com/a/egypt-reforms-school-textbooks-to-counter-extremism/2730247.html; J. M. Determann's tremendous study 'The Crusades in Arabic Schoolbooks' from the University of Vienna in 2007 is also published in an abbreviated form as 'The Crusades in Arab School Textbooks', *Islam and Christian–Muslim Relations* 19, no. 2 (2008), pp. 199–214.

15   Computer gaming is yet a further forum in which the crusades and Saladin loom large, notably the *Assassin's Creed* series taking place at the time of the Third Crusade. There is an emerging literature on this subject – see a forthcoming volume in the 'Engaging the Crusades' series. Major exhibitions on Saladin in Paris (2001–2) and across Germany in 2005 should also be noted as part of the wider interest in him.

1 The Muslim Near East and the First Crusade

1   T. el-Azhari, *Zengi and the Muslim Response to the Crusades: The Politics of Jihad* (Abingdon, 2016), pp. 10–39; C. Hillenbrand, '"Abominable Acts": The Career of Zengi' in J. P. Phillips and M. Hoch (eds.), *The Second Crusade: Scope and Consequences* (Manchester, 2001), pp. 111–32; IA, 1.291–3.

2   C. Hillenbrand, *Islam: A New Historical Introduction* (London, 2015), pp. 144–67, 180–3.

3   Ibid., pp. 150–3.

4   A. C. S. Peacock, *The Great Seljuk Empire* (Edinburgh, 2015), pp. 1–9, 61–88; R. Ellenblum, *The Collapse of the Eastern Mediterranean: Climate Change and the Decline of the East, 950–1072* (Cambridge, 2012), pp. 61–108; P. M. Cobb, *The Race for Paradise: An Islamic History of the Crusades* (New York, 2014), pp. 78–88; C. Hillenbrand, 'The First Crusade: The Muslim Perspective' in *The First Crusade: Origins and Impact* (Manchester, 1997), pp. 131–5; T. el-Azhari, *The Saljuqs of Syria during the Crusades, 463–549 AH / 1070–1154 AD* (Berlin, 1997). On the revival of Harran and al-Raqqa in this period see S. Heidemann, *Die Renaissance der Städte in Nordsyrien und Nordmesopotamien: städtische Entwicklung und wirtschaftliche Bedingungen in ar-Raqqa und Harran van der Zeit der beduinischen Vorherrschaft bis zu den Seldschuken* (Leiden, 2002).

5   V. Minorsky, *Studies in Caucasian History* (London, 1953), pp. 107–39; R. S. Humphreys, *From Saladin to the Mongols* (Albany, NY, 1977), pp. 28–31. On Turkish–Kurdish tensions, see below, p. 286.

6   IK, 1.244–5.

7   H. Möhring, 'Zwischen Joseph-Legende und Mahdi-Erwartung: Erfolge und Ziele Sultan Saladins im Spiegel zeitgenössicher Dichtung und Weissagung' in Y. Lev (ed.), *War and Society in the Eastern Mediterranean, 7th–15th Centuries* (Leiden, 1997), pp. 177–223; A-M. Eddé, *Saladin*, tr. J. M. Todd (Cambridge, MA, 2011), pp. 158–60.

8   N. Christie, *Muslims and Crusaders: Christianity's Wars in the Middle East, 1095–1382, From the Islamic Sources* (Abingdon, 2014), p. xxxii.

9   Hillenbrand, *Islam*, pp. 219–43; al-Sulami, *The Book of the Jihad of Ali ibn Tahir al-Sulami (d.1106): Text, Translation and Commentary*, N. Christie (Farnham, 2015), pp. 2–3.

10   O. Latiff, *The Cutting Edge of the Poet's Sword: Muslim Poetic Responses to the Crusades* (Leiden, 2018), pp. 27–30.

11   Al-Sulami, *The Book of the Jihad*, pp. 1–34.

12   Anonymous poet, quoted in Hillenbrand, 'The First Crusade', pp. 137–8.

13   Mu'izzi, in Peacock, *Great Seljuk Empire*, p. 84.

14   C. Hillenbrand, *The Crusades: Islamic Perspectives* (Edinburgh, 1999), pp. 100–12; N. E. Morton, *The Field of Blood: The Battle for Aleppo and the Remaking of the Medieval Middle East* (New York, 2018); Cobb, *Race for Paradise*, pp. 122–3; Christie, *Muslims and Crusaders*, pp. 24–7.

15   Hillenbrand, 'The Career of Zengi', p. 124.
16   Ibn al-Athir, al-Bahir, tr. El-Azhari, Zengi, p. 162.
17   Ibid., p. 168.
18   C. MacEvitt, The Crusades and the Christian Worlds of the East: Rough Tolerance (Philadelphia, PA, 2008), pp. 50–78.
19   Ibn al-Athir, al-Bahir, tr. El-Azhari, Zengi, pp. 168–9.
20   Gregory the Priest, Armenia and the Crusades, 10th to 12th Centuries, ed. and tr. A. E. Dostaurian (Lanham, MI, 1993), pp. 243–4; WT, 2.140–4; J. P. Phillips, The Second Crusade: Extending the Frontiers of Christendom (London, 2007), pp. xvi–xvii.
21   Ibn al-Athir, al-Bahir, tr. El-Azhari, Zengi, p. 170.
22   Ibn al-Furat, in Hillenbrand, 'Career of Zengi', p. 119.
23   Ibn al-Athir, al-Bahir, tr. El-Azhari, Zengi, p. 1.
24   IQ, pp. 269–70.
25   Ibid., p. 271; Ibn al'Adim, tr. El-Azhari, Zengi, p. 155; IA, 1.382.
26   Ibn al-Athir, al-Bahir, tr. El-Azhari, Zengi, p. 167.
27   Phillips, Second Crusade, pp. 168–208.
28   IA, 2.16.
29   Phillips, Second Crusade, pp. 37–79, 207–27; IA, 2.21–2.
30   WT, 2.196–7.
31   IK, 1.615.
32   The major work on Nur al-Din is N. Elisséeff, Nur ad-Din un grand prince musulman de Syrie au temps des croisades (511–569 H. /1118–74), 3 vols. (Damascus, 1967).

2 Nur al-Din and the City of Damascus

1   IA, 2.222–3; WT, 2.394.
2   Lev offers an important analysis of Nur ad-Din laying emphasis on his dynastic ambitions: Y. Lev, 'The "jihad" of Sultan Nur al-Din of Syria (1146–1174): History and Discourse', Jerusalem Studies in Arabic and Islam 35 (2008), pp. 228–84; Elisséeff, Nur ad-Din, 2.436–42; Qutb al-Din acquired Mosul, Sinjar and part of the Jazira. After November 1149, Nur al-Din was able to take over Homs and the family treasury.
3   IQ, 292; WT, 2.197–9; Y. Tabbaa, 'Monuments with a Message: Propagation of Jihad under Nur ad-Din (1146–1174)' in V. P. Goss (ed.), The Meeting of Two Worlds: Cultural Exchange between East and West during the Period of the Crusades (Kalamazoo, MI, 1986), pp. 224–9; N. Elisséeff, 'The Reaction of the Syrian Muslims after the Foundation of the First Latin Kingdom of Jerusalem' in M. Shatzmiller (ed.), Crusaders and Muslims in Twelfth-Century Syria (Leiden, 1993), p. 169.
4   IQ, p. 298.
5   Ibid., pp. 309–10; Christie, Muslims and Crusaders, pp. 31–2.
6   D. Talmon-Heller, B. Z. Kedar, Y. Reitel, 'Vicissitudes of a Holy Place: Construction, Destruction and Commemoration of Mashad Husayn in Ascalon', Der Islam 93 (2016), pp. 182–215.
7   M. Brett, The Fatimid Empire (Edinburgh, 2017), pp. 281–3.
8   IQ, pp. 314–17; M. C. Barber, The Crusader States (London, 2012), pp. 200–6.
9   Gibb's English translation of Ibn al-Qalanisi [IQ] omits some of the material on the internal politics of Damascus. For these events see the French translation: Damas de 1075 à 1154, tr. R. Le Tourneau (Damascus, 1952), pp. 332–3. N. Christie, 'Ibn al-Qalanisi', Medieval Muslim Historians and the Franks in the Levant (Leiden, 2014), pp. 7–28.
10   IQ, pp. 318–20.
11   Ibid., p. 321.
12   Peacock, Great Seljuk Empire, p. 7; J-M. Mouton, Damas et sa principauté sous les Saljoukides et les Bourides, 468–549/1076–1154 (Cairo, 1994), pp. 21–93.

13   On Saladin's attachment to Damascus, see M. C. Lyons and D. E. P. Jackson, *Saladin: The Politics of the Holy War* (Cambridge, 1982) p. 3.

14   IJ, pp. 271–2. Note, however, the scepticism about some of these claims expressed in the late twelfth century account of al-Harawi, *A Lonely Wayfarer's Guide to Pilgrimage*, tr. J. W. Meri (Princeton, NJ, 2004), pp. 26–30. The most detailed contemporary information about Damascus is in Ibn Asakir's monumental seventy-volume history, although one section explicitly describes the physical city; see *La description de Damas d'Ibn Asakir*, tr. N. Elisséeff, second edition (Damascus, 2008); Z. Antrim, 'Ibn Asakir's Representations of Syria and Damascus in the Introduction to the *Ta'rikh Madinat Dimashq*', *International Journal of Middle Eastern Studies* 38 (2006), pp. 109–29.

15   IJ, pp. 271, 287, 295; J. W. Meri, *The Cult of Saints amongst Muslims and Jews in Medieval Syria* (Oxford, 2002), pp. 29–56, 195–8.

16   Humphreys, *From Saladin to the Mongols*, p. 12.

17   IJ, p. 272; Ibn Asakir, *Description*, pp. 9–73; G. Degeorge, *Damascus* (Paris, 2004), pp. 33–42.

18   Meri, *Cult of Saints*, pp. 38, 44, 200–1; IJ, p. 279.

19   IJ, pp. 305–8; L. Richter-Bernberg, 'Between Marvel and Trial: al-Harawi and Ibn Jubayr on Architecture' in U. Vermeulen and K. D'Hulster (eds.), *Egypt and Syria in the Fatimid, Ayyubid and Mamluk Eras VI* (Leuven, 2010), pp. 115–46.

20   The life associated with mosques, their place in society, the societies within and around mosques, the preachers and the processes of communication are wonderfully brought out in D. Talmon-Heller, *Islamic Piety in Medieval Syria: Mosques, Cemeteries and Sermons under the Zangids and Ayyubids (1146–1250)* (Leiden, 2007).

21   J. Berkey, *Popular Preaching and Authority in the Medieval Islamic Near East* (Seattle, WA, 2001), pp. 53–6. See IQ, p. 321 for an example of public communication from the pulpit.

22   Ibn Asakir, *Description*, pp. 84–139; Talmon-Heller, *Islamic Piety*, p. 43.

23   IJ, p. 297; Elisséeff, *Nur ad-Din*, 3.919–30; Degeorge, *Damascus*, pp. 62–7.

24   Elisséeff, *Nur ad-Din*, 3.714–15.

25   Ibn Asakir, *Description*, pp. 247–95; Degeorge, *Damascus*, pp. 68–9.

26   Elisséeff, *Nur ad-Din*, 3.847–51; M. Ecochard, 'Trois Bains Ayyoubides de Damas' in *Les Monuments Ayyoubides de Damas, Volume II* (Paris, 1940), pp. 51–112; figs. 29–61; plates 13–20.

27   IJ, p. 302.

28   W. F. Spengler and W. G. Sayles, *Turkmen Figural Bronze Coins and their Iconography*, 2 vols. (Lodi, WI, 1992–6).

29   IJ, p. 302; N. Elisséeff, 'Corporations de Damas sous Nur al-Din: Matériaux pour une topographie économique de Damas au xiie siècle', *Arabica* 3 (1956), pp. 61–79.

30   Ibid., pp. 283–4.

31   IA, 2.263; M. Chamberlain, *Knowledge and Social Practice in Medieval Damascus, 1190–1350* (Cambridge, 1994), pp. 135–7; K. Hirschler, *The Written Word in the Medieval Arabic Lands: A Social and Cultural History of Reading Practices* (Edinburgh, 2012); idem, *Medieval Damascus: Plurality and Diversity in an Arabic Library. The Ashrafiya Library Catalogue* (Edinburgh, 2016).

32   Y. Tabbaa, *The Transformation of Islamic Art during the Sunni Revival* (Washington DC, 2001), p. 88.

33   A. Ragab, *The Medieval Islamic Hospital: Medicine, Religion and Charity* (Cambridge, 2015), pp. 51–9.

34   Imad al-Din, quoted in D. S. Richards, 'The Early History of Saladin', *Islamic Quarterly* 17 (1973), p. 146.

35   IJ, pp. 301–2.

36   IQ, p. 326.

37   Ibid., p. 329.

38 Ibid., pp. 330–2.
39 AS, 4.86; IQ, p. 337.
40 IQ, p. 333.
41 Elisséeff, *Nur ad-Din*, 2.517–25; IQ, pp. 341–4.
42 A. D. Buck, *The Principality of Antioch and its Frontiers in the Twelfth Century* (Woodbridge, 2017), pp. 198–208.
43 IQ, pp. 354–6. The author backs down from his by-now strident holy-war rhetoric to praise Nur al-Din for his sure judgement in making an agreement with the Greeks.
44 IQ, pp. 355–6.
45 Brett, *Fatimid Empire*, pp. 280–87; Peacock, *Great Seljuk Empire*, pp. 111–13.
46 WT, 2.335.
47 Brett, *Fatimid Empire*, pp. 287–91; Barber, *Crusader States*, pp. 231–8.
48 IA, 2.118.

3 Nur al-Din and the Rise of the Jihad

1 Latiff, *Cutting Edge*, p. 159.
2 Ibn ad-Adim, in Elisséeff, *Nur ad-Din*, 2.577.
3 IA, 2.144, 176.
4 P. W. Edbury and J. G. Rowe, *William of Tyre: Historian of the Latin East* (Cambridge, 1988), pp. 13–31.
5 WT, 2.303.
6 *Letters from the East: Crusaders, Pilgrims and Settlers in the 12th–13th Centuries*, tr. M. C. Barber and K. Bate, Crusade Texts in Translation 18 (Farnham, 2010), p. 60.
7 IA, 2.146.
8 WT, 2.305; *Letters from the East*, p. 59.
9 BaD, p. 41.
10 IA, 2.147.
11 K. J. Lewis, *The Counts of Tripoli and Lebanon in the Twelfth Century: Sons of Saint-Gilles* (Abingdon, 2017), pp. 203–4.
12 *Letters from the East*, p. 61. On the fall of Banyas, see WT, 2.308–10.
13 The *mi'raj* – Muhammad's Night Journey from Mecca to Jerusalem, and then his ascent 'from there into heaven where he met the prophets of old and gazed upon God', Hillenbrand, *Islam*, p. 299.
14 H. Dajani-Shakeel, 'Al-Quds: Jerusalem in the Consciousness of the Counter Crusader' in V. P. Goss (ed.), *The Meeting of Two Worlds: Cultural Exchange between East and West during the Period of the Crusades* (Kalamazoo, MI, 1986), pp. 201–21; Latiff, *Cutting Edge*, pp. 4–8.
15 Y. Tabbaa, *The Transformation of Islamic Art during the Sunni Revival* (Washington DC, 2001), pp. 53–64.
16 Y. Tabbaa, *The Ayyubid Era: Art and Architecture in Medieval Syria* (Vienna, 2015), pp. 164–9.
17 Tabbaa, *Transformation of Islamic Art*, pp. 93–6.
18 Tabbaa, 'Monuments with a Message', pp. 232–5.
19 IJ, pp. 262–3.
20 Tabbaa, *Transformation of Islamic Art*, pp. 87–93.
21 Ibid., p.25. For Nur al-Din as a calligrapher, see AS, 4.17.
22 B. Boehm and N. Holcomb, *Jerusalem 1000–1400: Every People under Heaven* (New York, 2016), pp. 173–4.
23 Ibn Asakir's text is elegantly discussed, edited and translated in S. A. Mourad and J. E. Lindsay, *The Intensification and Reorientation of Sunni Jihad Ideology in the Crusader Period: Ibn Asakir of Damascus (1105–1176) and His Age, with an Edition and Translation of Ibn Asakir's The Forty Hadiths for Inciting Jihad* (Leiden, 2013).
24 Ibid., p. 65.

25 Ibid., pp. 65–81.
26 Elisséeff, *Nur ad-Din*, 3.763. On the 'Merits of Jerusalem' texts, see particularly Latiff, *Cutting Edge*, pp. 30–9.
27 Latiff, *Cutting Edge*, pp. 158–9.
28 *The Sea of Precious Virtues*, tr. J. S. Meisami (Salt Lake City, UT, 1991), pp. 296–7; on this text it is important to see also G. J. van Gelder, 'Mirror for Princes or Vizor for Viziers: the Twelfth-Century Arabic Popular Encyclopaedia *Mufīd al-ulum* and its Relationship with the Anonymous Persian *Bahr al-fawa'id'*, *Bulletin of the School of Oriental and African Studies* 64 (2001), pp. 313–38.
29 Elisséeff, *Nur ad-Din*, 3.844; Latiff, *Cutting Edge*, p. 22.
30 D. S. Richards, 'Imad al-Din al-Isfahani: Administrator, Littérateur and Historian' in M. Shatzmiller (ed.), *Crusaders and Muslims in Twelfth Century Syria* (Leiden, 1993), pp. 133–46; L. Richter-Bernburg, 'Imad al-Din al-Isfahani' in A. Mallett (ed.), *Medieval Muslim Historians and the Franks in the Levant* (Leiden, 2014), pp. 29–51; N. O. Rabbat, 'My Life with Salah al-Din: The Memoirs of Imad al-Din al-Katib al-Isfahani', *Edebiyat* 7 (1997), pp. 267–87; Y. Lev, *Saladin in Egypt* (Leiden, 1999), pp. 30–3.
31 Richards, 'Imad al-Din al-Isfahani', p. 136; Latiff, *Cutting Edge*, pp. 152–3.
32 Ibn Abi Tayy, in Richards, 'Early History of Saladin', p. 145; S. England, *Medieval Empires and the Culture of Competition. Literary Duels at Islamic and Christian Courts* (Edinburgh, 2017), p. 75.
33 *Itinerarium*, pp. 27–8.

4 Shirkuh, Saladin and the Conquest of Egypt

1 WT, 2.313–14; BaD, p. 42; IK, 4.487. See also IA, 2.163. Edbury and Rowe, *William of Tyre*, pp. 26, 167–9.
2 IA, 2.163.
3 Ibn al-Athir, 'Atabegs', *Recueil des historiens des croisades. Historiens orientaux*, 5 vols. (Paris, 1872–1906), 2.ii.305. Perhaps wishing to smooth over subsequent tensions, a later writer commented that Saladin told him Nur al-Din always consulted Shirkuh about his policy-making: Abu Shama cited in Lev, *Saladin in Egypt*, p. 135.
4 N. D. MacKenzie, *Ayyubid Cairo: A Topographical Study* (Cairo, 1992), pp. 2–9; Brett, *Fatimid Empire*, pp. 99–102.
5 WT, 2.318. The Latin is 'vetera innovare pacta pacisque perpetue federa inviolabili stabilitate inter dominum regem et calipham firmare', William of Tyre, *Chronicon*, ed. R. B. C. Huygens, 2 vols., *Corpus Christianorum continuatio mediaevalis* 63, (Turnhout, 1986), 2.886. G. Weigert 'A Note on *Hudna*: Peacemaking in Islam' in Lev (ed.), *War and Society in the Eastern Mediterranean*, pp. 399–405; M. Köhler, *Alliances and Treaties between Frankish and Muslim Rulers in the Middle East* trs. P. M. Holt and K. Hirschler (Leiden, 2013), pp. 297–300.
6 W. S. Murrell, 'Dragomans and Crusaders: The Role of Translators and Translation in the Medieval Eastern Mediterranean, 1098–1291', unpublished doctoral thesis (Vanderbilt University, TN, 2018).
7 WT, 2.315–25.
8 Although the sultan had taken part in the previous expedition to Egypt.
9 WT, 2.331–4; BaD, p. 41.
10 From the chronicle, 'Al-Bustan al-Jami', quoted in Richards, 'Early History of Saladin', p. 152.
11 WT, 2.339.
12 Ibid., 2.338–43; IA, 2.164–65; E. Harvey, 'Saladin Consoles Baldwin IV over the Death of his Father', *Crusades* 15 (2016), pp. 27–34.
13 IA, 2.165; BaD, pp. 41–2.

14   IA, 2.172; BaD, p. 42.

15   WT, 2.347–51; IA, 2.171–2; Barber, *Crusader States*, pp. 248–51.

16   WT, 2.351–2; *History of the Patriarchs of the Egyptian Church, Volume 3*, trs. A. Khater and O. H. E. Burmester (Cairo, 1968), pp. 104–5.

17   IA, 2.172.

18   W. Kubiak, 'The Burning of Misr al-Fustat in 1168. A Reconsideration of Historical Evidence', *Africana Bulletin* 25 (1976), pp. 51–64; A. Ehrenkreutz, 'The Place of Saladin in the Naval History of the Mediterranean Sea in the Middle Ages', *Journal of the American Oriental Society* 75 (1955), pp. 102–3.

19   H. A. R. Gibb, 'The Armies of Saladin' in *Saladin: Studies in Islamic History* (Beirut, 1972), pp. 138–9.

20   BaD, p. 43; IA, 2.174; IK, 4.489.

21   WT, 2.356.

22   Lev, *Saladin in Egypt*, pp. 60–5; 'Un document contemporain de Nur ad-Din. Sa notice biographique par Ibn Asakir', tr. N. Elisséeff, *Bulletin d'études orientales* 25 (1972), p. 131; IK, 4.489–91; Bar Hebraeus, *The Chronography of Bar Hebraeus, Volume* I, tr. E. A. Wallis Budge (Oxford, 1932), pp. 294–5.

23   IA, 2.175.

24   Imad al-Din, in Ibn Wasil, *Mufarrij, Volume 1*, pp. 165–7, tr. Latiff, *Cutting Edge*, p. 203.

25   WT, 2.357–8.

26   Ibn Abi Tayy cited in Lev, *Saladin in Egypt*, p. 94, n. 134.

27   BaD, p. 45; IK, 4.492.

28   AS, 4.143.

29   Elisséeff, *Nur ad-Din*, 3.926–7.

30   IK, 1.626.

5 Saladin's Succession in Egypt

1   Ibn Abi Tayy, in Richards, 'Early History of Saladin', p. 156; see also Lev, *Saladin in Egypt*, pp. 49, 79–81.

2   Al-Wahrani, in G. J. Van Gelder, 'A Conversation on Contemporary Politics in the Twelfth Century: "al-Maqama al-Baghdadiyya" by al-Wahrani (D. 575/1179)' in C. F. Robinson (ed.), *Texts, Documents and Artefacts: Islamic Studies in Honour of D. S. Richards* (Leiden, 2003), pp. 103–19, quote at p. 112.

3   BaD, p. 44.

4   IA, 2.177; IK, 4.494–5; Lev, *Saladin in Egypt*, p. 49.

5   IK, 2.430, 520–1; D. Ayalon, *Eunuchs, Caliphs and Sultans: A Study in Power Relationships* (Jerusalem, 1999), pp. 178–9.

6   IK, 4.494–6; IA, 2.176–8; Minorsky, 'Prehistory of Saladin', 137–46.

7   IK, 4.479.

8   M. Strickland, *Henry the Young King, 1155–1183* (London, 2016), pp. 119–205, 282–305; Peacock, *Great Seljuk Empire*, pp. 107–23.

9   IA, 2.177.

10   IK, 4.495; *History of the Patriarchs of the Egyptian Church*, p. 106 from where the details of the garment and neck-band are derived using the description of Shirkuh's investiture a couple of months earlier; Christie, *Muslims and Crusaders*, p. xl.

11   Eddé, *Saladin*, pp. 36–7 and Lev, *Saladin in Egypt*, pp. 66–81 disagree sharply here – the latter suggests that Saladin was given the right to pass the title on to his descendants.

12   Al-Wahrani, in Gelder, 'Conversation on Contemporary Politics', p. 112.

13   England, *Medieval Empires*, pp. 82–5, 94–5.

14   BaD, p. 45.

15   IA, 2.178.

16   For example, *The Sea of Precious Virtues*, pp. 295–6.

17   IK, 4.496.
18   WT, 2.359.
19   IK, 4.497.
20   IA, 2.179–80; Ayalon, *Eunuchs*, p. 178.
21   C. Cahen, 'L'administration financière de l'armée fatimide d'après al-Makhzumi', *Makhzumiyyat: Études sur l'histoire économique et financière de l'Égypte médiévale* (Leiden, 1977), pp. 155–63; Tibble, *Crusader Armies*, pp. 212–22.
22   IA, 2.179–80; Brett, *Fatimid Empire*, pp. 292–3.
23   Al-Wahrani, in Van Gelder, 'A Conversation', pp. 112–13.
24   H. Rabie, *The Financial System of Egypt, A. H. 564–741/A. D. 1169–1341* (Cambridge, 1972), pp. 29–30; Humphreys, *From Saladin to the Mongols*, pp. 15–18; Christie, *Muslims and Crusaders*, p. xxxii; Lev, *Saladin in Egypt*, pp. 158–60.
25   Y. Lev, 'The Dismemberment of the Fatimid State and the Emergence of a New Ayyubid Elite in Egypt' in U. Vermeulen and K. D'Hulster (eds.), *Egypt and Syria in the Fatimid, Ayyubid and Mamluk Eras V* (Leuven, 2007), pp. 147–51.
26   P. Smoor, 'Fatimid Poets and the "Takhallus" that Bridges the Nights of Time to the Imams of Time', *Der Islam* 68 (1991), p. 259.
27   Lev, *Saladin in Egypt*, pp. 14–25.
28   IK, 2.111–12. See also: D. E. P. Jackson, 'Some Preliminary Reflections on the Chancery Correspondence of the Qadi al-Fadil' in U. Vermeulen and D. de Smet (eds.), *Egypt and Syria in the Fatimid, Ayyubid and Mamluk Eras I* (Leuven, 1995), pp. 207–17.
29   C. Cahen, 'Un traité financier inédit d'époque fatimide-ayyubide' in *Makhzumiyyat: Études sur l'histoire économique et financière de l'Égypte médiévale* (Leiden, 1977), pp. 1–21; Rabie, *Financial System of Egypt*, pp. 11–12.
30   Humphreys, *From Saladin to the Mongols*, p. 74.
31   Rabie, *Financial System of Egypt*, pp. 73–9.
32   C. Cahen, 'Douanes et commerce dans les ports Méditerranéens de l'Égypte médiévale d'après le *minhadj* d'al-Makhzumi' in *Makhzumiyyat*, pp. 57–152.
33   Rabie, *Financial System of Egypt*, pp. 133–5.
34   Phillips, *Defenders of the Holy Land*, pp. 168–208.
35   WT, 2.360–70.
36   IA, 2.183–4.
37   Ibid., 2.183. For the campaign, see also WT, 2.361–70.
38   BaD, p. 47; J-M. Mouton, D. Sourdel and J. Sourdel-Thomine (eds. and trs.), *Gouvernance et libéralités de Saladin d'après les données inédites de six documents arabes* (Paris, 2015), pp. 30–1.
39   Al-Wahrani, 'A Conversation', p.114, n. 56.
40   IA, 2.194.
41   Y. Frenkel, 'Political and Social Aspects of Islamic Religious Endowments (*awqaf*): Saladin in Cairo (1169–73) and Jerusalem (1187–93)', *Bulletin of the School of Oriental and African Studies* 62 (1999), pp. 2–5; G. Leiser, 'The Madrasa and the Islamization of the Middle East: The Case of Egypt', *Journal of the American Research Center in Egypt* 22 (1985), pp. 41–2; Brett, *Fatimid Empire*, p. 293.
42   Mouton, Sourdel and Sourdel-Thomine (eds. and trs.), *Gouvernance et libéralités*, pp. 17–35, 101–3.
43   MacKenzie, *Ayyubid Cairo*, pp. 51–3.
44   J-M. Mouton, *Sadr: Une forteresse de Saladin au Sinaï. Histoire et archéologie*, 2 vols. (Paris, 2010).
45   IA, 2.194; WT, 2.371–7.
46   D. Pringle, 'The Castles of Ayla (al-Aqaba) in the Crusader, Ayyubid and Mamluk Periods' in U. Vermeulen and J. Van Steenbergen (eds.), *Egypt and Syria in the Fatimid, Ayyubid and Mamluk Eras IV* (Leuven, 2005), pp. 333–53; J-M. Mouton and S. Abd al-Malik, 'La forteresse de l'Ile de Graye (Qal'at Ayla) à l'époque de Saladin: Étude épigraphique et historique', *Annales Islamologiques* 29 (1995), pp. 75–90.
47   Lyons and Jackson, *Saladin*, p. 45.

48   M. El-Moctar, 'Saladin in Sunni and Shi'a Memories' in N. Paul and S. Yeager (eds.), *Remembering the Crusades: Myth, Image and Reality* (Baltimore, 2012), pp. 198–201. On the other hand, an example of a positive Nizari Isma'ili engagement with the memory of Saladin was the Aga Khan's support of the restoration of Qa'alat Saladin, known to the Franks as Saone, in north-western Syria.

49   Lyons and Jackson, *Saladin*, p. 46; Gibb, 'Armies of Saladin', pp. 143–4.

50   Brett, *Fatimid Empire*, p. 293.

51   This is elegantly brought out by P. Sanders, 'From Court Ceremony to Urban Language: Ceremonial in Fatimid Cairo and Fustat' in C. E. Bosworth et al. (eds.), *The Islamic World from Classical to Modern Times: Essays in Honour of Bernard Lewis* (Princeton, NJ, 1989), pp. 311–21, quote at p. 318.

52   Ibid., p. 319.

53   IK, 4.497–9. A later Christian writer offers three different accounts of al-Adid's death, all of which place the Ayyubids, and particularly Turanshah, Saladin's brother, as active participants in the caliph's demise. William of Tyre suggested that Saladin himself was responsible. WT, 2.359.

54   P. E. Walker, 'Succession to Rule in the Shi'ite caliphate', *Journal of the American Research Center in Egypt* 32 (1995), p. 264.

55   AM, p. 37; IA, 2.198.

56   Imad al-Din, tr. O. Latiff, *Cutting Edge*, pp. 207–8.

6 Steps Towards Independence: The Break with Nur al-Din

1   AM, p. 151; *History of the Patriarchs of the Eastern Church*, p. 113; Walker, 'Succession to Rule in the Shi'ite caliphate', pp. 249, 264, n. 136.

2   IA, 2.197.

3   Reynolds, *Interpreting the Self*, pp. 145, 151; MacKenzie, *Ayyubid Cairo*, pp. 67–8, 117; F. Bora, 'Did Salah al-Din Destroy the Fatimids' Books? An Historiographical Enquiry', *Journal of the Royal Asiatic Society* 25 (2015), pp. 21–39.

4   Sanders, *Ritual, Politics and the City*, p. 193, n. 96.

5   Frenkel, 'Islamic Religious Endowments in Cairo and Jerusalem', pp. 1–16; Lev, *Saladin in Egypt*, pp. 108–13.

6   AS, 4.196 indicates the detour required.

7   IA, 2.198–9; AM, pp. 41–2.

8   IA, 2.199.

9   Ibid.; AM, pp. 42–3.

10   IA, 2.200.

11   Ibid.

12   AM, p. 43.

13   Ibid., p. 39; Sanders, *Ritual, Politics and the City*, pp. 42, 213.

14   Rabie, *Financial System of Egypt*, pp. 11–12, 95–100; Quran, 9:60.

15   Lev, *Saladin in Egypt*, pp. 132–5; Frenkel, 'Islamic Religious Endowments in Cairo and Jerusalem', pp. 2–3; *The Book of Government or Rules for Kings*, pp. 9–10.

16   AM, pp. 38–9; A. Ehrenkreutz, 'The Crisis of the Dinar in the Egypt of Saladin', *Journal of the American Oriental Society* 76 (1956), pp. 178–84.

17   A. S. Baadj, *Saladin, the Almohads and the Banū Ghāniya: The Contest for North Africa (12th and 13th Centuries)* (Leiden, 2015), pp. 110–27.

18   AM, pp. 40–1; Lev, *Saladin in Egypt*, pp. 186–9. Note that Christian–Muslim tensions were an ongoing feature of the Egyptian administrative scene and are illustrated from the time of Shawar and Saladin down to the mid-thirteenth century in Uthman ibn Ibrahim al-Nablusi, *The Sword of Ambition: Bureaucratic Rivalry in Medieval Egypt*, ed. and tr. L. Yarborough (New York, 2016), pp. 85–97.

19   J. B. Freed, *Frederick Barbarossa: The Prince and the Myth* (London, 2016), pp. 355, 480–1; J. P. Phillips, 'The Third Crusade in Context: Contradiction, Curiosity and Survival' in C. Methuen, A. Spicer and J. Wolffe (eds.), *Christianity and Religious Plurality, Studies in Church History* 51 (Woodbridge, 2015), pp. 102–3; B. Z. Kedar, 'Convergence of Oriental Christian, Muslim and Frankish Worshippers: the Case of Saidnaya and the Knights Templar' in Z. Hunyadi and J. Laslovszky (eds.), *The Crusades and the Military Orders: Expanding the Frontiers of Medieval Latin Christianity* (Budapest, 2001), pp. 89–92.

20   AM, p. 45.

21   Ibid., p. 44.

22   Ibid.

23   IK, 1.245–6.

24   AM, p. 46.

25   Hillenbrand, *Islam*, pp, 229–30.

26   IA, 2.217–18; AM, pp. 45–7; G. R. Smith, *Ayyubids and Early Rasulids in the Yemen (567–694/1173–1295)*, 2 vols. (London, 1978), 2.32–49.

27   Lev, *Saladin in Egypt*, pp. 86–94.

28   IA, 2.219.

29   Lev, *Saladin in Egypt*, pp. 86–94.

30   IA, 2.218–21; AM, pp. 46–8.

31   Reynolds, *Interpreting the Self*, pp. 95–6; Imad al-Din, quoted in IK, 2.370–1.

32   On *adab* see P. M. Cobb, *Usama ibn Munqidh: Warrior Poet of the Age of the Crusades* (Oxford, 2005), pp. xx, 59–69.

33   For substantial coverage of holy war, see Latiff, *Cutting Edge, passim*; for the more satirical aspects, see J. Rikabi, *La poésie profane sous les Ayyubides et ses principaux représentants* (Paris, 1949), pp. 78–80, n. 4; Lyons and Jackson, *Saladin*, pp. 119–20; Eddé, *Saladin*, pp. 344–6.

34   Latiff, *Cutting Edge*, p. 40.

35   IJ, p. 311.

36   England, *Medieval Empires*, pp. 86–7.

37   Reynolds, *Interpreting the Self*, pp. 93–4.

38   Rabie, *Financial System of Egypt*, p. 63.

39   Ibn Abi Usaybi'ah, *A Literary History of Medicine: 'Uyūn al-anbā' fī ṭabaqāt al-aṭibbā' of Ibn Abī Uṣaybi'ah (d.1270)*, eds., trs. and analysed by E. Savage-Smith, S. Swain and G. J. van Gelder, with I. Sánchez, N. P. Joosse, A. Watson, B. Inksetter and F. Hilloowalla (Brill, 2019), 15.8.2.

40   IK, 3.95.

41   Eddé, *Saladin*, pp. 345–6.

42   Latiff, *Cutting Edge*, p. 167.

43   K. Abu Deeb and D. Bakhsh (eds.), *Abd al-Mun'im ibn Umar ibn Ḥassān al-Jilyānī al-Andalusī, Dīwān al-tadbīj: Fitnat al-ibdā wa-dhurwat al-imtā* (London and Oxford, 2010) contains both text and many fine images of the poems; J. Bray, 'Picture Poems for Saladin: Abd al-Mun'im al-Jilyani's *mudabbajat*' in *Syria in Crusader Times: Conflict and Co-existence*, ed. C. Hillenbrand (Edinburgh, 2019); J. Bray, 'From Spain to Syria: What did al-Jilyani bring with him?', in *Re-Defining a Space of Encounter. Islam and Mediterranean: Identity, Alterity and Interactions: Proceedings of the 28th Congress of the Union Européenne des Arabisants et Islamisants, Palermo 2016*, eds. A. Pelliterri, N. Elsakaan, M. G. Sciortino, D. Sicari (Leuven, forthcoming).

44   Al-Wahrani, 'A Conversation', p. 106.

45   Umara, quoted in Reynolds, *Interpreting the Self*, p. 95. On Umara, see also IK, 2.367–72.

46   AM, p. 48.

47   IK, 3.338–42; IA, 2.221–3; Tabbaa, *Ayyubid Era: Art and Architecture in Medieval Syria*, pp. 89–90; Elisséeff, *Nur ad-Din*, 2.691–4.

48   The fine eulogy by the Damascene Ibn Asakir is in 'Un document contemporain de Nur ad-Din', pp. 126–33.

49   WT, 2.394.
50   Lev, 'The "jihad" of Sultan Nur al-Din', pp. 252–64; Christie, *Muslims and Crusaders*, pp. 39–40 also outlines some of the more negative assessments of Nur al-Din.
51   Al-Harawi, *A Lonely Wayfarer's Guide to Pilgrimage*, pp. 34, 59–60; Meri, *Cult of Saints*, pp. 81, 188; IK, 3.341.

7 Saladin's Takeover of Damascus: Open Ambitions

1   There was a strong Byzantine influence apparent as well. Brett, *Fatimid Empire*, pp. 270–80; A. Metcalfe, *The Muslims of Medieval Italy* (Edinburgh, 2009), pp. 235–64. For trade, see Cahen, 'Douanes et commerce dans les ports Méditerranéens de l'Égypte médiévale', pp. 223–4.
2   P. D. Mitchell, 'An Evaluation of the Leprosy of King Baldwin IV of Jerusalem in the context of the medieval world' in B. Hamilton (ed.), *The Leper King and His Heirs: Baldwin IV and the Crusader Kingdom of Jerusalem* (Cambridge, 2000), pp. 245–58.
3   Harvey, 'Saladin Consoles Baldwin IV', pp. 27–34.
4   H. Möhring, *Saladin: The Sultan and His Times, 1138–93*, tr. B. S. Bachrach, introduction, P. M. Cobb (Baltimore, MD, 2008), pp. 43–6.
5   WT, 2.399–400; IA, 2.229–30; AS, 4.164–7; Ehrenkreutz, 'Place of Saladin in Naval History', p. 104; Stanton, *Norman Naval Operations*, pp. 146–8.
6   BaD, p. 49; IA, 2.229–30; Minorsky, *Studies in Caucasian History*, p. 143, n. 1.
7   BaD, pp. 51–2; IA, 2.231–2.
8   IA, 2.231–2. Kumushtakin had been a senior figure in Nur al-Din's administration, notably in Mosul; IA, 2.193.
9   C. Yovitchitch, 'Bosra: Eine Zitadelle des Fürstentums Damaskus' in M. Piana (ed.), *Burgen und Städte der Kreuzzugszeit* (Petersberg, 2008), pp. 169–77.
10   IA, 2.232.
11   Ibid., 2.233.
12   AS, 4.169–81.
13   Mouton, Sourdel and Sourdel-Thomine (eds. and trs.), *Gouvernance et libéralités*, pp. 37–46, 103; BaD, pp. 22–3; D. Ayalon, *Eunuchs, Caliphs and Sultans: A Study in Power Relationships* (Jerusalem, 1999), pp. 178–80.
14   Mouton, Sourdel and Sourdel-Thomine (eds. and trs.), *Gouvernance et libéralités*, pp. 46–61, 103–4; Beha al-Din noted that those who entered Saladin's service were well rewarded; BaD, p. 26.
15   Hamilton, *Leper King*, pp. 84–93.
16   IA, 2.233.
17   Ibid., 2.233–4.
18   M. G. S. Hodgson, *The Secret Order of Assassins: The Struggle of the Early Nizârî Ismâ'îlîs against the Islamic World* (Philadelphia, PA, 1955) is the most authoritative work on this group.
19   Hillenbrand, *Islam*, pp. 150–5; Christie, *Muslims and Crusaders*, pp. xxxiv–xxxv, 13–14; Hodgson, *Secret Order*, pp. 62–78. The Nizaris are today the largest Isma'ili group in the world, led by their living Imam, the Aga Khan.
20   Mouton, *Damas et sa principauté*, pp. 129–35, 341–50.
21   William of Tyre, *Chronicon*, 2.953; F. Daftary, *The Assassin Legends: Myths of the Isma'ilis* (London, 1995), pp. 88–105; B. Lewis, *The Assassins* (London, 1967), pp. 40–9, 97–111; Hodgson, *Secret Order*, pp. 84–109; K. J. Lewis, *Counts of Tripoli and Lebanon in the Twelfth Century*, pp. 170–2.
22   IJ, p. 264.
23   Daftary, *The Assassin Legends*, pp. 88–101.
24   WT, 2.391–2.

25 While they were no friends of the Fatimid Isma'ili regime in Cairo, there is a suggestion that they might have linked up with the 1174 rebellion in Egypt had it gained traction; Hodgson, *Secret Order*, pp. 198–9.

26 IA, 2.234.

27 Hamilton, *Leper King*, pp. 88–94; Lewis, *Tripoli*, pp. 219–24, 233–40.

28 WT, 2.405; see also 2.407–8.

29 Al-Jilyani, 'The Jewelled Precious Gift', in Ibn Abi Usaybi'ah, *A Literary History of Medicine*, 15.11.2.1, tr. G. J. van Gelder.

30 Hillenbrand, *Islam*, pp. 99–101.

31 BaD, pp. 25, 36; *Sea of Precious Virtues*, pp. 295–6; *Rules and Regulations of the Abbasid Courts*, tr. E. Salem (Beirut, 1977); *Book of Gifts and Rarities*, tr. G. H. al-Qaddumi (Harvard, 1996). In the West see, for example, Walther von der Vogelweide's poem to his patron Philip of Swabia, quoted in M. H. Jones, 'Richard the Lionheart in German Literature of the Middle Ages' in J. L. Nelson (ed.), *Richard Coeur de Lion in History and Myth* (London, 1992), pp. 86–8.

32 Bar Hebraeus, *Chronography*, pp. 341–2, cited by Eddé, *Saladin*, pp. 152–3.

33 Cited in R. P. Mottahedeh, *Loyalty and Leadership in an Early Islamic Society*, revised edition (London, 2001), p. 72.

34 J. P. Phillips, 'Saladin and Gift-Giving' in C. Hillenbrand (ed.), *Syria in Crusader Times: Conflict and Co-existence* (Edinburgh, 2019).

35 IA, 2.178. For the context Saladin moved into, see P. Sanders, 'Robes of Honor in Fatimid Egypt' in S. Gordon (ed.), *Robes and Honor: The Medieval World of Investiture* (Basingstoke, 2001), pp. 225–39.

36 R. S. Humphreys, 'Women as Patrons of Religious Architecture in Ayyubid Damascus', *Muqarnas* 11 (1994), pp. 35–54.

37 IA, 2.236.

8 *Progress Stalls*

1 AM, p. 52.

2 Ibid.; Lyons and Jackson, *Saladin*, p. 98.

3 WT, 2.410.

4 See N. O. Rabbat, 'My Life with Salah al-Din, The Memoirs of Imad al-Din al-Katib al-Isfahani', *Edebiyat* 7 (1997), pp. 267–87; Richter-Bernburg, 'Imad al-Din al-Isfahani', pp. 29–51; H. A. R. Gibb, 'Al-Barq al-Shami: The History of Saladin by the Katib Imad ad-Din al-Isfahani', *Wiener Zeitschrift für die Kunde des Morgenlandes* 52 (1953), pp. 93–115; D. S. Richards, 'A Consideration of Two Sources for the Life of Saladin', *Journal of Semitic Studies* 25 (1980), pp. 46–65.

5 IA, 2.241–2; Imad al-Din, from Lyons and Jackson, *Saladin*, p. 105.

6 Ibn Asakir is keen to assert that Nur al-Din behaved in this way too: 'Un document contemporain de Nur ad-Din', p. 132. See also Ibn al-Qalanisi's comments in Chapter 2 above, pp. 22–3.

7 AS, 4.181–2.

8 Lewis, 'Saladin and the Assassins', pp. 239–40.

9 Mouton, Sourdel and Sourdel-Thomine (eds. and trs.), *Gouvernance et libéralités*, pp. 56–7.

10 Kemal al-Din, tr. B. Lewis, 'Kamal al-Din's biography of Rasid al-Din Sinan', *Arabica* 13 (1966), pp. 236–7.

11 IA, 2.249.

12 AS, 4.183–4.

13 Lyons and Jackson, *Saladin*, p. 110.

14 IA, 2.409; *History of the Patriarchs of the Egyptian Church*, pp. 160–1 lists and names fifteen of the sons.

15 Lyons and Jackson, *Saladin*, pp. 135, 236; Rabbat, 'My Life with Saladin', pp. 277–8; J. B. Gillingham, *Richard I* (London, 1999), p. 264.

16 Imad al-Din, *Barq al-Sham*, tr. Reynolds, *Interpreting the Self*, pp. 150–1.

17 S. Pradines, 'Burj al-Zafar: Architecture de passage des fatimides aux ayyoubides' in *Egypt and Syria in the Fatimid, Ayyubid and Mamluk Eras VIII*, eds. U. Vermeulen, K. D'Hulster and J. Van Steenbergen (Leuven, 2016), pp. 51–119; N. O. Rabbat, *The Citadel of Cairo: A New Interpretation of Royal Mamluk Architecture* (Leiden, 1995).

18 Al-Maqrizi, in MacKenzie, *Ayyubid Cairo*, p. 59.

19 Abd al-Latif al-Baghdadi, *The Eastern Key: Kitab al-ifadah wa'l-l'tibar of 'Abd al-Latif al-Baghdâdi*, tr. K. Hafuth Zand, J. A. and I. E. Videan (London, 1965), p. 109.

20 J. Gonella, 'Die Ayyubidische und Mamlukische zitadelle von Aleppo' in Piana (ed.), *Burgen und Städte*, pp. 139–47.

21 IJ, p. 43.

22 MacKenzie, *Ayyubid Cairo*, pp. 60–2; Rabbat, *Citadel of Cairo*, pp. 63–4.

23 Ibn Jubayr, *Travels*, p. 45; Abd al-Latif al-Baghdadi, *Eastern Key*, p. 109.

24 Rabbat, *Citadel of Cairo*, pp. 68–9.

25 Lyons and Jackson, *Saladin*, pp. 121–6.

26 WT, 2.426–34; Letter of Raymond, a Hospitaller, to the Christian faithful, in *Letters from the East*, pp. 72–3; AS, 4.184–9; IA, 2.253–5; BaD, pp. 54–5. See also M. Ehrlich, 'St Catherine's Day Miracle: The Battle of Montgisard', *Journal of Medieval Military History* 11 (2013), pp. 95–106; Lyons and Jackson, *Saladin*, pp. 120–6; Hamilton, *Leper King*, pp. 133–6; Tibble, *Crusader Armies*, pp. 300–17.

27 M. Benvenisti, *The Crusaders in the Holy Land* (New York, 1970), pp. 114–30.

28 Hillenbrand, 'Captivity of Reynald of Châtillon', pp. 79–101.

29 CCKJ, 2.9–27.

30 WT, 2.427–32.

31 A. V. Murray, 'Mighty against the enemies of Christ' in J. France and W. Zajac (eds.), *The Crusades and their Sources: Essays presented to Bernard Hamilton* (Aldershot, 1998), pp. 217–38.

32 Ehrlich, 'St Catherine's Day Miracle', pp. 96–102; Tibble, *Crusader Armies*, pp. 300–13.

33 AS, 4.185.

34 Ibid., 4.186.

35 Letter of Raymond, a Hospitaller, to the Christian faithful, in *Letters from the East*, pp. 72–3. On the Hospital in Jerusalem, see P. D. Mitchell, *Medicine in the Crusades: Warfare, Wounds and the Medieval Surgeon* (Cambridge, 2004), pp. 61–75.

36 Brother Raymond's claim of 30,000 Muslims killed and 15,000 captured is far-fetched, but makes the broad point that the casualties on Saladin's side were significant. Letter of Raymond, a Hospitaller, to the Christian faithful, in *Letters from the East*, p. 73.

37 IA, 2.253–4. For an interesting story connected with Isa's captivity, see below, p. 198.

38 BaD, p.54; AS, 4.184–9; WT, 2.432–3.

39 AM, p. 57.

40 Phillips, *Defenders of the Holy Land*, pp. 237–65; Hamilton, *Leper King*, pp. 243–4; M. Staunton, *The Historians of Angevin England* (Oxford, 2017), pp. 261–2.

41 BaD, p. 54.

42 AS, 4.191–2; IA, 2.254–5.

43 IA, 2.255–6; WT, 2.425–6, 434–5; Lewis, *Counts of Tripoli*, pp. 242–3.

44 AM, p. 58.

45 Lyons and Jackson, *Saladin*, p. 129.

46 IA, 2.254, n. 10.

47 Piana (ed.), *Burgen und Städte*, pp. 169–77.

48 IA, 2.232, 260–1; A. Azzam, *Saladin* (Harlow, 2009), pp. 238–9 discusses this episode in the context of Saladin's diplomatic skills.

49 Imad al-Din quoted in Reynolds, *Interpreting the Self*, pp. 152–3.

9 Victory at Jacob's Ford

1   R. Ellenblum, *Crusader Castles and Modern Histories* (Cambridge, 2007), pp. 261–74; M. Barber, 'Frontier Warfare in the Latin Kingdom of Jerusalem: The Campaign of Jacob's Ford, 1178–9' in J. France and W. G. Zajac (eds.), *The Crusades and their Sources: Essays presented to Bernard Hamilton* (Aldershot, 1998), pp. 9–22.

2   R. Ellenblum, 'Frontier Activities: the Transformation of a Muslim Sacred Site into the Frankish Castle of Vadum Iacob', *Crusades* 2 (2003), pp. 83–98.

3   R. Kool, 'Coins at Vadum Jacob: New Evidence on the Circulation of Money in the Latin Kingdom of Jerusalem during the Second Half of the Twelfth Century', *Crusades* 1 (2002), pp. 73–88.

4   WT, 2.439–40.

5   AS, 4.195–6; D. Nicolle, *Saladin and the Saracens* (Botley, 1986), pp. 15–21; Tibble, *Crusader Armies*, pp. 255–61.

6   IA, 2.262.

7   Al-M, pp. 57–8; IA, 2.261; Lyons and Jackson, *Saladin*, p. 133.

8   AS, 4.206.

9   Ibid., 4.198–200; WT, 2.439–40.

10   AS, 4.198–9.

11   Ibid., 4.203–9; IA, 2.265–6; WT, 2.436–9, 444.

12   P. D. Mitchell, Y. Nagar and R. Ellenblum, 'Weapon Injuries in the 12th Century Crusader Garrison of Vadum Iacob Castle, Galilee', *International Journal of Osteoarchaeology* 16 (2006), pp. 145–55.

13   Although for an important discussion of the limited numbers of actual Turks within such a force by this time, see Tibble, *Crusader Armies*, pp. 117–24.

14   IA, 2.266.

15   AS, 4.209–11; Ehrenkreutz, 'Place of Saladin in Naval History', pp. 106–7.

16   IA, 2.271–2.

17   Ibid., 2.272–3.

18   AM, pp. 61–2. On the death of Caliph al-Mustadi (1170–80), see Mason, *Two Statesmen of Medieval Islam*, pp. 76–81.

19   IA, 2.268.

20   Barber, *Crusader States*, pp. 274–5.

21   WT, 2.447.

10 Saladin, Cairo and the River Nile

1   Al-Mas'udi, quoted in al-Maqrizi, in J. P. Cooper, *The Medieval Nile: Route, Navigation and Landscape in Islamic Egypt* (Cairo, 2014), p. 107.

2   See above, p. 65.

3   Sanders, *Ritual, Politics and the City in Fatimid Cairo*, pp. 104–19.

4   Cooper, *Medieval Nile*, pp. 117–23.

5   Imad al-Din, *Barq*, tr. O. Latiff, p. 144.

6   Al-Qalqashandi, *Selections from Subh al-A'sha by al-Qalqashandi, Clerk of the Mamluk Court*, eds. and trs. H. El-Toudy and T. G. Abdelhamid (London, 2017), p. 211, n. 1446; Cooper, *Medieval Nile*, pp. 107–17.

7   M. Chamberlain, 'The Crusader Era and the Ayyubid Dynasty' in C. F. Petry (ed.), *The Cambridge History of Egypt, Volume 1, Islamic Egypt, 640–1517* (Cambridge, 1998), p. 219.

8   Ibn Tubayr al-Qaysarani, *Nuzhat al-muqlatayn fī akhbār al-dawlatayn Ibn aṭ-Ṭuwayr*, ed. A. F. Sayyid (Beirut, 1992), tr. O. Latiff, pp. 190–1.

9   AM, pp. 64–5.

10   Ibid., p. 61.

11   Ibid.
12   Al-Qalqashandi, *Selections*, pp. 210–14; Sanders, *Ritual, Politics and the City*, pp. 112–14.
13   Sanders, *Ritual, Politics and the City*, pp. 100–14; Cooper, *Medieval Nile*, pp. 117–23.
14   Mouton, Sourdel and Sourdel-Thomine (eds. and trs.), *Gouvernance et libéralités*, p. 56.
15   AM, p. 65; Sanders, *Ritual, Politics and the City*, pp. 104–9; Cooper, *Medieval Nile*, pp. 117–23; al-Qalqashandi, *Selections*, pp. 214–19. See also S. D. Gotein, *A Mediterranean Society: The Jewish Communities of the World as Portrayed in the Documents of the Cairo Geniza* (Berkeley CA, 2000), 2.356–7.
16   AS, 4.212–17; IA, 2.277–8; Lyons and Jackson, *Saladin*, pp. 162–3.
17   AM, p. 64; Ehrenkreutz, 'Place of Saladin in Naval History', p. 100; Lev, *Saladin in Egypt*, pp. 166–8.
18   AM, pp. 63–6; AS, 4.214; IA, 2.276; Barber, *Crusader States*, p. 265.
19   For an overview of his career, see R. S. Cooper, 'Ibn Mammati's Rules for the Ministries: Translation with Commentary of the Qawanin al-Dawawin', unpublished doctoral thesis (University of California, Berkeley, CA, 1973), pp. 10–18. Rabie, *Financial System of Egypt* makes frequent reference to Ibn Mammati.
20   AM, pp. 64–6; IJ, pp. 50–8; Y. Lev, 'Saladin's Economic Policies and the Economy of Ayyubid Egypt' in U. Vermeulen and K. D'Hulster (eds.), *Egypt and Syria in the Fatimid, Ayyubid and Mamluk Eras V* (Leuven, 2007), pp. 309–20.
21   AM, p. 67; MacKenzie, *Ayyubid Cairo*, pp. 143–4; L. Korn, '"Die Bauten Saladins": Kairo, Damaskus, und Jerusalem in der Baupolitik des an-Nasir Salah ad-Din Yusuf Ibn Ayyub' in U. Vermeulen and D. de Smet (eds.), *Egypt and Syria in the Fatimid, Ayyubid and Mamluk Eras II* (Leuven, 1998), pp. 212–17, 226.
22   AM, p. 63.
23   IA, 2.281; AM, p. 68. *Najd* means 'uplands', referring to the central area of the Arabian peninsula.

11 *Progress in Syria and Reynald's Red Sea Raid*

1   WT, 2.473–5; M. Ehrlich, 'The Battle of Hattin: A Chronicle of a Defeat Foretold?', *Journal of Medieval Military History* 5 (2007), pp. 17–27.
2   Ehrenkreutz, 'Place of Saladin in Naval History', pp. 108–9.
3   WT, 2.475–9.
4   See, for example, IA, 2.277–80.
5   IK, 2.537–40.
6   Abu Shama quoted in Ibn Khallikan, 2.543, n. 5.
7   IA, 2.284–5; BaD, pp. 56–7.
8   WT, 2.480.
9   Imad al-din, 'Al-Barq al-Shami', tr. Gibb, p. 103.
10   Ibid., pp. 103–6.
11   Ibid., pp. 100–1; WT, 2.490.
12   IA, 2.294; BaD, pp. 59–60.
13   WT, 2.490.
14   IA, 2.294.
15   BaD, 60; WT, 2.491.
16   Latiff, *Cutting Edge*, pp. 104–6.
17   BaD, p. 62.
18   WT, 2.485–6.
19   G. Leiser, 'The Crusader Raid on the Red Sea in 578/1182–3', *Journal of the American Research Center in Egypt* 14 (1977), p. 97.
20   Hillenbrand, 'The Imprisonment of Reynald of Châtillon', p. 97. On the influence of Reynald's imprisonment and its possible influence on his understanding of

Muslim ritual practices, see M. Milwright, 'Reynald of Châtillon and the Red Sea Expedition' in N. Christie and M. Yazigi (eds.), *Noble Ideas and Bloody Realities: Warfare in the Middle Ages* (Leiden, 2006), pp. 235–57.

21 Barber, *Crusader States*, p. 209.

22 WT, 2.277.

23 Several historians have analysed this episode, notably: A. Mallett, 'A Trip Down the Red Sea with Reynald of Châtillon', *Journal of the Royal Asiatic Society* 18 (2008), pp. 141–53; Leiser, 'Crusader Raid', pp. 87–100; Hamilton, *Leper King*, pp. 180–4.

24 Imad al-Din, 'Al-Barq al-Shami', tr. in Leiser, 'Crusader Raid', p. 89; IA, 2.289.

25 Tr. in Lyons and Jackson, *Saladin*, pp. 186–7.

26 IA, 2.289–90; Imad al-Din, 'Al-Barq al-Shami', tr. in Leiser, 'Crusader Raid', pp. 89–90.

27 IJ, p. 52; al-Maqrizi, tr. in Leiser, 'Crusader Raid', p. 94.

28 Latiff, *Cutting Edge*, p. 182.

29 Al-Qadi al-Fadil, tr. Latiff, *Cutting Edge*, pp. 179–80.

30 B. Hamilton, 'The Elephant of Christ: Reynald of Châtillon', *Religious Motivation: Biographical and Sociological Problems for the Church Historian*, ed. D. Baker, *Studies in Church History* 15 (1978), pp. 97–108.

31 Leiser, 'Crusader Raid', p. 91.

32 IA, 2.297; WT, 2.492–8; R. C. Smail, 'The Predicaments of Guy of Lusignan, 1183–87' in B. Z. Kedar, H. E. Mayer and R. C. Smail (eds.), *Outremer. Studies in the History of the Crusading Kingdom of Jerusalem presented to Joshua Prawer* (Jerusalem, 1982), pp. 159–76; Tibble, *Crusader Armies*, pp. 317, 323.

33 Hamilton, *Leper King*, pp. 192–3; see also WT, 2.498–504.

34 M. Milwright, *The Fortress of the Raven: Karak in the Middle Islamic Period (1100–1650)* (Leiden, 2008), pp. 61–4; H. Kennedy, *Crusader Castles* (Cambridge, 1994), pp. 45–52.

35 WT, 2.503–4.

36 IA, 2.297–8; BaD, p. 63.

37 IK, 4.417–35; Lev, *Saladin in Egypt*, pp. 33–6; Richards, 'Consideration of Two Sources', pp. 50–5.

38 BaD, pp. 63–4.

12 *Final Preparations: The Sieges of Kerak and Mosul*

1 AS, 4.251.

2 BaD, pp. 64–6.

3 IA, 2.300–1; BaD, pp. 64–5; AS, 4.252–5.

4 AM, pp. 74–5; IJ, pp. 313–14; IA, 2.300–1; BaD, pp. 64–5.

5 IJ, pp. 300–1.

6 Ibid., pp. 322–4.

7 Ibid., pp. 317–18; CCKJ, 4.36; E. Bach, *La cité de Gênes au xii siècle* (Copenhagen, 1955), pp. 55–70; D. Abulafia, *The Two Italies: Economic Relations between the Norman Kingdom of Sicily and the Northern Communes* (Cambridge, 1977), pp. 96–122; S. A. Epstein, *Genoa and the Genoese, 958–1528* (Chapel Hill, NC, 1996), pp. 55–62, 158–69.

8 Phillips, *Defenders of the Holy Land*, pp. 251–63.

9 AM, p. 78.

10 IJ, p. 190.

11 Rabbat, *Citadel of Cairo*, pp. 68–9.

12 BaD, p. 65; IA, 2.303.

13 AM, p. 76.

14 OFCWT, pp. 16–17; Barber, *Crusader States*, pp. 290–1.

15   Hamilton, *Leper King*, p. 210; J. Harris, *Byzantium and the Crusades*, second edition (London, 2014), pp. 132–5. The construction of the castle of Ajlun was another decision of note: C. N. Johns, 'Medieval Ajlun', *Quarterly of the Department of Antiquaries in Palestine* 1 (1931), pp. 21–33; K. Raphael, *Muslim Fortresses in the Levant: Between Crusaders and Mongols* (Abingdon, 2011), pp. 27–51.

16   BaD, p. 66; IA, 2.304.

17   Lyons and Jackson, *Saladin*, pp. 222–23; Baadj, *Saladin, the Almohads and the Banu Ghaniya*, pp. 8, 178; Bennison, *Almoravid and Almohad Empires*, pp. 104–5.

18   Peacock, *Great Seljuk Empire*, pp. 115–21, 153–5; Mason, *Two Statesmen of Medieval Islam*, pp. 70–88; E. Sivan, 'Saladin et le calife al-Nasir', *Scripta Hierosolymitana* 23, *Studies in History* (Jerusalem, 1972), pp. 126–36.

19   BaD, p. 66; Lyons and Jackson, *Saladin*, p. 227.

20   IA, 2.304–5.

21   Ibid., 2.305–6.

22   Ibid.

23   BaD, p. 68; P. E. Pormann and E. Savage-Smith, *Medieval Islamic Medicine* (Edinburgh, 2010), p. 48.

24   BaD, p. 68; IA, 2.308; Sivan, 'Saladin et le calife al-Nasir', p. 131.

25   BaD, p. 69; IA, 2.309, 315; H. A. R. Gibb, 'Arabic Sources for the Life of Saladin', *Speculum* 25 (1950), interrogates the evidence, pp. 68–70.

26   IaD, *Barq*, p. 154, fol. 120–4, tr. O. Latiff.

27   IA, 2.313–14.

28   BaD, pp. 69–71; IA, 2.313–15; AM, pp. 80–1.

29   BaD, p. 70; IA, 2.313–15.

30   C. De Vasselot, 'A Crusader Lineage from Spain to the Throne of Jerusalem: The Lusignan', *Crusades* 16 (2017), pp. 95–114.

31   IJ, p. 324; OFCWT, p. 26; interestingly, Imad al-Din knew of these events as well, IaDM, p. 19.

32   IaD, p. 19; IA, 2.316.

33   AS, 4.258; OFCWT, pp. 29–30.

34   IA, 2.316.

35   Ibid.; OFCWT, p. 29.

36   BaD, pp. 37–8; IA, 2.317.

37   Lyons and Jackson, *Saladin*, p. 241.

38   See letter in *Conquest of Jerusalem and the Third Crusade*, tr. Edbury, pp. 156–7; Barber, *Crusader States*, pp. 297–9.

39   IA, 2.319; H. J. Nicholson, '"Martyrum collegio sociandus haberet": Depictions of the Military Orders' Martyrs in the Holy Land, 1187–1291' in S. John and N. E. Morton (eds.), *Crusading and Warfare in the Middle Ages: Realities and Representations. Essays in Honour of John France* (Farnham, 2014), pp. 105–9.

40   IA, 2.319.

41   AS, 4.262.

13 *The Battle of Hattin*

1   BaD, pp. 37–8.

2   *Libellus*, 'De Expugnatione Terra Sanctae per Saladinum' in Ralph of Coggeshall, *Chronicon Anglicanum*, ed J. Stevenson, Rolls Series, no. 66 (London, 1875), p. 217.

3   'Saladin's Hattin Letter', p. 210; IA, 2.319.

4   Lyons and Jackson, *Saladin*, pp. 252–3.

5   IaDG, pp. 127–8.

6   Ibid., pp. 126–7.

7   IA, 2.320.

8   AS, Arabic text, *Kitāb al-rawḍatayn*, tr. O. Latiff, pp. 191–2.

9   Ehrlich, 'The Battle of Hattin', pp. 25–6.

10   *Libellus*, p. 218.

11   Tibble, *Crusader Armies*, pp. 323–4.

12   *Libellus*, p. 218; OFCWT, pp. 35–7; Letter of Abd-Allāh bin Aḥmad al-Maqdisī in AS, Arabic text, *Kitāb al-rawḍatayn*, tr. O. Latiff, pp. 191–2.

13   B. Z. Kedar, 'The Battle of Hattin Revisited' in B. Z. Kedar (ed.), *The Horns of Hattin* (Jerusalem, 1992), pp. 193–4; Ehrlich, 'Battle of Hattin', pp. 26–8.

14   Ehrlich, 'Battle of Hattin', p. 25.

15   IA, 2.321.

16   AS, Arabic text, *Kitāb al-rawḍatayn*, tr. O. Latiff, pp. 191–2.

17   OFCWT, pp. 38–9; M. Barber, 'The Reputation of Gerard of Ridefort' in J. Upton-Ward (ed.), *Military Orders Volume 4: On Land and by Sea* (Aldershot, 2008), pp. 111–20.

18   Ibid., pp. 39–40.

19   AS, Arabic text, *Kitāb al-rawḍatayn*, tr. O. Latiff, pp. 191–2.

20   IA, 2.321.

21   R. Y. Lewis, 'Crusader Battlefields: Environmental and Archaeological Perspectives' in A. Boas (ed.), *The Crusader World* (Abingdon, 2016), pp. 460–89.

22   J. France, *Hattin* (Oxford, 2015), pp. 89–90; Tibble, *Crusader Armies*, pp. 327–30.

23   IaDM, p. 25; IaDG, p. 131.

24   IK, 2.535–43.

25   'Saladin's Hattin Letter', p. 211.

26   IaDM, p. 25; IaDG, p. 131.

27   BaD, p. 73.

28   Kedar, 'Battle of Hattin Revisited', pp. 198–203; France, *Hattin*, pp. 92–5; Tibble, *Crusader Armies*, pp. 330–1.

29   Lewis, 'Crusader Battlefields', pp. 474–5.

30   Ibid., pp. 471–2.

31   IaDM, p. 26.

32   Lewis, 'Crusader Battlefields', pp. 475–6.

33   AS, Arabic text, *Kitāb al-rawḍatayn*, tr. O. Latiff, pp. 191–2; *Libellus*, pp. 224–6.

34   Lewis, 'Crusader Battlefields', pp. 480–2.

35   IA, 2.323.

36   IaDG, p. 133.

37   AS, Arabic text, *Kitāb al-rawḍatayn*, tr. O. Latiff, pp. 191–2.

38   BaD, pp. 37–8, 74–5; IaDM, pp. 27–8; IaDG, pp. 133–4; IA, 2.323; 'Saladin's Hattin Letter', p. 212.

39   IaDM, p. 30; IaDG, pp. 137–8.

40   *Itinerarium*, p. 78; BaD, p. 74.

41   IaDM, pp. 30–1; IaDG, pp. 138–9.

42   IA, 2.324.

43   IaDM, p. 29; IaDG, p. 137; Murray, '"Mighty against the Enemies of Christ": The Relic of the True Cross in the Armies of the Kingdom of Jerusalem', pp. 232–8.

44   For numerous examples during the thirteenth century see the references in J. Bird, E. Peters and J. M. Powell (eds.), *Crusade and Christendom: Annotated Documents in Translation from Innocent III to the Fall of Acre, 1187–1291* (Philadelphia, PA, 2013).

45   AS, 4.271; Z. Gal, 'Saladin's Dome of Victory at the Horns of Hattin' in B. Z. Kedar (ed.), *The Horns of Hattin* (Jerusalem, 1992), pp. 213–15.

14   *The Capture of Jerusalem*

1   AS, 4.293–9; *Libellus*, pp. 234–6.; IA, 2.324–5; *History of the Patriarchs*, p. 154; CCKJ, 4.35–40.

2 *Libellus*, pp. 236–8.

3 Niketas Choniates, *O City of Byzantium*, tr. H. J. Magoulias (Detroit, 1984), p. 210.

4 See for example the Al Jazeera *Arab History of the Crusades* (2016), Episode 4.

5 Imad al-Din, quoted in Lyons and Jackson, *Saladin*, p. 271.

6 *Libellus*, pp. 241–3; IA, 2.330–1.

7 J. Seligman, 'A Wall Painting, a Crusader Flood Diversion Facility and other Archaeological Gleanings from the Abbey of the Virgin Mary in the Valley of Jehoshaphat, Jerusalem' in L. D. Chrupcala (ed.), *Christ is Here! Studies in Biblical and Christian Archaeology in Memory of Michele Piccirillo ofm* (Jerusalem, 2012), pp. 185–220.

8 Y. Natsheh, 'The Architecture of Ottoman Jerusalem' in S. Auld and R. Hillenbrand (eds.), *Ottoman Jerusalem: The Living City, 1517–1917* 2 vols (London, 2000), 1.600–4; D. Myers, 'An Overview of the Islamic Architecture of Ottoman Jerusalem' in ibid., 1.326–38.

9 O. Grabar and B. Z. Kedar (eds.), *Where Heaven and Earth Meet: Jerusalem's Holy Esplanade* (Jerusalem, 2009); CCKJ, 3.397–435.

10 *Itinerarium*, p. 38; *Libellus*, pp. 241–3.

11 AS, 4.323–4; IaDG, p. 151.

12 There is some mild variation in the texts as to the location of the final assault. Some Muslim sources state it was near the Damascus Gate to the north, although Beha al-Din goes for the northern corner of the side facing the valley of Jehoshaphat. The eyewitness Latin writer of the *Libellus* indicates that it was a corner on the northern side with the Old French Continuation of William of Tyre giving the stretch from the Damascus Gate to Jehoshaphat Gate. *Libellus*, pp. 243–5; IaDM, p. 45; IaDG, p. 154, IA, 2.331, BaD, p. 77; OFCWT, p. 56.

13 *History of the Patriarchs*, pp. 132–3.

14 *Libellus*, pp. 245–6.

15 AS, 4.328; Latiff, *Cutting Edge*, pp. 67–78, 86–8.

16 On vengeance, see the sermon of Muhyi al-Din on 9 October 1187, IK, 2.639. On Ibn Asakir, see *Intensification and Reorientation of Sunni Jihad Ideology*, pp. 38–40.

17 K. Hirschler, 'The Jerusalem Conquest of 492/1099 in the Medieval Arabic Historiography of the Crusades: From Regional Plurality to Islamic Narrative', *Crusades* 13 (2014), pp. 37–76.

18 IaDG, pp. 156–8; IA, 2.331–2.

19 IA, 2.332; BaD, p.78; *Libellus*, pp. 246–7; OFCWT, pp. 60–1.

20 BaD, p. 77. By way of parallel, once the Franks had finished their major reconstruction of the Church of the Holy Sepulchre they chose to rededicate it on 15 July 1149, fifty years to the day of their capture of Jerusalem on the First Crusade. M. C. Gaposchkin, *Invisible Weapons: Liturgy and the Making of Crusade Ideology* (Ithaca, 2017), p. 134.

21 Nizam al-Mulk, *The Book of Government or Rules for Kings*, tr. H. Darke (London, 1960), pp. 143–4.

22 *Sea of Precious Virtues*, p. 299; see also p. 173 for a further instance of this advice.

23 J. Sourdel-Thomine, 'Les Conseils du Shayh al-Harawi à un prince Ayyubide', *Bulletin des études orientales* 16 (1961–2), pp. 205–66, with reference here to pp. 234–5; W. J. Hamblin, 'Saladin and Muslim Military Theory' in B. Z. Kedar (ed.), *The Horns of Hattin* (Jerusalem, 1992), pp. 228–38.

24 IA, 2.333; IaDG, p. 159; OFCWT, p. 64. The OFCWT indicates that the queen was freed after the siege of Ascalon because Saladin did not want to besiege Jerusalem with her inside, OFCWT, p. 54. The eyewitness *Libellus* does not list Sibylla as one of those liberated at this time.

25 IA, 2.332–5; OFCWT, pp. 60–7; AS, 4.329–30. Imad al-Din suggested 100,000 Franks were in the city; IaDG, pp. 157–60. On Eastern Christians, see J. Pahlitzsch, 'The

People of the Book' in R. Hillenbrand and S. Auld (eds.), *Ayyubid Jerusalem: The Holy City in Context 1187–1250* (London, 2009), pp. 435–40.

26   Ibn Abi Usaybi'ah, *A Literary History of Medicine*, 14.49, trs. E. Savage-Smith and F. Hilloowala.

27   B. Z. Kedar, 'The Jerusalem Massacre of 1099 in the Western Historiography of the Crusades', *Crusades* 3 (2004), pp. 15–76. Similar images are used by contemporary Muslim writers in describing killing Frankish knights, such as Imad al-Din writing after the battle outside Acre on 4 October 1189; IaDM, p. 184.

28   IA, 2.334; *Libellus*, pp. 250–1.

29   *CCKJ*, 3.397–417.

30   IaDG, pp. 168–72; M. Hawari, 'Ayyubid Monuments in Jerusalem' in Hillenbrand and Auld (eds.), *Ayyubid Jerusalem*, pp. 217–18.

31   IaDG, p. 160.

32   IK, 2.635.

33   Ibid., 2.636–7.

34   Ibid., 638–41.

35   IaDG, p. 168.

36   Imad al-Din quoted in Reynolds, *Interpreting the Self*, p. 155; IaDM, pp. 47–8; AS, 4.335.

37   IK, 4.520–8.

38   *CCKJ*, 3.143.

39   C. Hillenbrand, 'Ayyubid Jerusalem: A Historical Perspective' in Hillenbrand and Auld (eds.), *Ayyubid Jerusalem*, pp. 5–8; IaDM, pp. 58–9. A *waqf* is property declared inalienable by its owner who assigns its revenues to support a pious or charitable foundation. D. Sourdel and J. Sourdel-Thomine, *A Glossary of Islam* (Edinburgh, 2007), p. 181.

40   L. Singer (ed.), *The Minbar of Saladin: Reconstructing a Jewel of Islamic Art* (London, 2008).

41   R. Hillenbrand, 'The Ayyubid Aqsa: Decorative Aspects' in Hillenbrand and Auld (eds.), *Ayyubid Jerusalem*, pp. 301–26, esp. 307–10.

42   Analysed by L. Korn, 'Ayyubid Mosaics in Jerusalem' in ibid., pp. 379–82.

43   Letter of Grand Preceptor of the Templars to Henry II of England, January 1188, in *Letters from the East*, p. 84.

15 *The Siege of Tyre*

1   *Conquest of Jerusalem*, pp. 168–9.

2   *CCKJ*, 4.178–9.

3   Lyons and Jackson, *Saladin*, p. 277.

4   IA, 2.336; IaDM, pp. 68–71; OFCWT, pp. 67–8; Letter of Terricus, a Templar, in *Letters from the East*, pp. 83–4.

5   *Itinerarium*, pp. 39–40.

6   Sivan, 'Saladin et le calife al-Nasir', pp. 136–7.

7   IA, 2.340, 357–8; Mason, *Two Statesmen of Mediaeval Islam*, pp. 89–90, 96; Peacock, *Great Seljuk Empire*, pp. 118–20.

8   IaDM, pp. 85–91.

9   BaD, pp. 78–9; IaDM, pp. 76–80.

10   IA, 2.337; Barber, *Crusader States*, pp. 138–42.

11   BaD, p. 90; IaDM, pp. 107–9.

12   IaDM, pp. 84–5, 109; *CCKJ*, 4.6, 54–5, 83; AS 4.346.

13   IaDM, pp. 83–4, 110–12; AS, 4.347.

14   IaDM, pp. 112–13.

15   BaD, p. 81.

16   IA, 2.293–4.

17   BaD, pp. 135–6, 138, 140.

18   IaDM, pp. 116–21.

19   Al-Harawi, 'Stratagems' in Sourdel-Thomine, 'Les Conseils du Sayh al-Harawi à un prince Ayyubide', p. 227.

20   J. Mesqui, 'Die Burg Saône' in Piana (ed.), *Burgen und Städte*, pp. 356–66.

21   The siege is described in detail in al-Harawi's 'Stratagems' and discussed in Hamblin, 'Saladin and Muslim Military Theory', pp. 231–4.

22   IA, 2.345; J. Mesqui, 'Bourzey, une forteresse anonyme de l'Oronte' in N. Faucherre, J. Mesqui and N. Proteau (eds.), *La Fortification au temps des croisades* (Rennes, 2004), pp. 95–133.

23   OFCWT, pp. 76–7, 83–4 has Guy's explanations as to why he was released from the vow; Ambroise, pp. 69–70.

24   BaD, p. 83, claims that it was destroyed but see D. Pringle, *Pilgrimage to Jerusalem and the Holy Land, 1187–1291, Crusade Texts in Translation* 23 (Aldershot, 2012), pp. 69, 252, 359.

25   IaDM, pp. 144–5; BaD, pp. 82–8; IA, 2.349–54; Buck, *Principality of Antioch*, pp. 55–7.

26   Lyons and Jackson, *Saladin*, p. 291.

27   BaD, p. 88.

28   IaDM, pp. 148–54.

29   Ibid., pp. 149–50; BaD, pp. 88–9.

30   IA, 2.356.

31   IaDM, pp. 148–9; IA, 2.354–5. Scurvy through lack of vitamin C is the more likely cause of blindness. Shaubak surrendered in May 1189. For Shaubak and Petra, see G. Vannini and M. Nucciotti (eds.), *Da Petra a Shawbak: Archeologia di una frontiera* (Florence, 2009).

32   IaDM, pp. 150–3; IA, 2.355–6.

33   Al-M, pp. 89–90.

34   J. H. Pryor (ed.), 'Two *excitationes* for the Third Crusade: The Letters of Brother Thierry of the Temple', *Mediterranean Historical Review* 25 (2010), pp. 147–68 and those from the post-Hattin period in *Letters from the East*, pp. 82–7.

35   *Libellus*, p. 243.

36   Peter of Blois, 'Passio Reginaldi principis Antiochie' in *Tractatus duo*, ed. R. B. C. Huygens, *Corpus Christianorum continuatio mediaevalis* 194 (Turnhout, 2002), pp. 40, 57.

37   BaD, p. 90. The story is also in AS, 4.396–7. Imad al-Din included these events too, although the text is not in Massé's translation which cites a reference from Beha al-Din that is contained in the later chronicle of Abu Shama, IaDM, pp. 159–61.

38   BaD, p. 91.

39   Cobb, *Usama ibn Munqidh*, pp. 59–62.

40   There is a western account of this siege in the OFCWT, pp. 70–3. See also IaDM, p. 162.

41   A. Mallett, 'Ibn al-Jawzi' in D. Thomas and A. Mallett (eds.), *Christian–Muslim Relations: A Bibliographical History, Volume 3 (1050–1200)* (Leiden, 2011), p. 733.

42   P. Masri and M. N. Swanson, 'Apologetic Commentary on the Creed' in ibid., pp. 671–5.

43   B. Z. Kedar, 'Croisade et jihad vus par l'ennemi: une étude des perceptions mutuelles des motivations' in M. Balard (ed.), *Autour de la première croisade* (Paris, 1996), pp. 345–55.

44   H. E. Mayer (ed.), *Die Urkunden der lateinischen Könige von Jerusalem*, 4 vols. (Hanover, 2010), 2.859–85.

45   IaDM, pp. 160–1; IA, 2.360–1; BaD, p. 35.

46   BaD, p. 97.

47   Ibid., pp. 96–7.

48 Known to the Muslims as Tell al-Fukhkhar or Tell al-Musallabin; BaD, p. 97, n. 2; IaDM, p. 170. See also IA, 2.364–5; J. H. Pryor, 'A Medieval Siege of Troy: The Fight to the Death at Acre, 1189–91, or the Tears of Salah al-Din' in G. I. Halfond (ed.), *The Medieval Way of War: Studies in Medieval Military History in Honor of Bernard S. Bachrach* (Aldershot, 2015), pp. 97–115; J. D. Hosler, *The Siege of Acre, 1189–91: Saladin, Richard the Lionheart and the Battle that decided the Third Crusade* (London, 2018), pp. 15–17.

49 IaDM, pp. 168–71; BaD, pp. 96–8; OFCWT, pp. 81–2; Ambroise, pp. 71–3.

16 The Siege of Acre, Part I: 1189–90

1   *Itinerarium*, p. 83.
2   Ibid., calls it a triangle. The various elements of the description of Acre are synthesised from: D. Pringle, 'Town Defences in the Crusader Kingdom of Jerusalem' in I. A. Corfis and M. Wolfe (eds.), *The Medieval City under Siege* (Woodbridge, 1995), pp. 81–4; D. Jacoby, 'Aspects of Everyday Life in Frankish Acre', *Crusades* 4 (2005), pp. 73–105; R. Gertwagen, 'The Crusader Port of Acre: Layout and problems of maintenance' in M. Balard (ed.), *Autour de la première croisade* (Paris, 1996), pp. 553–82; M. Benvenisti, *The Crusaders in the Holy Land* (New York, 1970), pp. 93–113; Pryor, 'Medieval Siege of Troy', pp. 97–115.
3   *Itinerarium*, p. 71.
4   E. Stern (ed.), *Encyclopaedia of Archaeological Excavations in the Holy Land*, 4 vols. (New York, 1993), 3.862–7.
5   Minorsky, *Studies in Caucasian History*, p. 143.
6   IA, 2.365–6; BaD, pp. 98–100.
7   *Itinerarium*, p. 74.
8   Hosler, *Siege of Acre*, pp. 27–41.
9   IA, 2.367, IaDM, pp. 179–80.
10 Minorsky, *Studies in Caucasian History*, pp. 139–41; BaD, pp. 101–2. See also B. Z. Kedar, 'A Western Survey of Saladin's Forces at the Siege of Acre' in B. Z. Kedar, J. S. C. Riley-Smith and R. Hiestand (eds.), *Montjoie: Studies in Crusade History in Honour of Hans Eberhard Mayer* (Aldershot, 1997), pp. 113–22. On the *Asadiyya*, see Humphreys, *From Saladin to the Mongols*, p. 415, n. 6.
11 IA, 2.367–8.
12 An interesting parallel to the imagery associated with the crusader capture of Jerusalem in 1099.
13 IaDM, pp. 182–8; IA, 2.368; Ambroise, pp. 74–6; *Itinerarium*, pp. 77–81.
14 Quoted in Lyons and Jackson, *Saladin*, p. 304.
15 IaDM, pp. 178–83.
16 Ibid., pp. 185–6.
17 BaD, pp. 102–5; IA, 2.366–8; IaDM, pp. 187–90.
18 Ambroise, pp. 76–7; *Itinerarium*, pp. 81–3.
19 IaDM, p. 191; Milan 1158 reference, see Freed, *Frederick Barbarossa*, pp. 224–5.
20 Hosler, *Siege of Acre*, pp. 41–4; *History of the Patriarchs*, p. 144; R. Rogers, *Latin Siege Warfare in the Twelfth Century* (Oxford, 1992), pp. 217–36.
21 BaD, pp. 100–1.
22 Harris, *Byzantium and the Crusades*, pp. 132–6; 'History of the Expedition of the Emperor Frederick', *Crusade of Frederick Barbarossa*, pp. 58–81.
23 BaD, p. 106.
24 IaDM, p. 198.
25 Baadj, *Saladin, the Almohads and the Banū Ghāniya*, pp. 142–53; Bennison, *Almoravid and Almohad Empires*, pp. 99–106; Ehrenkreutz, 'Place of Saladin in Naval History', pp. 114–15.
26 IaDM, pp. 205–7; Lyons and Jackson, *Saladin*, p. 309.

27   IA, 2.370; Pryor, 'Siege of Acre', p. 104.

28   IK, 2.431; IaDM, p. 207.

29   A-M. Eddé, 'Religious Circles in Jerusalem in the Ayyubid Period' in Hillenbrand and Auld (eds.), *Ayyubid Jerusalem*, p. 200. Also in the autumn of 1189 Saladin changed the patriarch of Jerusalem's house into a Sufi convent, showing his ongoing concern for spiritual matters in the holy city. J. Pahlitzsch, 'The Transformation of Latin Religious Institutions into Islamic Endowments by Saladin in Jerusalem' in L. Korn and J. Pahlitzsch (eds.), *Governing the Holy City: The Interaction of Social Groups in Medieval Jerusalem* (Wiesbaden, 2004), pp. 47–69.

30   The French translator of Imad al-Din broke off his text claiming that the details that followed were 'too shocking' to be reproduced; IaDM, p. 203. The Italian translator, Gabrieli had no such qualms and his rendition of the text is at IaDG, pp. 204–7.

31   IaDM, pp. 211–12.

32   IA, 2.372–4; BaD, pp. 110–11; IaDM, pp. 217–20. The contemporary Coptic source, *History of the Patriarchs* has a further version of this story as well, pp. 150–1.

33   BaD, p. 111; IaDM, pp. 221–2.

34   IaDM, pp. 215–17, 221–6; IA, 2.374.

35   BaD, p. 109; IaDM, p. 214.

36   Sivan, 'Saladin et le calife al-Nasir', pp. 141–3.

37   *Idem, L'Islam et la croisade*, pp. 120–3.

17 *The Siege of Acre, Part II: The Threat from the North*

1   'History of the Expedition of the Emperor Frederick' in *The Crusade of Frederick Barbarossa: The History of the Expedition of the Emperor Frederick and Related Texts*, tr. G. A. Loud, *Crusade Texts in Translation* 19 (Aldershot, 2010), pp. 80–115; 'Chronicle of Magnus of Reichersberg', *Crusade of Frederick Barbarossa*, pp. 156–63; Freed, *Frederick Barbarossa*, pp. 494–511; A. V. Murray, 'Finance and Logistics of the Crusade of Frederick Barbarossa' in I. Shagrir, R. Ellenblum and J. S. C. Riley-Smith (eds.), *In Laudem Hierosolymitani: Studies in Crusades and Medieval Culture in Honour of Benjamin Z. Kedar*, Crusades Subsidia 1 (Aldershot, 2007), pp. 357–68; Harris, *Byzantium and the Crusaders*, pp. 141–52.

2   BaD, p. 115; IaDM, pp. 226–30.

3   'History of the Expedition of the Emperor Frederick', *Crusade of Frederick Barbarossa*, pp. 115–16; 'Chronicle of Magnus of Reichersberg', *Crusade of Frederick Barbarossa*, pp. 164–5; 'A Letter Concerning the Death of Emperor Frederick', *Crusade of Frederick Barbarossa*, pp. 169–72; Freed, *Frederick Barbarossa*, pp. 512–13.

4   IA, 2.376.

5   IaDM, pp. 232–7.

6   BaD, pp. 118–20; IaDM, pp. 237–40; *Itinerarium*, pp. 94–6; Hosler, *Siege of Acre*, pp. 67–72.

7   IaDM, pp. 243–7; a letter from the chaplain of the archbishop of Canterbury gives a list: *Conquest of Jerusalem and the Third Crusade*, p. 171.

8   OFCWT, p. 95; Ambroise, p. 86.

9   BaD, pp. 126–7; IaDM, pp. 248–9.

10   Qadi al-Fadil in Lyons and Jackson, *Saladin*, pp. 317–18.

11   Ehrenkreutz, 'Place of Saladin in Naval History', p. 114.

12   BaD, p. 126.

13   Ibid., p. 180.

14   Ibid., pp. 96–9, 105–6; IA, 2.369.

15   An ideal consideration of contemporary medicine in the Muslim world is Pormann and Savage-Smith, *Medieval Islamic Medicine*; Al-Razi, *Kitab al-Qulang (Le livre de colique)*, ed. and tr. S. M. Hammami (Aleppo, 1983) which also includes an edition,

but not a translation, of Ibn Sina's text. A detailed discussion of colic is: W. Webb, *An Inaugural Dissertation on Colic* (Philadelphia, PA, 1798).

16   IJ, p. 311.

17   BaD, p. 68; IA, 2.309. The near-fatal illness at Mosul and Harran in late 1185 and early 1186 may have included an episode of stomach troubles; see Lyons and Jackson, *Saladin*, p. 235.

18   BaD, pp. 29–31, 130; IA, 2.379.

19   Eddé, *Saladin*, p. 356.

20   Ibid., p. 359.

21   Ibn Abi Usaybi'ah, *A Literary History of Medicine*.

22   Ibid., 15.36, tr. N. P. Joosse.

23   Ibid., 15.23, tr. N. P. Joosse.

24   Ibid., 15.11, trs. G. J. van Gelder and N. P. Joosse.

25   Ibid., 15.11.2.1, tr. G. J. van Gelder.

26   IA, 2.384–5; BaD, pp. 133–4.

27   BaD, p. 135; IaDM, pp. 261–2.

28   Quoted in Lyons and Jackson, *Saladin*, p. 320.

29   BaD, pp. 128–9; IaDM, pp. 250–2; CCKJ, 4.187.

30   BaD, pp. 130–1; IaDM, pp. 253–7.

31   BaD, pp. 123–4; IA, 2.379; *Itinerarium*, pp. 125–37.

32   Al-Maqrizi in Lyons and Jackson, *Saladin*, p. 329.

33   BaD, p. 136; IaDM, p. 264; Minorsky, *Studies in Caucasian History*, pp. 141–2. Eyewitness sources again give us the Muslim army's battle order so it is possible to see who still actively supported the sultan at this stage. The army stretched from the hill of al-Kharruba to the River Belus near the sea, south of Acre. The left wing was a combination of the Turkmen under Imad al-Din Zengi and Sanjar Shah, as well as the Kurdish contingents of the Hakkari and Mihrani forces, led by al-Mashtub and other Kurdish emirs, along with Saladin's nephew, Taqi al-Din. In the centre stood the royal guard and on the right, three of his sons, the rulers of Damascus, Aleppo and Bosra; then contingents from Saladin's vassal the Zengid lord of Mosul, Izz al-Din Mas'ud. Next stood Arab and Turkish emirs who commanded men from the Syrian fiefs of Banyas and Tell Bashir, with at the extreme right, Saphadin (presumably with troops from Egypt) and other important Mamluk emirs and northern Syrian nobles. A number of these men had not figured in the previous year's listing, although in some cases, such as Isa al-Hakkari, they had died in the interim. Broadly speaking this combination of Kurds, coupled with fief-holders from Saladin's Syrian lands and conquests, as well as external help from Sanjar and the Jazira gave Saladin just about enough men to deal with the current constitution of the Christian forces.

34   BaD, pp. 136–8; Ambroise, pp. 87–8; J. D. Hosler, 'Clausewitz's Wounded Lion: A Fighting Retreat at the Siege of Acre, November 1190' in J. France (ed.), *Acre and its Falls* (Leiden, 2018), pp. 30–48.

35   IaDM, pp. 268–70; BaD, pp. 139–40.

36   IaDM, pp. 272–3.

37   Ibid., pp. 273–8; BaD, pp. 141–2; IA, 2.380.

18 *The Arrival of Philip Augustus and Richard the Lionheart: The Fall of Acre*

1   Ambroise, pp. 89–93.

2   Letters to the caliph cited in Lyons and Jackson, *Saladin*, pp. 324–5; IaDM, pp. 288–9.

3   IK, 2.391–2; IaDM, pp. 283–6; IA, 2.385–6; BaD, p. 133; Humphreys, *From Saladin to the Mongols*, p. 64.

4   BaD, pp. 144–5.

5   Ibid., pp. 147–8; IaDM, pp. 294–5.

6   The text of this agreement is in *Caffaro of Genoa and the Twelfth-Century Crusades*, tr. M. A. Hall and J. P. Phillips, *Crusade Texts in Translation 26* (Farnham, 2013), pp. 218–20.

7   Gillingham, *Richard I*, pp. 140–54.

8   IaDM, pp. 295–7.

9   OFCWT, pp. 98–9.

10   BaD, p. 150. For the size of Richard's army, see Gillingham, *Richard I*, pp. 143–4. For varying assessments of Richard's performance on the crusade see ibid., pp. 140–221; J. Flori, *Richard the Lionheart: King and Knight*, tr. J. Birrell (Edinburgh, 2006), pp. 83–154; Asbridge, *Crusades*, pp. 430–513; Rogers, *Latin Siege Warfare*, pp. 225–36 outlines the technical details of the siege machinery employed by Richard. These historians, along with Staunton, *Historians of Angevin England*, pp. 242–59, draw out the contribution of writers favourable to Richard, such as Roger of Howden, Richard of Devizes, and William of Newburgh.

11   IaDM, p. 308.

12   IaDM, p. 299; BaD, p. 151.

13   T. S. Asbridge, 'Talking to the enemy: the role and purpose of negotiations between Saladin and Richard the Lionheart during the Third Crusade', *Journal of Medieval History* 39 (2013), pp. 275–96.

14   BaD, p. 153.

15   IA, 2.387; Ehrenkreutz, 'Place of Saladin in Naval History', pp. 114–15; Gillingham, *Richard I*, pp. 144, 159.

16   T. G. Wagner and P. D. Mitchell, 'The Illnesses of King Richard and King Philippe on the Third Crusade: An Understanding of 'arnaldia' and 'leonardie', *Crusades* 10 (2011), pp. 23–44.

17   Ambroise, 2.95–8; IaDM, pp. 306–7.

18   BaD, p. 155; IaDM, p. 305.

19   IaDM, p. 307; BaD, pp. 156–7; Ambroise, pp. 98–100.

20   BaD, p. 157.

21   IaDM, pp. 312–13; BaD, p. 158.

22   IaDM, p. 315.

23   BaD, p. 159.

24   IaDM, pp. 309–10; BaD, pp. 155–60.

25   BaD, p. 159; IA, 2.388.

26   BaD, p. 160.

27   The sources adduce some variation in the precise terms here with Hosler, *Siege of Acre*, pp. 134–35 running through the options.

28   BaD, pp. 161–2.

29   Ibid., p. 162.

30   IaDM, pp. 318–19.

31   Ibid., pp. 323–4.

32   Ibid., p. 326.

33   BaD, pp. 161–5; IaDM, pp. 327–31; Ambroise, pp. 103–8; Letter of Richard I, in *Conquest of Jerusalem*, pp. 179–80; Hosler, *Siege of Acre*, pp. 143–57.

34   Ehrenkreutz, 'Place of Saladin in Naval History', p. 116.

35   Al Jazeera, *Arab History of the Crusades* (2016), Episode 3.

19 *Battles of Sword and Words: Arsuf and Diplomacy*

1   *Tell Keisan (1971–1976): une cité phénicienne en Galilée*, eds. J. Briend and J-B. Humbert (Fribourg, 1980), pp. 46–9. The crusaders killed during the raid towards the River Belus and Haifa in November 1190 were buried in holes dug during the march, BaD, p. 136.

2   BaD, p. 168; IaDM, p. 333; Ambroise, p. 110.

3   IA, 2.364; J. F. Verbruggen, *The Art of Warfare in Western Europe during the Middle Ages* (Woodbridge, 1997), pp. 232–9; J. H. Pryor, *Geography, Technology and War: Studies in the Maritime History of the Mediterranean, 649–1571* (Cambridge, 1988).

4   *Itinerarium*, pp. 236–45; Ambroise, pp. 109–15.

5   BaD, p. 169; IaDM, pp. 337–8.

6   IaDM, p. 337; Ambroise, p. 114.

7   Lewis, 'Crusader Battlefields', pp. 463–8, 477–8; M. Ehrlich, 'The Battle of Arsur: A Short-Lived Victory', *Journal of Medieval Military History* 12 (2014), pp. 109–18.

8   Ambroise, pp. 115–22; BaD, pp. 174–6; IaDM, pp. 340–4; Letter of King Richard, in *Conquest of Jerusalem*, p. 180; Gillingham, *Richard I*, pp. 174–8; B. Z. Kedar, 'King Richard's Plan for the Battle of Arsuf/Arsur, 1191', in G. I. Halfond (ed.), *The Medieval Way of War: Studies in Medieval Military History in Honor of Bernard S. Bachrach* (Farnham, 2015), pp. 117–32.

9   BaD, pp. 176–7; Ambroise, pp. 125–6.

10   Ambroise, p. 126; BaD, pp. 178–80.

11   Letters of King Richard, *Conquest of Jerusalem*, pp. 180–2.

12   IA, 2.395.

13   BaD, pp. 184, 190–1; Sivan, 'Saladin et le calife al-Nasir', p. 143.

14   Asbridge, 'Talking to the enemy', p. 281.

15   In a literary context see England, *Medieval Empires*, pp. 67–104.

16   BaD, p. 38; Gillingham, *Richard I*, pp. 40, 44–6, 208.

17   BaD, p. 186.

18   Ibid.

19   Ibid., pp. 187–8.

20   'Chronica regia Coloniensis', *MGH* 18.121–25. The source also notes that Saladin was prepared to convert his lands to Christianity which suggests a rather optimistic reading of the situation. On marriages between Eastern Christians and Muslims, see Minorsky, *Studies in Caucasian History*, pp. 134–36. For Iberian examples, see S. Barton, 'Marriage across frontiers: sexual mixing, power and identity in medieval Iberia', *Journal of Medieval Iberian Studies* 3 (2011), pp. 1–25.

21   BaD, pp. 186–7.

22   Ibid., pp. 32, 190.

23   Ibid., pp. 184, 190–1.

24   IaDM, pp. 348–9; Sivan, 'Saladin et le calife al-Nasir', p. 143.

25   IaDM, pp. 353; BaD, pp. 192–3; Ambroise, pp. 130–1; IA, 2.392; *Itinerarium*, pp. 272–4.

26   IaDM, pp. 353–4.

27   BaD, pp. 194–5.

28   Köhler, *Alliances and Treaties*, pp. 263–7, 312–19.

29   IaDM, pp. 353–4.

30   Ibid., pp. 356–7, 367–8, 372–3; IA, 2.393–4.

31   Ambroise, p. 135; IA, 2.394.

32   Ambroise, p. 135.

33   IA, 2.393.

20 1192: Family Feuding, the Battle of Jaffa and the End of the Third Crusade

1   IA, 2.393; *CCKJ*, 3.125–9; Frenkel, 'Islamic religious endowments', pp. 7–8.

2   AM, pp. 95, 98; D. Abulafia, *The Great Sea: A Human History of the Mediterranean* (London, 2011), pp. 296–9.

3   Ambroise, pp. 138–9; *Itinerarium*, pp. 283–9.

4   BaD, p. 198.

5   Humphreys, *From Saladin to the Mongols*, pp. 65–6.
6   IaDM, p. 382.
7   BaD, p. 201.
8   Ibid., p. 202.
9   Humphreys, *From Saladin to the Mongols*, pp. 65–6.
10   IA, 2.399–400.
11   Ambroise, pp. 141–7.
12   OFCWT, pp. 112–13; Gillingham, *Richard I*, pp. 148–9.
13   Gillingham, *Richard I*, pp. 199–201, 233–7.
14   IA, 2.396–7; Ambroise, pp. 150–1.
15   OFCWT, pp. 114–15.
16   Ambroise, pp. 152–5. IaDM, p. 377 voices disgust at the treatment of the widowed, pregnant princess.
17   IaDM, p. 377.
18   IaDM, pp. 378–9.
19   Ambroise, pp. 162–3, 167–8.
20   BaD, pp. 206–8; IA, 2.399; IaDM, pp. 380–2; Ambroise, pp. 170–2.
21   Al-Harawi, *Lonely Wayfarer's Guide to Pilgrimage*, pp. xxii–xxiii, 4, 78.
22   A. J. Boas, *Crusader Archaeology: The Material Culture of the Latin East*, second edition (Abingdon, 2017), p. 31.
23   BaD, p. 209.
24   Ibid., pp. 209–11.
25   IaDM, pp. 375–6; Bar Hebraeus, *Chronography*, p. 321.
26   Added to this, at some point in 1192 a group of Shi'ite troops in Cairo staged a revolt, even freeing Frankish prisoners, although the uprising was soon quelled. A. Mallett, *Popular Muslim Reactions to the Franks in the Levant, 1097–1291* (Farnham, 2014), p. 132.
27   BaD, pp. 211–12; Ambroise, pp. 173–4.
28   Ambroise, p. 159; Gillingham, *Richard I*, pp. 195, 204.
29   Pringle, 'Richard I and the Walls of Ascalon', pp. 133–47.
30   BaD, p. 215.
31   Ibid., p. 216; Ambroise, p. 175.
32   IA, 2.401; BaD, pp. 217–21; Ambroise, pp. 175–7.
33   BaD, p. 220.
34   Ambroise, p. 180; OFCWT, pp. 116–17.
35   Asbridge, 'Talking to the enemy', pp. 285–90.
36   OFCWT, pp. 117–18 has a variation on this tale with the suggestion that the first horse was knowingly unsafe to ride, but Saphadin then felt shamed and sent a second, more amenable mount. Gillingham, *Richard I*, pp. 216–17.
37   BaD, p. 225; IA, 2.401 gives a similar phrase.
38   BaD, p. 33.
39   *Sea of Precious Virtues*, p. 185.
40   BaD, p. 106.
41   Eddé, *Saladin*, pp. 387–8.
42   Ambroise, p. 186.
43   BaD, pp. 227–8.
44   IaDM, p. 391.
45   Ibid., pp. 390–2; BaD, p. 231; Ambroise, pp. 186–7.
46   BaD, p. 231.
47   IaDM, pp. 389–90, 394.
48   Ibid., pp. 392–3.
49   BaD, pp. 233–4.
50   Abd al-Latif al-Baghdadi quoted in Reynolds, *Interpreting the Self*, p. 162.
51   Ambroise, p. 191.

52 Gillingham, *Richard I*, pp. 15–23; Flori, *Richard the Lionheart*, pp. 315–31.
53 IaDM, pp. 396–400; Bar Hebraeus, *Chronography*, p. 341; BaD, p. 35; Buck, *Principality of Antioch*, pp. 57–60.
54 BaD, p. 236.
55 Bar Hebraeus, *Chronography*, p. 340 suggests 60,000 dinars.
56 IaDM, p. 401.
57 Humphreys, *From Saladin to the Mongols*, p. 89.
58 IaDM, pp. 401–2, 407–8.
59 Mouton, Sourdel and Sourdel-Thomine (eds. and trs.), *Gouvernance et libéralités*, pp. 63–71, 108–9, 116–17.

21 Peace at Last

1 BaD, pp. 240–2; IK, 4.543; Abd al-Latif al-Baghdadi, in Reynolds, *Interpreting the Self*, p. 163.
2 IaDM, p. 410.
3 Ibid., pp. 408–9.
4 BaD, p. 244.
5 IA, 2.409.
6 Ibid.; IK, 4.545.
7 The essential monograph on this period is Humphreys, *From Saladin to the Mongols*. Much of what follows here is also derived from K. Hirschler, 'Frankish–Muslim Relations in the Ayyubid Period, *c*.1193–*c*.1250' in A. Jotischky and J. P. Phillips (eds.), *The Cambridge History of the Crusades, Volume 2* (Cambridge, 2020); Chamberlain, 'Crusader Era and the Ayyubid Dynasty' in Petry (ed.), *Cambridge History of Egypt, Volume 1*, pp. 219–26.
8 Humphreys, *From Saladin to the Mongols*, pp. 88–97.
9 J. Richard, 'Les esclaves franques de Saladin' in Mouton, Sourdel and Sourdel-Thomine (eds. and trs.), *Gouvernance et libéralitiés*, pp. 123–5.
10 Hirschler, 'Frankish–Muslim Relations'; Humphreys, 'Women as Patrons'.
11 D. P. Little, 'Historiography of the Ayyubid and Mamluk epochs' in Petry (ed.), *Cambridge History of Egypt, Volume 1*, pp. 414–20.
12 L. S. Northrup, 'The Bahri Mamluk Sultanate, 1250–1390' in ibid., pp. 244–51.
13 Humphreys, *From Saladin to the Mongols*, pp. 333–63.
14 Ehrenkreutz, *Saladin*, pp. 234–5.

Part II: Afterlife

1 J. C. G. Röhl, *Wilhelm II: The Kaiser's Personal Monarchy, 1888–1900*, tr. S. de Bellaigue (Cambridge, 2003), pp. 951–5; J. Krüger, 'William II's Perception of Sacrality' in H. Sadler, T. Scheffler and A. Neuwirth (eds.), *Baalbek: Image and Monument, 1898–1998* (Beirut, 1998), pp. 89–95; B. Isphording, *Germans in Jerusalem, 1830–1914* (Jerusalem, 2009), pp. 25–47.
2 S. Weber, *Damascus: Ottoman Modernity and Urban Transformation (1808–1918)*, 2 vols. (Aarhus, 2009), 2.241–2; S. Heidemann, 'Memory and Ideology: Images of Saladin in Syria and Iraq' in C. Gruber and S. Haugbolle (eds.), *Visual Culture in the Modern Middle East* (Bloomington, IN, 2013), pp. 60–2.
3 C. Hillenbrand, 'The Sultan, the Kaiser, the Colonel, and the Purloined Wreath', in *The Making of Crusading Heroes and Villains: Engaging the Crusades*, eds. M. Horswell and K. Skottki (Abingdon, forthcoming).
4 When in Jerusalem, Wilhelm reportedly criticised the aggression of the medieval crusaders, again, contrasting his own peaceful intentions. A-R. Sinno, 'The

Emperor's Visit to the East as Reflected in Contemporary Arabic Journalism' in H. Sader, T. Scheffler and A. Neuwirth (eds.), *Baalbek Image and Monument, 1898–1998* (Beirut, 1998), pp. 129–33.

5   FO 195/2024, report of Consul William Shortland Richards, November 1898, TNA. The phrase cited by Ende, 'a knight without fear or blame, who often had to teach his adversaries the right way to practice the Art of knighthood [i.e. chivalry]', conveys the same message; W. Ende, 'Wer ist ein Glaubensheld, wer ist ein Ketzer? Konkurrierende Geschichtsbilder in der modernen Literatur islamischer Länder', *Die Welt des Islams* 23–4 (1984), p. 83.

6   Sinno, 'Emperor's Visit', pp. 132–3. As Sinno notes, several writers also voiced suspicion about German intentions as well; ibid., pp. 115–19.

7   Ende, 'Wer ist ein Glaubensheld', p. 84; P. Wien, *Arab Nationalism: The Politics of History and Culture in the Modern Middle East* (Abingdon, 2017), pp. 38, 61. A. Boudot-Lamotte, *Ahmad Sawqi, l'homme et l'oeuvre* (Damascus, 1977), pp. 93–4, 418. On Shawqi see also A. J. Arberry, 'Hafiz Ibrahim and Shauqi', *Journal of the Royal Asiatic Society* 35 (1937), pp. 50–8.

8   Kansteiner suggests this is 'the result of the interaction among three different types of historical factors: the intellectual and cultural traditions that frame all our representations of the past, the memory makers who selectively adopt and manipulate those traditions, and the memory consumers who use, ignore, or transform such artefacts according to their own interests'. W. Kansteiner, 'Finding Meaning in Memory: A Methodological Critique of Collective Memory Studies', *History and Theory* 41 (2002), p. 128.

9   K. Skottki, 'The Dead, the Revived and the Re-created Pasts: "Structural Amnesia" in Representations of Crusade History' in *Perceptions of the Crusades from the Nineteenth to the Twenty-First Century,* M. Horswell and J. P. Phillips (eds.), *Engaging the Crusades 1* (Abingdon, 2018), pp. 116–18.

10 J. Assmann, 'Collective Memory and Cultural Identity', *New German Critique* 65 (1995), p. 130.

22 Saladin's Reputation in the West

1   *Letters from the East*, p. 72; Phillips, *Defenders of the Holy Land*, pp. 251–64.

2   Tolan, *Saracens*, pp. xx, 105–34; Morton, *Encountering Islam on the First Crusade* gives a much more nuanced picture.

3   *Gesta Francorum, The Deeds of the Franks and the Other Pilgrims to Jerusalem*, ed. R. Mynors, tr. R. M. T. Hill (London, 1962), p. 21.

4   Rubenstein, *Nebuchadnezzar's Dream*, p. 175; *Letters from the East*, pp. 79, 81, 84–6.

5   The impact and understanding of the fall of Jerusalem as expressed by England's historians is expertly set out in Staunton, *Historians of Angevin England*, pp. 216–27.

6   Rubenstein, *Nebuchadnezzar's Dream*, pp. 181–207; Cole, *Preaching the Crusades*, pp. 63–71; Jubb, *Legend of Saladin*, pp. 7–11; *Passio Reginaldi*, pp. 40, 46, 50–1, 58.

7   C. J. Tyerman, *England and the Crusades, 1095–1588*, (Chicago, 1988) pp. 75–80.

8   M. Rajohnson, 'L'Occident au regret de Jérusalem. L'image de la Ville sainte en chrétienité latine (1187–fin du xiv s.)', unpublished doctoral thesis (University of Paris, Nanterre, 2017).

9   See above, p. 291.

10 Rubenstein, *Nebuchadnezzar's Dream*, pp. 161–4, 209.

11 Cobb, *Usama ibn Munqidh*, pp. xx–xxi. For an indication of some of the literary constraints and influences on Ambroise's depiction of Saladin and Saphadin, see M. J. Ailes, 'The Admirable Enemy? Saladin and Saphadin in Ambroise's *Estoire de la guerre sainte*' in N. Housley (ed.), *Knighthoods of Christ: Essays on the History of the Crusades and the Knights Templar presented to Malcolm Barber* (Aldershot, 2007), pp. 51–64.

12   Although the broader elites of the Muslim Near East were not accorded such generous treatment: Cole, *Preaching the Crusades*.

13   M. H. Jones, 'Richard the Lionheart in German Literature in the Middle Ages' in J. L. Nelson (ed.), *Richard Coeur de Lion in History and Myth* (London, 1992), pp. 85–7.

14   D. von Güttner-Sporzynski, *Poland, Holy War and the Piast Monarchy, 1100–1230* (Turnhout, 2014), pp. 174–9; *idem*, 'Bishop Vincentius of Cracow and his *Chronica Polonorum*' in D. von Güttner-Sporzynski (ed.), *Writing History in Medieval Poland: Bishop Vincentius of Cracow and the Chronica Polonorum* (Leiden, 2017), pp. 1–17.

15   J. France, 'Saladin, from Memory towards Myth in the Continuations' in S. B. Edgington and H. J. Nicholson (eds.), *Deeds done Beyond the Sea: Essays on William of Tyre, Cyprus and the Military Orders Presented to Peter Edbury*, Crusades Subsidia 6 (2014), pp. 69–82.

16   G. Heng, *The Invention of Race in the European Middle Ages* (Cambridge, 2018).

17   R. S. Loomis, 'The "Pas Saladin" in Art and Heraldry' in D. Milner (ed.), *Studies in Art and Literature for Belle da Costa Greene* (Princeton, NJ, 1954), pp. 83–91.

18   *La fille du comte de Ponthieu. Nouvelle du xiii s.: 'Roman' du xv s.*, ed. and tr. R. Dubois (Paris, 2010), pp. 27–77; Jubb, *Legend of Saladin*, pp. 55–65.

19   M. Keen, *Chivalry* (London, 1984), pp. 6–8.

20   M. A. Jubb, 'Enemies in Holy War, but Brothers in Chivalry: The Crusaders' View of their Saracen Opponents' in H. van Dijk and W. Noomen (eds.), *Aspects de l'épopée romane: mentalités, idéologies, intertextualités* (Groningen, 1995), pp. 251–9.

21   J. V. Tolan, 'Saladin in the Medieval European Imagination', *Sons of Ishmael: Muslims through European Eyes in the Middle Ages* (Gainesville, FL, 2008), pp. 95–6.

22   P. McCracken, 'Scandalizing Desire: Eleanor of Aquitaine and the Chroniclers' in B. Wheeler and J. C. Parsons (eds.), *Eleanor of Aquitaine: Lord and Lady* (Basingstoke, 2002), pp. 250–5. Another admirer was said to be the wife of King Philip Augustus, who died before the Third Crusade; Jubb, *Legend of Saladin*, pp. 125–31. The Middle Dutch text adds a strongly anti-French tone as well as blending in chivalry, an invasion of England, and a deathbed conversion, ibid., pp. 185–7.

23   Jubb, *Legend of Saladin*, pp. 90–109; the *Pas Saladin* story offered another variant with twelve valiant English knights holding off Saladin on a mountain pass. Froissart witnessed a French variant on this in 1396. Tolan, 'Saladin in the Medieval European Imagination', pp. 89–91.

24   Dante Alighieri, *Il Convivio*, tr. R. H. Lansing (New York, 1990), 4:11; England, *Medieval Empires*, p. 185; Tolan, 'Saladin in the Medieval European Imagination', pp. 79–80.

25   Giovanni Boccaccio, *Tutte le opere 4: Decameron*, ed. V. Branca (Milan, 1976), pp. 54–7, 921–41; idem, *Tutte le opere 9: De casibus virorum illustrium*, eds. P. G. Ricci and V. Zaccaria (Milan, 1983), p. 800–4; Jubb, *Legend of Saladin*, pp. 120–1.

26   England, *Medieval Empires*, pp. 142–70.

27   F. Petrarca, *Trionfi, Rime estravaganti, Codice degli abbozi*, eds. V. Pacca, L. Paolino and M. Santagata (Milan, 2013), lines 148–51.

28   BaD, pp. 25, 244.

29   Jacques de Vitry, *Exempla, or Illustrative Stories from the Sermones Vulgares of Jacques de Vitry*, ed. T. F. Crane (London, 1890), pp. 54–5; Jubb, *Legend of Saladin*, pp. 42–4; J. Bird, 'Memory and the Crusades: Sermons as Vectors for Commemoration and Contextualization' (forthcoming).

30   R. Porter, *Enlightenment: Britain and the Creation of the Modern World* (London, 2000), pp. 72–6.

31   EEBO 1586. https://data-historicaltexts-jisc-ac-uk.ezproxy01.rhul.ac.uk/view?pubId=eebo-99844109e&terms=saladin%20shirt&pageTerms=saladin%20shirt ; see also N. Vienne-Guerrin, *The Unruly Tongue in Early Modern England: Three Treatises* (New York, 2012) who notes the influence of Coignet's text.

32   EEBO 1653. https://data-historicaltexts-jisc-ac-uk.ezproxy01.rhul.ac.uk/view?pubId=eebo-ocm12404310e&terms=saladin%20shirt&pageTerms=saladin%20shirt&pageId=eebo-ocm12404310e-61337–1.

33   ECCO 1781. https://data-historicaltexts-jisc-ac-uk.ezproxy01.rhul.ac.uk/view?pubId=ecco-0386401200&terms=saladin%20shirt&pageTerms=saladin%20shirt&pageId=ecco-0386401200–10.

34   EEBO 1695. https://data-historicaltexts-jisc-ac-uk.ezproxy01.rhul.ac.uk/view?pubId=eebo-ocm12075953e&terms=saladin&date=1695&undated=exclude&pageTerms=saladin&pageId=eebo-ocm12075953e-53606–75.

35   T. Fuller, *Historie of the Holy Warre* (Cambridge, 1639), p. 132; Tyerman, *Debate on the Crusades*, pp. 37–66.

36   *Calendar of the Fine Rolls of the Reign of Henry III. Volume III: 1234–42*, eds. P. Dryburgh and B. Hartland, technical eds. A. Ciula and J. M. Vieira (Woodbridge, 2009), 25/463, 21 June 1241, pp. 421–2.

37   B. Z. Kedar, 'Noms de saints et mentalité populaire à Gênes au XIVe siècle', *Moyen Age* 73 (1967), p. 442; A. Rovere et al. (eds.), *I Libri Iurium della Repubblica di Genova*, 9 vols. (Rome, 1992–2002), 1.347, 6.242–4.

38   Jubb, *Legend of Saladin*, pp. 40–1; Tolan, 'Saladin in the Medieval European Imagination', pp. 80–1. North of Avignon is a fine vineyard, the Domaine Saladin, in existence since 1422, now in its twenty-first generation and worth investigation.

39   Rifa'a Rafi al-Tahtawi, *An Imam in Paris: Account of a Stay in Paris by an Egyptian Cleric (1826–31)*, tr. D. L. Newman, second edition (London, 2011), pp. 289–90.

40   ECCO 1777. https://data-historicaltexts-jisc-ac-uk.ezproxy01.rhul.ac.uk/view?pubId=eccoii-1383800600&terms=saladin&date=1777&undated=exclude&pageTerms=saladin&pageId=eccoii-1383800600–130; on Defoe, see: Porter, *Enlightenment*, pp. 383–4.

41   https://www.bl.uk/collection-items/the-political-history-of-the-devil-by-daniel-defoe

42   Jubb, *Legend of Saladin*, p. 209; R. Irwin, 'Orientalism and the Development of Crusader Studies' in P. W. Edbury and J. P. Phillips (eds.), *The Experience of Crusading 2. Defining the Crusader Kingdom*, 2 vols. (Cambridge, 2003), 2.219–29.

43   Tyerman, *Debate on the Crusades*, pp. 100–10.

44   F-L-C. Marin, *Histoire du Saladin*, 2 vols. (Paris, 1758); 'History of Saladin' in R. Schechter (ed. and tr.), *Nathan the Wise with Related Documents* (Boston, 2004), pp. 139–50; Jubb, *Legend of Saladin*, pp. 207–11; Tyerman, *Debate on the Crusades*, pp. 70–1.

45   Tyerman, *Debate on the Crusades*, pp. 77–80; Jubb, *Legend of Saladin*, pp. 206–7.

46   Gotthold Ephraim Lessing, *Nathan the Wise with Related Documents*, ed. and tr. R. Schechter (Boston, 2004), extract from p. 88; Jubb, *Legend of Saladin*, pp. 197–9.

47   On Scott, see M. Girouard, *The Age of Camelot* (London, 1981), pp. 29–39; Porter, *Enlightenment*, pp. 76–77; E. Siberry, 'The Crusades: Nineteenth Century Readers' Perspectives' in M. Horswell and J. P. Phillips (eds.), *Perceptions of the Crusades from the Nineteenth to the Twenty-First Century: Engaging the Crusades 1* (Abingdon, 2018), p. 7. Quote from D. Coward, introduction to A. Dumas, *The Black Tulip*, tr. D. Coward (Oxford, 1993), p. vii.

48   W. Scott, *The Talisman* (London, 1832), p. 2; Siberry, *New Crusaders*, pp. 100–10, 130; M. J. Horswell, *The Rise and Fall of British Crusader Medievalism, c.1825–1945* (Abingdon, 2018), pp. 35–6, 44–9, 69–78. Saladin and Richard both appear in statues adorning the Scott Monument in Edinburgh, started in 1840 with the figures added in the 1870s. On Kaiser Wilhelm reading Scott's works, see J. C. G. Röhl, *Young Wilhelm: The Kaiser's Early Life, 1859–1888*, tr. J. Gaines and R. Wallach (Cambridge, 1988), p. 163.

49   Siberry, *New Crusaders*, pp. 65–8, 147–63.

50   Tyerman, *Debate on the Crusades*, pp. 77–8.

23 The View from the East: From the Medieval Age to the late Nineteenth Century

1   L. V. Thomas, *A Study of Naima*, ed. N. Itzkowitz (New York, 1972), pp. 45–6, 112; see also pp. 5–6, 78–85, 100–3; Lewis, *Muslim Discovery of Europe*, pp. 164–6.

2   C. H. Fleischer, *Bureaucrat and Intellectual in the Ottoman Empire: The Historian Mustafa Ali (1541–1600)* (Princeton, NJ, 1986); Naima's work was widely copied as a manuscript and came to be printed in 1733, boosting its circulation further. Note also that he made use of writings by al-Maqrizi and Mustafa Ali and see further Thomas, *Study of Naima*, p. 78.

3   B. Lewis, *History Remembered, Recovered, Invented* (Princeton, NJ, 1975), p. 84: 'After the final defeat and withdrawal of the Crusaders, the whole affair was forgotten and it was only in modern times, once again drawing from European sources, that Muslim interest revived.' E. Sivan suggested this latter point in his 'Modern Arab Historiography of the Crusades', *Asian and African Studies* 8 (1972), pp. 109–49. Ende, 'Wer ist ein Glaubensheld', pp. 70–94. J. S. C. Riley-Smith takes the matter further, 'Islam and the Crusades in History and Imagination, 8 November 1898–11 September 2001', *Crusades* 2 (2003), pp. 151–67. Repeated in, for example, Möhring, *Saladin*, pp. 101–2; J. Man, *Saladin: The Life, the Legend and the Islamic Empire* (London, 2015), pp. 333–7. This assertion has then seeped into other areas of study, e.g. P. Connerton, *How Societies Remember* (Cambridge, 1989), pp. 15–16.

4   N. Housley, *The Later Crusades: From Lyons to Alcazar, 1274–1580* (Oxford, 1992); A. Leopold, *How to Recover the Holy Land: The Crusade Proposals of the Late Thirteenth and Fourteenth Centuries* (Aldershot, 2000).

5   D. P. Little, *An Introduction to Mamluk Historiography* (Wiesbaden, 1970); idem, 'Historiography of the Ayyubid and Mamluk epochs' in Petry (ed.), *Cambridge History of Egypt, Volume 1*, pp. 412–44.

6   P. Nora. 'Between Memory and History: Les Lieux de Mémoire', *Representations* 26 (1989), pp. 7–24.

7   Hillenbrand, *The Crusades: Islamic Perspectives*, pp. 263–7; M. C. Lyons, 'The Crusading Stratum in the Arabic Hero Cycles' in M. Shatzmiller (ed.), *Crusaders and Muslims in Twelfth Century Syria* (Leiden, 1993), pp. 147–61; idem, *The Arabic Epic: Heroic and Oral Story-Telling*, 3 vols. (Cambridge, 1995), volume 1, see esp. pp. 1–28, 105–7. R. Irwin, *The Arabian Nights: A Companion* (London, 1994), pp. 103–19 provides a helpful background to the storytelling genre. For the western travellers, see A. Russell, *The Natural History of Aleppo*, 2 vols. (London, 1794), pp. 148–9; E. W. Lane, *An Account of the Manners and Customs of the Modern Egyptians* (London, 1860), pp. 360–91.

8   R. Irwin, *Ibn Khaldun: An Intellectual Biography* (Princeton, NJ, 2018).

9   Ibn Khaldun, *The Muqaddimah: An Introduction to History*, tr. F. Rosenthal, second edition, 3 vols. (London, 1967), 2.43–5, 82, 101, 263, 435; 3.11. See also W. J. Fischel, *Ibn Khaldun in Egypt: His Public Functions and His Historical Research (1382–1406): A Study in Islamic Historiography* (Berkeley, CA, 1967), pp. 72–3.

10   A. J. Fromherz, *Ibn Khaldun, Life and Times* (Edinburgh, 2010), p. 99; on the institution itself see MacKenzie, *Ayyubid Cairo*, pp. 110–11.

11   Irwin, *Ibn Khaldun*, pp. 162–70.

12   J. Garcin, 'Histoire, opposition politique at piétisme traditionaliste dans le Husn al-Muhadarat de Suyûti', *Annales Islamologiques* 7 (1967), pp. 33–89, esp. pp. 43–7; E. M. Sartain, *Jalal al-din Suyuti*, 2 vols. (Cambridge, 1975), 1.47–51; M. J. Saleh, 'Al-Suyuti and His Works: Their Place in Islamic Scholarship from Mamluk Times to the Present', *Mamluk Studies Review* 5 (2001), pp. 73–89.

13   D. P. Little, 'Mujir al-Din al-Ulaymi's vision of Jerusalem in the ninth/fifteenth century', *Journal of the American Oriental Society* 115 (1995), pp. 237–47. There is a partial translation into French: *Histoire de Jérusalem et d'Hébron depuis Abraham jusqu'à la fin du xv s.*, tr. H. Sauvaire (Paris, 1876).

14   Quote from Little, 'Mujir al-Din', p. 241; Gerber, *Remembering and Imagining Palestine*,
      pp. 62–4; Little, 'Mujir al-Din', p. 240 indicates that Mujir al-Din used Ibn al-Jawzi
      and Ibn al-Athir; it seems apparent that he also had Imad al-Din's 'Conquest of
      Jerusalem' with him, see the Sauvaire translation, pp. 81–3, as against IaDM, pp.
      394–6.

15   P. Walker, 'Al-Maqrizi and the Fatimids', *Mamluk Studies Review* 7 (2003), pp. 83–97;
      F. Bauden, 'Taqi al-Din Ahmad ibn Ali al-Maqrizi' in A. Mallett (ed.), *Medieval Muslim
      Historians and the Franks in the Levant* (Leiden, 2014), pp. 161–200, esp. 185–8.

16   H. Laoust, 'Ibn Katir, historien', *Arabica* 2 (1955), pp. 63–4, 69, 81–3.

17   Ahmad al-Hariri, *al-I'I'lām wa-al-tabyīn fī khurūj al-Firanj al-malā'īn 'alā diyār
      al-muslimīn* ('The Exposition and Explanation of the Cursed Franks' Departure to
      the Muslim Lands'), ed. S. Zakkar (Damascus, 1981), tr. O. Latiff (2017).

18   A. Rafeq, 'Ottoman Jerusalem in the Writings of Arab Travellers' in S. Auld and
      R. Hillenbrand (eds.), *Ottoman Jerusalem: The Living City, 1517–1917*, 2 vols. (London,
      2000), 1.63–72.

19   Even al-Maqrizi voiced a more critical tone towards the sultan in his earlier works
      on the Fatimids, although this changed in later decades as his focus moved towards
      the Ayyubids: Walker, 'Al-Maqrizi and the Fatimids'.

20   *Mustafa Ali's Description of Cairo of 1599*, ed. and tr. A. Tietze (Vienna, 1975), p. 68.
      This anecdote aside, the Ottoman historian Naima suggests that Mustafa Ali did
      offer admiration of Saladin through his summary of the writings; see note 1 for
      this chapter, above.

21   Sharaf al-Dîn Bitlîsî, *The Sharafnâma: Or the History of the Kurdish Nation – 1597, Book
      One*, tr. M. R. Izady (Costa Mesa, CA, 2005), pp. xxi–xxxi, 170–208.

22   D. Beben, 'Remembering Saladin: The Crusades and the Politics of Heresy in
      Persian Historiography', *Journal of the Royal Asiatic Society*, Series 3, 28 (2018), pp.
      231–53.

23   P. Jackson, *The Mongols and The Islamic World: From Conquest to Conversion* (London,
      2017).

24   Ata-Malik Juvaini, *Genghis Khan: The History of the World Conqueror*, ed. and tr. J. A.
      Boyle (Manchester, 1997), pp. 664–5.

25   D. Abouali, 'Saladin's Legacy in the Middle East before the Nineteenth Century',
      Crusades 10 (2011), pp. 175–89.

26   R. Dankoff, *An Ottoman Mentality: The World of Evliya Çelebi (revised second edition)*
      (Leiden, 2006); R. Dankoff and S. Kim, *An Ottoman Traveller: Selections from the Book
      of Travels of Evliya Çelebi* (London, 2010); *Ottoman Explorations of the Nile: Evliya
      Çelebi's 'Matchless Pearl These Reports of the Nile' map and his accounts of the Nile and
      the Horn of Africa in "The Book of Travels"*, eds. and trs. R. Dankoff, N. Tezcan and
      M. D. Sheridan (London, 2018), p. 94.

27   *Evliya Tshelebi's Travels in Palestine (1648–1650)*, tr. St H. Stephan (Jerusalem, 1980),
      pp. 30–1, 38–9, 48, 59.

28   *Ottoman Explorations of the Nile*, pp. 100–2. For other episodes involving Saladin see
      idem, pp. 165, 182 and map. Around the same time as Çelebi lived, a scholar from
      Medina, Ibrahim al-Khiyari (d.1672) passed through Jerusalem on a journey from his
      home to Istanbul. When he entered the al-Aqsa Mosque he engaged in discussion
      with the custodian about the order of precedence and the exact locations of the
      prayer leaders of the four great Sunni law schools. In answering, the local man stated
      that when Saladin had conquered Jerusalem the *imams* were asked to agree on their
      mutual rankings and what they had decided back in 1187 (AH 583) still prevailed.
      Rafeq, 'Ottoman Jerusalem in the Writings of Arab Travellers', 64–5; B. Masters, *Arabs
      of the Ottoman Empire, 1516–1918* (Cambridge, 2013), pp. 55–7, 103, 109.

29   A. Olsaretti, 'Political Dynamics in the Rise of Fakhr al-Din, 1590–1633: Crusade,
      Trade, and State Formation along the Levantine Coast', *International History Review*
      30 (2008), pp. 709–22; National Archives SP97, p. 94 (16 May 1614); D. Ze'evi, *An*

Ottoman Century: The District of Jerusalem in the 1600s (New York, 1996), pp. 20–1; Marco Gemignani (ed.), Le bandiere della Chiesa di Santo Stefano dei Cavalieri di Pisa: Loro storia, significato e restauro / The Flags of the Church of Saint Stephen of the Knights in Pisa: Their History, Meaning and Restoration (Pisa, 2015).

30   Rashid, Khalidi, 'Contrasting Narratives of Palestinian Identity' in P. Yaeger (ed.), The Geography of Identity (Ann Arbor, MI, 1996), pp. 215–17.

31   Abouali, 'Saladin's Legacy in the Middle East', pp. 179–80; Asali, 'Jerusalem under the Ottomans', p. 219.

32   E. L. Menchinger, First of the Modern Ottomans: The Intellectual History of Ahmed Vasif (Cambridge, 2017), p. 89, n. 60.

33   P. Strathern, Napoleon in Egypt: 'The Greatest Glory' (London, 2008), pp. 106–28, quotes at p. 122.

34   D. Zeevi, 'Back to Napoleon: Thoughts on the beginning of the Modern Era in the Middle East', Mediterranean Historical Review 19 (2007), pp. 73–94.

35   Al-Jabarti, Napoleon in Egypt: Al-Jabarti's Chronicle of the French Occupation, tr. S. Moreh, introduction R. Tignor, expanded edition (Princeton, NJ, 2004), p. 83.

36   Gerber, Remembering and Imagining Palestine, p. 66; A. Manna. 'The Sijill as a Source for the Study of Palestine' in D. Kushner (ed.), Palestine in the Late Ottoman Period: Political, Social and Economic Transformation (Jerusalem and Leiden, 1986), p. 358; Khalidi, 'Contrasting Narratives of Palestinian Identity', pp. 41–2. A. Layish, 'The Sijill of Jaffa and Nazareth Shari'a courts as a source for the Political and Social History of Ottoman Palestine' in M. Ma'oz (ed.), Studies on Palestine during the Ottoman Period (Jerusalem, 1975), pp. 526–7, writes of the assaults of 'the covetous French sect'.

37   M. Broers, Napoleon, Soldier of Destiny (London, 2014), pp. 169–202; J. Cole, Napoleon's Egypt: Invading the Middle East (New York, 2007).

38   L. Bjørneboe, In Search of the True Political Position of the Ulama: An analysis of the aims and perspectives of the chronicles of Abd al-Rahman al-Jabarti (1753–1825) (Aarhus, 2007), pp. 89–98, 211–15; T. Philipp, 'The French and the French Revolution in the Works of al-Jabarti' in D. Crecelius (ed.), Eighteenth-Century Egypt: The Arabic Manuscript Sources (Claremont, CA, 1990), pp. 127–40. E. Prusskaya, 'Arab Chronicles as a Source for Studying Bonaparte's Expedition to Egypt', Napoleonica. La Revue 24 (2015), pp. 48–60.

39   Bjørneboe, In Search of the True Political Position of the Ulama, pp. 197, 252.

40   Al-Jabarti, Napoleon in Egypt, p. 36.

41   Nicolas Turc, Chronique d'Égypte 1798–1804, ed. and tr. G. Wiet (Cairo, 1950), pp. 35–6, 44–5; G. M. Haddad, 'The Historical Works of Niqula El-Turk 1763–1828', Journal of the American Oriental Society 81 (1961), pp. 247–51; A. Sayyid Marsot, 'A Comparative Study of 'Abd al-Rahman al-Jabarti and Niqula al-Turk' in Crecelius (ed.), Eighteenth-Century Egypt, pp. 115–26.

42   Broers, Napoleon, Soldier of Destiny, p. 200.

43   R. Mazza, Jerusalem from the Ottomans to the British (London, 2009), pp. 84–5.

44   Ibid.

45   Y. Shalit, The European Powers' Plans regarding Jerusalem towards the Middle of the 19th Century (Berlin, 2004), pp. 5–11, 35–9.

46   M. Mo'az, Ottoman Reform in Syria and Palestine, 1840–1861: The Influence of the Tanzimat on Politics and Society (Oxford, 1968), pp. 210–40.

47   H. Temperley, England and the Near East: The Crimea (London, 1936), esp. pp. 28off.

48   J. Finn, Stirring Times: Or, Records from Jerusalem Consular Chronicles of 1853 to 1856, 2 vols. (London, 1878), 1.337.

49   Ibid., 1.xix, 340; see also 1.488–9.

50   Ibid., 2.127.

51   Ibid., 1.58–9; 2.15, 381.

52 Mo'az, *Ottoman Reform in Syria and Palestine*, pp. 227–30.

53 L. Fawaz, *An Occasion for War: Civil Conflict in Lebanon and Damascus in 1860* (London, 1994), pp. 101–22; J. Spagnolo, *France and Ottoman Lebanon 1861–1914* (London, 1977), pp. 3–25; Mo'az, *Ottoman Reform in Syria and Palestine*, pp. 231–5.

54 Fawaz, *An Occasion for War*, pp. 108–31, quotes at pp. 115, 119.

55 Siberry, *The New Crusaders*, pp. 64–72; Mazza, *Jerusalem from the Ottomans to the British*, pp. 78–80.

56 J. Porter, *Five Years in Damascus: With Travels and Researches in Palmyra, Lebanon, the Giant Cities of Bashan and the Hauran*, second edition (London, 1870), pp. 17, 35.

57 Finn, *Stirring Times*, 1.455–6.

58 R. Amitai, 'Some Remarks on the Inscription of Baybars at Maqam Nabi Musa' in D. Wasserstein and A. Ayalon (eds.), *Mamluks and Ottomans: Studies in Honour of Michael Winter* (Abingdon, 2006), p. 47.

59 Mujir al-Din, *Histoire de Jérusalem et d'Hébron*, pp. 25–7; A. Cohen, 'Al-Nabi Musa – an Ottoman festival (*mawsim*) resurrected?', in D. Wasserstein and A. Ayalon (eds.), *Mamluks and Ottomans: Studies in Honour of Michael Winter* (Abingdon, 2006), pp. 38–9.

60 Finn, *Stirring Times*, 1.455–6; Gerber, *Remembering and Imagining Palestine*, pp. 71–5.

24 Early Arab Nationalism Expressed Through Theatre, Books and Newspapers

1 A further spur to the spread of this narrative came in 1860 with an advertisement for a printed version, with another edition produced in Egypt in 1871. K. Hirschler, *Medieval Arabic Historiography: Authors as Actors* (Abingdon, 2006), pp. 118–21; for more on newspapers at this time, see A. Ayalon, *The Press in the Arab Middle East: A History* (Oxford, 1995), pp. 29–34.

2 Texts by al-Maqrizi emerged in 1853–4, in 1881 Ibn Khallikan's mighty thirteenth-century *Biographical Dictionary*; four years later the influential *Perfect Work of History* by Ibn al-Athir was produced as well. R. Khalidi, *Palestinian Identity: The Construction of Modern National Consciousness* (New York, 2009), pp. 43–4, p. 223, n. 20; Bauden, 'Al-Maqrizi', p. 171.

3 B. Anderson, *Imagined Communities: Reflections on the Origins and Spread of Nationalism*, revised edition (London, 2016), pp. 37–46, discusses the effect of print culture on the origins of nationalism, albeit in a broader context.

4 Polk, *Crusade and Jihad*, pp. 119–25; R. Woltering, *Occidentalisms in the Arab World: Ideology and Images of the West in the Egyptian Media* (London, 2011). p. 49.

5 Gerber, *Remembering and Imagining Palestine*, p. 52.

6 Hillenbrand, *The Crusades: Islamic Perspectives*, p. 593.

7 I. Shagrir and N. Amitai-Preiss, 'Michaud, Montrond, Mazloum and the First History of the Crusades in Arabic', *al-Masaq* 24 (2012), pp. 309–12; Sivan, 'Modern Arab Historiography of the Crusades', pp. 109–13.

8 Sivan, 'Modern Arab Historiography of the Crusades', p. 112.

9 On the St Louis Hospital, still a working hospice run by the Sisters of St Joseph of the Apparition, see (in Hebrew) E. Schiller, *Wall Paintings at the St Louis Hospital in Jerusalem* (Jerusalem, 2016); my thanks to Joab Simon for kindly translating this text for me. C. Nicault, 'Foi et politique: les pèlerinages français en Terre Sainte' in D. Trimbur and A. Aaronsohn (eds.), *De Bonaparte à Balfour: La France, L'Europe occidentale et la Palestine, 1799–1917* (Paris, 2001), pp. 311–20.

10 N. R. Keddie, *An Islamic Response to Imperialism: Political and Religious Writings of Sayyid Jamal al-Din 'al-Afghani'* (Berkeley, CA, 1983), pp. xv–xvi, 3–11; Woltering, *Occidentalisms in the Arab World*, pp. 50–2; *Revue du monde musulman* 22 (March, 1913), pp. 183–5; N. R. Keddie, 'The Pan-Islamic Appeal: Afghani and Abdülhamid II',

Middle Eastern Studies 3 (1966), p. 55; J. P. Montada, 'Al-Afghânî, a Case of Religious Unbelief?', *Studia Islamica* 100/101 (2005), p. 215.

11 M. Abduh, *The Theology of Unity*, tr. I. Musa and K. Cragg (New York, 1980), pp. 9–23, 149; M. Sedgewick, *Muhammad Abduh* (Oxford, 2010), pp. 16–17; Woltering, *Occidentalisms in the Arab World*, pp. 53–4.

12 The role of Al-Tahtawi's 'Open Ways for Egyptian Hearts to be Followed in the Embellishment of Contemporary Culture' with its emphasis on a 'love of the *watan*', an Arabic word meaning originally village or town, but now employed to be understood as a nation should be noted. Wien, *Arab Nationalism*, pp. 1–10; Woltering, *Occidentalisms in the Arab World*, pp. 43–8.

13 Zaydan quoted in M. Moosa, *The Origins of Modern Arabic Fiction*, p. 158; W. Hamarneh, 'Jurji Zaydan', in *Essays in Arabic Literary Biography, 1850–1950*, ed. R. Allen (Wiesbaden, 2010), pp. 389–92.

14 Ayalon, *The Press in the Arab Middle East*, pp. 53–54; P. Starkey, 'Romances of History: Jurji Zaydan and the Rise of the Historical Novel' in M. Booth and A. Gorman (eds.), *The Long 1890s in Egypt: Colonial Quiescence, Subterranean Resistance* (Edinburgh, 2014), pp. 343–53; A-L, Dupont, 'Le grand homme, figure de la "Renaissance arabe"' in C. Mayeur-Jaouen (ed.), *Saints et héros du Moyen-Orient contemporain* (Paris, 2002), pp. 62–3, 70–1.

15 T. D. Philipp, 'Approaches to History in the Work of Jurji Zaydan', *Asian and African Studies* 9 (1973), pp. 63–85; M. Nammour, 'La perception des croisades chez Jurjy Zaidan (1861–1914)' in L. Pouzet and L. Boisset (eds.), *Chrétiens et Musulmans au temps des croisades: Entre l'affrontement et la rencontre* (Beirut, 2007), pp. 141–61.

16 Translated into English as *Tree of Pearls, Queen of Egypt*, tr. S. Selim (Syracuse, 2012); Jurji Zaidan, *Saladin and the Assassins*, tr. P. Starkey (Bethesda, MA, 2011); Starkey, 'Romances of History: Jurji Zaydan and the Rise of the Historical Novel', pp. 355–9.

17 O. Bashkin, 'My Sister Esther: Reflections on Judaism, Ottomanism and Empire in the Works of Farun Antun' in M. Booth and A. Gorman (eds.), *The Long 1890s in Egypt: Colonial Quiescence, Subterranean Resistance* (Edinburgh, 2014), pp. 315–19.

18 D. M. Reid, *The Odyssey of Farah Antun: A Syrian Christian's Quest for Secularism* (Minneapolis, MN, 1975), pp. 98–101; M. M. Badawi (ed.), *Modern Arabic Literature* (Cambridge, 1992), pp. 343–4.

19 M. M. Badawi, *Early Arabic Drama* (Cambridge, 1988), pp. 1–67; J. Landau, *Studies in the Arab Theatre and Cinema* (Philadelphia, PA, 1958).

20 L-W. Deheuvels, 'Le Saladin de Farah Antun du mythe littérraire arabe au mythe politique', *Revue des mondes musulmans et de la Méditerranée* 89–90 (2000), pp. 189–203.

21 Wien, *Arab Nationalism*, pp. 41–2; G. Meynier, *L'Algérie révélée: la guerre de 1914–1918 et le premier quart du XXe* (Geneva, 1981), p. 174; Badawi (ed.), *Modern Arabic Literature*, p. 402; K. Amine and M. Carlson, 'Islam and the Colonial Stage in North Africa', *Performance and Spirituality* 3 (2012), pp. 1–12; N. Barbour, 'The Arabic Theatre in Egypt', *Bulletin of the School of Oriental Studies* 8 (1935), p. 173. It is not clear whether the play by Antun or Haddad was the Saladin-themed drama performed in Damascus in 1919. J. L. Gelvin, *Divided Loyalties: Nationalism and Mass Politics in Syria at the Close of Empire* (Berkeley, CA, 1998), pp. 254–6. For other plays that recall the history of the crusades at this time, see J. P. Phillips, 'Unity! Unity between all the inhabitants of our lands!' in M. J. Horswell and J. P. Phillips (eds.), *Engaging the Crusades* (Abingdon, 2018), pp. 79–106.

22 A. Rihani, *The Book of Khalid*, afterword by T. Fine (Brooklyn, NY, 2012), pp. 275–6, 317–25.

23 M. Strohmeier, *Crucial Images in the Presentation of a Kurdish National Identity: Heroes, Patriots, Traitors and Foes* (Leiden, 2003), pp. 18–26, 42–6; *Rojë Kurd* (1913).

24 Sheikh Riza Talabani, 'The Baran Land', tr. in C. J. Edmonds, *Kurds, Turks and Arabs: Politics, Travel and Research in North-Eastern Iraq, 1919–1925* (London, 1957), pp. 56–7.

25   R. Khalidi, 'The Role of the Press in the Early Arab Reaction to Zionism', *Peuples Méditerranéens* 20 (1982), pp. 116–17.

26   N. Mandel, *The Arabs and Zionism before World War I* (Berkeley, CA, 1978), pp. 88–92; B. Z. Kedar and D. Pringle, 'La Fève: A Crusader Castle in the Jezreel valley', *Israel Exploration Journal* 35 (1985), pp. 164–79.

25 Struggles for Independence in Syria, Egypt and Palestine

1   M. Provence, *The Last Ottoman Generation and the Making of the Modern Middle East* (Cambridge, 2017), p. 3, citing the book by P. La Mazière, *Partant pour la Syrie* (Paris, 1926). La Mazière was a journalist who visited Syria in 1925–6 and was scathing about Gouraud, describing him as having the mentality of a crusader, invoking Godfrey of Bouillon and Baldwin I of Jerusalem, and acting as if he was on a new crusade. He reported that Saladin was a man 'whose memory all the Muslims venerate' and that Gouraud said at the tomb 'My presence here consecrates the victory of the cross over the crescent.' La Mazière wrote (p. 193) that making such a statement, and doing so at Saladin's tomb, 'appalled' all the Muslims of Syria. See also J. Barr, for 'Syria Comment', 27 May 2016, www.joshualandis.com/blog/general-gouraud-saladin-back-really-say, accessed 19 February 2018.

2   FO 371/4186, December 1919, TNA; J. Barr, *A Line in the Sand: The Anglo-French Struggle for the Middle East, 1914–1918* (New York, 2012), pp. 87–8; see more generally, E. Tauber, *The Formation of Modern Syria and Iraq* (London, 1995); J. Richard, 'National Feeling and the Legacy of the Crusades' in H. Nicholson (ed.), *The Crusades* (Basingstoke, 2005), pp. 209–18.

3   Sayyid Qutb, in W. E. Shepard, *Sayyid Qutb and Islamic Activism: A Translation and Critical Analysis of 'Social Justice in Islam'* (Leiden, 1996), p. 216; M. Maqdsi, 'Charter of the Islamic Resistance Movement (Hamas) of Palestine', *Journal of Palestine Studies* 22 (1993), pp. 122–34; *President Gamal Abdel Nasser's Speeches and Press Interviews 1958* (Cairo, 1959), p. 129. For the 1938 reference, see Abd al-Fattah M. el-Awassi, *The Muslim Brothers and the Palestine Question, 1928–1947* (London, 1988), p. 50; F. Hinz and J. Mayer-Hamme, *Controversial Histories – Contemporary International Views on the Crusades: Engaging the Crusades* (Abingdon, forthcoming).

4   Harun Hashim Rashid's poem was first published in Arabic in his 'Ship of Anger', in Kuwait in 1968. It is in Salih Jawad al-Tu'ma, 'Salah al-Din al-Ayyubi fil-Shi'r al'Arabi al-Mu'asir', *al-Adab* 11 (November, 1970), unpublished translation here by O. Latiff, 2018.

5   N. Faulkner, *Lawrence of Arabia's War* (London, 2016), pp. 24–5.

6   Polk, *Crusade and Jihad*, pp. 197–202.

7   See E. Bar-Yosef, *The Holy Land in English Culture, 1797–1917: Palestine and the Question of Orientalism* (Oxford, 2005), pp. 251–69. Note also, in some comparison to the struggles of Richard the Lionheart in reaching Jerusalem, the troubles Allenby had in approaching the city: D. P. Woodward, *Hell in the Holy Land: World War I in the Middle East* (Lexington, KY, 2006), pp. 138–57.

8   M. Strohmeier, 'Al-Kulliyya al-Salahiyya: A Late Ottoman University in Jerusalem' in R. Hillenbrand and S. Auld (eds.), *Ottoman Jerusalem: The Living City, 1517–1917*, 2 vols. (London, 2000), 1.157–62.

9   FO 686/38, November 1917, TNA; A. L. Tibawi, *Anglo-Arab Relations and the Question of Palestine, 1914–1921* (London, 1978), pp. 242–5; E. Tauber, *Arab Movements in World War I* (London, 1993), pp. 152–5.

10   D. Pipes, *Greater Syria: The History of an Ambition* (Oxford, 1990), pp. 23–8; Gelvin, *Divided Loyalties*, esp. p. 242 for the removal of the kaiser's wreath.

11   'The First Call', FO 371/4185, 20 November 1919, TNA, pp. 139–42.

12   Ibid., p. 142.

13   FO 371/4185, WAAP 17, 19–23 December 1919, TNA.

14 Riots at the 1920 Nebi Musa festival showed how the situation in Syria was exacerbating tensions, spilling over to draw in Jerusalem's Jews as well; Provence, *Last Ottoman Generation*, p. 115.

15 Barr, *Line in the Sand*, pp. 103–4. See also comments made to Churchill in 1921, H. Gerber, *Remembering and Imagining Palestine: Identity and Nationalism from the Crusades to the Present* (Basingstoke, 2008), p. 180; P. S. Khoury, *Syria and the French Mandate: The Politics of Arab Nationalism, 1920–1945* (London, 1987), pp. 27–70, 97–126; Bhatia, *Forgetting Osama bin Munqidh, Remembering Osama bin Laden*, pp. 13–14.

16 Ibid., p. 21

17 A. P. Burdett, *Islamic Movements in the Arab World, 1913–66*, 4 vols. (Slough, 1998), 1, pp. 373–5.

18 Ibid.

19 FO 141/514/2, 1922, TNA.

20 I. Gershoni and J. P. Jankowski, *Egypt, Islam and the Arabs: The Search for Egyptian Nationhood, 1900–1930* (Oxford, 1986), pp. 46–7.

21 Gershoni and Jankowski, *Egypt, Islam and the Arabs*, pp. 158–9; I. Gershoni and J. P. Jankowski, *Redefining the Egyptian Nation, 1930–1945* (Cambridge, 1995), pp. 138–41.

22 Ibid., pp. 88–91.

23 Hasan al-Banna, *Five Tracts of Hasan al-Banna (1906–1949)*, tr. C. Wendell (Berkeley, CA, 1978), p. 96; G. Krämer, *Hasan al-Banna* (Oxford, 2010); R. Bonney, *Jihad: From Qu'ran to bin Laden* (Basingstoke, 2004), pp. 211–15.

24 Sayyid Qutb, in Shepard, *Sayyid Qutb and Islamic Activism*; A. A. Musallam, 'Sayyid Qutb and Social Justice, 1945–1948', *Journal of Islamic Studies* 4 (1993), pp. 52–70; Mitchell, *Society of the Muslim Brothers*, pp. 209–24.

25 Sayyid Qutb, in Shepard, *Sayyid Qutb and Islamic Activism*, pp. 216, 282–9, 326–7; Mitchell, *Society of the Muslim Brothers*, pp. 229–31.

26 Muhammad Asad, *Islam at the Crossroads* (Delhi, 1934), pp. 69–77.

27 Sayyid Qutb, *Milestones* (repr. New Delhi, 2002), pp. 159–60; Bonney, *Jihad*, pp. 215–23.

28 Wien, *Arab Nationalism*, pp. 48–79. One with a crusading link was the 1492 expulsion of the Muslims of al-Andalus, medieval Spain, a fate that the Palestinians feared they might suffer as well.

29 K. A. Sulaiman, *Palestine and Modern Arab Poetry* (London, 1984), p. 59.

30 Ibid., pp. 23, 38–9.

31 Ibid., p. 60. Speaking at the Bludan Conference the bishop of Homs praised the Arabs for their guardianship of the Christian holy places, notably during the time of Umar or the reign of Saladin, a comment noted as drawing cheers and applause; FO 684/10.

32 N. Gertz and G. Khleifi, *Palestinian Cinema: Landscape, Trauma and Memory* (Edinburgh, 2008), pp. 16–17.

33 G. Ankori, *Palestinian Art* (London, 2006), pp. 39–41; FO 371/16926.

34 D. Matthews, *Confronting an Empire, Constructing a Nation: Arab Nationalists and Popular Politics in Mandate Palestine* (London, 2006), pp. 148–57; U. M. Kupferschmidt, *The Supreme Muslim Council. Islam under the British Mandate for Palestine* (Leiden, 1987), p. 236; FO 371/16926; *Palestine and Transjordan Administration Reports 1918–1948, Volume 4, 1932–3* (Gerrards Cross, 1995), p. 13.

35 Khalidi, *Palestinian Identity*, pp. 189–90; Gerber, *Remembering and Imagining Palestine*, pp. 180–1; Bonney, *Jihad*, p. 271.

36 P. Wien, 'The Long and Intricate Funeral of Yasim al-Hashimi: Pan-Arabism, Civil Religion, and Popular Nationalism in Damascus, 1937', *International Journal of Middle East Studies* 43 (2011), pp. 271–92; *idem, Arab Nationalism*, pp. 39–40, 121–9; FO 684/10, 'an occasion for Pan-Arab display ... as an outstanding Arab patriot was buried in the garden near Saladin's tomb'. On al-Hashimi's role more generally, see Provence, *Last Ottoman Generation*.

26 *Looking for a New Saladin, c.1950–2001*

1   M. Khouri, *The Arab National Project in Yousef Chahine's Cinema* (Cairo, 2010), pp. 47, 51; P. B. Sturtevant, 'SaladiNasser: Nasser's Political Crusade in *El Naser Salah Ad-Din*' in N. Haydock and E. L. Risden (eds.), *Hollywood in the Holy Land: Essays on Film Depictions of the Crusades and Muslim–Christian Clashes* (Jefferson, NC, 2009), p. 143; E. Sivan, *Mythes politiques arabes* (Paris, 1995), pp. 23–4.

2   Commemorations and parades were central in establishing the authority of the new regime. An important occasion was the reburial of Mustafa Kamil (d.1908), seen as a leader of the Egyptian national movement, in a mausoleum in Salah al-Din Square, neatly linking the two heroes. E. Podeh, *The Decline of Arab Unity: The Rise and Fall of the United Arab Republic* (Eastbourne, 1999), p. 78.

3   G. A. Nasser, *Egypt's Liberation: The Philosophy of the Revolution* (New York, 1956), pp. 61–67, 87–8.

4   M. N. Belli, *An Incurable Past: Nasser's Egypt Then and Now* (Gainesville, FL, 2013), pp. 123–4.

5   Podeh, *Decline of Arab Unity*, pp. 1–7, 42–57.

6   *President Gamal Abdel Nasser's Speeches and Press Interviews 1958* (Cairo, 1959), p. 63.

7   Ibid., pp. 125–6.

8   Ibid., p. 27; also 19 September 1959, *President Gamal Abdel Nasser's Speeches and Press Interviews 1959* (Cairo, 1960), pp. 427–8.

9   For example, between October–December 1960, see *President Gamal Abdel Nasser's Speeches and Press Interviews October to December 1960* (Cairo, 1961), pp. 42, 47–9, 71, 104–5, 107–8, 183–4. Other references of note include the resistance of Damietta during the Fifth Crusade in 1219–21, May 1960, pp. 101–2.

10 8 May 1960, pp. 108–9; 7 May 1960, pp. 81–4; 1959, p. 140.

11 19 September 1959, pp. 428–9.

12 8 May 1960, p. 104; also 7 May 1960, p. 85; 20 March 1958, p. 129. For Allenby, 19 September 1959, p. 429.

13 Podeh, *Decline of Arab Unity*, p. 78; Sivan, 'Modern Arab Historiography of the Crusades', pp. 113–14.

14 I. Fawal, *Youssef Chahine* (London, 2001), p. 156.

15 Khouri, *Arab National Project*; V. Shafik, *Popular Egyptian Cinema: Gender, Class and Nation* (Cairo, 2007), pp. 105–7; Sturtevant, 'SaladiNasser' in Haydock and Risden (eds.), pp. 123–46; J. Aberth, *A Knight at the Movies: Medieval History on Film* (New York, 2003), pp. 91–107; H. Halim, 'The Signs of Saladin: A Modern Cinematic Rendition of Medieval Heroism', *Alif* 12 (1992), pp. 78–94; J. M. Ganim, 'Reversing the Crusades: Hegemony, Orientalism and Film Language in Youssef Chahine's *Saladin*' in L. T. Ramey and T. Pugh (eds.), *Race, Class and Gender in 'Medieval' Cinema* (Basingstoke, 2007), pp. 45–58. Chahine talks about the film and the crusades in C. Bossémo, *Youssef Chahine l'Alexandrin: CinémAction* 33 (1985), p. 143.

16 Nasser was also involved in Arab Nationalist movements elsewhere, such as Operation Saladin in the Yemen; L. James, *Nasser at War: Arab Images of the Enemy* (Basingstoke, 2008), p. 86, n. 686; Reiter, *Jerusalem and its Role in Islamic Solidarity*, pp. 120–1; Sivan, 'Modern Arab Historiography of the Crusades', p. 114.

17 R. Israeli (ed.), *The Public Diary of President Sadat, Part One: The Road to War (October 1970–October 1973* (Leiden, 1978), 14 May 1971, p. 57.

18 Ibid., 23 July 1971, p. 92; 30 August, 1971, p. 103; 24 April 1972, p. 182; 1 May 1972, pp. 198, 201; 14 May 1972, p. 211; *The Public Diary of President Sadat, Part Two: The Road of Diplomacy (November 1973 – May 1975)*, ed. R. Israeli (Leiden, 1979), 23 March 1975, pp. 810–11.

19 A. El-Sadat, *Speech by President Anwar el-Sadat to the Knesset, 20th November 1977* (Cairo, 1978), p. 20.

20 M. M. Badawi, *Modern Arabic Drama in Egypt* (Cambridge, 1988), pp. 196–7.

21 Badawi (ed.), *Modern Arabic Literature*, pp. 389–90.

22 Badawi, *Modern Arabic Drama in Egypt*, pp. 219–20.

23 Thatcher Archive, Churchill College, Cambridge, THCR 1/17/123.

24 R. S. Simon, 'The Teaching of History in Iraq before the Rashid Ali coup of 1941', *Middle Eastern Studies* 22 (1986), pp. 41–2, 49.

25 J. Nixon, *Debriefing the President: The Interrogation of Saddam Hussein* (London, 2016), p. 75.

26 O. Bengio, *Saddam's Word: Political Discourse in Iraq* (Oxford, 1998).

27 M. Thatcher, 6 September 1990, Hansard 177/734–43.

28 Heidemann, 'Memory and Ideology: Images of Saladin in Syria and Iraq', pp. 64–7; E. Podeh, *The Politics of National Celebrations in the Arab Middle East* (Cambridge, 2011), p. 148; A. La Guardia, *Holy Land, Unholy War: Israelis and Palestinians* (London, 2001), p. 55.

29 Nixon, *Debriefing the President*, pp. 75–6, 86.

30 Personal correspondence between the author and John Nixon, February 2017.

31 R. French, 'The Religion of Sir Walter Scott', *Studies in Scottish Literature* 2 (1964), pp. 32–44.

32 M. Mo'az, *Asad: The Sphinx of Damascus: A Political Biography* (New York, 1988), p. 44; M. Kedar, *Asad in Search of Legitimacy: Message and Rhetoric in the Syrian Press under Hafiz and Bashar* (Brighton, 2005), pp. 132–3.

33 L. Weedon, *Ambiguities of Domination: Politics, Rhetoric and Symbols in Contemporary Syria* (Chicago, 1999), pp. 1–3; Kedar, *Asad in Search of Legitimacy*, pp. 133–4.

34 U. Freitag, 'In Search of "Historical Correctness": The Ba'ath Party in Syria', *Middle Eastern Politics* 3 (1999), pp. 3–10.

35 Kedar, *Asad in Search of Legitimacy*, pp. 140–1.

36 Ibid., pp. 133–41.

37 Heidemann, 'Memory and Ideology: Images of Saladin in Syria and Iraq', pp. 68–73; Hillenbrand, *The Crusades: Islamic Perspectives*, pp. 595–600; Mo'az, *Asad: The Sphinx of Damascus*, p. 44.

38 Weedon, *Ambiguities of Domination*, p. 10.

39 Mo'az, *Asad: The Sphinx of Damascus*, pp. 44–5.

40 L. Hilsum, *Sandstorm: Libya from Gaddafi to Revolution* (London, 2012), p. 123. For more on Gaddafi and the crusades, see Hillenbrand, *The Crusades: Islamic Perspectives*, pp. 609–11. See also comments by the British ambassador in FCO 93/351, Diplomatic Report no. 213/74 and in Determann, 'Crusades in Arabic Schoolbooks', pp. 64–71.

41 Polk, *Crusade and Jihad*, pp. 388–96.

42 E. Karsh, *Arafat's War: The Man and his Battle for Israeli Conquest* (New York, 2004), p. 65.

43 Gerber, *Remembering and Imagining Palestine*, pp. 1–13; M. Litvak, 'Constructing a National Past: The Palestinian Case' in M. Litvak (ed.), *Palestinian Collective Memory and National Identity* (Basingstoke, 2009), pp. 97–133; Y. Reiter, *Jerusalem and its Role in Islamic Solidarity* (Basingstoke, 2008), p. 121.

44 S. Birnbaum, 'Historical Discourse in the Media of the Palestinian National Authority' in Litvak (ed.), *Palestinian Collective Memory*, pp. 135–41.

45 La Guardia, *Holy Land, Unholy War*, pp. 55–6.

46 E. Aubin-Boltanski, 'Salāh al-Dīn, un héros à l'épreuve: Mythe et pèlerinage en Palestine', *Annales. Histoire, Sciences Sociales* 60 (2005), pp. 91–107; I. Zilberman, 'The Renewal of the Pilgrimage to Nabi Musa' in M. Breger, Y. Reiter and L. Hammer (eds.), *Sacred Space in Israel and Palestine: Religion and Politics* (Abingdon, 2012), pp. 103–15.

47 Singer (ed.), *The Minbar of Saladin*; Karsh, *Arafat's War*, p. 65.

48 C. Yovitchitch, 'Die Aiyubidische burg Aglun [Ajlun]' in Piana (ed.), *Burgen und Städte*, pp. 118–25; Determann, 'The Crusades in Arabic Schoolbooks', pp. 29–34.

49 M. Darwish, *If I Were Another*, tr. F. Joudah (New York, 2011), p. 36; *idem, Memory for Forgetfulness: August, Beirut, 1982*, tr. I. Muhawi (Berkeley, CA, 2013), pp. 111–17; M. Abu Eid, *Mahmoud Darwish: Literature and the Politics of Palestinian Identity*

(London, 2016), p. 84; K. Abdel-Malik, *The Rhetoric of Violence: Arab-Jewish Encounters in Contemporary Palestinian Literature and Film* (Basingstoke, 2016), pp. 59–62.

50   N. Gertz and G. Khleifi, 'A Chronicle of Palestinian Cinema' in J. Gugler (ed.), *Film in the Middle East: Creative Dissidence* (Austin, TX, 2011), pp. 192–3; *idem*, 'Tale of the Three Jewels: Children Living and Dreaming Amid Violence in Gaza' in ibid., pp. 208–17; *idem, Palestinian Cinema*, pp. 93–7; E. Black, *Parallel Realities: A Jewish/Arab History of Israel/Palestine* (Minneapolis, MN, 1992), pp. 137–45; D. Ohana, *The Origins of Israeli Mythology: Neither Canaanites nor Crusaders* (Cambridge, 2012), p. 174; A. Elad-Bouskila, *Modern Palestinian Literature and Culture* (London, 1999), pp. 120, 133–4. One might also note theatre as another continuing medium with the El-Hakawati Theatre (the Palestinian National Theatre) in Jerusalem staging 'In Search of Omar Khayyum while passing through the Crusades and the story of the Assassins' written by François Abu Salem in 1989.

51   Y. Reiter, *Contested Holy Places in Israel-Palestine: Sharing and Conflict Resolution* (Abingdon, 2017), pp. 132–55.

52   Maqdsi, 'Charter of the Islamic Resistance Movement (Hamas) of Palestine', pp. 126, 130.

53   M. I. Jensen, *The Political Ideology of Hamas: A Grassroots Perspective* (London, 2008), pp. 53–9, 172, n. 141.

54   G. Keppel and J-P. Milelli (eds.), *Al-Qaeda in its own Words*, tr. P. Ghazaleh (Cambridge, MA, 2008). On bin Laden's background, see pp. 17–40, on al-Zawahiri, see pp. 147–70; Polk, *Crusade and Jihad*, pp. 472–86.

55   Osama bin Laden, *Messages to the World: The Statements of Osama bin Laden*, ed. B. Lawrence, tr. J. Howarth (London, 2005), p. 28.

56   https://georgewbush-whitehouse.archives.gov/news/releases/2001/09/20010916-2.html

57   https://georgewbush-whitehouse.archives.gov/news/releases/2001/09/20010918-5.html. A further, more recent example, of a western politician using the word 'crusade' in an inappropriate context was in March 2011, when the French interior minister, Claude Guéant, described President Nicolas Sarkozy's role in Libya as 'leading the crusade to mobilise the UN Security Council, the Arab League and the African Union', a comment that provoked widespread condemnation.

58   Bin Laden, *Messages to the World*, pp. 134–8.

59   Ibid., pp. 212–32. An earlier communication, in the form of a sermon, made a similar point, giving a deeply historical and global basis for his arguments to resist 'the Bush–Blair axis, which has the same banner and objective, namely the banner of the Cross and the objective of destroying and looting our beloved Prophet's *umma*', ibid., p. 187.

60   M. Scheuer, *Osama bin Laden* (New York, 2011), p. 30. See also p. 158 for one of bin Laden's associates discussing Nur al-Din and his 'student' Saladin.

61   Ayman al-Zawahiri, 'Knights under the Prophet's Banner' in *Al-Qaeda in its own Words*, p. 199.

62   M. Scheuer, *Imperial Hubris: Why the West is Losing the War on Terror* (Lincoln, NE, 2007) pp. 103–4.

Conclusion

1   P. Centlivres, D. Fabre, F. Zonabend, *La Fabrique des héros* (Paris, 1999), pp. 1–8.

2   Ehrenkreutz, *Saladin*, p. 97.

3   IaDG, p. 161.

4   IK, 3.238.

5   D. S. Richards, 'Biographies of Ayyubid Sultans' in Hillenbrand and Auld (eds.), *Ayyubid Jerusalem*, p. 443.

6   Abd al-Latif al-Baghdadi, cited in Ibn Abi Usaybi'ah, tr. in B. Lewis, *Islam from the Prophet Muhammad to the Capture of Constantinople* (New York, 1974), pp. 66–67.
7   http://americanradioworks.publicradio.org/features/resentment/angryprint.html

Writing the History of Saladin

1   Ehrenkreutz, *Saladin* takes the most aggressive stance; Eddé, *Saladin* applies an intensive analysis throughout.
2   Lambton, 'Islamic Mirrors for Princes'; see, for example, *The Sea of Precious Virtues*, or the work by Nizam al-Mulk, *Book of Government*.
3   Gibb, 'Arabic Sources for the Life of Saladin', and Lev, *Saladin in Egypt*, are just two of the historians to outline the other contemporary, or near-contemporary, writers of note, such as Ibn Abi Tayy and Ibn Wasil.
4   See the entries in the bibliography.
5   H. A. R. Gibb, 'The Achievement of Saladin', *Bulletin of the John Rylands Library* 35 (1952), p. 60.
6   Ehrenkreutz, *Saladin*, pp. 234–8.
7   Richards, 'A Consideration of Two Sources'; P. M. Holt, 'Saladin and his Admirers: A Biographical Reassessment', *Bulletin of the School of Oriental and African Studies* 46 (1983), pp. 235–9.
8   See the entries in the bibliography.
9   See the entries in the bibliography.
10 A. Maalouf, *The Crusades Through Arab Eyes* (London, 1986).

Index